Re-creating the Circle

RE-CREATING THE CIRCLE

The Renewal of American Indian Self-Determination

LaDonna Harris,
Editor and Mentor

Stephen M. Sachs *and* Barbara Morris,
General Authors

Deborah Esquibel Hunt, Gregory A. Cajete,
Benjamin Broome, Phyllis M. Gagnier,
and Jonodev Chaudhuri,
Contributing Authors

University of New Mexico Press
Albuquerque

First paperback edition, 2020
Paperback ISBN: 978-0-8263-5058-9

Library of Congress Cataloging-in-Publication Data

Re-creating the circle : the renewal of American Indian self-determination /
edited by LaDonna Harris, Stephen M. Sachs, and Barbara Morris.
    p. cm.
  Includes bibliographical references and index.
    ISBN 978-0-8263-5057-2 (cloth : alk. paper) — ISBN 978-0-8263-5059-6
(electronic)
    1. Indians of North America—Politics and government. 2. Indians of North
America—Government relations. 3. Indians of North America—Social
conditions. 4. Self-determination, National—North America. 5. Political
participation—North America. I. Harris, LaDonna. II. Sachs, Stephen M.,
1938– III. Morris, Barbara, 1959–
  E98.T77R45 2011
  323.1197—dc22
                                    2011005734

Contents

INTRODUCTION AND ACKNOWLEDGMENTS   vii

PART ONE
The Harmony of the Circle and the Impact of Colonialism   1

CHAPTER ONE: The Harmony of the Circle: American Indian Traditions
and Their Relevance for the Twenty-First Century   2

1. Traditional American Indian Politics, Society, and Culture   5
2. Contemporary Lessons from American Indian Traditional
Politics   24
Notes   39

CHAPTER TWO: The Circle Under Siege: The Impact of Colonialism on
American Indian Communities   52

1. Introduction: The Harmony of the Circle   52
2. Fracturing of the Circle: The Legacy of Physical and Cultural
Genocide   53
3. The Long Path to Re-creating the Circle   56
4. What Must Be Healed to Re-create the Circle   92
Notes   93

PART TWO
Re-creating the Circle   105

CHAPTER THREE: Honoring Indian Nations' Sovereignty: Building
Government-to-Government Relations Between Tribal
Governments and Federal, State, and Local Governments   106

1. Re-creating the Circle of Tribal–Federal Government Relations   106
2. Completing the Circle of Tribal–State and Local Government
Relations   151
Acknolwedgments   184
Notes   184

CHAPTER FOUR: Returning to Harmony Through the Wisdom of the
People: Applying Traditional Principles to Develop Appropriate and
Effective Indian Tribal Governance   201

1. Returning Indian Nations to Culturally Appropriate Forms of
Decision Making   201
2. Completing the Circle in Resolving and Transforming Disputes:
Indigenizing Legal Codes and Judicial Processes   250
3. Conclusion: Successful Governance and Peacemaking Requires
Inclusive Participation   269
Notes   270

CHAPTER FIVE: Rebuilding the Circle: Reestablishing Appropriate Means for Overcoming the Economic, Educational, Psychological, and Social Problems of Physical and Cultural Genocide 281

    1. Nurturing the Circle: American Indian Nation Sovereignty and Economic Development 282

    2. The Spiral of Renewal: Appropriate Indian Education 317

    3. Re-creating the Circle: Healing the Wounds and Returning to Harmony: Healing Historical Trauma and Grief: Transforming the Wound to Medicine 378

    Notes 395

PART THREE

Completing the Circle Through Appropriate Leadership and Collaboration and an Overview of the Re-creation Process 407

CHAPTER SIX: Working in the Circle: Appropriate Leadership, Collaboration, and Consulting to Apply Traditional Values Appropriately for the Twenty-First Century 408

    1. Returning to Traditional Leadership in Indian Nations: The Example of LaDonna Harris 410

    2. Facilitators and Resource Persons for the People: Consulting with Indian Nations as Collaborators 419

    3. Completing the Re-creation of the Circle: An Overview of the Process 436

    Notes 445

BIBLIOGRAPHY 451

INDEX 488

Introduction and Acknowledgments

LaDonna Harris, Stephen M. Sachs,
Barbara Morris, Deborah Esquibel Hunt,
Gregory A. Cajete, Benjamin Broome,
Phyllis M. Gagnier, and Jonodev Chaudhuri

Re-creating the Circle is a collective undertaking by Indian people and their allies that focuses on American Indian and Alaska Native self-determination: the returning of Indigenous peoples and people to effective sovereignty, self-sufficiency, and harmony, that they may revert to living well in their own communities while partnering with their neighbors, the nation, and the world for mutual advancement. We have carried out this project in an Indigenous way, by weaving the perspectives and styles of individual contributors into a larger whole that provides a broader understanding of the issues and events than we could have achieved if we had compiled separate statements. We took this approach because American Indian affairs are extremely complex—so much so, in fact, that no one person can have a complete perspective or full understanding of them. We can provide a thorough analysis only through a dialogue of multiple voices. This traditional Native way of approaching life's important issues, as chapter 1 shows, is increasingly being taken in the contemporary world, where, for example, participatory workplaces increase quality, productivity, and efficiency though team process, and physicians and other technical experts find functioning in teams necessary to produce satisfactory results.

This book arose from a series of collaborations that began in 1992 to develop articles and papers on a variety of interrelated topics. Our elder and advisor has been LaDonna Harris (Comanche), founder and president of Americans for Indian Opportunity (AIO) and a leading catalyst of progress in Native American affairs and policy for more than four decades. This volume is offered as a tribute to her continuing contribution to improving the lives of Native and other peoples; the issues the book discusses are among those in which she has played an important collaborative role in attaining major advances. Stephen Sachs presents a perspective on her career and approach in chapter 6. Harris took the lead in developing the theme of each chapter in consultation with the volume editors, and she provided guidance and specific input on their revisions. Thus, we designate her as this volume's "mentor and editor."

Two volume editors were involved in drafting the book and, along with Harris, in editing the entire work. Stephen Sachs, professor emeritus of political science at Indiana University–Purdue University Indianapolis and editor of the online journal *Indigenous Policy*, served as coordinating editor of the project and was involved in the drafting of all of the chapters. Barbara Morris (Comanche and Cherokee) served as a coauthor of chapter 3 and shared in the editing of the entire volume. She is professor of government and provost and vice president for academic affairs at Fort Lewis College in Durango, Colorado, and has long been involved in the leadership of the American Political Science Association's (APSA) Race, Ethnicity and Politics section, including serving as co-president in 1998–1999.

Five contributing authors were involved in the writing and editing of one or more sections of the book. Deborah Esquibel Hunt (whose maternal grandmothers are Cherokee) is a project officer at the American Indian College Fund. She has served Jefferson County Schools as program coordinator of the Title VII Indian Education Program at the Office of Educational Equity in Golden, Colorado, and is a former assistant professor of social work at Highlands University in Las Vegas, New Mexico. She partnered in drafting and editing parts of chapters 2, 5, and 6 and was the initial drafter of the section of a paper that was developed into section 3 of chapter 5, concerning healing individual and community dysfunction resulting from colonialism and appropriately working with and serving Indian communities and people.[1]

Gregory A. Cajete (Tewa), Santa Clara Pueblo, New Mexico, director of Native American Studies and associate professor in the College of Education at the University of New Mexico, drafted the major portion of the Indian education section in chapter 5 and shared in editing the entire section. Benjamin J. Broome, currently professor of communications at Arizona State University, while on the faculty of George Mason University was one of the facilitators in the inclusive participatory strategic planning process the Comanche used to build harmonizing community consensus that is discussed in chapter 4, section 1, and he cooperated in the drafting of that section. Phyllis Gagnier (Algonquin) provided the first portion of the title of this book ("Re-creating the Circle"), coauthored part of the education section in chapter 5, and assisted with editing several parts of the book. She is the creator of From the Heart Training and Consulting. She has worked with numerous Indian nations on educational development, nonviolent conflict resolution, and cultural projects, including the development of the Telly Award–winning video production *From the Heart of a Child*, about substance-abuse intervention, and the video production *Awee Sha No Tsa* (My Child Will Return to Me). Jonodev Osceola Chaudhuri (Muscogee), chief justice of the Muscogee (Creek) Nation Supreme Court and an appellate judge for the San Manuel Band of Serrano Mission Indians, as well as a practicing attorney and former judge for two other tribes, collaborated in writing chapter 4, section 2, concerning Indian nations indigenizing their dispute resolution, legal process, and law.

We are extremely appreciative of the assistance of several people in developing *Re-creating the Circle*. Michael Chapman, former special assistant to the assistant secretary of the interior for Indian affairs, and Faith Roessel, former coordinator of the Administration Working Group on American Indians and Alaska Natives, made extremely helpful comments and provided much useful information concerning the building of government-to-government relations between the federal government and Indian tribes, discussed in chapter 3. Jeff Corntassel, associate professor in the Indigenous Governance Programs at the University of Victoria, in Victoria, British Columbia, contributed important research and editing ideas to the drafting and revising of chapter 3 and made useful comments for the development of several sections of the book. Sharon O'Brien, professor of Indigenous Native Studies at the University of Kansas, undertook a thorough reading of the entire manuscript and contributed many helpful comments for improving the text. Edgar Sachs read the various drafts of all the chapters, providing numerous editing suggestions throughout this volume. Leah Ingraham assisted us in obtaining American Indian and Alaska Native health statistics and made a number of useful suggestions. Dianne Russell copyedited the manuscript, improving the presentation, and Bonnie Cobb compiled the bibliography. Robert Swanson compiled the index.

Re-creating the Circle is a holistic consideration of the ongoing process of returning American Indian and Alaska Native peoples to sovereignty, self-sufficiency, and harmony, enabling them to collaborate with their neighbors and tribal governments to be effective partners in the practice of federalism in the United States for the betterment of the country and the planet. The phrase "Re-creating the Circle" reflects the importance of the circle as a symbol of wholeness in Native American cultures (a topic chapter 1 develops), a quality that needs continuous renewal in the life of the people. In 1931, during the depths of the depredations that colonialism visited on Indians, Black Elk commented that "the nation's hoop is broken and scattered."[2] Today the hoop, or circle, of many Native nations is in the process of rejuvenation.

As a work on Indigenous renewal, this volume begins discussing in chapter 1 just what is being renewed: Native American traditions and how those ways are increasingly relevant today, both for Indigenous people and for the wider world. The underlying lesson of the chapter, and of the entire book, is how traditional Native values can be appropriately applied to the circumstances of the twenty-first century in ways that enhance continuing positive development.

Chapter 2 briefly examines the serious and continuing impact of colonialism on Indigenous North Americans and includes an outline of improvements that have been made over the last century, with indications of what yet needs to be overcome. This consideration sets the groundwork for the detailed analysis of the chapters that follow.

Because the basis for fostering Native renewal is self-determination and sovereignty (which we discuss further below), chapter 3 focuses on the re-creation of tribal governments and governance. It discusses how recognizing tribal governments as partners in U.S. federalism—partners that enjoy true government-to-government relations with federal, state, and local governments and agencies—is mutually beneficial to all the parties politically, economically, and socially. Chapter 3 examines the development of relations between tribal governments and other governments, showing what has been achieved to date and what the major pitfalls and promises are for further collaborative work.

Because tribal communities cannot effectively develop themselves or partner well with others unless their own decision-making and adjudication processes are well functioning, chapter 4 examines the problem of overcoming inappropriate forms of government that were imposed on Indian nations by the U.S. government and that clash with community culture. The discussion looks at what some Indian communities have done to bring back governance that is consistent with traditional values in ways that are effective in current circumstances, first in community consensus building and decision making, and second in adjudication.

Because the project of Indigenous renewal is an integral whole whose interrelated aspects must be advanced simultaneously to achieve success, the sections that make up chapter 5 look at the other areas of Indigenous advancement. First, sovereignty, well-being, and partnership with others require adequate economic development, including sufficient infrastructure and services. But experience demonstrates that to be effective, economic development must be appropriate to the needs and culture of the community, which, at the very least, must guide economic activity to ensure that it appropriately enhances the whole of tribal development, of which it is an integral part. This discussion shows that, indeed, the normal Western view of economics must be expanded to encompass living well in harmonious relationship with the environment, human and physical.

Second, a crucial key to Indian renewal is proper education, from preschool through higher education to lifelong learning. This is partly a matter of gaining sufficient funding, but, more important, it is a problem of developing ways of learning and teaching that are relevant to the culture and learning style of the specific Native people concerned and that empower them to become who they are and to act effectively in their own communities and the wider world. Finally, much healing must be undertaken by many Indigenous people and communities in order to return to wholeness. Such healing involves the undertaking of activities and services that fit the particular individuals and communities and partner with them to honor the value of their survival as individuals and as peoples and to emphasize that, despite colonialist put-downs, they have much to be proud of in their traditions. It should also provide means for overcoming and transforming historical and ongoing grief and guilt. In many cases, this work can be carried out with the assistance of traditional or equivalent contemporary processes.

Finally, chapter 6 explores how the paths to renewal that chapters 3 through 5 detail might be undertaken. This exploration involves an examination of what constitutes appropriate Native leadership for the twenty-first century and what are appropriate ways for working with Indian nations and people. The last section of the chapter provides a short integrative conclusion to the book. The section also points out that American Indian renewal has global implications in the time of the United Nations' (UN) Second International Decade of the World's Indigenous People, the UN's Declaration on the Rights of Indigenous Peoples, and the rise of Native movements in Latin America that have had a significant impact on the region. Indeed, the book illuminates numerous lessons for development in other contexts from Native American experience.

In the course of the discussions in this volume, two questions of terminology raise broader concerns. First, the focus of this volume is on Native peoples and people in what is now the United States, although some of those Native nations and many of their relatives live outside the country's current borders. Indeed, the basic problems of colonialism and what needs to be done to overcome it, to differing degrees and in varying ways are fundamentally the same for Indigenous people around the world. In general, Indigenous people prefer to be referred to as members of their own nation. We do that in this book when we are speaking of specific peoples. But the question of which term is best to use to refer to Native people collectively in the United States does not have a simple answer.

During the 1960s it became popular to say "Native American" both because the term includes the officially named groupings of Alaska (and Hawaii) Natives and American Indians and because the word "Indian" had been imposed by colonial Europeans. It is widely believed, even among Indigenous Americans, that naming the original inhabitants of the Americas "Indians" was an error by Columbus, who thought he had arrived in India, making that name inappropriate on its face. It seems more likely, however, that the origin of "Indian" is the Spanish *en Dios*, or "in God," which stems from the positive things Columbus had to say about those he is credited with "discovering" on arriving in the New World. In any event, it has turned out that many Native people in the continental United States prefer "Indian" to "Native American." Other terms, such as "Indigenous," are sometimes used for collective reference. In our discourses here, we wish to be respectful of those of whom we speak, while at the same time we believe that some variety and avoidance of overcomplexity in language is a benefit to the reader. Therefore, although we sometimes use the official U.S. government term, "American

Indian and Alaska Native," as the most general collective term (and either "Native" or "Indian" as the more geographically specific collective), we often rotate among Native, Indian, and Indigenous when speaking intertribally.

Second, we are not entirely happy with the term "sovereignty" as defined in the Western lexicon. But because of its wide use, particularly in Indian affairs, we cannot avoid it. From the perspective of most Indigenous people, what is involved in sovereignty is a natural right to autonomy, or self-determination, that people have as individuals and as members of collective entities such as clans, bands, tribes, and federations. But because actions (and nonactions) have consequences and we are all related ("all" traditionally including not only human beings but all beings), autonomy is not absolute but exists within an agreed-to set of relationships, traditionally often seen as involving respect, responsibility, reciprocity, and redistribution in order to keep everything in harmony and balance or, as the Diné, say, beauty. This definition is not far from the way sovereignty is viewed in U.S. federalism, in which both the states and the federal government are often referred to as "sovereign," meaning they each have independent spheres of jurisdiction within a larger relationship. As we consider that tribal governments are governments within the system of American federalism (a major focus of chapter 3), this definition of sovereignty is appropriate. However, we also note that the entire history of federalism has involved arguments about what the proper extents of jurisdiction are. Some would find the term "self-determination" more appropriate than "sovereignty," and indeed "self-determination" has been a key legal term in Indian affairs since the 1970s. The problem with it for many Native people is that the actions of the federal government in relation to Indian nations have not always corresponded with the common meaning of "self-determination." We argue in this work that Native self-determination would benefit all Americans if its full meaning were honored.

It is important to note that in speaking of federalism and tribal governments in this work, we do not give full treatment to two important issues. First, although the territorial jurisdictions of tribal governments are on tribal lands, mostly in rural areas, today, both as a matter of economics and past U.S. government policy, almost two-thirds of tribal members live off reservations, whereas most services for Native Americans are delivered on usually distant reservations. Thus, there is a pressing need to provide adequate services and a voice in how they are delivered to urban

Native people. In addition, there is a need to ensure that off-reservation tribal members have an appropriate voice at home, for example, by including Comanches in some cities in deliberations of tribal policy (which we discuss in chapter 4), and by considering the proposal that Navajos in Albuquerque be empowered to organize their own Navajo governance chapter.[3]

Second, in focusing on federally recognized tribes (and to some extent state-recognized tribes) and their members, along with their relations with federal, state, and local governments, we do not develop the major questions concerning which nations are officially recognized and how the recognition process works. Similarly, crucial questions exist regarding who is and is not a tribal member and how such decisions are made. Unless these sets of concerns are equitably and appropriately resolved according to the principles set forth in the unfolding of this volume, the Indigenous restoration that we promote in these pages will be incomplete at best.

It is our hope that the discussion in the following chapters in some small way will assist in returning American Indian nations to sovereignty, self-sufficiency, and harmony as full partners in American federalism and society. More broadly, we hope these pages will be helpful in improving the condition of Indigenous people around the Earth and in bringing into being a better approach to development in general and improved ways of doing many things, for the benefit of all.

Notes

1. Sachs et al., "Recreating the Circle." Hunt drafted Part 3, Section A.
2. Neihardt, *Black Elk Speaks*, 230.
3. "Indian and Indigenous Developments: U.S. Developments," "Tribal Developments," and "States, Localities, and Indian Nations," Indigenous Policy 17, no. 1.

Part One
The Harmony of the Circle and the Impact of Colonialism

One

The Harmony of the Circle

AMERICAN INDIAN TRADITIONS AND THEIR RELEVANCE FOR THE
TWENTY-FIRST CENTURY

Stephen M. Sachs

American Indian people today are struggling to return to effective sovereignty, harmony, and self-sufficiency after more than five hundred years of colonialism. Before the European invasion brought devastating physical and cultural genocide, the tribal and band societies of what is now the United States were in general quite harmonious and democratic, providing mutually supportive relationships and a relatively high quality of life for virtually all of their members. The more than five hundred Indian nations were each unique in the details of their quite varied cultures but shared a common set of core values.[1] These basic values, applied in different ways and to differing degrees by each people, and by the same peoples in changing circumstances, provided the basis for good lives in usually well-functioning societies. The heart of the struggle for renewal by Indian nations and people today is to find the freedom, resources, and ways to return to these traditional principles in the context of the twenty-first century. Thus, a reexamination of traditional ways is necessary to recover what many Indian people no longer remember due to cultural genocide. Revitalizing Indian traditions and developing ways to apply and integrate them appropriately to the circumstances of contemporary life with an eye to building a positive future is not only essential for Indian people but is also relevant to the entire world at the dawn of a new millennium.

In this period of both troubling and hopeful change, with all too often violent conflict in the United States and throughout the world, there is a growing concern for rediscovering community on all levels that will renew harmony among human beings and between humanity and the Earth. The collapse of so-called Communism in Eastern Europe (although it involves much more than this, and only partially involves this problem) reminds us that extremely collectivist approaches to human affairs generally fail to achieve the good lives for everyone at which they aim, because these unitary approaches deny the diversity of interest and outlook upon which any true community must be based.[2] At the same time, the current U.S. experience suggests that overreliance upon individualism as the basis of social relations may create the very war of all against all within society that Thomas Hobbes and other prudent liberals sought to escape through the social contract.[3] John Locke tells us that in forming a social contract, people escape the scarcity of the state of nature in order to enter a society that offers the opportunity for potentially unlimited abundance.[4] Yet at the opening of the twenty-first century, we are approaching the carrying capacity of the terrestrial environment. We find that our lust for unending economic development threatens our very existence. Thus, the laws of the state of nature that require us to consume no more than we need now apply within society.[5]

In the midst of contemporary crises, it seems wise to reexamine our basic concepts of politics and public policy in hope of avoiding the dangers, while also grasping opportunities to move ahead in the best way possible. Although the places to which we can look for assistance in this enterprise are virtually unlimited, it is important to note that a great deal can be learned from societies whose members lived quite successfully in considerable harmony with one another and with nature on this continent on which we live. Traditional Native American societies, although not perfect, enjoyed a generally high quality of life, with virtually no poverty or crime, and with mechanisms to provide for those who were not well off. These societies furnished a great deal of emotional and physical support through the members of extended families, as well as a sufficient variety of choices of social roles, so that almost everyone could find acceptance and develop self-esteem. The virtues of these societies are attested to in numerous ethnographies and commentaries.[6]

Christopher Columbus's first impression recorded in his diary of the

Native people he encountered is relevant: "They are loving people, without covetness. . . . They love their neighbors as themselves, and their speech is the sweetest and gentlest in the world."[7] More to the point is a statement in 1782 by Hector St. John Crevecoeur in *Letters of an American Farmer*: "There must be in their [the Indians'] social bond something singularly captivating, and far superior to anything to be boasted among us; for thousands of Europeans are [have become] Indians, and we have no example of even one of those Aborigines having from choice become Europeans."[8] This is not to say that Indigenous North American societies were perfect in conception or fully lived up to their basic values. No society is or does. Rather, it is to say that as imperfect human beings, we all have a great deal to learn from one another.

Indeed, there is a long history in Western political thought of learning from Native American traditions, although those traditions were generally misunderstood by those who commented on them.[9] It is clear from reading *The Second Treatise on Civil Government* that Locke was influenced by reports of tribal life in North America.[10] Several places in *The Social Contract* and the discourses indicate that the Indian experience had an effect upon Rousseau.[11] Much of Marx's theory of social evolution follows from Locke's and Rousseau's understanding of Indigenous society and was later confirmed in his reading of Morgan's studies of the life of the Six Nations, which we call the Iroquois.[12] Marx and Friedrich Engels found the quality of life and the level of interpersonal relations of what appeared to be earlier forms of society so fine when compared with those of their own time that they came to believe that those natural human relations could return in a new form once the problem of scarcity was solved by the development of capital to a sufficiently high level.

Moreover, new scholarship now makes clear that the Indian experience with democracy and federation had a profound impact upon the framers of the U.S. Constitution.[13] However, the framers did not go as far in developing democracy as had the Indigenous people they learned from. Although we need not repeat the analyses of prior social thinkers, their positive reaction to North American tribal societies is an indication that surveying the Indigenous experience might be helpful in finding good ways to deal with our present difficulties. At the same time, it is useful for Indian people to do so in order to revitalize their traditional roots as they renew their own lives and societies in the context of the twenty-first century. Therefore, section 1 of this chapter surveys that tradition, and section 2 continues the survey to show the relevance of North

American Native tradition to dealing with problems in contemporary American and world societies.

1. Traditional American Indian Politics, Society, and Culture

When we examine traditional (before the impact of European contact) politics among Native American tribes and bands, we see that politics had a somewhat different character than has been accepted by the main-stream of Western political theory beginning with Hobbes and, perhaps, Machiavelli.[14] Traditional American Indian politics is primarily about finding consensus within a community.[15] The primary function of tra-ditional Native American political leaders is to facilitate the building of consensus.[16] Power is an important resource for doing this, but it is not the central element for determining "the authoritative allocation of values" (or for determining "who gets what, when, where, how").[17] Moreover, power in American Indian tribal and band societies is only partly a vehicle for control. It is also a source of empowerment. Tribal and band politics have very important cooperative elements along with competitive aspects. At the heart of this politics is a set of communal relationships based upon mutual respect, emphasizing both the com-munity and the individual, so that in a very important sense, the whole is equal to the part.

The principle of respect for all people and indeed all beings (includ-ing the Earth, which was considered to be alive) was developed from practical experience, which taught that unresolved conflict was very dan-gerous to everyone, and that to live decently—and often to survive—required cooperation among the people in the community. This could best be obtained through an inclusiveness that emphasized honoring each person in the community (including all those affected by a deci-sion, who were given a say in processes that built consensus) and a gen-erosity that ensured that the basic economic needs of everyone in the community were met. (Similarly, one needed to respect the nonhuman beings in the environment to keep nature in balance, so that there would be enough food and other products for the people to survive and live well over time.) Therefore, the aim of life and of the natural order was har-mony and balance in all relations. But from this perspective, harmony and balance are not seen as automatic. One has to work continually to attain and maintain them at every level. As the Chaudhuris, who have long been involved with the Muscogee, say of them: "Given the unpredictable elements of nature and the quirks of human nature, the search for harmony takes sustained effort in all social institutions."[18] Hence, in personal inner work and in all relationships, including with the natural environment and all its nations of plants, animals, and other forms, one continually participates in processes for returning to harmony. Each Native culture did this in a different manner, but almost all followed the same general principles (at least until they become too large or events put them out of balance), an important aspect of which was working to build and maintain community consensus.[19]

We can see the consensus-building nature of traditional Native American politics consistently by surveying what is known about the life of tribes and bands in North America before European contact.[20] For example, among the Inuit, Unalit, and other Arctic bands that are commonly called Eskimos, there was no formal leadership or governmental process.[21] Through an informal consensus, a man (often the best hunter) was deferred to for leadership of the community. So long as he was considered a good leader (i.e., he was wise and acted effectively in accordance with community values), people would follow his advice in community affairs (such as when and where to move the encampment or when and how to undertake a hunt). But as soon as people were not satisfied with him, they would no longer follow his leadership. If someone in the community acted sufficiently outrageously to be considered a danger or serious problem to the group, the community needed to reach consensus before action could be taken against the alleged offender. Often the leader, or headman, of the community would initiate the discussion (in effect, a trial), but nothing would be done unless and until general agreement was reached as to the propriety of any action.[22]

The Yakimas of the Columbia River area in the Pacific Northwest also lived in small groups (of from 50 to 1,500 people, generally averaging from 100 to 150 people).[23] Residents of each village met together daily in a general council to discuss and decide important matters. Leadership was exercised by elders respected for their wisdom, outstanding individuals renowned for their virtue (particularly generosity, fairness, and bravery), and those who were skilled in activities of importance to the community, such as fishing and hunting. Leaders advised the group as a whole and held considerable influence, but decisions were made by consensus. Villages generally were led by a headman and a small council. These individuals held their positions only so long as they retained the ongoing support of the community. When such support was withheld, they ceased to be leaders and new leaders arose according to the needs of the village. Closely connected villages formed bands, and in times of stress, several bands or villages might temporarily come together, but no regular structures existed for formal collaboration.

Similarly, the Chiricahua Apache of the Southwest lived in small bands, each with its own consensus-based governance.[24] They lived by hunting, gathering, raiding, and agriculture. Each band and, within it, each local group, was guided by one or more recognized leaders assisted by a number of subordinates. Important decisions were made at band or local group meetings at which all adults were present and male heads of household usually spoke to represent their families, although wives and unmarried sons and daughters might contribute to the discussion. A man would become a leader if enough people respected him sufficiently to give him their loyalty, and he would maintain that leadership role only so long as he maintained that respect and loyalty. People dissatisfied with a local or band leader could simply move away to another band or group. As in many bands and tribes, being of good family was an advantage in gaining the respect necessary to become a leader, and a leader was almost always the head of an extended family. But the primary basis of leadership was being respected for ability and good qualities, as demonstrated by an individual's achievements. He must be wise, respectful of others, able in war, capable in managing his own and his family's affairs, and generous. Thus wealth was an aspect of qualification for leadership as a sign of ability and as a source of the generosity that leaders were expected to exhibit by hosting prominent people, putting on feasts, and providing for those less well off.

The functions of a leader included being an advisor in community affairs, a peacemaker, and a leader in war. Although leaders could command in combat, they had no power of control in civil governance beyond what was supported by public opinion. To the extent that they were respected and were persuasive (a quality contributing to respect), leaders exercised influence in the forming of community views. However, even in the peacemaker role, leaders had only the authority of mediators when deviant acts or major disputes occurred. Because Chiricahua individuals needed one another's help in a variety of economic and social activities (as is normally the case in band and tribal societies), the main influence for following social norms, including reaching settlement when necessary, was the pressure of public opinion (in which women played an important role in traditional Indian societies, as we will discuss later). Thus, leaders were under continuing scrutiny to act well and needed to be concerned for the needs and views of the members of the community.

In particular, the band leader needed to listen carefully to and take into account the advice of the local group leaders. They, in turn, had to be especially responsive to the leading heads of family, who were obligated to be responsive to the adult members of their family. Thus, power and influence were widely disbursed in Chiricahua society. Respected elders had the most political influence, but this influence and respect itself rested upon the opinions of the community members in a culture that emphasized respect for all community members (and indeed all beings). This dynamic is typical in band societies, including the more dispersed Ojibwa, who lived generally in single-family units engaged in hunting and gathering in the woodland and lake country of what is now the northern Midwest and adjacent Canada; the hunting and gathering Utes of the Rocky Mountains; and the Comanches, who we will discuss below in connection with overcoming contemporary disharmony through returning to institutions and processes that apply traditional values in contemporary context.[25]

The basic values and underlying pattern of consensus-based decision making of band societies were also found in the larger and more complicated tribal societies in North America who had not yet begun to develop the attributes of states. For example, the Diné, popularly known as Navajo, were a society governed largely at the band level with somewhat more complexity in their social organization owing to their strong clan structure.[26] Clans (extended family units) were important in public affairs in part because they were responsible for the behavior of their own members (e.g., regarding debts, torts, and crimes). Because clans gave considerable emotional and economic support to their members, pressure from kinsmen, especially elders, was likely to have exerted a strong influence. In speaking of more contemporary local governance, Kluckhohn and Leighton describe what oral history shows was true of the old band government and which was typical of traditional Native American government in general:

> Headmen have no powers of coercion, save possibly that some people fear them as potential witches, but they have responsibilities. They are often expected, for example, to look after the interests of the needy who are without close relatives or whose

relatives neglect them [a rare occurrence in traditional times], but all they can do with the neglectful ones is talk to them. No program put forward by a headman is practicable unless it wins public endorsement or has the tacit backing of a high proportion of the influential men and women of the area.[27]

The two authors go on to say that at meetings, "the Navaho pattern was for discussion to be continued until unanimity was reached, or at least until those in opposition felt it was useless or impolitic to express disagreement."[28] They point out, however, that although public meetings provided an occasion for free voicing of sentiments and the thrashing out of disagreements, the most important part of traditional Diné political decision making took place informally in negotiations among clan and other leaders representing their respective groups, who regularly discussed community concerns face to face. (We discuss the important role of women in traditional politics later.)

The underlying principles of consensus politics based upon mutual respect can be seen in somewhat different forms in two upper Plains tribes who lived quite differently from the Diné: the Hidatsa and the Lakota. The Hidatsa were a relatively sedentary people who farmed, hunted, fished, and gathered along the Upper Missouri River in the eighteenth and nineteenth centuries.[29] Formed from a mix of peoples, their exact living arrangements varied over time. From the late eighteenth century until 1845, they constituted three villages, which in one period were independent and in another politically linked. In 1845, they moved into a single new village. However, at various periods the Hidatsa moved annually from their summer residences to winter camps. Social organization was complex, with a system of clans and moieties and an age-grade system that emphasized the influence of elders in political life beyond the universal attributes of age (e.g., as relating to wisdom, developing an even temperament, having a proven record) as a factor in qualification for political leadership in traditional North American societies.[30] All else being equal, a person in a higher age grade would be chosen for a leadership position. If a young man of good record attempted to assert leadership, the elders would usually tell him to be patient: "When you are older and have demonstrated your ability in other things, the people will want you to be their leader. . . ."[31]

Indeed, it was thought that capable people of good character should have a chance at leadership when they were ready for it. Therefore, it was the custom that many civil positions—such as leader of the summer hunt, manager of the winter camp, or leader of ventures beyond the summer village—were held for short duration. This practice diversified power and fostered an equality following from the principle of mutual respect. War leaders might be more permanent, but they could lead only to the extent that other men were willing to follow them. Thus, upon finding dissatisfaction with their leadership, many war leaders had the tact (good manners were required by mutual respect) to invite discussion of the issues and attempt to satisfy the complainers. If they could not, they would suggest that someone else lead.

The same was true of civil leaders. A Hidatsa camp or village leader, advised by a council of elders, might be able to enforce decisions with the help of the men of the Black Mouth age grade (a partially senior grade below that of elder), who acted as police. But any family or person who wished to move elsewhere could do so. Moreover, important civil decisions and questions of war and peace were not made by leaders (although leaders were influential) but rather at council meetings where everyone was represented. Normally, considerable time was taken in making decisions so that every household and subgroup had a chance to consider the matter and have an elder male member express its views. No decision could be made until it was unanimously accepted, which might take extensive negotiation.

Religion was an important factor in all aspects of Hidatsa life, including politics (as it was in different ways and to different degrees in all traditional Indian nations, as we discuss later). Every village and village ward had a prominent spiritual protector, with a powerful bundle, and all top civil and military leaders were those of spiritual ability and often were leaders of important religious rites. Because spiritual leaders were not an organized priesthood, or hierarchy, in a society in which all members had medicine, religion sanctioned and did not diminish Hidatsa democracy on the basis of mutual respect. Thus, religion was a strong force in supporting and maintaining tribal values and ways with which, as a rule, it was fully consistent.

The Hidatsa's neighbors, the Lakota (Western Sioux), functioned in the late eighteenth to mid-nineteenth century on the basis of essentially the same political principles, despite differences of social organization and economics.[32] The Lakota were primarily wide-ranging hunters and gatherers. They had no clans, moieties, or age grades, and descent was effectively bilateral. The more varied life of the Lakota made more explicit the fluidity of governance common to the Hidatsa and a great many other Native peoples. The Lakota were widespread over the northern plains, with the buffalo the mainstay of their economy and hence central to life. They were one of an association of seven tribes that may once have been a federation. The Lakota themselves were composed of seven bands, whose members lived in independent camps, or *tiyospaye*, for much of the year.

A *tiyospaye*, in effect and sometimes in fact an extended family, could be formed any time enough people came together in a camp or related camps to establish a council of several categories of office. As was the case in units in quite a number of Indigenous societies, membership in a *tiyospaye* was voluntary. People could join and leave the camp at will. This placed a restraining influence upon political authority, pressuring leaders to treat people respectfully and keep them happy. Among the men of the council was the *itancan*, the symbolic father or titular leader of the *tiyospaye*. He acted as facilitator at council meetings, and through his moral and persuasive leadership and personal generosity, he carried out his responsibility for seeing to the welfare of the members of the *tiyospaye*. This responsibility included the heavy burden of caring for the sick, orphaned, and indigent. An *itancan* was chosen by his fellow council members, following the consensus feeling of the community. He was expected to be kind, generous, wise, patient, diplomatic, and brave. He would be removed by the council (if he did not resign) if he became ineffective or acted improperly. Typically, an *itancan* appointed two trusted friends, often younger warriors, to keep him informed of the affairs of the community and to act as his diplomats.

Major decision making was undertaken at council meetings at which anyone, including elder women, could speak. No decision could be made until a consensus was reached. Often the *itancan* would simply listen to the discussion, but he could be influential in commenting at key moments. Unlike many small bands, in which decisions were enforced by pressure of public opinion or on occasion by community members after a community leader had facilitated the making of a consensus on a course of action (in effect, a trial), the Lakota did have a regular mechanism for enforcing council decisions and established customary norms of behavior (as did many Indian societies that were larger than small bands). The *Wakiconza* was a committee of two to six men chosen every spring to oversee the movement of the camp, arbitrate disputes, supervise the community buffalo hunt, umpire games, and oversee all wagers. The

Wakiconza was assisted by the *Akicita*, who were responsible for enforcement and carrying messages. The *Akicita* had sufficient independence to require anyone, including leaders, to obey their orders. The *Akicita* were kept within the limits of their job by careful selection, a limited term of office, and pressure of public opinion. Any *Akicita* who became tyrannical was taken in hand by the military societies, which played an important role in the warrior life of Lakota society. Thus checks and balances were built into social organization. That these checks and balances were devised deliberately is made clear by the traditional story of "The Festival of the Little People," whose moral states: "It is not wise to put the strong in authority over the weak."[33]

When the camp moved, responsibility for governance rotated with the circumstances. The *Wakiconza* decided the route and led the line of travel. When movement began, the *Akicita* encircled the people, watching for signs of external danger while making sure no one fell behind, strayed from the chosen route, or acted improperly. If the people were threatened by enemies, the war leader (*blotahunca*) and his warriors took charge, just as they would if the camp were threatened. Once the people reached their destination, the *Akicita* of the march were dismissed and a more relaxed camp life returned. Similarly, when a buffalo hunt was undertaken, the *Wakiconza* sent out scouts and planned the hunt. Then the *Akicita* were put in charge to coordinate the movement of the hunters.

Although there was regularly cooperation among Lakota in different groups, each *tiyospaye* made its own decisions independently about whether to join in some larger activity. Furthermore, during the years when difficulties with the U.S. government became more intense, warriors in a *tiyospaye* sometimes acted on their own, without the agreement of the civil leaders or the consensus of the community. However, at times, particularly during the winter, several Lakota bands would come together in a single camp with governance following the pattern of the *tiyospaye* but adjusted for the larger community circumstance.

The band *itancan* and *Wakiconza* formed a multiband council with one of each of the *tiyospaye* types of officials performing his particular function for the multiband camp. *Akicita* were then appointed to police the camp, with any appeals resulting from their actions referred to the council. In addition, four warriors with the best character and achievements were selected as head shirtwearers to act as peacemakers in the camp. Shirtwearers served a life tenure but could be deposed by the council for major infractions. Although some of the details are different, camp governance was essentially the same for an annual Sun Dance as for other occasions, with the difference that spiritual leaders played the leadership roles. The Sun Dance was a major summer religious ritual for the renewal of the Earth and the people, and often attended by Lakota from more than one band. However, within the ceremony itself, spiritual leaders governed completely (although they were subject to the same pressures of public opinion as the secular leadership was, with the possibility that they could lose prestige and ceremony participants should they be seen as acting improperly).

Major decisions by the council in multiband Lakota camps involved the band leaders on the council acting in accordance with the consensus of their own *tiyospaye* and discussion moving back and forth between informal discussions among *tiyospaye* members and council meetings until a general consensus could be reached. This is the principle on which the larger federations of tribes typically operated. Examination of one such case presents helpful insight into the general nature of the power of leaders and the process of decision making that in different ways and to different degrees pervaded traditional North American Indigenous societies. Bruce G. Trigger describes the traditional ways of the Wendat, more widely known as the Huron, who lived around Lakes Huron and Erie.[34]

The Huron were a confederation of several tribes numbering from thirty to forty thousand people in 1634. They lived partially intermingled with one another in settlements of as many as two thousand people that consisted of a central town and surrounding villages. Their social organization included a clan structure. In each community, each clan segment had two formal chiefs, known as *Yarihawa* ("he is a great voice"), who were chosen from among the men of the clan that held the right to serve in that office. Their primary functions were to announce decisions arrived at by a process of consensus formation that involved discussion by all the adult men and women of their group and to facilitate the discussion process. Chiefs could advise and persuade, but they could not decide. No action could be taken until it had been acceded to by every person who was affected by it. In practice, that meant that decision making tended to include the concerns of everyone involved. To reach consensus on a proposal, the group would continue to modify it to take into account each person's concerns until almost everyone supported the decision, and the few who did not, having been heard and seeing nothing to gain by further discussion, accepted the view of the group.

The chief's first duty was to assist his own group to come to a consensus and then to represent his people in negotiating with the chiefs of other groups. Trigger states:

> Huron Chiefs had no constitutional authority to coerce their followers or force their will on anyone. Moreover, individual Huron were sensitive about their honor and intolerant of external constraints, and friends and relatives would rally to the support of someone who believed himself insulted by a chief. Overbearing behavior by a chief might, therefore, encourage a violent reaction and lead to conflicts within or between lineages. In the long run, chiefs who behaved arrogantly or foolishly tended to alienate support and would be deposed by their own lineages. The ideal Huron Chief was a wise and brave man who understood his followers and won their support by means of his generosity, persuasiveness, and balanced judgment.[35]

The two chiefs of each clan segment at the local level were the civil chief and the war chief. The civil or peace chiefs, who were primary, were concerned with matters of everyday life, from settling disputes to arranging feasts, dances, and games to negotiating foreign treaties. The separation of peace and war chiefs, and the primacy of the civil chief, was typical of many tribes. Among the Cheyenne, for example, a chief of one of the military societies, upon becoming one of the forty-four peace chiefs, would have to resign his chieftainship of the military society.[36] This primacy of civilian over military leadership is similar to the U.S. Constitution having the president, a civilian, as commander in chief of the armed forces. It may well be that the older tribal practice is the basis, or at least a contributing source, for the U.S. practice.

The national government of each Huron tribe consisted of a council made up of chiefs of the clan segments in each community. (The one exception was the Tahontaenrat Tribe, which lived in a single settlement, so that its community and national governments were coterminous.) The confederacy council appears to have been composed of the civil chiefs of the various national councils. The national and confederacy councils had no power to compel the groups whom their members represented.

Their function was to develop consensus through dialogue and mutual exchange among all the parties involved in the matters they considered. In order for the decisions of these councils to be effective, they had to be accepted by the constituents of the chiefs. This meant that national and confederacy affairs were discussed by citizens at the local level to a far greater extent than is true in modern federal republican governments, with the result that chiefs were usually far more representative of their constituency than elected representatives in the United States and many other Western and non-Western countries are today.

Underlying Huron politics was a culture that balanced strong concern for individual (e.g., person, family, clan) autonomy with a rigorous equalitarian moral sense of the good of all (e.g., family, clan, tribe) and respect for the views of others. Thus, there was an abhorrence of compelling action of anyone. But, at the same time, both by upbringing and ongoing experience, Huron people were very sensitive to the views of others and to the pressure of public opinion. If one acted improperly, one would lose honor and, eventually, necessary economic and social support if she or he went too far. In the Huron case, as in the case of many (but not all) Native North American peoples, this meant that, through honoring generosity, no one was allowed to be either poor or rich. Similarly, although certain political and social positions of authority might belong to specific clans or clan segments (but filled on the basis of perceived merit within that clan or segment), authority, and hence power, was widely dispersed so that individual offices carried limited authority. This system worked to keep effective the primary limitation on power: public opinion. This widespread arrangement in traditional North America is somewhat similar in effect to, although it is less formal and more extensive than, the later use of the combination of separation of powers, checks and balances, and direct and indirect elections by the framers of the U.S. Constitution, who almost surely were influenced by Indian practice (both directly and indirectly, as through influential English thinkers such as John Locke, who clearly incorporated Indian ideas and practice in their theories).

The Huron cultural and related structural basis of politics is in many ways typical of traditional Indian societies. In some way or other, virtually every North American culture developed its own unique way of dynamically balancing a set of seemingly opposite values to produce a harmonious unity (e pluribus unum?).

Beginning in terms of what we have been discussing, the first pair of opposites consists of freedom and autonomy for the individual (person and group) harmonized with the primacy of the whole (family, clan, working group or party, village, tribe, world, or whatever level of wholeness was relevant in a particular context). This balance is illustrated by the broad range of societies we briefly referred to above and can be seen in others representing additional geographic areas and ways of economic and social living.[37] The general principles applied even in the most diverse of cultures. For example, the collection of cultures in the Southwest referred to as Pueblos were strongly formal in their governance (particularly in contrast to the informality of their Diné neighbors).[38] Perhaps more than any other traditional North American societies, the Pueblos formally emphasized the spiritual nature of life. Life in the Pueblo cultures was tightly integrated with an emphasis upon unity that was perhaps the strongest of any traditional North American societies. Yet the individuality of person and group remained. In the cycle of the year's highly organized rituals, each individual had a distinct role.[39]

From what we know about them from the period of the Spanish Conquest of North America, Pueblos at first glance appear to be governed by a theocracy, which mostly follows their precontact practice. But the leading priests only set the spiritual and philosophical tone for government, and the governor (*cacique*, following the Spanish nomenclature) chosen by the council of priests, like chiefs elsewhere, could advise only, not command. The cacique and his assistants oversaw executive process and, like the European formal head of state, he announced decisions of the Pueblo council. But in legislative and judicial matters, including oversight of executions, decision making was undertaken through consensus by the council along the same general lines typical of Native American traditional government that we have discussed.[40] The consensus basis of Pueblo decision making can be seen to this day in a modernized form at Laguna Pueblo, where, over an extended period, discussion of issues goes back and forth between the members of the elected council and constituents until general consensus is reached and then made official by a unanimous council vote.[41]

Similarly, a number of traditional Native societies had strong hierarchical aspects that contrast with the general equalitarian nature of some of the Indian nations we have discussed. However, hierarchy in almost all of these societies did not carry so far as to negate the essential roles of participation and consensus building, although it might somewhat diminish them. The Kiowa, for example, had distinct socioeconomic classes, with strong competition for position and status, in which band leaders could give orders.[42] Yet neither political nor social position were hereditary (although good parentage was an advantage), for both had to be attained and maintained by achievement and a reputation for right living. Moreover, as in some of the other cases previously discussed, band leaders were strongly restrained by the fact that their followers were at liberty to leave them at will and join or form another band.

This was the case even in Kwakiutl (and other Pacific Northwest Coast) society, where amidst huge natural bounty, there was a more permanent hierarchy of largely inherited positions with leaders competing to outdo one another in huge giveaways (potlatches).[43] But, in matters of subsistence for living and many other aspects of life, participation and the need for consensus based upon the dignity of each person remained, even as collaboration and sharing ensured that persons with the lowest status had enough to live comfortably.

Along with uniting the principles of individuality and wholeness in traditional North American society, there was a harmonizing of competitiveness (among individuals and groups) and cooperation. Among the Plains Indians, such as the Lakota, for example, there were numerous opportunities to compete for honor by undertaking socially desirable actions and exhibiting the four virtues: bravery, fortitude, generosity, and wisdom.[44] Such might take place in warfare in which a man would be recognized for being among the first in a battle to touch an enemy or for leading a raid to steal horses from an enemy camp. When a young Lakota man went on his first buffalo hunt or undertook some honorable action, his father would often have the camp crier go round the village announcing that the father was giving away a horse to a poor family in honor of his son's deed.[45] Giving to those less fortunate was honorable and increased the community opinion of the benefactor. A woman would be honored for making beautiful articles of clothing and sharing them with others. Conversely, hoarding goods for oneself was dishonorable, and indeed any improper act reduced one's standing.

By channeling competitiveness into promoting helpfulness, American Indian societies tended to encourage collaboration.[46] This was accomplished more directly in other ways, however. One of the most important of these was inclusiveness, by providing everyone with a role in community affairs, as exemplified by the consensus decision-making processes discussed above. An essential element in the development and maintenance of cooperation was the acculturation to collaborative values, stressing the well-being of the whole before everything else while also providing continuing opportunities to participate in supporting the whole through activities involving mutual support.[47]

Extended family relations were also an important aspect of the maintenance of harmony and balance in community affairs. As Ella Deloria says of the Dakota:

> Kinship was the all-important matter. Its demands and dictates for all phases of social life were relentless and exact; but on the other hand, its privileges and honorings and rewarding prestige were not only tolerable but downright pleasant for all who conformed. By kinship all Dakota people were held together in a great relationship that was theoretically all-inclusive and co-extensive with the Dakota Domain. Everyone who was born a Dakota belonged in it; nobody need be left outside. [And since being Dakota, as with Indian societies generally, was more a matter of participation in the community than blood, kinship included all who effectively joined the community, whether they married in or were adopted, a common practice throughout traditional Native America.]
>
> ❧
>
> I can safely say that the ultimate aim of Dakota life, stripped of accessories, was quite simple: One must obey kinship rules: One must be a good relative. No Dakota who has participated in that life will dispute that. In the last analysis every other consideration was secondary—property, personal ambition, glory, good times, life itself. Without that aim and the constant struggle to attain it, the people would no longer be Dakota in truth. They would no longer be even human. To be a good Dakota then was to be humanized, civilized. And to be civilized was to keep the rules imposed by kinship for achieving civility, good manners, and a sense of responsibility toward every individual dealt with. Thus only was it possible to live communally with success; that is to say, with a minimum of friction and a maximum of good will.[48]

Deloria goes on to point out that kinship, like all the other principles we have been discussing, while not functioning perfectly, worked quite well in Indian society:

What I have given here is, of course, an ideal picture. But I can honestly say that hardly one in a hundred dared to be thought of as deviating from its rule, although there were always a few naturally heedless persons who persistently or occasionally disregarded it. But that at once classified them as with the *witko*—the naughty, irresponsible child, the outlaw adult, the mentally foolish, the drunk. No adult in his right mind cared to be so classed.[49]

A similar view of family is expressed about Cherokee ways, and beyond that about traditional Native Americans in general, by Michael Garrett:

> Because the survival and well-being of the individual is synonymous with that of the community, family plays a prominent role in our lives, . . . Many Native American people *are* a family in a real sense, because they identify themselves not by their own accomplishments, but by the nature of their relations and the energy they draw from those connections.[50]

Garrett goes on to point out that for the Cherokee, as for other traditional Indian peoples, the concept of "family" was part of larger metaphysical and spiritual concerns:

> The traditional view of family is universal in scope. "Family" extends well beyond immediate relatives to extended family relatives through the second cousin, members of the clan, members of the community or tribe, all other living creatures in this world, the natural environment and the universe itself. The entire universe is thought of as "a family" with each and every one of its members having a useful and necessary place in the Circle of Life, just as each strand creates the beauty and strength of the Web [of life].[51]
>
> [And,] In the traditional way, the prevalence of cooperation and sharing in the spirit of community is essential for harmony and balance.[52]

In Indian societies, the harmony of the individual within the whole was reinforced by a spirituality that pervaded all of life. This spirituality was consistent with the social values of each people and was an important building block in the development of individual and social integration.[53] For instance, if you go to a Lakota (or Dakota or Nakota) Sun Dance and ask the dancers why they endure four grueling days dancing beneath the hot sun without food or drink, they will not tell you that it is to gain prestige or to receive personal spiritual power, although those things may come to them. The dancers will tell you that they give themselves away that "the people may live."[54] Their giveaway is first to the Great Spirit, second to the people, and only last for themselves (and even so, only so that they can play their proper part in the greater whole).

Indeed, in different ways, as we will discuss further, every Native American society functioned under spiritual principles of harmony (or as the Diné say, beauty) that involved harmonizing the individual and the whole. In some more individualistic band societies, such as the Comanche, which had individual and small-group ceremonies and spiritual practices but no overarching rituals, both the religion and the sociopolitical practice put more responsibility on the individual to find his or her place in the larger whole than did societies with strong collective rituals, such as the Pueblos.[55] Yet, these latter societies, as we discussed above, still provided spiritual as well as social roles for each individual. Many societies, such as the Lakota and the Cheyenne, had both individual ceremonies, such as when a person seeking a deeper understanding of her or his purpose in life embarked on a vision quest (an individual retreat), and one or more collective rituals of renewal of the Earth and the people, such as the Sun Dance.[56] Moreover, the individual rituals and spiritual experiences had important societal aspects, even as there were unique individual roles in the collective rituals. For example, for Plains tribes, the visions one might receive on a vision quest, in a dream, in a Sun Dance, or at any time, often contained important information for the society as well as for the individual.[57] Thus, there were dream societies to help interpret a person's dreams and, when proper, to help that person share her or his dreams in appropriate ways with the community.

A very important aspect of the principle of inclusiveness is mutual empowerment of the individual person and group and of the larger group and society. By giving each person and group continual opportunity to participate, in his or her own unique way, in decision making and in the work of providing for the welfare of the larger group and community, Native cultures provided each person and social unit the freedom, sense of purpose, and opportunity for self-actualization and development necessary for their own realization in ways that directly provided for the needs of the community. As we are beginning to learn in the contemporary workplace with the rise of employee involvement and team process, this method of harmonizing individual freedom with social purpose is exceedingly efficient, effective, and productive.[58]

Unity through diversity also provides for a high level of equality while allowing for differences in prestige. Whereas in hierarchical social systems, differences of function tend to be marked by significant differences in status, participatory systems tend to minimize status differences. For example, in differing ways in each society, men and women in Native American cultures carried out their separate functions and had a greater say in differing areas of social life. But this division of labor did not produce the difference in status and value that accompanied the dichotomy of social roles in Western society.[59] To the extent that in Western societies it could be said that a man's home is his castle, among traditional Native Americans, one might say that a man's home was her castle. Among the Haudenosaunee, for example, only men served as chiefs (sachems) on the intertribal council, but women held considerable power. In certain clans, the women, speaking through the Clan Mother, nominated the chiefs and had the power to remove them for misconduct.[60] In some tribes, women served as chiefs, but regardless of their formal role, women in traditional Native American societies held sway over their own affairs and wielded great influence in public affairs.[61] Indeed, a study of thirteen North American societies and multiple society culture areas north of what is now Mexico found that, traditionally, in all but one case, there was a balanced reciprocity between men and women.[62] Further research indicates that even that one case involved balanced reciprocity.[63]

A number of factors appear to account for the difference between Indian societies and pre-twentieth-century European society concerning the status and authority of women. One important reason was that Native American societies were based on mutual respect and individual autonomy. A related factor is that Indian economies usually involved women working at least partly autonomously and owning property, which was inherent to their autonomous economic roles.[64] Another reason seems to be related to the importance of the feminine in societies closely connected to nature (as appears to have been the case also in very early Europe and Asia).[65] The great Haudenosaunee prophet Deganawidah, founder of the Six Nation Confederation, is reported to have said, "[God] caused the body of our mother, the woman, to be of great worth and honor. He proposed that she shall be endowed and entrusted with birth and the upbringing of men, and that she shall have the care of all that is planted by which life is sustained and supported and the power to breathe is fortified: and moreover that the warriors shall be her assistants."[66] It is important to note that there were a large number of important positive female mythical figures throughout Indian societies who indicate the importance of, and respect for, the feminine. Among them are White Buffalo Calf Woman, who brought the Sacred Pipe to the Lakota;[67] Woman Who Changes and White Shell Woman of the Diné;[68] and Holy Woman and Woman Who Married the Morning Star of the Blackfoot.[69]

The extent to which the feminine was a primary cultural principle and how that principle was applied varied from tribe to tribe, but it was universally important. Often, it was especially strong in agricultural societies in which descent was primarily matrilineal. Among the Wendat or Huron, an Iroquoian people, for example, residence, clan membership, and inheritance of office were determined matrilineally, with the division of labor overwhelmingly along gender lines and a strong emphasis on same-sex work teams.[70] Thus, women shared their concerns on public policy and other matters with one another, and men did the same, providing a basis for collective voices that gave men and women essentially equal influence and control over decisions that affected them. Respected older women were often the ones to voice women's concerns, but individual women had a direct say in many matters.

In Great Plains societies, which, after the coming of the horse, engaged primarily in hunting and were quite mobile, there was somewhat less emphasis upon the feminine than among Iroquoian farmers. Still, mutual respect remained central to all relationships. Among the Lakota, for example, kinship relations, though in a sense bilateral, were essentially nonlateral or variable, since a nuclear family could choose which extended family to live among.[71] In addition, either party to a marriage could dissolve it: a man by taking his personal items out of the lodge, and a woman by placing her husband's personal items outside the lodge. The lodge belonged to her, as she was primarily responsible for child care. Among the Comanche, as with the Lakota, either a husband or wife could initiate a divorce.[72] Women had considerable influence individually and collectively, and their opinions were occasionally voiced in council meetings by older women. Indeed, in these societies, in which descent was matrilineal, women set much of the moral standard of behavior, which they could enforce collectively by shaming anyone who violated the mores.

The collective voice of women, especially elders, was extremely important in traditional Native American societies, particularly because of the emphasis on honor and shame in those cultures, and it remains important, even with all the changes in American Indian ways that have occurred with the arrival of Europeans and others. This reality is illustrated by an experience author Stephen Sachs had one evening at the Sun Dance of the Southern Utes. In that sacred ceremony, the men at the drum start the song, but the women around them join in harmonizing the song and "have the last word." That night, after a visiting group of singers finished their turn, no regulars were available, so a few part-time singers and apprentices filled in under the direction of a young man who just that afternoon had been taught how to lead by the elder singers. While for the most part the young man's fine spirit made up for the singers' technical weakness, on one occasion the singers lost the song and were ready to let it go and go on to the next. But the women singers would not allow the indiscretion. They picked up the song and gave it back. And when that song was properly completed, they let the men at the drum know quite clearly how they were expected to do their job correctly in that sacred space. Thus the women functioned not merely as protectors of traditional ways but as teachers of those values and how to apply them—a traditional woman's role.

The relative traditional balance of men and women, each dominant in their own spheres, can also be seen today at the Southern Ute reservation in the continuance of the ancient Bear Dance each spring.[73] When, in the dance, the two facing lines of men and of women break into couples (or trios), the partners are side by side, with the men facing east and the women facing west. As a couple makes the long prance east, the man guides the couple. When the couple makes the long prance west, the woman guides.

At least in some cases, the strong emphasis upon the entire community in Indigenous North American cultures was developed to counter the dangers of unrestrained individuality in the person, family, or other group. For the Cheyenne, for example, Hoebel reports that the centralization of political authority in the forty-four tribal peace chiefs, the predominance of public over private law, and the very strong prohibition against killing another Cheyenne, all arose to counter the threat of internal disintegration.[74] For the Lakota, the Sacred Pipe, often referred to as the "peace pipe," is central to all religious rituals and was smoked to sanctify and affirm the reaching of agreements (or the willingness to come to agreement), including the settlement of disputes.[75] In at least some versions of the story of the White Buffalo Calf Woman's bringing of the Pipe to the people, her arrival came at a time of great trouble and disharmony, which was healed by the coming of the Pipe.[76] The history is quite clear among the Six Nations. Their current ways, including their confederation (the Great Peace), arose to overcome internal dissension.[77] It was a time of blood feud among clan units and fighting between tribes reminiscent in our own time of the civil war in Lebanon and gang wars in Los Angeles. Thanks to the vision and work of the Peacemaker (Deganawidah) assisted by Hayanwatah (or Hiawatha), the Great Peace was achieved and an extremely participatory government based upon principles of equality and justice was installed, with the attendant responsibility that each decision and action the people made be beneficial in its results to the seventh generation yet to come. That government and numerous others across traditional North America were able to guide, in a most democratic manner, societies that, whatever their imperfections, were remarkably peaceful, prosperous, and happy for virtually all of their citizens.

2. Contemporary Lessons from American Indian Traditional Politics

In looking at our own politics in light of Native American experience, it is important to ask whether we in Western culture have traditionally overemphasized power (particularly as control), competition, and the state as the core of our politics. Many people, including this writer, believe that we have and that this overemphasis has contributed to the growth of fragmentation and alienation experienced by citizens in Western societies.[78] For instance, in looking at the operation of federalism in the United States, it is now well recognized that whereas in legal theory federalism constitutes a system based on separation of powers, in practice federalism operates as a cooperative system (with competitive elements), with the federal government more often carrying out policy by empowering the states and localities through grants in aid with varying degrees of discretion by the recipient, than by exercising control.[79] In regulating within its own sphere of powers, the federal government has always been aware that there are limits to the extent to which it can successfully achieve desired results entirely by command. Thus, gaining voluntary compliance from those regulated is a traditional element in American regulatory activity. The problem is that we have not fully recognized the extent to which politics in principle involves the harmonization of cooperation and conflict, requiring empowerment in consensus building, which is central to the process of governance.

Indeed, despite considerable collaboration in many aspects of public affairs, the dominant mind-set driving a large portion of politics in the United States is highly competitive, viewing public affairs largely as a zero-sum game. As many recent critics of the U.S. Congress, for example, have stated, the result is that numerous opportunities to cooperate are missed, making it difficult to pass legislation and accomplish other work. Measures taken are often unbalanced or otherwise defective because they are the result of which personalities or groups are able to have part of their program included, not the result of the careful working out of what the situation actually demands, taking into account all of the relevant concerns. A more inclusive, collaborative approach to decision making along traditional Native lines would be much more efficient, produce far better policy, and would result in more harmonious relations among citizens. One factor involved in bringing a shift to a more harmonious perspective is for people to realize, as Native people traditionally do, that in the long term, it is in one's interest to be collaborative, because the results are better when we can find common ground. In chapter 3, section 2, we offer examples that involve collaborative settlement of complex water rights issues that maintain better working relationships for people and organizations that need to work together on an ongoing basis.

Regarding the process of regulation, protection of the environment offers a useful example. For many years, the United States has regulated environmental protection at both the federal and state levels, primarily through a command system requiring a large bureaucracy.[80] The Environmental Protection Agency (EPA) in particular, but the state agencies as well, have been very slow to develop regulations. They are inefficient in gaining compliance and expensive to operate, in large part because the command-driven bureaucracy is far more inefficient than are cooperative, mission-driven systems.[81] Moreover, the command system of regulation fosters competitiveness, encouraging a fragmentation of interests with a premium on the power of individual interests to influence the process. This is not to say that disproportionate power is not a problem in any political process or system, but rather that strongly competitive systems emphasize power differences.

In recent years, prior to the administration of George W. Bush (which was exceedingly unilateral and competitive), more collaborative and inclusive approaches were taken in the field of environmental policy. The EPA, for instance, developed a process for developing regulation by bringing all the interested parties (primarily representatives of environmental groups, business, and the agency) together to participate in consensus decision making. Any of the parties could withdraw from the process at any time, but after they accepted the final agreement, they could not later challenge it in court. As in traditional tribal governance, the process of dialogue takes time but usually results in better decisions than competitive processes because of the effort made to accommodate all of the concerns and interests of those affected to create a viable policy. By contrast, decisions in competitive processes tend to be the result of the ability of individual contenders to force the inclusion of as much of their position as possible in the final outcome, with compromises determined more in terms of including the diverse agendas of strong pressure groups than in achieving a well-working policy as a whole.

The setting of new standards for the contents of gasoline in 1991 used this new inclusive process.[82] Often even when this process fails to produce a consensus, it is still useful because agreement is invariably reached on many of the issues, leaving only a narrow range of questions, which have already been well framed by the discussion of the concerned parties, to be decided by the agency. Several states, including Indiana, California, and Florida, have taken such an inclusive approach to promoting energy conservation and pollution reduction in the generation of electric power.[83]

In the past, there have been no incentives for power companies to operate efficiently or to encourage customers to conserve energy.[84] Using an inclusive process, power-company, environmental-group, and consumer-group representatives have sat down together with state officials to develop regulations that meet the primary concerns of all the parties. This process has resulted in measures that save consumers money and reduce energy use (thereby reducing pollution) by allowing power producers to benefit financially from encouraging consumers to be energy-efficient.

Instituting such a process involves re-creating one of the strengths of traditional Indigenous societies: finding the means or incentives (which can be moral, political, and social, as well as economic) to encourage people to act in the general interest by making it in their personal interest to do so. But doing so can only be effective to the extent that the structure and functioning of the incentives in practice actually encourage the socially desirable behavior (or in an organization, organizationally desirable behavior). Sometimes common apprehension of not finding a solution to a major problem can be an effective inducement to take part in a consensus-building process, if all the concerned parties understand that their views and interests will be respected and included in the outcome. For example, Search for Common Ground assisted some communities in the United States in defusing the very divisive issue of abortion by bringing together the full range of concerned people in each community in problem-solving dialogues.[85]

For such inclusive processes to function properly, particularly in government, a number of requirements exist. First, the process must be truly inclusive, involving all the interested parties on an equal basis. Otherwise, the process will be only a vehicle of hierarchical, competitive government driven by special interests. For example, during the presidency of George H. W. Bush, Vice President Dan Quayle's Competitiveness Council involved only big-business leaders and government personnel in blocking new federal regulation that business did not want, regardless of the impact of such action on the rest of the country.[86] Equally pernicious was the older practice of regular meetings between the Business Advisory Council, which was composed of leaders of large corporations, and top officials in the Department of Commerce and various cabinet members in exclusive sessions at The Homestead in Hot Springs, Virginia, and other expensive resorts—sessions paid for by the Department of Commerce.[87] The George W. Bush administration was widely known for including only a narrow range of interests and actors—including oil companies—in its decisions, and of exacerbating divisiveness in U.S. politics.

Second, the power between the parties in the process needs to be reasonably equal, to the extent of their interest, in order for the outcome to be equitable. If, for example, in the early 1990s EPA gasoline-content decision-making process, the oil industry could have gotten most of what it wanted by going directly to Congress, then it could have perverted the consensus process in its favor by threatening to pull out of the discussions if it did not receive most of what it wanted at the expense of everyone else.

Third, there need to be reasons, or incentives, for those interested to participate, and the consciousness of the parties must be such that they are open to participating. For example, if the petroleum companies had had sufficient power to secure the regulations they wanted within a satisfactory time frame through the EPA and didn't care about the well-being of the other parties, the companies would not have bothered to join in the consensus process. However, even if they were generally significantly more powerful politically than the other parties, the oil companies would have joined in the consensus-decision process with only a small advantage if the delay in or uncertainty of the outcome produced by not participating had been sufficient.

Where parties are in an ongoing relationship, as were members of traditional Indian communities, they may well find it to their long-term advantage to join in a collaborative problem-solving process by consensus, rather than to bargain competitively. Thus, employers and labor unions, having gained sufficient trust in each other through jointly managing team process for mutual benefit (learning, for example, that the resulting greater productivity leads to increased profits and wages), sometimes now find it advantageous to work out labor contracts by mutual problem solving. Such may be useful not only for obtaining a better deal for both parties, but also for maintaining the trust necessary to continue to carry out effective team process in the workplace.[88]

The point is that well-working consensus decision making involves the creation of a close relationship between the parties in which each party gains its own ends by helping the other parties attain their goals. It also involves people really listening to one another and engaging in dialogue to produce a flow of meaning rather than shouting to drown out divergent points of view, which constitutes too much of contemporary discourse over issues, solves nothing, and has a tendency to escalate, even to violence. Experience taught Native peoples the value of inclusive decision making and reharmonizing processes to keep the peace, and nonviolent conflict resolution and training has been successfully applied in the United States, particularly with young people, to reduce violence. Experience with nonviolent conflict resolution, and with instituting team process in workplaces, demonstrates that what is necessary to get people to appreciate and use mutually respectful means of communication and decision in contemporary society is cultural and educational. Most people prefer such modes of interrelating once they come to understand them and learn the skills involved in using them.[89]

Currently, government in the United States and much of the world faces a series of related crises both in internal operations and external relations. Some of these difficulties relate to the way in which we conceptualize and operate government processes. By failing to recognize the extent to which governance is, in principle, a collaborative and empowering enterprise, we have greatly increased the costs of its operation, limited its effectiveness, and distanced it from the people.[90] Thus, reforms that equitably increase citizen and employee participation in the operation of government bodies, build teamwork among government agencies, and in other ways debureaucratize government operations are useful developments consistent with traditional principles of band and tribal governance.[91]

The second level of the problem has to do with relations among people. A shrinking and rapidly changing world has increased the level of cross-cultural interaction externally while magnifying the diversity of populations internally. Just as the Haudenosaunee and other Native American societies developed inclusive processes that achieved unity through honoring diversity in order to overcome the dangers of divisiveness, so we, too, need to develop inclusive relations that create community through empowering individuality in socially useful ways.

The principle of diversity itself tells us that we cannot simply copy from others in order to develop a politics of harmony. Each people and generation is unique and needs to develop creatively on its own terms. Traditional Indian societies were generally smaller and more homogeneous than our own but, as we have indicated, shared many of the same types of problems we face, and increasingly we are finding the application of the same basic values and approaches helpful in meeting those problems when undertaken appropriately for current circumstances. If we are to achieve community, we must remember that in our uniqueness we are not so much independent as interdependent. Although the cultural age and situation are our own, they are sufficiently similar to others that there is much we can learn from those who struggled with the same problems. Indeed, the very differences are virtues when we understand them, for they give us a useful perspective that we would otherwise be denied. Given our current condition, there is a great deal that we can learn by looking further into the depths of the traditions of some of those who have preceded us on this continent and are still very much with us.

In order to attain productive and harmonious relations within and between communities, it is essential that human interaction be based upon mutual respect.[92] Unless people deal with one another as equal partners in a mutual relationship, interaction is likely to lead to injustice and dangerous dominance. This in turn will most probably lead to an ongoing struggle marked by open or structural violence. To break out of the recurring cycles of repression and violence, it is necessary that we build human relationships upon the principle of unity in diversity, so that each of us respects the interests, views, and ways of all individuals, groups, and cultures. Doing so is important not only to avoid causing harm to others but also because we each have something to learn from every person, group, and culture. Moreover, repression is costly and inefficient in comparison with collaboration, which is also far more emotionally rewarding to everyone. Thus, it is mutually advantageous for all of us to move from relations founded upon cultural hegemony to relations centered upon cultural sharing and exchange. For example, following the events of 9/11, the Bush administration would have been far more effective in limiting international terrorism if it had called for collaborative international action based upon inclusive discussions among nations rather than acting and cajoling largely through unilaterally exercising and threatening to exercise U.S. military, economic, and diplomatic power.[93]

The principle that relationships need to be based upon mutual respect was central to traditional Native American cultures. Although in practice many traditional tribal members fully applied that principle only to members of their own society, the more thoughtful and more spiritual realized its universality, as, clearly, is necessary in the world today.[94] It may be that we cannot always obtain mutually respectful relations, even as Native American societies were not free from war. But as both Thomas Hobbes and traditional Native American leaders saw, it is necessary to make considerable effort and to take calculated risks to create them.

At a fundamental level, virtually all of the traditional peoples of North America saw human beings as part of the natural harmony of the whole of nature. For example, in all important ceremonies, the Lakota people respectfully acknowledge *mitakye oyasin*, "all my relations."[95] Thus they signify their respect for all they are integrally connected to—not only their immediate family but all the human beings, the animal nations, the creepy crawlies, the bird nations, the grass nations, the rock nations—all that share this world. There is respect for the environment; one never takes more than one needs. One is careful never to deplete the resources of any place, always leaving enough of a species to allow for natural renewal in the next cycle of seasons. And even then, one harvests a plant or kills an animal respectfully, after asking its permission and forgiveness. The current world environmental crisis, most particularly human-created global warming causing climate change, is the result of Western cultural thinking that is reductionist, not taking into account the full range of effects over time of decisions and actions. If the world's decision makers for the past three centuries had been Indigenous thinkers, the planet would not currently be suffering from increasingly dangerous environmental degradation. If we are to have real progress now in restoring the environment and in preventing the worst potential effects of climate change—avoiding making the problem worse through well-meaning ameliorative actions or creating serious new problems—it is imperative that we mirror traditional Indigenous thinking in carefully considering the full range of the impacts of actions in relation to the environment.[96]

The principle of harmony with nature and with other people is expressed by the Diné in their traditional statement of farewell, "May you walk in Beauty."[97] It is important to live in balance with all one's relations. Many of the tribal renewal rituals of Plains and Rocky Mountain peoples emphasize maintaining and renewing harmony. The Sun Dance of the Southern Utes, for example, is undertaken to "court Grandmother Earth that She will be bountiful to us again next season," and to renew accord in relations within the community and the world.[98] When one is out of harmony, action must be taken to restore appropriate balance and order. The Diné have many rituals for returning a suffering person to the path of beauty. If two Lakota boys are continually in conflict, the lesson of social harmony is often taught by tying their braids together until they learn how to get along. Indeed, the very name Lakota (or Dakota, or Nakota) means a state or condition of peace.[99]

These traditional values of harmony with nature and among people have a special importance for us today regarding developing environmental consciousness and the positive cross-cultural and transnational relationships that the world needs for survival and a high quality of life for all people. What traditional Native Americans understood experientially about the interrelationship of all people, beings, and things is today being discovered by the cutting edge of postmodern science.[100] But the concern for maintenance and reestablishment of harmony has additional contemporary value.

Hoebel describes a case in which two young Cheyenne men were caught hunting buffalo on their own. Solo hunting was prohibited because single or a few hunters might scare a herd away. To insure an adequate food supply, buffalo hunting had to be undertaken by the whole tribe in a coordinated action. When members of the military society policing the hunt came upon the offenders, they shot the hunters' horses and broke their weapons in the course of inflicting a beating that the two men did not resist. After the miscreants had listened silently to a reproach for their dangerous behavior, one of the chiefs of the military society called out, "Look how these two boys are here in our midst. Now they have no horses and no weapons. What do you men want to do about it?" One of the police patrol spoke up, "Well, I have some extra horses. I will give one of them to them." Another member of the military society did the same. Then a third member of the patrol declared, "We broke those guns they had. I have two guns. I will give them one." All the others responded, "Ipewa" ("good"). In this case, the police enforced the law quickly and firmly. But once it was clear that the violators had learned their lesson, they were reintegrated with the group through the generous acts of those who had administered the punishment.[101]

The value of restoring harmony in terms of learning that is exemplified by the Cheyenne case has relevance to the contemporary world. In the United States, the primary approach to crime, often based upon the principle of retribution, consists of punishment by removing convicted felons from society and locking them away in prisons with other offenders. This system often creates more capable criminals but has a relatively small effect in reducing repeated criminal behavior. Thus, there has been a growing interest in what are often more effective alternative approaches to corrections, which to varying degrees bring back the Indigenous focus on building and restoring harmony. These include programs that reintegrate convicts with society, such as halfway houses with job programs, and various forms of restorative justice that involve the lawbreaker doing work in the community. Sometimes this work is undertaken among those injured by the criminal's act, to repay at least some of the damage done and to return the criminal to a good relationship with the community.[102] These approaches are reflective of traditional tribal ways, which, traditional elders would say, when applicable are the wise way to deal with destructive acts in order to lessen their likelihood of reoccurrence and to bring those involved into inner as well as relational harmony. Such is especially the case with a growing movement to bring young offenders face to face with their victims, when appropriate. After one such mediation, the juvenile wrongdoer stated, "I now realize I hurt them a lot. . . . To understand how the victim feels makes me feel a lot different." Hearing that in a meaningful dialogue is often healing to the victim.[103]

Restoring harmony is relevant not only for correcting deviant behavior but also is important for keeping up with the rapidly changing world. It helps people to develop their positive potentials more fully in those areas of life that are relatively stable, as well as in relation to changing circumstances. To the extent that each of us can see life—in the family, the workplace, in society, and in the world—as an ongoing learning experience, we will be open to participating affirmatively in the changes that we need to make in adapting to new circumstances, as well as in improving our responses to ongoing situations.[104] Evidence for these outcomes is provided by the success of many of the leading companies taking part in the current worldwide revolution in management and work relations.[105] The development by everyone in the workplace of the view that life is experimental, which provides a continual set of opportunities for learning and improvement, has been a very important element in these companies' success. These firms, along with numerous public sector and nonprofit organizations, have been significantly improving productivity and the quality of working life through instituting participatory team process. On the most successful of these teams, every member is continually learning from other members and from the ongoing work experience. The result of this mutual empowerment is continual improvement of operations, relations, and personal satisfaction by virtually every standard that one might suggest.[106]

Adaptability to new situations was another important aspect of traditional tribal culture, although the rate of change was not as great before European contact as it has been in the postmodern world. The key to dealing with new circumstances is the flexible application of core values to meet new situations in appropriate ways. An interesting case of this involved the Cheyenne. Traditionally, generosity was a very important Cheyenne value. It was customary that one might borrow something from a friend without asking permission, with the borrower often leaving an identifiable item to let the absent owner know the borrower's identity.

The coming of the horse presented a new situation to the Cheyenne, however. Horses, unlike inanimate things, were seen as having personalities, and a warrior established a personal relationship with his favorite horses. Borrowing horses for extended periods without permission, then, became annoying to many Cheyenne. In one recounting, when a favorite horse was borrowed from a warrior by a friend without asking, and the friend did not return to camp for a long time, the warrior took the matter to his military society, the Elk Soldiers. The society leaders sent a message to the friend at a distant camp. The friend immediately returned and made a satisfactory explanation and a handsome gift in addition to returning the horse, whereupon the friends made each other blood brothers in acceptance of the settlement. The leaders said, "Now we have settled this thing." But, they went on, "Now we shall make a new rule. There shall be no more borrowing without asking. If any man takes another man's goods without asking, we will go over and get them back for him. More than that, if the taker tries to keep them, we will give him a whipping."[107] Thus, in a fashion typical to traditional North American societies generally, the Cheyenne changed their practice to apply their core values appropriately to changing circumstances. They avoided the fixed ideological approaches that some people and leaders in Western culture take to problems and issues, approaches that do not take into account the varying situations that one needs to honor to be successful in applying valid principles to varying situations. (For more on this topic, see the discussion of working and consulting appropriately with Indian Nations in chapter 6.)

Adapting traditional values to developing circumstances remains an important task for Indian nations today in overcoming problems of community disharmony and for the development of positive futures. The Northern Arapaho Tribe has consistently done this successfully in dealing with postcontact difficulties. As a result, the tribe has, remarkably, avoided the infighting that has beset many Indian communities and has been unusual in never having had elections contested or the actions of its Business Council complained about by tribal members. The key has been the adaptability of the Northern Arapaho elders in approving and encouraging change consistent with traditional principles.[108] For example, when the Ghost Dance and peyote rituals came to the Arapaho, the elders said that it was good to participate in these things, but that the people must keep their own Sacred Pipe ceremonies first in their hearts. By contrast, in another tribal community, a split developed between those who accepted and those who opposed the introduction of peyote rituals (associated with the Native American Church), a disagreement that continues to divide people in that community.[109]

Although adaptability is important for Indian nations, even as it has been a factor in the success of participatory working groups, perhaps even more important to the successful team, and to contemporary thinking in general, is a balancing of the values of unity and diversity in a manner analogous to traditional North American ways of seeing. In the Native cultures we are considering, there is an emphasis upon the whole: the whole family, clan, tribe, and world. Being is understood as relational, so that one's meaning comes from participating in the whole at many levels.[110] Most ceremonies are undertaken with all the participants sitting in a circle, which represents wholeness. But within the bond of unity there is a respect for diversity based upon the uniqueness and individuality of each person, group, and people. Together we form the Medicine Wheel, the circle of life.[111] Our purpose is in filling our place in the circle. But there is no circle without all of the individual places in it, each of which has a different quality as seen in each of the four directions. Each direction provides a different way of seeing the whole. Therefore, no decision can be made without consulting everyone to understand how the situation looks from their place in the circle. Moreover, since everything is related, all sides of a matter need to be considered in making a decision, including short- and long-run consequences of any action. As contemporary life becomes more complex and the effects of actions in one sphere are strongly felt in others, we need to return to the kinds of holistic thinking and problem solving that were central to Native cultures.

Traditional Native North Americans had practical methodologies for realizing the principle that everyone needs to be heard and their views included in a decision. In general, each person in turn was considered the center of the circle and given the chance to speak with everyone's full attention. In some cases, this was formalized with a circulating talking stick that indicated whose turn it was to speak. This practice was found in some religious ceremonies, such as the Pipe ceremony of many of the Plains tribes, in which a pipe circulates so that each person in turn has the opportunity to pray. In this way, the practicing of living on the basis of mutual respect was reinforced. Today, this practice of people speaking in turn to assure that all participants are involved and their contributions really heard, is increasingly being used around the world by participatory work teams and other groups applying consensus decision making.

For traditional Indian people, the principle of the circle was not just a convenient methodology but was a fundamental aspect of living. Everyone is born into a given place in the circle. If one lives well, she or he will explore the circle and come to know the other places. Traditionally, the circle consisted of the four cardinal compass points, to which are added the Sky above and the Earth below. In addition, there is also the often unspoken seventh direction, the Center, which is everywhere. The idea of the seventh direction is an ancient view quite consistent with Heisenberg's uncertainty principle and today's cutting-edge physics.[112]

There are some interesting parallels between traditional views of the Four Directions and psychologist Carl Jung's quarternio of modes of perceiving and mental processing. These are thought, feeling, intuition, and sensation. According to Jung and Meyers-Briggs personality typing, different people employ these four functions in differing degrees in mental processing, with one function tending to be dominant.[113] Although there are differences in the two systems, in working with both the Four Directions and Jung's quarternio (e.g., Meyers-Briggs), it is clear that different people perceive and process information differently, a reality we need to understand, whether in education, decision making, designing and assigning jobs, putting together working groups, or relating to one another. Moreover, we need people with different qualities and different ways of seeing. It would be unfortunate if we had no one with the aptitude and perspective to be an accountant. And it would be equally bad if everyone's aptitude and way of seeing was that of an accountant. As the complexity of postindustrial technology and society is making increasingly clear, no one can manage a complex situation or organization alone. A variety of skills and perspectives are needed, therefore teamwork and team-based organizations are becoming more and more necessary. The perspective of the Medicine Wheel is becoming more and more relevant to the contemporary world.

The Native American way of seeing life as relational had further consequences that are increasingly relevant in the development of contemporary society and culture. Each individual and each social group has a responsibility to every other person and social entity, and indeed to all beings, seen and unseen, since even the rocks are perceived as living and pervaded by spirit.[114] Each can be helpful to each other if they will be friends. In this relational view, each has a responsibility to all, including oneself; however, precisely because each individual is to be respected as an independent entity in an interdependent relationship, ultimate responsibility is to oneself, and it is up to each one to make her or his own decisions on the basis of individual understanding. This principle is somewhat similar to the Quaker emphasis upon morality through personal conscience and inner strength. People are urged to have and act upon moral values, but the emphasis is upon each person developing appropriate answers through deep inner reflection. Doing so leads to the development of a strong character with tolerance based upon mutual respect and produces individuated people who are strong and flexible partners in dialogue, because each comes from his or her own inner strength in giving support to others in a dialectic of mutual assistance.[115] Perhaps the expanding interaction on the virtual web of the Internet will help people to realize that they are participating partners in the web of life.

This kind of mutual respect is precisely what we need to develop in the world today if a culture of peace and positive human interaction is to arise. To be realized, mutual respect needs to be more than a good idea. Friendship, relational consciousness, begins in the heart rather than in the mind. How we feel toward one another is crucial. When we feel good about others, we are generous with them. In traditional Native American cultures, giving of oneself is highly valued, leading to an emphasis upon sharing as opposed to trading. The latter follows from a focus upon acquiring. At the end of major ceremonies, there is usually a "giveaway" in which at least one central person in the event gives to all, though sometimes everyone gives to each of the others.

For example, at the end of the annual Sun Dance, the Southern Utes place a blanket in the Sun Dance lodge upon which everyone in the community, and anyone else who wishes to do so, is invited to place a gift. When the dancing concludes, the women coordinating the giveaway choose a gift from the blanket for each visitor present. Because the Southern Ute Sun Dance is one of a cycle of annual Ute and Shoshone Sun Dances, there is reciprocity, as those who give at their home dance receive when they travel to the other dances.[116] The giveaway is followed by a feast. Indeed, the feast, sharing at least water and usually food, is an integral part of virtually all Plains and Rocky Mountain ceremonies. Moreover, various forms of generosity, or "giveaway," producing reciprocity are central to all Native American societies. The sharing from the heart in the feast and giveaway produces a reciprocity with a high degree of compassion, in contrast to the reciprocity of the market based upon calculated fairness.

As recent trends in the world emphasize, markets and the market consciousness necessary to make them function effectively have an important practical value. But if markets are to attain their end of enhancing the quality of human life as a whole, markets and market consciousness need to be balanced by concerns for harmony, including both ecological consciousness and compassion for all people and beings. John Locke wrote in the seventeenth century about society arising out of, and being separate from, the state of nature.[117] At the close of the twentieth century, we are rediscovering that society exists within nature and that we must synthesize our understanding of the states of society and of nature.

Synthesis is the problem of the day. We cannot survive and prosper unless there is a place in our circle for all. Every person, every culture, has a place. But how is that place to be defined? And how are institutions best structured and resources allocated? Each person has her or his own view, which has some legitimate basis in reality. No one alone can produce viable solutions. The problem now is to develop processes for dialogue based upon mutual respect. As we have indicated, traditional Native American societies can give us examples of how this can be achieved. In addition, some of the more successful current workplace teams, and broader collaborative efforts based on the same principles, provide hopeful models.[118] In turn, the current developments in teamwork and collaboration in many settings can be an encouragement for tribal people to break out of imposed inappropriate institutions and ways of thinking and find appropriate methods to apply their core traditional values in building their own ways in the twenty-first century.[119]

To develop and operate successfully, processes for human interaction require an appropriate culture. In learning to create and operate new forms of interrelating so that we can get to peace in ourselves, our families, our friendships, our workplaces, our communities, and our world, we do not need to reinvent the wheel. In evolving a harmonious culture, we would do well to learn from and build upon the traditions of those who have preceded us in living as participants in the whole. We suggest here that there is a great deal that is helpful that we can learn from traditional Native American culture and that we can use in educating for better ways of living and relating. In proposing this, we do not suggest that we try to become Native Americans. Our problem is to become ourselves more fully. But in doing so, we can learn from one another.

In undertaking this task, we need to be careful not to romanticize Native American ways, contemporary models, or possibly helpful ideas or systems from any culture. None are perfect. Moreover, of that which is clearly positive in a culture, only a part is transferable or usefully suggestive to other settings. Just as all good principles will be helpful in practice only if they are applied in ways appropriate to the whole of a given circumstance, so one must be careful in transferring anything from one cultural setting to another.

Any method or institution is likely to function differently in another setting, and its transfer may have unintended and unforeseen side effects and consequences. Thus, as we will consider more fully in the last chapter of this book, successful adaptation generally can occur only when the people who are going to live and work with it participate fully and inclusively in thoughtful dialogue about what to do, and in ongoing review and adjustment of unfolding development. Whether the context is ancient or postmodern, such would seem fundamental to the principles we have been discussing.

Notes

1. Several authors have delineated a set of "pan-Indian" values. These have included generosity, respect for elders, respect for women as life givers, regarding children as sacred, harmony with nature, self-reliance, respect for the choices of others, accountability to the collective, courage, sacrifice for the collective in humility, recognizing powers in the unseen world, and stewardship of the Earth. See Tolman and Reedy, "Implementation," 382–93.

   It should be understood that different cultures operationalized those values in diverse ways and in varying degrees and did so differently over time, just as the method and extent of their inclusiveness and participativeness varied. Moreover, in stating that, in general, precontact Native peoples enjoyed relatively high levels of democracy and harmony, the authors do not intend to assert that these were anywhere near perfect societies. We believe, as did Native people traditionally, that in the nature of things there is always conflict in societies and among people. The question is how well that conflict is managed. As we will discuss below, for traditional American Indians, the goal is harmony, but to even approach harmony momentarily requires continual effort, and to maintain and regain a reasonably high level of good relations requires continual work and timely appropriate efforts at restoration. (See Chaudhuri and Chaudhuri, *A Sacred Path*, chaps. 4, 5, 9, and 10; and Sachs, "Returning the World.") We find that from experience, North American tribal societies (which were small enough that they were not beginning to become states) generally developed relatively effective ways of working toward achieving harmony. Their small size and relative cultural homogeneity gave them an advantage in doing so. However, as we develop in section 2 of this chapter, the growing application by contemporary Western society of the same kinds of methods Indigenous peoples use to build, maintain, and re-create reasonably good relations among people is a strong indication that there is merit to the underlying values and principles of Native cultures.

   Some critics may object that traditional North American Indian societies cannot have been relatively good societies because they had wars and, to some extent, slavery. Our answer is that when one compares Native societies with those of Europe, at least since the time of ancient Rome, American Indian nations look rather good. As the various studies of traditional North American tribal societies cited in his volume show, war, battles, and raids were usually not as lethal as many of those in European history. Casualties were relatively few and honor in facing the enemy was more important than killing or wounding an enemy (one example is the honor a warrior received in many nations from merely touching an enemy—

counting coups), so that Indian fights were most often like very rough games in comparison with the human, social, and environmental devastation of modern warfare. Indeed, as war was usually entered into only after careful consideration by the tribe after diplomacy failed, intertribal disputes were often settled by games as an alternative to going to war (for example, see Chaudhuri and Chaudhuri, *A Sacred Path*, chap. 5). Furthermore, as we will see below, individual captives and defeated enemy villages or tribes were not uncommonly adopted as tribal members by the victors.

Similarly, some tribes in what is now the United States did keep a few individual captured enemies as slaves (who usually could eventually become tribal members), but as French, *Legislating Indian Country*, 1–2, points out, this practice was insignificant when compared to the institutionalized slavery Europeans brought to North America and that was brutally inflicted by Europeans on many tribal peoples. Fortunately, slavery is no longer a legal institution in the West, although illegal slavery still exists in the prostitution trade and in the forced labor of some immigrants.

2. Whether or not the Communist governments of Eastern Europe were, in fact, communist or socialist in Marx's sense is a question that has been subject to considerable debate. It should be noted that in speaking of extremely collectivist governments, we refer only to those that are collectivist at the expense of individualism and do not include those, such as Israel's kibbutzim or the Paris Commune, that mix collectivism and individualism through participatory democracy (as did virtually all traditional Native American governments, as discussed below). The problem of emphasizing the collective good without leaving room for the happiness (and one could say interests) of all individuals is ancient, and was considered by Plato in *The Republic*, including at 465a–467a. Although the extent to which Communist societies actually attempted to operate this way is only a small part of their experience, some of the problems of a regime asserting the collective good in order to suppress individual interest is considered in Rusmich and Sachs, *Lessons from the Failure*, part I and part II.

3. Barber, *Strong Democracy*, part I, provides a good critique of the Liberal tradition. It should be noted that we do not claim that political and social conditions have been progressively worsening. As the opening sentence of this chapter indicates, this is a particularly troubling period in the complex evolution of the world that exhibits a combination of negative and positive trends. Although there is not space to provide a full analysis of this point in this chapter, it is our contention that at this moment in history, applying some ancient and modern approaches to political and social problems is useful. Furthermore, in objecting to carrying the individualism in Lockian and similar Liberal thought to its extreme, we are neither denying the positive contribution of Locke in his own time to human development nor denying that Liberalism has something to contribute to current social dialogue. Rather, we suggest that it is important to take notice of the fact that one of Locke's aims was to develop individualism to counter the statist tendencies of his day (he did not argue for it in a vacuum) and also to note that, whatever the difficulties that had been occurring in England, Locke was writing in a context in which there existed a sense of community that we need to regain in multicultural America and in a world of increasing intercultural interaction. Concerning the need to integrate a variety of approaches to deal with contemporary problems, see Gebser, *The Ever-Present Origin*, particularly chap. 1.

4. Locke, *Second Treatise*, chap. 5.

5. Ibid.

6. For example, E. Adamson Hoebel gives a good brief picture of many of the virtues (and problems) of Eskimo, Comanche, Kiowa, and Cheyenne life in *Law of Primitive Man*, chaps. 5 and 7.

7. O'Brien, *American Indian Tribal Governments*, 37. Angie Debo, in *History of the Indians*, 19, explains that when Columbus returned to Spain, he reported that the inhabitants of the lands he had discovered were "gentle people." That Columbus came to exploit this gentleness is clear from history. Extracts from his diary at and just after first contact follow.

On October 12, 1492, after landing and first contact, Columbus recorded:

> As I saw that they were very friendly to us, and perceived that they could be much more easily converted to our holy faith by gentle means than by force, I presented them with some red caps, and strings of beads to wear upon the neck, and many other trifles of small value, wherewith they were much delighted, and became wonderfully attached to us. Afterwards they came swimming to the boats, bringing parrots, balls of cotton thread, javelins, and many other things which they exchanged for articles we gave them, such as glass beads, and hawk's bells; which trade was carried on with the utmost good will. But they seemed on the whole to me, to be a very poor people. They all go completely naked, even the women, though I saw but one girl. All whom I saw were young, not above thirty years of age, well made, with fine shapes and faces; their hair short, and coarse like that of a horse's tail, combed toward the forehead, except a small portion which they suffer to hang down behind, and never cut. Some paint themselves with black, which makes them appear like those of the Canaries, neither black nor white; others with white, others with red, and others with such colors as they can find. Some paint the face, and some the whole body; others only the eyes, and others the nose. Weapons they have none, nor are acquainted with them, for I showed them swords which they grasped by the blades, and cut themselves through ignorance. They have no iron, their javelins being without it, and nothing more than sticks, though some have fish-bones or other things at the ends. They are all of a good size and stature, and handsomely formed. I saw some with scars of wounds upon their bodies, . . . they answered me in the same way, that there came people from the other islands in the neighborhood who endeavored to make prisoners of them, and they defended themselves. I thought then, and still believe, that these were from the continent. It appears to me, that the people are ingenious, and would be good servants and I am of opinion that they would very readily become Christians, as they appear to have no religion. They very quickly learn such words as are spoken to them. If it please our Lord, I intend at my return to carry home six of them to your Highnesses, that they may learn our language . . .

On October 13, 1492, Columbus recorded: "The natives are an inoffensive people, and so desirous to possess any thing they saw with us, that they kept swimming off to the ships with whatever they could find . . ."

And on October 14, 1492:

I discovered a tongue of land which appeared like an island though it was not, but might be cut through and made so in two days; it contained six houses. I do not, however, see the necessity of fortifying the place, as the people here are simple in war-like matters, as your Highnesses will see by those seven which I have ordered to be taken and carried to Spain in order to learn our language and return, unless your Highnesses should choose to have them all transported to Castile, or held captive in the island. I could conquer the whole of them with fifty men, and govern them as I pleased. ("Christopher Columbus: Extracts from Journal," *Internet Medieval Sourcebook*, http://www.fordham.edu/halsall/source/ Columbus1.html.)

8. O'Brien, *American Indian Tribal Governments*, 40.
9. Mohawk, "Indians and Democracy."
10. Locke, *Second Treatise*, 61, 102. For an analysis of the effect of American Indian ways upon Locke as shown in the *Second Treatise*, see Sachs, "Acknowledging the Circle."
11. Rousseau, *The Social Contract*, book 3, chap. 5, 67, and indirectly on the topic of confederacy as a new subject in reference to the Six Nations, or Iroquois League, and other Native American confederations, including the Huron (*The Social Contract*, book 3, chap. 15, 96–97 in the footnote). Rousseau also commented favorably on Native American life in "A Discourse on the Origin of Inequality," published in the same volume. An analysis of the effect American Indian ways had on Rousseau as seen in *The Social Contract* and the Discourses is in Sachs, "Acknowledging the Circle."
12. Bottomore, *Marx: Selected Writings*, 39. Marx and Friedrich Engels had read L. H. Morgan's *Ancient Society*. For a discussion of the limitations of Morgan's understanding, see Bilharz, "First Among Equals?," 107.
13. See Johnson, *Forgotten Founders*; Grinde and Johnson, *Exemplar of Liberty*, including Vine Deloria Jr.'s Introduction discussing the issues of scholarship on this question; Barreiro, *Indian Roots*; Mohawk, "Indians and Democracy"; Venables, "American Indian Influences"; and Grinde, "Iroquois Political Theory."
14. Although it is impossible to have direct knowledge of Native American ways before contact with Europeans, a great deal of information is available about various North American societies at the time of contact and shortly thereafter. Because the spread of Europeans in large numbers across the continent was not sufficient to disrupt the traditional ways of some tribes until well into the nineteenth century, a long period existed during which Europeans and their descendants collected information on traditional Native American ways. In addition, interviews of older people who themselves remembered traditional ways exist, and much has been preserved in tribal and band oral history (or was preserved long enough to be set down in writing), so that it is possible in many cases to distinguish traditional from later ways. There are, of course, many holes in contemporary knowledge of traditional ways, and many points about which there is uncertainty. In some cases, aspects of traditional ways relating to governance continue to this day, as pointed out by O'Brien in *American Indian Tribal Governments*, 17. In considering Native American ways, it is important to note the breadth of variety and the individuality of the many cultures. Some idea of this variety is given in Driver, *Indians of North America*; and Brown, *Spiritual Legacy*.

Note that the tribes and bands in what is now the United States in 1492 were all societies that were small enough that they were not beginning to become states, as were some of the Native empires at that time in Latin America. These larger-scale societies, at least in their central governments, often developed political, social, and economic hierarchies and began to move away from some of the basic values of the smaller-scale tribal societies described here, although aspects of those values tended to remain in operation, particularly at the local level. For example, see Page, *In the Hands*, 99, 95–96, and 100–101; and Saunders, *Ancient Americas*, 110–12.

15. O'Brien, *American Indian Tribal Governments*, chap. 2.

16. Ibid., and also shown in Hoebel, *Law of Primitive Man*, chaps. 5 and 7.

17. The concept of politics as the "authoritative allocation of values (when sanctions are available)" was introduced by Easton, *The Political System*, 131–32. The definition of politics as the determination of "who gets what, when, where, how" is from Lasswell, *Politics*.

18. Chaudhuri and Chaudhuri, *A Sacred Path*, 68.

19. The practical experience leading to the primacy of respect, and the inclusiveness that follows from it to build and maintain harmony, is very clearly seen in the history and myth of the forming of the Great Peace by the Haudenosaunee (Iroquois) and its application in governance in Morgan, *League of the Iroquois*. See also Wall, *To Become a Human*.

The importance of balance and harmony following from respect, is exemplified by the Muscogee in their creation story and in all their related stories showing how everything is interrelated and must be kept in balance, as set forth in Chaudhuri and Chaudhuri, *A Sacred Path*. The Chaudhuris tell us, for example, that

> The beautiful astronomical legends give us a picture of the balance of male and female energies, thereby showing the patch of darkness in light and light in darkness, all circling in the search for harmony in motion. The legends provide a humanities parallel of the science of the Creeks which also sees the search for balance between the four elements and the synergy linking the cycles of dynamic energies of the earth, the water, the sun (fire), and the sky (air). This is no romantic pipe dream, but the vision of an earth-centered culture with sacred trust responsibilities. The Earth centered physics involves exchanges between and transformations of various forms of energy and the cycles of energy among soil, water, nutrients, animals, sunlight, air and rain in an environmentally balanced manner. (19)

This dynamic balancing, which is necessary in the physical sphere, is also necessary in society, in which all the elements: men, women, the different clans, and the two moieties—indeed all individuals—each have their unique and essential functions that must be kept in, and returned to, balance. The same is true of the individual, who, if internally out of balance cannot act socially in a balanced way. "In the Muscogee Creek cosmos, all things consist of particular combinations of body, mind and spirit. When these are not in harmony, one is truly lost and healing becomes necessary for the entity to continue" (23). For a discussion of a similar approach by the Diné (Navajo), see Kluckhohn and Leighton, *The Navaho*; Downes, *The Navajo*, particularly chaps. 2, 3, and 8; Young, *Political History of Navajo*; and Reichard, *Navaho Religion*. Something of the Lakota approach to these principles can be found in Mohatt and Eagle Elk, *Price of a Gift*, 3, 35, 145–46, and 298–99; and Marshall, *The Lakota Way*, 211, 227. The central place of respect in harmony and balance, as such requiring inclusiveness and related values, is developed with reference to various Indian nations in Sachs, "Returning the World."

20. O'Brien, *American Indian Tribal Governments*, chap. 2.

21. Hoebel, *Law of Primitive Man*, chap. 5, see particularly 81–83.

22. Ibid., 88–89.

23. O'Brien, *American Indian Tribal Governments*, 16–17, 29–33.

24. See Opler, *Apache Way of Life* on politics, particularly 460–71. The Chiricahuas are typical of the Apaches generally in the nature of their politics. For example, see Tiler, *The Jicarilla Apache Tribe*.

25. For the Ojibwa, see Landes, "The Ojibwa of Canada," chap. 3, particularly 93–96. Landes discusses how individual families, or some of their members, come together in common endeavors for a limited time. On those occasions, one of their number is accepted as the informal leader. Anyone not happy with the leadership goes elsewhere. For the Utes, see Young, *Ute Indians of Colorado*, 73, 255. Young discusses the consensus-building style of traditional Ute leaders. See also Osburn, *Southern Ute Women*, 21–23.

26. Kluckhohn and Leighton, *The Navaho*, 111–23. Young, in *Political History of Navajo*, 15–16, 25–27, reports that according to Diné legend, the people lived in independent, self-sufficient camps in which, like other band societies we discuss, decisions were made by the community by consensus. The headman (*Hozhooli Naat'aah*) acted only as an advisor. He usually was proficient in leading at least one ceremony, governed by persuasion, and

> expounded on moral and ethical subjects, admonishing the people to live in peace and harmony. With his assistants he planned and organized the workday life of his community, gave instruction in the arts of farming and stock raising and supervised the planting, cultivating and harvesting of the crops. As an aspect of his community relations function, it was his responsibility to arbitrate disputes, resolve family difficulties, try to reform wrong doers and represent his group in its relations with other communities, tribes and governments. He had no functions whatsoever relating to war because the conduct of hostilities was the province of War Chiefs.

> A headman was a man of high prestige chosen for his good qualities and remained a leader only "so long as his leadership enlisted public confidence or resulted in public benefit."

27. Kluckhohn and Leighton, *The Navaho*, 118.

28. Ibid., 120.

29. Bowers, *Hidatsa Social and Ceremonial*. See particularly 26–64.

30. Fowler, *Arapahoe Politics*. Throughout the work, Fowler shows that age grades in Arapaho society essentially had the same effects as in Hidatsa society.

31. Bowers, *Hidatsa Social and Ceremonial*, 33. The young man was also given advice for how to act to gain the respect necessary to become a leader.

32. For Lakota political life, see Price, *The Oglala People*. Price drew on many sources, including the Walker papers, particularly pages 7–21, 33–34, 60–62, 98–99, 156, 168, and 172–73. See also the second of the three edited volumes of the James R.

Walker papers published by the University of Nebraska Press: *Lakota Society* part 1, particularly documents 6–16; O'Brien, *American Indian Tribal Governments*, 23–26; and Mirsky, "The Dakota."

33. Eastman and Eastman, *Wigwam Evenings*, 99–105.

34. Trigger, *The Huron*. See especially chap. 6, "Government and Law."

35. Ibid., 84.

36. Hoebel, *The Cheyennes*, 37.

37. O'Brien, *American Indian Tribal Governments*, chap. 2, "Traditional Governments," gives a brief overview of a geographically and in other ways diverse sample of traditional Native American governments.

38. Ibid., 27–29. On Pueblo politics and society, see also Goodman, "Zuni of New Mexico."

39. Frank Waters presents a feeling for the cycle of annual ceremonies in the life of Taos Pueblo in his novel, *The Man Who Killed the Deer*.

40. Waters gives a feeling for the process of the Taos Pueblo Council in a description of a meeting in *The Man Who Killed the Deer*, 12–25.

41. Reported in a private communication to author Stephen Sachs by Laguna Pueblo member Lee Francis, and by an attorney for the Pueblo.

42. Richardson, *Law and Status*, 5–16. A good impression of the relevant workings of Kiowa society can be glimpsed in the novels of Mardi Oakley Medawar: *Death at Rainy Mountain*, *The Witch of Palo Duro*, and *Murder at Medicine Lodge*.

43. Goldman, "Kwakiutl of Vancouver Island," 180–209. See the discussion of the extent of and limitation on Kwakiutl hierarchy on 181, 202, and 205–8.

44. Hassrick, *The Sioux*, chaps. 2 and 13. Note that some Lakota consider a longer list of positive qualities essential virtues. The English word "virtue" can only approximate the Lakota concept. A number of Lakota have told author Stephen Sachs that they do not think of good qualities exactly in the classical sense of virtue.

45. Standing Bear, *My People the Sioux*, chap. 5.

46. For discussion of collaboration and competition in other Native North American societies, see the discussions of the Ojibwa, Kwakiutl, Iroquois, and Zuni (as well as the Dakota) in Mead, *Cooperation and Competition*.

47. There is some discussion of this in O'Brien, *American Indian Tribal Governments*, chap. 2.

48. Ella Deloria, *Speaking of Indians*, 24–25.

49. Ibid., 37.

50. Garrett, "To Walk in Beauty," 165.

51. Ibid., 166.

52. Ibid., 165.

53. The underlying metaphysics of traditional American Indian political systems is discussed in Barsh, "Nature and Spirit," 181–98.

54. Author Stephen Sachs's personal observation and discussion with Lakota Sun Dancers.

55. See Hoebel, *Law of Primitive Man*, chap. 7; and Wallace and Hoebel, *The Comanches*.

56. See Hoebel, *Law of Primitive Man*, chap. 7, and Hoebel, *The Cheyennes*, chaps. 1–5.

57. See Irwin, *The Dream Seekers*, chaps. 1, 2, and 8.

58. Simmons and Mares, *Working Together*; Sachs, "The Cutting Edge"; and Sachs, "Employee Participation." Sachs, "Interest and Goal Structure," 59, discusses the advantages of collaborative organizations as compared with hierarchical

organizations, including the tendency of collaborative organizations to minimize status differences stemming from the division of labor.

59. Klein and Ackerman, *Women and Power*, 3–16, 230–49.

60. O'Brien, *American Indian Tribal Governments*, 17–20.

61. Mathes, "Native American Women," 44.

62. Klein and Ackerman, *Women and Power*. The one exception in the study was the case of the Muscogee, and this case was a partial exception concerning both the place of women in particular and the relative lack of hierarchy in Indian societies in general.

63. As explained more fully in Klein and Ackerman, *Women and Power*, although men and women did not do the same things or have the same authority and power, a balance in their relations referred to as "balanced reciprocity" existed. Concerning the case of the Muscogee reported in *Women and Power*, Joyotpaul Chaudhuri, who was married to a Muscogee woman and lived among the Muscogee and studied their tradition for forty years, communicated to author Stephen Sachs that that conclusion is accurate only for postcontact times—not for the precontact Muscogee. For an understanding that the traditional Muscogee maintained a balance between men and women, see Chaudhuri and Chaudhuri, *A Sacred Path*.

64. Sattler, "Women's Status," points out differences in these factors as likely reasons for differences in the status of women between the Cherokee and the Muscogee.

65. See Campbell, *Transformations of Myth*, particularly chap. 3. There appears to be an evolution of the place of the feminine and masculine in human life relating to general social and psychological development. In Western society, an early emphasis upon the feminine was later replaced by a preeminence of the masculine. Currently, the feminine is returning, but this time (it is to be hoped) in integration with the masculine, moving toward a dynamically balanced androgyny. This dynamic makes aspects of the feminine in traditional Native American culture (and in other Indigenous and older periods of "modern" cultures) of contemporary relevance. Campbell discusses many Native American myths with reference to the feminine in *Masks of God: Primitive Mythology*. Note that what seems to speak strongly to us today is the need for balanced integration of the masculine and feminine energies, rather than the elimination of differences. In equalizing the rights of women and men, the aim ought not to be to compel women to be like men, as our society has traditionally characterized men (e.g., women ought not be acculturated to overwork without paying attention to their feelings, leading to increased risk of heart attacks). What is needed is for the qualities that traditionally have been allowed only to men and only to women to be allowed equally in both men and women.

66. Allen, *The Sacred Hoop*, 213. The reference to women as mothers parallels the importance of the Earth as Mother, who gives birth to all that makes human life possible. Many important mythical heroes in Native American cultures were women (e.g., the White Buffalo Calf Woman who brought the Sacred Pipe to the Lakota), and a great many (perhaps 70 percent) of traditional North American societies were organized on the basis of matrilineal descent (Allen, 22). Note that men and women were not considered the same and hence were not precisely equal, nor did they have the same rights and duties in traditional North American societies, but neither gender was dominant generally. The details of the roles and relations of men and women varied from tribe to tribe. Some interesting comments about the roles of men and women in Lakota Society are put forth by Beatrice Medicine in "Indian Women," 159–71.

67. See Dooling and Jordan-Smith, "White Buffalo Woman: Lakota," 204–5; and Powers, *Oglala Religion*, 49, 50, 64, 82–83, 86, 89, 101, 116, 131, 169, 179–81, and 196–98.

68. Dooling and Jordan-Smith, "The Return: Navajo," 233–39.

69. Kehoe, "Blackfoot Persons," 116–20.

70. Trigger, *The Huron*, 68–70, 87, and 141–42.

71. DeMallie, *Lakota Society*, 4–8 and documents 19–21.

72. It has sometimes been argued that men had more rights than women in Comanche society. However, although there were differences in what was proper behavior for men and women, there was balance between the genders. Wallace and Hoebel, in *The Comanches*, 214 and 234–35, report that, in the mid- to late nineteenth century, a Comanche husband had the right to use various methods, including torture, to interrogate his wife if he thought she were having a secret affair with another man, and the wife had no equivalent right against her husband. They report that he could punish her, including killing her, without fear of retaliation. These reports need to be put into context. Author LaDonna Harris, a knowledgeable Comanche, states that there was considerable sexual freedom among traditional Comanches, as well as the mutual ability to dissolve marriages. Only in the rare instances in which one partner acted very outrageously in dishonoring the other were there grounds for either party or his or her supporters to act against the other. Normally, a woman's family, supported by community opinion, would require her husband to pay damages if he injured or killed her, unless it was clear that she had acted well beyond the bounds of propriety. Moreover, if a man dishonored his wife, she had considerable ability to shame him in the eyes of the community. This is a powerful sanction in a society in which honor and shame are fundamental. Thus, except in some rare instances after contact with Europeans had broken down some of the old ways, what Wallace and Hoebel report should be seen as more the exception than the rule. Moreover, this exception involved only a very limited area of Comanche life.

73. Osburn, in *Southern Ute Women*, 23, writes:

> In short, before confinement to the reservation, the Utes recognized significant differences in gender roles but did not value one gender more highly than the other. Women were equal members of their families and bands. They did not restrict their activities to the home and allow men to rule in the public realm. Rather, they participated in councils, were active in warfare, and provided leadership and power in spiritual matters. After relocation to the reservation, women continued to insist on participation in public affairs.

74. Hoebel, *The Cheyennes*, chaps. 4 and 5.

75. Hassrick, *The Sioux*, 50–51, 66; Stolzman, *The Pipe and Christ*, chap. 12.

76. Hassrick, *The Sioux*, 253–64. Author Stephen Sachs has heard the story of the coming of the Pipe told with the indication that White Buffalo Calf Woman brought the Pipe at a time of great difficulty and disharmony.

77. Lyons, "The American Indian"; and Grinde, "Iroquois Political Theory."

78. An excellent critique of traditional Liberal theory along the lines suggested here appears in Barber, *Strong Democracy*.

79. The cooperative nature of federalism is discussed at length by Elizar in *American Federalism*.

80. Smith, *The Environmental Paradox*; Davis, *Politics of Hazardous Waste*.

81. Osborne and Gaebler, *Reinventing Government:* see the Introduction, "An American Perestroika," and chap. 4, "Mission Driven Government: Transforming Rule-Driven Organizations."

82. Smith, "Traditional Foes Agree," 1, 7.

83. Citizens Action Coalition, *Citizens Power*, contains several articles on this topic. Osborne and Gaebler, *Reinventing Government*, 299–395 touches on this issue in environmental regulation and discusses some other incentive-based approaches to environmental regulation.

84. Clark, *Energy for Survival*, chap. 3. Other examples and suggestions for developing incentives to promote socially desirable activity are discussed in Osborne and Gaebler, *Reinventing Government*, chap. 10.

85. For more about Search for Common Ground's defusing of the abortion issue, see Search for Common Ground's "Search Results" page, keyword "abortion," http://search.freefind.com/find.html?id=77561039&pageid=r&mode=ALL&n=0&_charset_=&bcd=%C3%B7&query=Abortion.

86. *Indianapolis News*, "EPA, Quale."

87. Fritschler, *Smoking and Politics*, 46.

88. Numerous examples exist of effective employee-involvement programs collapsing because of bad feelings arising over collective bargaining. A classic example is that of the Armco Steel plant in Ashland, Kentucky. The collaborative effort of the plant's team process was a major factor in its achieving the lowest cost in the world for steel production. But because management failed to appreciate and take into account labor's concern on a major issue, the team-process arrangement fell apart, reducing the plant's ability to keep production costs low and product quality high. See, U.S. Department of Labor, *ARMCO*.

89. On nonviolent conflict resolution and training, see Search for Common Ground's "Search Results" page, keywords "nonviolent training," http://search.freefind.com/find.html?oq=Abortion&id=77561039&pageid=r&_charset_=&bcd=%C3%B7&scs=1&query=nonviolent+training&Find=Search&mode=ALL. See also the Fellowship of Reconciliation's "Peacemaker Training Institute" page, http://www.forusa.org/programs/pti/default.html. For parallel development of respectful interpersonal relations and decision making in participatory workplaces, see Bernstein, *Workplace Democratization*; Sachs, "Building Trust"; and Sachs, "Workplace Democracy."

90. Osborne and Gaebler, *Reinventing Government*.

91. Ibid. See the discussion of reforming government, which grows out of the movement for workplace democratization, involving institutions in a modern context of the traditional tribal and band principles of inclusive consensus decision making.

92. For a discussion of this necessity and of the process of building a culture of peace based upon mutual respect and unity in diversity, see Sachs, "Building the World Team," and Sachs, "Learning the Pedagogy."

93. See, for example, the discussions and reports concerning U.S. policy related to terrorism in issues of *Nonviolent Change* from 2003 to the present, available through www.nonviolentchangejournal.org.

94. Deloria, *Speaking of Indians*, 76.

95. Most of the points concerning spiritual aspects of Lakota, or Western Sioux, culture that we discuss in this chapter are considered at greater length in Deloria, *Speaking*

of *Indians*, 49–62; Powers, *Oglala Religion*; DeMallie and Parks, *Sioux Indian Religion*; and Stolzman, *The Pipe and Christ*. Additional information on the Lakota, including spirituality and religion, can be found in Neihardt, *Black Elk Speaks*; Brown, *The Sacred Pipe*; Lame Deer and Erdoes, *Lame Deer*; Black Elk and Lyon, *Black Elk*; Eastman, *Soul of the Indian*; Hassrick, *The Sioux*; and the three edited volumes of the James R. Walker papers published by the University of Nebraska Press: Walker, *Lakota Belief and Ritual*; Walker, *Lakota Society*; and Walker, *Lakota Myth*. Much understanding of the traditional Lakota can also be gleaned from Mari Sandoz's biographical novel, *Crazy Horse: The Strange Man of the Oglalas*.

96. Concerning dealing appropriately with the environment by applying traditional Native thinking, see Sachs, "Climate Change."

97. For more information on the Diné, or Navajo, see Kluckhohn and Leighton, *The Navaho*; Downes, *The Navajo*, especially chaps. 2, 3 and 8; Young, *Political History of Navajo*; and Reichard, *Navaho Religion*. A very enjoyable way to become familiar with Diné culture (although there are some inaccuracies, especially in the earlier volumes) is through the mystery novels of Tony Hillerman, including *Listening Woman*, *The Blessing Way*, *Skinwalkers*, *The Ghostway*, *The Dark Wind*, *Dance Hall of the Dead*, *People of Darkness*, *The Fallen Man*, and *A Thief of Time*.

98. Discussion of the Southern Utes in this chapter is based on author Stephen Sachs's support in 1986 to 2006 of the annual Southern Ute Sun Dance held on the tribal Sun Dance Ground near Ignacio, Colorado, and on his consulting with the Southern Ute Tribe in 2000. Sachs participated in the singing for the Sun Dance in 1989 through 1991. Information about the Utes is available in Young, *Ute Indians of Colorado*; Marsh, *The Utes of Colorado*; Simmons, *Ute Indians of Utah*; Pettit, *Utes: The Mountain People*; and Jefferson et al., *Southern Utes*, which contains a useful bibliograhical essay. An excellent study of the Ute and Shoshone cycle of Sun Dances in historical, social, economic, and political perspective to 1969 is Jorgensen, *Sun Dance Religion*.

99. Deloria, *Speaking of Indians*, 32–37, discusses the traditional ways of maintaining and re-creating harmony among the people.

100. The presence of ancient North American (and also ancient Asian) metaphysical understanding in contemporary science can be seen by comparing Indian ways of seeing (on such points as the interrelationship of all that is) with developing physics discussed in such works as Capra, *Tao of Physics* and Sachs, "Cutting Edge of Physics." See also note 112 below.

101. Hoebel, *Law of Primitive Man*, 150–53. An excellent short ethnography of the Cheyennes with additional bibliography is Hoebel, *The Cheyennes*. A longer ethnographic work focusing on traditional law, and therefore saying much about governance and something of other aspects of Cheyenne life, is Llewellyn and Hoebel, *The Cheyenne Way*. George Bird Grinnell's longer two-volume classic, *The Cheyenne Indians*, was reprinted by the University of Nebraska Press in 1972, and his collection of Cheyenne mythology, *By Cheyenne Campfires*, was reprinted by the University of Nebraska Press in 1971. A picture of traditional Plains culture in general, and Cheyenne ways in particular, is Heyemeyohsts Storm's novel, *Seven Arrows*. The work was written as a teaching, and the first three chapters are explanations of core cultural principles.

102. For discussion of the problems with punitive approaches to corrections and the value of restorative and related alternative approaches, see Branegan, "Restoring Community." See also Zehr, *Changing Lenses*. Zehr's historical work on restorative

justice finds that knowledge of American Indian peacemaking tradition played an important role in the rise of restorative justice in the mainstream U.S. justice system (160). See also Metoui, "Returning to the Circle," 517–40. Additional writings on restorative justice are listed on the "Resources" page of The Centre for Restorative Justice website, http://www.sfu.ca/crj/resources.html. The Missouri Restorative Justice Coalition has compiled "Restorative Justice Bibliography and Resources," available as a PDF file at http://www.dps.mo.gov/dir/programs/jj/documents/rj/Restorative_Justice_Bibiliography-Nina_Balsam%5B1%5D.pdf.

103. Wilson, "Real Justice," 58–62, 60.

104. Sachs, "Building the World Team," 20–21.

105. For discussion of the worldwide revolution in management and work relations, see Simmons and Mares, *Working Together*; Sachs, "The Cutting Edge"; and Sachs, "Employee Participation."

106. Simmons and Mares, *Working Together*; and New York Stock Exchange, *People and Productivity*.

107. Story recounted in Hoebel, *Law of Primitive Man*, 24–25.

108. Fowler, *Arapahoe Politics*, Introduction, and 122. The theme of adaptability in applying traditional values runs throughout Fowler's book. Rebecca Moore, a member of the Northern Arapaho Tribe, in a personal communication with author Stephen Sachs in July 2000, commented that the basic situation at the Northern Arapaho Tribe remains essentially the same, in this regard, as it was in 1971, although the social structure, with the leading role of the elders, is weaker than it was when Fowler wrote in 1982.

109. Young, *Ute Indians of Colorado*, 97–98, 169, and 274–75.

110. Stolzman, *The Pipe and Christ*, discusses this from a Lakota point of view. Toelken, "Demands of Harmony," considers relationship and relational thinking from a Diné perspective. Sam Gill's discussion across several cultures, "It's Where You Put Your Eyes," is also relevant.

111. Excellent discussions of the Medicine Wheel, or the Four Directions, are to be found in Stolzman, *The Pipe and Christ*, chap. 14; Storm, *Seven Arrows*, 3–27; and Freesoul, *Breath of the Invisible*, chaps. 7, 8, and 9.

112. The idea of the seventh direction is an ancient view quite consistent with Werner Heisenberg's uncertainty principle. For in a sense, the uncertainty principle can be understood as saying that the center is nowhere and hence everywhere in a universe in which everything is interrelated. (See Bohm and Hiley, *The Undivided Universe*, especially chap. 7.) This principle holds true both for American Indian and a variety of traditional Eastern ways of seeing. For a discussion of the uncertainty principle in the course of a consideration of the parallels between contemporary physics and ancient Eastern metaphysics, see Capra, *Tao of Physics*, 125–29, 143–46, 178–79, 207–9, and 251–53. A number of Lakota examples of the application of the principle of the seventh direction show its parallels to the uncertainty principle and equivalent views in Eastern traditions, as discussed by Capra. The seventh direction is within and around everything (it is everywhere), yet it is the center of the world (or universe or all that is). Thus, wherever a Sun Dance may be held, the circle of the world is re-created in the ceremonial circle with the Tree of Life in the center being the center of the world, where spiritual energy made present by the ceremony enters the world. Similarly, in a Lakota Pipe ceremony or talking circle, wherever it may be held, whoever holds the pipe or the talking stick is the center of the circle. Thus it is that Joseph Campbell reports that, as recorded in *Black Elk*

Speaks, Black Elk states, "'In my vision, I saw myself on the central mountain of the world, Mount Harmon [Harney Peak].' But he said, 'The center of the world is everywhere.'" (Toms, *Wisdom of Joseph Campbell*, tape 1, side 2). See also Sachs, "Cutting Edge of Physics."

113. Jung, *Psychological Types*. Application of Jung's understanding in Western culture can be seen in Meyers, *Gifts Differing*, and Keirsey and Bates, *Please Understand Me*. Duran and Duran, *Native American Postcolonial Psychology*, 65–83, demonstrates that although Jung's perspective is essentially correct, his model needs to be adjusted for different cultures, and the authors posit a Native American model.

114. Stolzman, *The Pipe and Christ*, 180.

115. Individuation is discussed in Laszlo, *Carl Gustav Jung*, 143–88. An explanation with reference to various sources in Jung is in Hopcke, *Guided Tour*, 63–65. On the importance of inner strength for participants in dialoguing processes, see Sachs, "Learning the Pedagogy," 1.

116. Jorgensen, *Sun Dance Religion*, chap. 6. Indian societies engaged in what Marshall Sahlins, in *Stone Age Economics*, calls "generalized" as opposed to "balanced" reciprocity. There is some interesting discussion of this concept in Patterson, "Evolving Gender Roles," 128–29.

117. Locke, *Second Treatise*.

118. For a discussion of the implications of workplace democratization for developing a culture of peace, see Sachs, "Global Focus."

119. A few examples are the increased use of consensus decision making for solving a wide variety of public and private problems, the building of interorganizational teamwork—including its use in conjunction with more participatory approaches to public problem solving, including community policing—and the spread of various forms of conflict resolution, prevention, and transformation based on building mutual understanding and respect.

Two
The Circle Under Siege
THE IMPACT OF COLONIALISM ON AMERICAN INDIAN
COMMUNITIES

*Stephen M. Sachs, LaDonna Harris, Barbara Morris, and
Deborah Esquibel Hunt*

1. Introduction: The Harmony of the Circle

As we have seen, traditionally, most American Indian communities in
what is now the United States lived well and governed themselves harmoniously by building consensus democratically on the basis of mutual
respect. Traditionally, American Indian societies balanced a strong individualism with an equally strong sense of communal unity by giving
everyone a say in building consensus toward reaching decisions and by
channeling individual interest toward the meeting of community needs.
This process occurred in a context in which a broad agreement on fundamental values was maintained in a slowly evolving culture. Thus,
although numerous viewpoints and factions existed in Indian communities, through mutual respect and participation in consensus decision making, these differences became strengths that harmonized into a
whole in which everyone enjoyed a valued place.

However, after five hundred years of devastating contact with
Europeans and European Americans that brought physical and cultural
genocide, many American Indian communities are struggling to overcome the destructive infighting among many of their members that has
become a serious problem.[1] These communities are attempting to re-create

traditional harmonious relations and governance internally while also returning externally to having their sovereignty honored as partners in American federalism. Before individual and community healing can be achieved, ameliorative action must be taken to counteract the causes of the disruptive, dysfunctional behavior of too many tribal members.

2. Fracturing of the Circle: The Legacy of Physical and Cultural Genocide

Physical Genocide

Given differences in worldview and focus that technological development engenders, contact with Europeans would have been somewhat disruptive to tribal life in North America even if Europeans had come to "Turtle Island" in an entirely friendly and respectful way.[2] Contact with Native Americans also had a significant impact on European culture and civilization.[3] However, because contact brought with it wave after wave of destructive, imperialistic intrusion, Indigenous people's lives and ways of life were seriously disrupted. Repeatedly, Indian populations were decimated by war, by imported disease (on occasion deliberately inflicted), and by harsh living conditions resulting from relocation, reduction of the land base, and destruction of traditional ways of living. By 1850, the Indian population in the United States, which had been estimated at 5 million in 1492, was reduced by 95 percent to 250,000.[4] By 1930, tribes that were still recognized by the federal or state governments lived on vastly reduced territory often far from their traditional lands, and on land of poor quality for providing a living, either directly through agriculture or hunting and gathering, or indirectly from economic development.

Once proudly independent people were thus left dependent on the U.S. government, which, while accepting vast cessions of land, consistently failed to keep its treaty promises and trust responsibilities to provide Indian people a reasonable standard of living and furnish adequate material and educational assistance so that Indians could regain self-sufficiency. The government's failure to even remotely meet its trust obligations, combined with a lack of opportunity stemming from racist discrimination and the isolation of reservations, left Indians in extreme poverty. As the Meriam Report, published in 1928, shows, Indian people were in dire economic need to the point of starvation, with poor housing, high rates of ill health, and a declining population.[5]

Cultural Genocide

The repeated waves of military pressure, conquest, relocation, and other aspects of physical genocide inflicted upon Indian nations from the sixteenth through the nineteenth centuries frequently caused divisions in Indian communities. Faced with nearly impossible situations, Indian nations frequently were divided in their attempts to identify and choose the least destructive of the available harsh, high-risk alternatives. The fracturing of communities continued under later U.S. Indian policy that pushed Indigenous people toward assimilation, although little meaningful assimilation was possible given the prevalence of poverty, limited education, and racism. This situation furthered the destruction of the physical basis of traditional life and of any potential for a simple return to traditional ways. However, difficult as the problem of intensified factionalism was, if they had been left free to do so, it is likely that Indian nations eventually would have returned to community harmony in developing their own ways to adapt to the new conditions. Although dialogue would have been more intense than usual, the traditional values of mutual respect and the cultural mechanisms for building consensus among diverse factions and viewpoints would have been available to re-create unity within the increased fragmentation.[6] At the same time, traditional methods of spiritual and psychological healing and of returning individuals to inner harmony—such as the Sweat Lodge and Sun Dance of many Plains tribes and the various healing ceremonies for returning people to beauty or harmony of the Navajo Nation—would have provided effective means for Indian people to process and transcend feelings of historical loss and grief.[7]

Destructive U.S. Government Policy

U.S. government policy, to a considerable extent, destroyed the means Native nations had for harmonizing individuals and communities, and thus greatly exacerbated community fracturing, furthering the real and perceived loss that individuals suffered. This destruction occurred through a variety of measures that undermined traditional leaders and governance while repressing traditional culture, including traditional religion and spiritual practice, with the aim of assimilating Indians into white culture.[8] Perhaps the most pernicious of these actions was the forced taking of Indian children from their families and communities and placing them in boarding schools to drive their traditions out of them.[9] Because this "schooling" cut young Indians off from their own culture, in most cases without providing them with the ability to function effectively in

European American society, it left many American Indians alienated both from the larger culture and from their own people.[10] Often, it disrupted family relationships, which were the primary supports of traditional Indian societies and cultures. Furthermore, the boarding school experience was widely marked by physical, sexual, and emotional abuse, initiating a vicious cycle of poor parenting and repeated child abuse in addition to creating low self- and community esteem and anger in many who suffered it.[11]

Moreover, the cultural genocide created new factions in many Native communities. For example, the disruption of traditional spiritual practice by government policy accompanied by the imposition of Christianity—with different denominations assigning missionaries and running schools on various reservations—resulted in a diversification of approaches to spiritual and religious thought and practice. Although some Native people have integrated traditional and newer ways or continue to be accepting of diversity, in many cases, this imposition created conflicts in values and identity. Instances of this include dissonance among those who focus on being "Christian" (even if they continue in some traditional spiritual beliefs and practices) and those who focus on following traditional ways (even if they accept some Christian beliefs or practices), and between those who follow traditional tribal religious ways and those who participate in newer pan-Indian spiritual practices, such as the Native American Church. This conflict has also happened more broadly, leading to the development of a variety of ways of approaching traditional and adaptive cultural values and identity by different people, sometimes leading to factional conflict in Native communities. In addition, the imposition of Western culture in general and Christianity in particular has caused numerous Indian people to experience conflict in their personal values and confusion in their sense of identity, which has contributed to dysfunctional behavior.

A major aspect of the destruction of the old methods for creating community harmony amid a diversity of views was the U.S. government's general disavowal of tribal self-governance and placement of the governance of tribal affairs in the hands of Indian agents who, as a general rule, intentionally undermined traditional leadership and culture. This took place to some extent under the administration of the army but happened primarily under the Bureau of Indian Affairs (BIA), which became part of the Department of the Interior in 1849.[12] Although how the BIA operated varied according to time and place and its efforts to undermine traditional culture and values were resisted by a great many Indians, there is no question that the BIA's administration of Indian affairs had numerous destructive effects, including increasing the degree of community fragmentation by largely destroying the traditional vehicles for social integration and consensus building.

A variety of quantitative and qualitative studies attest to and describe the impact of colonialism on Native people and peoples in the United States and their as yet far from complete progress in overcoming it. However, reporting on the developing condition of Indigenous people here is of necessity fragmented because American Indians often have not been specifically measured in many government and other studies, and when specific studies of Native people do exist, the data has often been collected for only a limited time period.[13] In addition, frequently, studies made at different times have been undertaken with differing methods or measures, including variation as to whom the definitions of "Indian" and "Alaska Native" include. Despite these problems, the general consistency of the picture provided by the somewhat rough and incomplete statistical data, when combined with descriptions from observations, indicates that, overall, the data is fairly representative of the reality of Native American life.

3. The Long Path to Re-creating the Circle

Slowly Overcoming Persistent Poverty and Beginning
Economic Development
The conditions of life for Indians both on and off reservations have improved since 1928. The Indian population has rebounded from less than 240,000 in 1900 to almost 2 million in 1990 and at least 2.476 million in 2000.[14] However, economic recovery has been slow, partly because of lack of opportunity in isolated areas, and partly as a result of ineffective government economic programs combined with a conflict of interest in the Department of the Interior (which we discuss in chapters 3 and 5), which until very recently disadvantaged tribes in their business dealings with private corporations and people. This situation has left Indian nations highly dependent on federal government money for jobs, economic development, and social services. A critical difficulty is that federal spending has remained inadequate to approach meeting Native needs, even in recent years. Since 1986, per capita spending for Indians has been less than that for the U.S. population as a whole, and the gap

has been widening. In 1998, on all U.S. government domestic programs, federal spending per Indian was less than 65 percent of federal spending per American, and Jonathan Taylor and Joseph Kalt report that in the period between the 1990 and 2000 U.S. census, federal Indian funding lost ground against non-Indian domestic spending.[15] Thus, regarding health care, Tex Hall, president of the National Congress of American Indians (NCAI), stated in the third annual State of Indian Nations Address on February 3, 2005, that "per capita expenditure for American Indian and Alaska Native medical services is less than one-third of the average annual expenditure for individual Medicaid assistance, and is even less than our per capita health expenditure for federal prisoners."[16]

The result has been that Indigenous Americans have remained deeply mired in poverty, with some ups and downs over time, although recently there has been some improvement. From 1980 to 1990, the percentage of Native Americans below the poverty line increased from 27.5 percent to 30.9 percent, making them the second poorest ethnic group in the United States.[17] Furthermore, the percentage of Indian children below the poverty level rose from 32.5 percent to 37.6 percent during that time. It should be noted that because of large average sizes of households, Native Americans were the only group to have household income (adjusted for inflation) *decline* during the decade. Indians were the measured group with the second largest percentage of children below the poverty line in both 1980 and 1990, with only African American children suffering a higher poverty rate. However, although the percentage of African American children below the poverty line increased over the decade (from 37.8 to 38.8 percent), the percentage of Indian children below the poverty line during the same time period increased even more (from 32.5 to 37.6 percent).[18]

From 1990 to 2000, and where data has been available since, the situation has improved somewhat. Yet, following an increase in employment and income for Native people with a general rise in economic development (which we discuss in chapter 5), the 2000 census indicated that the American Indian and Alaska Native population was second lowest, just ahead of Hispanics, in per capita income, but still last, below African Americans and Hispanics, in median family income. The American Indian and Alaska Native population was unequivocally at the bottom in the proportion of the population below the poverty level, with more than a quarter of the Indigenous population officially in poverty. However, that figure is clearly an improvement from 1990, when 30.9 percent of the Indigenous population was below the poverty line—even considering measurement differences between the 1990 and 2000 census. Table 1 details the figures.

Table 1.

U.S. 2000 census data for single-race identifiers

Category	Total population	American Indian	Asian	Black	Hispanic	White
Population	281,421,906	1,865,118	10,242,998	34,658,190	35,305,818	211,460,626
Per capita income	$21,587	$12,923	$21,823	$14,437	$12,111	$23,918
Median family income	$50,046	$33,116	$59,324	$33,255	$34,397	$53,356
No. of individuals below poverty level	33,899,812	475,118	1,257,237	8,146,146	7,797,874	18,847,674
Percentage of population below poverty level	12.05%	25.47%	12.27%	23.50%	22.09%	8.91%
No. of families below poverty level	6,620,945	98,434	226,915	1,777,105	1,495,297	3,548,532

Source: Data from U.S. Census Bureau, Census 2000 Demographic Profile Highlights.

The Census Bureau yearly report "Income, Poverty, and Health Insurance Coverage in the United States" for 2003 reported that 23 percent of single-race Native families lived below the poverty line, which was double the national rate, and 28 percent of single-race Native Americans were without health insurance, compared with 15.1 percent of all Americans. Because this census data is based on people identifying themselves as American Indians and Alaska Natives—thus including those of Native ancestry who are not members of federally recognized tribes as well as tribal members who are provided medical care by the Indian Health Service—this data indicates that a very high percentage of Indigenous people who are not members of federally recognized tribes had no health insurance in 2003. It also suggests that Indians who are not members of federally recognized tribes may in general have less access to services than do tribal members. Mean Native American income dropped 1.6 percent from 2001 to 2003, to $33,024, whereas nationally, median family income fell 0.6 percent, to $43,527.[19]

Jonathan Taylor and Joseph Kalt found that although American Indians remained the poorest group in the United States, American Indians in Indian country experienced substantial growth in income per capita, so that even with the Indian population increasing by more than 20 percent between 1990 and 2000, real (i.e., inflation-adjusted) per capita Indian income rose by about one-third.[20] For both gaming and nongaming tribes, the overall rate of income growth substantially outstripped the 11 percent increase in real per capita income for the United States as a whole. From 1990 to 2000, Indian family poverty rates dropped by 7 percent or more in nongaming areas, and by about 10 percent in gaming areas. For the United States as a whole, family poverty dropped 0.8 percent. Meanwhile, between 1990 and 2000, Indian unemployment rates dropped by about 2.5 percent in nongaming areas and by more than 5 percent in gaming areas, while overall U.S. unemployment dropped by 0.5 percent.

Urban versus Reservation Indian Poverty and Service Deficiency

Because of lack of economic opportunity on and near reservations, a large number of Indians have moved to urban areas (with government encouragement to do so during the termination period of the 1950s), so that more than 60 percent of Native Americans lived off-reservation by 2000. The Harvard Project on American Indian Economic Development issued a report in July 2005 showing that census data indicates that urban Native Americans experience a 17 percent poverty rate as compared with a 35 percent poverty rate on reservations.[21] Urban Indians have difficulty accessing health care, for although more than 60 percent of Native people live off-reservation, only 1 percent of Indian Health Service (IHS) funding is off-reservation, and various eligibility requirements prevent many Indigenous people from using what health services are available. Among other things, this means that urban Indian children often suffer from substance abuse without supportive services. With most Indian incomes low and urban rents high, the vast majority of urban Indians are forced to live in questionable neighborhoods. Although the number of Natives buying houses is increasing, very few can afford to do so. This is especially so in San Francisco, which has the nation's most costly housing and the fourth largest urban Indian population.

Underfunding and Continuing Low Native American Educational Achievement Rates

The underfunding of school, housing, health, and other services, combined with the fact that such services are often supplied in culturally inappropriate ways (which we discuss in chapter 5), continues to make it difficult for Indians to break out of the poverty cycle. Thus Indians have long suffered the lowest overall rate of educational achievement of any measured group in the United States. The 1990 census reported that only 65.3 percent of Native American residents twenty-five years or older and residing on reservations completed high school, as compared with 75.2 percent of all Americans over the age of twenty-five. Only 8.9 percent of the same Native American population obtained a four-year college degree, compared with 20.3 percent of the U.S. population older than twenty-five. Similarly, in 1989, Native Americans suffered the highest high school dropout rate of any ethnic group measured and had the lowest rate of achievement in mathematics, as the following tables show.

Table 2.

High school dropout rates by ethnic group in 1989

Ethnic Group	Dropout Rate (%)
Asian	8
White	15
Black	22
Hispanic	28
Native American	36

Source: Trends in Indian Health, 1993 (Rockville, MD: IHS): 1993, p. 28; U.S. Department of Health and Human Services, Public Health Service, Indian Health Service, Office of Planning, Evaluation, and Legislation, Division of Program Statistics.

Jonathan Taylor and Joseph Kalt found that from 1990 to 2000, the proportion of adult Indians on reservations with less than a ninth-grade education declined substantially. In Indian areas with gaming, the proportion placed adult Indians approximately on par with overall U.S. levels.[22] By using a different measuring method, the Urban Institute reported in a February 2004 study that in 2001, Native American students at public high schools had only a fifty-fifty chance of graduating. By looking at student enrollment per year, the Institute came up with a way of

Table 3.

Distribution of eighth-grade students by level of performance in mathematics in 1988

	White (%)	Asian (%)	Hispanic (%)	Black (%)	Native American (%)
Advanced	22.4	34.7	8.7	5.3	4.8
Intermediate	24.3	21.2	16.9	16.5	13.0
Basic	37.9	37.0	46.8	49.4	49.8
Below basic	15.5	13.4	27.6	28.9	28.9

Source: Final Report, Indian Nations at Risk: An Education Strategy for Action (Washington, D.C.: U.S. Department of Education): 1991, pp. 7, 9; U.S. Department of Education, Indian Nations at Risk Taskforce.

determining the graduation rates of the nation's students that in many cases differ widely from the numbers reported by states. But regardless of the method used, American Indians and Alaska Natives finish school at rates far below their white and Asian counterparts. In the Institute's study, only 51 percent of Native students graduated in 2001, compared with 74.9 percent of whites and 76.8 percent of Asians. The national average was 68 percent. Although the exact percentage of graduates varies slightly with the data used, by 2007, the situation remained essentially unchanged, with two reports stating that compared to a overall national graduation rate of 70 percent, either 54 percent or 47 percent of American Indian young people were graduating from high school.[23]

The low graduation rates for Indigenous students suggest that average levels of academic achievement in grades K through 12 for Indians are also low. This conclusion is supported by reports from schools. In South Dakota in 2007, for example, where American Indians constituted 12 percent of the state's school population of twenty thousand, only two schools had consistently failed over several years to achieve federally mandated Adequate Yearly Progress achievement rates, and these were on the Pine Ridge and Rosebud reservations. However, although the average statewide Indian achievement rates were below the overall rate, Native school achievement varied from school to school. Some schools that had previously experienced achievement rates below Adequate Yearly Progress for Indian students had risen above the required minimum achievement level through a variety of approaches—from after-school academic programs to applying culturally appropriate teaching methods for Indian students. (Chapter 5, section 2 includes an extensive discussion of the problems involved in low Indigenous student academic accomplishment and what can be done to bring improvement. This discussion includes consideration of difficulties with the Bush administration's "No Child Left Behind" approach to education and testing.) BIA schools have also experienced difficulty in developing high rates of success. For instance, for the period of 2004 to 2005, 37 (25.2 percent) BIA schools attained an Adequate Yearly Progress rating of student achievement, and 110 (74.8 percent) failed to do so. During this period, BIA schools were experiencing a 57.05 percent graduation rate and an 11.31 percent high school dropout rate.[24]

Discrimination as a Factor in Low Native High School Graduation and College-Entry Rates

Recent research by Eileen M. Luna-Firebaugh and Delphine Redshirt finds that a major factor in the high numbers of American Indians who fail to finish high school, and thus are unable to go on to college, is discrimination leading to differential treatment.[25] Their data shows that although a smaller percentage of Native school students get into trouble over behavior than non-Indian students, a far higher percentage of Indigenous students are suspended from school or expelled. Similarly, a far higher percentage of Indian youth are incarcerated or sent to juvenile detention centers (which takes them out of school), than are non-Native students for the same offenses. Once removed from school for an extensive period, it is difficult for many Native young people to return, especially if they are from impoverished families. This prevents them from going on to college directly and may keep them from ever entering higher education. However, as Taylor and Kalt's findings partially reflect, a great many Indian people eventually obtain high school equivalency degrees (such as a GED), so that in the longer term, the number of Indian people who finish high school or attain an equivalent degree becomes close to that for the country as a whole.

A number of specific legal cases illustrate Luna-Firebaugh and Redshirt's general research results. The Winner, South Dakota, school district, on nontribal land within the boundaries of the Rosebud Reservation, for example, in 2007 settled a lawsuit brought in federal district court by the American Civil Liberties Union (ACLU) on behalf of the parents of Indian students. The suit alleged (according to an

ACLU study) that schools in the district sent only Native students to law enforcement authorities over disciplinary issues. The settlement required, among other things, that any American Indian student who is called into a principal's office must be accompanied by a parent or tribal official. The ACLU study, which was the basis of its suit, showed that the "school-to-prison pipeline" caused many Native students to drop out of school.[26]

Similarly, a settlement was reached on September 12, 2007, between two Paiute parents, backed by the Bishop Paiute Tribe and supported by the ACLU, and the Bishop Union Elementary School District. The settlement was designed to end what families claimed was a pattern of discrimination that was driving Paiute children away from the school system.[27] An ACLU investigation of the school's records on suspensions and expulsions from 2000 to 2006 found that American Indian students, who make up about 17 percent of the student body, comprised 67 percent of the students who were punished for subjective offenses such as "defiance" and "being disrespectful/argumentative." A review of school records found American Indian students were suspended for minor infractions such as dress code violations, having candy in class, chewing gum, and being late to class, although the state's education code establishes suspension as a last resort for such offenses. Repeated suspension forced some of these students to attend continuation school, which was designed for students unable to meet the standards of the traditional school system, thus depriving the Native students of educational opportunities. In the 2005–2006 school year, half of the American Indian students in the sixth grade were in the continuation school, as were seven of the twenty-six American Indians in the eighth grade. The settlement expunges from student records suspensions that were in violation of state rules and calls for diversity training for teachers, students, and administrators. The district also will keep discipline records available for ACLU review. Because the plaintiffs alleged that improper police actions were part of the problem, the settlement stipulates that a police officer will no longer be assigned to patrol the schools. Shortly after the settlement was reached, the complaining families stated that the situation was improving. And the ACLU reported that suspensions had decreased significantly, and the district had begun to implement a cultural awareness program.

Continued Struggle for Native Advancement in Higher Education

Concerning college accomplishment, Jonathan Taylor and Joseph Kalt report that in 1990 to 2000, the proportion of Indian adults with college degrees rose substantially, although not enough to keep pace with the very substantial gains in overall U.S. college-degree attainment. In his first State of Indian Nations Address in 2003, NCAI President Tex Hall stated that only 17 percent of Native American young people go on to college in a nation where, overall, 62 percent of young people do so.[28] Table 4 shows the increase in Native participation in postsecondary education from 1990 to 2001.

Table 4.

American Indian and Alaska Native college enrollment from 1990 to 2001 (in thousands)

	1990	1995	2000	2001
Total	102.8	131.3	151.2	158.2
Undergraduate	95.5	120.7	138.5	144.8
Graduate	8.2	8.5	10.3	11.2
Professional	1.1	2.1	2.3	2.1

Source: Data from U.S. Census Bureau Educational Attainment Tables.

Reasons for Low American Indian School Performance

There are a number of reasons why Native Americans have not performed well in school. To begin, it is important to note that American Indian school-age children, who, in 1990, made up about 1 percent of the total U.S. school population but constitute a much higher percentage in the areas in which they are concentrated, attend a variety of school types. In 1990, at least 9 percent of the student population in Alaska, New Mexico, and Oklahoma was Native American. During 1989 to 1990, 10 percent of Native students attended BIA-funded schools, and another 3 percent attended private schools under contract with the BIA. Eighty-seven percent were enrolled in public schools. The website of the Bureau of Indian Education, BIE (formerly the Office of Indian Education Programs), reported in February 2008 that "[t]he BIE has responsibility for 184 elementary and secondary schools and dormitories as well as 24 colleges, and our Bureau-operated Haskell Indian Nations University and Southwest Indian Polytechnic Institute. Our post-secondary institutions, schools and dormitories are located on 63 reservations in 23 states across the United States serving approximately 60,000 students representing 238 different tribes."

Particularly for American Indian young people attending public schools, a persistent problem has been the lack of accommodation of their cultural background, combined with an element of prejudice against them both in the views and attitudes of school staff and in the available teaching materials (e.g., history texts omit the accomplishments and virtues of Native people while discussing them primarily as enemies in war and troublemakers). Little opportunity is given for Indian students to study their own languages and cultures, or to develop a basis for pride in their heritage. This situation engenders low self-esteem in Native students, which is compounded by the fact that, particularly in public schools, teaching methods are in general appropriate for many European Americans, but not often for young people raised in American Indian cultures (we discuss this issue further in chapter 5, section 2).

Improvement in this aspect of the educational problem has begun in recent years in schools on reservations, especially since the passage of the Tribally Controlled Schools Act of 1988, which assists Indian nations to realize the autonomy that was the theoretical basis of the Indian Self-Determination and Education Assistance Act of 1975 (but which largely was not put into practice because of BIA bureaucratic conservatism).[29] Also, the development of culturally appropriate curricula requires time and resources and therefore has not been fully realized, although in recent years, some gains have been made, as we discuss in chapter 5.

Clearly, the conditions of poverty and underdevelopment in which Native Americans often grow up, especially on, but also off, reservations are an important part of the educational problem.[30] But there are other difficulties as well, including low expectations of Indians in school and relegation to low-ability tracks that result in poor achievement; a lack of Native American educators as role models; a lack of opportunity for parents and communities to develop a real sense of participation; limited library and learning resources to meet the academic and cultural needs of the community; limited availability of computers and other technological tools, principles, and research; unequal and unpredictable funding for many schools at all levels (from preschool through tribal colleges); and limited access to colleges and universities because of insufficient funding.[31]

Concerning the problems of funding, tribal colleges are a good example. Although tribal college enrollments increased steadily from 1981 to 1991, federal funding per student dropped each year until 1989, finally increasing by 50 percent in 1990; however, the resulting figure was still less than two-thirds of the 1981 level.[32] This difference has never been made up, and indeed there were some program cuts for the colleges between 1990 and 1996. Under the Bush administration, at least until 2006, Native American education programs, including tribal college funding, continued to fall financially further behind education funding for the rest of the United States. Meg Goetz, congressional liaison for the American Indian Higher Education Consortium, stated in February 2005 that although Congress provided $52.8 million in fiscal year 2005 for tribal colleges, full funding would have been $67 million. She commented that because tribal colleges are funded only year to year, they cannot plan, and when funding is delayed, as it was from October to December 2004, the schools have to find a way to operate without federal money in the meantime. To break even, tribal colleges need to have their authorized funding at $6,000 per student, but currently they receive only $447 per student. Moreover, where state community and university colleges can rely upon state funding and endowments, tribal colleges usually cannot.

In addition, many tribal college physical facilities are significantly substandard. Many continue to operate in overcrowded, abandoned BIA building and trailers. One school has a building known as the Hall of Many Buckets because of the numerous leaks in the roof. Some say they have enough computers but cannot use them because wiring is not up to code. Meanwhile, the American Indian College Fund provides scholarships of $3.4 million a year, which covers about 15 percent of need. The Navajo Nation in 2005 received $10.7 million, $547,000 less than in 2004, from the federal government for the operation of its higher education grant and student aid programs.[33]

Tribal colleges have been particularly important in American Indian higher education because they have been able to achieve far higher completion rates than the dismal 15 percent completion rate for Indians at state-supported institutions of higher learning.[34] Only 10 percent of Native Americans who enter mainstream four-year colleges and universities directly from high school earn a degree, whereas the graduation rate jumps to more than 90 percent for those who have first attended a two-year tribal college.[35]

The lack of adequate funding for American Indian education is visible on many reservations. For example, the Loneman School on the Pine Ridge Reservation was built in the 1950s for 160 students but continued to operate through the end of the twentieth century.[36] In 1995, almost 400 students were jammed into the crumbling building and a couple of trailers. Space was at such a premium that even unventilated spaces without windows, such as a basement shower room, had to be used for classes. Forty-eight students were stuffed into a trailer more than twenty years old with no bathroom. In 1995, a trailer ceiling fell in. As of 1999, money continued to be unavailable for new construction or additional trailers or for adequate maintenance, which was cut by 34 percent in 1996. The school building itself was in such bad shape that it was condemned in 1991. The two boilers in the basement had to be continually turned on and off to keep them from exploding. Teacher's salaries were low: Teachers with six years of experience and an excellent record were paid $20,000 per school year. Supplies of all kinds were in short supply. With no lab equipment, science was taught solely from a textbook. Lack of funds also dictated fewer bus runs, reducing extracurricular activities to the few that could be squeezed into regular school hours. When the average allowance for school transportation nationally was $3.00 a mile, Loneman had $1.50 a mile to cover unusually high transportation costs of long runs over very bad roads. Under these circumstances, the school had to transfer $900 per day from other budget categories to maintain the daily 683-mile minimum bus runs. Loneman's financial, educational, and safety situation was one of the worst in the country, but it is not unique. The school was finally replaced, but BIA officials remain concerned that crumbling and dangerous schools across Indian Country are "a major, major problem."[37] A $650 million backlog in funding for 187 schools existed in 1995, and although federal funding for school construction has since increased, there was still a considerable backlog as of 2006, and school-building maintenance remains underfunded.[38] For example, in March 2004, Delegate Wallace Charley stated that Navajo Nation schools are always underfunded by the federal government, and seven of the fourteen schools listed on the BIA construction list with serious deficiencies—to the point that they are literally crumbling—are located in Navajo Nation, where only one new school building had been completed in 2004.[39] Even worse, by spring 2005, at the Crow Creek tribal high school, the gymnasium had been locked for more than a year after being declared unsafe in a state inspection that recommended that the high school building no longer be used. Later, the three-story brick dormitory at the school was reduced to a blackened hulk in a fire. Tribal officials state that the entire campus should have been rebuilt years ago.[40]

Inadequate funding for Indian education is not only a problem in every aspect of BIA-financed schools but also in the levels of federal funding for Indian primary and secondary school programs through the U.S. Department of Education. Table 5 shows that from 1980 to 1999, the budget for Indian primary and secondary education was below its inadequate 1980 level in fifteen of those twenty years and has consistently surpassed the 1980 level only since 2000. There was a significant rise from 2000 to 2001, followed by rises through 2003. But the Indian Education budget then declined in each of the next three years, and remained level from 2006 to 2007. At first glance, the 56.4 percent rise in budget from 1980 to 2007 may appear reasonably large, but when one considers that it took place over twenty-seven years, it is clear that it is not sufficient to keep up with inflation, much less the growth in Native school population, which has been much faster than the expansion of school-age population for the nation as a whole. Just adding up all the annual inflation rates for each year (as stated by "The U.S. Misery Index" at http://www.miseryindex.us, and not compounding the result) leads to a total rise of 107.93 percent over the twenty-seven years, which is 191.4 percent of the budget increase.

Table 5.

Department of Education Indian primary and secondary education budget for fiscal years 1980–2007 (in millions of U.S. dollars)

Year	Amount	Year	Amount	Year	Amount	Year	Amount	Year	Amount
1980	$75.9	1986	$64.2	1992	$76.6	1998	$59.8	2004	$120.9
1981	$81.7	1987	$64.0	1993	$80.6	1999	$66.0	2005	$119.9
1982	$77.9	1988	$66.3	1994	$83.5	2000	$77.0	2006	$118.7
1983	$69.2	1989	$71.6	1995	$81.0	2001	$115.5	2007	$118.7
1984	$68.8	1990	$73.6	1996	$52.5	2002	$120.4		
1985	$67.4	1991	$75.4	1997	$58.1	2003	$121.6		

Source: Education Department Budget History Tables, published April 26, 2007, U.S. Department of Education, http://www.ed.gov/about/overview/budget/history/index.html. Note: Not adjusted for inflation.

Greater Victimization from Crime, Less Protection from Law Enforcement

American Indians and Alaska Natives also suffer a violent crime rate more than twice the national average, but dissimilarly to all other measured groups, most crimes against Native Americans are committed by non-Natives (even with high Native domestic violence rates, as we will discuss).[41] At the same time, Native Americans generally have less protection from law enforcement than do other groups. On isolated reservations, this is particularly the case because low rates of funding provide for only a few officers to patrol long distances, which makes it more difficult to investigate many crimes adequately. As we discuss in chapter 3, section 2, Indian nations have limited criminal jurisdiction, extending only to misdemeanors committed by members of Indian tribes. Prosecution for most Indian country crime rests with federal attorneys. However, federal prosecutors are more likely to decline cases that involve crime in Indian country than to prosecute: 76 percent of all potential cases are declined by U.S. attorneys who have jurisdictions in Indian country. The situation exists for a variety of reasons, notwithstanding incomplete investigations.[42]

In addition, in some areas around reservations, local law enforcement often has acted prejudicially toward American Indians. In 2006, Barbara Perry interviewed 278 Native Americans from seven states representing eight American Indian nations that revealed "startling patterns of racial violence against this community. In part, this may be accounted for by the enabling climate created by law enforcement in these communities. Of particular concern in this paper are patterns of police activity, which simultaneously represent both the under-enforcement and over-enforcement of the law with respect to Native American communities. Participants have reported activities ranging from willful blindness toward Native American victimization at one extreme, to police brutality at the other."[43]

Improper police behavior toward Indigenous people is part of a broader pattern of racism that has been lessening over at least the last thirty years but that still constitutes a major problem. A reasonably representative example is Farmington, New Mexico, a city bordering the Navajo reservation. A 2006 research report of the Harvard Project on Pluralism reported:

> Farmington, New Mexico is a border town of about 37,000 people, adjacent to the Navajo Nation and not far from the Jicarilla Apache nation. In 1974, three Navajo men were savagely beaten to death by teenagers from Farmington High School. The teens may have been "Indian rolling," a slang term for abusing homeless Navajo inebriates. Controversy over how widespread "Indian rolling" was and is continues today. The

Native American community began holding peaceful protest marches in Farmington throughout the spring of 1974; until the day after the teenagers were sentenced to terms at the New Mexico Boys School. The protest march was denied a permit for that day, and the Sheriff's Posse parade marched instead. Several members of the Coalition for Navajo Liberation found the Sheriff's Posse march offensive, and tried to stop the parade. The meeting between the protesters and the parade turned into a riot, and over 30 people were arrested.

The following year, the U.S. Civil Rights Commission produced a report on the state of affairs in Farmington. The town was reprimanded for the state of interracial relations: a failure on the part of elected officials to assume responsibility for connecting the different populations in Farmington, police prejudice, lack of access to health care, minority underrepresentation in government and business, and economic discrimination were all reported. Farmington had gained the unofficial nickname of "the Selma, Alabama of the Southwest."

Thirty Years Later

In November 2005, the same U.S. Civil Rights Commission produced a report on "Civil Rights for Native Americans, 30 Years Later." The "report card" grade had raised to a B-, but only with a great deal of effort. An earlier lawsuit had led to redistricting, which resulted in two Navajo county commissioners, the first in San Juan County. (4) The local political and business leaders were engaged in addressing the issue of racism and discrimination, in contrast to a fairly disinterested and defensive stance in 1974. More Navajo entrepreneurs joined the ranks of local businesses, and two Navajo-owned and operated stores exist in the center of downtown Farmington.

Although changes have been made in Farmington, conflicts and discrimination still exist. Unscrupulous business and lending practices were cited in the report of the Civil Rights Commission as a continuing problem, one that seems to target Native Americans. Allegations of law enforcement bias remain. Many of the institutions of the town seek to become more multicultural, albeit with slow results. Minority representation in the police force had increased since 1974, but Farmington still lacks a Navajo councilman or mayor. The Better Business Bureau and the Chamber of Commerce had implemented programs to improve business and consumer relations, but did not yet have Navajo employees. The Farmington education system was praised, although the nearby Shiprock system was rebuked for a failure to incorporate Navajo culture and values into its curriculum. In many ways, those institutions within Farmington that have been able to integrate the concerns of all the different citizens have been most successful.

As a result of the Civil Rights Commission Report, and pressure from American Indians and others, the mayor of Farmington established a steering committee with Native American representation to shape community relations and hear citizens' complaints against police and other municipal employees.[44]

A particularly serious aspect of the problem of racism spawning violence and diminishing law enforcement protection has been an epidemic of rape against Native women in Alaska. Amnesty International reported in May 2007 that "[s]exual violence against Indigenous women in the USA is widespread and especially brutal." Native American and Alaska Native women are more than 2.5 times more likely to be raped or sexually assaulted than other women in the United States, and one in three American Indian or Alaska Native women are raped at some point in their lives. Most do not seek justice because they know they will be met with inaction or indifference. The Amnesty International report found that the violence has been compounded by the federal government's steady erosion of tribal government authority and its chronic underfunding of those law enforcement agencies that should protect Indigenous women from sexual violence. Amnesty International stated that the first steps to stopping the violence are undertaking comprehensive data collection to establish the extent of the problem and making available adequate law enforcement and access to forensic examinations.[45]

On July 23, 2008, after five hearings and more than a year of development by the Senate Committee on Indian Affairs, Senator Byron Dorgan of North Dakota introduced the Tribal Law and Order Act of 2008 (S. 3320; H.R. 6583) to attempt to overcome many of the problems in tribal law enforcement with a major overhaul of federal agency law enforcement in Indian Country.[46] The bill had not come up for a vote as of November 2008. However, the act does not address lack of funding for adequate Native law enforcement, which would have to be dealt with separately by increased appropriations.

The Slow Recovery of American Indian Health

American Indian health has also long been substandard for the United States. Although significant improvement in the health of Indigenous Americans has occurred over the past three-quarters of a century, Native Americans continue to have a higher mortality rate than the U.S. population at large due to poor living conditions and inadequate access to health care.[47] The death rate for Native Americans, although it is improving, remains higher than for the entire population for selected causes. In 1988, Native Americans experienced disease, accident, and murder and suicide rates that were greater than those of the general population: for example, tuberculosis, 520 percent greater; pneumonia and influenza, 44 percent greater; diabetes mellitus, 188 percent greater; alcoholism, 433 percent greater; accidents, 166 percent greater; homicide, 71 percent greater; and suicide, 54 percent greater.[48]

Maternal death rates and infant mortality rates remained somewhat higher for Native Americans than for Americans generally. With considerably more fluctuation than any other group experienced, maternal death rates for Native Americans have improved, as have maternal death rates for the population as a whole, since 1973 but have risen more sharply than have those of other groups since 1985, when all groups suffered some increase. Indian infant mortality rates have always been higher than have those of the population as a whole but fell further between 1973 and 1988 than the rates for any other group did. The number of infant deaths per 1,000 were as follows in 1988: Native Americans, 11; whites, 8.5; and the general population, 10. Life expectancy for Native Americans has improved. It trailed the population as a whole by 10 years in 1972; in 1988, Native Americans had come to within 3.4 years of the population as a whole and to within 4.1 years of whites.[49]

The Centers for Disease Control and Prevention (CDC) reported in July 2005 that although the national public health goal of reducing infant mortality rates by the year 2000 had been achieved for the general population, American Indians had not experienced the same rate of reduction. For the country as a whole, the proportion of babies who died in their first year of life declined between 1995 and 2002 to a rate of seven deaths per one thousand live births. In Montana, the general population infant mortality rate for the same period was the same as the nation's, but the death rate for Indian babies in the state was 9.8 deaths per 1,000. During the seven-year study period, 610 Montana babies died: 100 of those infants were Indian, although only about 12.5 percent of births in Montana during the period were Indian. The Indian infant mortality rate was worse in surrounding states: in Wyoming it was 12 per 1,000; in South Dakota, 13.6 per 1,000; in North Dakota, 12.9 per 1,000; and in Idaho, 12.4 per 1,000.[50]

A related set of findings appeared in an epidemiological study conducted at two IHS clinics in Montana in 2005–2006 and written by IHS epidemiologist Christine Dubray that uncovered a hepatitis C infection rate among women who went to the clinics for prenatal care that is six times higher than is found in the general population.[51] The finding surprised tribal and state health officials, who responded by creating an educational brochure that targets young American Indians.

On January 31, 2003, NCAI President Tex Hall, in the first State of Indian Nations Address, reported that American Indian life expectancy was five years shorter than for any other race. American Indians are three times more likely to die from diabetes and are disproportionately affected by other diseases, yet Indians receive fewer health care services than the average American does, and development of Indian health services is exceedingly slow. However, the IHS found in 2007 that its Special Diabetes Program for Indians was producing an ongoing reduction of diabetes and its complications among Indians and Alaska Natives, indicating that the program was making significant progress, although the incidence rates remained very high. The NCAI communicated in 2005 that life expectancy for Native Americans is almost six years less than for any other group measured in the United States. Thirteen percent of Native deaths occur in those younger than twenty-five, a rate three times higher than for the U.S. population as a whole. The U.S. Commission on Civil Rights reported in 2003 that "American Indian youths are twice as likely to commit suicide . . ." Native Americans are 630 percent more likely to die from tuberculosis, 650 percent more likely to die from diabetes, and 204 percent more likely to suffer accidental death as compared with other racial and ethnic groups. In 2007, the IHS found that the rate of suicide for American Indians from 15 to 24 years of age is more than three times the national average.[52]

The report *American Indians and Alaska Natives with Cancer*, published in April 2008 by the Intercultural Cancer Council, noted that cancer is the second leading cause of death among American Indians and Alaska Natives over the age of forty-five and that American Indians with cancer are largely "invisible" to policy makers, making it difficult for many Native people to receive high-quality treatment and prevention assistance.[53] Lovell Jones, cofounder of ICC, states in the report that because American Indians as a group tend to be younger than other racial populations in the United States, traditional research has previously suggested that cancer is less common in Native communities. However, Jones indicates that better health data collection in Indian country now shows that such research is not correct. "Cancer rates were previously reported to be lower in American Indians," Jones said, "but they have actually been increasing over the past twenty years." Compared with other racial groups, Indians have the lowest survival rate for all cancers, and there are many cancers that disproportionately affect Indian populations. Death from lung cancer was found to be the most common type of cancer death in eight of the nine IHS areas. Incidence and death rates from kidney cancer among Natives were also found to be higher than for any other racial or ethnic groups. Poverty, discrepancies between rural and urban health care, and lack of access to prevention strategies such as screening tests are all contributors to the alarming trends, according to IHS officials. The ICC study noted that a report released on October 15, 2007, by the American Cancer Society found the cancer death rate declined by almost twice the previous rate in the general U.S. population, and cancer incidence among all races and both sexes declined slightly. A special section of the American Cancer Society report examined the most full and accurate cancer data ever compiled for American Indians and Alaska Natives, and the key finding was that cancer incidence varies regionally and by cancer type. Although Native cancer incidence rates were higher for cancers of the stomach, liver, kidney, gallbladder, and cervix, the incidence rate for all cancers among Native Americans was lower than for non-Hispanic whites from 1999 to 2004. Judith Salmon Kaur, a professor of oncology and the director of Native American programs at the Mayo Clinic, stated in the report that nationally and for Native people: "I think the nugget is that screening really can make a difference. . . . I'd rather prevent cancer than have people coming to me for radiation, chemotherapy, operations. . . . We're not there yet, but we can be doing a lot more to prevent cancer." The variety in regional rates—with lung and kidney cancer showing a higher incidence in the northern and southern Plains, Alaska, and urban areas than in the Southwest, where cigarette smoking is more constrained—in effect targets the higher-incidence regions for antismoking intervention, Kaur said. The same holds true for many of the cancers that vary in regional incidence.

A study led by Dartmouth Medical School and published in June 2004 found that American Indians and Alaska Natives have a greater chance of death within thirty days of surgery and suffer more from several preoperative risks than do white patients.[54] The study showed a significant difference in mortality rates after surgery, with 3.1 percent of American Indians dying, compared with 2.2 percent of white patients. The research also indicated higher rates of some preoperative risk factors among Native Americans as compared with whites. These findings confirm previous reports that nearly twice as many older American Indians as whites experience some type of functional impairment. The higher risk factors found in the study include wound infections, low platelet counts, and diabetes. The Dartmouth research cited related studies that found that American Indian patients received fewer kidney transplants than whites and experienced a greater delay from onset of treated end-stage renal disease to transplantation. Another study found that the Native population underwent coronary revascularization procedures less often than whites, although their need for the procedure was at least as great.[55]

Meanwhile, HIV/AIDS infection rates for Indians continue to rise, especially compared with the rates for whites. In 1995, the Native American rate of HIV infection surpassed that for whites and by 2003 was 40 percent higher than the white rate, at 11.5 per 100,000, compared with 8.1 per 100,000. More than a million Americans were reported to have HIV/AIDS, nineteen hundred of whom were Native, with more than half of those cases in California, Oklahoma, Arizona, Washington, and Alaska.[56]

A report commissioned by International Relief and Development, a food and welfare advocacy organization, and made public in April 2008, found that although overall American Indian health continues to improve, it remains well below that of all other groups and poverty clusters in the United States, with some particular areas of concern, including malnutrition on some reservations with levels comparable to those seen in underdeveloped countries.[57] Thoric Cederstrom, director of International Relief and Development's sustainable food and agriculture program, notes in the report that "American Indian/Alaska Native populations are facing a number of serious challenges, including poverty and health-related issues. . . . Many of these problems have, at their root cause, a lack of sufficient and consistent access to nutritious foods." The report notes that in many cases, Indians living on reservations do not have sufficient funds to buy nutritious foods, and food subsidy programs often do not provide incentives to help people purchase healthy foods, which tend to be more expensive than junk food. Recent studies indicate that 23 percent of American Indian households report being food insecure, compared to 11 percent of all U.S. households, and the percentage is much higher for some tribal populations. A 2002 study of high-needs groups of Northern Cheyenne tribal members found that as many as 70 percent of the population experienced food insecurity and 35 percent experienced persistent hunger. Poverty also contributes to obesity, sometimes because it is related to overeating and sedentary lifestyles, but also, according to Cederstrom, because "[s]ome Indian people are not getting enough of the right kinds of food, and too many Indian people are over consuming the wrong sort of nutrients, like refined carbohydrates and fats." According to Michele Companion, a researcher with the University of Colorado who wrote the International Relief and Development report, unhealthy food choices have become a part of the collective taste preferences of many Indian cultures. She believes the historical process of colonization, assimilation, and acculturation all played into this contemporary effect. One project Companion highlighted in the report that promotes healthy eating originates in a partnership between Tohono O'odham Community College and the Tohono O'odham Community Action grassroots organization to rekindle traditional food-production systems and reincorporate elements of traditional diet to address nutrition-related illnesses: "To make these foods more easily and readily available, they established a traditional agriculture project in 2002 as a learning laboratory and training area for traditional practices." The groups have established community gardens in locations across the Tohono O'odham reservation in Arizona that serve as learning and teaching centers for youth and elders. They also organize numerous trips to collect wild foods that not only provide exercise but also encourage healthier diets and provide opportunities for cultural revitalization and knowledge transfer.

Substance abuse, including an extensive problem with crystal meth, continues to be a major problem for Native Americans, although there have been some gains in combating it. The 2004 National Survey on Drug Use and Health of the Substance Abuse and Mental Health Services Administration, found that illicit drug use among Americans between the ages of twelve and seventeen dropped 9 percent from 2002 to 2004; 10.6 percent of people in that age group had used an illicit drug in the last month before the survey. However, some minority groups saw higher drug-use rates than the general population, with the highest rates, 26 percent, among American Indian or Alaska Native youths, compared with 12.2 percent for youths reporting two or more races, 11.1 percent for white youths, 10.2 percent for Hispanic youths, 9.3 percent for African American youths, and 6 percent for Asian youths. The high rate of substance abuse includes very high rates of alcohol abuse, which in turn contributes considerably to a number of major health problems. Among these is that the fetal alcohol syndrome rate among American Indians is thirty times higher than the rate among whites.[58]

A similar and in some ways more troubling pattern of substance abuse and often-related problems was indicated in one of the first studies of urban Indians, who now make up the majority of Native Americans in the United States, *Reported Health and Health-Influencing Behaviors Among Urban American Indians and Alaska Natives*, released on March 5, 2008, by the Seattle-based Urban Indian Health Institute.[59] The report found that, rich or poor, American Indians in cities across the country are facing health challenges unlike those of any other urban population. Researchers found that in urban areas across the country, even as American Indians move up the income ladder, rates of binge drinking and tobacco use in the Native community are staying the same and sometimes even increasing, which is not the case for any other measured group. According to the report, overall, fewer Indian respondents reported drinking than people of other races. But among those who did drink, more American Indians reported an episode of binge drinking— or consuming five or more drinks in one sitting—at least once in the previous month. Among higher-income respondents—defined as those earning more than $38,700 for a family of four—46 percent of American Indians reported one episode of binge drinking in the previous month, compared with 25.3 percent among people of other ethnic backgrounds. The study also found that diabetes and obesity rates were about the same for urban Indians, whether they were rich or poor. Among other ethnic groups, people with higher incomes tend to have fewer of those health problems. Maile Taualii, scientific director at the Urban Indian Health Institute, stated in the report that, "[t]here seems to be a sense of hopelessness, a sense that diabetes, alcoholism and other health problems are inevitable in the community."

Researchers also concluded that, unlike the general population, rates of diabetes, obesity, and smoking remained about the same among low-income and wealthy urban Indians. According to Taualii, those results—and data showing that Native people in some cities reported having more difficulty getting health care than urbanites of other backgrounds—show that special attention must be paid to the health disparities for urban Indians. Newman Washington, who runs drug and alcohol programs at a government-funded Indian clinic in Wichita, Kansas, was quoted in the report as saying that tight finances already make it difficult to meet the needs of patients from the Kickapoo, Potawatomi, and other nearby tribes. Alcoholic clients wanting to detox often have to wait two months to be admitted to a hospital bed or travel seventy-five miles to Ponca City, Oklahoma, to be treated in an inpatient facility. Washington stated that "[p]eople go away and get an education, but then they come back home and have a really hard time changing their behavior. Whenever you start looking at the core, there's some shame and guilt that people are carrying around from past generations." One difficulty is that in many urban areas, it is difficult for Native people to find culturally competent health care. The report also showed that more data is needed to quantify the special needs of urban Indians and more united action between urban Natives and tribes is needed "to achieve a better future for all Native people." The report notes that "[t]here is a critical lack of research on the issues facing Native families residing in urban areas," and that the need exists "to make sure that the needs of reservation-based and urban Native people are not a cause for division but instead for united action."

An overall measure of health that reflects the collective impact of various factors is the set of the surveys that the CDC uses to determine Health-Related Quality of Life. HRQOL data has a high correlation to economic and living-condition levels that have been found to affect health. Because Native people in the United States rank at or near the bottom in measures of these factors as well as in access to high quality health care, it is not surprising that Indians rank at the bottom, and one case next to the bottom, of the measured groups in the HRQOL surveys. Participants in the study self-reported for thirty days prior to each of the surveys undertaken from 1993 to 2002. Analysis of the results found:

> Compared with non-Hispanic whites (12.8%), more Hispanics (21.9%), American Indians/Alaska Natives (21.1%), and non-Hispanic blacks (19.8%) reported fair or poor health, and fewer Asians/Pacific Islanders (9.0%) reported fair or poor

health. The percentages of Hispanic men (19.6%), American Indian/Alaska Native men (19.2%), and black men (17.3%) with fair or poor health were higher and the percentage of Asian/Pacific Islander men (8.8%) with fair or poor health was lower than that of white men (12.0%). Similarly for women, percentages of Hispanic women (24.2%), American Indian/ Alaska Native women (23.1%), and black women (21.6%) with fair or poor health were higher and the percentage of Asian/ Pacific Islander women (9.2%) with fair or poor health was lower than that of white women (13.6%).

Reported mean number of physically unhealthy days was higher among American Indian/Alaska Native men (3.9) than among men of "other races" (3.1), and black (3.0), white (2.7), and Hispanic (2.7) men. American Indian/Alaska Native women (4.9) and women of "other races" (4.1) reported more mean number of physically unhealthy days than black (3.8), Hispanic (3.8), and white (3.5) women. Asian/Pacific Islander men and women reported the fewest physically unhealthy days (1.8 and 2.2, respectively).

Reported mean number of mentally unhealthy days was higher among American Indian/Alaska Native men (4.1) and men of "other races" (3.5) than Hispanic (2.9), black (2.7), and white (2.4) men. American Indian/Alaska Native women (5.0) and women of "other races" (4.9) reported more mentally unhealthy days than Hispanic (4.0), black (3.8), and white (3.5) women. Asian/Pacific Islander men and women reported the fewest mentally unhealthy days (2.1 and 2.6, respectively).

In addition, American Indian/Alaska Native men (6.7) and men of "other races" (5.8) reported more overall unhealthy days than black (4.9), Hispanic (4.9), and white (4.5) men. American Indian/Alaska Native women (8.4) and women of "other races" (7.9) reported more overall unhealthy days than black (6.7), Hispanic (6.7), and white (6.2) women. Asian/ Pacific Islander men and women reported the fewest overall unhealthy days (3.6 and 4.5, respectively).

Reported activity limitation days were higher among American Indian/Alaska Native men (2.6) than among men of "other races" (2.1), and black (1.9), white (1.6), and Hispanic (1.6) men. American Indian/Alaska Native women (3.1) and women of "other races" (2.9) also reported more activity limitation days than black (2.4), Hispanic (2.1), and white (1.9) women. Asian/Pacific Islander men and women reported the fewest activity limitation days (1.1 and 1.2, respectively).

More American Indians/Alaska Natives (13.5%) reported >14 physically unhealthy days and fewer Asians/Pacific Islanders (5.1%) reported >14 physically unhealthy days than persons of "other races" (10.9%), blacks (10.5%), Hispanics (10.0%), and whites (9.3%). More American Indians/Alaska Natives (14.4%) and persons of "other races" (12.9%) reported >14 mentally unhealthy days and fewer Asians/Pacific Islanders (6.2%) reported >14 mentally unhealthy days than whites (8.6%), blacks (10.3%), and Hispanics (10.5%). In addition, more American Indians/Alaska Natives (23.8%) and persons of "other races" (20.4%) reported >14 overall unhealthy days and fewer Asians/Pacific Islanders (10.6%) reported >14 overall unhealthy days than Hispanics (18.1%), blacks (18.0%), and whites (16.0%).

The percentages of persons who reported >14 activity limitation days were higher among American Indians/Alaska Natives (9.2%), persons of "other races" (7.6%), and blacks (6.9%) and were lower among Asians/Pacific Islanders (2.9%) than Hispanics (5.7%) and whites (5.2%). In comparison, the percentages of blacks and Hispanics with >14 physically unhealthy days, mentally unhealthy days, and overall unhealthy days did not differ but were higher than whites.[60]

The Long-Term Problem of Insufficient and Substandard Housing
A factor in health and general well-being is the condition of housing and infrastructure on reservations. Although conditions vary from reservation to reservation, in general, insufficient housing is the rule, leading to the crowding of many people into small structures. At the Pine Ridge Reservation in South Dakota, for example, as of 1995, only 1,500 units for 26,000 people existed—an average of seventeen people per house, which might measure only twenty feet by twenty feet.[61] About one thousand Pine Ridge residents were then on the waiting list for housing, and some of them had been waiting for two decades. Much of the housing was substandard, without insulation (thus very hot in summer and quite cold in winter), plumbing, or an adequate kitchen. Houses were aging and in

serious need of repair (the BIA housing repair program was backlogged with a documented $600 million need in 1996).[62]

Stephanie M. Schwartz reported in 2007 that the small BIA/Tribal Housing Authority homes on the Pine Ridge Reservation are overcrowded and scarce, resulting in many homeless families who often use tents or cars for shelter. Many families live in old cabins and dilapidated mobile homes and trailers. Schwartz stated that a 2003 report from South Dakota State University found that the majority of the current Tribal Housing Authority homes were built by the BIA from 1970 to 1979 and that a large percentage of the original construction was "shoddy and substandard." Twenty-six percent of the housing units on the reservation are mobile homes, often purchased or obtained through donations as used, low-value units with negative-value equity. At least 60 percent of the homes on the Pine Ridge Reservation are infested with black mold (*Stachybotrys* species), which causes a number of serious health problems, including an often-fatal condition affecting high-risk individuals such as infants, children, the elderly, those with damaged immune systems, and those with lung and pulmonary conditions. Exposure to this mold can cause hemorrhaging of the lungs and brain as well as cancer. The mold infestations on the reservation are so serious that the only solution is to destroy infected houses, but there are no insurance or assistance programs to replace them. Even though there is a large homeless population on the reservation, most families never turn away a relative no matter how distant the blood relation, so many homes are extremely overcrowded: many homes, which might have only two or three rooms, shelter approximately seventeen people. Some larger homes, originally built for six to eight people, have as many as thirty people living in them. Schwartz stated that the tribal council had recently estimated a need for at least four thousand new homes to combat the homeless situation. Overall, 59 percent of the reservation homes are substandard, more than 33 percent lack basic water and sewage systems, and 39 percent have no electricity. Water systems are inadequate, so that many residents must carry water, which is often contaminated, from local rivers daily for their personal needs. Some reservation families are forced to sleep on dirt floors.[63]

The Inter Tribal Council of Arizona, which runs an indoor air quality environmental education program funded by the EPA, reported in 2004 that substandard housing, inadequate maintenance, and mold can cause major health problems, even in desert areas. The council also reported that secondhand smoke is also a major problem, introducing a cancer threat to many Native buildings, especially on many reservations where there are no smoking policies. Some Native nations have been taking action against mold and other indoor air pollutants, including the Makah in very wet Washington state.[64] The IHS and other agencies have been working to reduce Indigenous smoking rates, which are the highest in the country.

The housing situation was somewhat improved on many reservations by 2006, due to increases in tribal economic development and because many Indian nations took over housing programs from the federal government and have been able to build housing faster and more cheaply, as we discuss in chapter 3. However, federal funding for Indian housing remains inadequate, and growth of tribal economies has not brought an equivalent expansion of Native housing. This situation exists in part because as Native incomes rise, many Indians become ineligible for federally subsidized housing, and despite considerable improvement, it is still far more difficult for reservation Indians to acquire mortgages than it is for the general public.[65]

The Ongoing Need for Modern Infrastructure

Infrastructure, including roads, is in general seriously underdeveloped in Indian country. On the vast Navajo Nation reservation, which spans three states and is home to the largest Native American population in the country, many areas are linked only by hundreds of miles of extremely poor unpaved roads. Anyone who wants to enjoy Chaco Canyon National Monument inside the reservation by the shortest route from a paved highway must drive more than twenty miles on an unimproved road that is almost entirely washboard and threatens to shake to pieces any vehicle traveling more than three miles per hour. Other infrastructure, such as electric power, sewage treatment, and telephone communications (to say nothing of fiber optic cables) is also underdeveloped in Indian country.

An NCAI study of the Bureau of Indian Affairs Road Program in 2003 showed that although Indian country contains 3 percent of the nation's roads, only 1 percent of U.S. highway funding was spent on them. Of the fifty thousand miles of reservation roads, three-quarters were unpaved. Hazardous road conditions were a significant factor in Indian highway fatalities, which were four times the national rate. Bridges across Indian country were equally in need of improvement, repair, and maintenance.[66] NCAI President Tex Hall pointed out in his January 31, 2003, State of Indian Nations Address that 25 percent of American Indians have no telephones, and more than 14 percent of reservation homes have no electricity and 8 percent have no running water.[67]

Research conducted by the CDC's Arctic Investigations Program in conjunction with the Alaska Native Tribal Health Consortium found that the lack of infrastructure development connected with Indian housing, and particularly the absence of water services to homes, was a major source of health problems.[68] The research showed that the lack of running water in the home is linked to severe respiratory infections and lung and skin infections among Alaska Natives. Infants who live in villages with the lowest rates of in-home water service are hospitalized for lower respiratory tract infections and respiratory syncytial virus at a rate five times higher than for infants who live in homes with water service. Compared with the overall U.S. population, these infants experience a rate of hospitalization for pneumonia that is eleven times higher. These findings may help explain why the rates of respiratory illness among Alaska Native infants are extremely high: 75 percent of all hospitalizations among Alaska Native and American Indian children in Alaska are due to respiratory problems. The study also found that elders sixty-five years old and older living in areas with low rates of water service were twice as likely to be hospitalized for pneumonia or influenza. For all age groups, skin infections were significantly higher in areas with lower water service rates. Alaska Natives without in-home water have no easy way to take a shower, wash their clothes, or even go to the bathroom. Families in rural areas regularly make lengthy treks via snowmobile to fill up five-gallon buckets of water to bring home, heat up, and use to wash their dishes. Troy Ritter, a senior environmental health consultant for Alaska Native Tribal Health Consortium who helped conduct the study, notes that people who have to haul water in a bucket from a remote point use about 1.8 gallons of water per person each day. The average American uses between eighty and one hundred gallons of water each day. According to census data for 2000, 99.4 percent of all American homes have complete sanitation service. In Alaska, 93.7 percent of homes have complete sanitation, and the proportion of homes without such service was much higher in rural Alaskan villages. The state ranks last in the proportion of homes with in-home water service. Between forty and fifty Native communities throughout Alaska still lack modern sanitation facilities, including running water, bathrooms, and flush toilets. The estimated cost for bringing running water to all Native homes in the state currently is at least $600 million. The price has been falling as more houses have plumbing installed and technology costs decrease. Water projects costing between $60 million and $70 million are currently underway in rural areas.

Finally Beginning to Reduce Continuing High Native Unemployment
The lack of adequate and appropriate education, health and other services, and infrastructure and economic development have contributed to very high unemployment and underemployment for American Indians. For many years, most of the available jobs around many reservations have been with the tribes and have been at least partially funded by the federal government. This situation is changing with advances in Native economic development, which we discuss in chapter 5, but is still well behind that of the rest of the country. Relatively few Indians, either on or off reservations, hold high-paying, professional jobs. But off-reservation Native Americans have better job opportunities than do Indians who live on reservations, as figures from 1970 that are still generally relevant show: 48 percent of employed Native Americans in cities worked as white collar workers, technicians, craftsmen, and foremen, as compared with 35 percent of employed Native Americans on reservations.[69]

Although situations vary from reservation to reservation and are improving on many reservations, unemployment generally runs high, driving down wage levels for those who can find jobs. For example, at the Pine Ridge reservation in South Dakota, which still has had little economic development, conditions are not much better than in the late 1990s, when unemployment ran from a low of 45 percent in the summer months when seasonal work, such as construction, was available, to a high of 90 percent in the winter, averaging about 80 percent over the year. In 2006, Pine Ridge unemployment was estimated at about 83 to 85 percent but ran higher during the winter months when travel to work is difficult to impossible.[70] William Kindle, president of the Rosebud Sioux Tribe, in a letter dated January 24, 1996, to Alex. J. Lumberman Sr. of the American Heritage Association, reported an 80 percent unemployment rate on the Rosebud reservation, which is near the Pine Ridge reservation and has similar conditions. Overall, unemployment for Native Americans averaged 16.2 percent for males and 13.5 percent for females in 1989, compared with 6.4 percent for males and 6.2 percent for females in the U.S. population as a whole that year.[71]

Unemployment remains a serious problem for Indians, despite

improvements. Stephen Cornell and Joseph Kalt found that between 1990 and 2000, Indian unemployment rates dropped by about 2.5 percentage points in nongaming areas and by more than 5 percentage points in gaming areas, whereas overall U.S. unemployment dropped by half a percentage point during the same time period.[72] However,

> Between 1994 and 2003, the unemployment rate for American Indians/Alaska Natives, ages 16 and over, fluctuated but did not significantly increase or decrease overall. The unemployment rate for American Indians/Alaska Natives has remained higher than the rate for the general population. In 2003, the American Indian/Alaska Native unemployment rate (15 percent) was 9 percentage points higher than the general population's rate (6 percent). Whites, Asian/Pacific Islanders, and Hispanics had lower unemployment rates than American Indians/Alaska Natives in 2003 (5, 6, and 8 percent, respectively, vs. 15 percent). In 2003, the American Indian/Alaska Native unemployment rate was three times as high as the unemployment rate for the White population.[73]

An examination of table 6 shows that Native American and Alaska Native official unemployment from 1994 to 2003 was the highest of any group measured, and was tied for the highest rate only once, in 1994, with black, non-Hispanic unemployment. Over the course of the period surveyed, Native unemployment actually worsened. In 1994, Native unemployment (at 11.7 percent) was 221 percent of the white, non-Hispanic rate (at 5.3 percent), and 180 percent of the total rate. With a surge in Indian unemployment from 2002 to 2003, in 2003, the difference increased so that Native unemployment rose to 328 percent of the white, non-Hispanic rate and 256 percent of the total rate. Just prior to the 2002–2003 Native unemployment surge, Indian unemployment in comparison with white, non-Hispanic unemployment had risen only slightly, to 239 percent, and 198 percent of the national average. Without further data, it is impossible to know whether the increase in Native unemployment in 2003 was a trend or a singular occurrence. Because official rates of unemployment vary in their indication of actual unemployment, it is possible to conclude only that despite the increases in employment due to economic development that Cornell and Kalt reported, American Indian joblessness remains a major problem.

Table 6.

Comparison of U.S. unemployment rates

Year	Total (%)	White, non-Hispanic (%)	Black, non-Hispanic (%)	Hispanic (%)	Asian/Pacific Islander (%)	American Indian/ Alaska Native (%)
1994	6.5	5.3	11.7	9.9	5.8	11.7
1995	5.4	4.5	8.8	9.0	4.4	12.9
1996	5.5	4.3	10.2	9.4	4.2	12.0
1997	5.1	4.0	10.0	8.2	4.4	10.3
1998	4.7	3.7	8.5	6.9	4.0	9.1
1999	4.2	3.4	7.8	6.2	3.7	11.1
2000	4.1	3.3	7.1	6.2	3.4	9.6
2001	4.4	3.5	8.2	6.5	2.8	9.5
2002	5.8	4.8	10.4	7.5	5.5	11.5
2003	5.9	4.9	9.8	7.8	6.3	15.1

Source: U.S. Census Bureau, March Current Population Survey (CPS), 1994 to 2003.

The Ongoing Need for Economic Development

A major factor in high rates of Indian poverty and unemployment is the lack of economic development on reservations. Economic improvement has been made difficult by the isolated locations of reservations and their lack of infrastructure of all kinds, including a scarcity of adequate roads, electric power, telephone lines, water mains, and sewage lines and treatment. The generally low levels of education among Native Americans is also a difficulty. Moreover, until recently, most of the limited attempts that were made at economic development on reservations were undertaken in culturally inappropriate ways that ensured a high degree of failure. However, significant but not yet adequate improvement in living conditions and tribal economies has taken place in recent years, some with federal government assistance, largely as a result of Indian nations gaining control of economic and other decision making. But although the situation is improving for many nations, most tribes lack the capital and income necessary for expanding tribal business and individual-member entrepreneurship.[74] Thus, there is a need for further provision of resources for investment, education, and services until the reservations become self-sufficient and can prepare their youth to succeed in the job market both on and off tribal lands.

The possible sources of capital necessary for the needed development of tribes and their members are generally limited. Reservation land consists of tracts that were considered least desirable by the mostly European American populations that displaced tribal peoples; thus, reservation land often has limited potential for gainful agriculture or ranching. In many instances, the tapping of natural resources on reservation land has been possible but must be balanced with environmental and other concerns. Moreover, natural resources such as oil, natural gas, coal, and other minerals are nonrenewable and can be profitably exploited only for a limited time. Resource development has been an important source of income for tribes and can be increased by educating tribal members to run their own resource managing operations (as the Southern Utes have done in developing their own natural gas company) rather than merely receive royalties from outside corporations. Some tribes have been able to attract some manufacturing business or start their own businesses in various fields, either on their own or in collaboration with external entities.[75] However, given the isolated geographic location of many Indian nations and the need for increased education and other development and services required to overcome long-term poverty and to provide adequate infrastructure to support development, economic advancement can take place only over a long period of time. We discuss advancements in overcoming these difficulties and what is needed for further improvement in chapter 5, section 1.

One recent development that has been helpful is the rise of casino gambling on reservations. However, except for a handful of the 40 percent of the more than 550 Indian nations that have gambling, gaming revenue, although it has been an important source of capital and income, has been far from adequate to provide self-sufficiency. The National Indian Gaming Commission announced in July 2004 that total Indian casino revenue in 2003 was $16.7 billion. The forty-three most profitable casinos each produced more than $100 million in revenue, which enriched the top 7.8 percent of Indian nations, which did not include any of the most populous tribes. The seventy-three least profitable casinos each generated less than $3 million, and the average income of the seventy-three was just over $1 million. The National Indian Gaming Commission reported that Indian gaming grossed $25.08 billion in 2006.[76]

Most casinos do not make huge profits. Some gaming operations are extremely limited and because of location are likely to remain so. Others have been important both in creating jobs for tribal and nontribal members and for bringing in funds and creating opportunities for further economic development, but the needs of the tribes are so great that this revenue, while significant, is only a small portion of what is required. Moreover, largely because of increasing competition, the rate of increase of revenue from Indian gaming is declining, with an 11 percent increase in 2006 over 2005, down from a 15 percent increase in 2005 over 2004, and a 16.7 percent increase from 2004 over 2003.[77] Therefore, although Indian gaming is a significant source of capital for tribes, additional sources are needed if Indian nations are to become economically viable, and continued federal funding is clearly essential for tribal development, as are other measures that we discuss in chapter 5.

The experience and long memory of physical and cultural genocide and still widespread poverty with inadequate health, education, and other services is, of itself, a major cause of disharmony in Indian communities.[78] This factor has not been adequately addressed even for the relatively few now-well-off Native Americans. Unresolved feelings of historical loss and deprivation have produced low self-esteem and anger in a considerable number of American Indians, in many cases leading to a variety of patterns of disruptive behavior. These include alcoholism and other substance abuse and a variety of disrespectful and abusive behaviors towards self and others, which, in many instances, become secondary causes of further inharmonious feelings and behavior. The considerable negative impact of physical and cultural genocide are compounded by a number of other factors.

Imposition of Culturally Inappropriate Government

When Indian nations finally were given the opportunity to return to governing themselves, the Indian Reorganization Act of 1934 and the Oklahoma Indian Welfare Act of 1936 imposed a European American form of representative government on many Indian nations that then had no say as to how those governments would be structured.[79] The Western form of government generally imposed upon the tribes most often so clashed with traditional values that it created significant additional problems for the communities involved. People who were used to having a direct say in their governance had to choose those who would decide for them. Thus, citizens were denied the basic respect of being heard directly, which undermined their sense of self as participating members of their societies.

The current practices of holding elections in which there are winners and losers and of electing councils that make decisions rather than announce decisions made by the people as a whole, are divisive. Those who lose an election often feel that they have been rejected by the community and feel that their honor has been impugned. Often, tribal officials defeated in a recall or a reelection bid, will spend the rest of their lives attacking the tribal government. In addition, people who are not included in the making of a decision, even if they are invited to a meeting to state their opinion to the decision makers, tend to feel left out.

Indeed, today many people are in fact left out because their interests are not effectively represented in the tribal electoral systems. Communication about public issues has become fragmented, with a considerable number of tribal members unaware of, or holding distorted perceptions about, what tribal government is considering and doing. A good example of how communication has tended to break down, so that even key people may not know what tribal government is doing, was observed by author Stephen Sachs on a relatively small reservation in the late 1990s. The tribe had long held a single Sun Dance, which was the most important spiritual ceremony for traditional tribal members. One year, a spiritual leader and longtime helper at Sun Dances and a member of a tribal faction that felt left out of certain aspects of community affairs went to the Elder's Committee to request permission to start a second Sun Dance. According to tradition, everyone concerned, most particularly the chief of the existing Sun Dance, should have been invited to a meeting to share their views on the proposal and have a say in deciding whether, and how, to accept or reject the proposition. In the contemporary setting, however, that did not happen. Indeed, it was not until several weeks after the decision had been made by the Elder's Committee and acknowledged by the tribal chair with the knowledge of the Tribal Council, that the chief of the existing Sun Dance found out—from someone who was not a tribal member and did not even live in the area—about the proposal and subsequent decision to have a second Sun Dance.

The breakdown of communications in this example is directly related to the generally low level of participation in elections and public meetings on many reservations that is accompanied by a great deal of disrespectful and at times vicious gossip and a considerable amount of often tenacious infighting. In addition, when combined with the history of Indian people having to resist destructive initiatives by the U.S. government, the necessity in the present of resisting seemingly and sometimes actually unrepresentative and illegitimate actions (according to traditional values) by contemporary tribal governments has tended to make many Indian people reactive, when what is needed to regain their personal and tribal sovereignty is a return to being proactive. Moreover, since the 1960s, tribal government has frequently been fractured by the development of separate services that originally reported to various federal agencies with disparate regulations and reporting requirements. This situation tended to create competing fiefdoms that were sometimes at odds with the elected leadership.

The overall effect of these factors has often made it difficult for tribal governments to get business done, and in some cases, it has led to one faction coming to power, often temporarily, only to face extremely acrimonious conflict over its legitimacy.[80] In a number of cases, these conflicts have escalated to physical violence.[81] These difficulties are a result of the innate nature of the system itself rather than of who the particular leaders happen to be at the moment. Paradoxically, these problems have been growing worse as one of their initial causes is being removed. In the 1970s, the federal government began implementing a policy of self-determination for Indian people. As self-determination has developed, there has been an accompanying growth of government-to-government relations between tribal governments and federal, state, and local governments.[82] Therefore, what tribal governments do has become more important, which provides a growing focus for contention in what is often a fractious political atmosphere.[83] We discuss overcoming this set of problems in chapter 4.

Unresolved Historical Grief: The Dark Side of Honor and the Frustrated Warrior

Behind the statistics of poverty, poor living conditions, inadequate and sometimes degrading services, and inappropriate governance and community processes are people who have been devastated by the long experience of colonial repression—overt, structural, and resultant. This devastation has been the source of psychological and social ills for many Native people that we have discussed in this chapter. In addition, the combined effects of physical and cultural genocide have been compounded for many Indians by what we might call the "dark side of honor." In traditional American Indian and other cultures in which honor and shame are major aspects, a sense of honor is a major impetus toward positive behavior and self- and community esteem whereby the community recognizes diverse ways to gain honor, and there is plenty of honor available to be attained.[84] But when such people are regularly treated as being shameful and there is little honor available for anyone to earn, the sense of honor tends to put people in a destructive double bind. To begin with, it is difficult for people who do not respect themselves to act respectfully to others. Then, the importance of honor makes it difficult for shamed people to cope with their condition, to accurately assess when the causes of their situation are external, and to take responsibility when they are internal. Even for people without a concept of honor, the natural tendency in such circumstances to externalize one's pain and blame others who are in reach is magnified. This tendency is further enabled where people have learned to be reactive, and thus often defensive, rather than proactive in adapting to powerful external pressures in the past and culturally inappropriate forms of government in the present. Moreover, especially in societies that have been equalitarian, as were the Indigenous tribes and bands of North America, this constant internal struggle leads to envy of others who are succeeding and a tendency to attack and undercut those who are getting ahead. Unfortunately, when such states of mind and behaviors become sufficiently widespread, they tend to reinforce and escalate one another.

In some instances, the set of problems relating to the dark side of honor may be intensified by what we might call the difficulty of the frustrated warrior. In pre-Columbian times, the peoples of North America to varying degrees engaged in some level of internation warfare. For many tribes, the frequency and intensity of military conflict was greatly increased by the arrival of Europeans. This increase resulted directly from conflict with the invading and expanding European and European American population and indirectly from intertribal conflicts created by the European incursion that pushed Indian nations from their own lands onto the lands of other nations.[85] Changes brought about by the European introduction of such things as new weapons and the horse also had an impact. This set of developments increased the importance of the role of the warrior and of warrior ways of thinking and acting for some Indigenous people. It appears that for some tribal members today, a significant remnant of the warrior's penchant to attack problems remains, but because few positive channels are open to it, it has become frustrated, and thus is at times misdirected to infighting and other destructive action.[86]

4. What Must Be Healed to Re-create the Circle

Although many Indians are able to cope internally with the complex of difficult, repressive, and degrading experiences they must endure (often because of the surviving elements of their traditional cultures, including a strong and pervasive spirituality), others are sufficiently negatively impacted psychologically that they display dysfunctional behavior that generally adds to individual and community difficulties. So, in seeking to return to harmony, Indian communities must overcome a number of interrelated difficulties occurring on different levels. First, there are a variety of psychological problems, including unresolved historical loss and grief, low individual and community esteem, a damaged sense of honor, and a number of patterns of thinking and associating developed as adaptations to destructive conditions that are in need of transformation.[87] All of these wounds must be healed for a return to individual and community wholeness and harmony, which we consider in chapter 5. Second are a number of social problems, including the highest rate of alcoholism and other forms of substance abuse of any ethnic group in the United States, various forms of abuse of self (including very high suicide rates) and others (both physical and emotional), a violent crime rate more than twice the national average, and the lowest rate of educational achievement and the highest school dropout rate of any U.S. ethnic group.[88] We discuss overcoming this set of problems in chapter 5. Third are a set of political problems including lack of appropriate forms and processes of self-government, an incomplete honoring of sovereignty and self-determination in relation to other governments, and often a lack of a sufficient number of adequately educated people to ensure full self-determination with well-operating self-governance.[89] Meeting these problems is the focus of chapters 3 and 4. Fourth is a set of economic problems, including a lack of sufficient resources for creating individual and community self-reliance and for providing the appropriate educational and other services that are necessary to solve the entire set of difficulties confronting Indian communities and their members.[90] We discuss this set of concerns in chapter 5, section 1.

Only by fully and appropriately addressing all of these problems can American Indian communities return to harmony, self-sufficiency, and sovereignty as partners in American federalism. The accomplishment of this task will not benefit Indian people alone. As chapters 3 and 5 show, the development of Indian communities since 1960 demonstrates clearly that as Indian people take control of their lives, they improve the condition of their lives, which allows them to contribute economically, socially, politically, and spiritually to the well-being of the people living around them and of the entire nation. The struggle to complete the renewal of American Indian self-determination is the topic of the following chapters.

Notes

1. For example, see Norell, "Chaos Continues for San Carlos," A6; Norell, "The Power that Divides," C1; Rector, "Comanche Nation Conflict Question," B1, B9; Gray and Kelley, "Critics: BIA Too Slow," 1A, 4A; Castile, *To Show Heart*, 129–33; and Alfred, "From Bad to Worse." See also Fowler, *Arapahoe Politics*, Foreword, 15, Introduction, 1.

    For a history of the physical and cultural American Indian genocide, see Page, *In the Hands*, parts 2–4; Venables, *American Indian History*, chaps. 1–7; Nichols, *American Indians in U.S.*, chaps. 2–6; Debo, *History of the Indians*, chaps. 2–19; O'Brien, *American Indian Tribal Governments*, part 2, and the histories of several specific tribes in part 3; and French, *Legislating Indian Country*, chaps. 1–5.

2. Contact between vastly different cultures, even when friendly, almost always creates some difficulties. An example of this is described in Sharp, "Steel Axes for Stone," 17–22. A good case in point in North America is that of the French (and other Europeans) trading for furs in exchange for items that were technologically new to Native Americans, including more powerful weapons. The new trade induced the Indigenous trading partners to overhunt their own lands, and then, being suddenly more powerful, to invade the lands of their neighbors. So began an expanding wave of displacements and cultural disruptions. See Eccles, *The Canadian Frontier*.

3. The impact of American Indian ways on the development of European American political institutions and political thought is discussed in Johnson, *Forgotten Founders*; Grinde and Johnson, *Exemplar of Liberty* (including Vine Deloria's Introduction discussing the issues of scholarship on this question); Barreiro, *Indian Roots of American Democracy*; Mohawk, "Indians and Democracy"; Venables, "American Indian Influences"; and Grinde, "Iroquois Political Theory." That observation of American Indian experience had a profound effect on European political thinkers is evident in reading Locke, *Second Treatise*, 61, 102, where, in addition to including several Indian ideas and practices in the theory, Locke makes direct references to Indians, indicating the source of those ideas.

    Similarly, Jean Jacques Rousseau makes a number of references to American Indians, demonstrating that reports of their ways (regardless of the reports' accuracy) had a strong effect upon his thinking. For example, in *The Social Contract*, Rousseau makes references to Indians, supporting a number of his main points in book 3, chap. 5 (67), and book 3, chap. 15 (96–97n), indirectly in referring to the subject of confederacy as a "new subject" (based on the French experience with the Wendat, usually called the Huron). See Trigger, *The Huron*, chaps. 1–3, 6, 7, and 10. Similarly, Rousseau comments favorably on Native American life in "A Discourse on the Origin of Inequality," published in the same volume as *The Social Contract*.

    In the case of Karl Marx and Friedrich Engels, reading the reports of Six Nation, or Iroquois, society in the anthropologist L. H. Morgan's *Ancient Society* affirmed their view, developed from reading Locke and Rousseau, of what human nature and society are like in the absence of scarcity and exploitation: that is, both at the beginning of human social-political-economic development, and in the far future in the ultimate attainment of communism, or the second stage of socialism. See Bottomore, *Karl Marx, Selected Writings*, 39.

4. O'Brien, *American Indian Tribal Governments*, 77. Other estimates of Indian population in 1492 in what is now the United States range from one million to more than eighteen million people (for example, see Stiffarm and Lane, "Demography of Native North America"). Regardless of the exact figure, the population loss since 1492 is an immense number.

5. Meriam et al., *Problem of Indian Administration*, discussed in Debo, *History of the Indians*, 336–37; and Olson and Wilson, *Native Americans in the Twentieth Century*, 100–112, 193. A representative excerpt is published in Prucha, *United States Indian Policy*, 219–21.

6. Evidence for this assertion can be found in the successes that have been attained when such processes have been reinstituted, as we will discuss. See Harris, Sachs, and Broome, "Recreating Harmony," "Returning to Harmony," and "Wisdom of the People." We believe current experience gives evidence that traditional consensus-building methods were likely to have been successful even though reduced living space and mobility would have lessened the availability of one way of maintaining consensus, that of people changing communities; for example, Comanches were free to move from one band or village to another. See Wallace and Hoebel, *The Comanches*, 22. Similarly, among the Hopi in 1906, a group of traditional people who did not want to participate in certain modern adaptations of living left Orabi and founded a new village at Hotevilla. See Mails and Evehema, *Hotevilla*, 280. Such moves did not break tribal and kinship relations and thus were but one method for respectfully allowing for individual (whether person or group) freedom and difference harmoniously within a larger whole or community.

    As Ella Deloria points out in *Speaking of Indians*, 131, if, after militarily defeating Indian nations, the U.S. government had worked with the tribes respectfully to help them adapt to the new difficult conditions, the results would have been far better than what resulted from policies of cultural genocide: "[I]f the missionaries and government officials had studied the problem with the chiefs and leaders, together they might have been able to reinterpret the [traditional Indian] ideal and revamp the customs in a workable form acceptable to the people."

7. Recent successes using these methods to resolve historical grief have proven their efficacy, as we will discuss. The impact of the loss of traditional ceremonies and the need for bringing back traditional ceremonies or their equivalents is discussed in Duran and Duran, *Native American Postcolonial Psychology*, 42–53, 55–83, and 180. For discussion of Plains ceremonies as practiced by the Lakota, see DeMallie and Parks, *Sioux Indian Religion*. An interesting discussion of the Shoshone/Ute Sun Dance, also practiced by the Crow, and how it was adopted around 1890 for the difficult times brought on by European American oppression, is presented in Jorgensen, *Sun Dance Religion*. For a discussion of Diné ceremonies, see Kluckhohn and Leighton, *The Navaho*.

8. There is some discussion of this in Debo, *History of the Indians*, chaps. 15–17.

9. For a discussion of the problems of Indian education, including in boarding schools prior to 1928, see Szasz, *Road to Self-Determination*, 2–3, 10–11, 18–27, and

67. A more detailed critique of the boarding school experience is found in Adams, *Education for Extinction.*

10. Weaver and Brave Heart, "Examining Two Facets"; and Weaver, "Indigenous People," 205–6.

11. Morrisette, "Holocaust of First Nation," 381–92.

12. See Deloria and Wilkins, *Tribes, Treaties,* 39–41; and Prucha, *United States Indian Policy,* 37–38.

One commentator summed up the BIA's control of the lives of Indians as follows:

> The Indian is never alone. The life he leads is not his to control. Every aspect of his being is affected and defined by his relationship to the federal government—and primarily to one agency of the federal government: the Bureau of Indian Affairs. . . .
>
> Even when exercised illegally, the total power of the Bureau is virtually unchallengeable and unreviewable. Where the normal citizen has three avenues of redress political, judicial, administrative—the Indian has none. . . .
>
> Through the perverseness of the Bureau's role, the exercise of power and administration of programs by the BIA have come to ensure that every effort by the Indian to achieve self-realization is frustrated and penalized; that the Indian is kept in a state of permanent dependency as his price for survival; and that alienation from his people and past is rewarded and encouraged for the Indian.

Quoted by Nelson and Sheley, "Bureau of Indian Affairs," 178. See also Cahn, *Our Brother's Keeper,* 5, 10, 13.

13. The problem of the lack of research and data on American Indians for at least one area of concern is shown in Archambault, "Government Reductionism."

14. The 1990 census data is from Davis, *Native America,* 233. The 2000 data is from *U.S. Census 2000 Profiles: Table DP-1 Profiles of General Demographics Characteristics 2000,* available as a PDF file at http://www.census.gov/prod/cen2000/dp1/2kh00. pdf. This was the first census that allowed people to identify themselves as belonging either to a single race or to more than one race. Counting the Indians who identified themselves as belonging to a single race—which likely loses some Indians who would have been included in the older system of people listing only one race—and excluding those who included American Indian or Alaska Native in answers identifying multiple races, the 2000 census found 2,475,956 people identifying as American Indian and Alaska Native, or 0.9 percent of the entire U.S. population. Adding to this figure individuals who included American Indian and Alaska Native in answers identifying multiple races, the total of American Indian and Alaska Native people grew to 4,119,301, or 1.5 percent of the total U.S. population.

15. Friends Committee on National Legislation, "Federal Indian Spending," 1, 3; Taylor and Kalt, *American Indians on Reservations.* The overall inadequacy of federal spending for Indians is discussed in Sachs, "Termination by Budget."

16. Tex Hall's third annual State of Indian Nations Address is reported on in "Indian and Indigenous Developments: U.S. Developments" and "Ongoing Activities," *Indigenous Policy* 16, no. 1. That federal spending for Indians has been inadequate,

even since the beginning of policies aimed at Indian self-development with the Indian New Deal in the Roosevelt administration (which we outline in chapter 3), can be seen in former BIA head John Collier's complaints about Congress providing insufficient funding for Indian programs, including for technical assistance, while "Land acquisition for Indians authorized by Congress, is blocked through the appropriation bills; the situation is similar with regard to the expansion of the Indian Cooperative Credit System" (Collier, *Indians of the Americas*, 166–77, quoted and further discussed by French, *Legislating Indian Country*, 100).

17. "Poverty Status, By Race/Ethnicity, 1980 and 1990," 814.

18. Ibid.

19. The 2003 "Income, Poverty and Health Insurance Coverage in the United States," report was reported on in "Indian and Indigenous Developments: U.S. Developments" and "Tribal Developments," *Indigenous Policy* 15, no 1. Also see Gray, "Indians Remain Poorest," 7; and Gray, "Weak Economy Hurting," A6. For further economic discussion on American Indians, see Rosser, "This Land," 6nn31–32; and "Poverty Status, By Race/Ethnicity, 1980 and 1990," 814.

20. Taylor and Kalt, *American Indians on Reservations*. Taylor and Kalt also report that in the period between the 1990 to 2000 census, federal Indian funding levels lost ground against non-Indian domestic spending.

21. Hensen and Taylor, *Indians at the Millennium*. For this and other Harvard Project reports, visit The Harvard Project on American Indian Economic Development Publications Search site at http://hpaied.org/publications-and-research/search-publications. The Harvard Project announced in late 2005 that the report would soon be available in book form.

22. Taylor and Kalt, *American Indians on Reservations*.

23. The Urban Institute Study is available in full at the Indianz.com "News Headlines" page: http://www.indianz.com/News/archive/000355.asp. *Indigenous Policy* reported on the study in brief in "Indian and Indigenous Developments: U.S. Developments" and "Educational and Cultural Developments," *Indigenous Policy* 15, no. 1. The 2007 reports, respectively, are from Gouras, "American Indian Legislators"; and *News from Indian Country*, "Study Says."

24. South Dakota school information is from "Indian and Indigenous Developments" and "Educational and Cultural Developments," *Indigenous Policy* 18, no. 3. BIA school data is from U.S. Bureau of Indian Affairs, Office of Indian Education Programs, "Bureau Wide Annual Report Card, 2004–2005." Proficiency levels are listed in the reports. However, because no comparable data exists with which to compare them for non-Indian students or students outside the BIA system (the BIA has its own standards, although some BIA schools use individual state standards), we haven't included those figures here.

25. Luna-Firebaugh and Redshirt, "Impact of Criminal Justice." A short abstract of this paper is available from the Western Social Science Association's website on the "Past Conferences" page, under the "2008 Conference Abstracts" link at http://wssa.asu.edu/conferences/past.htm.

26. The case was *Antoine et al v. Winner School District*, filed in 2006. See Melmer, "School District Settles Lawsuit"; and "Native American Families and Winner School District Announce Settlement in Case Alleging Discrimination," available on the ACLU "Racial Justice, Education" web page: http://www.aclu.org/crimjustice/juv/30155prs20070618.html.

27. "Indian and Indigenous Developments: U.S. Developments" and "Tribal Developments" *Indigenous Policy* 18, no. 3; and "ACLU Protects Native American Children in Landmark School Settlement," available on the ACLU of Northern California "Racial Justice" web page: http://www.aclunc.org/issues/racial_justice/aclu_protects_native_american_children_in_landmark_school_settlement.shtml.

28. Taylor and Kalt, *American Indians on* Reservations. Tex Hall's address is reported in "Indigenous Developments: Economic Developments" and "Ongoing Activities," *Native American Policy* 14, no. 1.

29. The Tribally Controlled Schools Act of 1988 is partially reproduced in Prucha, *United States Indian Policy*, 314–17. The findings section of the act includes a critique of BIA policy and denial in practice of the autonomy promised in the 1975 act. The Indian Self-Determination and Education Act of 1975 is partially reproduced in Prucha, 274–76, 30. See Olson and Wilson, *Native Americans in Twentieth Century*, 185–86.

30. Indian Nations at Risk Taskforce, *Final Report*, 6–10.

31. Ibid., 5–6.

32. Fisher, "Haskall, Tribal Colleges," 4.

33. Ibid.

34. "Indian and Indigenous Developments: U.S. Developments," *Indigenous Policy* 14, no. 1.

35. "Indian and Indigenous Developments: U.S. Developments" and "Educational and Cultural Developments," *Indigenous Policy* 14, no. 2.

36. Hamilton, "$28 Million Turned Back," 10A; and Kelley, "Tribal Schools—Decaying," 7.

37. Ibid., 7: the quote is from John Tippeconic, director of the BIA Office of Indian Education Programs.

38. Brokaw, "Indian Tribes Allege."

39. The one new building was the Tse Ho Tso Intermediate Learning Center, dedicated on April 30, 2004, to begin functioning in the 2004–2005 school year in Fort Defiance, Arizona ("Indian and Indigenous Developments: U.S. Developments" and "Educational and Cultural Developments," *Indigenous Policy* 15, no. 1).

40. Brokaw, "Indian Tribes Allege."

41. See Brasher, "Indians' Crime Risk," section A, as reported by the U.S. Department of Justice.

42. Melmer, "Statistics Show."

43. Perry, "Nobody Trusts Them!," 411–44.

44. Wheeler and Ronald, "Navajo Community and Farmington." See also "Native Americans Find"; Frosch, "In Shadow"; and Jackson, "A Summer of Violence," which discusses the mayor of Farmington setting up a community-relations steering committee. *The Farmington Report: Civil Rights for Native Americans 30 Years Later*, is available in a PDF file at http://www.usccr.gov/pubs/122705_FarmingtonReport.pdf.

45. The online Amnesty International report "United States of America: Maze of Injustice: The failure to Protect Indigenous Women from Sexual Violence in the USA: End Injustice—Indigenous Voices Must be Heard" is available at http://www.amnesty.org/en/library/info/AMR51/059/2007/en. See also, "Indian and Indigenous Developments: U.S. Developments," "Ongoing Activities," and "U.S. Activities," *Indigenous Policy* 18, no. 1.

46. The Tribal Law and Order Act of 2008 (S. 3320; H.R. 6583) was introduced in the Senate by Senator Byron Dorgan, Democrat from North Dakota, on July 23, 2008, after five hearings and more than a year of development. The bill envisions a comprehensive reorganization of federal agency law enforcement responsibilities in Indian country and would increase tribal access to law enforcement resources while enhancing tribal and federal jurisdictional authority in Indian country. The changes proposed are substantial. Title I would substantially reorganize the Department of Justice (DOJ) and the Department of the Interior offices relating to crime prevention and prosecution in Indian country. It would require the attorney general to make the DOJ's Office of Tribal Justice a permanent division of the DOJ; create an Office of Indian Country Crime (OICC) within the DOJ's Criminal Division to develop, enforce, and administer the federal criminal laws applicable to Indian country; coordinate with U.S. attorneys to prosecute federal crimes; require each U.S. attorney whose district includes Indian country to appoint at least one assistant U.S. attorney to serve as a tribal liaison for the district; and allow for the appointment of qualified tribal prosecutors and other qualified attorneys to aid in prosecuting federal offenses committed in Indian country. Title I would also establish a nine-member Indian Law and Order Commission to conduct a comprehensive study of law enforcement and criminal justice in tribal communities and recommend changes to federal, state, and tribal justice systems. The Indian Law and Order Commission would appoint a Tribal Advisory Committee to assist in its work. The title would create an Office of Indian Alcohol and Substance Abuse within the Substance Abuse and Mental Health Services Administration to coordinate with and monitor the performance of other federal agencies' efforts to combat alcohol and substance abuse in tribal communities. The DOJ would be required to report data regarding crimes in Indian country annually. Any federal law enforcement official or employee who declines or terminates an investigation of an alleged violation of federal law in Indian country would be required to file a report with tribal officials and submit data to the OICC. Similarly, U.S. attorneys who declined or terminated prosecution of a case would be required to coordinate and communicate with tribal officials and provide reasonable details to permit a tribal prosecutor to pursue the case in tribal court. Title VI includes the following requirements: The BIA Division of Law Enforcement Service would be required to provide training for how to interview victims of domestic and sexual violence and how to collect, preserve, and present evidence to federal and tribal prosecutors. The secretary of the Interior, the U.S. attorney general, and the IHS would develop services for domestic violence and sexual assault victims and advocate training programs. The IHS, in consultation with tribes, would develop standardized sexual assault policies and protocols similar to those used by the DOJ. Notices would be provided to tribal law enforcement officials when prisoners are released and relocated to areas under tribal jurisdiction. Titles III, IV, and V would increase tribal access to resources for crime prevention, data collection, and incarceration of convicted tribal offenders. Title III would allow tribal and BIA law enforcement agencies and officials to access and enter information into federal criminal information databases without the limitations on subject matter in existing law that focuses on crimes against women. Title III would also allow tribes to enter into agreements with the Federal Bureau of Prisons to transfer tribal offenders convicted of violent crimes, crimes involving sexual abuse, and serious drug offenses to Bureau of Prison facilities. Title IV would require the attorney general to reserve $35 million annually for grants to

construct and maintain tribal jails; enter into contracts for the construction of tribal facilities; provide alternatives to incarceration; increase federal funding for alcohol and substance abuse emergency shelters; extend the Community Oriented Policing Services program to allow tribal governments receiving direct law enforcement services from the BIA to access the program on the federal government's behalf. Title IV would also authorize the attorney general to waive the Community Oriented Policing Services matching-funds requirement and expand the sources of funds that could be used to meet the match requirement for tribes. The bill would also authorize the attorney general to extend the project period of a grant to tribes to the time necessary to carry out the project purpose. Title V would authorize the secretary of the Interior to provide grants to improve tribal data collection systems.

Some of the most important jurisdictional provisions in the act are to increase tribal court sentencing authority to three years and/or a fine of $15,000. In exercising the enhanced sentencing authority, a tribal court must provide defense counsel for indigent defendants, and tribal court judges must be licensed to practice law. The federal government, at a tribe's request, could assume concurrent jurisdiction to prosecute federal crimes. The DOJ would be authorized to provide grants and technical assistance to states, tribes, and local governments who wish to enter into cooperative agreements to improve law enforcement services and reduce crime in Indian country and neighboring communities. The bill would enhance the secretary's authority to enter into agreements with federal, tribal, and state agencies to aid in law enforcement efforts in Indian country; require the secretary and the attorney general to develop a plan to "enhance the certification and provision of special law enforcement commissions to tribal, state and local law enforcement officials"; require the secretary to consult with tribes to develop minimum requirements for special law enforcement commissions; and prohibit the use of nonfederal law enforcement personnel if a tribe objects to their use. Although the Findings in the Tribal Law and Order Act legislation recognizes as a problem that "tribal courts have no criminal jurisdiction over non-Indian persons," the bill would not extend tribal jurisdiction over non-Indians, as many tribal representatives urged. More information on S. 3320 and H.R. 6583 is available from the website of the law firm Hobbs, Straus, Dean and Walker, LLP, at http://www.hobbsstraus.com/, General Memorandum 08–095, August 5, 2008. The foregoing summary was published in "Indian and Indigenous Developments: U.S. Developments" and "In the Courts," *Indigenous Policy* 19, no. 3.

47. Indian Health Service, *Trends in Indian Health*, 5.
48. Ibid., 35, 36.
49. Ibid., 71.
50. As reported in the *Billings Gazette*, July 6, 2005.
51. The IHS hepatitis C infection rate study is reported in "Indian and Indigenous Developments: U.S. Developments" and "Tribal Developments," *Indigenous Policy* 19, no. 1.
52. *Native American Times*, "Trifecta," 3. The 2007 IHS finding of improvement in diabetes rates is reported in "Indian and Indigenous Developments: U.S. Developments" and "Tribal Developments," *Indigenous Policy* 19, no. 1. Information about infant mortality is available from the CDC by searching on the National Center for Health Statistics web portal, using the keywords "American Indian infant mortality," http://www.cdc.gov/nchs/index.htm. IHS suicide data is reported in Jawort, "Tribes Work Together."

53. *American Indians and Alaska Natives with Cancer* is no longer available from the ICC. See the following reports and articles with similar and related information: "Cancer Incidence in American Indians and Alaska Natives," http://www.cdc.gov/cancer/healthdisparities/what_cdc_is_doing/aiansupplement.htm; "CDC Media Advisory: Report Shows High Regional Lung and Colorectal Cancer Rates in American Indians and Alaska Natives in the United States, 1999–2004," http://www.cdc.gov/media/pressrel/2008/a080820.htm; "Annual Report to the Nation on the Status of Cancer, 1975–2004, Featuring Cancer in American Indians and Alaska Natives," http://onlinelibrary.wiley.com/doi/10.1002/cncr.23044/abstract; "An Update on Cancer in American Indians and Alaska Natives," 1999–2004, http://onlinelibrary.wiley.com/doi/10.1002/cncr.v113:5+/issuetoc; "U of M Study Shows Cancer Hits American Indians at Higher Rates," http://minnesota.publicradio.org/display/web/2008/08/20/indiancancer; "U of M Researcher Finds Higher Cancer Rates Among American Indians Living in Minnesota, Northern Plains," http://www.cancer.umn.edu/news/releases/2008/americanindiancancerrates.html; "Challenges for American Indians and Alaska Natives Attaining Health Equality," http://natamcancer.org/handouts/ChallengesHlthEquality_06–26–08_HND.pdf; and "Cancer in Multicultural Groups," http://www.lilly.com/pdf/2391_Cancer_in_Multi_FS_V2.pdf.

54. The study was published in *Journal of the American College of Surgeons,* June 2004.

55. See *Native American Times,* "Study: Natives Suffer More." The study, released in February 2005 by the National Kidney Foundation, shows that Native Americans are 60 percent less likely, and Hispanics 40 percent less likely, than whites to receive kidney transplants, although American Indians and Hispanics are twice as likely to develop end-stage kidney disease as are whites, and those rates are increasing.

56. "Indian and Indigenous Developments: U.S. Developments" and "Tribal Developments," *Indigenous Policy* 16, no. 2.

57. The April 2008 International Relief and Development report on Indian health, including the study on nutrition, is described in "Indian and Indigenous Developments: U.S. Developments" and "Tribal Developments," *Indigenous* Policy 19, no. 1. The International Relief and Development website is available at http://www.ird.or.id.

58. "Indian and Indigenous Developments: U.S. Developments" and "Tribal Developments," *Indigenous Policy* 16, no. 2. For 1991 statistics on Native American high school students, see the online *MMWR Weekly* article "Tobacco, Alcohol, and Other Drug Use Among High School Students in Bureau of Indian Affairs–Funded Schools—United States, 2001," 1070–72, available at http://www.cdc.gov/mmwr/preview/mmwrhtml/mm5244a3.htm. The information about fetal alcohol syndrome is from the October 22, 2007, broadcast of the six-part series "Fetal Alcohol Syndrome: The Invisible Disorder," Minnesota Public Radio.

59. The 2008 Urban Indian Health Institute report is available in a PDF file at http://www.uihi.org/wp-content/uploads/2009/01/health_health-influencing_behaviors_among_urban_indiansupdate-121020081.pdf.

60. Zahran et al., *Quality of Life Surveillance.* The material in this report originated in the National Center for Chronic Disease Prevention and Health Promotion, Janet Collins, PhD, director, and the Division of Adult and Community Health, Wayne H. Giles, MD, acting director.

61. Van Biema, "Bury My Heart," 48, 50. See also *Indian Country Today,* "Tribal Housing Susceptible,"A10, for an overview of the tribal housing situation. The article reports that the situation today would be much worse if there had not been

a significant increase in new housing construction in recent years and that housing construction has become more efficient in terms of cost and construction time.

62. On the long wait for tribal housing, see Haase, "Tribal Housing," A9. On the condition of tribal housing, see Deer, "1997 Budget," A7. It should be noted that U.S. Department of Housing and Urban Developmont, *Annual Report to Congress: FY1979*, in commenting that much progress had been made during 1979 made a statement that remains largely true today:

> The condition of Indian housing is generally poor, and the needs for community development assistance enormous. Units needing replacement often lack normal water, sewage, and electrical services, or effective weatherproofing. Almost half of all Indian housing is substandard, as measured by relatively conservative BIA standards. Over 25% of existing structures have severe structural deficiencies, are unsuitable for even basic rehabilitation and require replacement.
>
> Housing and community development needs are closely interrelated on Indian reservations. Lack of water and sewer systems, electricity, all-weather roads (paved or unpaved), and fire fighting equipment are as much of a problem and a priority for communities as a whole as they are for those interested in the provision of new housing. Unfortunately, Indian communities are almost uniformly of very low income, and lack the income tax base to finance such improvements (6).

63. Reported in "Indian and Indigenous Developments: U.S. Developments" and "Tribal Developments," *Indigenous Policy* 18, no. 1.

64. Krol, "Tribes Work," 9.

65. National Indian Housing Council, *Sustaining Indian Housing*, indicates that increasing economic development on reservations does not bring the same level of increase in housing development. In some instances, economic development has had an adverse effect on housing improvement because increased income has made many Native people ineligible for federal housing assistance. (This is a problem with many government assistance programs that cut off completely at certain income levels, rather than reduce assistance in stages as income rises.) But on the other side of the coin, higher incomes (together with increased availability of mortgages to reservation residents) have increased the number of Indians who can obtain conventional financing for mortgages. Also, as tribal incomes have risen, more money has become available for infrastructure development, including housing. (However, as occurred at the Southern Ute reservation in Ignacio, Colorado, in 2004, tribal members with sufficiently high income cannot reside in tribal housing constructed with federal financial assistance, so federally assisted tribal housing may remain vacant, or tribes with wealthier members increasingly have to undertake housing construction without federal money.) At the same time, reservations with very little development (as is the case with the Walker River Paiute Tribe in Nevada) have found their members moving away to find work, and tribal members who stay find it increasingly difficult to maintain their housing. But in cases of extremely strong economic development, such as with the Eastern Band of the Cherokee Nation, housing conditions have improved strikingly. Although well-paying employment has become widespread for Eastern Band Cherokees, the tribe has placed 1.5 percent of its sizable gaming revenues into infrastructure improvement,

and an additional 0.5 percent into the Tribal Housing Improvement Program. However, even when tribal economic development is strong, allowing significant investment in new and improved housing, in many instances, there is such a backlog of overcrowded and substandard housing to overcome that providing decent living space for all is a long-term project.

Improvement in the availability of home mortgages for Native Americans has been the result of tribal, federal, and private action (as reported in "Indian and Indigenous Developments: U.S. Developments" and "Economic Developments," *Indigenous Policy* 16, no. 1). For example, at the end of 2004, Microsoft Corporation deposited $1 million in the Native American Bank in Denver, and Fannie Mae deposited $1.5 million in Chickasaw-owned Bank2 in Oklahoma City, which is helping make mortgages available to American Indians. In 2004, three of the largest U.S. home-loan banks granted $2.6 million to help fund Indian housing projects: Federal Home Loan Bank of Seattle with $1.7 million, Federal Home Loan Bank of Dallas with $547,000, and Home Loan Bank of San Francisco with $466,000. Despite continuing difficulties in obtaining mortgages for American Indians and Alaska Natives, lending to Native people in the United States for housing increased from $4.5 billion in 2002 to $6.7 billion in 2003. However, data from the Federal Financial Institution Examination Council shows that the number of mortgages awarded to Native Americans fell 5 percent from 2002 to 2004, whereas the number of housing loans to whites and other minorities increased during the same time from 11 percent to 18 percent (as reported in "Indigenous Developments: Tribal Developments," *Native American Policy* 13).

66. "Indigenous Developments: Economic Developments" and "Ongoing Activities," *Native American Policy* 14.

67. Ibid.

68. Reported in *Mukluk Telegraph*, April–June 2008. See also "Groundbreaking Study Links Respiratory Disease with Inadequate Water Service," http://anthc.org/upload/08–04–03Study_links_respiratory_Disease-2-1.pdf.

69. Olson and Wilson, *Native Americans*, 164.

70. Ibid., 185. The 2006 estimates are from the Schwartz report included in "Indian and Indigenous Developments: U.S. Developments" and "Tribal Developments," *Indigenous Policy* 18, no. 1.

71. Indian Health Service, *Trends in Indian Health*, 29.

72. Cornell and Kalt, *Successful Economic Development*.

73. U.S. Census Bureau, *March Current Population Survey*.

74. Corporation for Enterprise Development, *Effective State Policy*, 2.

75. A particularly interesting example of joint economic development is that of the Mississippi Choctaw, who collaborated with the city of Philadelphia, Mississippi, to make possible the expansion of the tribe's General Motors plant, which created many new jobs, most of which were filled by nontribal members. See Mississippi Band of Choctaw Indians, *Choctaw Industrial Park*; and Peterson, "Three Efforts at Development."

76. Wanamaker, "NIGC Numbers, C1–C2." According to the National Indian Gaming Commission, as reported in Melmer, "Casino Tax Shelved," 1, the number of tribal casinos continues to rise somewhat but remains limited, in part because under current law, casino gaming is legal only when it is legal in the state in which the reservation is located, and then only after a compact has been signed between the

tribe and the state. Some additional casinos may be established, but given the legal requirements alone, expansion of gambling to additional reservations is likely to be slow and may be quite limited in the future. The 2006 financial report is available from the National Indian Gaming Commission website at http://www.nigc.gov.

77. *Indian Country Today*, "NIGC Numbers." Declining casino profits have been the case for some time, as reported in *Indian Country Today*, "Casino Profits Going Down," A4. We calculated declining casino profit increase figures from the "Growth in Indian Gaming Graph 1996–2006," available on the "Gaming Revenue Reports" page on the National Tribal Gaming Commission website at http://www.nigc.gov/Default.aspx?tabid=67.

78. Bachman, "An Analysis," shows that poverty on reservations is a cause of violent and other disharmonious behavior.

79. See Harris, Sachs, and Broome, "Recreating Harmony."

80. This was a consistent problem among the Comanche in Oklahoma in the early 1990s, as "Recreating Harmony" discusses.

81. For example, see the discussion of conflict at Pine Ridge, South Dakota, in the 1970s in Castile, *To Show Heart*, 129–33.

82. See Harris, Sachs, and Morris, "Native American Tribes"; and Harris, Sachs, and Broome, "Strategy and Choice."

83. Castile, *To Show Heart*, 34–35, 132.

84. Honor and shame are major aspects of a number of cultures. They function differently in different societies, although on the deepest psychological and cultural levels, there are major similarities in how they function across cultures. Some picture of the functioning of honor among the traditional Dakota in North America is portrayed in Part 2, "A Scheme of Life that Worked" in Deloria, *Speaking of Indians*, 35–37, 39, 40–48, 51–52, 54–55, and 63–67. The functioning of honor and shame in Mediterranean society is discussed in Peristiany, *Honour and Shame*; and Campbell, *Honour, Family and Patronage*, chap. 10.

85. For example, in the 1740s and 1750s, Comanche bands, armed with guns provided by French traders farther east, pushed increasingly west into what is now New Mexico, putting them into increasing conflict with Apache bands. As Apaches moved westward as a result of this pressure, they increasingly raided Pueblos (and Spanish settlements) in the Rio Abajo (see Bayer, *Santa Ana*, 106). Similarly, as part of the long chain of displacements beginning with European movement into the East Coast of North America, by 1850, a century of migration caused by the movement of the better-armed (thanks to European and American traders) Chippewa to their east (and encouraged with the arrival of the horse by the lure of huge buffalo herds) found the Lakotas moving out onto the Great Plains and clashing with the Crow, who in turn undertook a fighting retreat westward (see Utley, *Lance and the Shield*, 3, 8). The increase in warfare resulting from the pressure of migration and technological change (e.g., the introduction of guns and horses) in turn affected Lakota society and culture, increasing the role and value of the warrior (see Price, *The Oglala People*, 17, 107–9, 127–29, 134, 145, and 173–75; and Utley, *Lance and the Shield*, chap. 1).

86. See the discussion of the turning inward and of the misdirected warrior in Duran and Duran, *Native American Postcolonial Psychology*, 35–42.

87. An indicator of the low cultural esteem that many Indians have come to feel is the report by a member of an Indian community to author Stephen Sachs about

childhood games. The tribal member said that when she was a child, she and her friends often played Cowboys and Indians, but everyone wanted to be a cowboy, and no one wanted to be an Indian.

88. Native Americans have an alcoholism rate that is 433 percent of the national average (see Indian Health Service, *Trends in Indian Health*, 5). Indian children are more likely to be abused than are children of any other ethnic group, although family abuse among Indians overall is about the same as the national average, according to a DOJ report. Although it is not clear whether the figures represent an actual increase or merely an improvement in reporting, the study shows an increase of child abuse and neglect of 18 percent among Indians from 1992 to 1995, while the national average fell by 8 percent (see Brasher, "Indians' Crime Risk"). The American Indian suicide rate is 54 percent higher than the national average (see Indian Health Service, *Trends in Indian Health*, 5). For an analysis of the causes of suicide among Indians, see the consideration of internalized oppression in Duran and Duran, *Native American Postcolonial Psychology*, 27–30. The estimate of the violent crime rate among Indians is reported by the DOJ (see Brasher, "Indians' Crime Risk").

89. The need for education and training to make self-determination viable for many tribes is discussed in Sachs, Harris, and Morris, "Devolution of Federal Authority," parts 2 and 4; and in Harris, Sachs, and Morris, "Native American Tribes." More general discussions of the need to improve Indian education and of what is necessary to make Indian education adequate and appropriate are found in Szasz, *Road to Self-Determination*; and Indian Nations at Risk Taskforce, *Indian Nations at Risk*.

90. The considerable need for economic resources by many Indian nations is discussed in Sachs, "Termination by Budget."

Part Two
Re-creating the Circle

Three
Honoring Indian Nations' Sovereignty

BUILDING GOVERNMENT-TO-GOVERNMENT RELATIONS BETWEEN
TRIBAL GOVERNMENTS AND FEDERAL, STATE, AND LOCAL
GOVERNMENTS

LaDonna Harris, Stephen M. Sachs, and Barbara Morris

At the heart of the American Indian struggle for renewal is self-determination: the rebuilding of government-to-government relations between Indian tribal governments and the federal, state, and local governments based upon recognition of the inherent sovereignty of Indian nations. Completing the return to self-sufficiency and harmony through community and economic development requires that Native people run their own affairs. As Indian communities have increased in prosperity according to their own values, the surrounding communities have benefited significantly. In an age in which the affairs of all people are becoming increasingly interrelated and interdependent, it is appropriate that Indian tribal governments be full partners in American federalism.

1. Re-creating the Circle of Tribal–Federal Government Relations

The relationship between Indian nations and the U.S. government has undergone many changes and been influenced by many factors that have often affected parallel shifts in the nature and functioning of U.S. federalism. Although the concept of federalism evokes many different perceptions and connotations in different historical and cultural contexts, the central tenet is one of self-rule combined with shared rule. Federalism has been employed as a means to accommodate diversity in plural societies. It is a means for relatively autonomous constituents to come together for common purposes. At its core, federalism may be viewed as a covenant. This implies that there is an agreement between parties to enter into an allegiance, a relationship built on trust. The United States has experienced many models of shared rule. The country has gone through periods of dual federalism, cooperative and creative federalism, and new federalism, to the current model of devolution federalism.[1]

The tribal–federal relationship began as an equal relationship between independent sovereign states and has since evolved through many stages and substages, given the complexity of an ever-changing federalism in a large country with many regional and local variations, and more than five hundred Indian nations, each with somewhat different cultures and histories, spread across a wide range of localities. Because of the complex nature of tribal–U.S. government interactions, we open this chapter with an outline of the early general history of those relations before switching to a problem-oriented approach to their development. This analysis first considers federal–tribal government relationships, beginning with the general shift in policy in Congress and the executive branch starting in the 1960s to self-determination. Then it examines the problem of Bureau of Indian Affairs (BIA) dominance of Indian affairs and of overcoming that dominance both through the transformation of the bureau and the breaking of the BIA's policy monopoly by involving Indian nations in the programs of a wide range of federal agencies. Then the discussion takes up the problem of developing appropriate mechanisms for the relationships between tribal governments and federal agencies at various levels within federal agencies and departments, culminating in a consideration of agencies with more appropriately developed tribal relationships. Next, the discussion focuses on proper methods with which the federal government can coordinate Indian policy, consulting appropriately with Native nations, and concludes with an overview of what has been accomplished and what remains to be done in establishing properly functioning federal–tribal government relations overall. The second section of this chapter examines the problem of creating appropriate tribal, state, and local government relations, showing some of the progress, looking at problems and developments in specific policy areas, and exploring promising examples of tribal, state, and local government collaboration.

*The Unfolding of Relations Between Indian Nations and the
United States*

The United States was born in a situation in which a number of European powers were contending for position and territory. Until the United States obtained hegemony in North America, it often joined in the competition to gain Indian nations as allies. At the same time, it sought to keep formerly tribal lands and gain new territories from Indian nations. At least in theory, and, for a while sometimes in fact, the relationship of the United States to Native tribes was one of sovereign nation to sovereign nation. It was based upon treaties, with agreements binding both parties. As the United States became the stronger party, it began treating Indian nations as protectorates. By treaty, and under related acts such as provisions of the Northwest Ordinance, in return for friendship, land, and sometimes military help, the United States had an obligation to protect Indian lands from incursion and to provide goods and money. Although the federal government has often failed to live up to its treaties and at times has used subterfuge and coercion to obtain agreement from Indian nations to change treaty provisions, at least formally, the U.S. government has always recognized the inherent sovereignty of Indian nations and the need to obtain their agreement to change treaty arrangements and obligations.[2]

From the outset, the United States promised to protect tribal lands and to provide education, health, and other services to Indians in exchange for tribes ceding land and ending hostilities. This was the beginning of the trust relationship between the federal and tribal governments that continues to be fundamental to U.S.–Indian relations. Similarly, the inherent sovereignty of Indian nations, with the right of self-governance, has never been extinguished, even though it was violated in fact by the U.S. government for many years. Some argue that treaties are not a proper basis for Indian affairs and the continuing authority of tribal governments because many of the treaties were forced upon Indian nations.[3] However, if one considers the treaties invalid, then it follows that the United States has no right to anything it has obtained by them. Because it would be improper for a nation that purports to base its institutions and actions on underlying democratic principles of consent and inalienable rights to argue the legitimacy of acts based solely on force, it would seem that, at a minimum, the United States ought to live up to its agreements.

The relationship between Indian nations and the United States has undergone many changes.[4] From the 1770s until the 1820s, prior to the

United States becoming the preeminent power in North America, Indian nations were treated as protectorates constituting sovereign nations. The United States dealt with them as legally equal political entities in international relations. As U.S. power on the continent grew and the government pursued policies of manifest destiny, that relationship shifted, bringing Indian displacement and removal from the 1830s to 1850s under a variety of treaties and congressional acts.[5] During this period, the U.S. government treated Indian nations as dependent domestic nations in a government-to-government relationship, with the United States accepting a trust responsibility to protect Indian rights and interests. However, the United States, as a colonial power dealing with those it colonized, interpreted the trust relationship primarily according to its own interests. During this period, many Indian people were forced to give up their lands to settlement by European Americans and to move west, often on terribly destructive trails of tears.[6]

Beginning in the 1850s and until the 1930s, the United States began to treat Indians as wards in need of protection and interpreted the trust relationship as empowering the government to act in whatever way Congress decided was in the interest of Indians (regardless of the actual impact of congressional action on Native people).[7] From the 1850s to the 1870s, as the U.S. government waged deadly wars against Indians who resisted U.S. policy, the practice of displacing Indians from their homelands shifted to a new policy of colonization that practiced relocating tribes onto reservations under treaties. In 1871, Congress ended treaty-making, replacing it until 1921 with a process of negotiated executive agreements as the United States changed from a policy of relocating Indians with some effort at assimilation to a policy focused upon assimilating them into the mainstream culture. The new policy was carried out under the domination of the BIA. The policy became fully realized with the Dawes Allotment Act in 1887, which began the general practice of allotting 160-acre parcels of reservation land to individual Indians and selling the remainder of the reservation land to settlers (and in some cases, as in Oklahoma, terminating reservations).[8] As part of the process of assimilation, Indian children were forced to attend boarding schools to learn European American customs, mores, and trades. These schools, which often treated their students brutally, were destructive of Indian culture and failed to integrate Indian young people into the dominant European American society and economy. The result was that many Native young people were left alienated from both their own culture and mainstream society.[9]

By 1928, the Meriam Report made clear that assimilation had not been achieved and that U.S. policy had left Indian people in dire economic need to the point of starvation, with poor housing, ill health, declining populations, and justifiable discontent.[10] Indian people and their leaders had long complained about their treatment, but as they were only a small portion of the U.S. population, generally did not have the vote until 1924, and did not gain a full knowledge of how the American political system functioned until World War II, they had had little power to change their situation.[11]

Moreover, the Department of the Interior, which had oversight of Indian affairs through the BIA, suffered from a conflict of interest because it also handled a variety of land and resource issues concerning which, its primary constituents, who often exercised considerable economic and political power, were often in direct conflict with Indian nations. Thus, Indians were subjected to misguided, incompetent, and often corrupt administration of their affairs.

Roosevelt and Collier: The Preliminary Round in a Renewal of Honoring Sovereignty

Thus it was that the administration of Franklin Roosevelt initiated a policy of Indian self-government as part of national recovery that was accompanied by the renewal of government-to-government relations between the federal government and Indian tribes, who were now considered quasi-sovereign entities. With John Collier leading the BIA, significant steps were taken toward returning Indians to self-governance and improved living conditions.[12] In practice, these actions were limited and developed very slowly, for several reasons. First, political limitations and pressures hampered Collier's efforts. Indians and their supporters had little political power and were opposed by contrary interests, including economic interests, religious groups who ran Indian missions and schools—that to a considerable degree supported the existing thrust of Indian policy—and bureaucrats in Indian administration whose organizational culture and sense of institutional interest most often supported the status quo.

Both in Congress and on the part of the general public, little support existed for going beyond the prior mistreatment of Indians in what most continued to consider a program of assimilation in melting-pot America. Multiculturalism, with its roots in the civil rights movement in the 1960s, did not reach mainstream discourse among Americans until the 1970s.

Second, as we will discuss in detail in the chapter 4, whether as a result of political constraints, limitations in Collier's vision, or problems in administration, the form of self-government that was forced upon most Indian tribes ran counter to their traditional cultural practice, often making it difficult to reach decisions and contributing greatly to community fracturing.[13] As a result, Indian nations were limited in their ability to participate in tribal–federal relations. Third, overcoming the entrenched bureaucracy of the BIA presented a variety of difficulties.[14]

"Our Brother's Keeper": Overcoming the Bureaucratic Morass at the BIA

The history of the BIA as a colonial agency to 1933 made it an inappropriate vehicle for empowering Indian self-governance and autonomy. In 1865, as part of government policy that considered Indians wards in need of protection, Congress passed legislation that removed control of tribal affairs from the War Department and consolidated it completely in the Department of the Interior. All supervisory and appellate powers and duties were given to the secretary of the interior. The commissioner of Indian affairs, along with the secretary of the interior, had sole discretion in administering federal tribal policy. Both offices had, in fact, had a great deal of power prior to 1865, and this legislation institutionalized that authority. From that time until recently, the BIA has exercised virtual total control in applying Indian policy, for the most part with little administrative or congressional oversight. In the past, the Department of the Interior usually has had more pressing concerns to attend to than overseeing the BIA, and until the formation of the originally temporary Select Committee on Indian Affairs in the Senate and the rise of both a more favorable public opinion and a significant increase in Native American political activity in the 1970s, Congress did not regularly scrutinize the BIA's operations.[15]

These conditions contributed to making the BIA a large bureaucracy operating under a control-minded culture that generally was resistant to change (although many individuals within the agency were exceptions to this rule). Moreover, decentralization of the bureau made it even more difficult to reform. The problems of reforming the culture under which large organizations operate can be seen in the difficulties of the last few years in attempts to change the way the U.S. military treats women and gays.[16] John Collier, as commissioner of Indian affairs, had difficulty enough dealing with the political opposition to his attempts to change

Indian policy and its administration: "More serious was what Oliver La Farge once called 'cotton wool resistance,' the capacity of insensitive, dictatorial Indian Bureau employees, secure in their civil service tenure, to lie low until a reform dies down. There was also the lag between policy and performance due to bureaucratic inertia."[17]

An important part of this lag was cultural. Bureaucratic organizations develop a perspective, philosophy, and approach to their mission and task that are based on the perceived reasons for their founding and on the views of the founding staff (which are usually directly connected to the rationale for launching the organization). As new personnel come into the organization, they are generally acculturated to the views and ways of the organization. (Those who are not so acculturated tend not to remain.) Acculturation is never complete, and many of those acculturated do change their views and modes of operating in the face of new experiences. But such cultural development tends to be slow, especially when it is not supported by strong and consistent energy for change, and imposed new ways of doing things tend to be assimilated into the traditions of the organization. Therefore, actual change tends to be considerably reduced and delayed.[18] Thus, the preferential hiring of Native Americans at the BIA in the 1930s (and increased by the Nixon administration), which by the late 1980s meant that more than 75 percent of the bureau's staff was Native American, was not sufficient to bring about rapid change in the functioning of the bureau.[19]

In addition to these difficulties, as a low-priority agency within the government, the BIA has long struggled with insufficient resources for modernizing its training and equipment and thus has been unable to update its operations sufficiently to carry out its job (which is necessarily a large and difficult one, given the very wide range of concerns and the large number of tribes with which it must deal), even as defined in its own traditions. A review initiated by the chairman of the Senate Select Committee on Indian Affairs for 1992–1995 showed that the BIA had been unable to act quickly enough to encumber a significant portion of the funds appropriated to it each year.[20] As a result, millions of dollars for seriously underfunded and essential programs have been lost, and other spending for badly needed projects has been delayed. For fiscal year 1995, for example, the total of unobligated funds at the end of the fiscal year was $91 million, $28 million of which was lost to tribal programs. Moreover, an audit of the bureau's bookkeeping initiated by the Senate Select Committee on Indian Affairs showed that because the BIA had not been given the necessary computers, staff, and training to carry out the vast accounting necessitated by tribal and individual accounts, the bureau was unable to account for $2.4 billion in tribal trust funds that it had inherited from first, the War Department, then the Department of the Treasury, and, finally, the Minerals Management Service of the Department of the Interior (any or all of which agencies may have had difficulty keeping their records up to date).[21]

Given the complex of problems with the BIA, the thrust of reform concerning relations between the federal government and the tribes began with decentralizing authority away from that agency. This decentralization was initiated by Commissioner of Indian Affairs John Collier with the support of the Roosevelt administration. The strategy of decentralization was initiated in recognition of the fact that the BIA was originally created to control Indians and had continued, to a considerable extent, to do so. As one student of the bureau observed:

> The Indian is never alone. The life he leads is not his to control. Every aspect of his being is affected and defined by his relationship to the federal government—and primarily to one agency of the federal government: the Bureau of Indian Affairs.
>
> Even when exercised illegally, the total power of the Bureau is virtually unchallengeable and unreviewable. Where the normal citizen has three avenues of redress—political, judicial, administrative—the Indian has none.
>
> Through the perverseness of the Bureau's role, the exercise of power and administration of programs by the BIA have come to ensure that every effort by the Indian to achieve self-realization is frustrated and penalized; that the Indian is kept in a state of permanent dependency as his price for survival; and that alienation from his people and past is rewarded and encouraged for the Indian.[22]

The initiatives Collier launched involved giving decision-making authority to the tribes and contracting for services that previously had been run directly by the BIA, in the hope that the bureau would shift from a supervisory to an advisory role.[23] Some devolution of authority did occur with these measures, but to a large extent, the bureau frustrated the intent of the reforms by manipulating the processes under the guise of providing expert assistance to the tribes, a tactic the BIA continued to employ well into the 1970s to slow the impact of more recent reforms in the name of carrying out its trust responsibilities.[24]

Collier's efforts at reform of the BIA did make slow progress so long as he and his political allies (including the tribes and Native American organizations) were able to place consistent pressure on BIA personnel for change. The entrance of the United States into World War II substantially reduced those efforts, as fighting the war became the prime concern of the government and the country. The federal government's shift in policy toward terminating its relationships with the tribes in the name of acculturation (which was disastrous for Native Americans) in 1950, effectively halted reform at the bureau for a decade.[25]

Indian Renewal Renewed: The 1960s to the Present

The next wave of devolution of BIA power came in the 1960s, first with a renewal of reform during the Johnson administration's War on Poverty.[26] This reform involved the creation of new, decentralized federal programs whose tribal variants were carried out at the local level directly by tribally run organizations under a grant-administration process with the relevant federal agency. The process was overseen by the newly created National Indian Opportunity Council, and for the first time in a century, an Indian was appointed to head the BIA. Johnson's breaking of the BIA monopoly on Indian administration brought with it considerable "nation building" for the tribes through providing hands-on administrative experience to a new generation of tribal leaders. This development was extremely important, for it is only with such experience that people who have been kept dependent can develop the capability to be partners in government-to-government relationships. Paternalistic bureaucratic rule from afar is doubly destructive, for it leads not only to bad decisions that are in themselves harmful to those governed, but it also denies the people concerned the opportunity to learn from their mistakes and to gain confidence from their successes, allowing them a way to break out of the dysfunctionality that accompanies dependency. The extensive record of tribal successes since the late 1960s clearly shows that Indian nations have regained considerable capability in self-governance and in being effective partners in intergovernmental relationships.[27] These gains need to be further enhanced through continued empowering development, as we will discuss.

At the same time that opportunities for tribal participation in governance were expanding, Native American political activity was increasing nationwide. The military experience of many Indians in World War II and their subsequent education under the G.I. Bill of Rights produced a new group of Indian leaders and the founding of the National Congress of American Indians (NCAI). Some of these leaders, and a younger cadre whom they helped inspire, became galvanized by the federal policy of terminating Indian tribes in the 1950s, and they played a major role in stopping the policy by the decade's end. An NCAI conference of more than five hundred Native Americans from sixty-seven tribes held at the University of Chicago in 1961 generated a new burst of political activism and a greater spirit of unity that affected both the Johnson and Nixon administrations.[28]

Among the results of this activity were three major developments: the federal government's return of the sacred site of Blue Lake to Taos Pueblo, the restoration of the Menominee Tribe (which had been terminated by the federal government during the 1950s and 1960s), and passage of the Alaska Native Claims Settlement Act recognizing Alaska Native land ownership and compensating Alaska Natives for the taking of their land (though much was put into the act that Alaska Natives did not favor).[29] These successes, fortified by increased Indian activism and more favorable public opinion (including the helpful impact of the civil rights movement), energized friendly members of Congress on Indian issues, including Senators Fred Harris, James Abourezk, and Robert Kennedy, leading to a number of pieces of Indian reform legislation and the formation of the Indian Policy Review Commission. The commission's report helped publicize the need for further reforms favored by many Native Americans.

By the mid-1970s, the new energy (in some cases supported by limited federal funding during the early stages of the War on Poverty) had led to the rise of a host of new Indian organizations.[30] These organizations have provided an essential vehicle for carrying Native American concerns to government at various levels, as well as to the public, despite the fact that the organizations are limited in actual and potential funding, given the relatively small and financially poor population they represent. Nevertheless, in the 1996 presidential campaign, Native Americans donated well over a million dollars to the Democratic Party, and in that campaign, for the first time, there was a Native American Desk at both the Committee to Reelect the President and the Democratic National Committee. In 2000, Indian money and activity was crucial in the defeat of Washington Senator Slade Gorton. Clearly, Indians have political power concerning issues on which they are not directly opposed by other strong interests, which is regularly the case concerning the development of government-to-government relations.[31] Indeed, constant pressure from Native Americans and their allies on intergovernmental relations issues has kept the development process in motion. (We discuss the impact of improving Indian nation economic development in further increasing Native American political power in the opening of the twenty-first century in chapter 5, section 1.)

In addition, the shift in federal Indian policy toward developing self-determination brought with it a number of pieces of legislation (including the Indian Self-Determination and Education Assistance Act of January 1975) that increased tribal autonomy in decision making, as well as expanded the number of relationships between tribal authorities and federal agencies other than the BIA.[32] This growth of relationships has been further enhanced by the creation of additional federal agencies, such as the Environmental Protection Agency (EPA), that deal directly with tribes. Meanwhile, the BIA continued to play a major role in Native American affairs, again diluting the impact of some of the reforms, as it did in the 1930s.[33] More recently, the reformation of the bureau and the reacculturation of its staff has finally brought it very close to catching up with current policy. It is now only one of a number of federal agencies dealing with the tribes, and its role continues to diminish.[34] As a result of all these efforts, by fiscal year 1987, the Office of Management and Budget reported that the $3.1 billion in federal funding for Native American programs was administered through twelve federal departments and agencies and involved some seventy-three programs.[35] This dispersion of federal relationships with the tribes raised a new set of problems (while some of the older difficulties remained) in developing a government-to-government partnership between federal agencies and Indian nations. Overcoming them has required significant effort that has had both institutional (or structural) and cultural aspects. The fundamental difficulty has been that most federal agency personnel who deal with Indians and Indian tribes have had little, if any, knowledge of them and have failed to pay attention to Indians and their specific concerns because Indians are but one of numerous constituencies affected by the policies of the agencies.

Institutional Problems in Recognizing Self-Determination
On the institutional/structural side, this problem has manifested in the lack of clear channels through which Indian concerns and interests can

be expressed to administrative policy makers. Two primary aspects of this problem are important. First is the necessity of developing mechanisms within larger departments of federal agencies for making appropriate policy in communication with tribes; second is the need for the federal government to coordinate appropriate policy with consultation with tribal governments. The difficulty lies in a lack of cultural awareness (and hence a considerable amount of misperception and miscommunication) on the part of administrators in dealing with those in a milieu outside their experience (a problem not only for Indians). Recognition of these problems has been acknowledged from time to time by members of the federal administration as part of the continuing effort to overcome them. In a draft statement on "Government-Wide Responsibility to Native Americans: An Implementation Strategy," the Intra-Departmental Council on Indian Affairs, Administration for Native Americans, Office of Human Developmental Services, wrote in 1989:

> The self-sufficiency of Indian people has been hampered and inhibited by a lack of implementation policy by the very Federal agencies charged with working with tribes on a government-to-government basis. Rather than working together to enrich scarce resources, it can be said that currently, federal agencies operate alone, in a narrow categorical fashion, entirely lacking in a "futuristic world view," and an overall complementary approach that should dovetail and enhance the mission of sister agencies.
>
> It is well documented that Federal implementation policies, by and large, have inhibited the political and economic development of tribes. The absence of mechanisms permitting agencies to share or exchange basic demographic, social, economic and tribal governance information has caused the further implementation or interpretation of program goals in an unnecessarily restrictive or exclusionary fashion.
>
> The lack of a Federal focal point at the highest policy levels results in excessive regulation and self-perpetuating bureaucracies that stifle local decision making, thwart Indian control of Indian resources, and promote dependence rather than self-sufficiency.
>
> As a corollary to Federal agencies' categorical approach, those which lack an explicit legislative mandate to serve

Native Americans tend to ignore their responsibilities to them entirely, viewing services, resources and opportunities to this population as the purview only of the Indian "Programs."[36]

A prevalent aspect of these problems is expressed in letters accompanying "Red Alert" emergency newsletters that Americans for Indian Opportunity (AIO) sent to the assistant, under, and deputy secretaries of several federal departments in March and June 1978:

> Too often federal agencies, such as yours, develop and perpetuate a service delivery system to tribal governments based upon the premise that Indians are categorized as minority, racial or other types of disadvantaged groups. Barriers to service to Indians are developed when federal programs do not recognize the governmental nature of tribes. In the end, you end up depriving Indian citizens of services your agency is responsible to deliver.[37]

The practical impact of these problems becomes readily apparent when considering specific cases. For example, in May 1985, Congressman Mike Synar wrote to Secretary of the Interior Donald Hodel:

> It has come to my attention that the Department of the Interior is considering the abolition of the Board of Indian Appeals and placing its function with the Board of Land Appeals. . . .
> My primary concern is that the Board of Land Appeals is comprised of experts with backgrounds primarily in public law. Does the Department of the Interior intend to provide the Board of Land Appeals with experts in the field of Indian Law? If not, this proposal would appear to defeat the purpose of providing an avenue of appeal of BIA decisions.
> My second concern is that the transfer of cases to the Board of Land Appeals could add to a considerable backlog of cases already pending before that board and create a lengthy delay in decisions. Several federal court decisions have indicated that failure to deal with Indian cases expeditiously is a violation of the trust responsibility of the BIA.[38]

Further illumination of some of the problems that have developed in the area of land, water, and mineral rights is found in the March 1977 letter to President Carter from the president of AIO.

> We want to reaffirm our telegram of March 2nd commending your decision to suspend your operations on several water development programs until the programs have been reviewed by your administration. These proposed water projects will be devastating to the Indian community. In the past Native Americans have been ignored during the planning and construction of federal water projects. Indian land has been flooded when viable alternatives existed in such projects. Indian water needs have been ignored or given low priority in irrigation systems and no consideration has been given to economic development needs, especially in the area of energy development. There is case after case of the destruction of the small amounts of land still owned by Native peoples by these projects, and equally devastating, is the infringement on the tribes' rightful claim to water by certain projects.
>
> As you know, there is no national Indian Policy, and as mentioned before, Native American rights and needs are never taken into consideration when state, regional and national projects like these are being considered. Because of lack of policy, individual tribes have had to fight to survive, taking on the Corps of Engineers, the Bureau of Reclamation, the Department of Interior, and state and local governments with little chance of winning their fight. We're hoping that in reconsidering these federal water development programs that the Department of Interior will fulfill its trust responsibility in protecting the last of the land holdings of these tribes and their indigenous and legal right to these waters.
>
> Indian tribes are just on the threshold of using their natural resources—coal, timber, farm lands, etc.—to achieve economic self sufficiency. To deprive them of both lands and water at this point would be totally unconscionable.
>
> We are hoping that with the good judgment you have used in selecting Secretary Andrus and your renewed efforts in rights of minority people, and recognizing the legal responsibility the federal government has toward Native peoples, you will right these wrongs.[39]

Similar problems have occurred in virtually every area of policy. For example, one of the key difficulties that Indians have had is that much of the education provided to them is inappropriate and ineffective, causing them to have the lowest level of achievement and highest dropout rate of any measured ethnic group in the United States.[40] Experience has shown that to make Native American education effective, it is important to involve Native Americans in the design, implementation, and evaluation of educational programs. Although this need had been recognized within the federal government, the president of AIO found it necessary to write in January 1975 to Morris Thompson, commissioner of the BIA: "I was disturbed to learn of an invitation to bid on a contract to conduct Oklahoma Indian Education Needs Assessment several days after the bids were due. I was even more disturbed to learn that other national Indian Organizations were unaware of such a proposal."[41]

Similarly, a month later, Patricia Locke wrote to Special Assistant to the President Dr. Ted Maarse,

> As an American Indian enrolled as a Standing Rock Sioux and as a citizen of the United States, I am concerned that there be compliance with P.L. 92–318, Title IV—the Indian Education Act.
>
> Specifically, I am concerned that members of the National Advisory Council on Indian Education hereafter be selected from recommendations made by Indian Tribes and Indian organizations as the Act requires. The present 15-member Council, whose terms expire in May of 1975, was not selected from recommendations made by Indian tribes and organizations but for two or three exceptions.
>
> It has come to my attention that the present Council has written a letter to the White House requesting that its term be extended. It is my strong conviction that this would be a disservice to American Indians concerned with the education of their children because we Indian people insist that we have a voice in the selection of those who represent us. This is the essence of Indian self-determination. Title IV, in its language, recognizes this concern and provides for this process in the legislation.[42]

Developments Within Federal Agencies

The solution to these problems requires two levels of structural reform. The first involves providing a means to ensure that individual federal agencies act knowledgeably on issues of Indian policy with appropriate consultation with Indian people. The second involves providing a means to coordinate Indian policy and communication within the executive branch as a whole, ensuring that individual agencies are properly handling such issues and dealing with Indian tribes on a government-to-government basis. At the agency level, the first in a long series of steps to improve the handling of matters affecting Indians was undertaken during the Johnson administration at the initiation of the National Council on Indian Opportunity. This involved the establishment of what were in essence a series of advisory committees in various federal agencies dealing with tribes.[43] Additional bodies of this kind, with various titles and status levels, have since been created, and a number are still in existence. Among these are the National Advisory Council on Indian Education (of the U.S. Office of Education in the U.S. Department of Health, Education, and Welfare—HEW), the American Indian Advisory Group (of HEW), the Indian Health Service Advisory Board, the National Indian Health Board, The National Council on Indian Opportunity (of the Office of Economic Opportunity), and the Presidential Commission on Reservation Economies. In some cases, Native Americans were included in broader advisory groups such as the Advisory Committee on Minority Enterprise Development (of the Department of Commerce).

Although these entities produced positive improvements in the making and carrying out of Indian policy, they did not go far enough. First, they were not always properly constituted, as the letter from Patricia Locke indicates. Second, they were only advisory bodies, and as is often the case with such entities, there was no assurance that they would be paid serious attention by policy makers and administrators. Even if they were, such attention was often temporary, as new administrators might not be interested in them and might not even reconstitute them. Moreover, where such groups technically were "advisory committees," their duration was legally limited to a few years. Such groups did and can continue to play an important role, but they are generally insufficient unless connected to permanent and more authoritative vehicles within agencies, as have been developed more recently.

The next step in attempting to provide appropriate and effective Native American input into federal policy making and implementation at the agency level was made by the Nixon administration, which undertook a strong Indian policy of "self-determination without termination," which included the right of American Indians to operate and control federal programs.[44] Nixon initiated "Indian Desks" in each of the human resource departments of the federal government to help coordinate and accelerate Indian programs.[45] (Nixon also proposed, and President Carter established by department order, elevating the head of the BIA from commissioner of Indian affairs, reporting to the secretary of the interior through the assistant secretary for public land management, to assistant secretary for Indian and territorial affairs, reporting directly to the secretary of the interior.) Nixon also proposed an independent Indian Trust Counsel Authority "to assure independent legal representation for the Indian's natural resource rights with a presidentially appointed membership of three, two of whom must be Indians." However, Congress was slow to act on it, and it was ultimately lost amid the throes of Watergate.[46]

Some of the people appointed to the new Indian Desks were extremely active and made great strides toward fulfilling their intended functions.[47] However, the assignment of a contact person for the tribes often meant little, because the tribal liaison assignment was added to already existing primary duties of staff members who frequently had a low level of commitment to tribal relations to begin with. Even when the agency officer did significant work as tribal liaison, the function was carried out by that particular individual and not attached to a permanent position. Given the relative lack of political resources by the tribes to continuously maintain a high level of agency and administrative attention, when the liaison person left the agency, the function was generally not reassigned and was lost. This was especially the case with the arrival of new department heads or new administrations, who were either unaware of, or not greatly interested in, the position and its functions. Some improvements in appropriately institutionalizing tribal liaisons came later in the Clinton administration's revitalizing of Indian Desks, and in the actions of some agencies, such as the EPA.

Coordination of Indian Policy at the Department Level

In departments in which there were numerous agencies with programs relating to Native Americans, a single part-time person was incapable of providing a basis for coordinating policy or of keeping up with the amount of communication necessary to adequately inform tribes in a timely manner or to ascertain tribal views and concerns and communicate them to the relevant agencies and program personnel. Therefore, in the spring of 1975, the extremely complex Department of Health, Education, and Welfare (HEW, currently the U.S. Department of Health and Human Services—HHS) established the Intradepartmental Council on Native American Affairs, supplementing it in 1979 with the American Indian Advisory Group, chartered to function for two years.[48] Similarly, in January 1979, the Department of Agriculture established an agency-wide Native American Task Force.[49] The purpose was to improve the effectiveness of the department's programs as they apply to Indians. The task force was chaired by the assistant secretary for rural development, and included the assistant secretaries for conservation, research and education, food and consumer services, and international affairs and commodity programs. The task force reported to the secretary quarterly, beginning in March 1978. Policy issues that the chairman believed to be beyond the role of the task force were referred to the secretary for consideration by the Program and Budget Review Board. All agencies of the department were authorized and directed to cooperate with the task force and to detail personnel on a temporary basis, as might be requested by the chairman.

In principle, coordinating bodies of this kind can be extremely helpful if they are permanently institutionalized. However, to be effective, the leading members (or a sufficient number of the members) of the coordinating body must have an understanding of the legal status of tribes as governmental entities, the concerns and cultures of Indians, the situations of the tribes, and the relation of the relevant programs to the developing situations of the Indian nations.

In the case of the Department of Agriculture task force, the relatively powerful position of the members provided them with appropriate organizational authority to be effective, but because each of the members had a number of concerns, of which Native American affairs were but a small part, there was no assurance that the understanding and orientation of the task force members would be appropriate (and would not merely strengthen the perpetuation of misguided paternalistic policy and implementation). Although appropriate staffing might have corrected this situation, the possibility of that occurring, and continuing, depended upon who the secretary, chair, or other key members happened to be. Experience with Indian Desks shows, as organizational common sense would hypothesize, that this crucial matter needed to be institutionalized in the official makeup and formal charge to the coordinating body.

Although such formal statements do not assure the appropriate operation of any entity, they can greatly increase the likelihood that it will operate as intended and provide a touchstone for review and correction of its functioning.

As we will discuss, this became much more the case. Moreover, continued concern about this issue in the White House and the institution of higher-level coordinating bodies that have a sharp focus on Indian issues has brought about a significantly higher level of awareness at higher levels of administration. As a result, at least by the end of the Clinton administration, the likelihood that members of bodies such as the HHS task force would have an appropriate orientation and understanding was significantly greater than it had been when the task force was first organized. The key to this improvement is a proper education in Indian affairs for all personnel whose work touches upon Native American issues, which will assure that good people will not take misguided action simply because of a lack of knowledge and experience. Indian people in government can play, and often have played, an important role in providing such education.

EPA: Moving Toward a Better Model of Approaching Indian Affairs

A third stage of enhancing government-to-government relationships that linked structural and cultural development holistically began in the 1980s at the EPA. The agency became the leading edge in the development of cooperative relationships between the tribes and federal agencies. Many factors may have led to the EPA's leadership role. Being a newer, smaller, and less cumbersome agency than the BIA or HEW, it was organizationally more flexible, and its culture wasn't held hostage by stereotypes about how to work with those who were affected by its policies. This was especially so with Indians, whose public perception had been improving, at least since the 1960s. There were also important parallels between the agency's goal to protect the environment and the relatively broad approach doing so required (as contrasted with the traditional narrow scope of providing categorical grants) and traditional Native American concern for harmony, including respect for the environment and the holistic seeing and thinking that went with along it. Also of importance was the fact that in the early 1980s, the EPA was experiencing a renaissance in the backlash against the Reagan administration's attempts to weaken and redirect the agency's focus.[50]

By 1980, during the Carter administration, the EPA had become aware that "our state implemented regulatory programs often fail to sufficiently address the facts of tribal sovereignty and the jurisdictional status of Indian lands." The agency had created an Indian Work Group to "develop a policy for the administration of EPA programs on American Indian Reservations," seeking "appropriate ways in which tribal governments can play a more central regulatory role in implementing EPA programs on reservation lands."[51] The orientation of the EPA and its Indian Work Group toward developing government-to-government relationships was enhanced by President Reagan's 1983 Indian Policy Statement, which was quoted in the opening of the EPA Indian Work Group's July 1983 Discussion Paper, *Administration of Environmental Programs on Indian Lands:*

> Our policy is to reaffirm dealing with Indian tribes on a government-to-government basis and to pursue the policy of self-government for Indian tribes without threatening termination.
>
> Tribal governments, like state and local governments, are more aware of the needs and desires of their citizens than is the federal government and should, therefore, have the primary responsibility for meeting those needs.
>
> This Administration affirms the right of tribes to determine the best way to meet the needs of their members and establish and run programs which best meet their needs.
>
> This Administration intends to restore tribal governments to their rightful place among the governments of this nation and to enable tribal governments, along with state and local governments, to resume control over their own affairs.[52]

In 1983, the EPA, initially through its Indian Work Group and several of its regional and program offices, began a discussion and then a series of collaborations with tribes and Native American organizations (including AIO) to develop an environmental policy for Native American lands that would

> ensure that our programs to protect the environment and human health operate as effectively on Indian reservations as they do elsewhere.
>
> . . . incorporate Tribal governments into the operation and management of the Agency's programs, as follows:

1. EPA will recognize Tribal Governments as the primary parties for policy formulation and implementation on Indian lands, consistent with Agency standards and regulations. The Agency is prepared to work directly with Indian Tribal Governments on a one-to-one basis, rather than as subdivisions of other governments.
2. EPA will take affirmative steps to encourage and assist Tribes in assuming regulatory and program management responsibilities for reservation lands.
3. EPA will take appropriate steps to remove existing legal and procedural impediments to working directly and effectively with Tribal Governments on reservation programs.
4. EPA will ensure that Tribal concerns and interests are fully considered whenever EPA's actions and/or decisions may impact reservation environments.
5. EPA will encourage cooperation between Tribal and State governments to resolve environmental problems of mutual concern.
6. EPA will work with other Federal agencies which have related responsibilities on Indian lands, to enlist their interest and support in cooperative efforts to help Tribes assume environmental program responsibilities for reservations. [This primarily concerns the IHS, which has responsibility for sanitation and drinking water on many reservations, and secondarily concerns the BIA.[53]]
7. EPA will incorporate its Indian Policy goals into its planning and management activities.[54]

The EPA realized that this policy required considerable development over time. Both environmental conditions and the ability of tribes to manage them varied widely from reservation to reservation, and detailed information about the extent of the situation was not available. Hence, early on, the EPA contracted with AIO to survey actual conditions.[55] In some cases, tribes already had environmental management capability from ongoing projects of their own or in partnership with the EPA that could be enhanced to broaden their programs. In other cases, tribal environmental management capability had to be created, sometimes with the EPA temporarily managing reservation environmental programs with tribal input and ongoing dialogue until the tribe was able and willing to manage the programs.[56] Because air and water pollution flow across jurisdictional boundaries, in a number of cases, the EPA facilitated the organization of tribal–state collaboration, including the formation of area regulatory bodies, such as in protecting salmon and regulating the waters of the Columbia River ecosystem with numerous tribes (through the Columbia River Inter-Tribal Fish Commission) and local, state, and federal agencies.[57] The EPA also had to arrange for some procedural changes to accomplish all this, including obtaining from Congress legal modifications of existing regulations.[58] This EPA initiative brought a number of additional concerns to the attention of Congress, on which it took action.

The entire process of development involved enhancing new relationships and capabilities among all involved, including interchange at numerous meetings and workshops. In addition, the EPA trained its own staff in the new collaborative process and in various aspects of interacting with tribes on a government-to-government basis. The EPA also increased its own ability to work with tribes by bringing into the ranks of its administrators experienced tribal environmental professionals and by making structural changes to facilitate its collaborative relationships with tribes.[59] These changes are exemplified by the creation of the American Indian Environmental Office, whose administrative director reports directly to the administrator of the EPA. The office was established to coordinate all EPA Indian programs and to cooperate with other agencies involved with tribal environmental programs. The office had oversight of EPA personnel training on trust responsibilities and related environmental concerns, culture, and legal issues. In 1994, these efforts were augmented by the establishment of the EPA Office of Tribal Operations to address critical gaps in environmental protection and improve the EPA's government-to-government relationship with tribal governments.[60] The office's first director had previously been the executive director of the Tulalip Tribe's Fisheries and Natural Resources.

The rise of collaborative action on the environment between the EPA and tribal governments led Congress to include in the Water Quality Act of 1987 a provision that the EPA treat qualifying tribes as if they are states for the purpose of setting water-quality standards. After establishing new regulations for resolving "any unreasonable consequences that may arise from an Indian tribe and a State adopting differing water quality standards for common bodies of water" in 1984, in a proposal originally drafted by three tribes, three states, and the EPA, the agency began authorizing a growing list of selected tribes to set standards for water quality on their own reservation, which required compliance by jurisdictions upstream of the tribe.[61] The EPA's way of working with tribes as if they are states is increasingly becoming the standard method with which that agency deals with Indian nations, as exemplified by the EPA extending that approach to air-quality programs in late 1994.[62] By mid-1996, approximately a hundred tribes had received EPA approval to administer 150 surface water, drinking water, and solid waste programs as if they are states, and some twenty tribes operated pesticide programs under cooperative agreements with the EPA.[63]

Although the EPA's relations with the tribes is still not perfect, and the tribes (as well as state and local governments) are not always happy with the EPA, the agency's approach to developing government-to-government relations with Indian nations is an excellent model for the kind of development of collaborative relations between federal agencies and tribal governments that by the late 1990s was emerging throughout the national executive branch.[64] For example, the Department of Energy (DOE), also a more recently established agency, began acting collaboratively with tribes, negotiating comprehensive cooperative agreements with a number of them that allowed the tribes to develop the ability to address health and safety issues and tribal cultural concerns resulting from environmental management activities.[65]

The DOE's nuclear waste division, perhaps because of its strong interest in finding nuclear storage sites, regularly dialogues with tribes and tribal organizations, such as NCAI, on policy and implementation questions. Under a collaborative agreement between DOE and NCAI, the NCAI Nuclear Waste Program has been monitoring commercial spent-fuel activities and potential programmatic impacts in Indian country since 1983.[66] The project is assisting tribal governments to develop their own programs to monitor the passage of nuclear waste through their lands. The program acts as a vehicle for the DOE to provide legally required training to any tribe on whose land radioactive waste may pass at least three years prior to the first transshipment.

Similarly, with encouragement from the Clinton administration, the DOJ established an office to deal directly with the tribal governments and has instituted a number of partnership programs with tribes to improve their justice system. Moreover, U.S. attorney's offices with significant Indian country jurisdiction have worked with tribal, federal, and state agencies to develop memoranda of understanding to address problems of overlapping jurisdiction. A more recent example is the collaboration between the NCAI Homeland Security Working Group and the U.S. Department of Homeland Security in a wide-ranging effort to improve the department's relationship with Indian country.[67] This collaboration has led, for example, to the department announcing on April 28, 2008, that beginning May 26, 2008, airport security in the United States would accept as identification at checkpoints U.S. tribal photo ID cards and Canadian Indian and Northern Affairs cards that meet Department of Homeland Security standards.

Decentralizing Programs to States, Localities, and Tribes: Forced Federalism—Expanding or Limiting Tribal Sovereignty?

Meanwhile, the U.S. Department of Housing and Urban Development (HUD) decentralized all tribal housing programs to tribal authorities through direct block grants under the United States Housing Act of 1996, which went into effect October 1, 1997. The act recognizes the government-to-government relationship between the federal government and the tribes, acknowledging that "providing affordable and healthy homes is an essential element in the federal government's role in helping the tribes and their members to achieve a socio-economic status comparable to their non-Indian neighbors."[68] The act separates Native American housing from other public housing, so that beginning in 1997, each tribe received, directly, one block grant to its Tribally Designated Housing Entity to be used for development, rehabilitation, acquisitions, housing support and management services, crime prevention and safety activities, and for initiation of model housing programs.

The act allows tribes a great deal of flexibility within the bounds of accountability and frees them from the current inappropriate housing program design created for urban areas. The act eliminates the need for Indian nations to apply for a myriad of separate grants, empowering them to create strategies appropriate for development in their own communities. Experience has shown that community-appropriate development can often be undertaken much more cheaply (e.g., at San Juan Pueblo at one-third the cost) than has been typical of HUD's single approach to all communities.[69] The bill also attempts to make it easier for tribes to attract private mortgage financing by extending the maximum lease-hold provision from twenty to forty years. In addition, the bill allows tribal housing authorities to borrow or issue debt equal to five years' worth of their allotment, payable over twenty years with the full backing of the U.S. Treasury. By way of acknowledgement of the government-to-government relationship, in December 1996, HUD brought tribal housing leaders from around the United States to a meeting in Scottsdale, Arizona, to begin writing compliance regulations for the new housing program.

The decentralizing of federal programs to tribes through block grants was continued as a general policy at least through the George W. Bush administration. In enacting welfare reform under Public Law 104–193 in 1996, which altered welfare financing and administration to provide direct block grants to the states, Congress provided that in many instances, tribes can take over programs, receiving federal funding directly (although this often leads to a reduction in program funding to the tribe), and included incentives for states to make compacts with tribes to provide programs to the tribes, most likely at the same level, or close to the same level, as is provided to the rest of the state. Generally, welfare reform results in reduced assistance to low-income persons. In some cases, the reductions in the act affect at least some tribes less severely, but in general, the effect is more severe for tribes, depending on how the reform is implemented in practice.[70]

Welfare reform for the tribes is exceedingly complex, but some general conclusions can be made.[71] Although tribes can run their own welfare programs, only a few have chosen to do so, for two reasons. One, doing so frequently leads to lower benefits, because tribes receive only the federal portion of the funding and do not receive and usually do not have the tax or financial basis to provide the equivalent of the state's share of the benefits (which is provided in state programs by state matching funds). Two, tribes often do not have the training or administrative resources to run welfare programs, and the federal government provides no funding or other resources (including training) for doing so. This is a common problem with the devolution of federal programs, as we will discuss.

Welfare reform does include some incentives for state (and sometimes local) governments to communicate and collaborate with tribal governments to ensure that tribal members are well and fairly served by welfare programs. Although there are excellent examples of such collaboration, the incentives have not always been sufficient to ensure well-working collaboration and equity. To ensure equity and well-functioning government-to-government relations, the federal government must include adequate incentives to the states to collaborate with tribal governments as partners in the programs, with appropriate procedures to resolve disputes (as the EPA has provided in some environmental programs).

Decentralization Requires Education and Guidance to Realize Empowerment

In considering federal block grants to tribes as a method of realizing government-to-government relationships, it is important to note that they can work effectively only to the extent that the on-site administrative authority has the competence to appropriately and properly carry out the program. Experience with HUD programs indicates that this has occasionally been a problem with local programs under the block grant system initiated under the Nixon administration (and given increased local administrative autonomy under the Reagan administration), as well as in tribal programs. Although many local governments have functioned extremely well when given autonomy, because of incompetence, numerous instances of inappropriate projects have been carried out by municipalities under HUD programs, some of which made conditions worse.[72]

Similarly, a combination of investigative reporting in 1996 and subsequent review by HUD of tribal housing programs showed that, although many housing programs ran very well, numerous instances of mismanagement, abuse, and fraud existed in some reservation programs (which had the effect of lowering the quality of the program as a whole).[73] The HUD experience makes clear that the federal government and involved federal agencies have the duty to provide adequate and appropriate empowerment to the tribe (or other local entity) and to ensure that there are proper procedures for carrying out the programs with appropriate oversight. The EPA's developmental approach is one example of a method for doing this. Clearly, the involvement of tribal housing officers in writing regulations for the new housing program is an important aspect of carrying out this responsibility on a government-to-government basis. Furthermore, given the federal government's traditional disallowance of tribal governance, followed by the initiation of often-inappropriate tribal government under the Indian Reorganization Act of 1934 beginning in the 1930s, and the fact that much federal regulation runs counter to traditional Indigenous ways of proceeding, it is also often necessary to provide adequate education and training so that tribal personnel understand the principle and detail of regulations and have the skills necessary to carry them out.

The imposition of federal standards and regulations on tribes does create a difficulty for tribal sovereignty, including the possibility that acculturating Native people to mainstream bureaucracy might undermine traditional culture. Because colonialism destroyed Indian nation self-sufficiency, tribes cannot simply be left to operate on their own if they are to attain renewal—as the experience with termination in the 1950s and 1960s demonstrated. To empower Indian nations to return to effective sovereignty, self-sufficiency, and harmony requires the federal government to provide sufficient services as part of its trust responsibility, including appropriate guidance encompassing apt regulation. What is most often needed is to involve tribal people in making the regulations, so far as is pertinent, while providing the resources (including appropriate education) for tribes to be able to run, or contract out under their competent supervision, their own programs. It is also necessary to provide appropriate education to Indian nations and people so that they can reinforce and develop their own culture in their own terms and also deal easily and effectively with people and institutions from other cultures.

Other Aspects of Decentralization for Empowerment

A parallel development to decentralization in the housing program that allows tribes to combine related programs from different agencies has been experimented with in the field of job training under Public Law 102–477 (1992). This arrangement allows tribes to set their own job-training goals and to combine programs, with simplified paperwork, from the BIA, the Department of Labor, and HHS into a single tribally designed program and to remain directly involved in setting policies and developing their own programs. By mid-1996, this vehicle had allowed the twelve participating tribes to design much more effective programs with the same amount of money they had previously.[74]

An attempt to carry decentralization of federal programs to the tribes to the greatest degree possible was initiated under the Tribal Shares Process.[75] The BIA, acting under the Indian Self-Determination and Education Assistance Act and Fiscal Year 1997 Appropriations Language for the Department of the Interior, worked with every federal agency to develop a list of functions in Indian programs that are inherently federal and can only be carried out by the federal government and functions that are not inherently federal and can be carried out by tribes directly or, if the tribes are unable or unwilling to carry them out themselves, can be contracted out by the tribes. The preliminary list published in May 1997 was circulated for comment. In addition, top BIA personnel met with tribal leaders around the United States to discuss the list. The final product is a list of functions remaining with the federal government and the "tribal shares" to be carried out or contracted out by the tribes, with the federal budget showing the specific monies that are "the share" of each tribe. It remains to be seen if this division of functions is appropriate. Moreover, the federal government needs to provide the resources to realize the potential of this approach.

Do the Myriad Indian Policy Mechanisms in a Plethora of Federal Agencies Increase or Decrease Sovereignty and the Understanding that Native Americans Are Not Just Another Interest Group?

Some commentators may believe that although all of the advisory committees, Indian Desks, and myriad programs in a range of federal agencies may have some practical benefit for Indian nations, their multiplicity dilutes tribal sovereignty in principle while contributing to the impression that Native Americans are just another interest group. Although almost all actions have multiple effects in a variety of directions and dimensions so that it seems likely to the authors that there are some effects along these lines, we believe that for the most part, the opposite is true.

Perhaps, if Europeans had come to the Americas in a cooperative manner and Indian nations had joined (or associated with) the United States voluntarily as autonomous commonwealths (or in some similar arrangement), the concentrating of U.S. government–Indian relations in a collaborative BIA might have been a very positive vehicle for expressing and enhancing tribal sovereignty. However, even if contact had unfolded in such a friendly manner, there is no reason why sovereignty would necessarily have had to express through a single body or suffer diminishment if it expressed through multiple vehicles. Forced limitation of relations to a single agency might have reduced collaborative action, and hence the exercise of sovereignty, which in reality is nothing more than the ability or power to act freely and independently as one wills. In reality, a limitation upon the exercise of sovereignty—except when self-imposed—is a limitation upon or reduction of sovereignty. Indeed, by mutual agreement, nations often arrange for particular affairs to be carried out between them by a number of agents and agencies. Although the State Department is usually the lead agency in U.S. negotiations with other counties and international organizations, Congress and the president have authorized a large number of agencies and officials to act directly with foreign counterparts to carry out official business. Moreover, the idea that everything has to go through a single "sovereign" head of state is a hierarchical Western idea that never reflected regular European practice and that is foreign to the more polyarchic (or equalitarian in principle) way of most Indigenous traditions.

Given the actual history of the development of U.S.–Indian relations, it is clear that the BIA acted, until very recently, as an agent for controlling Indian nations and people and suppressing their sovereignty. As we have seen, it was only with considerable effort over time that sufficient reform was achieved that the bureau might become a vehicle to empowering Native sovereignty—and to achieve that end, the bureau's monopoly in Indian affairs had to be broken. Moreover, the BIA's location within a department below the top of the federal government—one with a conflict of interest regarding Indian affairs—made it an inappropriate agency for taking leadership toward enhancing Indian sovereignty or self-determination (in its true sense, and not merely the limited self-determination of U.S. Indian policy), as we have seen.

If they function properly, many channels of interconnection between Indian nations and the federal government can be, and indeed do constitute, a necessary set of vehicles for the mutually beneficial development of complex policy to a reasonably high degree. But to operate well as agents of empowerment and mutual benefit, the set of agencies functioning in Indian affairs requires appropriate coordination, with proper tribal input—not at a lower level, but at the center or top of the government. The effort to create such responsive coordination at the presidential level is the next topic we will examine.

First, however, it is necessary to meet the objection that having multiple agencies with their own tribal liaisons promotes the perception that Indian tribes are just another set of interest groups with no special status, arising out of unbroken tribal sovereignty. It does seem likely that some people, particularly in government, have gotten the impression from the multitude of tribal liaisons that Indians are a special interest—probably because the sheer number of liaisons signaled Indians as an interest, rather than as a nation with a unique status. But the idea was widely held before the breaking of the BIA monopoly, when some would have perceived that Indians were just another interest group and that the agency that served them was the BIA. The most important aspect of this misperception is lack of correct information, the solution to which is education. The greater the number of people in government (as well as in the general public) who are educated about the special legal status of Native Americans (as well as about their status as an interest group), the more effective the education will be. Thus, when more agency personnel are correctly educated in a larger number of agencies (e.g., see the discussion of "Indian 101" below), the likelihood that the false impression will be overcome will increase.

Developing Coordination of Policy and Communication Within the White House

All of the attempts we have discussed so far to develop relations between Indian nations and the federal government on a government-to-government basis focus on individual agencies and departments. Even if one or more of them functioned exceedingly well and continued to do so, as of 1960, there was nothing in the operation or the structure of the federal government to encourage others to do so. And even if each entity functioned perfectly in its own terms, that does nothing to overcome the common problems of duplication of effort, contradiction of purpose, and failure to address broad problems properly that the lack of coordination between separate programs in the U.S. federal system perpetuates. It would seem then that some mechanism is necessary at the highest level to ensure the proper orientation of each operation, provide appropriate coordination of effort (including in holistic strategic planning), and provide a focal point for discussion of issues with the Native American community.

Development of such mechanisms has taken place over the course of a number of presidential administrations. Initially, under Lyndon Johnson in March 1968, a solid basis was laid by the establishment of the National Council on Indian Opportunity (chaired by the vice president), to "bring the problems of the Indians to the highest level of government."[76] The council was composed of six cabinet members, the director of the Office of Economic Opportunity, and six Native Americans. But the council did not meet for almost two years after its inception, and because it was established by presidential order and not statute, it did not last long.[77]

The next several presidents attempted to provide coordination and communication with the White House strictly on an ad hoc basis. For example, President Nixon generally relied on White House advisor ("Kitchen Cabinet Member") Leonard Garment to coordinate and troubleshoot Indian affairs, and Garment often worked with Bradley Patterson, Bobbie Kilburg, and Bob Robertson, director of the Vice

President's National Council on Indian Opportunity. However, there was nothing formal or permanent about this role, which was but one of Garment's assignments.[78]

Nixon initiated a strong policy that the federal government increase its efforts to carry out its trust relationship with the tribes by moving toward government-to-government relationships. But without Garment and other staff members who were committed to this policy and knowledgeable about Native American affairs implementing and developing the policy and informing the president when his attention was needed, Nixon's policy statements would have been mostly empty rhetoric.

On coming to office, President Ford chose to continue Nixon's approach. In August 1976, a White House memo was sent to the heads of all federal departments and other key agencies:

> I am today designating Bradley H. Patterson, Jr., of the White House Office to assist me in the area of American Indian Affairs. It will be Mr. Patterson's specific responsibility to work with each of you to improve coordination among the Federal agencies with programs that serve the Indian people.
>
> It is important that you insure the effective delivery and efficient operation of Federal Indian programs and services. I request that priority attention be given to coordination of these efforts among the Departments and Agencies and within the Executive Office of the President.
>
> In addition, I request that you continue to ensure that when Federal actions are planned which affect Indian communities, the responsible Indian leaders are consulted in the planning process.[79]

Other presidents have taken different approaches. The Reagan administration created a White House liaison for federally recognized tribes in the Office of Public Liaison. The position was moved early in 1983 to the Office of Intergovernmental Affairs.[80] This would seem to be a particularly appropriate place to provide a coordinator to ensure appropriate government-to-government relations between the tribes and the federal and other governments. However, to be effective, such an office would need to be made permanent, with a clear legal and institutional charter, and sufficient staff and other resources.

The issue of adequate resources was clearly raised by President Reagan, who made a strong commitment in principle

> that the traditional 'government-to-government' relationship between the federal government and Indian government should be continued. In my view that would include consulting with tribes and their leaders in the development of federal Indians and tribal governments. I believe that the people whose lives are most affected should play a larger role in influencing federal policy and personnel, so that the federal government can become more sensitive and responsible.[81]

But in practice, this policy was undermined when Reagan cut the federal budget, the consequences of which fell particularly heavily upon the tribes whose programs were already far from adequately funded, so that Reagan was criticized by many in the American Indian community for instituting "termination by budget." The cuts adversely affected government-to-government relations in some instances. For example, the Department of Labor, in the course of reducing staff in 1983, transferred decision making concerning American Indian employment programs away from the division of Native American Programs to other agencies not familiar with Native Americans and their needs. In one instance, rather than operating an Indian employment program locally through a tribal government or Indian organization, prime sponsorship and administration for the program, located in San Diego County, California, was awarded to a program in Sacramento that was geographically distant from the site and had no direct involvement with Indians.[82]

Although a more detailed examination of budget and related financial issues is more appropriately considered in chapter 5, we can point out here that the major reductions in funding for Indians in the 1996 federal budget illuminates the fact that adequate provision of resources is a prerequisite for the successful functioning of any effort to develop and carry out government-to-government relations.[83] This is not only a matter of direct funding but also involves making a variety of resources available for this purpose. For example, one of the provisions of the Indian Self-Determination and Educational Assistance Act (P.L. 93–638) was to extend to Indian tribes and tribal organizations eligibility to participate in the Intergovernmental Personnel Act (IPA: P.L. 91–648) Title IV program, which allows the interchange of personnel between federal, state, and local governments and institutions of higher learning.[84] This provision was used in the mid-1990s to enhance the establishment and administration of the tribal issues communication website INDIANnet.

The Clinton Administration's White House Working Group and National Indian Meetings

More recently, the Clinton administration, beginning in 1994, established what appears to be a fairly adequate and appropriate set of mechanisms for coordination and mutual communication of concerns. This began with what is believed to be the first meeting in which all federally recognized tribes were invited to the White House to discuss Indian affairs.[85] This meeting became an annual event, forming a useful vehicle for enhancing government-to-government relations. It would be beneficial to use this event as a means to focus on the field of Indian affairs as a whole and to include representatives of "urban Indians," since more than 60 percent of the Native American population now lives off reservations, mostly in cities (whereas most federal agencies and programs are primarily focused on the reservations).

The first White House conference was followed up by the National Indian Listening Conference, jointly sponsored by the Department of the Interior and DOJ, with participation from HUD. The heads of all three departments were in attendance.[86] This meeting with tribal leaders led directly to a series of reforms both within departments (e.g., the creation of the Office of Tribal Justice in the DOJ) and at the top of the administration that have institutionalized Indian relations.

The most important of these initiatives was the establishment of the Working Group on American Indian and Alaska Natives within the Domestic Policy Council. As of January 1997, the council was composed of twenty high-ranking members of executive departments (such as the undersecretary of agriculture for rural development, the chief of staff of the Department of Commerce, and the principle deputy assistant secretary for congressional and intergovernmental affairs of the Department of Energy) and other agencies (such as the Office of Management and Budget), along with designated staff from each agency.[87] The secretary of the interior chaired the working group.

There was one major problem with the organization of the working group as it was constituted at the end of the Clinton administration. Its being headed by the secretary of the interior presented the secretary with a conflict of interest between his responsibilities to his department and the requirements for coordinating Indian policy as a whole. He had to contend with pressures from a number of constituencies in his department, along with the necessity to maintain his power and authority to function effectively as department head. Moreover, the secretary, as an official of equal status with other department heads, had to work cautiously and diplomatically with other departments. As a result of this dual difficulty, energy was drawn away from the secretary's ability to ensure that the BIA and other Interior Department agencies dealt adequately with current major issues while communicating well with the tribes. As a result, the working group was unable to move swiftly or effectively to solve major problems that crossed department and agency jurisdictional boundaries in such crucial fields as gaming and the handling of toxic waste.

Moreover, little was done to improve the extremely varied quality of tribal communications so that all tribal governments and their members could receive up-to-date information from, and provide timely input to, all federal agencies (as could be achieved by developing adequate Internet linkages). What needed to be done was to move the coordination (and chairing) of the Indian Working Group entirely into the White House as part of the Intergovernmental Working Group, with equal status given to tribal governments vis-à-vis state and other government entities. There it would be able to operate from above the level of the departments with the full authority to effectively coordinate Indian policy and its implementation in dialogue with the tribes.

As it was, the working group was the initiator, after appropriate consultation, of a number of reforms, and it took steps to see that government-to-government relations were operating on a regular and proper basis throughout the executive branch. These steps included the establishment of permanent Indian Desks or offices in all agencies that regularly dealt with, or had an impact on, Native Americans, and the drafting of several presidential memoranda for the heads of agencies and departments, first "directing them to engage in continuing government-to-government relations with federally recognized tribal governments," then requesting the departments and agencies to report what government-to-government procedures they had instituted, as a step in "insuring that the President's directive is properly implemented."[88]

This initiative continued to encourage expansion of agency consideration of Indian interests and consultation with tribal governments in the early months of the Bush Administration.[89] However, although there were many fine examples of real dialogue between federal agencies and tribal governments and officials, there were, and continue to be, numerous complaints from tribal officials that federal agency staff often claim to "consult," when they are merely lecturing.[90] This complaint is also voiced by state and local government staff.[91]

The working group issued annual reports of developments since the first White House conference. Among the developments reported in August 1996 were the continuing increase of the share of the BIA's budget (then over 50 percent) for Tribal Priority Allocation.[92] This allowed tribes to prioritize programs and shape them according to their unique needs. The BIA had been involved in about fifteen hundred self-determination contracts totaling some $650 million. This development signaled the increasing level of freedom tribes had to run or contract out their own programs in virtually every area even prior to the implementation of the Tribal Shares process.

Similarly, the number of self-governance annual funding agreements had extended to 180, or about one-third, of recognized tribes, and rules for administering the self-governance program were being developed by a joint federal and tribal negotiating team including the Department of the Interior, HHS, and tribal representatives. The number of tribes directly carrying out their own programs or overseeing their contracting or compacting slowly expanded, even through the George W. Bush administration, so that by late 2007, about 40 percent of federally recognized tribes were involved in self-governance. For those nations, the results were generally positive, although there were continuing problems to overcome, as both tribal representatives and Department of the Interior personnel testified before the Senate Committee on Indian Affairs on May 13, 2008, during a hearing on shortfalls in congressional appropriations for federal Indian agencies. Witnesses were consistent in stating that self-governance had been a success. Funding agreements between tribes and the Department of the Interior under the program numbered ninety-four, according to Associate Deputy Secretary for Indian Affairs James Cason, and provided approximately $380 million annually to 234 tribes and tribal consortia. Agreements between the IHS and 320 tribes provided another $1 billion for self-governance programs. With funding that used to go to the federal agencies, tribes then executed a full range of social and resource management services for their citizens. "The self-governance program has spurred an important transition from bureaucratic one-size-fits-all programs to flexible, tribally designed and administered programs," said Clifford Lyle Marshall, chairman of the Hoopa Valley Indian Tribe, which he described as the first self-governance tribe. "Self-governance afforded tribes the opportunity to take over the planning and development of these programs. At that point they became based on the priorities and needs of Indian communities as determined by the tribes, and for this reason they work." However, Marshall and James Steele of the Confederated Salish and Kootenai Tribes, indicating one of the remaining difficulties with self-governance, testified that allowable costs that have always been acceptable under realistic management are now found "illegal," and agreed with Chairman W. Ron Allen of the Jamestown S'Klallam Tribe that new interpretations of "allowable costs" at the Office of the Special Trustee within the Interior Department have stymied the program.

Thus, by the end of the Clinton presidency, it would appear that the transformation of the BIA had become considerably advanced, as the entire executive branch appeared to be attaining a high level of government-to-government interaction with the tribes. The process is not yet complete, for although the official rhetoric throughout the executive branch at the end of the Clinton administration was consistent with the philosophy of government-to-government relationships, and the higher levels of the administration, departments, and agencies in general were acting in a collaborative manner, providing leadership to carry that thinking and behavior to all levels of the federal bureaucracy, the extent to which the government-to-government way of proceeding in Indian affairs has become part of the working culture varies from agency to agency, within the same agency, and among different regions, offices, and working groups.

Some indication of this variation in acculturation emerged in discussions with officials of two Southwest tribes by author Stephen Sachs in July 1997. Two Southern Ute officials commented that their tribe's relations with the BIA were vastly improved, and one of them stated, "Things turned around about five years ago. The BIA works for us now." By contrast, Navajo Nation officials said that, although BIA personnel currently worked more collaboratively with their tribe than had been the case in the past, they still experienced bureaucratic difficulties in trying to work with the BIA.[93]

In addition, since 1997, there has been little increase in the number of Indian nations running their own programs, which as of fall 2007 was about 40 percent of federally recognized tribes. The problem, as was the case with welfare reform, is that many tribal governments do not have the funding, experience, or trained personnel to run federal programs that they could take over legally, and for the most part, the federal government does not provide the training or resources for training, starting up, or administering programs. This failure, even at the end of the Clinton administration, was continuing to be a major constraint on the realization of fully developed tribal government empowerment and tribal–federal government partnership. Lack of adequate resources also seriously limits Indian community and personal development, a concern we will discuss in chapter 5.

A Step Backward: Developments in the Bush Administration

In January 2001, George W. Bush assumed the office of president of the United States. A newly elected president has a great deal of latitude in organizing the Executive Office of the Presidency. The Executive Office was originally established in 1939 upon recommendation from the Brownlow Committee. The committee had determined that, with existing staffing, presidents could not adequately discharge the job of chief administrator. Thus, the committee recommended additional administrative support separate from the existing bureaucracy. Agencies, task forces, desks, and offices may be placed under the aegis of the Executive Office of the Presidency by congressional statute, executive order, and presidential directive. The Executive Office of the Presidency, unlike other executive branch offices and agencies, is composed of political appointees rather than civil servants, most of whom are not subject to Senate confirmation.[94]

As we have described, presidents since Nixon have created either a task force, commission, or work group, or at least have appointed an individual to serve as a liaison or coordinating body to focus on American Indian interests. These positions are ad hoc in nature and mainly symbolic in practice. However, they did at times serve as a much needed focal point between agencies in the executive branch and American Indian peoples and tribal governments.

Author Barbara Morris contacted the Bush administration transition team in the fall of 2001 to determine the status of the working group President Clinton had established. After a number of phone calls, the question still remained unanswered. In fact, so many calls were diverted to so many different individuals that it appeared as if no one within the Executive Office of the Presidency had any clear understanding or commitment to Indian policy.

In January 2002, Barbara Morris went to Washington to meet with senior officials in the White House and the Republican Senatorial Committee. During this visit, she met with a senior official in the White House office and asked for assistance in determining, first, whether the working group still existed, and second, if it did not, whether anyone was working in Indian policy or serving as a tribal liaison. The official stated at the outset that "this sounds like something we would get rid of."[95] Various staffers both within the White House and from the Republican Senatorial Committee helped investigate this matter. As of June 2002, Barbara Morris had received no information regarding any person, agency, task force, or commission within the Executive Office of the Presidency that was designated to work on Indian policy.

One individual in the White House did suggest that the BIA was the agency in charge of all Indian matters. Under the new strategic plan that the BIA developed, there are directives to determine which agencies and bureaus might be involved in delivering particular services to Native Americans. The plan specifies that, if multiple agencies or bureaus are involved, cross-cutting relationships should be established. However, within the strategic plan, there is no discussion or example of how these relationships will be established and maintained in practice.[96]

The result was that the Bush administration, which especially after September 11, 2001, generally considered Indian policy a minor concern, dealt with Native issues on an ad hoc basis. In a few instances, where Indian policy related to major Bush administration initiatives, as in education, the president did take new steps on Native issues. For example, in June 2003, the administration acted on a long-standing tribal request to elevate Indian issues within the Department of Education, and Acting Secretary of Education Rod Paige elevated the department's Office of Indian Education to report to Undersecretary Eugene Hickok rather than an assistant secretary. Similarly, in July 2003, President Bush established the President's Board of Advisors on Tribal Colleges and Universities to make recommendations to the White House and the secretary of education on ways the federal government and the private sector can help tribal colleges strengthen and expand their resources, programs, facilities, and use of technologies, and to provide advice on the progress federal agencies are making toward fulfilling the purposes and objectives of Presidential Executive Order 13270 to improve Native American education. The order calls for executive agencies to develop three-year plans to provide programs for tribal colleges and universities in such areas as preserving native languages. Then, on April 30, 2004, President Bush issued an executive order establishing the Interagency Working Group on American Indian and Alaska Native Education, consisting of the heads of the Departments of Education, Interior, Health and Human Services, Agriculture, Justice, and Labor and such other executive branch departments, agencies, or offices as the co-chairs of the working group may designate. The working group was charged to develop a federal interagency plan within ninety days that recommends initiatives, strategies, and ideas for future interagency actions to assist American Indian and Alaska Native students in meeting the student academic standards of the No Child Left Behind Act of 2001 in a manner that is consistent with tribal traditions, languages, and cultures. In addition, the secretary of education, in coordination with the working group, was charged to conduct a multiyear study of American Indian and Alaska Native education with the purpose of improving American Indian and Alaska Native students' ability to meet the student academic standards of the No Child Left Behind Act.[97] (We analyze the problems for American Indians with the No Child Left Behind initiative in chapter 5.)

The White House, however, undercut these advances, and Native American programs in general, by constantly proposing cuts in Indian budgets as part of broader efforts to reduce domestic spending. Congress acted to restore many of the reductions and made some important increases. Meanwhile, the administration worked in a number of areas, generally without tribal consultation, to interpret legislation or change rules in order to reduce the eligibility of Indian nations or people for a variety of federal programs.[98] For instance, in 2003, the Bush administration sought to restrict entitlement services to Indians to those who are tribal members, denying the services to currently eligible children of tribal members who themselves are not members.[99] An initiative to this effect from the Justice Department stalled reauthorization of the Indian Health Services Act, while Kanaka Maoli (Native Hawaiians who have received services as descendants of Native people) were eliminated from the proposal for reauthorization of the Indian Housing Act. At the same time, the Office of Management and Budget moved toward using a Program Assessment Rating Tool for funding for tribes that would reduce funding for BIA programs that the servicing agency rated poorly for management.

Also that year, the administration sent a proposal to the House to reauthorize the Workforce Investment Act, formerly known as the Job

Training Partnership Act. The act provides for job training and placement and some related support services that would force Indian grantees to turn over a portion of their Section 166 funds to the state, and also would require every One-Stop partner, including tribal governments and other Indian grantees under Section 166, to provide funds to the state for the operation of the state Workforce Investment Act One-Stop centers. The funds would be used to pay for costs, such as rent and utilities, for centers that many Indian clients have no access to because of the remote rural location of their communities. The centers provide few, if any, of the services Indian people need. The proposed bill set no limit on the amount of funds that states could demand from tribes and other Indian grantees. The proposal would force Indian grantees to turn over a portion of their Section 166 funds to local Workforce Investment Boards. In addition to providing funds to the state, Indian grantees could be required to make financial contributions to local Workforce Investment Boards through provisions in the Memorandum of Understanding that each One-Stop partner must negotiate with the board. Although Indian grantees would be forced to pay for the state One-Stop centers, the administration's proposal did not provide for any increase in Section 166 Comprehensive Services funds. All payments to the state and the local Workforce Investment Boards would have to come out of existing Section 166 funds, reducing services for Indian clients. In addition, the administration's proposal would delete the language in Section 166 that allowed people who were eligible for Indian Job Training Partnership Act services to remain eligible for Indian Workforce Investment Act services, a change that would restrict the program to members of federally recognized tribes, with the result that Alaska Natives, Native Hawaiians, and members of tribes that are not federally recognized could no longer be served.[100]

It was revealed in 2007 that the Office of Management and Budget—which reviews the planned text of executive branch officials' upcoming testimony—had twice in the early months of that year removed reference to the Snyder Act and the Indian Health Care Improvement Act that were "at the core of the federal government responsibility for meeting the health needs of American Indians and Alaska Natives" and implied that there is a trust responsibility rooted in law for the health care for Native Americans. Greg Smith of the law firm Johnston and Associates in Washington, D.C., said that the two excisions were not coincidental or unrelated when considered in light of the Justice Department's characterization in 2006 of programs in the Indian Health Care Improvement Act reauthorization as race-based. He stated that, from the earliest weeks of the 110th Congress, Capitol Hill staff and Indian-issue lobbyists willing to speak with candor only on condition of anonymity had warned of an arch-conservative agenda in Congress to challenge any federal benefit for nontribal Native groups as a way of chipping away at the trust relationship.[101]

In the meantime, the Bush administration generally allowed collaboration between federal agencies and tribes to continue, with some expansion: for example, in certain DOJ programs and in discussions between the Department of Homeland Security and the Homeland Security Taskforce of the NCAI following numerous complaints from tribes along U.S. borders that they were not being consulted in matters of security, and as a result, they and border security operations were negatively affected.

Although during the Bush administration some increases in discussions between federal agencies and tribes occurred, tribal complaints that executive-branch agencies were not consulting the tribes increased overall. For instance, in November 2003, NCAI President Tex Hall told the organization's fifty-ninth annual convention that he was troubled by the administration's proposal to move Head Start from HHS to the Department of Education and shift the majority of Head Start funding and decision making to the states, a proposal that was made without consultation with Indian nations and people. Similarly, in early 2008, Executive Director of the National Indian Gaming Association Mark Van Norman, on hearing that the Department of the Interior had changed policy and essentially rejected twenty-two applications for new off-reservation casinos by requiring that they not be distant from the reservation, stated, "We were shocked by the lack of due process involved. The Department of Interior created a new regulatory standard one day, didn't notify anybody and applied it the next day."[102]

What Is Still Needed to Complete the Circle of Federal–Tribal Relations?

Although the U.S. Constitution provides no clear statement about the place of tribal governments in American federalism, more than forty years of practical development, including congressional acts, presidential orders and practices, and administrative agency policies and actions signal that Indian tribal governments are now partners in American federalism in principle and are becoming so in practice. Certainly, if one accepts that Indian nations are today domestic, rather than foreign, sovereign nations and are moving away from being "domestic dependent nations" (as Chief Justice John Marshall termed them in *Cherokee Nation v. Georgia*), as the federal government meets its trust responsibility to return them to self-sufficiency, it is appropriate that they should have such status and position.[103] Because of their international origins, federally recognized tribes are in some ways equivalent to, and in some ways superior to, states.[104]

By the end of the Clinton administration, a great deal had been accomplished toward developing effective arrangements and practices to realize an appropriate tribal–federal government relationship; unfortunately, the Bush administration backed away from these gains. If we use the Clinton administration arrangements as a model, several additional steps are still necessary to complete the task those arrangements began. First, the top-level body for coordinating federal Indian policy with appropriate Indian input, informing the president of Indian concerns, and serving as a vehicle for presidential leadership in Indian affairs needs to be headed by an appropriate person above the cabinet level. Tribal relations could certainly benefit by establishing a formal unit within the Executive Office of the President. Perhaps the most appropriate place is within the Office of Intergovernmental Relations, a subunit of the Domestic Policy Council within the Office of Policy Development of the Executive Office of the President. During the Clinton administration, an official of the Office of Intergovernmental Relations who represented the Working Group on American Indian and Alaska Natives in the office had as part of her job description the investigation and coordination of policies dealing with Native Americans. If the holder of this position were also the head of the working group, and the position and the working group were institutionalized both by congressional statute and executive order, the formal arrangements at the top of the U.S. government would be appropriately completed.

However, a unit is only effective if it is adequately supported with funding for a sufficient staff and if the president uses it. At the same time, an entity established by law cannot be eliminated simply by executive order, and if it is underutilized or effectively deactivated in one administration, it can be reenergized in a subsequent administration that has the will to do so. As a practical matter, in order for an office to be effective, both Congress and the president need to be convinced of its utility.

Therefore, it is a necessity that Indian nations have the political energy (generated both of their own initiative and through that of allies and public opinion) to make possible the creation and maintenance of such arrangements.

Second, because most of the necessary structural arrangements at the national, department, agency, and subordinate levels now appear to be in place, they need to be evaluated on an ongoing basis to refine and adapt them to developing circumstances so that they can continue with enough energy to become firmly established and penetrate effectively throughout the federal system. At the same time, examining other models and methods may bring useful improvement. Similarly, cultural development now seems to be in place, or developing, throughout the federal government for all whose work touches on Native American affairs and policy, and this momentum needs to continue vigorously until the current transformation of bureaucratic outlook is complete. After that, cultural development can be continued at a modest level to maintain awareness and perspective, and to educate new personnel. This is necessary not only as regards agency staff working with Indian policy and people: all agency personnel ought to understand the needs of, and be able to communicate readily with, the people whom their work affects.

Any evaluation of arrangements as they function in practice must include consideration of whether, at the highest level, institutionalization of appropriate arrangements has been sufficiently realized in order to coordinate the making and carrying out of Indian policy. This involves informing the president and keeping his or her attention on Indian policy matters as is necessary and proper, providing oversight and encouragement to ensure that government-to-government arrangements are functioning properly at lower levels, and providing top-level input from, and dialogue with, the Indian community about policy formation and administration needs and concerns.

Given the breadth of American Indian policy and the large number of departments and agencies involved with it, it would be advisable to ensure that the working group is indeed adequately and appropriately staffed and that communication with the tribes (as well as with federal and, as appropriate, state and local agencies concerned with Indian affairs) is functioning adequately. It should be noted that although such arrangements, however perfected, cannot be effective with a truly disinterested president, they should be effective in gaining appropriate attention from a president who is at least open-minded; if such arrangements have considerable political support, they might be able to cause even an unfriendly president to move favorably.

At department and agency levels, it is appropriate to examine whether the vehicles for coordination of Indian policy are working effectively, whether those within the department are operating on an appropriate government-to-government basis with the tribes, and whether there is appropriate ongoing dialogue with tribal governments (and, as warranted, representatives of urban Indians). A good model for such communication is the EPA's example of frequently engaging in all kinds of interaction with tribes and Native American organizations (including meetings, conferences, and workshops, as well as exchanges of memoranda, newsletters, one-to-one electronic or paper mailings, and conversations).[105]

To date, the collaborative government-to-government way of thinking and acting in federal administration has developed to differing extents among the various agencies, programs, and offices of the federal bureaucracy. In order to ensure that federal government personnel are competent to undertake activities involving the government-to-government relation with the tribes, appropriate education and access to needed information is required. Appropriate education includes understanding and knowledge of the nature of the relationship (including the requirements of the trust responsibility of the federal government), of the processes through which the government-to-government relationship operates, and of how to work appropriately within those processes. It also includes understanding the culture and views of American Indians and the relevant conditions for the tribes and their members, as well as the relevant policies. Since changes in personnel frequently occur, particularly at the higher levels, in addition to changes in conditions, the educational process needs to be ongoing.

To begin with, an initial orientation needs to be provided for new personnel that is adjusted to each person's background. For example, someone coming to a Native American policy–related position in an agency with tribal government or organization experience will need to be oriented to the ways of the agency and its policy principles, including how these have been applied in working with tribal governments. Someone with long experience in a federal agency in matters not relating to Native Americans would primarily need orientation on how to work well with Native Americans and the conditions to which the agency's policies apply.

Once there is an initial orientation to the government-to-government process as it relates to a particular position, much of the ongoing process of education can be undertaken in the course of dialogue and direct experience with the agency's programs. This includes dialogue regarding feedback from and evaluation of the programs' operation, along with updated information and sharing of broader information about the events and development of the government-to-government process. This kind of education, which prepares incoming staff to understand their policy areas and the people affected by their work and keeps them abreast of developments, ought to be provided for all federal personnel.

An example of such education was undertaken in the DOE during the Clinton administration. A team led by LaDonna Harris provided "Indian 101" for the secretary of the DOE and top agency staff. The plan was for them to train personnel below them, who, in turn, were to educate their own subordinates, with each level below the top reporting back to the staff member who was coordinating department intergovernmental relations that the instruction had been completed. The full plan was not fulfilled before the administration changed. But had it been institutionalized as regular procedure, it would have been a most helpful practice.

These measures are not a matter for the executive branch of government alone. Congress has an important role in legislating the basis for this kind of process, providing appropriate policy statements and funding, and undertaking proper oversight. Some structural concerns exist on the congressional side as well. Prior to the establishment of the Senate Select Committee on Indian Affairs, the committees of the House and Senate that included Indian affairs in their much larger areas of policy concern rarely paid much attention to Indian policy and exercised virtually no oversight over the administration of Indian programs. The American Indian Policy Review Commission was authorized by Congress in 1975 (under Public Law 93–580) to report in 1977 on what needed to be done in the field of Indian affairs.[106] Staffed by interested and knowledgeable members of the Senate and House and Native American leaders, the commission produced an extensive overview of the problems of Indian policy at that time, along with two hundred proposals for action that were generally well received by the tribes.[107] The impact of the commission's report was important in giving impetus to initiating policy changes that would have to be made incrementally (and that Congress was not ready to go very far with at that moment). It led directly to the establishment of the Senate Select Committee on Indian Affairs as an ongoing body to develop and review policy and oversee its implementation. The establishment of such temporary review and strategic planning bodies as the commission can be very helpful at key moments. The active and helpful role of the Senate Select Committee on Indian Affairs in policy development and administrative oversight is testimony to the desirability of having a permanent committee directly involved with Native American affairs.

It is important to note, however, that neither that committee nor Congress in general operates in a political vacuum. The membership, focus, and energy of the committee are very much dependent upon the political climate and specific input from political groups, which makes the extent and effectiveness of American Indians, the tribes, and Native American organizations as actors in the political arena a critical element in what government will do.[108] Similarly, since the courts play an important role in ultimately determining policy, it matters very much who the judges are. But because Indian affairs are generally not a concern at the moment of making judicial appointments and Native American political strength is unlikely to be a significant factor in influencing such appointments or the Senate confirmation process, in general, the most that the Indian community can do to encourage helpful judicial attitudes is to continue to promote favorable attitudes by the general public.

In making the above proposals, we seek to have policy makers and administrators continue to move away from treating Native Americans and tribes as special interests and continue to move toward dealing with tribes as they would other government bodies in the U.S. system of federalism, treating Native Americans as participants in dialogue with government entities in the making and administration of policy, as all citizens should be treated. Thus, the thrust of these proposals are broader than the field of American Indian policy. Rather, by showing how Native American policy can be better carried out, they exemplify the benefits of a more collaborative federalism and a more participatory political process.[109]

2. Completing the Circle of Tribal–State and Local Government Relations

The development of government-to-government relations between tribal governments and the federal government has had a profound impact on the growth of cooperative relations between tribal governments and state and local governments, to the extent that tribal governments have realized self-determination. This has been extremely important for all concerned.

If there had been no achievement of tribal self-determination, the current devolution of federal authority and responsibility to the states would have continued the unfortunate situation of Indian nations prior to 1933, with mounting costs for the rest of the nation. The federal government would either have persisted in carrying out that administration or it would have fully or partially transferred administration to the states.

Turning over authority in Indian affairs to the states would probably have been more disadvantageous to Indian nations (it would also have violated federal trust responsibility) than continued federal domination, because the conflict of interest in Indian affairs becomes more intense as one moves from the national to the state and local level. Many of the people with short-term interests that are most opposed to those of Indian nations are often their immediate neighbors whose political power is stronger at the state and local level than in Washington.[110] (In general, although it varies with the particular case or situation, large corporations interested in extracting natural resources on reservations have considerable political power at both state and national levels.) This situation has begun to change in direct relation to the extent that Indian nations have attained self-governance and self-sufficiency, which allows them to integrate more fully into the economic and political life of the area in which they are located.

Without independent and well-functioning tribal governments, the substantial though still insufficient economic and other development that Indian nations have achieved would not have occurred. The historical record shows a close relationship between the growth of Indian self-governance and economic and other development. Indeed, studies of economic development on reservations show that programs imposed from the outside have largely failed, whereas programs that have been successful have almost always been undertaken by Indian people themselves or in full partnership with others.[111] Today, with the economic advancement that has occurred as self-determination has grown, many Indian nations are experiencing an economic and more general resurgence, while their rural neighbors have been experiencing a decline. Indian people and reservation economic activity now play a significant role in many state economies by producing considerable income, tax revenues, and jobs, and Indian people pay more in state taxes than they receive in state benefits.[112]

Appreciation of this growing interrelationship is contributing toward the rise in government-to-government relations between tribal, state, and local governments, although in most instances, state and local governments do not yet see tribal governments as equal partners. Instances of tribal government–state and local government cooperation are numerous and cover many fields, with mutual benefits for all parties.[113]

Collaboration between tribal, state, and local governments is a relatively new development. Although it is occurring more frequently, it is not yet the norm. Initially, the national government maintained an almost exclusive relationship with Indian nations.[114] Indeed, one condition of becoming a state for eleven western states was to include a clause in their constitution renouncing all jurisdiction and taxing authority over Indians and Indian lands.[115] Prior to Congress adopting a policy of attempting to assimilate Indians into mainstream U.S. society in the mid- to late nineteenth century, most of the few instances of tribal–state relations stemmed from agreements that some of the thirteen original states had made with Indigenous nations prior to the writing of the U.S. Constitution. Especially after the passage of the Dawes Act in 1887, as Indians accepted allotments of land as individuals, they came under state jurisdiction when off the reservation, and some reservations were terminated, particularly in Oklahoma. The federal government, however, through the administration of the BIA, continued to be responsible for governing reservations and for providing services to Indians, including education.[116]

Beginning in the late nineteenth century, the BIA contracted with individual school boards for some Indian education in public schools and in the 1930s began contracting for Indian education with individual states, which Congress authorized in the Johnson-O'Mally Act of 1934.[117] Because Indian tribes and people had no formal say (and almost no informal influence) in how this education was carried out, it was most often culturally inappropriate, sometimes racist, and largely ineffective, contributing directly to the high dropout rates and low average levels of achievement that Indian people continue to suffer, in part because they still often have little say concerning the education of Indian young people in public schools.

With Congress providing limited tribal self-government with some contracting authority subject to BIA approval in the 1934 Indian Reorganization Act and related legislation, some modest instances of tribal–state relations occurred.[118] However, the small amount of tribal government authority in practice precluded the development of significant tribal–state government relations at the time.

Congress precipitated a major entrance of states into Indian relations without direct tribal participation with the movement to terminate Indian tribes and end the federal trust responsibility in the 1950s.[119] For example, during the termination period, the BIA made a series of transfers of responsibility for maintaining reservation roads to counties, so that in 1972, 42 percent of the roads on Indian lands were maintained by counties. Similarly, during the 1950s, the BIA contracted most Indian agricultural extension work to states that carry out federal extension programs. In addition, beginning in the 1950s and to a greater extent in the following decade, the BIA emphasized state and local government collaboration with tribal governments in economic development. Of particular importance, in 1953, Congress passed Public Law 280, which gave five states (California, Minnesota, Nebraska, Oregon, and Wisconsin) criminal and civil judicial authority over Indians.[120] However, budget considerations restrained these states from fully exercising this authority, and more recent congressional action prevents these states from exerting new authority in this area without the permission of tribal governments. Moreover, in most of these states, tribal pressure has led state legislatures to return Public Law 280 powers to tribal governments.

The congressionally initiated movement toward termination was accompanied by an increase in state government interest in Indian affairs, for which the states would have had a major responsibility if termination had been fully carried out. One aspect of this increase was a first movement toward tribal–state government dialogue.[121] In 1950, Governor Luther Youngdahl of Minnesota held a conference to develop a long-term program on Indian affairs with top officials, including four governors, representatives from fifteen states, Indian leaders, and BIA officials. This resulted in the formation of the Governors' Interstate Indian Council with state executive and Indian members. Several states subsequently formed Indian commissions. The Governors' Interstate Indian Council remained an active forum at least until 1970 but faded in importance as the self-determination era developed, and the original state Indian commissions, while undertaking some significant projects, have never been consistently effective. Thus, the end of the termination era, when Congress launched a policy of Indian self-determination, found only a modest increase in tribal–state and local government relations but an expanded concern on the part of states and localities regarding Indian affairs.

Despite the initial efforts of the 1950s, when tribal governments first began to gain some autonomy from federal domination, they received little respect from most state and local governments. Unfortunately, extremely costly jurisdictional confusion, lack of adequate understanding and communication, and competition and conflict have long been major features of many of the relations between tribal and state and local governmental entities. In too many instances, perceived social, political, and economic inequalities among neighbors, fueled by racism and competition for valuable resources, have turned in a vicious cycle with hazy areas of responsibility, mistrust, and misunderstanding between jurisdictions that continues to block cooperation for mutual advancement.

This situation has been changing in recent years, in large part as a result of the rise of government-to-government relations between tribal governments and the federal government. This is especially the case now that, increasingly though unevenly, federal agencies, including a much transformed and still-developing BIA, have begun to deal with Indian nations as governments, giving them a high level of autonomy in running their own programs and including Indian input in federal-agency decision making, and at times encouraging tribal–state and local government collaboration. As Indian tribal governments have increased activity and gained experience, state and local authorities have increasingly come to see that tribal governments can be capable partners in collaborative activity.

In addition, there is some indication that the combination of the change in general public perception of Native Americans, increased Indian political power, increased use of collaborative rather than competitive ways of approaching issues in the United States, and the rising understanding that tribes contribute significantly to area and state economies and thus share common interests with the rest of the population, are having some effect in increasing cooperation between state and local governments and tribes.[122]

For example, a study by the Oklahoma Indian Affairs Commission shows that the state's Native American population (252,519 or 8.03 percent of the total state population) contributed to the state economy and to state and local revenues in five ways in 1990. Direct spending by the tribes was estimated at $317.93 million, of which $181.22 million originated from tribal taxes, and $136.71 million originated from federal assistance paid directly to tribal governments. The tribes did not rely on state or local taxes for income. Federal funding to tribes, as part of the federal government's obligation to the tribes for cession of lands, generated increased revenues for Oklahoma. The overall impact of tribal spending was estimated at between $413.9 million and $667 million (depending on the multiplier used), and represented between 0.83 and 1.33 percent of gross state product (GSP). Jobs supported by this spending represented between 0.68 and 1.13 percent of total Oklahoma employment. This spending generated between $3.9 and $4.8 million in state income tax and between $2.2 and $2.7 million in sales tax. Overall, the thirty-six Oklahoma tribes and their members, although possessing a relatively low mean personal income, had a considerable impact on the economy and revenues of Oklahoma in 1990. Combining the five revenue sources above, the tribal presence might have been responsible for $3.534 billion in gross expenditure, generating $44.8 million, or 6.5 percent, of state income tax and $24.8 million, or 5.16 percent, of state sales tax, contributing $5.983 billion, or 11.94 percent, of GSP and generating 150,600 jobs. Because there is some overlap in the impact of each of the five sources of income, jobs, and revenue, the actual results will be somewhat less than the apparent results of simply adding the five sets of figures together. This will be somewhat offset by, first, the conservative nature of some estimates, and second, by additional Native American and tribal contributions to the Oklahoma economy that were not identified in the study.

Less inclusive studies of Arizona and New Mexico produced similar results. In Arizona, twenty-one tribes with 166,282 enrolled tribal members resided in the state in 1990. In that year, tribal governments made off-reservation expenditures of $178.29 million, and on-reservation enterprises made $100 million in off-reservation expenditures; the federal government made $479.5 million in expenditures attributable to the Native American population. Total median household income of tribal members was $415.9 million, with a total off-reservation consumption of $208 million. Statewide employment attributable to the Native American population was 34,546, with statewide income attributable to the Native American population totaling $828 million. Visitors to Arizona spent $62.5 million on the reservation and $479 million off-reservation. It is estimated that the state gained $93 million in revenue from Native American consumer expenditures and enterprises, whereas the state spent only $21.9 million on behalf of the tribal population. The New Mexico study shows that there were 134,002 Native Americans, or 8.92 percent of the state population, in twenty-five tribes in 1990. The 1991–1992 revenues of the tribes totaled $39.26 million, of which $2.18 million was federal money, $6.89 million originated from tribal enterprises, and $17.11 million originated from tribal taxes. Tribes and tribal enterprises employed

12,708 people in 1990–1991 (of whom about 23.7 percent were not Native American). These employees earned a mean annual salary of $26,000, which was higher than the mean state income in 1991 of $20,185. The total state tax contribution of Native Americans was $75.8 million in 1990 and $80.6 million in 1991, or 4.5 percent of total revenues in each year. In contrast, it is estimated that Native Americans receive less than 4 percent of state-program benefits.[123]

It appears that the New Mexico and Arizona studies have facilitated increased tribal and state government cooperation in the field of tourism. In May 1992, representatives of tribes, neighboring communities, state and federal officials, and entrepreneurs came together in a Southwest American Indian Tourism Conference to collaborate in developing "strategies for environmentally and culturally appropriate, economically sustainable tourism" relating to the tribes in the Southwest.[124]

Another move to increased collaboration involved South Dakota Governor Bill Janklow, who had quite acrimonious relations with the state's tribes during his first two terms. After his return to the governorship in July 1995, he brought the tribes together for a collaborative discussion that tribal leaders found to be a most pleasant surprise. At the open-ended session, which allowed anyone to raise issues for discussion, Janklow stated, "We can work together. If it's on the reservation it's yours. If it's off the reservation, its ours. If it's in the checkerboard areas, we have trouble. Let's forget the past and work on the future."[125] The meeting was followed by an improvement in state–tribal relations during Janklow's second term, although the extent of his administration's cooperation and acting in agreement with the state's Native nations varied with the issue.

The extent to which state and local governments and tribes cooperate will depend upon a number of factors beyond those already mentioned. Where decision making is rational (rather than based upon habit, prejudice, or emotional reaction), the choice to cooperate or compete typically will be based upon estimations of the short- and long-term costs and benefits of cooperating rather than competing. These estimations include both political considerations of the probable reactions of the public (and government bodies) to whom the actors are directly or indirectly responsible, and the policy and financial results that are likely to accrue from taking either course (or using a mixed approach). The extent of information available about the other party's situation, decision-making authority and process, and record of past actions is an important determinant of how to proceed. The lack of this information, particularly about tribal governments, has often deterred collaboration. A related factor in making estimations of likely outcomes is the trust one has in the intentions (and the ability to make good on and continue to keep agreements) and competence of the other party. Since, to a considerable extent, trust is based upon prior experience (as well as the general climate and the specific immediate factors in the circumstances at hand), it tends to be built or undermined by ongoing behavior.

Expanding Experience in Tribal–State and Local Government Cooperation

We can see the impact of these factors by looking at some experiences in the field of law enforcement. A major problem in state and local–tribal government relations concerning law enforcement is confusion over jurisdiction, which often involves considerable complexity.[126] Tribal police (and courts, in criminal cases) have authority only on reservations, and only in cases in which the suspect is a Native American. (Even then, tribal courts can only try misdemeanors; major crimes are tried in federal court, and the FBI has jurisdiction to investigate and arrest.) Except in the few instances where state and local police have limited authority on reservations (generally under the limited continuation of Public Law 280), they cannot make an arrest on a reservation unless both the victim and the suspect are non-Indian.

This already confusing situation is compounded by the fact that many reservations are checkerboards of property owned both by Native Americans and non-Native Americans. This not only creates serious difficulties in carrying out investigations and making arrests, but it also prevents the giving of timely assistance when a crime or dangerous situation is in progress. In a threatening circumstance, the nearest police authorities may have no jurisdiction and those who do may be a considerable distance away, while citizens wishing to summon assistance may not know whom to call. Moreover, because jurisdiction in part depends on the identity of the suspect, which might not be determinable in the midst of an ongoing situation, even a well-informed citizen or officer might not know how to proceed.

Given these circumstances, in situations in which state and local authorities have little trust in tribal members or the competence of tribal police, state and local authorities have often attempted to gain as much jurisdiction as possible at the expense of the tribes. In turn, having had bad experiences with state and local justice in particular and decision making in general, tribes have fought to keep and extend as much "sovereignty" as possible, including in the field of law enforcement. With some important exceptions, this competitive approach to jurisdictional questions has been the historical norm. With neither side able to eliminate the jurisdiction of the other, the relatively small gains achieved through the competitive approach, with the accompanying problems of continuing complexity, seemed to be preferable to attempts by either side to gain more cooperation than is absolutely necessary.

The state and local governments would not trust the tribes with jurisdiction, and the tribes saw cooperation as giving away sovereignty. Indeed, in the past, when tribal members were isolated from the surrounding communities and had little relevant technical expertise and few financial, political, or other resources available to help them deal with outside jurisdictions, the relative inequalities between the parties often turned even genuinely intended cooperation into co-option by the outside authority.

Building enough trust to develop a cooperative approach to jurisdictional problems through collaboration has often been difficult and slow. However, some successes in this area that have been consistently carried out over time provide precedents and open opportunities whereby other groups can build trust. For example, a number of Indian nations, including the Southern Utes in Colorado; the Miccosukees in Florida; the Blackfeet, Assiniboines, and Flatheads in Montana; the Yakimas in Washington; and the Wind River Reservation Northern Arapaho and Eastern Shoshone Tribes in Wyoming, have found effective solutions to these difficulties by coming together with neighboring local and state police to cross-deputize one another's officers (so that they have authority in all jurisdictions) and to engage in close communication and collaboration. The Poarch Band of Creek Indians in Alabama not only have cross-deputizing arrangements with neighboring police, but also provide fire and emergency services to nearby areas. Meanwhile, the police of the city of Albuquerque, New Mexico, and the adjacent pueblos have arranged that when Pueblo members are arrested for misdemeanors in the city, the police will turn them over to their Pueblo authorities for trial.[127]

The result of agreements to take such cooperative approaches depends upon how the relationships among the individuals participating in the new arrangements are initiated and fostered, as has been shown by extensive experience with developing teamwork in workplaces.[128] Collaboration involves an ongoing relationship, and the quality of the interaction in any such relationship follows from the attitudes and skills of the participants. Having a common goal, such as effective and fair law enforcement, is an important element in launching successful cooperation, but it is not sufficient to make a cooperative effort successful.

To enable participants in any collaborative effort to work together effectively and cordially so that the experience of collaborating is a positive one, sufficient mutual trust to communicate freely and work cooperatively, sufficient understanding of other participants (which is especially important to take into account in developing cross-cultural collaboration), and sufficiently developed collaborative attitudes and skills must already exist or be created by education or team-building exercises. More care needs to be taken to ensure that participants are able to collaborate well when they work closely together on an ongoing basis—as with employees on the same production team—rather than in cases in which people only occasionally work together, such as in the case of cross-deputized police officers.

Nevertheless, the ability to communicate and collaborate easily is still important, although this will be easier to attain where participants, even though they are from differing cultural backgrounds, have similar professional and other education. With tribal members increasingly receiving higher levels of formal education, especially those, such as tribal police officers, who are likely to serve in skilled professional roles, high-quality collaboration is becoming easier to achieve. Indeed, there are now a considerable number of tribal members with college and professional education, and the number of highly skilled tribal professionals such as lawyers and college professors is significant and growing. Recent increases in the training of tribal police and the expansion of their numbers that the DOJ initiated under Janet Reno during the Clinton administration have enhanced the ability of tribal officers and police departments to work with neighboring law enforcement agencies.

Typically, if the beginning is good, positive relations will tend to follow. But often competent facilitation and troubleshooting (either by the participants themselves, if they have sufficient skill and willingness to do so, or by joint or outside facilitators) are necessary, especially in the early stages, to overcome difficulties that are likely to arise in human interaction. As successful collaboration is built in one area, such as law enforcement, sufficient trust tends to build between the parties to encourage collaboration in other areas. Conversely, failure at, or difficulty with cooperation tends to build distrust.

Several current trends are increasing the likelihood that collaborative initiatives between tribes and state and local governments will be more successful. These include increasing knowledge in the United States of how to collaborate and make collaboration effective. Such knowledge follows from the broader use of collaboration, especially in workplaces, together with increases in the level of education and technical training among Native Americans.

Given the history of a lack of collaboration between state and local governments and tribes, however, developing cooperation is often difficult. In many cases, institutionalized mechanisms to begin joint efforts must be discovered or created. A recent example in the field of law enforcement is illustrative both of the problem and of the making of such a beginning. The state of New Mexico became concerned that the existence of separate jurisdictions that did not share records meant that the state was limited in acting against drunk driving because it had no information concerning drunk-driving arrests on the considerable extent of reservation land within New Mexico. Not knowing how to initiate collaboration with the several tribes in the state, New Mexico officials contacted the University of New Mexico Institute of Law and Policy. The institute did not know how to go about initiating such arrangements either, but it was aware of AIO in Bernalillo, whose work includes improving both tribal governance and government-to-government relations. AIO was able to bring state and tribal officials together to develop a means for sharing records and assisting each other with enforcement.[129] Now that the point has been reached where there is increasing interest in developing tribal–state and local collaboration, it is essential that appropriate mechanisms be established for doing so, as we will discuss.

Developments similar to those in law enforcement are taking place in other areas where jurisdictional confusion affects regulation and service delivery. Although the difficulties are often less complex than in law enforcement, in some cases, they arise over determining who has authority to regulate or who is eligible to receive which services from whom. Often, the tribes understand their jurisdictional authority, but other governments do not. And sometimes, because of negative experience, tribes have trouble trusting that collaborating with neighboring governments will strengthen rather than weaken their sovereign authority. In the area of environmental protection, for example, there are frequently questions as to who has jurisdiction to regulate and take preventive or restorative action. When state and tribal authorities argue over the authority to act in a particular situation, there are long and expensive delays in redressing pollution problems that continue to expand. Where tribal, state, and local (and sometimes federal) authorities can negotiate a joint approach, the jurisdictional questions become moot, and vitally needed action can be taken expeditiously.

Such was the case in New York, where the state realized it had an ally in the St. Regis Mohawk Tribe in obtaining a toxic waste cleanup at the General Motors Superfund site on the St. Lawrence River and in limiting pollution of the river by nearby Alcoa and Reynolds Aluminum operations.[130] The state of New York entered into a cooperative agreement with the Mohawks (who have a similar agreement with the EPA) to act to protect the fishery that is an important resource of both the tribe and the state.

Environmental protection has been a particularly strong area of cooperation because the tribes have begun receiving training and other support from the federal government (particularly under the 1986 amendments to the Safe Drinking Water Act, the 1977 amendments to the Clean Water Act, and amendments to the Superfund statute) that empowers federally recognized Indian nations to undertake environmental planning and regulation.[131] Often, surrounding counties do not have the necessary resources to plan and regulate on their own, which encourages them to join with the tribes to plan and act together to enhance the quality of a jointly shared environment, for pollution does not stop at jurisdictional boundaries.

In other areas in which the tribes do not have the resources to participate and federal sources of assistance are not available, pressure on concerned governments to move on environmental issues, together with the growth of more favorable perceptions of tribes by the wider public, have at times brought state and local governments to perceive that it is to their advantage to assist the tribes to act. In doing so, strong partnerships develop in which, typically, everyone wins.

In other instances, questions exist as to how regulation can best be undertaken or services delivered. The case of the San Carlos Apache high school students in Arizona is a good example of the latter.[132] In the 1970s, the dropout rate among San Carlos students attending high school in Globe, Arizona, was 50 percent. The reasons for this were complex but appeared to be related to the fact that the Globe high school program did not relate well to the cultural background of the Apache students, who had attended grade school on the reservation. To increase the effectiveness of education for those students, in 1977, the Globe school district and the San Carlos Apache Council agreed to open an alternative high school on the reservation to provide a more appropriate educational program, including the teaching of useful skills for employment in tribal enterprises. The program teaches vocational classes on a cooperative basis, and students can earn money in related apprentice programs as they complete their education. The tribe provides the school facilities, most of the teachers and staff, farmland for agricultural education, equipment, and supplies. The Globe school district provides supplies, a counselor, and an agricultural and a diversified occupation teacher.

Similar mutual benefits can be achieved through tribal–state collaboration, as will likely become increasingly necessary as federal programs devolve. The Northern Ute Indian Tribe and the state of Utah, for example, both have a concern about the welfare of children living on the Uintah and Ouray Indian Reservation.[133] The tribe is better equipped than the state to provide culturally appropriate child services, but it lacks the necessary funding and technical ability, which the state has. As a result, the state and the Uintah Utes reached a cooperative agreement for the tribe to provide the services, with technical and financial support from the Utah Division of Child and Family Services. The agreement includes a provision for the state to make foster care payments to low-income Ute families who take in relatives' children, thus overcoming a primary obstacle for finding appropriate foster care on the reservation.

Moving from Competition to Collaboration over Scarce Resources
Traditionally, the greatest conflict between tribal governments and state and local governments has been over scarce resources. Although this will continue to be an area of conflict, at least to some degree, experience shows that under certain circumstances, collaboration will replace competition. Two areas in which resource competition has been strong are in the areas of water and fishing and hunting.[134] In many states, most notably in the Pacific Northwest and the upper Midwest, tribes, in ceding lands to the federal government by treaty, retained off-reservation fishing and hunting rights. At the time of the treaty signing, these rights were necessary for tribal members' survival, and for low-income reservation residents this food supply remains essential.

The Indian population has always been extremely conscious of conservation, never taking more fish or game than needed and always leaving enough for fish and animal populations to reproduce. Pollution resulting from clear-cutting timber and building dams by non-Indians has significantly reduced the availability of fish, whereas non-Indian development has diminished the game population. In addition, many of the non-Native people who have moved into or visit these states have not been so conservation-oriented and have overfished and overhunted, causing shortages that the states must contend with. Uninformed sports and commercial anglers and hunters have often blamed the tribal population for the shortages, while states, in carrying out conservation programs, have attempted to interfere with tribal members exercising their right to provide necessary food for themselves. This has often led to serious harassment of Indians attempting to feed their families by state officials and local citizens (some of whom, at times, have acted violently).

The situation has also led to expensive litigation, with federal courts fairly consistently upholding Native American fishing and hunting rights under existing treaties. In the last few years, some of the newer appointees to the Supreme Court have led it to be less favorable to the tribes than had been the case for some time previously, leading to speculation that if future Supreme Court appointees continue to rule in a similar direction, the legal situation concerning hunting and fishing might change. So long as it is fairly clear that the courts will uphold tribal fishing and hunting rights (and Congress does not weaken or end them) and the general political climate is reasonably supportive of the tribes, there is an incentive for state governments to work with tribes to conserve and increase available fish and game, rather than take legal action against tribes and their members for that purpose. For tribes, joining with state governments in jointly maintaining and expanding resources may be advantageous in building and maintaining a climate of good relations with surrounding communities while attaining a greater availability of resources at less cost to their members than could be achieved through fighting through the courts.

An example of this kind of cooperation in dealing with wildlife conservation has occurred in western Washington. There, tribes established the Northwest Indian Fisheries Commission to work with state and federal game officials.[135] Collaborating closely with state officials, the tribes have created their own fishing regulations and enforcement programs. The commission employs fisheries biologists who work closely with state fisheries biologists to monitor and regulate all fisheries. The tribes also have developed more than sixty fish hatcheries that as of the late 1980s were producing sixty-six million fish a year and providing jobs for more than eight hundred specialists.

More recently, the Northwest Indian Fisheries Commission has been collaborating with local, state, federal, and tribal governments and nonprofit and private organizations to preserve and restore endangered salmon.[136] This is a case where relations have developed from confrontation to cooperation, and from cooperation to collaboration, because all parties have the resources to come together on an equal basis as partners in a joint undertaking of great mutual interest. An important factor in the case of the Northwest fisheries is that collaborative action led to a significant increase for all parties in the availability of the resource concerned. A strong incentive for collaborating is the realization that without it such increases would not occur.

The Difficult Case of Western Water

A somewhat different case is that of water, an even more important resource that is becoming increasingly scarce in dry western states as populations increase and businesses expand.[137] The problem is not only one of the availability of water per se, but also of maintaining supplies of water of sufficient quality for consumption by people and animals and for commercial purposes. Therefore, it is a problem partly of pollution prevention and partly of conservation. In the western states, water rights typically are the property of the first user of a source of water (whether or not that source is on or adjacent to the user's property), so long as that user continues to make use of what he, she, or it is entitled to. In the case of Indian nations, water rights originate in the moment a reservation was created by treaty and continue regardless of whether the tribes use the water. Water issues are made especially difficult by the lack of a general national or broad regional policy. Consequently, each case is decided on its own merits.

Water issues are often extremely complex and involve pressures both for collaboration and competition. On the one hand, with water, and especially high-quality water, becoming an increasingly scarce necessity in the West, it behooves all the users and concerned governmental entities, including the tribes, to engage in collaborative problem solving to preserve the quantity and quality of the resource. On the other hand, collaboration is rarely likely to increase the availability of water, or good-quality water, and often a wide variety of users are seeking to maintain and increase the amount available to them, regardless of the impact on others. Given the complexity of the situation, there are problems in reaching solutions by both cooperative and competitive strategies.[138] Because of the large number of concerns and parties involved, negotiations and litigation are extremely time-consuming and expensive.

Typically, to be taken seriously in negotiation, a party must have made the same preparations as for litigation, using the possibility of going to court as a lever to pressure the other parties to negotiate, or to negotiate on an equal basis. Given the complexities and the length of time involved to complete negotiations or litigation, there are great uncertainties in undertaking either route toward settlement. The law, the climate of political and public opinion, and even the views of the parties involved can change before a final settlement can be achieved. In recent years, however, two factors have been significant in causing parties to prefer negotiations over litigation. The first is the general move toward collaborative approaches and the rise of government-to-government cooperation in many areas we have discussed. The second is that negotiated settlement tends to make for better relations among parties who must continue to relate to one another over numerous ongoing concerns.

It should be noted, however, that the combination of the complexity of many water rights issues, which often affect many people and jurisdictions over a wide area, and the limits of what can be achieved politically often make for less than ideal settlements from almost everyone's point of view. Given this situation, negotiated settlements may not turn out to be final once achieved (though a settlement usually will be both the starting point for, and a strong influence upon, renegotiations). Often the whole process takes many years to complete.

An example of such a protracted negotiation that has had to undergo some amendment since its original settlement, and whose ultimate completion long remained in doubt, is the Animas–LaPlata Project, which involves parties in Colorado and New Mexico.[139] The completion of the project was the result of years of negotiation to settle the water rights of the Southern Ute and Ute Mountain Ute Tribes of southwest Colorado. Prior to the settlement, the water rights of the tribes had never been quantified, and water for any reasonable settlement was no longer directly available to the reservations when the negotiating process first began in the 1960s.

As in many other cases, members of the tribes involved have been and continue to be divided in opinion over whether it was best to accept a settlement that quantified the tribe's water rights and provided a means for the tribe to exercise them—even if the tribe might receive less than its members believed it was entitled to (on the basis of fairly sound historical evidence)—or to hold out for a possible settlement that would more closely provide the tribe with all of what it was in theory entitled to (even though until such a settlement could be achieved and carried out, these rights could not be enjoyed and might be reduced). This meant that a change in the membership of any of the government bodies concerned could have changed the position of that body in the course of a negotiation that required many years to complete. Similarly, changes in the dominant views of other parties over time may also affect the negotiation. The other leading parties in this negotiation have been the Jicarilla Apache Tribe, the states of Colorado and New Mexico (and some of their local governmental entities), and the federal government, with the outcome of the negotiations affecting many people over an extensive area of southern Colorado and northern New Mexico.

Theoretically, the easiest, most economically efficient and environmentally sound solution probably would have been to allow the tribes to sell or lease rights to whatever water they were entitled that did not flow directly onto the reservations. However, an important aspect of this negotiation was that any settlement would have to be approved, and in this case funded, by Congress. Given congressional politics (including the politics of pressure influencing congressional action), that was not feasible. The agreement reached in 1988 was to make the water available by diverting it from one river basin to another over a mountain range. The electricity required for pumping the water would be sufficient for the needs of a town of thirty thousand people. However, while Congress authorized the project in 1988, it had not begun to fund it by 1994, and with a general shift in national sentiment away from funding such water projects in the meantime, there was by then a serious question as to whether Congress would ever begin appropriating money for the construction work. In the meantime, environmental issues that were secondary in federal policy at the time of settlement came to the forefront, requiring changes in plans for the project.

Finally, with the election of a Republican majority in both houses of Congress in 1994, the situation changed. Although the Republican majority generally favors reducing federal spending, the members of Congress representing the areas that would receive the water (and the benefits of initiating the construction) were Republicans who as members of the majority had gained sufficient influence that as of fall 2002 the twice-altered (since 1988) Animas–La Plata water project had begun to receive funding, and by 2009, much of a reduced version of the project had been constructed and was in operation.[140] Congress eventually approving and funding a version of this project likely encouraged parties to engage in negotiated settlements since 2000 that require federal action. Clearly, one factor affecting the likelihood of the use of collaborative problem solving is the perception by the parties involved that the process can lead to a realizable result.

Another factor affecting the willingness of parties to participate in any process is their trust in it. The effective, equitable, and efficient resolution of concerns by negotiation requires the use of an appropriate and well-carried-out collaborative process. This is especially the case where issues are as complex as tribal water rights. When the issues are so difficult to settle, collaboration and problem solving by all the parties concerned is essential in order to initiate timely and appropriate action. Since collaborative processes are currently being used in an increasing number of areas, knowledge of how to undertake them and the availability of skilled personnel to carry them out is growing, making it more likely that good process will be available in intergovernmental affairs involving Indian nations.

A suggestive example of such collaboration in the area of Indian water rights is the Truckee-Carson-Pyramid Lake Water Settlement, involving the Pyramid Lake Paiute Reservation; the state of California (primarily representing area ranchers); the state of Nevada (primarily representing the cities of Reno and Sparks); the Sierra Pacific Power Company, which provides the water supply for the two municipalities and generates electricity hydroelectrically; and several other parties.[141] The dispute over the water of the Truckee and Carson Rivers had been unresolved for eighty years. It involved conflicting demands for water for municipalities; ranching; power generation; protection of two endangered species of fish in Pyramid Lake, which were essential to the Paiutes for subsistence and income; and protection of wetlands.

In 1987, Nevada Senator Harry Reid brought the four main parties together to begin a consensus decision-making process aimed at including the fundamental interests of all the parties in the eventual outcome. Constructive dialogue was achieved by limiting the initial negotiations to the four primary parties (who had agreed that any agreement by all the parties was binding and could not be contested in court). The consideration of issues was broken down into subdiscussions by issues, with the parties meeting with a trained facilitator from Senator Reid's staff, who assisted them in developing alternative solutions that would meet everyone's primary needs.

The most contentious issues were approached first, making it easier to deal with the other issues later. As agreement was neared on an issue, additional parties were brought into the problem-solving discussion. The result was an agreement reached by most of the parties in less than two years, in which all those who participated in the final agreement gained what was essential to them and yielded on secondary desires.

The agreement was ratified by Congress in August 1989 and signed into law by the president in November 1990. The provisions are currently being implemented. However, although the Pyramid Lake case is suggestive of what good process might be, the result was not perfect. One of the parties, the Truckee-Carson Irrigation District, a major water user in the area, dropped out of the negotiations, leaving its water rights unresolved in the agreement and the ratifying legislation.[142]

Building Collaboration on Taxation and Economic Development
One area of economic-resource concern that often leads to conflict and in which collaborative problem solving may be applied is taxes. The limited extension of state government concern to reservation affairs during the termination period, combined with an interest in increasing sources of revenue and preempting tax avoidance, tended to increase state interest in on-reservation taxation.[143] In Oklahoma, for example, the state tax commission long argued that it had the right and duty to levy sales taxes against Indian-owned businesses within the state. The commission contended that, following from certain agreements and congressional actions, protections usually granted to reservations do not apply to Oklahoma: "Although there are remnants of the form of tribal sovereignty, these Indians have no effective tribal autonomy and they are actually citizens of the state with little to distinguish them from all other citizens."[144] The commission admitted that "[t]his conflict has almost exclusively been the subject of litigation, rather than legislation or cooperation, to the end that the various courts hearing the matter have neither settled the law, resolved the dispute, nor satisfied any of the litigants."[145] (A lawsuit brought by the Sac and Fox Nation concerning these questions has recently been decided against the state of Oklahoma.)

Among the commission's concerns was the loss of revenue from cigarette taxes. The state tax rate in 1991 was twenty-three cents a pack. There were then more than 350 tribally owned or licensed smoke shops in Oklahoma selling items such as groceries and souvenirs in addition to tobacco. Tribal tax rates ranged from zero to fifteen cents a pack, which encouraged smokers to travel to tribal land to buy their cigarettes. How much revenue was lost by the state is debatable. A study of all smoke shops in the Tulsa metropolitan area indicates that 65 percent of the customers came from within a four-mile radius of the shop, suggesting that substitution of tribal for nontribal shops was less extensive than was feared by state tax officials. Nevertheless, the commission discouraged in-state wholesalers from supplying the smoke shops, so that the wholesale purchase income from these shops did not go to Oklahoma wholesalers. This meant that $90 million of wholesale business was lost annually to the state, resulting in a reduction of nearly $198 million in income to state citizens, costing some two thousand jobs, and reducing state revenues by almost $1.4 million.[146]

By contrast, in South Dakota, the state and the Oglala Sioux Tribe have worked out an agreement on the tribal sale of cigarettes. Legally, the state can tax only sales to non-Indians, whereas the tribe can tax all sales. In this case, the state and the tribe have set equal taxes. The state collects all the cigarette taxes on the reservation and then, after deducting a small administrative fee, passes the tribe's share on to the Oglala Sioux. A number of other tribes have made similar agreements with states.[147]

Given the precedent of the South Dakota collaboration, Oklahoma's failure to succeed in the courts, and the results of studies indicating that Oklahoma's attempted use of other means of discouraging sales of non-taxed cigarettes has reduced the income of state citizens and state revenues, it would seem that there are practical incentives for states to seek collaboration with Indian nations in at least some taxation matters, provided that the legal situation remains unchanged. Oklahoma has come to understand this, recently making a compact with Indian nations in the state under which each tribe receives a rebate for its share of fuel taxes the state collects.[148] A growing number of such tribal–state tax arrangements have been occurring in recent years.[149]

Similar concerns about loss of tax revenue have been expressed about the growth of gambling casinos on reservations. The issues involved include both whether casinos on existing reservations should pay state taxes and whether purchase of land outside of the reservation for a gambling casino or for other commercial purposes incorporates that land into the reservation (and thus removes it from state and local taxation). A number of factors, beyond those we've discussed, influence the approach that state and local governments can take in relating to tribes concerning these issues.

First is the lobbying and related action of competing interests. Wealthy professional gambling interests seeking to preempt and reduce competition have attempted to portray reservation gambling as an isolated phenomenon at odds with American public policy and economic trends. These interests have encouraged a variety of limitations on tribal casinos, including having them taxed. In fact, the rise of gambling on reservations is part of a national trend: numerous communities with limited possibilities for economic development have initiated various types of gambling, including casino and riverboat gambling and pari-mutuel racetrack betting, as vehicles to create jobs and increase local income. Moreover, many states have initiated lotteries. The lobbying and public relations campaigns by professional gambling interests have been enhanced by the remarks of commentators who see the great financial success of two small tribes in Connecticut (all of whose members have become wealthy) as typical of tribes in general, which is not the case.

Second, a number of studies, including the three state studies of the impact of Indians on state economies we discussed above and one study of the impact of gambling on two reservations in Minnesota, have shown that the loss in state taxes (and increased cost for services, such as additional requirements for police and highway maintenance) is more than offset by the economic and revenue benefits to the locality and state as a whole that are generated by increased business activity.[150] The publication of these studies is increasing the likelihood that localities and states, which often give tax abatements and other advantages to private businesses to induce them to move to their jurisdiction or to remain there, perceive casinos and other businesses on reservations as economic development in which the reservations and surrounding communities and their governmental entities are mutually involved. Indeed, state and local governments have one advantage in working on economic development with the tribes that they do not have in dealing with private business. Whereas private businesses are becoming increasingly mobile and may decide to move an operation out of an area, no matter how great the benefits public authorities have provided for them, the tribes are firmly rooted to their land and will not move away.

For this reason, at least nineteen states have made compacts with tribes to allow for tribal operation of gambling casinos.[151] In some cases, these compacts provide for revenue sharing by the casinos with state and local governments, and in other cases, tribes have contracted with state and local authorities for the provision of services (such as additional policing) related to the opening of casinos. It remains to be seen exactly how the taxation concerns surrounding tribal gambling will be resolved, but among the factors that affect the resolution of these concerns is the nature of the relationships between the tribes and the state and local governments and how those relationships are perceived. To the extent that the economic development of the tribes is able to continue, their interrelationships with the surrounding communities will grow, as will the occasions for interaction with neighboring governmental authorities where there is a mutual interest in collaboration. An example of this is an agreement among the Southern Ute Indian Tribe, La Plata County, and the state of Colorado to partially compensate the county from tribal and state funds for loss of property taxes as the tribe acquires private land within the boundaries of its reservation.[152] The Southern Utes will also help the county make up for lost revenue by providing assessment information that the county does not have about private land within the reservation. The agreement was based on a mutual understanding of shared interests and took into account the separate concerns in the case.

As the county and the tribe interact in many areas, they have a need to maintain a good working relationship. The county and state benefit from economic development and activity by the Utes and from services (such as emergency and sewer services) the tribe provides to some area non-Indian residents for significantly less than the county could provide them.[153]

The tribe needs to cooperate with the county and state on many issues, such as water use, wildlife, road building and maintenance, and law enforcement. For example, the county has provided space in its jail to the tribe for a fee. This has been necessary because of an increase in arrests that have resulted from a growth in business activity on the reservation. The renting of jail space later ceased as arrests increased and the Southern Utes opened a new justice center, which offered detention space to the county. The tribal justice system works with the county to provide protection against drunk driving, as per a tribal–state agreement that allows area municipal and state law officers to suspend tribal members' licenses on reservation land.[154] The Southern Ute Tribal Council, the La Plata County Board of Commissioners, and the city of Ignacio now hold joint planning and brainstorming sessions. Because of similar common concerns, the Southern Ute Tribal Council recently began holding informal meetings with the Archuleta County commissioner, and the county has added a seat on its planning commission for a representative of the Southern Ute Tribe.[155]

The economic development that gambling has enabled for some tribes is starting to change the positions of those tribes as they relate with other governments. (We will discuss this further in chapter 5.) For the first time, these Indian nations have some economic power, which makes it easier for them to participate as partners in the relationships that constitute federalism. On the one hand, the increased tribal wealth is a source of power. On the other hand, the economic development that is taking place increases the role of these tribes in the economies and life of the areas in which they are located, increasing their interdependence with surrounding communities and governments and thus making collaborative rather than competitive relations generally more desirable.

This interdependence is intensified by the fact that reservations currently contain few retail (or wholesale) enterprises. Tribal members and entities must do the majority of their shopping outside the reservation; 95 percent of money coming onto a reservation flows out to the surrounding community.[156] To the extent that this fact is appreciated, neighboring communities have good reason to support tribal economic development, in contrast to earlier periods when the primary interest of many tribal neighbors was to gain greater access to Indian lands (or the resources connected with them).

As tribes see increases in their economic development, it is to be expected that joint efforts at economic development between tribes and neighboring political entities will also increase. The case of the Mississippi Band of Choctaw Indians and the city of Philadelphia, Mississippi, is a good model of what can happen when a tribe, which typically has a small population within its locality, has a viable economic enterprise worthy of expansion. In this instance, the city, primarily by passing a bond issue to provide funding, assisted the Choctaw in expanding their General Motors transmission plant to become the fourth largest employer in the state, knowing that most of the new jobs would go to nontribal members and that many of the new dollars brought in by the expansion would flow through the city.[157]

Gambling (and other business activity) engaged in by tribes will inevitably raise concerns for the surrounding communities to whom the reservations are directly and indirectly linked. As we have shown, it is often advantageous for state and local government entities to engage with Indian nations on these issues by employing mutual dialogue and joint problem solving. Such is very much in keeping with the traditions of all the Indian nations, whose ancient cultures were extremely cooperative, democratic, and inclusive. Based on mutual respect for the uniqueness of each individual and group, traditional Native American cultures emphasize the need to include everyone affected by a decision and to act in accordance with the long-run interests of all involved ("to the seventh generation"). Moreover, it was traditional for Indian communities to function on the basis of developing personal relations with people with whom one needed to interact. Since the world was perceived as complex and uncertain (along the lines of contemporary chaos and uncertainty theory), one did not know who might be a good ally in the future, and it was better to have as few enemies as possible. Therefore, it was prudent for Native people to develop a broad range of positive personal relationships, especially with people in important positions, whether formal or informal.[158] (We discuss this point further in chapter 6.)

The development of gambling facilities by the Southern Ute Indian Tribe is a fine example of what can happen when Indigenous people are given the opportunity to interrelate on the basis of mutual respect, cooperating with their neighbors, and developing good personal relations. The Southern Ute Reservation near Durango, Colorado, has long been a checkerboard of tribal land with individual tribal member allotments and land (much of which is ranched) owned by whites and Hispanics.[159] Along with intercultural conflicts, misunderstandings, and resentments, a great many strong cross-cultural relationships have developed that have produced a "tricultural" sense of interrelationship in much of the greater reservation area. Against this background, a former Southern Ute administrator helped to build cooperative, usually personal, relationships between tribal and area state and local agencies as he assisted the development of Southern Ute administration over a number of years. The administrator was naturally outgoing and, as the son of a successful rancher, built contacts in the surrounding communities that he could call upon in his efforts to improve tribal operations.[160] The Southern Utes have benefited from collaboration between their own agencies and those of surrounding government entities, and the tribe has generally been seen as gaining from progressive, innovative policies.

The development of gambling facilities by the Utes has been a heated issue on the reservation and also a concern in the surrounding area. In deciding to go ahead with the project, the tribe had the legal authority to build a gambling casino adjacent to a main highway away from the center of the reservation, which was the best of the proposed locations both in terms of bringing in customers and in being the least intrusive upon tribal life. Instead, the Tribal Gaming Coordinating Committee decided upon a location in the center of the reservation after taking into account the concerns of people living in the area, local agencies, and Southern Utes.[161] (We discuss Southern Ute–local government collaborative relations further in chapter 5.)

Similarly, the Cherokee Nation in Oklahoma has a long history of collaboration with state and local governments in a wide variety of policy areas.[162] In one of many joint economic development projects, the Cherokees worked with city and county government to build an industrial park for which the tribe was successful in bringing in a plant that manufactures filters for the airline industry. In a number of the Cherokee business operations that are legally exempt from direct state taxation, the tribe has voluntarily paid corporate, sales, and other taxes. In several cases, the tribe has cooperated in constructing municipal buildings for joint use with county and municipal officials (at least in one case with the construction financing supplied entirely by Cherokee money and federal funds passed through the tribe), and the Cherokees have built many miles of general-use water systems. The tribe works jointly with state and local entities on regulatory matters such as environmental protection and operates a number of services for both tribal and nontribal members in the community, including a youth shelter, elderly and handicapped housing projects, two health clinics, and an ambulance service staffed by paramedics.

As Cherokee Principal Chief Wilma Mankiller said, "Our approach to tribal government has always been—I've been here twelve years—that we do not operate tribal government in a vacuum. Our people are citizens of the Cherokee Nation, but we're also citizens of Oklahoma, and we're citizens of the United States. So the way we have chosen to do business is to work collaboratively with the state of Oklahoma and its communities."[163] The Cherokee Nation has been able to be a strong partner with the state and local governments of Oklahoma because it is a strong government whose sovereignty is respected by those it deals with. The Cherokees do not have to defend themselves in their intergovernmental relations and are free to collaborate in the mutual interest of all involved, which in the long run, the Cherokees understand, is in their own best interest.

This does not mean that there are no differences of interest between the tribe and the neighboring jurisdictions, or that all issues between jurisdictions can be resolved easily or quickly. Indeed, where relations are always smooth on the surface, it may mean that important concerns are not being addressed and that what is occurring may be more akin to co-option than cooperation. Good collaborative relations are those where there is sufficient mutual respect and trust combined with adequate problem-solving and communication skills, so that the parties have the orientation and ability to approach difficult issues constructively. Even in the best relationship, how quickly and easily resolution can be found will vary with the issue and the circumstances. Moreover, cooperative relations are never perfect, and can always be improved. Even the best of working relationships need effort and attention to maintain, and must continually be renewed. An occasional crisis or conflict may be an opportunity for such renewal.

Building Coordination for Developing and Maintaining Cooperation
All of the studies and cases considered in this chapter show that the tribes and surrounding state and local governments are tightly bound together by a web of economic, social, political, and legal relationships. Their problems are interrelated and require mutual understanding and cooperative action. Competition and lack of coordination between tribal and state and local agencies very often has been humanly and economically costly. By contrast, in numerous cases where good communication and understandings have been developed, mutually beneficial collaboration has resulted. What is needed is an increase of communication on the basis of mutual respect from government to government, agency to agency, and public servant to public servant.

Most of the detailed work of collaboration needs to be carried out by direct dialogue and mutual action by parallel tribal and state and local agencies and personnel, because those who work directly on particular concerns need to interact closely without being separated, confused, and delayed by having to communicate roundabout through distant hierarchical structures, except where higher or broader considerations are involved.[164] However, to develop and maintain that direct dialogue and coordinate Indian-related policy with the input of all concerned parties requires appropriate higher-level vehicles.

Several interrelated, advanced models for developing, maintaining, and carrying out tribal–state collaboration are now functioning in the Pacific Northwest. The first of these is an intertribal Indian organization for coordinating and enhancing collaboration concerning health policy with multiple state agencies in the three states that constitute the Portland Area of the IHS. The Northwest Portland Area Indian Health

Board discusses problems common to its several member tribes and works to develop appropriate policy and implementation with the states of Idaho, Oregon, and Washington.[165] The board, representing many of the tribes in the three states since 1974, has a professional staff and actively communicates with member tribes; state, regional, and national Indian organizations concerned with health issues; and health-related agencies in the three states. By providing professional staff and an active information and dialoguing network, a well-functioning relationship for the mutual development of policy and resolution of problems has been established. Clearly, well-staffed and adequately funded intertribal policy organizations can greatly help tribes identify and analyze common concerns and coordinate tribal communication with other government entities. A major factor in the success of the Northwest collaboration is that each state has developed its own vehicles for coordinating Indian health policy and Indian policy generally in dialogue with the tribes in the state.

In Oregon and Idaho, representatives of tribal governments meet regularly with the state's health personnel and the coordinating institution. In Oregon, the Commission on Indian Services was created by statute in 1975.[166] The commission is an organ of the state legislature, consisting of one representative each from the Oregon Senate, the Oregon House, and the eleven federally recognized tribes in the state. The Commission on Indian Services acts as a resource and advisory board to the legislature, the governor, and state agencies, recommending ways for the state to improve all areas of services to Indians and the state's relationship with Oregon's Indian tribes and people.

The commission holds regular meetings to consider how issues of concern to Indian people can best be addressed, often with the participation of state and local government and agency personnel. Meetings include an annual government-to-government summit of tribal and state legislative and executive branch leaders, and three or four sets of "cluster" meetings of issue-oriented work groups that focus on the details of government-to-government work in various policy areas involving all twenty-six executive departments. The commission evaluates legislation that affects Indian people both in its drafting stage and after implementation, notifying interested parties about the legislation and coordinating legislative testimony. The commission also acts as a clearinghouse and source of information for state, local, and tribal governments and the general public on Indian laws, programs, issues, demographics and economics, and tribal government.

The executive branch of Oregon state government also is well developed to handle Indian affairs, in collaboration with the Commission on Indian Services. Under a 1996 executive order from the governor and a 2001 statute, an official in the governor's office designated by the governor oversees the coordination of executive-branch Indian policy and communication.[167] Each cabinet-level department head is responsible for seeing that the agency he or she leads communicates regularly in a government-to-government manner with the Oregon tribes on all matters that affect them, making a reasonable effort to cooperate with the tribes in the development and implementation of Indian-related policy. The department designates and publishes a list of "key contact" staff members who dialogue with tribes and are responsible for overseeing areas of Indian-related policy in their agencies. Each department produces an annual report of its Indian-related policy developments and government-to-government relationship with Oregon tribes. At least once a year, the Department of Administrative Services in consultation with the Commission on Indian Services provides training to state agency managers and other personnel who regularly communicate with tribes.

In Washington, concerned tribes formed the American Indian Health Commission for Washington State to provide policy advice and collective communication with the state on health matters. The commission communicates regularly with a variety of state and local health agencies, and each Washington tribe appoints its own representative to the Indian Policy Advisory Committee in the Washington Department of Social and Health Services. The department also has appointed a liaison for Native American and Alaska Native concerns who is actively involved with the commission and plays an instrumental role in avoiding and solving problems.

In Washington, as in Oregon, Indian policy as a whole is coordinated from the top of the executive branch by the Governor's Office of Indian Affairs.[168] The office recognizes that tribes have different needs, priorities, and objectives that are broader in purpose than economic development. It acknowledges that two-way communication and training are essential to its many efforts. The Governor's Office of Indian Affairs has enhanced government-to-government relations between state agencies and tribes through promoting dialogue, increasing the number of qualified Native Americans employed in state government, and providing education to agency staff on Indian issues and communication. The resulting collaboration has brought about advances in policy in economic development, natural resources management, and social and cultural issues.

Other vehicles for carrying on dialogue are also possible. In Oklahoma, the State Supreme Court has sponsored an annual Sovereignty Symposium that brings together state, federal, and tribal judges; legislators; and executive branch and administrative personnel to discuss mutual concerns and share information.[169] This body has no decision-making authority, but it can help develop relationships and understanding that enhance collaboration.

Local governments and agencies may also come together on their own initiative with tribal governments. On February 14–15, 2000, the first Minnesota Tribal and County Government Summit took place on the Mille Lacs Band of Ojibwe Reservation under the sponsorship of the Minnesota Indian Affairs Council and the Association of Minnesota Counties to identify and begin working on common problems.[170] The top five concerns were economic development, education, child welfare, housing, and health care. Leaders agreed that improved reservation economics would help reduce crime, substance abuse, child abuse, poor health, and other social problems that trouble reservations and the surrounding communities. Several examples of existing tribal–county collaboration were discussed, including sharing the costs and responsibilities of road construction and repair, waste disposal, law enforcement, and other services. Scott County Public Affairs Coordinator Lisa Kohner commented, "We're learning that what binds us together is much stronger than what divides us, and that it's our differences that make us interesting."

The use of special-focus coordination at the state level is also appropriate, as has recently occurred in California, where the state attorney general opened the Office of Native American Affairs within his department to foster government-to-government relations on issues of law enforcement and crime prevention. The office works collaboratively with tribal governments on issues of crime prevention and empowering Indian nations to "create law enforcement capability to police their own reservations and enterprises." The office also services all Californians of Native American heritage, because the majority of Indians in California are from other states.[171]

In addition, the federal government can promote tribal–state and local government cooperation in several ways, as we have discussed. First, federal agencies can come together to work with tribal, state, and local agencies on common problems, as has occurred to preserve salmon in the Pacific Northwest. Second, devolving federal programs to states and tribes can include encouragement of tribal–state collaboration and mechanisms to equitably resolve disputes—for example, as the EPA has done. As we have seen in discussing welfare reform, it is important that in devolving programs that affect tribes to the states, the federal government include sufficient incentives to the states or localities to bring about cooperation that will lead to the equitable provision of services or carrying out of regulations. Third, because many problems are common concerns of federal, state, local, and tribal governments, the federal government can initiate intergovernmental meetings to engage in joint problem solving and facilitate collaboration. One example of this kind of interchange occurred in 1996, when federal, state, local, and tribal officials came together in Helena, Montana, to discuss problems, exchange information, and share approaches and ideas for improving highway safety.[172]

An important vehicle encouraging the development of tribal-state government collaboration is the joint task force of NCAI and the National Conference of State Legislatures.[173] Both organizations had been concerned about the need for such cooperation for a number of years and had communicated with each other about it when welfare reform was passed by Congress in 1996. The devolution of welfare reform to states and tribes, as part of the federal government's growing reform policy delegating program authority downward, thus increased the necessity for tribes and states to work together and prompted NCAI and the National Conference of State Legislatures to launch the task force. The task force has researched the problems of tribal–state relations, documented instances of collaboration, analyzed what makes for effective collaboration, and produced a number of publications and held several conferences.

Thus, many tribal and government vehicles provide an effective means for realizing government-to-government relations among tribal and other governments. One of the key elements, which is often missing when tribal and state and local governments would like to collaborate, is the institutionalization of effective means of communication and policy coordination. A number of states that lack such institutions currently have bodies that could be developed to adequately fulfill that purpose.

State Indian affairs commissions, or their equivalents in a number of states, could be energized and further empowered by legislation or executive order to fulfill this role. At least three of the economic studies that have shown the extent to which Indian people and reservation economics are important contributors to the larger economies of their states were undertaken by or in collaboration with these commissions, providing evidence that these bodies can undertake or sponsor research and publish reports that are appropriate to the necessary leadership role. To be effective, the commission membership must be fully representative of the tribes and the agencies, and the agency members in particular must be sufficiently empowered, informed, and concerned so that they can speak freely and act effectively as liaisons between the agencies and the tribes, as has been occurring in Oregon and Washington. Unfortunately, such is currently not always the case. Appointments to these commissions have often been haphazard and based on convenience or politics, rather than on careful consideration of representativeness and ability. This practice must change, and the commissions, or their equivalents, be given a larger role to play to ensure that they can appropriately fill their needed function. It should be noted that in recent years, a growing number of governors have initiated meetings and initial cooperative agreements with tribes that form a basis for creating high-level state Indian policy and communication coordinating bodies.[174]

Whatever the state-level Indian affairs coordinating body is called, and regardless of its formal location in state government, as long as it is located centrally enough to be effective (e.g., as a legislative commission in Oregon, as a staff organization in the governor's office in Washington), it must meet several requirements: it must have adequate legal and informal administrative-political authority, and it must have adequate funding and a sufficient number of dedicated, competent, and appropriately oriented staff to properly carry out the coordinating function. That function will, first and most directly, involve tribal–state government collaboration. In addition, as exemplified by actions of the Oregon Commission on Indian Services, there is much that the coordinating body can do to promote good and effective relations between tribal and local governments: through conferences and meetings, by undertaking surveys and providing information, and in offering education and training.

The coordinating agency staff needs to understand that Indian people in various tribes, often have varying needs, values, concerns, and styles of communicating than do other citizens and people in government, and the agency must therefore be oriented toward, and adequately prepared to, dialogue effectively with Indian people and tribal officials. It should facilitate and effectively encourage high-quality dialogue, when necessary, between state and local and tribal people and agencies. To do so, the agency must necessarily include an educational function to ensure that government personnel primarily, and citizens in the state secondarily, are aware of their common interest in engaging in such dialogue, and the agency must take steps to ensure that government personnel who make or carry out policy that affects Indians are aware of Indian concerns and able to work well with Indian people (both as individuals and on a government-to-government basis). This is simply a specific application of the general principle in a diverse society that people generally, but most especially in public service, ought to understand diversity and work respectfully with it. It will often be helpful if the coordinating agency promotes understanding of Indian concerns and issues among the general public, as well as within government.

It is essential that the coordinating agency promotes mutual understanding and dialogue regarding Indian issues between tribal governments (and, as appropriate, representatives of off-reservation Indians) and state and local government agencies and officials. It will be most helpful if such discussion occurs proactively, before issues come to a head or need immediate decision, as well as during the official decision-making process. It is also important to periodically review how, and how well, policy affecting Indians is being carried out. Perhaps most important of all, the coordinating body needs to facilitate the building and maintenance of a good working relationship, based upon mutual respect and trust, among tribal and state and local governments and agencies throughout the state.

Conclusion: Factors in the Future of Tribal–State and Local Government Relations

Just how the tribal–state and local government relationship continues to develop is likely to be greatly influenced by how the federal government continues to relate to Indian nations. First, will Congress and the administration, at all levels, continue to develop and maintain the government-to-government relationship with tribal governments? Second, will the federal government, in a time of fiscal conservatism, provide adequate resources to Indian nations for self-determination and the development of self-sufficiency, when tribes have never received adequate resources for their needs, or even an equitable per capita share of federal funding? Third, in the course of devolving programs, will the federal government provide enough autonomy to tribal governments and enough incentive to state governments to promote tribal and state and local government-to-government relations?

The continued development of tribal governments' ability to function as equal partners with state and local governments clearly requires the federal government to continue to respect tribal governments as governments in the federal system while also expanding and maintaining its orientation toward Indian self-governance. The necessary empowerment includes: (1) continuing to expand recognition of existing legal authority and in some cases creating additional legal provisions for Indian self-government; (2) providing financial and other incentives to exercise that legal authority, and; (3) more broadly, providing the necessary resources for Indian nations to be self-sufficient, and thus self-determining, in finances, education, training, and other culturally appropriate services (as we discuss in chapter 5). These resources can be provided directly, or the federal government can promote the ability of Indian nations to provide them for themselves through economic and other development.

Internally, the federal government needs to continue to develop appropriate structures for coordinating and carrying out Indian policy in the course of representative consultation with Indian people (both on and off reservations) while furthering the ability of federal employees (through appropriate staffing, education, training) to function in Indian affairs and related matters knowledgeably in an appropriate government-to-government manner.

In addition, if tribal–state and local government relations are to develop fully, the federal government must structure devolution of federal functions to the states appropriately to encourage, with adequate incentives, promotion of tribal–state and local government cooperation. Moreover, in matters where the federal and lower levels of government are involved, the federal government can enhance the development of such collaboration by providing appropriate means for facilitating tribal–state and local government negotiations and dispute resolution, as exemplified by the mechanisms established by the EPA.

The goal of Indian nations acting as full partners in federalism, with full government-to-government relations between tribal and state and local governments, will only be realized if neighboring governments: (1) come to appreciate the mutual benefits of relating with Indian nations on a government-to-government basis; (2) create adequate and appropriate structures for government-to-government relations (including appropriate means of communication and coordination); and (3) develop their personnel (e.g., through appropriate hiring, education, and training) to function fully in government-to-government relationships. Further discussion by those concerned may produce additional alternatives for enhancing and coordinating collaboration. Regardless of which specific approach is taken, the development of a fully collaborative and highly communicative government-to-government relationship among tribal and state and local entities will be a most progressive and beneficial process for all the citizens and members of the concerned states and tribes. Fortunately, current trends indicate continued movement in that direction.

Acknowledgments

The authors are indebted to Michael Chapman, former special assistant to the assistant secretary of the interior for Indian affairs, and Faith Roessel, former coordinator of the Administration Working Group on American Indians and Alaska Natives, for extremely helpful comments and much useful information concerning the building of government-to-government relations between the federal government and Indian tribes. We also are most appreciative of the research and editing work that Jeff Corntassel, associate professor in the Indigenous Governance Programs at the University of Victoria in Victoria, British Columbia, contributed to the development of this chapter.

Notes

1. For a history of the various forms and stages of American federalism, see Walker, *Rebirth of Federalism*. Part 1 discusses what federalism is and presents a number of models and interpretations of federalism. Part 2 provides a history of U.S. federalism and its various stages and variations since before the writing of the U.S. Constitution up to and through the Clinton administration.
2. Deloria and Wilkins, *Tribes, Treaties*, particularly chap. 3; see page 61 for a discussion of the basic standards for valid treaties, and acts following from them, between the United States and Indian nations.
3. Morris, Sachs, and Harris, "Placing Tribes," responding to Lilias Jones, "Neither Fish Nor Fowl."
4. The related history is discussed in O'Brien, *American Indian Tribal Governments*, part 2, chap. 12. Debo presents a more detailed history in *History of the Indians*, 2–21. See also Page, *In the Hands*, parts 2–5; and Nichols, *American Indians in U.S.*
5. O'Brien, *American Indian Tribal Governments*, chap. 4; and Debo, *History of the Indians*, chaps. 4–7.
6. As with the Cherokees (see Debo, *History of the Indians*, 120–25) and the Muscogees, or Creeks, and Seminoles (*History of the Indians*, 116–20, 125–26; Chaudhuri and Chaudhuri, *Way of the Muscogee*, 146–57). See also Nichols, *American Indians in U.S.*, 106–11; and Page, *In the Hands*, 250–65.
7. O'Brien, *American Indian Tribal Governments*, 259–61. A legal critique of this approach is presented in Deloria and Wilkins, *Tribes, Treaties*, 68–70.
8. O'Brien, *American Indian Tribal Governments*, chap.3; and Debo, *History of the Indians*, chap. 15–17. A detailed account of allotment appears in McDonnell, *The*

Dispossession. See also Page, *In the Hands*, 327–33; and Nichols, *American Indians in U.S.*, 164–72. Note that although the roots of allotment, and examples of its use in certain cases, date back to the early days of European settlement in what is now the United States, allotment became general federal Indian policy with the Dawes Act of 1887 (see *The Dispossession*, 1).

9. For a discussion of the problems of Indian education, including in boarding schools prior to 1928, see Szasz, *Road to Self-Determination*, particularly 2–3, 10–11, 18–27, and 67. A more detailed critique of the boarding-school experience is to be found in Adams, *Education for Extinction*; and Child and Lomawama, *A Hard Lesson*.

10. Meriam et al., *Problem of Indian Administration*, discussed in Debo, *History of the Indians*, 336–37; and Olson and Wilson, *Native Americans in Twentieth Century*, 100–112 and 193. A representative excerpt is published in Prucha, *United States Indian Policy*, 219–21. A history of Indian policy and its impact under the Dawes Act is also provided in McDonnell, *The Dispossession*.

11. O'Brien, *American Indian Tribal Governments*, 79–82; Debo, *History of the Indians*, 335; and Szasz, *Road to Self-Determination*, 5, 6, and 113–14.

12. The developments of this period are discussed in Debo, *History of the* Indians, chap. 18; Olson and Wilson, *Native Americans in Twentieth Century*, chap. 6; Page, *In the Hands*, 358–63; and Nichols, *American Indians in U.S.*, 178–84.

13. Problems with the imposed forms of tribal governments are briefly discussed in Olson and Wilson, *Native Americans in Twentieth Century*, 122–23; and Castile, *To Show Heart*, 129–31. See also Foster, *Being Comanche*, 60, 138, 161, and 204n79. With assistance from Americans for Indian Opportunity (AIO), the Comanches, and to a lesser extent three other Oklahoma tribes, initiated community-building processes to overcome some of the difficulties arising from this imposition. A consideration, in short form, of the difficulties is included in a discussion of the steps taken toward overcoming them in Harris, Sachs, and Broome, "Returning to Harmony"; for a more detailed discussion, see Harris, Sachs, and Broome, "Recreating Harmony"; and Harris, Sachs, and Broome, "Wisdom of the People."

14. Cahn, *Our Brother's Keeper*; Nelson and Sheley, "Influence on Indian Self-Determination," 177–97; and Deloria and Lytle, *Nations Within*. On the BIA in the Kennedy, Johnson, and Nixon administrations, see Castile, *To Show Heart*, 87–91, 94–97, 102, and 147–48. For the BIA under Carter and Reagan, see Castile, *Taking Charge*, 9, 10, 14, 18–20, 29, 36, 39–41, 52, 53, 56, 74, 95, 96, 103–4, 112–13, and 116.

15. The Senate Select Committee on Indian Affairs was formed after the termination of the Senate Subcommittee on Indian Affairs of the Senate Committee on Interior and Insular Affairs, in order to sort out the more than two hundred proposals of the American Indian Policy Review Commission that was created in 1975 following the occupation at Wounded Knee, South Dakota. See Holm, "Crises in Tribal Government"; and Deloria, "Federal Indian Policy Making," 139–43, 253–54.

Both the Senate subcommittee and its counterpart, the Subcommittee on Indian Affairs of the House Interior Committee, were charged with examining issues of Indian policy and overseeing its administration in the executive branch (see Champagne, "Organizational Change and Conflict," 38–40, 50–52). But without pressure from public opinion or powerful pressure groups, the subcommittees generally gave little energy to that function, as the fact that it is difficult to find reference to them in works about the history of Indian policy indicates. Moreover, because most of the members of the subcommittees were conservative westerners generally favorable to the assimilationist thrust of traditional BIA policy and more responsive to Anglo-American constituents than to the tribes, the subcommittees produced little that proceeded to the full committees or the chamber floor for debate. Most of the important reform legislation on Indian Affairs of the 1970s was written and supported by a coalition of liberal congressmen and senators who did not sustain interest in Indian affairs. Most important, committee and subcommittee focus was primarily on legislation, not on oversight of administration (at least until the 1970s; oversight hearings of operations in California were held in 1974). See *California Indian Oversight Hearings*. In 1979, the committee began two years of oversight review, including hearings, on economic development on Indian reservations. See Udall to Harris, May 3, 1979, LaDonna Harris Papers.

Certainly, especially in the House, some processing of constituent complaints concerning the BIA was undertaken by members of Congress prior to the 1970s. However, until the rise of sustained Native American political activism, it appears that members of Congress were far more responsive to non-Native Americans in such matters (e.g., the leasing of reservation land or mineral rights) than to tribes and their members. In 1978 and 1979, the House and Senate appropriations committees raised serious questions about BIA operations, but until the 1970s, the BIA was not required to justify its operations to any legislative body.

For sixteen years, through most of the Hoover and Roosevelt administrations, a Senate special investigating subcommittee was concerned with Indian affairs and was a staunch critic of the BIA. However, the subcommittee's focus—as part of a general ideological thrust, which during the FDR years was anti–New Deal—was opposition to policy reform and not oversight to improve administration. BIA Commissioner Collier and his agency were targeted, in part, because of the commissioner's strong support for the New Deal beyond the scope of Indian Affairs. See Freeman, *The Political Process*, 43–46.

16. Such treatment is seen in the Navy Tailhook scandal, the sexual abuse of female (and some male) officers by U.S. Navy and Marine Corps officers that became public in 1996, and in other continuing revelations of sexual misconduct in the military. See Dishneau, "Drill Sergeant," A4; and Priest, "Admiral, Army Lawyer," A5). A long-term picture of the difficulties in bringing change to the military in relation to issues of gender and sexuality is presented by Francke in *Ground Zero*. For information about homosexuality and the armed forces, see Allenan, "Homosexuality in the Navy," 94–98; Bardy, "Improvement Strategy for Homosexuals," 221–34; and Kier, "Homosexuality in U.S. Military," 36–56.

17. Debo, *History of the Indians*, 340.

18. This tendency can be seen in some of the classic cases reported in Stein, *Public Administration*, particularly in "The Transfer of the Children's Bureau," 15–29, and in the behavior of the Army Corps of Engineers in "Kings River Project," 533–37.

19. O'Brien, *Native American Tribal Governments*, 275. On the Nixon administration increase in Indian hiring preference, especially at the higher levels, see Castile, *To Show Heart*, 88–89.

20. Melmer, "BIA Financial Reports," A1, A2.

21. "Trust Funds Gone," A1–A3. It should be noted that most, if not all, of the money, is in the BIA. The problem is mostly one of inadequate bookkeeping, so that it is impossible to know where all of the money is, how much has actually been given to tribes and tribal members, and how accurate current accounts are. As of October 2007, the issue was still unsettled and was brought to federal court in 1996 in *Cobell*

v. Kempthorne, with a second case filed by 250 tribes on January 2, 2007. Congress has been debating settlement of the cases, but as of June 2008 no legislation was close to being passed. Meanwhile, U.S. District Judge James Robertson in January 2008 ruled in a 165-page decision in the *Cobell v. Kempthorne* federal lawsuit alleging mismanagement of Indian trust funds that the Department of the Interior had "unreasonably delayed" its accounting for billions of dollars owed to Indian landholders, and that the federal agency "has not, and cannot, remedy the breach" of its responsibilities to account for the Indian money: "Indeed, it is now clear that completion of the required accounting is an impossible task." Robertson said he would schedule a hearing during February to discuss ways to solve the problem. He added that his conclusion that the Interior Department is unable to perform an adequate accounting does not mean that the task is hopeless: "It does mean that a remedy must be found for the department's unrepaired, and irreparable, breach of its fiduciary duty over the last century. And it does mean that the time has come to bring this suit to a close." The suit, first filed in 1996 by Blackfeet Indian Elouise Cobell, claims the government has mismanaged more than $100 billion in oil, gas, timber, and other royalties held in trust from Indian lands dating back to 1887. Judge Robertson declared from the bench at a March 5, 2008, hearing that he expected the case to finally be completed by the end of summer, if not before. Summaries of the developments concerning the Indian trust fund suits are carried in the "U.S. Developments" section of spring and fall issues of *Indigenous Policy*, available on the journal's website at http://www.indigenouspolicy.org.

22. Cahn, *Our Brother's Keeper*, 5, 10, and 13. The passage is also quoted in Nelson and Sheley, "Influence on Indian Self-Determination," 178.

23. A discussion of the Collier reforms is presented in Olson and Wilson, *Native Americans in Twentieth Century*, chap. 5. See also, Debo, *History of the Indians*, chap. 18; Page, *In the Hands*, 358–63; and Nichols, *American Indians in U.S.*, 177–88.

24. Nelson and Sheley, "Influence on Indian Self-Determination," 180–94. The authors comment on page 182:

> The trustee role afforded the BIA the opportunity to make its presence felt in Indian affairs and, though less formally, to maintain roughly the same degree of sovereignty over Indians as it held prior to the passage of Public Law 93–638 [the Indian Self-Determination and Educational Assistance Act of 1975]. More to the point, the BIA has retained its powerful position through increased bureaucratization, a tactic relatively unnecessary prior to Public Law 93–638. During the past seven years, the BIA has maintained and increased its dominance over Indians through 1) a planning orientation suited more to its bureaucratic needs than to tribal needs, and 2) the conversion of tribes themselves to a bureaucratic planning orientation.

The authors' last point is extremely important, for it illustrates one of the ways that the BIA has continually acted to subvert tribal governments for its own purposes. As LaDonna Harris, president of AIO, wrote to Congressman Morris Udall: "Tribal governments have become extensions of the Federal Government and are not functioning to take care of the needs of their specific communities. They are being required to spend their time administering rather than governing" (Harris to Udall, October 12, 1979, LaDonna Harris Papers).

25. O'Brien, *American Indian Tribal Governments*, 83–86; and Debo, *History of the Indians*, chap. 19. On termination, see Wilkinson, *Blood Struggle*, chap. 3; Castile, *To Show Heart*, Introduction; Page, *In the Hands*, 368–78; and Nichols, *American Indians in U.S.*, 187–94.

26. The commencement of the era of self-determination policy is outlined in O'Brien, *American Indian Tribal Governments*, 86–91, 261–75. See also Debo, *History of the Indians*, chaps. 20 and 21; Olson and Wilson, *Native Americans in Twentieth Century*, chaps. 7 and 8; Wilkinson, *Blood Struggle*, chaps. 6–10; Castile, *To Show Heart*; Page, *In the Hands*, 379–403; and Nichols, *American Indians in U.S.*, 194–304. Although the Kennedy administration ceased supporting termination, backing away from it on an ad hoc basis, it did not repudiate it. Even during the Nixon administration, there remained sizable support for termination.

27. There are numerous examples of tribal successes both in self-government and in partnerships with other government agencies. A striking example of the former is the San Juan Pueblo housing program, which has been able to build housing much faster than the U.S. Department of Housing and Urban Development (HUD) at one-third the HUD cost. The housing is also of higher quality and employs a locally appropriate design, rather than HUD's generic design that is based on average U.S. urban conditions that are very different from those at the pueblo. (See Brambach, "Building for Bertha," C7, C8.) Similarly, a 1995 Department of the Interior audit showed that ten tribes that had contracted to take over programs all did a better job of running them than had the BIA. (See Brasher, "Audit Finds," 1, 2.) One of the strongest areas of tribal collaboration with other government entities has been in the area of environmental protection, specifically, the relatively good relationships that have developed between the EPA and the tribes. As we will discuss, the EPA has now delegated considerable regulatory autonomy to a number of tribes, and in a number of cases, tribes with more environmental protection expertise than surrounding counties have worked with those neighboring governments to plan and act together to enhance the quality of a jointly shared resource.

28. Olson and Wilson, *Native Americans in Twentieth Century*, 158–59; Wilkinson, *Blood Struggle*, part 2; Nagel, *American Indian Ethnic Renewal*, parts 2 and 3; and Smith and Warrior, *Like a Hurricane*, 194–204.

29. This period of Indian history and the three acts are discussed in Olson and Wilson, *Native Americans in Twentieth Century*, chap. 8; Wilkinson, *Blood Struggle*, 262–68; Castile, *To Show Heart*, chaps. 6 and 7; Castile, *Taking Charge*, chap. 2; and very briefly in Debo, *History of the Indians*, addenda. On termination of the Menominee Nation and the movement to overcome and reverse it, see Peroff, *Menominee Drums*. The three acts of Congress are included in Prucha, *United States Indian Policy*, 258–62, 264–66. Concerning the Alaska Native Claims Settlement Act, LaDonna Harris states that the use of Native corporations was written into the bill against the wishes of Native Alaskans. The Supreme Court has since interpreted the act as providing Alaska Native village governments less power than tribal governments have in Indian country. See *Alaska v. Village of Venetie Tribal Government*, 118 S. Ct. 948 (1998).

30. Olson and Wilson, *Native Americans in Twentieth Century*, chap. 8. Examples of such organizations are the American Indian Movement, AIO, the Coalition of Indian Controlled School Boards, the Navajo Indian Education Association, the National Advisory Council on Indian Education, the National Indian Leadership

Training Program, the National Tribal Chairmen's Association, Native American Rights Fund, and Oklahomans for Indian Opportunity (OIO). On federal funding helping Indian organizations, see Nagel, *American Indian Ethnic Renewal*, 122–31.

31. More recently, American Indians have enjoyed a number of important political successes and some losses. A high percentage of Indians vote, and vote knowledgeably, in states with high concentrations of Indians: if important Indian issues are involved, Indians often have influence as a swing constituency. Indian organizations overall now have more money available for political purposes than they did some years ago, which has been important for funding political advertising on certain key issues, such as on propositions concerning Indian gaming in California. The organizations also have more funding available for campaign donations than they did a decade ago but have reduced the amount of money they spend on campaign donations because they have found that donation money buys only access to candidates and officials, so spending beyond a certain level is not helpful. See "Indian and Indigenous Developments," *Native American Policy Network Newsletter* 17.

32. Ibid.; and O'Brien, *Native American Tribal Governments*, 86–91, 258. The Indian Self-Determination and Education Assistance Act of 1975 (Public Law 93–638) is partially presented in Prucha, *United States Indian Policy*, 274–76. Legislative developments and congressional–administration relations on Indian affairs from 1960 to the Reagan administration are set out in Castile, *To Show Heart*; and Castile, *Taking Charge*.

33. This is discussed at length in Champagne, "Organizational Change and Conflict," especially 44–57.

34. For example, a bill has been introduced in Congress to remove financing of Indian school construction, repair, and maintenance from the BIA (which is unable to keep up with the task to the extent that, currently, badly needed repairs alone would take two hundred years at the BIA's current rate of approving funding) and give it to a National Indian bonding authority that would provide money directly to the tribal schools. See Melmer, "$850 Million Needed," B6, B7.

35. Members of the Special Committee on Investigations of the Senate Select Committee on Indian Affairs to President George H. W. Bush, February 23, 1989, LaDonna Harris Papers.

36. Draft of December 1, 1989, LaDonna Harris Papers.

37. The letters of June 2, 1998, to John C. White, deputy secretary of the Department of Agriculture, and James Alfred Joseph, undersecretary of the Department of the Interior, concerning the Red Alerts are in the LaDonna Harris Papers.

38. Mike Synar to Donald Hodel, May 3, 1985, LaDonna Harris Papers.

39. LaDonna Harris to President Jimmy Carter, March 4, 1977, LaDonna Harris Papers.

40. For statistics and an analysis of the problem, see Indian Nations at Risk Taskforce, *Final Report*. 41. LaDonna Harris to Morris Thompson, January 27, 1975, LaDonna Harris Papers.

42. Patricia Locke to Dr. Ted Maarse, January 28, 1975, LaDonna Harris Papers.

43. For a discussion of advisory committees, See Fritschler and Hoefler, *Smoking and Politics*, 4.

44. See "Recommendations for Indian Policy."

45. Ibid., 11.

46. Ibid., 9–10. The elevating of the head of the BIA was intended to increase oversight of the agency as well as to increase the importance of Indian affairs in the

department and the federal government. The independent Indian Trust Authority was intended to overcome the problems stemming from having the secretary of the interior and the DOJ handle trust rights cases, and it would have authority to bring cases against the United States with an automatic waiver of sovereign immunity. A brief history of the fate of these provisions and of developments relating to Indian policy in the Nixon administration is contained in Garment, *Crazy Rhythm*, 223–47.

47. For example, see the letters in the LaDonna Harris Papers that Stuart Jamison, supervisor of the Indian Desk, Department of Agriculture, sent to AIO between February 1976 and February 1978.

48. See LaDonna Harris to Caspar Weinberger, May 30, 1975, LaDonna Harris Papers. Also see the December 19, 1978, "Note to National Indian Organizations" from A. David Lester, chairman of the Intradepartmental Council on Native American Affairs, attached to LaDonna Harris to A. David Lester, January 17, 1979, LaDonna Harris Papers.

49. See the "Secretary's Memorandum No. 1932: Native American Task Force of January 25, 1978," attached to Stuart Jamison to LaDonna Harris, April 4, 1978, LaDonna Harris Papers.

50. See Davies, "Environmental Institutions"; and Andrews, "Deregulation," 143–80.

51. B. Leigh Price to Ron Andrade, June 1990, LaDonna Harris Papers. The letter indicated that Price and Andrade had previously discussed the matter.

52. The complete "Indian Policy: Statement of Ronald Reagan, January 24, 1983" is reprinted in Prucha, *United States Indian Policy*, 301–2. Excerpts from this statement are included in the July 1983 EPA Indian Work Group Discussion Paper *Administration of Environmental Programs on Indian Lands*, and are referred to in other EPA documents concerning such programs in the 1980s in the LaDonna Harris Papers.

53. An example of such a collaboration between EPA, IHS, and the tribes is discussed in the EPA draft, *Report to Congress on Indian Waste Water Treatment Needs and Assistance*, 2, 3, attached to Robert J. Blanco to Tribal Organization Official, January 15, 1988, LaDonna Harris Papers.

54. Excerpts from July 18, 1984 EPA document "Indian Policy: Answers to Common Questions," LaDonna Harris Papers.

55. United States Environmental Protection Agency, "Request for Approval and Justification to Negotiate CERT Services Subcontract Requirements," August 28, 1986, LaDonna Harris Papers, concerns the AIO follow-up survey to the original AIO survey and the development of a database to catalogue survey data.

56. This included collaborating to help improve the general capability of tribal governments. Some of this work was achieved in connection with the Governance Project of AIO, "Work establishing governance with Native American Tribes to further self-sufficiency with American Indians," which was partially funded by grants from the Administration for Native Americans. See "A Proposal Submitted to the U.S. Environmental Protection Agency by Americans for Indian Opportunity, Inc.," January 8, 1985, LaDonna Harris Papers.

57. Singleton, "Dividing a Shared Resource."

58. "Summary of EPA Proposed Indian Programs FY 84–85," July 16, 1984, LaDonna Harris Papers, makes reference to four such cases. The summary shows that at that time, the EPA had ongoing programs with tribes involving air, radiation, water

quality, hazardous materials, pesticides, underground injection control, public water supply, and solid waste. The summary includes under "New Initiatives" that:

> The Agency will undertake a few, carefully selected pilot projects in the next year to enable us to work through the legal, procedural, and management issues faced by the Agency in dealing with Indian Tribes. Because most of EPA's statutes, regulations, and program-specific policies and strategies of the last thirteen years have been written without regard to Indian Tribes, Agency managers report widespread, significant obstacles and impediments to working with Tribal Governments in almost every program area. The pilot projects will begin to address these issues and obstacles.

A partial listing of existing collaborative programs between EPA regions and tribes as of 1983 is presented in the EPA Indian Work Group Discussion Paper, *Administration of Environmental Programs on Indian Lands*," 10–14, LaDonna Harris Papers. Indication of preparation to ask for additional funds to expand tribal programs is in the EPA memorandum of July 16, 1984 from Alvin L. Alm, deputy administrator, to assistant administrators, regional administrators, general counsel, LaDonna Harris Papers. Drafts dated July 18, 1984, of the proposed "EPA Policy for the Administration of Environmental Programs" and the memorandum "Indian Policy Implementation Guidance" are in the LaDonna Harris Papers.

59. For example, when the Office of Tribal Operations was established in 1994, Terry Williams, previously executive director of the Tulalip Tribe's Fisheries and Natural Resources, was appointed its first executive director (Hansen, "EPA Establishes Offices," 10). Then in 1997, Kathy Gorpospe, a member of the Laguna Pueblo tribe, for six years an executive assistant with the Columbia River Inter-Tribal Fish Commission, was appointed executive director of the Office of Tribal Relations (Swanson, "Oregon Natural Resources Specialist," B1, B2). Given the salmon decline, which recently has become serious, the collaboration has not always been easy, nor have completely satisfactory solutions to problems always been arrived at.

60. Hansen, "EPA Establishes Offices."

61. See David K, Sabock to To Whom It May Concern, January 9, 1988, LaDonna Harris Papers. This letter from the EPA's Office of Water Regulation Standards concerns continuing the proposed regulation and the Water Quality Act of 1987, Pub. L. No. 100–4, §131.7. Concerning authorizing tribes to set water-quality standards, see the remarks of Richard DuBay in Zelio, *Promoting Effective State-Tribal Relations*, 2–7; and O'Brien, *Native American Tribal Governments*, 223. The extension of this practice to a tribe in Wisconsin was accompanied by opposition from some state and local officials who feared increased costs for some of their constituents from potentially higher water-quality standards that might apply to their jurisdictions.

62. Clay, "EPA Proposes," 10.

63. *Two Years after*, 1996, 4.

64. For example, in spring 1997, Chippewa tribal officials in Wisconsin complained that the EPA was not living up to its trust responsibilities by rushing through the permit process to allow eleven million gallons of sulfuric acid to be used to leach copper from a mine near White Pine, Michigan, five miles from Lake Superior, the largest freshwater lake in the world, which is known for its pristine beauty.

Tribal leaders feared that the sulfuric acid, when added to exceedingly saline brine already in the mine, would cause overflow into the lake in fifty years. See Morrison, "Chippewa Rap EPA," A3.

65. *Two Years After*, 1996, 4.
66. National Congress of American Indians Nuclear Waste Program, "Tribal Radiological Emergency Preparedness."
67. *Two Years After*, 3, 22–23. The Department of Homeland Security–NCAI collaboration is reported in "Indian and Indigenous Developments: U.S. Developments," *Indigenous Policy* 19, no. 1.
68. Howell, "Tribes Writing Regs," B1, B5.
69. As reported in Brambach, "Building for Bertha."
70. The potential impact of the 1996 welfare reform on tribes is analyzed in the "George Waters and Tim Seward Legislative Update," from George Waters Consulting Service, "RE: Welfare Reform/Budget Reconciliation—P.L. 104–193, August 12, 1996." Note that the National Indian Policy Center in Washington, D.C., received an Administration for Native Americans grant to allow it to subcontract with NCAI to help defray costs of a national forum for tribal leaders to develop a plan to ensure the appropriate government-to-government dialogue between tribal governments and the federal officials responsible for initiating welfare reform. See "Policy Center to Participate," A3.
71. For an analysis of the impact of welfare reform on Indian nations and people as an intergovernmental concern, see Hunt, Sachs, and Morris, "Devolution of Welfare Programs."
72. This information was conveyed to author Stephen Sachs in discussions with HUD area office personnel in the early 1980s.
73. A five-part investigative series about serious irregularities in Native American housing programs appeared in the *Seattle Times* in November and December 1996 and was reprinted in the "Northwest Today" section of *Indian Country Today* in five consecutive weeks, from December 1996 to January 1997. In testimony before the Senate Committees on Indian Affairs and on Banking, Housing and Urban Affairs on March 12, 1997, HUD Inspector General Susan Gaffney testified that the *Seattle Times* reports of fraud, abuse, and mismanagement were generally accurate. Ms. Gaffney presented both an analysis of the factors that had allowed for fraud, abuse, and mismanagement and a set of recommendations for regulatory and administrative reform. The testimony is reprinted in *Indian Country Today*, "Housing and Urban Development," A2, A6.
74. "Tribes Set Own Goals," 15A.
75. See *Proposed List of Inherently Federal Functions and Non-Inherently Federal Functions of the Bureau of Indian Affairs* and "Department of the Interior, Bureau of Indian Affairs, Notice of Schedule of Regional Consultation Sessions on Tribal Shares," 62 Fed. Reg. 27064 (May 16, 1997).
76. President Johnson, Special Message to Congress, March 6, 1968, reported in part in Prucha, *United States Indian Policy*, 248–49.
77. Debo, *History of the Indians*, 411–12.
78. Garment, *Crazy Rhythm*, 145–49 and 223–47. For more detail on the coordination of Indian affairs from Johnson to Reagan, see Castile, *To Show Heart*, and *Taking Charge*.
79. White House Memorandum of August 26, 1976, attached to Bradley Patterson, Jr. to LaDonna Harris, August 30, 1976, LaDonna Harris Papers.

80. Pat Williams et al. to Ronald Reagan, April 22, 1983, LaDonna Harris Papers. This letter, on the stationery of Representative Pat Williams, was signed by sixty-one members of the House of Representatives.

81. See LaDonna Harris, "'Government To Government': Indian Tribal Governments and the Federal Government, A Discussion Paper," Americans for Indian Opportunity, May 1981, LaDonna Harris Papers.
82. The impact on the tribes of the Reagan budget cuts, including of employment programs, is discussed in Moris, "Termination by Accountants," 63–84.

83. For a discussion of issues concerning Native Americans in the federal budget, see Sachs, "Termination by Budget."

84. U.S. Civil Service Commission, "Discussion Paper: IPA Mobility Program Eligibility," January 26, 1976.

85. "Tribal Leaders Zero in," A2.

86. Michael Chapman, special assistant to the assistant secretary of the interior for Indian affairs, personal communication with author Stephen Sachs.

87. "Members of Working Group on American Indians and Alaska Natives of the White House Domestic Policy Council," revised January 27, 1997.

88. Erskine Bowles, chief of staff to the president and Bruce Reed, assistant to the president for domestic policy, White House Memorandum for Heads of Departments and Agencies concerning Executive Memorandum on Government-to-Government relations, May 23, 1997.

89. For example, the Department of Defense was engaged in 2001 in a new study of the possible impact of the operation of military bases upon Indian tribes. Sharon O'Brien, Indigenous Native Studies Program, University of Kansas, personal communication with author Stephen Sachs.

90. Rolo, "Tribes, Government Differ."

91. Staff of various Indian state agencies from 1980–2000, personal communications with author Stephen Sachs concerning the communications process at federal agency meetings for state agency staff.

92. *Two Years After*, 1996. For reasons we will discuss, there has been only a slow increase in the number of tribes that run or contract out their own programs since 1996, constituting about a third of federally recognized tribes. In a November 8, 2007, hearing by the House Committee on Natural Resources on Indian tribes and organizations, including Alaskan and Hawaiian Native organizations, on HR 3994, which would apply the rules and procedures of self-governance in use at the IHS to the Interior Department, department officials stated that 40 percent of tribes were managing their own BIA programs with federal funds that had been administered on their behalf by the BIA or the IHS in the past. Congress refined the program within the IHS in 2000. Nick Rahall of West Virginia noted that "Indian tribes have reported that those changes have immensely improved the administration of self-governance within the Indian Health Service." Similarly, a May 13 hearing before the Senate Committee on Indian Affairs showed similar general tribal and Department of the Interior satisfaction with self-governance for those tribes able to take advantage of it, despite some continuing and new problems with the policy. See "Indian and Indigenous Developments: U.S. Developments," *Indigenous Policy* 19, no. 1.

93. It should be noted that the Southern Ute Tribe is a small tribe that is relatively advantaged economically and that has been extremely progressive in taking its affairs into its own hands at every opportunity. By contrast, the Navajo Nation

is quite large in terms both of population and geographical size and spread, and it has a bureaucratized central tribal government that is only just beginning the process of decentralizing government functions to its 110 local chapters. Therefore, the relative readiness of a tribe to act autonomously (and the extent to which it has attempted to do so) may be a factor affecting how federal agency personnel relate to the tribe. This notion is supported by the fact that the Navajo Nation's Ramah Chapter, because of its geographical separation from the rest of the Navajo Nation, has developed a high degree of autonomy in running its own affairs, has taken an extremely large number of autonomous initiatives with considerable energy, and generally enjoys better government-to-government relations with federal agencies than is typically the case in Navajo government.

94. Hart, *The Presidential Branch*.
95. The official requested anonymity.
96. U.S. Department of the Interior, *Strategic Plan 2000–2005*.
97. For information about Indian education initiatives, see the "Indian and Indigenous Developments: U.S. Developments" section of *Indigenous Policy* 14, no. 2, and *Indigenous Policy* 15, no. 1.
98. The specific reports of complaints about lack of consultation are from "Indian and Indigenous Developments: U.S. Developments" and "U.S. Activities," *Indigenous Policy* 14, no. 1 and "Indian and Indigenous Developments: U.S. Developments," *Indigenous Policy* 18, no. 3.
99. For information about attempts at reducing eligibility for Indian programs, see "Indian and Indigenous Developments: U.S. Developments" and "U.S. Activities," *Indigenous Policy* 14, no. 1, and *Indigenous Policy* 18, no. 3.
100. Proposed changes in the Workforce Investment Act are detailed in "Indian and Indigenous Developments: U.S. Developments," *Indigenous Policy* 14, no. 2.
101. "Indian and Indigenous Developments: U.S. Developments," *Indigenous Policy* 18, no. 3.
102. Van Norman's statement was reported in "Indian and Indigenous Developments: U.S. Developments," *Indigenous Policy* 19, no. 1.
103. *Cherokee Nation v. Georgia*, 30 U.S. (5 Pet) 1 (1831).
104. Important concerns exist beyond the scope of the current discussion as to how federally recognized tribes are, and should be, determined. There are discussions of the status of Indian tribes in Deloria and Wilkins, *Tribes, Treaties*, chap. 19; and in Mason, "Tribal-State Relations."
105. Obviously, any such access and communication needs to be proper, appropriate, and ethically conducted so as to avoid improper favoritism to "special interests"—and ought to be so regulated. What is being sought here is the open communication that ought to exist between citizens and the government agencies whose actions affect them.
106. This is discussed in Holm, "The Crises in Tribal Government"; Vine Deloria Jr., "The Evolution of Federal Indian Policy Making"; Doss, *American Indian Policy Review*; and mailgram of May 9, 1977, to Mr. Ernie Stevens, director of the American Indian Policy Review Commission from the National Tribal Chairman's Association Special Committee for review of the findings and recommendations of the American Indian Policy Review Commission, Statement on the Commission's Final Report, April 20, 1977, LaDonna Harris Papers.
107. See Prucha, *United States Indian Policy*, 272–74, 281–83.
108. It is important to note that given the way in which Congress, and particularly

the Senate, operates, individual personalities often play key roles that, within the parameters of the politics of the moment, cannot easily be politically controlled by others. For example, in formulating the 1996 federal budget, when the House was generally much more stringent in cutting domestic programs than was the Senate, the Senate proposed much larger cuts in Indian programs than had the House (which ultimately made the final compromise appropriation significantly lower than it otherwise would have been) because of who the chairman of the relevant Senate appropriations subcommittee happened to be.

109. This is generally consistent with the proposals for improving the functioning of the government process set out in Osborne and Gaebler, *Reinventing Government*, particularly chaps. 2, 4, 5, 6, 8, and 9.

110. A good example of the problem of devolving Indian programs to the states without self-determination for Indian nations is to be found in the history of Indian education. Beginning in 1935, much of Indian primary and secondary education began to devolve to the states and local school boards. In general, this devolution has been a great failure, because local schools receiving federal funding for teaching reservation Indians simply added Indian children to existing programs without making any provisions for cultural differences, culturally appropriate education, or, in numerous instances, for eliminating racism in schools. The failure of local schools to make adequate provision for American Indian education is largely responsible for the fact that Indians have the lowest level of educational achievement and the highest school dropout rate of any ethnic group measured in the United States. See, Indian Nations at Risk Taskforce, *Final Report*, 7, 9; and Indian Health Service, *Trends in Indian Health*, 28. For discussion of two specific examples of this problem, see Young, *Ute Indians of Colorado*, 86–88, 234–35, 265–67, and 270. Because of the persistent problems faced by Southern Ute children in local public schools, the Southern Ute Tribe has developed its own school (Brown, "Family/Community Centers," 1). See also chapter 5.

111. Cornell, "Politics, Business." The one notable exception has been that some successful casino gambling has occurred on reservations without direct tribal participation in the development process. Even in this area, however, Indian nations have often been able to significantly increase their economic gain by having their members trained in how to run the gambling facilities, then taking over the casino operation.

112. For example, see Stringer and Blackwell, *Economic Impact*; Robinson, *Economic and Fiscal Importance*; Parker, *Indians in New Mexico*; and Rowley, "Dollar Impact of Tribes," 1. This topic in relation to the development of collaboration between tribal and state and local governments is discussed more broadly in Morris, Sachs, and Harris, "Strategy and Choice."

113. See Morris, Sachs, and Harris, "Strategy and Choice."

114. O'Brien, *American Indian Tribal Governments*, chaps. 4 and 5. See also Debo, *History of the Indians*, chaps. 4–20; and Olson and Wilson, *Native Americans in Twentieth Century*, chaps. 2–5. Note that prior to the forming of the United States, several colonies, which became eastern states, did have treaties with Indian nations, and this has led to a limited continuing relationship between certain states and tribes that includes state tribal recognition for certain Indian tribes that do not necessarily have federal recognition.

115. Wilkins, "Renouncing Jurisdiction."

116. Taylor, *Their Indian Citizens*, chap. 2.

117. Szasz, *Road to Self-Determination*, 5–6.

118. Taylor, *Their Indian Citizens*, chap. 3.

119. Ibid.

120. O'Brien, *American Indian Tribal Governments*, 85–86, 199–200, 203, 206, 225, 276–78, 280, 284, and 292. In November 2007, Carole Goldberg of the University of California, a legal expert on Public Law 280 and Duane Champagne completed the 568-page report, *Law Enforcement and Criminal Justice under Public Law 280*. At the time of publication, the report was the first and only comprehensive examination of the termination-era law. It details the shortcomings of the 1970 legislation, which transferred criminal jurisdiction on Indian reservations from the federal government to some states, offering a series of recommendations to improve the relationship between tribal governments and state law enforcement agencies to help deliver fair, efficient, and culturally appropriate law enforcement and justice systems in tribal communities. The researchers asked Congress to review and revise Public Law 280, none of whose problems have been evaluated and corrected, according to the report. The authors of this book find Public Law 280 to be a maze of complexity that pits state jurisdiction against tribal sovereignty and criminal laws against regulatory issues, and it has caused discontent, confusion, and, in some cases, tragedy in Indian country and among some state and local law enforcement and criminal justice officials. We recommend training police and court personnel in Public Law 280 and tribal cultures, enhancing communication between state law enforcement agencies and tribal communities, creating systems of accountability for police and justice systems, and enacting legislation to allow tribes to initiate retrocession from Public Law 280.

121. Taylor, *Their Indian Citizens*, 39–47.

122. See the discussion of this development in chapter 1, section 2.

123. For Oklahoma tribal economic impact study information, see Stringer and Blackwell, *Economic Impact*. For the Arizona study, see Robinson, *Economic and Fiscal*. For the New Mexico economic survey, see Parker, *Economic and Fiscal*. Other studies have shown similar results concerning tribal contributions to state economies. For example, a study by *Indian Country Today* finds that the tribes of South Dakota contributed more than $44.5 million to their state's economy in 1994 (Rowley, "Dollar Impact").

124. Stan Bindell, "Southwest Native Tourism," 11, 13.

125. Hamilton, "Governor Janklow Meets," 9. This is not to say that there were not significant later disagreements on issues between the governor and the tribes that at times became acrimonious. But the climate of discussion was changed by the governor's approach to tribal leaders in this meeting, and it remained better than it had been previously. Janklow, who earlier had been strongly anti–Native American, became willing to talk to the tribes on an equal basis and to collaborate with them on some issues. Similarly, the factors we have discussed, though they appear to us to be generally the most important, are not the only developments assisting the development of more collaborative relations between tribal governments and state and local governments. For example, in South Dakota, a number of individuals and groups have been working for reconciliation between the tribes and the non-Native American population at least since the 1960s, including the South Dakota Peace and Justice Center in Watertown.

126. O'Brien, *American Indian Tribal Governments*, 205–8, 279–81.

127. Ibid.; Young, *Ute Indians of Colorado*, 234; *News from Indian Country*, "Montana

Joint," 12A. The information on the Albuquerque–Pueblo arrangement was obtained by LaDonna Harris in discussions with Pueblo officials. Collaboration has also been attained between tribal and state and local authorities in other aspects of law enforcement. For example, Acoma Pueblo obtained increased law enforcement at its Sky City Casino in an arrangement with the New Mexico 13th Judicial District Attorney's office to prosecute crimes by non-Indians in the vicinity of the casino. Acoma Pueblo pays the district attorney's office for the service. See "DA Signs," C3.

128. See Sachs, "Building Trust."

129. The establishment of mutual assistance is important in allowing New Mexico governments to gain collaboration from the tribes. Such mutual assistance will assist the tribes in levying fines on motorists who violate traffic laws while passing through tribal lands. However, as of April 2000, New Mexico and the tribes had not yet instituted an effective reporting system (Mahesh, "Tribes Fail to Report," A1, A6).

130. From the remarks of Richard Du Bey in Zelio, *Promoting Effective State-Tribal Relations*, 2–7.

131. Zelio, *Promoting Effective State-Tribal Relations*, 289–90.

132. Ibid., 2–9.

133. "Ute Child Welfare Gains," B6.

134. O'Brien, *American Indian Tribal Governments*, 286–88.

135. Ibid., 287. Singleton, "Dividing a Shared Resource," 2, reports that tribes in Washington state join with state regulatory agencies to co-manage Pacific salmon: "The management of resource systems in general, and Pacific Salmon in particular, poses difficult problems. . . . Currently, co-management between the state and tribes functions relatively smoothly and the tribes have become active participants concerning land use development throughout the state."

136. Some of this preservation is being accomplished under the cooperative People for Salmon Project (see Hansen, "People for Salmon Project," 12). It should be noted that collaboration between the Northwest Indian Fisheries Commission and the agencies of other governments has not always been easy or smooth. There have been some contentious disagreements over some issues in this important area of economic and environmental concern. On some occasions, even if those from different governments who meet face to face reach personal agreement, it is sometimes difficult to obtain agreement from the governments of which they are a part to act in concert, given different constituencies and politics. The true test of the collaboration is not how smooth or rocky it may have been on occasion, but its ability to succeed over time, despite difficult moments dealing with tough problems. That, so far, has been the case here. It is notable that in 1998, the Northwest tribes and states and the federal government came together under the Three Sovereigns Fish and Wildlife Governance Process agreement to improve fish and wildlife management throughout the region. See Hansen, "Three Sovereigns Fish Management."

137. The complexities of water issues for the tribes and a detailed analysis of how they have been approached through the 1980s are provided in Burton, *American Indian Water Rights*.

138. McCool, "Intergovernmental Conflict," 85–101.

139. The history of the Animas–LaPlata Project, and the full range of interests and factors involved in it, are far too extensive to present here in full. The project is discussed in more detail in McCool, "Intergovernmental Conflict," 88–89, 93–94, 97, and 98; in Burton, *American Indian Water Rights*, 50–57, 75–76, 84, 85, and

127; and in numerous editions of *The Southern Ute Drum*, including the articles "Animas–La Plata Project Chronology," 1, 2; and Burch, "Briefing Paper," 8. Author Stephen Sachs has enhanced his understanding of the case through numerous discussions with members of the Southern Ute Tribe and academics with detailed knowledge of the project, including Daniel McCool and Richard Ellis, director of the Center of Southwest Studies, Fort Lewis College, Durango, Colorado.

140. In 1995, Congress appropriated an initial $10 million for Animas–La Plata. However, Congress was unwilling to spend the entire sum required to construct the original project and has twice reduced its scope. Because a number of years of funding were required to complete the work, the ultimate outcome of the project's fate in the political struggles over the federal budget was uncertain for many years. After a long and torturous road, on December 21, 2000, Congress passed Public Law 106–554, the Colorado Ute Settlement Act Amendments of 2000, authorizing a scaled-down Animas–La Plata water project. Public Law 106–554 provides for the construction of Ridges Basin Dam and Reservoir, Durango Pumping Plant, and Ridges Basin Inlet conduit, with an average annual depletion of 57,100 acre-feet. The law also provides for the construction of a pipeline to deliver water for domestic use on the Navajo Nation in Shiprock, New Mexico. Much of the construction has been completed, and the project was in operation by the end of 2009. The law's passage did not end all of the uncertainty, however, because construction, operation, and maintenance depend on annual congressional appropriation. See McCool and Kirwin, "Environmentalists, Tribes" for a general overview of Indian water rights settlements and issues and specifics of the Animas–La Plata negotiation to 1995. *The Southern Ute Drum* newspaper is an excellent source for following developments, debates, and discussions since 1995. Historical and current information on Animas–La Plata is available from the Bureau of Reclamation's Upper Colorado Region website, "Animas–La Plata Project: Implementation of the Colorado Ute Settlement Act Amendments of 2000," http://www.usbr.gov/uc/progact/animas/overview.html. Since 2000, a number of Indian water rights settlements have been in negotiation with some success at settlement. See Robert T. Anderson, "Symposium: Native American Natural Resources: Indian Water Rights: Litigation and Settlements," https://litigation-essentials.lexisnexis.com/webcd/app?action=DocumentDisplay&crawlid=1&srctype=smi&srcid=3B1 5&doctype=cite&docid=42+Tulsa+L.+Rev.+23&key=a4cd7997096037217d5b491 ae6796879; and Bonnie G. Colby, "Tribal Water Settlements in Arizona," http://ag.arizona.edu/azwater/publications/townhall/Chapter8.pdf.

141. Blomquist, "Improving Dispute Resolution"; and Wilds and Gonzales, "On the Cutting Edge."

142. McCool, "Intergovernmental Conflict," 94.

143. O'Brien, *American Indian Tribal Governments*, 276–78, 283–85.

144. Stringer and Blackwell, *Economic Impact*, 1–2.

145. Ibid.

146. Ibid., 3.

147. O'Brien, *American Indian Tribal Governments*, 284–85.

148. Melmer, "'Bribes for Tribe'" A1, A2. Some Indian people see this and other agreements between tribes and governments resulting in tribes being co-opted and giving away their sovereignty. Others see them as an exercise of sovereignty that strengthens tribal sovereignty and furthers tribal interest. Which is the case depends on what the agreement calls for and how trustworthy the other governments are. Past

history has justifiably created a great deal of mistrust among Indian people that needs to be overcome, but only with agreements that after careful consideration are shown to be of mutual benefit and in the course of a continuous trust-building process.

149. For example, see *Indian Country Today*, "Standing Rock-State Tax," B1; and *News from Indian Country*, "Dakota Agree to Split," 2A, and "Locke Signs."

150. Weise and Stewart, "Intergovernmental and Economic Impacts."

151. Reeves, "The Big Game Returns," D1, 4. The number of states signing gambling compacts with tribes has increased since 1994 and may increase somewhat over the next few years.

152. Rehorn, "Red Willow Branch," 1, 10; Rehorn, "Tax Talks," 3, 8; "SUIT, La Plata County Happy," 1; and Rehorn, "Tax Dispute Ends," 1, 8.

153. Rehorn, "Tribe Becomes Player," 1, 2; and Brown, "SUIT and Herald," 1.

154. Brown, "Colorado House Passes," 1.

155. "Good Neighbors Meet," 1, 3.

156. Americans for Indian Opportunity, *We the People*, 28–30.

157. See Mississippi Band of Choctaw Indians, *Choctaw Industrial Park*; and Peterson, "Three Efforts at Development."

158. Sachs, "Transformational Native American Gift." Concerning Native worldviews that see the world as complex and uncertain (along the lines of contemporary chaos and uncertainty theory), and thus encourage people, particularly leaders, to develop as wide a circle of good relations as possible, see the discussion of Indigenous leadership in chapter 6; Sachs, "Cutting Edge of Physics"; and Sachs, "Power and Sovereignty."

159. For background on the Southern Utes, see Jefferson et al., *The Southern Utes*; Petitt, *Utes: The Mountain People*; Marsh, *People of the Shining Mountains*; Young, *Ute Indians of Colorado*; and Simmons, *Ute Indians of Utah*.

160. Interviews with Southern Utes, July 1990 by author Stephen Sachs. Readers who have followed *The Southern Ute Drum*, at least since 1989, continually find references to collaboration between the Southern Ute Reservation and state and local agencies.

161. Rehorn, "The Tribal Gaming Controversy," 1–2, discusses some of the issues involved in the Southern Ute decision. The tribe may eventually build a facility out by U.S. Highway 550, but it did not choose to do so initially. The issues are more complicated than we can discuss here. The important point for this discussion is that the Tribal Gaming Coordinating Committee considered the outside community as well as tribal concerns in its decisions because the tribe understands itself to be part of the wider community, as illustrated by some of the remarks of Tribal Gaming Coordinating Committee Chair Archie Baker: "There's the highway issue and also the community problem. That corridor has many private owners and we Southern Utes are part of that. I believe we have just as much right to be involved in what happens there. Progress is happening all over the country and we are part of that progress. We believe it's everybody's responsibility to get together to pressure the state to do something about that highway."

162. Remarks of Wilma Mankiller in Zelio, *Promoting Effective State-Tribal Relations*, 10–18.

163. Ibid., 11.

164. The principles of delegating authority downward in an organization to the lowest level that is directly concerned with an issue and that includes everyone who is concerned with the issue, and the principles of networking (so that people directly

concerned with an issue can talk directly to one another) are now well-established in private business organizations and are increasingly being found essential in the public sector to providing efficiency and effectiveness that is consistent with accountability. See Osborne and Gaebler, *Reinventing Government.*

165. Fox, "Tribal/State Health Policymaking."

166. See the Oregon State Legislature Commission on Indian Services home page for more information: http://www.leg.state.or.us/cis, or the CIS pamphlet, "Legislative Commission on Indian Services." The Commission on Indian Services was enabled under Oregon Revised Statute 172.100 in 1975.

167. Executive Order No. EO-96-30 and Senate Bill 770. The Oregon Department of Administrative Services publishes an annual report, which includes the annual reports of all state departments, on Indian policy and communication with tribes. See, for example, *Government to Government 2000 Agency Memorandums*, obtainable from: Department of Administrative Services, Office of the Director, 155 Cottage Street NE U20, Salem, OR 97301.

168. The Governor's Office of Indian Affairs website is available at http://www.goia.wa.gov.

169. Justice Yvonne Kauger's remarks in Zelio, *Promoting Effective State-Tribal Relations,* 1.

170. *News from Indian Country*, late February 2001, 10a.

171. May, "California AG," 1, 2.

172. "Tribes Gather to Discuss," 16,

173. LaDonna Harris and AIO, of which she is founder and president, have long worked to improve relations between tribal and other governments and have been working with the task force. Author Stephen Sachs, working with AIO, participated in a task force meeting in 2000 and consulted with the task force in 2000 and 2001.

174. Examples of states that have created such bodies are North Dakota (*News from Indian Country*, "North Dakota and Lakota," 3A), Missouri (*News from Indian Country*, "Governor Invites Native Leaders," 12), Nebraska (Urbinato, "Nebraska Tribes, State Pledge," 4), and Montana (Jim Kent, "Montana Governor Wants Improved," 15A).

Four
Returning to Harmony Through the Wisdom of the People
APPLYING TRADITIONAL PRINCIPLES TO DEVELOP APPROPRIATE
AND EFFECTIVE INDIAN TRIBAL GOVERNANCE

*LaDonna Harris, Stephen M. Sachs, Benjamin J. Broome,
and Jondodev Chaudhuri*

1. Returning Indian Nations to Culturally Appropriate Forms of Decision Making

LaDonna Harris, Stephen M. Sachs, and Benjamin J. Broome

If Indian nations are to function effectively and harmoniously while relating efficaciously with other governments, it is essential that they enjoy governmental structures and processes that are compatible with the values of the people and institutional designs that are appropriate for current and developing needs. Today, many Indian nations are struggling to overcome considerable difficulties caused by the imposition of culturally inappropriate forms of tribal government.

Traditional versus Contemporary Tribal Governance
Traditionally, tribal and band societies in North America functioned mostly harmoniously through inclusive ways of building community consensus that balanced individual and community needs and concerns (as we discussed in detail in chapter 1).[1] Although each of the tribes had its own particular culture and way of governing, in all of the tribes and bands (so far as is now known), the general practice was that no decision was made without involving everyone who was concerned. Usually, issues were discussed until consensus was achieved.[2] Large tribes and

multitribal federations, such as that of the Huron, which in 1634 consisted of thirty to forty thousand people, attained consensus by employing consensus decision making in meetings at each organizational level (e.g., clan segment, village, tribe, federation), discussing back and forth across the levels until general consensus was reached.[3]

Leaders (who have mistakenly been called "chiefs") functioned primarily as facilitators, consensus builders, and announcers of decisions.[4] In general, they had little or no decision-making power of their own, although usually they had influence. They were chosen for positions of leadership on the basis of their high moral character and ability to represent the people and lead in the long-term interests of the community as a whole.[5]

As chapter 1 shows more fully, the inclusive process of egalitarian consensus decision making that normally limited civil leaders to being facilitators and advisors of the people was built upon cultural and structural foundations, that although varying in detail among Indian nations, generally followed the same basic principles. Culturally, people believed in, and related on the basis of, mutual respect, identifying with the band or tribe as an extended family in which members supported one another in their individual endeavors to the extent that they did not contradict the common good, at the same time that they collaborated out of mutual interest and a strong sense of shared consensus. Structurally, in different ways and to different extents among various peoples, political and social power and function were widely dispersed—generally beyond the division of powers and functions in the U.S. government (although for similar reasons). At the same time, economically as well as socially, the structure of living caused people to need one another's support, and economic power was at least not so concentrated as to upset egalitarian relations and was most often broadly dispersed in economies based upon reciprocity (usually even more so than is supposed to be the case, according to current mainstream economic theory, to maintain a "free" market economy). Thus, by developing cooperation and a sense of unity through honoring diversity on the basis of mutual respect, these communities usually maintained a very high quality of life.[6]

Today, most tribal and band societies in the United States suffer from considerable factionalism and disharmony as they struggle to emerge from the vestiges of repressive colonialism that inflicted physical and cultural genocide upon Indigenous people. Among the several factors contributing to today's disharmony is that the form of government imposed on most tribes by the U.S. government is not compatible with their traditional cultures.[7]

During the U.S. government's attempt to assimilate Native people into mainstream society from the late nineteenth century until the 1930s, most Indian nations were not permitted to govern themselves, and the federal government attempted to undermine traditional culture and leadership. When First Nations were again permitted to begin governing some of their own affairs, a less than optimal Western form of government was imposed on many tribes that contradicted traditional values and often suffered from structural difficulties.

Traditionally, inclusive forms of consensus helped to make community members more aware of their place within the community because direct participation in deciding about community affairs was a major source of each person's identity as a community member. The current practices of holding elections in which there are winners and losers and of electing councils that make decisions rather than announce decisions made by the people as a whole are divisive. Indeed, communication has broken down on a considerable number of reservations, so that people are often not aware of decisions, and in numerous instances have false impressions of how decisions have been made. This alienation is reflected in low levels of participation in elections and public meetings in many Native communities, accompanied by often vicious gossip and infighting. Those who lose an election often perceive that they have been rejected by the community and believe that their honor has been impugned (whereas, for non-Native Americans, this would not be the case). People who are not included in the making of a decision, even if they are invited to a meeting to state their opinion to the decision makers, tend to feel left out. Indeed, today many people are in fact left out, and their interests are not effectively represented in the tribal electoral systems. It is important to note that the effective exclusion of people from the electoral process is a result of the nature of the system itself, and usually not because of who the particular leaders happen to be.

Moreover, the concentration of legislative and executive, and sometimes judicial, authority in some tribal councils creates problems with the concentration of power that contradict not only Western principles of separation of powers but also the practice of wide dispersal of power that reflected traditional culture and was fundamental to inclusive, egalitarian consensus decision making.[8] When tribal government authority became more dispersed in the 1960s as the War on Poverty broke the

Bureau of Indian Affairs' (BIA's) monopoly in Indian affairs and each federal agency arranged the local implementation of its programs directly with each Indian nation, new programs were often not adequately integrated into tribal governments. The result was often a fracturing of the governance process by the development of separate services that reported to different federal agencies with disparate regulations and reporting requirements. This tended to create competing fiefdoms that were sometimes at odds with the elected leadership.

In addition, because of institutional racism, Indian people have not been taught in school the validity of their own ways, even though traditional Native American governance had a profound effect on the development of American democracy. Thus, Indian people have not been educated to formulate public policy from a tribal government perspective. As a result, tribes are often encouraged to create codes that mimic U.S. government statutes, rather than develop measures that fit their own tradition and circumstance. Because Indian people for generations were discouraged from following their own cultures, time and energy now often must be invested in order for tribal members to clarify how their traditions can be effectively applied in current circumstances. This is especially the case as a variety of perspectives have developed concerning what those traditions are, at the same time that new traditions have come into being, such as the rise of the Native American Church or the importation of some form of the Sun Dance by a number of Indian nations. Moreover, to varying degrees and in a range of ways, members of Indian communities have adopted, or been affected in their ways of seeing by, non-Indian ways and institutions (including churches, because most Indian people today are at least nominally Christians, regardless of the extent to which they may also follow traditional ways and be involved in traditional ceremonies).

In some instances, thinking through community values and developing culturally appropriate actions can be supported by external collaboration, as in the Comanche case we will discuss. However, external assistance can be helpful only if it is undertaken appropriately according to the needs, values, and situation of the nation in question and is carried out in an empowering fashion. This is especially the case currently; it is time for Indigenous people to shift from approaching situations reactively, which was a wise strategy during the long period of colonial imposition, to acting proactively, now that the U.S. government and much of mainstream society is accepting of Indian autonomy.

The development of current forms of tribal government has taken place over a considerable period and has gone through many stages.[9] More than half of federally recognized tribes have governments organized under the guidelines of the Indian Reorganization Act of 1934, the Oklahoma Indian Welfare Act of 1936, or the Alaska Reorganization Act of 1936. Some tribes, such as the Crow and the Yakima, have organized themselves through their own tribal agreements. Most tribes have an elected governing council of some kind (under a variety of names) that often combines legislative with executive (and sometimes judicial) authority. A few tribes, including the Onondaga, some Pueblo groups, many smaller bands in California, and most Native communities in Alaska, continue to use more traditional forms of tribal governance. Many of the Indian nations that do not have Indian Reorganization Act governments have been influenced by it in developing their own governmental forms or have developed other Western, rather than traditionally based, forms (as did the Navajo Nation) that mirror the federal government in establishing a three-branch system of government with checks and balances. Many of these tribal governments have suffered some of the same problems that have been typical of many Indian governments that were directly imposed by the U.S. government.

The problem of the inappropriateness of the more widely used general form of governance has increased in significance since the 1960s. Prior to that time (despite the intent of the 1930s legislation enacted under the leadership of BIA Commissioner John Collier), tribes and tribal governments had little autonomy, and much of the function of the elected council members was to act as brokers for the tribe and its members in dealing, first, with federal, and second, with state and local officials. With the civil rights movement and the War on Poverty came an increase in the authority of tribal governments to make significant decisions in their affairs that continues to expand.[10]

Thus, the difficulties that many Indian nations have experienced with inappropriate governmental processes have been intensifying over time. For some tribes, the problems have been relatively minor, whereas for others, they have been quite serious. In too many instances, infighting has left tribal governments deadlocked or quite unstable. In extreme cases, volatile conflict relating to governance has broken into violence or led to a takeover of tribal government by the Department of the Interior to restore or maintain peace.[11] Currently, tribal governments are facing increasing challenges that are making community disharmony more likely and more intense. These include demographic shifts; rapid cultural, social, and economic change; growing concern as to whether economic development is occurring compatibly with tribal values; and increasing responsibility for tribal governments as the federal government devolves authority to the tribes, states, and localities.

Re-creating the Circle: Indian Nations' Efforts to Apply Traditional Values to Improving Tribal Governance

In recent years, a growing number of Indian nations have been attempting to make their public-policy processes more effective by reshaping their systems of governance in accordance with the appropriate application of traditional values to contemporary circumstances. Such major change is necessarily an extended process that requires considerable effort and support over time. For example, the Navajo Nation, which has the largest population of any recognized Indian tribe in the United States and is spread over an extremely large reservation with poor roads and other infrastructure stretching across three states, found that attempting to govern almost all tribal matters from the tribal capital in Window Rock, Arizona, resulted in a cumbersome, bureaucratic tribal government that many Diné found to be unrepresentative and too geographically removed to act with an adequate understanding of conditions in its many varied local chapters or to be in communication with local citizens. Moreover, many aspects of the nation's three-branch government, which is modeled on the U.S. Constitution, did not fit with traditional Navajo ways, even though some traditional government practices were retained and the tribal courts incorporated a considerable amount of Navajo custom in tribal law.

Decentralization and Participation at Navajo Nation

Thus, in early 1998, the Navajo Nation acted to decentralize many aspects of government to its 110 local chapters, even as it was working to improve the quality of many chapter meetings by finding ways to incorporate relevant traditional values in contemporary governance.[12] A sales tax was established so that chapters certified in self-governing competence could obtain funding from retail sales in their jurisdiction. At the same time, the central government began taking steps to debureaucratize its operation and to improve the accessibility of, and communications with, each of its organs. Most of the planning and initial implementation of these efforts have been carried out by the Navajo Government Commission, an arm of the legislative branch, and its Office of Navajo Government

Development. The commission and the office have able staff and have been advised by traditional elders. A weak economy, however, has made it difficult for the nation to provide adequate resources for the immense and many-faceted task. The office has received some assistance for providing forums where local chapter officials can work out methods for improving chapter governance from the Leadership Program at Diné College. However, the program has not had the resources to move very quickly in working with the large number of geographically dispersed chapters.[13]

A similar problem exists concerning the technical competence of the chapters to carry out programs effectively and to handle finances with accountability. Thus, the nation's government established a process whereby chapters are approved on their competence to manage money, and thus can be certified to operate their own programs under the decentralization statute. At first, very few chapters became involved in the certification program because the paperwork involved was complex; also many of the chapters were understaffed, overworked, and inexperienced in the more complicated bookkeeping that the revenue-sharing process that applying tribal funds locally would involve. As a result, Navajo Nation developed methods to simplify accounting and maintain accountability while also finding affordable yet adequate ways to provide technical assistance to chapters on finance and other matters. This effort has begun to increase chapter certification. In October 2004, the Sweetwater Chapter became the first to have its Local Governance Act Community Land Use Plan approved by the Navajo Nation Council's Transportation and Community Development Committee. The Sweetwater Chapter obtained assistance from the Shiprock Agency Local Government Support Center, one of several regional centers set up to assist chapter governments. By April 2005, six more chapters achieved approval of land-use plans.[14]

At the same time, public participation in Navajo Nation national government has increased by several means, including the institution of representative focus groups to obtain input on important issues and the posting of proposed legislation on the legislature's website. Proposed legislation is posted in time to allow public (and Navajo executive agency) comment before issues come to a vote. In 2004, the Navajo Nation Supreme Court's chief justice called for public commentary in the regular evaluation of judges.[15] Also that year, the nation set up polling stations in tribal elections for its registered voters living off-reservation in Albuquerque, Denver, Salt Lake City, and Phoenix.

The Navajo Nation Constitutional Feasibility and Government Reform Project

Although the process of decentralization that was initiated in 1998 began to move toward its desired ends, many Navajo found it too limited and slow and brought a call to reexamine the entire system of the nation's government. The first step in doing this was undertaken by the Diné Policy Institute of Diné College, which issued the *Navajo Nation Constitutional Feasibility and Reform Projec*t report, September 2, 2008, which received its initial discussion by the Navajo Nation Council during its October 20–24 session.[16] The executive summary presents these findings about the Navajo Nation's existing three-branch national government, which mirrors the structure of the U.S. government:

> The concept of Nation-statism and constitutionalism is inappropriate and ineffective as applied to the Navajo Nation. Decentralization of government needs to be thoroughly examined. The current government originates from Western political history and carries a contrasting experience from that of the Diné. This has created a political system supporting a "strong man" which is historically incongruous. The Diné must rethink their government to reflect cultural values and norms. The Diné need to utilize new terminology when communicating governance ideas. We have adopted Western concepts of government that do not reflect our cultural knowledge. The prevailing institutions (norms and values) need to be addressed, understood, and deconstructed when examining governance and its implementation. The separation of powers is a problematic system—one codified on the basis mistrust—creates [sic] a multitude of limitations. An implicit, non-codified separation of powers, based in the Diné concept of trust, adequately reflects traditional concepts of cooperation and integration. Conversely, the current system only works within a model of mistrust and does not foster efficiency or confidence. Judicial review is an essential component to regulate government.[17]

The report acknowledges that the current Western-style structure has had some advantages, foremost among them stability, providing for community peace, and bringing a consistency that can foster economic development. But the report found that economic development, while desirable, must be balanced with other values, and that the national government in Window Rock at times acted contrarily to traditional values and to the will and needs of the people. This situation was found to occur partly because of Window Rock's geographical isolation and the alien Western values built into its structure, and partly because of the inefficiency and unwieldiness of its bureaucracy.

After examining the current Navajo government structure and the idea of having a formal constitution, the report proposes four "Alternative Governance Models," to provide a range of options for applying traditional values to the needs of the twenty-first century.[18] The traditional values focus on living in beauty, or in balance. This includes concern for the economic, social, familial, and environmental well-being of the Navajo Nation. As the author of the third model states, the first of four principles: "clearly safeguarded by historical Diné was an acknowledged ownership of goods and products of labor (however Lockian that appears to be). But more importantly was respect for others use of land and goods delineated by its use" (53). This involved reciprocity, and the responsibility of those with more to help those with less, as the third principle, below, indicates. Hence, all the proposed models express concern for distributive justice:

> Second, a respect for the moral order, that is in extreme cases there were moments of punitive measures meted out, but the rationale for those measures rested on a notion of restoring a sense of harmony among kin. Third, is a respect for the needs of others, to ensure that all needs of others were met as best as they could be by those who have. Fourth was an assurance of reciprocal security—that is one is assured that neighbors, often family, would be ready to protect against any encroachment, physical or spiritual. These four concepts appear to be the motivations of the historical Diné in their survival. Therefore, the four aspects include: rights and protection of property; respect and assurance of civil order; freedom to wealth with responsibilities; and, security from physical and spiritual dangers. Thus a government structure must be able to protect and safeguard these particular traditions of Diné, while also balancing and fulfilling its basic core function (53).

Other balances also needed to be preserved and restored according to tradition, most notably that between the male and female genders, a point directly addressed in two of the models. The report affirms the current functioning of the Navajo court system—none of the proposals suggest changing the judiciary. All of the models propose the need for education to decolonize the thinking of those in government and other institutions, and the people in general.

The Four Options for Revising Navajo Government

The four options the report puts forth range from adjusting the current system of government to totally changing it to returning to historic locally based governance. The first is a status quo model that emphasizes little change but alludes to efficiency in government. It would streamline bureaucracy, improving intergovernmental relationships: "These possible changes, not only should be within the system, but also as a social movement to deconstruct the existing cultural norms among the people and their reliance on the bureaucratic system" (41). This option calls for discussing whether (and if so, how and to what extent) privatization of collectively held land, as a means of promoting wealth generation, would be consistent with Navajo values. This approach asserts the need to move much further with decentralization: "Currently, and in all reality, the central Navajo government holds all real power with little emphasis placed on local governance (as seen with the dismal results of the Local Governance Act). Policy may be formulated which would emphasize local governance without sacrificing instability in the central government" (41).

The second option is a bicameral parliamentary model stressing the integration and cooperation of a traditional and legislative body to form and execute laws and decentralizing power by entrusting the Navajo people with the approval of all laws. The current model would be changed by eliminating the current executive branch and replacing it with an executive headed by a prime minister selected by the Navajo Council. The executive would then appoint a cabinet approved by the council. Elections for the council would be undertaken with a runoff election between the top two vote receivers in the initial voting. Terms would be for six years, with the possibility that incumbents could run for an additional two-year term. After an eight-year term, a council member would have to wait four years before running again, as would a person who was not elected to an additional two-year term after her or his initial six years in office. To maintain male–female balance, half the elected delegates would be men and half women, with a lottery determining which chapters would initially elect representatives of each gender. On completion of each six- or eight-year service, the gender of the chapter representative would switch. The second house would be a house of elders, appointed for life by the executive, whose function would be to advise the government to assist its acting consistently with Navajo values, and that would have no formal power. All laws passed by the council would be taken to the local chapters for approval. Effective channels would need to be constructed between the chapters and the council to maximize political stability. Educating the populace and those in government and the bureaucracy would be necessary to decolonize thinking and debureaucratize administration. This model would be developed over fifteen years.

The Third, Dialectical Option

The third model is a "dialectical model based in Navajo political philosophy," stressing the complete integration of Diné thinking as the premise behind all institutions in the governance system and critically calling into question each aspect of politics, deconstructed and succeeded by Navajo reasoning. Underlying this approach are four principles (50–51). The theory of representation requires full participation, open to all, with "the peoples' voice open to all aspects." "The peoples' will is a unified will that must be represented" in "a reciprocal arrangement that informs the relationship between representative and constituent." Thus "a leader who represents perfectly the will of the people is established." The theory of rights and duties involving reciprocity and equity holds that "there are certain rights, expectations, and duties that one can claim, demand and expect, while other things [*sic*] there is an obligation involved. Thus there is a theory of rights of access to the bounty of *Nahasdzaan Nihima* and *Nihiti'aa Yadilhil*." Notions of property begin with an "implicit recognition or respect of the ownership of others, songs, prayers, stories, material goods, and so forth. Yet, the notion of property here is not one that implies exclusive ownership where one is free to do as she pleases. Rather this concept of property, while under the individual use of one person is recognized as that, but also understood that it can be understood as communal property if certain criteria are fulfilled, such as familial criteria." The theory of the economic order "was that of constrained capitalism, where the onus of wealth was stressed. That is those who accumulated much were expected to be concerned and giving with their wealth to those who did not have much. This is a derivative of k'é, with the understanding that the knowledge and practice brings about both a spirit of constrained development, innovation, while having the struggles of the people at the forefront of any decision."

"The core functions of government derived from the Diné perspective include concern for the economic, social, familial, and environmental well-being of the Navajo Nation. Each of these areas corresponds to traditional notions of balance" (53).

> The purposes of the Navajo Nation are the protection and development of the individual and respect for the dignity of the individual, the democratic exercise of the will of the people, the building of a just and peace-loving society, the furtherance of the prosperity and welfare of the people and guaranteeing of the Fulfillment of the principles, rights, and duties of the Navajo Nation. Education and work are the fundamental processes for guaranteeing these purposes. The purpose of the Navajo Nation is to establish hozhoo [beauty or balance]. Hozhoo takes many forms in its economic, social, governmental, economic, political, educational, and environmental functions. Therefore the government must be able to provide effective governmental services to the people and to meet their dynamic needs (55).

This requires a government based upon trust: "To do so, there must a separation of powers based, not on the logic of distrust, but rather on the logic of trust, implicit trust of the institution and the people who occupy those institutions. This trust is extended so long as the people are able to give that trust status by upholding it through the continued practice of k'é. Thus the separation of powers must be an implicit shared power, not a legally bound separation of powers" (55–56). "Supervisory committees are needed to supervise the agencies and regulatory bodies; these oversight committees must be derived from the local levels. That is, a more democratic regime, than a republican regime. A single elected leader to serve as the voice of the nation, but not to retain much power, power to sign bills into law. Consistent with the Navajo Thinking, there must be a check of power, but not a codified separation of powers" (56):

> There should be a check on the powers of the leader—by the

Council of Elders, who have veto authority over the leader and the Council of the People; however, the Courts of Nahata have check on the powers of the leader, the Council of Elders, and the Council of the People. The leader will have two assistants—a Hozhoojii and Hashkejii Nataanii—these are appointed by the Council of Elders, with nomination from the leader, but confirmed by the Council of the People. The Council of Elders consist of 2 individuals from each agency—one Hozhoojii and one Hashkejii—these are appointed and approved by district, agency, and confirmed by the leader. The Council of the People consists of elected officials from the various electoral districts of the Navajo Nation. The Council of the People has non-voting status for community groups and NGOs, which are appointed by the chapter, districts, and agencies. These people are popularly elected. The Council of the People's acts are then checked by the chapters, the districts, and the agencies (56).

Ultimately, these reforms must be undertaken as a grassroots work, redesigning governance over a period of twelve years and beginning at the chapter level and working up.

The Fourth, Decentralized Option

The fourth proposal is a decentralization model stressing national and community concerns with greater empowerment to social subgroups and agencies. It outlines a government that reflects more fully traditional and customary laws and norms and replaces the president with an eleven-member executive board. The council remains nearly as is, with the exception of adding twelve nonvoting delegates who are specifically dedicated to certain social subgroups and nonprofit organizations. The decentralization will address the gender divide by balancing men, who predominate in positions in the central government, with women, who are predominantly leaders in chapters and the growing numbers of nongovernmental organizations (NGOs). "Our reasoning for this transition is based on Navajo history and current social behavior":

The Navajo Nation historically resembled a parliamentary system and had decentralized political units. We believe that our proposed model would move us back in this direction.

. . . Therefore, we have established four major steps to move our current system of governance from a presidential model to something more like the historic *naachid*. These steps are: 1) moderate the concentration of power in the executive branch; 2) restructure agency councils to balance power between legislative and chapter house members; 3) increase the power of the agency councils and 4) create new mechanisms through which nongovernmental organizations can influence formal governmental processes (63).

We would replace the Office of President and Vice President with an 11 person Executive Board, comprised of five female members, five male members, and the Navajo Nation Speaker who is the rotating chair. The members are elected, two from each of the five agencies, whereas the Speaker is a member of the Navajo Nation Council and therefore represents the interests of both the legislative branch and his or her particular community. Though the Speaker is a member of the 11 person Executive Board, he or she does not have ultimate authority over the rest of the council and therefore is a minor and not controlling member of it. . . . Secondly, the Agencies would gain more autonomy than what they have now. Each Agency addresses different concerns due to the surrounding topography. Therefore, the Chapters would address their concerns at Agency Council, and the Agencies would have more autonomy and more representation since they have elected representatives on the Executive Board.

Thirdly, the 88 Delegates would be elected in the same fashion as they are elected today . . . However, the major difference of the Legislative Branch would be the 12 Non-Voting Members of the Council. So, in total the Council would consist of 100 members. The Non-Voting Members would represent the non-profit sector on the Navajo Nation and the youth of the Nation. Since the youth population is growing at an astonishing rate and the role of women is needed, the implementation of the Non-Voting Members of Council will help eliminate some of the gender and age discrepancies. Lastly, with the removal of the entire Executive Branch, the Committees, Commissions and Divisions would have to be restructured. Therefore, we put into place four Committees:

the Social Committee, the Economic Committee, the Families Committee and the Environmental Committee. Under each Committee, we placed the appropriate Program or Division. For example, under the Environmental Committee, we place the Division of Natural Resources, the Navajo Environmental Protection Agency and the Navajo-Hopi Land Commission. Each Committee would consist of 12 members, which would include ten Delegates, and 2 Non-Voting Members of the Council. The Executive Board would appoint the Committee Members (65–66).

The proposal recommends that implementation take three years.

It will be very interesting to see how far, and in what ways, the Navajo Nation goes in reforming its government. The process of bringing back traditional values to fit present and future needs has been an extended one that has been unfolding in a series of expanding stages. The U.S. government, wishing to have a single leader and body to deal with, imposed a chairman-centered form of elected government, centralized at the national level, that is almost completely opposite of the traditional Diné participatory band government of regional associations and no national government. In 1989, a partial decentralization was undertaken, but it occurred almost entirely within the national government, instituting three branches of government with separation of powers. In 1998, a process of decentralization of some functions was initiated, with ongoing adjustments that have developed slowly and brought only limited control of governance back to the people in the chapters, while services remain bogged down in bureaucracy. To further and accelerate the process, the current deliberations we have described are now in motion. What the Navajos develop may also provide lessons and guidance for other nations struggling with inappropriate government systems.

Reviving Inclusiveness at Southern Ute

The Southern Ute Indian Tribe, consistent with the inclusive participatory decision making of its traditional bands, has also moved in stages to increase tribal-member involvement in government. First, in the late 1990s, the tribal council increased the number of general tribal meetings from quarterly to once a month. Shortly thereafter, it instituted monthly sessions where members with concerns or complaints about tribal government and services could meet individually with the tribal council.[19]

Next, in 1999, the Southern Utes became the first Indian nation to participate in a project, funded by the U.S. Department of Health and Human Services (HHS) Children's Bureau, to build coordination among social services that affected children, with ongoing community input. At the request of the tribal chair and council, a consulting team from the Social Research Institute at the University of Utah was brought in to help facilitate a design team. The team included administrators from a wide range of tribal services because, at least indirectly, all services and the community members they interact with have an impact on children. Community consultants, including former social service recipients and elders, collaborated in building teamwork and responsiveness to community needs and input among social services employees. The goal was to provide culturally relevant supportive and integrated services to ensure that all Southern Ute children are successful in school and in life.[20] The Southern Ute Indian Tribal Information Services Department, building upon interagency cooperation and coordination that began under the design team in 2000, called a meeting of Southern Ute and La Plata County, Colorado, social service agencies in February 2006 to renew and expand a 2003 memorandum of understanding, which included bringing in the community mental health center as a collaborator. The meeting focused on instituting working together as a consistent policy, the need to create a service directory, and the desire of nontribal entities to increase tribal awareness of efforts to create a La Plata County Health District. Thus inclusiveness and cooperation among tribal agencies continued to foster collaboration with outside entities for more appropriate and effective delivery of services to Southern Utes.

In 2001, when there was a heated dispute over who should lead the Southern Ute Indian Tribe's most important spiritual ceremony, the annual Sun Dance, including when it should be held and how it should be undertaken, the tribal chairman, for the first time, called for the Sun Dancers and any other interested community members to meet to resolve the problem.[21] After three contentious meetings, the issues were worked out. The previous Sun Dance chief resigned. Another experienced Sun Dance chief agreed to run the ceremony according to the wishes of the assembled Sun Dance community for one year, until a new Sun Dance chief could be chosen. After the meetings, people on each side of the major set of issues that had been discussed in the sessions, out of concern that they had been too harsh, went to some members of the other side to voice that concern. Thus, some significant reconciliation occurred before the year's Sun Dance, which ran smoothly. At the end of the ceremony, a new Sun Dance chief was announced. The new Sun Dance chief ran the 2002 ceremony, which ended with more harmony than the community had experienced in several years.

One widely experienced problem in instituting processes for reapplying traditional inclusive participatory values that arose at Southern Ute was that even though increased community involvement may bring tribal governance more into agreement with the basic mores of the culture, it takes time to firmly establish the new ways of doing so. Until that occurs, a new tribal chair or council majority may not appreciate them and may eliminate them. That occurred at Southern Ute when, even while initiating the design team, a new tribal chair led the council to discontinue monthly general meetings. However, that chairman was recalled by a vote of the tribe because he was seen as too unresponsive to the membership. His replacement returned momentum to expanding community participation by initiating the meetings to resolve the Sun Dance concerns. The Southern Ute Tribe has since begun using focus groups to provide member input on tribal issues (which also has become a regular practice at Navajo Nation) and in spring 2004 began holding "open forum" general meetings with no prior agenda to allow tribal members to raise concerns with the tribal council as the members see fit.[22]

Yurok and Alaska–British Columbia Inclusiveness

In another example of returning to inclusive participation, the Yurok Tribe in 2005 undertook a comprehensive, long-range Tribal Transportation Plan, "Taking Back a Traditional Trail." Under a grant from the California Department of Transportation, the tribe initiated an inclusive discussion process that involved tribal members, community residents, and other relevant stakeholders to identify community priorities, unmet needs, and the unique circumstances relating to tribal transportation.[23]

It was reported in May 2006 that a few Native nations in Alaska and in Western British Columbia have adopted the Bahá í Faith "consultation" method of decision making, which is essentially a consensus decision-making process.[24] This method requires an elected council that is trained to listen respectfully to all sides and views on an issue as expressed by community members, either in open community forums or by representatives of different ways of approaching an issue. Only after carefully hearing the full range of concerns on a question will the council move to craft a policy. It attempts to do so as inclusively as possible, balancing the full range of concerns in any decision. Policies can later be reviewed by the same process to take into account changing circumstances, or difficulties created or inadequately addressed, by the earlier action.

The Application of the Indigenous Leadership Interactive System by the Comanche and Three Other Nations

In February 1990, the Comanche Nation of Oklahoma began an especially interesting attempt to overcome problems of culturally unsuitable government by applying traditional values with contemporary means. The nation implemented the Indigenous Leadership Interactive System (ILIS—previously Tribal Issues Management System, or TIMS), a participatory strategic planning process that allowed the Comanche to re-create traditional ways of building consensus and maintaining harmony in the community.[25] This experience with the use of a particular dialoguing method in a single setting has implications for tribal people elsewhere and for renewing inclusive participatory democracy in forms that fit their particular traditions and circumstances.

Typical of most tribes in the United States, the Comanche felt themselves divided and often paralyzed in deciding major issues because of the clash between their traditional culture and the premises of their contemporary government processes, which were based on modern European American understandings. In order to overcome the problems caused by that cultural dissonance, the Oklahoma Comanche community, with the assistance of Americans for Indian Opportunity (AIO), Oklahomans for Indian Opportunity (OIO), the Department of Communication at George Mason University, and the consulting firm Christakis & Associates, decided to employ a collaborative process for tribal decision making by applying ILIS. As long as the Comanche used ILIS to create consensus on community issues, the process made significant contributions toward overcoming gridlock in tribal decision making and in initiating a beginning to restoring tribal harmony. In instances where neither ILIS nor any other method of broadly inclusive decision making was used, the nation continued to have difficulty reaching decisions. When the Comanche stopped using the process at the tribal level, considerable disharmony returned to the community. The Comanche experience with ILIS suggests that a process of inclusive participatory decision making, if appropriately designed and applied for a specific tribe or group and its unique circumstances, can be useful for other tribes in overcoming many of the remaining problems of colonialism if the process is used long enough to firmly establish it. The Comanche Nation is one of four tribes in Oklahoma that initially applied the ILIS process, and it has gone considerably further with the process than have any of the others.[26]

The Comanche Experience to 1990
The Comanche experience with tribal government is unique yet representative of the general pattern we have described. The Comanche people call themselves *Numunuh*, "The People."[27] Their present name was given them by the Spanish, who used a word derived from the Ute *Komantcia*, meaning "enemy" or, more precisely, "anyone who wants to fight me all the time."[28] Anthropologists consider the Comanche to be members of the Shoshonean group of peoples, which includes the Shoshone, Ute, Paiute, and Bannock tribes. Prior to 1700, the Comanche were mountain people living in what are now the states of Wyoming and Montana, although there is some speculation that their living area may have extended out onto the Great Plains.[29] Little is known of their history and customs before the first reported contact with them by the Spanish in 1705, but it is believed that the Comanche lived in small, autonomous family bands.[30] With the coming of the horse, life on the plains became feasible and the Comanche, at first alone, and then supported by their Kiowa allies, became "Lords of the Southern Plains" living in bands across what is now Kansas, Colorado, New Mexico, Oklahoma, and Texas.[31] They were extremely skilled horse handlers, adept at buffalo hunting, and masterful as warriors.

Social life involved a balance between strong autonomy for the individual and participation in the cooperative life of the people.[32] In terms of social organization, the Comanche were organized into a number of bands ranging from fifty to fifteen hundred people (the mid-nineteenth century total population is estimated at between twenty and thirty thousand).[33] Within each band, important civil decisions were made by consensus at council meetings of the men (women occasionally attended meetings and spoke on rare occasions).[34] Elder men, respected for their wisdom in community affairs, generosity, kindness, and, to a lesser degree, courage and physical fitness, had considerable influence. The most well-thought-of among them would be considered leaders, and one would become the band leader, or in European American terminology, the Peace Chief of the band.

There was no formal process for choosing the band leader; he simply became leader by consensus over time and would cease to hold that position if he lost the respect of the community. On matters of importance, he had no authority to decide anything but could influence decision making and mediate (but not arbitrate) disputes. His main job was to facilitate finding and maintaining consensus and harmony for the community. On minor daily matters, he could make decisions, but anyone who did not like a decision ignored it, and if enough people did so, he would no longer be a leader. Military leaders, who were separate from and subordinate to civil leaders, did have considerable dictatorial power when leading a war party. But they could only become and remain war leaders as long as men would join, and remain with, their parties.

These limits to the authority of leaders, combined with a strong belief in and practice of individual autonomy, did not lead to disruption in Comanche affairs. Practically, people needed one another, and the culture emphasized collaboration based upon mutual respect. Public opinion and consensus were major forces in a society with a strong emphasis upon honor. To a high degree, Comanches valued themselves by the extent to which they could contribute to the well-being of the community and be recognized for doing so. In the century and a half that followed the Lords of the Southern Plains period, many Comanches were adopted after having been captured as children on raids. Therefore, active participation in the community, rather than birth, defined one as a Comanche. Even today, being a "real Comanche" is an active relational concern and not just a biological matter, as is the case generally among Native Americans.[35]

The encroachment of whites onto the Great Plains effectively ended traditional plains life for the Comanche by 1875, when they were confined to a reservation of close to three million acres in southwest Oklahoma with their Kiowa and Apache allies.[36] The reservation was disbanded in 1901, and each Comanche was given 160 acres.[37] Although Comanche life and culture has undergone considerable change since 1875, the relational sense of "being Comanche" and a strong cooperative sense of community have persisted along with other elements of the traditional culture.[38]

Comanche governance has also continued in a way that is particular to the tribe yet consistent with the general pattern of tribal governance in the United States. Following their placement on a single reservation, the Kiowa, Comanche, and Apache tribes combined efforts to lobby for economic and other interests through the Kiowa-Comanche-Apache Business Committee, until the Comanches withdrew in 1966 to form the

Comanche Nation. (The Kiowa-Comanche-Apache Business Committee was largely disbanded with separation in 1966 but continues in a smaller role to handle matters concerning lands and businesses jointly owned by the three tribes).[39]

The Comanche Nation was formally established in 1969, under the constitution in force at the time ILIS was being applied, to allow the Comanches to manage their own funds and programs and participate more actively in the politics of Indian affairs and in the Anglo-American economy.[40] At that time, the Comanche largely adopted the previous BIA-style Kiowa-Comanche-Apache constitution to their own situation.[41] To be a member of the Comanche Tribe as of 1991, a person must be a direct descendent of a Comanche who received an original allotment of reservation land and must possess 25 percent Comanche blood. In 1991, the Comanche population, which numbered 8,690—the majority of whom were younger than forty years old—was divided geographically.[42] Approximately forty-five hundred Comanches lived in southwest Oklahoma, primarily in four communities: Lawton, Apache, Cache, and Walters. There were also sizable concentrations of Comanche in Texas and California.[43]

The governing body of the Comanche was the tribal council, which consisted of all tribal members eighteen years old or older. In 1991, there were approximately 6,100 eligible voters.[44] The tribal council elected seven members at large to staggered terms on the Comanche Business Committee. These include a chairman, vice chairman, and secretary treasurer, who also served as officers of the tribal council. Terms were for three years, and an individual could serve only two consecutive terms. Nominations for officers and other members of the Business Committee were made at the annual tribal council meeting in April. Polling places were provided for primary and runoff elections in the four communities, and absentee ballots were made available upon request for tribal members living outside the tribal area. The members of the Business Committee could be removed by the vote of any officially called Comanche meeting (such as a Business Committee meeting) at which 250 or more tribal members were present, and the Business Committee was required to receive the approval of a tribal council meeting to make any long-term commitment of tribal resources.[45]

The Business Committee's primary role was to regulate some important aspects of Anglo-Comanche economic relations, but it did not play a major part in directly regulating Comanche-to-Comanche relations.[46]

The committee was a combination executive and legislative body that oversaw a staff headed by an appointed tribal administrator, who managed the daily operation of tribal programs. The tribe had an annual budget of more than $3 million in fiscal year 1990 from a number of federal programs and tribal sources, including a bingo operation. The nation operated a number of social service programs (including a jobs program, a family violence program, aid to the elderly, and burial assistance), the Indian Child Welfare Program (offering counseling, crisis intervention, and foster homes recruitment), a food distribution program (providing U.S. Department of Agriculture [USDA] commodities), the Home Improvement Program, the Job Training Partnership Act program, a senior citizens center, the Community Health Representative Program, a nonemergency transport system, and a substance abuse program. The nation did not have sole ownership of any business in 1991 but shared ownership of two businesses with the Kiowa and the Apache: the Native Sun Winter Park and KCA Apparel, a clothing manufacturer.

The Business Committee's main problem in carrying out economic projects, aside from difficulty in arranging adequate financing, was resistance to forming and maintaining enough consensus to support long-term development.[47] This was partly because of continuing difficulties many Comanches had in acquiring sufficient resources for everyday life, but it was also because of the inappropriateness of the BIA-style government form for Comanche culture and society. The primary problem was the elected nature of the council as a body working separately from the various Comanche communities. This difficulty was compounded by electing all the council members at large, so there was no direct representation of the geographically dispersed communities. Foster reported that "there is considerable alienation among Comanches with respect to taking an active part in tribal government (as opposed to talking about tribal politics). Rumors of scandal and wrongdoing by tribal officials are common. In a recent election for chairman, less than one-fourth of the eligible voters cast ballots."[48] Moreover, because the use of elections with winners and losers runs counter to traditional Comanche culture, "there is a tendency for tribal leaders voted out of office to spend the rest of their lives being obstructive to leaders in power, no matter who the current leaders are. . . . These dynamics are not unique to Comanches, but are present in every tribal community attempting to make these imposed institutional structures work for them."[49]

The Indigenous Leadership Management System

ILIS was developed over two years as a collaborative effort involving AIO, OIO, and George Mason University, who met with Native Americans from a number of tribes. ILIS is based on Interactive Management (IM), a computer-assisted group-design process that identifies and resolves complex issues through consensus.[50] The collaborators worked during 1989 and 1990 to adapt IM for use with tribes, calling the resulting product Indigenous Leadership Interactive System.[51] The decision to develop ILIS was made after several successful experiences from 1987 to 1989 in applying IM to tribal concerns such as economic development and long-range planning.[52]

Following the initial development of ILIS, the Comanche Business Committee invited AIO and OIO to assist the tribe in setting up an ILIS process as a complement to its normal governance procedures. The invitation from the Business Committee and the active support from the tribal chairman were extremely important for legitimizing the process. Instituting a design process of this kind is likely to be seen as a threat to the status quo and opposed by the tribal leadership unless the leadership understands the advantages of introducing the process and is actively involved with it as it is carried out. If the process develops successfully with the support of the council, it can strengthen the position of the members. As harmony and consensus are created in the nation and tribal members no longer are, or feel, left out of the political process, complaints about tribal government and officials can be reduced even as they gain positive support. Moreover, as tribal members become empowered by participation to take charge of creating their own future and to focus less on receiving services, they tend to expand tribal resources. Infighting on the part of tribal members tends to give way to a return to focusing upon how each person can contribute to his or her community and make the tribe strong again.[53] Evidence supporting this analysis is given by the Comanche experience with ILIS and is well supported by the extensive existing experience with workplace participation.[54]

There are of course risks as well as opportunities for Business Committee or tribal council members in deciding to initiate a process like ILIS, just as there are with the making of any political decision (or nondecision). If the process works badly, its supporters may be blamed. If it works well, it might give rise to new leaders who challenge and even replace members of the committee or council, even if they support the new process. However, supporting a politically successful program usually enhances one's position. In the Comanche case, three members of the Business Committee who were not involved in the ILIS process were replaced by tribal members who were involved and had become active advocates for it, particularly at the local level, where they built strong bases of support as representatives of their local communities. (One of these committee members later resigned for health reasons, leaving two active ILIS participants on the Business Committee.) In addition, the more harmonious atmosphere created by the ILIS process was a major factor in the election of the first tribal chair since ILIS's initiation—also the first tribal chair in a decade to be reelected for a second term.

A related point is that both the principle of inclusion upon which ILIS is based and the necessity for developing broad support for it throughout the nation make it essential that all identifiable groups within the tribe be represented in the process from the beginning. Failure to be inclusive destroys the integrity of the process, and if this is not corrected, such failure will usually undermine the process's legitimacy and lead to its demise (as can be seen in numerous workplace cases where improperly executed employee participation has been short-lived). Just how to ensure that the process is and remains inclusive is a question that needs to be answered according to the particular situation. Inclusiveness was provided for in the Comanche case by inviting to the first session representatives from the four traditional rural Comanche communities (Lawton, Apache, Cache, and Walters), the newer urban Comanche communities, members of each living generation, tribal staff and employees, former council members, and members of old political divisions (e.g., those who voted "yes" and those who voted "no" on whether to establish a tribal government separate from the Kiowas and Apaches).

The Stages of ILIS

In general terms, the ILIS process begins with a problem-definition phase that enables the nation to develop a deeper understanding of its current situation. It then moves on to a second design phase that provides the tribe with a clearer vision of its direction for the future. In a third phase, participants proceed to define activities to bridge the gap between current reality and the desired future. This is followed by the assignment of roles and responsibilities for carrying out those activities. In this way, the tribe can create a vision of its own future and then empower itself to become that vision. The process is an ongoing one: in a sizable nation, it moves back and forth between general meetings, which usually involve members of the tribal council (or Business Committee in the Comanche case) and selected community representatives, and local meetings in each participating community, so that the results of all the forums are aggregated into a common vision statement and program. Once the first round of planning is completed, the tribe begins a new cycle to update its vision and program or to extend planning to new areas of concern.

ILIS is based on facilitated group interaction guided by trained group facilitators and supported by computer assistance. The process is designed to aid group participants with diverse viewpoints to get below the surface of discussion to explore the deeper logic of issues. During each of the phases of group work, ILIS takes the group through several stages, beginning with an idea-generation session in which responses are provided to a triggering question.[55] The triggering question, which is carefully worded to stimulate ideas about the primary issue of the participants' concern, is chosen prior to the beginning of the design sessions by the participants with the help of the facilitators. It is important that the participants develop the triggering question themselves so that the process is truly theirs and does not result in their being intentionally or accidentally manipulated by others in directions different from the collective will of the group.

In the opening stage and all of those that follow, the group sits in a circle, and each person in turn has the opportunity to respond or to pass, until everyone feels that they have contributed all that they wish at this stage.[56] With this process, each person becomes the center of the circle in turn, so that all have an equal chance to participate without having to fight to be heard, and all statements are valued as a contribution to the overall discussion. All of the ideas presented are recorded on large sheets of paper and posted on the wall for everyone to see.

Idea generation is followed by a round in which people can clarify their responses. In order to select the most important ideas for further group work, unit voting by secret ballot takes place, in which each participant votes for the five ideas she or he perceives as most important.[57] In the final stage, a computer-assisted methodology called Interpretive Structural Modeling helps the group explore the relationship between those ideas that received the most votes.[58] In both the problem-definition and the vision phases of group work, a structural map is developed that shows how the ideas influence one another. In the options phase, a field of possible activities is produced that consists of categories of options from which participants are asked to select those actions that are most appropriate for the purposes they have defined. Finally, key actors are identified and assigned responsibility for carrying out the options that the group has selected.

Before this kind of consensus decision-making process can be undertaken successfully with any group, sufficient team building needs to take place in order for participants to feel adequately connected to the group and its purpose, so that they will trust one another and the process enough to participate openly and freely.[59] Thus, as the opening part of an ILIS session with tribal people, a locally appropriate ceremony is carried out. This is the first of several mechanisms that recognize the crucial role tribal identity and values can play in discovering new ways out of complex and deeply rooted problems. Gift giving and public recognition of service in the interest of the tribe are appropriate additions that add to strengthening tribal identity. Blessings, pipe ceremonies, and prayers go much deeper than the typical greeting or statement of welcome. For tribal participants, attention is drawn to their common bond and all that it means. If outsiders are involved, the ceremony tends to elevate the status of tribal identity and values and places participants in a mode of mutual respect for one another.

The bonding necessary for a successful process can also be enhanced by calling on each participant to track her or his kinship ties to the rest of the group. Cross-links between individuals and their inherent relational obligations immediately begin drawing the group together and help make tribal values and tribal identity the focus of the group's attention. Often the strongest component of the tribal vision statement developed by the process is the continuation of "the people" (the *Numunuh* for the Comanche). Group identity is synonymous with being tribal, and where it is strong, preservation of the group and its value system become all-important.[60] The reiteration of kinship terms calls forth those values and practices that set the group apart and immediately bonds the group with a common cause.

In addition, asking participants to express what being a member of the nation means to them brings forth a deep affirmation of cultural values, often expressed subliminally. These values, if captured and clarified, become a useful reference point during all the subsequent steps of the process. In ILIS sessions, as much as one-third of the time spent together is absorbed with these preliminary activities, whose chief function is to bind the participants together into a single collaborative group. This amount of time is far greater than is the practice with other issue-management models, but it provides extremely crucial groundwork where participants have suffered from alienation and cultural dissonance. It tends to create a spirit of optimism about the potential for overcoming the immediate set of problems, given all that the participants and the tribe have overcome in the past. It is important to implement these bonding activities at the beginning of the work, but it is especially important to do so before the period of generating options for dealing with problems that the group has identified.

Key Roles in the Process

In many nations, much of the discussion that takes place during the early stages of public meetings involves strategizing by various participants to position themselves and establish a role in the group. This is partly a reflection of the importance of honor and of the relational sense of identity of traditional tribal cultures. It is also a reflection of the importance of feeling in Native American cultures and the fact that many people feel strongly about the issues under consideration (or about the background issues related to the discussion). Until they have the opportunity to vent their feelings, many participants will not be able to engage in open discussion and consensus building. Because ILIS forums separate the generation of issues from the generation of new options for dealing with those issues, and because each participant is awarded an opportunity to address the group in turn, posturing and venting become integrated with issue generation and become acceptable parts of the process that do not interfere with the more difficult generation of alternatives that takes place later on in the forum.

Two supporting roles are extremely important in ILIS forums. First, a tribal elder or visionary leader interjects statements, such as a historical overview, from time to time. This keeps the sights of the group high as the participants deal with a myriad of complex local problems that are very close to their everyday lives. These vision statements provide periodic reminders of the achievements and perseverance of the tribe and the meaning of tribal membership and tradition. They work to maintain the momentum of the session and are particularly helpful in preserving a sense of unity and purpose immediately before voting on prioritized issues or proposed activities.

Second, the facilitators play a key role in empowering the participants to take ownership of the process, for the success of ILIS in developing consensus and harmony rests on the ability of the participants to fully and actively come together as a unit, with full respect for the diversity of views and experiences of the members of the group. This is a delicate task, for the facilitators need to be active enough both to make sure the participants are clear about how the process works and to provide adequate guidance to keep the process proper and in balanced motion without ever being perceived as controlling it or as partial to any person, position, or outcome. This means, especially, that outside facilitators who serve initially as consultants to begin the process truly act as empowerers and quickly let go of the work, training local people to replace them so that the process fully belongs to the tribe.[61] Similarly, outside facilitators, while requiring the invitation of the tribal council or its equivalent, need to be clear that they are acting as consultants to the nation as a whole (and the participants as a group) and not to the members of the council as individuals.

The underlying point is that the dialoguing system must be established and operated in a way that gives ownership of it to the participants. There are numerous cases of supposedly participatory decision making that have failed to meet their potential because inappropriate forms or personnel were used or because appropriate participatory attitudes and skills were not developed. Even worse are instances in which pseudoparticipatory processes have been applied in deliberate attempts to manipulate people.[62] However, appropriate care in establishing and maintaining the discussion system can lead to very positive results in empowering the group and the larger community to meet concerns in ways that are extremely representative of all who are involved. Because the process is based upon mutual respect, and each participant is given a chance to be truly heard and to have his or her concerns included in the deliberations in very supportive ways, the tendency of this kind of interaction is to promote increasing levels of discussion, and it generates greater numbers of views in an extremely civil discourse that tends to reduce antagonism and infighting. Moreover, because the focus of the dialogue is on mutual problem solving, rather than on fighting for position, the process tends to be extremely creative as it encourages participants to react positively to, and build upon, one another's ideas (i.e., to produce synergy). Such a process tends to build community harmony, but not in the sense of limiting the range of expression or of channeling discourse along narrow lines. To the contrary, it tends to produce a polyphony of many diverse voices by working positively and creatively with conflict to harmonize the interests of each, so far as is possible, for the well-being of all.[63]

The Comanche Experience with the Indigenous Leadership Interactive System

The first Comanche ILIS session was held at Lawton, Oklahoma, in February 1990.[64] A broadly representative group of fifteen active participants supported by fourteen observers and nine staff members took part in the two-and-a-half-day meeting.[65] The deliberations began with a focus on the question, "What critical issues do you anticipate for the Comanche Tribe during the next decade?" The initial idea-generation session produced fifty-two ideas, from which twenty-one were selected in the unit voting process. Discussion about the relationship among these issues resulted in a critical issues map (see fig. 1). The item of greatest concern, the "trust period," involved a complex of problems that was created by the structures and arrangements, including form of government, that the U.S. government imposed on the Comanche Nation prior to the termination of the reservation and extending into the 1960s. The next two items of importance followed largely from the first: that is, the problems with the current Comanche constitutional structure and the difficulty the leadership experienced in defining their government role. The critical issues map revealed that many of the concerns that are often points of conflict in the community are primarily symptoms of the trust period difficulties (which the ILIS process had been initiated to overcome).

The meeting went on to generate thirty-nine proposed options and initiatives for dealing with the issues. Those that were perceived by the participants to be most important were superimposed on the critical issues map to highlight the objectives of each of the initiatives. Finally, sixteen key organizations and individuals were identified to carry out the initiatives.

As the closing comments of the participants make clear, the first Comanche experience with the ILIS process was extremely successful in building a spirit of collaboration and harmony—a unity based upon mutual respect. As one of the tribal elders said, "[W]e managed to disagree without being disagreeable," and it was generally appreciated that the disagreements, the differences in perspective, contributed significantly to the generation of better ideas. The session created a sense of vision among the participants as to the future of the tribe and produced a set of concrete plans to begin to realize that vision.

The process served as a vehicle for reestablishing Comanche values in several ways. This was accomplished, first, by the fact that ILIS consensus decision making expresses traditional values about discourse and

Fig. 1: Critical Issues Map (with Superposition of Options)

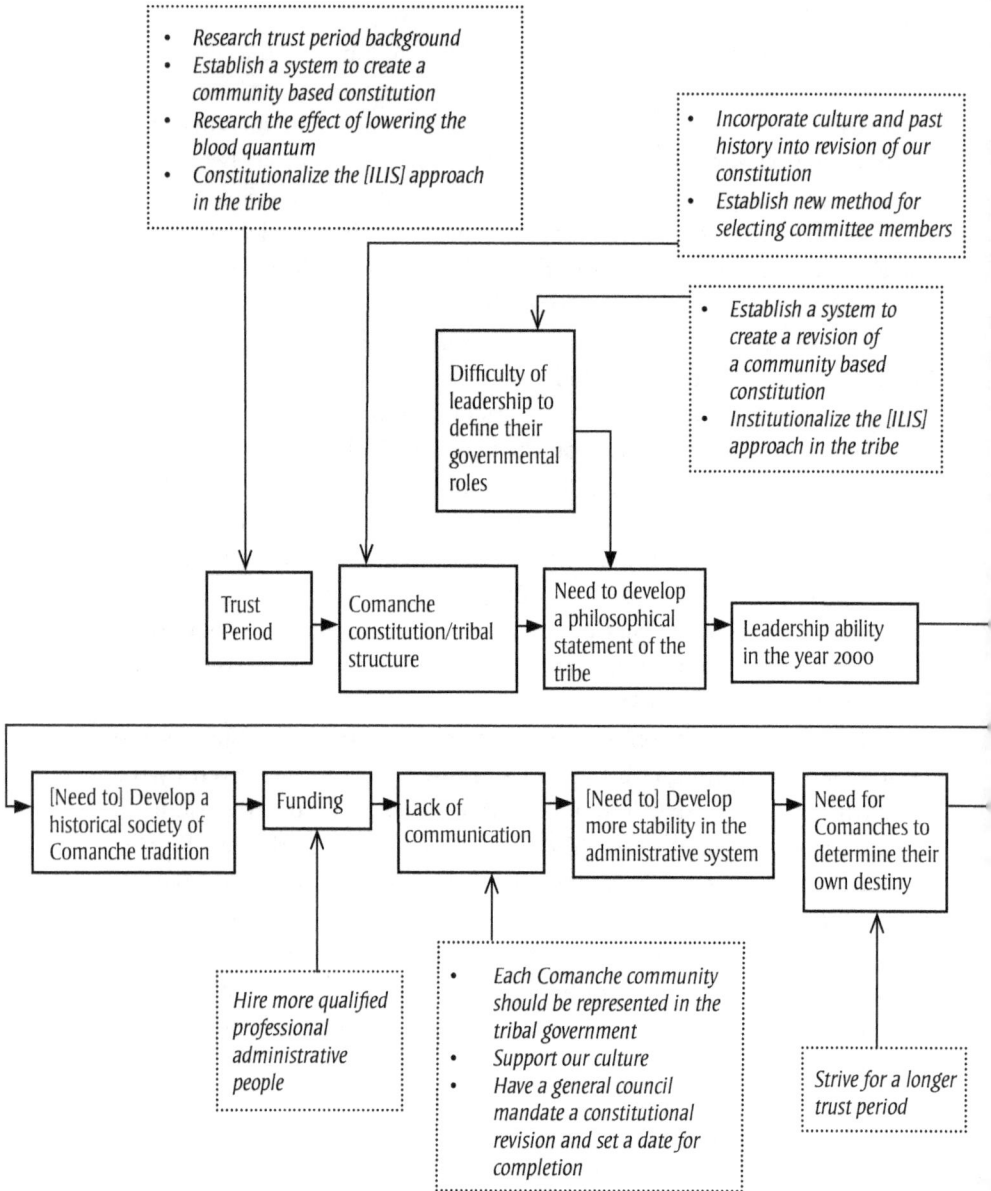

- Research trust period background
- Establish a system to create a community based constitution
- Research the effect of lowering the blood quantum
- Constitutionalize the [ILIS] approach in the tribe

- Incorporate culture and past history into revision of our constitution
- Establish new method for selecting committee members

- Establish a system to create a revision of a community based constitution
- Institutionalize the [ILIS] approach in the tribe

Difficulty of leadership to define their governmental roles

Trust Period

Comanche constitution/tribal structure

Need to develop a philosophical statement of the tribe

Leadership ability in the year 2000

[Need to] Develop a historical society of Comanche tradition

Funding

Lack of communication

[Need to] Develop more stability in the administrative system

Need for Comanches to determine their own destiny

Hire more qualified professional administrative people

- Each Comanche community should be represented in the tribal government
- Support our culture
- Have a general council mandate a constitutional revision and set a date for completion

Strive for a longer trust period

- *Establish a program for youth/elderly to exchange ideas*
- *Create a Comanche historical society by using volunteer elders*

Continue periodic reviews and amend constitution as needed

Need for restricting expenditure to budget items approved by tribe

Continue periodic reviews and amend constitution as needed

Reevaluate five-year restrictions

Need for changing the size of the governing body

Keeping our culture intact

Understanding how to work as a unit in the tribal government as a Comanche people

Lowering the blood quantum

Need to re-evaluate five-year restrictions on transactions by governing body

Conflict between committees

Need to develop an economic base

[Need for] More interest in minerals and royalties

[Need to] Develop system to create tribal jobs as a "career"

LEGEND

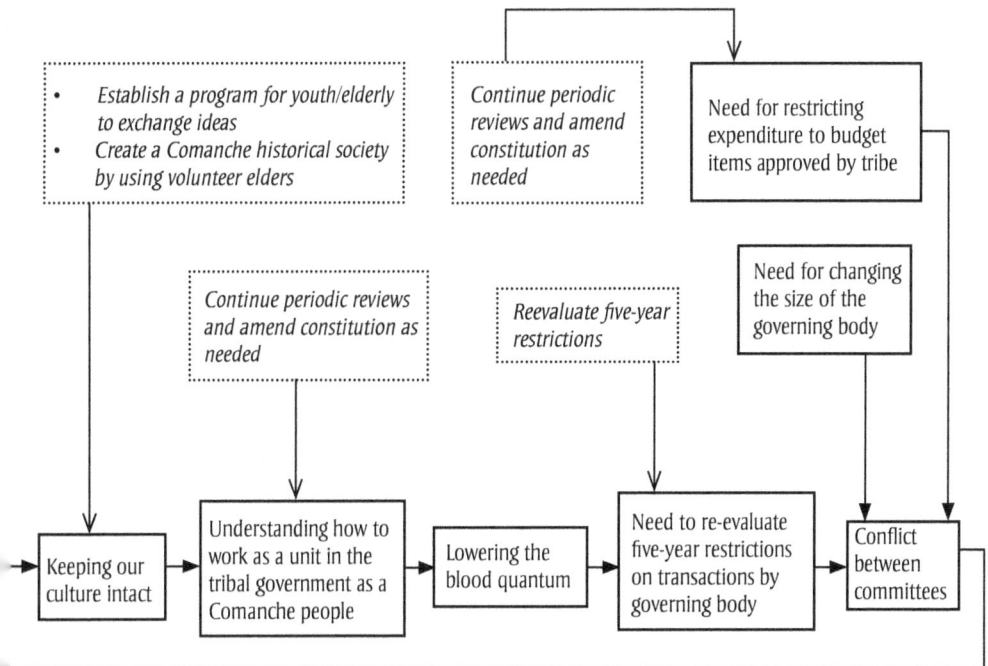

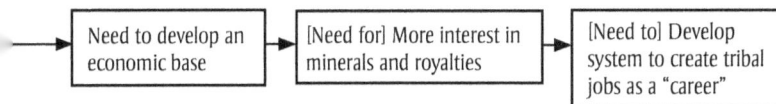

Plain text statements in closed boxes represent critical issues faced by the Comanche Tribe during the next decade. Their relationship is indicated by an arrow that indicates "should be of deeper concern" to the tribe. Issues on the left are deeper concern than those to their right.

Italicized items in dashed boxes represent options for dealing with the critical issues faced by the tribe. The relationship of the options to the critical issues is indicated by an arrow that indicates "helps resolve."

governance. "We rediscovered the joy of working together and valuing everyone's contribution. . . . We discovered the Comanche version of *demosophia*, or collective wisdom, the wisdom of kinsmen, which for us has always been the locus of true leadership, as expressed in persons who manifest that wisdom in their words and behavior."[66] Second, the enthusiasm for the renewal of traditional ways experienced in ILIS generated proposals to incorporate the process more widely in the discussion of community affairs and to revise the Comanche constitution. Third, it became clear that preserving traditional culture, including the Comanche language, is a function of tribal governance. A number of projects were initiated to work toward that end, including the establishment of a program for youth and elders to exchange ideas and the creation of a Comanche historical society.

The February ILIS session revealed an underlying circle of concern composed of three main areas that were intimately related to all the important issues in Comanche communities. First is the question of identity. Who are we and what will it mean to be a Comanche by the twenty-first century? How does the blood quantum requirement for tribal membership relate to who we are? Second is the issue of government and constitution. How do we institutionally structure ourselves so that our institutions make sense in Comanche terms? Third is the problem of communication/participation/contribution. How can we enable every person in our community to make a positive contribution to the life of the tribe by being both responsive and responsible? Not being able to contribute positively makes tribal people crazy and circles back around to negatively affect self-esteem and identity. ILIS has given the Comanche a way to address these central issues both in terms of process and concrete initiatives that have extended from the first meeting through the entire unfolding of ILIS meetings that have taken place to date.

The March and May 1991 Meetings
Following the February 1990 planning session, OIO, in collaboration with AIO, worked with the Comanche Nation to obtain funding from the Administration for Native Americans to train a Comanche facilitation team over seventeen months to conduct community meetings and tribal forums using the ILIS process. That training commenced at a pair of meetings, held on March 26–28, 1991, and May 13–15, 1991.[67] The spring 1991 sessions focused on the tribal governance concerns that were raised at the first planning session. The objective of these follow-up

sessions was to identify major barriers to community participation in Comanche tribal governance and to develop a plan for overcoming those barriers. A broadly representative group of sixteen active participants and ten supportive observers representing the various Comanche communities and the Business Committee took part in these discussions.

In answering the triggering question, "What are the barriers to greater participation in Comanche tribal governance?," the group at the March meeting generated sixty-four statements of problems of various kinds. Some of these involved attitudes, such as "a feeling that I cannot make a difference." Several statements concerned social problems, such as "influx of drugs and alcohol abuse." A number of statements referred to communications and educational difficulties, such as "no communication mechanisms in place to pass on information" and "lack of knowledge about tribal issues." A number of the statements focused upon structural barriers, including "inappropriate form of government laid out in the constitution." The map that the group produced showing the relationships among these barriers placed this latter item as the primary barrier to greater participation in tribal governance (see fig. 2). Two other leading barriers that are partially a result of the inappropriate form of government are "the lack of communication between leadership and tribal members" and "inadequate leadership." The problems that were perceived as resulting primarily from the three just mentioned were "failure to get involved" and "conflict between tribal members."

At the March and May meetings, the participants generated a list of ninety-nine options to deal with the problems, from which they selected twenty-nine actions for which specific groups and individuals were given responsibility in order to begin the first steps in revising the process of tribal governance (see fig. 3). Some of these were simple actions, such as "posting the tribal agenda" and encouraging tribal members "to read the constitution." Others were more complex, including "form a committee to get feedback on the constitution" and "developing a tribal vision statement." All but two of the options selected were objectives to be accomplished within a year. In general, the planning sessions identified ten major areas for action to be developed in three stages.

The initial stage was to focus on problem solving. Doing so entailed expanding the ILIS discussions through several measures: inviting "known" faction leaders to small group problem-solving sessions; requesting the Business Committee to organize a "Comanche vision commission" to develop a community-based vision statement; set goals and

Fig. 2: Influence Map of Major Barriers to Community Participation in Comanche Tribal Governance

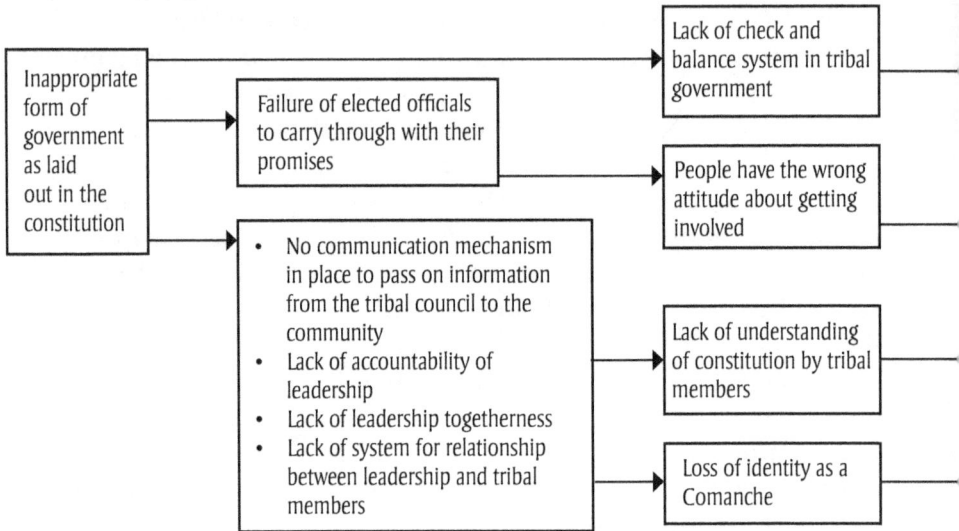

```
┌──────────────┐                                    ┌────────────────────┐
│ Inappropriate│                                    │ Lack of check and  │
│ form of      │   ┌─────────────────────┐          │ balance system in  │
│ government   │──▶│ Failure of elected  │          │ tribal government  │
│ as laid      │   │ officials to carry  │          └────────────────────┘
│ out in the   │   │ through with their  │          ┌────────────────────┐
│ constitution │   │ promises            │          │ People have the    │
└──────────────┘   └─────────────────────┘          │ wrong attitude     │
                                                     │ about getting      │
                   ┌─────────────────────────────┐  │ involved           │
                   │ • No communication          │  └────────────────────┘
                   │   mechanism in place to     │
                   │   pass on information from  │  ┌────────────────────┐
                   │   the tribal council to the │  │ Lack of            │
                   │   community                 │  │ understanding of   │
                   │ • Lack of accountability of │  │ constitution by    │
                   │   leadership                │  │ tribal members     │
                   │ • Lack of leadership        │  └────────────────────┘
                   │   togetherness              │  ┌────────────────────┐
                   │ • Lack of system for        │  │ Loss of identity   │
                   │   relationship between      │  │ as a Comanche      │
                   │   leadership and tribal     │  └────────────────────┘
                   │   members                   │
                   └─────────────────────────────┘
```

objectives for the tribe; and have Business Committee members participate at all levels of the issues-management process, including having community members invite the tribal council to an open-issues workshop.

Once sufficient community involvement was attained, the second stage of more particular projects was to be inaugurated. This involved a number of projects in the areas of constitutional education and discussion, development of internal and external media, cogenerational outreach, cultural enrichment, staff development, development of enhanced ability to tap external resources, and continued development of tribal involvement. After the process of constitutional education and discussion (and related second-stage projects) was sufficiently developed, the Comanche were to move to the third stage of constitutional revision.

Need for more involvement with today's problems of drugs and alcohol

Feeling that I cannot make a difference

- Factionalism
- Great deal of apathy on the part of the membership
- Jealousy and rivalry within the tribe as a whole
- Unaware of or a lack of vision/direction for the tribe

Legend

The arrow should be interpreted as: "Significantly Aggravates"

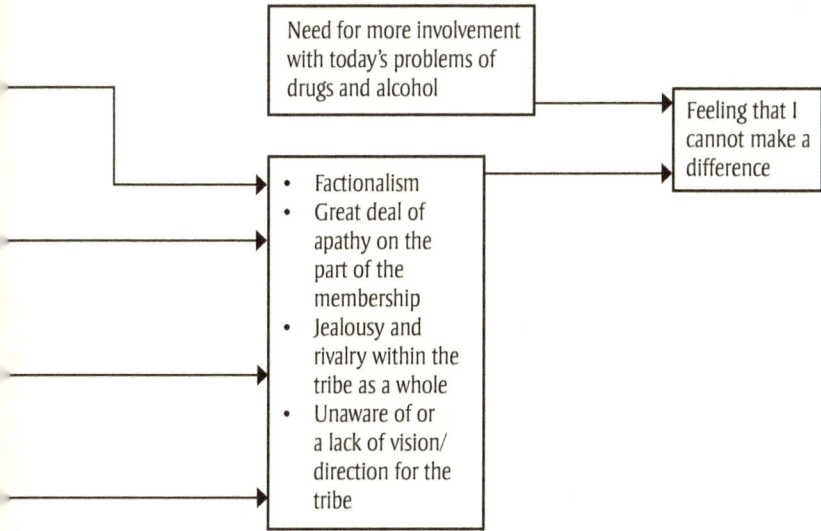

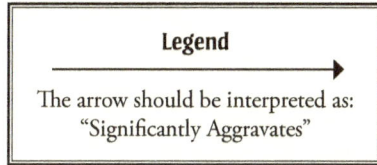

The participants' closing remarks in this second run of the ILIS process, as did those of the first session, exhibited considerable enthusiasm for the process and strong optimism for its role in enhancing tribal development. A few excerpts are revealing:

> I'd like to say that I'm really impressed. I really feel honored to be here because these are the concerns that I've had for a long time and they're not even voiced by most of us because you're not always able to say something for fear of stepping on someone's toe or saying something that's not reflecting something that you really feel, and someone misinterprets what you say a lot of times. And I just really appreciate being able to

Fig. 3: Options Selected for Implementation Promoting Greater Community Participation in Comanche Tribal Governance

A. Problem Solving
    - Invite known faction leaders to small group problem-solving settings
    - Request a Comanche Vision Commission to be organized by the Comanche Business Committee (CBC) to develop a community-based vision statement
    - Set goals and objectives for the tribe
    - Have CBC members participate in ILIS
    - Community members invite CBC to open issues workshop

B. Constitutional Education
    - Read constitution yourself for interpretation and understanding
    - Provide tribal members with historical perspective of the Comanche constitution
    - Form committee with community members to get feedback on constitution
    - Distribute copies of constitution (with survey) to all tribal households

C. Internal Media
    - Make information available on how to get involved in tribal governance
    - Provide tribal newsletter for all tribal members
    - Send minutes of CBC meeting out to communities for public posting
    - Request an increase in the tribal budget line item to cover cost of newsletter
    - Provide information to members on existing tribal programs
    - Mail or post tribal agenda

D. Cogenerational Outreach
- Investigate the feasibility of developing an Employee Assistance Program for the Comanche Tribe
- Increase senior citizens care
- Increase youth programs

E. Cultural Enrichment
- Establish tribal budget line item for teaching Comanche (language)
- Create and hold an annual Comanche holiday

F. External Media (no options selected in this category)

G. Tribal Involvement
- Encourage community meetings
- Promote interest in tribal meetings
- Increase Tribal Council's awareness in budgets

H. External Resources (no options selected in this category)

I. Staff Development
- Have workshops for the tribal staff on how to be more "service oriented"
- Establish a program designed to teach and train new Comanche business committee members about ins and outs of tribal affairs
- Develop orientation for new employees

J. Constitutional Revision
- Revise constitution based on Comanche identity
- Establish a community-based constitution revision committee
- Define role of all elected officials

deal with these things. I just feel the oneness that I've always wanted to feel about my culture.

I am impressed by all of the things that went on here the last few days. I'm surprised that we got as much done as we did. I've learned more about the way things are in the last few days . . . and I understand more about the way things work now. This is a very exciting time because we have the opportunity with this group to turn the corner and turn things in a different way. While it'll take a lot of work and a lot of time if we use the right effort and perseverance we have a chance to make things a lot better for the tribe.

Taking our skills and applying them back to the tribe and all these things are real good in that to me it's like some of the traditions that our tribe held like the Seven Arrows and the Four Directions. In the last few days we heard views with a lot of directions. . . . Sometimes like Roland, you know, he sees some things so big and can't do anything but with all of us working together coming from different directions like that, we all begin to see things from this point of view, things from that point of view. . . . This kind of helps us experience those kind of other things, like we might not of been able to see things in that kind of way. When I expressed myself, he was able to see it from a different point of view and accept it and see it in a different light. And with this, we're able to bring that back to our culture and we're not stuck in society's frame in going about things. We're getting back to the way our forefathers did things, processed out ideas and things. And I'm real glad to be able to be a part of this and I think we can conduct these meeting like Ben can and I think we can really do a great success with this program, with this process, out there in the communities and corporate it in our governments and it can really help our communities and our tribal members. . . .

Broadening the Process, July and September ILIS
The broadening of the tribal discussion process decided upon in the spring 1991 ILIS meetings was initiated shortly after that pair of meetings

concluded. An ongoing series of discussions and planning sessions commenced in each of the four primary Comanche communities. These meetings generally simplified the consensus discussion process, and eliminated the computer-assisted mapping. In conjunction with the community sessions, two tribal ILIS meetings were held in Lawton, on July 12–13, 1991, and September 27–28, 1991, with three representatives from each of the four communities reporting the findings from their local deliberations.[68] The objective of the Lawton sessions was to continue designing the future of the Comanche Tribe. Doing so consisted of further consideration of barriers to community participation and developing a tribal vision statement and additional options for the future of the nation ("What actions and initiatives can make the Comanche vision a reality?").[69] The process at the July and September meetings was essentially the same as that of the first two Comanche ILIS sessions, except that now the tribal-level discussions were directly linked to the deliberations in the local communities. Some of the decision-making process took place at each level, as discussion shifted back and forth between local and tribal meetings.

The consideration of barriers to community participation essentially ratified what had been decided at the previous sessions, and with this delineation of the structure of the barriers to effective tribal governance as a foundation, the process shifted to developing a tribal vision statement in the form of a set of objectives developed from considering the question, "What are your hopes, goals, and objectives for the Comanche Tribe of the future?" The two-level discussion produced a vision statement containing twenty goals organized in a map of seven support levels. Fig. 4 shows the "Collective Vision Statement for Comanche Future." In general terms, the first level focuses on the goal of improving communications throughout the tribe. The second level consists of two items, each of which is the initiation point for goals in the following levels, but the two separate tracks largely come together as sources for all the goals at the fifth level. One of the second-level goals is to strengthen tribal government. This supports, directly, a set of third-level goals aimed at improving the operation of tribal government, and these in turn contribute to the fourth-level goal of providing services to all Comanches.

The other goal at the second level is "to promote co-generational learning to teach respect and Comanche values." This supports, directly, a set of cultural goals at the third level as well as the goal "to change the enrollment qualification" (by changing the blood quantum requirement

Fig. 4: Collective Vision Statement for Comanche Future

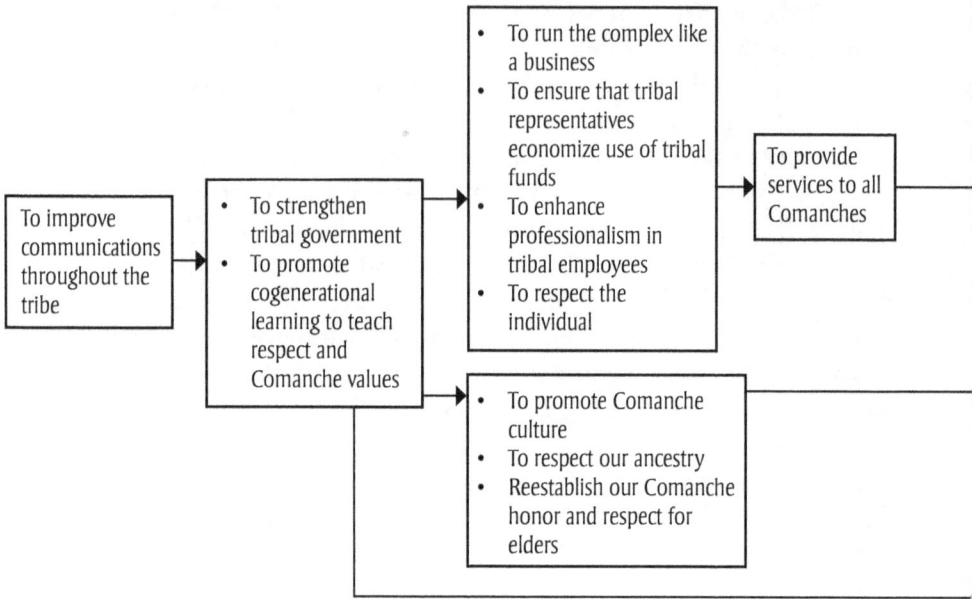

Fig. 4: Collective Vision Statement for Comanche Future

To improve communications throughout the tribe	→	• To strengthen tribal government • To promote cogenerational learning to teach respect and Comanche values	→	• To run the complex like a business • To ensure that tribal representatives economize use of tribal funds • To enhance professionalism in tribal employees • To respect the individual	→	To provide services to all Comanches

• To promote Comanche culture
• To respect our ancestry
• Reestablish our Comanche honor and respect for elders

for membership, with the feeling being that it should be made less restrictive). At the fifth level, the two tracks largely converge, producing a list of five goals: "To again become 'Lords of the Plains,'" "To eliminate favoritism," "To achieve more unity," "To prepare youth for leadership," and "To ensure equal access for Comanche services." These fifth-level goals lead to two at the sixth level: "To improve medical care" and "To improve educational services." This last goal was seen as providing significant support for the seventh-level goal: "To contribute to national and global issues." The last is important, for the sense of wholeness that is central to the Comanche (and other tribal people) includes first the individual's place in and contribution to the tribe, and then the tribe's place in and contribution to the nation and the world.

The process of identifying action options was begun at meetings in the four communities, each of which generated its own list of proposals. These were than shared at the September 27–28 session, which produced an extensive list from which each community and the tribal group might

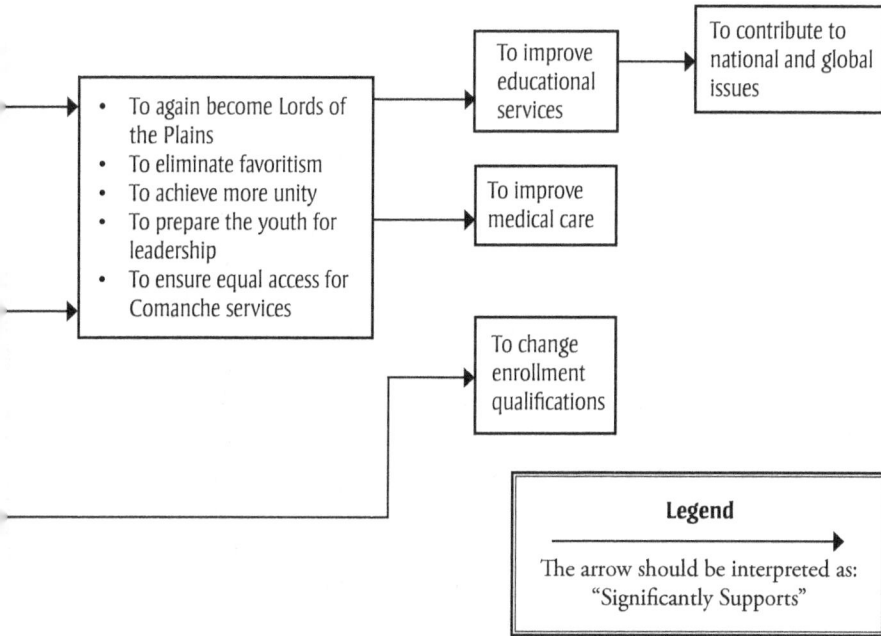

```
┌─────────────────────────┐      ┌──────────────┐      ┌──────────────────┐
│ • To again become Lords │ ───▶ │ To improve   │ ───▶ │ To contribute to │
│   of the Plains         │      │ educational  │      │ national and     │
│ • To eliminate favoritism│     │ services     │      │ global issues    │
│ • To achieve more unity │      └──────────────┘      └──────────────────┘
│ • To prepare the youth  │
│   for leadership        │      ┌──────────────┐
│ • To ensure equal access│ ───▶ │ To improve   │
│   for Comanche services │      │ medical care │
└─────────────────────────┘      └──────────────┘

                                 ┌──────────────┐
                            ───▶ │ To change    │
                                 │ enrollment   │
                                 │ qualifications│
                                 └──────────────┘
```

Legend

The arrow should be interpreted as:
"Significantly Supports"

choose for implementation. The list was defined as being open for further additions and would serve as a basis for choosing concrete actions at future meetings.

Once again, the closing statements by participants were extremely positive. These included affirmation that the process for the meetings and the mapping methodology and visual display were extremely appropriate and helpful. A number of constructive criticisms were produced from this first attempt at combined community–tribal process.[70] One of these was procedural. It was felt that it was important to involve the Business Committee in all of the tribal-level sessions, and that in future tribal-level meetings, the Business Committee, like each of the communities, should have three representatives.

The other suggestions were primarily technical. For example, it was decided that relevant cultural values need to be affirmed before vision statements are addressed by the group. This concern came about because the group was reluctant to deal with kinship obligations in the context of management problems of favoritism. However, it is likely that the group could have examined the problem in depth if the positive value of respect for kinship obligations had been discussed in more detail at an earlier stage.

Also noted were several problems in assuring that everyone's contributions were equally valued. For example, when the communities reported their lists of alternative actions, each community in turn presented its entire list. This created two problems. First, because some communities generated longer lists than others, this method of presentation tended to make some communities appear to be contributing more than others, and hence to be more valued. More important (because as was natural), considerable duplication existed in the proposals. As each succeeding group presented its lists, it appeared that groups who presented later were contributing less that was new than did groups that presented earlier. Thus, the last community to present had some feeling that its ideas were not considered seriously and were treated as less important than those of the others. This problem could be eliminated by taking ideas from each community in turn, noting where others have made the same finding (thus making duplication mutually supportive), and adding that idea to the growing general list.

Similarly, people not thoroughly used to this kind of strategic planning often confuse such things as a vision statement with a goal or an option for action. When this occurred in the process of visioning, action proposals were removed as not relevant at that moment, making the person proposing feel that she or he had made a mistake. If the generated list were considered in more neutral terms (and neutral language was used in the sorting process), then the group could consider which ideas should be considered at the moment and which shifted to a different list for later consideration. This would avoid the problem of people feeling that their contributions were less valued.

Developments in the Communities

A number of the participants took considerable initiative in developing the process in their own communities, and one participant was quite innovative in developing his own computer model for grouping the ideas from his community. He mentioned that once the Comanches have made the process fully their own, they would become so innovative with it that an outsider, knowing only the original process, would not recognize it after five years.

Following the July-to-September dialoguing, the four local communities, in their own meetings, began to develop some of the proposals generated in the two-level process.[71] The Lawton community launched a process of constitutional review that quickly became tribe wide. It also set up three tribal displays in libraries. The Cache community undertook the restoration of its cultural center, generating support from four agencies in the process. It also organized an evening of Comanche hymn singing.[72] The Walters community developed a collaborative effort involving the city, the county, and the tribe to plan an innovative community center for its area. It also organized several community dinners. The Apache community, after demonstrating grassroots support through a petition drive, succeeded in obtaining Comanche Business Committee approval for requesting an extension of the tribe's Job Training Partnership Act program into southern Caddo County (rather than relying upon the program from the Kiowa Tribe), and it appeared that this request would meet federal approval.

Impacts of ILIS at the Tribal Level

At the tribal level, increased community participation led to a turnout of more than three hundred tribal members at the next general council meeting, the largest number in attendance in a considerable time. Meanwhile, three of the community participants in the July–September 1991 ILIS sessions were elected to the Business Committee, strengthening the newly initiated liaison process between the Business Committee and the communities and among the communities (although the subsequent resignation of one of these members reduced the ILIS supporters on the committee to two). At the same time, the ILIS process was expanded to include Comanches living in Norman and Oklahoma City and began to include those living in concentrated numbers in other urban locations around the United States.

In June 1992 (at the completion of the pilot project funded by the Administration for Native Americans), the four communities formalized the two-level ILIS process in Comanche Community Participation Units Articles of Voluntary Association, which was officially made part of the tribal governance process in a resolution of the Comanche Business Committee meeting of July 11, 1992. A direct product of the ongoing process was the development of an internal list of tribal and community resources and a national external list of resources that the tribe can draw upon. In general, proposals to the Business Committee that came out of the ILIS process gained broad community support and were easily passed by the committee. In contrast, issues that have not been considered in broad community discussions continue to be difficult to build a consensus around. Thus, it is hard for the Business Committee to take any action on them. This situation is illustrated by the Business Committee's rejecting four successive proposals from the tribal council on economic development that appeared to be substantively strong, but for which there had not been broad participation in their development.[73] This experience of the Business Committee, combined with the fact that the calmer political climate that resulted from the initiation of inclusive community dialogue contributed significantly to the fact that the next-elected tribal chair was the first to be reelected to a second term in at least a decade, indicates the potential of the process to provide a means for ending deadlock in tribal decision making and to begin to lower the level of acrimony in the community, particularly relating to its political affairs.

Experience with participatory measures in other settings suggests that the full establishment of a process like ILIS requires considerable time. Building trust in the community that is necessary to transform long-existing bitterness and infighting into generally harmonious relations requires a long period during which consistently good experiences dealing with community issues result from working successfully with the process. Clearly, the reactions of participants, the spread of support for working with ILIS, and the unfolding of events indicate that movement toward such a change in feelings and ways of relating was beginning to occur among the Comanche by the end of 1992.

Even under the most favorable of circumstances, the integration of an innovative process like ILIS into the mainstream of community affairs is never smooth or entirely certain. As the new participatory way of deciding begins to generate enthusiasm in the community, it naturally stimulates people not yet acculturated to its ways to inject their own proposals into community deliberations from outside the new discussion process. If this happens too early or too forcefully (as may happen where there are strong factions that are not included in the process from the beginning, or at least from a very early stage), it can derail, or at least delay, the growth of the new consensus decision-making process.[74] If the new process is being developed in a sufficiently effective way, such incidents are merely part of the growing pains of making the process more inclusive.

An example of this kind of difficulty arose with the process of constitutional revision. The ILIS process set in motion a long-term discussion of the concerns aimed at the building of consensus over time before proposing a new document. In the midst of these deliberations, a former Business Committee member, who continued to feel alienated from the government process since his defeat in a reelection effort, proposed his own revision to the constitution that did not include the ILIS process. He managed to obtain enough signatures on a petition that a vote had to be taken on his proposal. His action at first created a great deal of confusion. Many people did not know whether the vote pertained to the revision that was being discussed in the community. However, the communication network and process that the introduction of ILIS set in motion had become sufficiently developed that most of the confusion was eventually straightened out. The proposal first passed but was quickly rescinded when people realized that what they had voted for was not the proposal being developed through the consensus-building dialogues.

Although this episode caused some delay, it did add to the inclusiveness of the process of constitutional revision. By mid-1996, sessions on drafting a new constitution had been held in the four communities and with Comanches in Norman, Oklahoma City, Albuquerque, Dallas, and Washington, D.C. A final tribal-level drafting session was then held with representatives of each of the communities, and a referendum appeared to be on the horizon. However, failure of the Comanche to maintain inclusive dialogue at the tribal level soon derailed the promising effort.

Failure to Fully Institutionalize ILIS

To maintain and further community discussion, it is necessary to institutionalize the process sufficiently that people will continue to use it consistently, regardless of changes in official personnel. This is true whether or not it continues to use the original format of its initiation, in this case ILIS, or is modified into some other form of inclusive participatory discussion. With the Comanche, that has happened in three of four communities, in which local meetings to discuss community affairs were still a regular occurrence as of 2002. In the fourth community, participatory discussions continued at least until mid-1996. At the tribal level, that has not been the case.

The chair of the tribal council, who came into office after the initial tribal-level work with ILIS had been completed, did not appreciate its importance in making the political climate favorable to his reelection. Thus, he made no use of the process and did not replace the ILIS liaison person to the council when the position became vacant, nor did he replace the tribal ILIS facilitators when they left the tribal staff. As the community at large was not yet sufficiently acculturated to returning to participatory dialogue of tribal issues, the chairman's lack of action concerning ILIS did not draw a significant response from the community. During the chairman's first term of office, no major controversial issues arose, so that the improved community climate resulting from the ILIS process remained, carrying the chair into a second term. Shortly after his reelection, however, two important issues surfaced that he believed required early action. When he undertook controversial initiatives concerning them without putting them before the communities for broad consideration, the result was political uproar.

In the first instance, the chair initiated plans for the building of a tribal casino. In the second, he attempted to create a health maintenance organization (HMO) in the face of a possible closing of the tribe's hospital. The latter action was threatening to some of the hospital's employees, who began to complain to others that the chairman was attempting to kill the hospital. This ignited a round of innuendo-laden gossip. Objection to being left out of the process was particularly voiced by those in the local communities who were now used to participating in the consideration of major issues in their local meetings.

Whatever the chair's concern may have been about the necessity for quick action, his initiating projects without prior consultation with the Comanche community through ILIS or an equivalent forum created a great deal of stormy controversy and raised considerable suspicion of the motives of those involved in developing the proposals, as was typical of Comanche politics prior to the launching of ILIS. Indeed, for some time, community turmoil was even more tumultuous than it had been prior to the initiation of ILIS because many Comanches were now used to being involved in community affairs and were angered at being left out of political decision making.

Although three of the four Comanche communities continued to have local participatory meetings at least into 2002, and there have been continued efforts to revise the nation's constitution—sometimes with fairly inclusive invitations to tribal members—author LaDonna Harris, an involved tribal member, reports that as of the summer of 2008, the Comanche had not adopted a new constitution. In January 1999, an attempt was made to improve tribal governance by restarting the ILIS process at the tribal level. However, the election of a new tribal chair shortly after ended the effort, and although Comanche politics have become more congenial, as of fall 2008, a tribal-level participatory process has not been reestablished.

Evidence for the Value of ILIS

Some may wonder if it is worth initiating a return to inclusive community discussion of issues in Indian communities, given that the Comanche community was even more disharmonious after its experience with ILIS than before its initiation. There is plenty of evidence, however, that ILIS was an appropriate and useful process. All of those who participated in it were moved by the experience and enthusiastically supported it. Whenever the community used inclusive participation, it built consensus over time for a plan of action and passed a program. It seems likely that a new constitution would have been enacted if community dialoguing had continued. The community became much more harmonious as long as many of its members were involved in meaningful consideration of community affairs, and the fact that many of them were angered at again being left out of policy making is an indication of the value of their participation. Overall, it would seem that as long as the Comanche used ILIS, it served as a creative vehicle of their empowerment. It has also provided a way to deal effectively with concerns for the mutual advancement of the members, the communities, and the tribe as a whole in a way that allows the Comanche to interact more effectively with the contemporary world through strengthening traditional values.

More recent applications of ILIS give further evidence that reinstituting inclusive participatory consensus decision-making processes such as ILIS is quite efficacious, when appropriately undertaken for the particular culture and situation, in bringing back a sense of identification with, and appreciation of, one's tribe and restoring a feeling of individual dignity among the members through fostering mutual respect and providing a means for all members to contribute positively to the wellbeing of the community. Several members of other tribes have participated in or observed the ILIS process and commented upon its broader applicability.

Former Winnebago Chairman Reuben Snake, a facilitator at the February 1990 ILIS meeting, commented that the process is a good match with traditional problem-solving strategies. This is because traditional people remain to this day holistic, systems thinkers, favoring the inclusion of many ideas into solutions rather than the adoption of one idea that overpowers all others.[75] Stanley Paytiamo, former governor of Acoma Pueblo, said that the ILIS process enables a group to accomplish in two-and-a-half days what it takes traditional decision makers two-and-a-half years to accomplish.[76]

Other Experiences with ILIS

Since its first use by the Comanches, ILIS has been applied successfully in a number of other settings.[77] AIO has used the process with a number of tribes and other organizations in Oklahoma, New Mexico, and Alaska. ILIS was instituted as an issues-management program for the Institute of American Indian Fine Arts. In addition, AIO has been using ILIS in its work in strengthening the government-to-government relationship between the tribal and federal governments. The process opens a nonconfrontational pathway for the interaction of government agencies and tribes. In several forums beginning in 1993, including a session with the Environmental Protection Agency (EPA) Office of Solid Waste Management, AIO has brought together local, state, regional, and national representatives to discuss concerns facing tribal governments. ILIS has promoted full and frank discussion, building coalitions for stronger tribes and more effective policy coordination. AIO also regularly makes use of ILIS in its work with the young people participating in the American Indian Ambassadors Program of leadership training. The process has helped the program participants understand the barriers to effective leadership, how issues are related to one another, and the roles that individuals can play in either creating or overcoming barriers. AIO has also found ILIS to be an exceedingly useful format in a number of international Indigenous meetings. Overall, the record indicates that ILIS-type processes can be extremely useful to tribes and tribal people in re-creating who they have always been as they move into the twenty-first century.

Conclusions on Renewing Tribal Participation

The main point is that most Indian nations are suffering from a clash between the values of their present forms of government and the surviving traditional values of the people that generally are quite participatory and cooperative. ILIS, however modified for specific circumstances, is only one method of initiating inclusive participatory decision making. Like all processes, ILIS has advantages and disadvantages. For example, the computer mapping is helpful in quickly showing the relationships among the ideas or issues under consideration. But using it requires expensive equipment and technically trained staff, which may make it impractical to use. Partly because of these requirements, in the Comanche case, the local communities usually did not use the computer equipment or the mapping. They simplified the procedures for their own needs, maintaining the procedures' inclusive participatory character.

Some Indian commentators have stated that they find consensus decision making too time-consuming to be generally practical, especially in larger tribes. As the Ute and Alaskan Bahá í–style cases demonstrate, it is still possible to involve people inclusively, regularly, and respectfully in tribal decision making without having everyone directly deciding by consensus. Indeed, as we discussed in chapter 1, a number of North American Native peoples, such as the Diné, traditionally used a brokering system to build consensus by representation in many of their affairs. Just what form or method is used needs to vary with the circumstances. What is important is to find appropriate ways to involve tribal members so that they are, and feel, involved.

As we have seen, even the best and most appropriate process of tribal decision making cannot instantly overcome many years of inappropriate governance and a host of other problems that have been exacerbated by the lack of a government that is appropriate to the culture and needs of the people. Properly initiating appropriate governance is an essential first step in beginning to return a community to harmony. Community involvement, then, has to be built in a good way, modifying the process as is necessary for community needs (but only on essential occasions in order not to undermine the confidence of the people in it), and maintaining it long enough to firmly establish it. Then, it can serve as a vehicle for developing policies to deal with the other problems that Indigenous communities must overcome to return to harmony and self-sufficiency. Consideration of what that may involve is the topic of the next chapter.

Developing policies that fit with tribal values often needs to be a patient and careful undertaking. Prior to colonialism, Indian peoples were adept at including a wide spectrum of views, interests, and concerns in building a consensus. Today the range of views has widened, particularly because tribal members have often assimilated varying amounts of mainstream or other external cultural values, and new traditions have developed differentially for different community members and memories of what is "traditional" have become more diverse. As one elder of a nation that used to hunt bison, elk, and deer but for a while got into ranching, commented to author Stephen Sachs: "I stopped going to elder's meetings when I realized they gave me a headache. Some of our elders complained, 'give us traditional food. We don't want these chicken dinners. We want beef.'" It is precisely in such diversified situations that respectful, inclusive dialogue is needed to build harmony and consensus.

So far in this chapter, we have been considering what may be needed to establish appropriate ways for Indian communities to create good policies concerning programs and regulations. This is essentially a matter of legislation. There remains the judicial question of what might be done to return Indian communities to deciding disputes and settling conflicts in ways that are consistent with their culture.

2. Completing the Circle in Resolving and Transforming Disputes: Indigenizing Legal Codes and Judicial Processes
Stephen M. Sachs and Jondodev Chaudhuri

One of the essential aspects of a community is how it resolves trouble cases and disputes among its members. This is a matter of the community's mores and rules of behavior and of the approach it takes and procedures it uses to settle or transform disputes. Historically, law for most Native communities was an outgrowth of the familial clan obligations and duties that were spelled out in tribal legends and oral histories. As a result, little distinction could be made between law and culture for Native communities. The imposition of an alien legal system on Indian nations with rules of behavior and principles for resolving conflicts that are different from their traditional ways of handling such issues has been the source of considerable confusion for Indian people and has contributed significantly to the disharmony in Native communities that we have discussed.

Traditionally, in differing ways, virtually all of the First Peoples of North America emphasized re-creating and maintaining harmony in dealing with disputes and commissions of harm by their members.[78] Doing so might involve punishment and often included some kind of compensation either in payment or service, but the emphasis was on restoring proper relationships among all concerned rather than on justice.

Thus, tribal people more often dealt with harm in ways that Western legal systems would consider torts (injuries to be dealt with by civil law) rather than crimes, with the emphasis on restoring the preexisting situation or set of relations. This might involve a gift or payment for damages: for example, when a Kiowa or Cheyenne man eloped with another man's wife, it was required that the absconder provide a suitable compensation to the injured husband, with a peace chief facilitating the resolution of the dispute between the parties.[79] In some instances of homicide, restoration went so far as to have the party causing the death (whether intentional or accidental) take on a role of the deceased. For example, an Inuit or Lakota man would marry the wife of the man he had killed in order to ensure that the deceased's family was cared for and, particularly if the killing was intentional, to restore harmony between the families involved in the dispute.[80] With the importance of familial relations in Native societies, an injury involved not only the individuals involved but also the familial group of which they were members. In some instances, the process of restoration even extended to warfare. Among the Wendat, for example, a captured enemy would sometimes be adopted to replace a family member whom the enemy had killed, with the adoptee taking on all of the lost person's roles, including leadership positions.[81]

The handling of disputes and trouble situations aimed to restore and maintain harmony in the community; therefore, working out a proper solution often encompassed considering the full range of relations between the parties and the whole catalogue of ill feeling, and its causes, between them. This approach contrasts with the narrow focus on what is specifically relevant to the case at hand in deciding fault or guilt in the U.S. judicial system (although the courts do consider wider concerns in deciding upon punishment in criminal cases).

Similarly, the emphasis on restoring harmony by traditional Native North Americans meant that acts of improper behavior were generally handled with a focus on rehabilitating the wrongdoer. Thus, as we earlier described, when some Cheyenne young men were caught hunting buffalo on their own, which might have stampeded the herd so that further hunting would have been impossible, the offenders were beaten and their horses killed and gear destroyed. But once it was clear that they accepted the punishment, the young men were resupplied and brought back into the ranks of the hunters.[82] It was generally only in extreme cases that a person who committed an offense was killed or exiled. Among the Aleuts, for instance, a man who killed community members several times, or someone who lied repeatedly, might be executed or forced out as a danger to the community.[83] Even in extreme cases, some rehabilitation might be possible. With the Cheyenne, for example, killing another tribal member was considered so serious that the whole tribe would be polluted by the act, requiring purification and renewal of the nation's most sacred objects and the expulsion of the murderer.[84] Yet, after several years the offender, if repentant, might be permitted to return with the permission of the family of the deceased—and there was usually social pressure on the family to give that permission.

U.S. Government Undermining of Traditional Peacemaking

So long as Indian nations were sovereign in fact, each tribe and band lived according to its own ways, dealing with disputes and violations of agreed-upon standards of proper behavior and following the varied particulars of its own culture. With the official subordination by the United States of Indian tribes as domestic sovereign nations, and its undermining of traditional ways and leaders in the attempt to assimilate Native people, the ability of Native nations to live under their own laws and their own judicial systems (or their equivalents in traditional terms) was severely limited.

Although some traditional dispute resolution continued unofficially, Indian agents began imposing their own systems of justice on reservations in the mid-nineteenth century, often with the agents acting as justices of the peace or appointing trusted Indians to do so.[85] In 1883, the commissioner of Indian affairs compiled and distributed to Indian agents a set of rules and guidelines for Courts of Indian Offenses (or CFR—Code of Federal Regulation—Courts) with a range of jurisdictional authority thought to be modeled on that of a justice of the peace in a state or territory where such a court would be located.[86] The only restriction for judges was that they not be "polygamists." With changes made by local agents and the BIA, these Courts of Indian Offenses continued to function until the passage of the Indian Reorganization Act in 1934, although about twenty-five CFR Courts continue, as based on these older courts.[87] Under the Indian Reorganization Act, tribes received constitutions, including provisions for tribal courts, which for the most part were imposed on the tribes by the act or the BIA. Although to varying degrees traditional values and procedures are included in their operation, most tribal courts function with processes and tribal codes that to a considerable degree are imposed Western forms that are not consistent with traditional values. Although their jurisdiction is limited to misdemeanors that take place on tribal land involving Indians and to civil cases in which they have subject-matter, personal, and geographic authority (including over non-Indians), tribal courts play an important role in the affairs of their communities.[88] Thus, the extent to which tribal court operation is consistent with community values has a significant impact upon the harmony and sense of well-being of their communities.

The Need for Tribal Courts with Independence

A major difficulty today is that many Indian nations do not have their own courts, making it extremely difficult to resolve quite divisive community issues. This has been particularly visible at the opening of the twenty-first century in questions of who should be tribal members. In the absence of tribal judicial processes, a number of tribes, particularly in California, have banished, often by disenrollment, tribal members, including entire families, with no effective recourse or review for fairness.[89] This was exemplified when the Pechanga Band of Luiseño Indians ejected about 90 descendents of Paulina Hunter in March 2006, bringing the number of banished Pechanga Band tribal members to more than 220, and the number has continued to grow since then. Across the United States, the use of banishment has been growing for various reasons, particularly economic, although voicing opposition to political leaders has also been a leading catalyst for banishment, demonstrating that fair and democratic tribal governments require a judiciary. Moreover, the judiciary must be independent to function properly, and this is not always the case. In many Indian nations, tribal councils can override their nation's courts. Thus, for instance, in a number of cases tribal court decisions that overturned banishment by tribal councils as improper have been reversed by the same council that made the original decision.

Fortunately, Native nations now have the authority to create and reorganize courts, and a number have done so. A good example is the Meskwaki Nation of Iowa, which introduced an independent tribal court in 2004 to settle civil disputes concerning tribal government, business (including the tribal casino) and contracts, family matters, and tribal customs and traditions. The step was taken to avoid a repetition of the problems that led to the closing of the tribal casino, which caused hundreds of layoffs and millions of dollars in lost revenue, in the previous year. The problems had occurred because there was no internal way for the nation to settle a dispute concerning the membership of the tribal council because the council held judicial as well as legislative authority.[90] The Meskwaki court includes a chief justice, three trial justices, and a community panel. The tribal executive director said about the setting up of the tribal judiciary: "It's about applying our traditional values or teachings, even determining what those interests are, and having a court that can render a decision based on those values."

Appropriately Developing Tribal Peacemaking

As we discussed in chapter 3 and the first section of this chapter, today Indian nations are freer to exercise their sovereignty, which includes developing tribal law and courts. Undertaking such development in ways that will be found legitimate by community members and that will enhance their welfare is a complex process that requires approaches that are appropriate for the particular tribe or band. Two general concerns need to be taken into account to do this successfully.[91] First, the legal process and the substance of the law need to be consistent with the values of community members. This is not only a matter of applying traditional values to changed and changing circumstances (itself a multifaceted matter), but of taking into account, appropriately, the fact that the worldviews and values of community members have changed and continue to change. Moreover, change has taken place differentially, so that Indian nations are far more diverse in their views and ways of seeing than they once were. Moreover, the suffering of Indian people caused by incompletely mourned physical and cultural genocide, together with the experience of living under imposed alien systems, has caused emotional and intellectual confusion within many Native people that compounds the difficulty of creating or reforming legal systems around which tribal consensus can form.

Second, rules of behavior and mechanisms for restoring and maintaining social harmony are more than expressions of values. To be effective, they must be pragmatic mechanisms adapted to the specifics of the relations and social dynamics of the community. Such systems need to be appropriate to the structure and substance of community conflicts so that they can appropriately and effectively resolve or transform them. Traditional mores and adjudicatory processes were well designed to provide a high degree of societal harmonization, as we discussed in chapter 1. Thus, understanding how these mores and processes functioned is a good starting place for approaching contemporary legal and judicial reform. To be successful in this endeavor requires understanding how tribal relations have changed and designing mechanisms that are appropriate for working with current and developing community dynamics.

Navajo Nation: Peacemaking Courts and Tribal Code Developments
A number of Indian nations have developed their codes and adjudicatory processes, which may be enlightening to examine. Among them
is the Navajo Nation, which for many years has included aspects of its
traditional ways in modifying its tribal code to meet developing problems, and whose common law is a developing continuation of traditional
principles. From 1892 until 1959, Navajo Nation's legal system functioned
under the U.S. government–imposed and culturally alien Navajo Court
of Indian Offenses, after which the nation adopted the 1934 BIA Law
and Order Code. These U.S.–originated codes required Navajos to judge
others and rely heavily on power and force for control, rather than apply
Navajo tradition, which relies on culturally specific versions of mediation and arbitration supported by family and clan opinion based on
Diné religion and related ways.[92] Having long used traditionally based
Navajo common law whenever applicable, the Navajo judicial system
consciously began a process of returning to traditional ways in 1981.[93]
Recently, the Navajo Nation Council has been considering whether and
how the nation might codify its common law.[94]

An example of Diné legal development to deal with new situations
is the rise of problems of domestic violence. In the old times, spouse
abuse was very rare. Women and men possessed equal dignity and essential equality (with women holding somewhat higher status and more
authority in certain settings).[95] Numerous ceremonies and stories taught
respectful and peaceful family relations. On the unusual occasions when
one spouse was abused by the other, family or clan would act to return
domestic life to harmony.

The U.S. government's undermining of Diné ways, including traditional family relations, both by direct action on the Navajo reservation
and by removing Diné children from their homes to face and learn abuse
in boarding schools, together with the effects of increasing exposure to
mainstream culture, have made Navajo spousal abuse a significant problem.[96] Thus, the Navajo Nation Council, having already recognized customary marriage and family planning by statute, placed an equal rights
amendment in the Navajo constitution in 1980.[97] Rising community
concern with domestic violence, particularly abuse of women, following the deaths of Diné women at the hands of their husbands, brought
subcommittees of the Navajo Nation Council and representatives of the
judicial branch to hold hearings on the problem in 1991.[98] Following the

hearings, the Navajo Nation Judicial Conference resolved to use conditions of release and act-specific sentences in criminal cases and civil restraining orders, which were detailed in an opinion of the solicitor of the judicial branch, as tools for combating domestic violence. The Navajo Supreme Court subsequently adopted domestic violence court rules based upon Navajo Nation common law, the Navajo Nation equal rights amendment, and applicable principles of the law of equity and English-American common law.

The Navajo Nation courts have increasingly been bringing traditional values and principles into their decisions. An interesting recent example is a December 2004 Navajo Nation Supreme Court ruling that the nation's tribal police do not have the right to mislead people in order to obtain a confession, nor may they act rudely. The justices found that Diné tradition requires acting with patience and respect. This is the traditional principle of *hazho'ogo*, the courteous way in which Diné treat one another. Accordingly, police need to ascertain that defendants understand their rights, which was not clear in the 2004 case because the defendant was not read his rights in the Navajo language.[99]

The Peacemaker Courts

Navajo Nation has also been using a modern adaptation of a traditional conflict resolution process, the Navajo Peacemaker Courts, to deal with domestic relations, including family violence.[100] These courts were created in each judicial district by the Navajo Judicial Conference in 1982 and operate under the supervision of the district courts, which enforce their decisions. The Peacemaker Courts function with a mix of traditional versions of mediation and arbitration. All the participants are thus placed on essentially the same footing, although elders and leaders have more prestige, in guiding the egalitarian process to a mutually acceptable solution. The process follows traditional values that are accepted by the participants, which prevents one of the parties from bargaining for a culturally unacceptable result. Thus, a husband who has beaten his wife cannot obtain allowance of some of his violence as part of the settlement.

The Peacemaker Court process is led by a *naat'aanii*, a Diné leader selected on the basis of his or her wisdom, ability, and persuasiveness to solve problems by working issues through with people. The *naat'aanii*, who may be related to the parties, functions by expressing traditional values, including that domestic violence is evil. He or she acts as an intervening leader in the troubled situation and uses prayer, lectures on values, and assessments of the parties' positions and values. The other participants are the parties and members of their families and clans. Thus, the process is essentially a mediated council meeting, in which the presence of relatives of both (or all) parties tends to equalize bargaining ability as the group finds a pragmatic solution and restores balance and harmony on the basis of community values. If one of the parties is psychologically unable to speak, family or clan members can speak for her or him. If the session becomes caught up in anger or recrimination, the *naat'aanii* may defuse the situation or call a recess so that emotions can cool. Legally, a wide variety of options are open toward which the peacemaker may guide the proceedings to a settlement that identifies and removes the sources of disharmony, practically returning the parties to a harmonious relationship in a process that has been called a justice and harmony ceremony. It is a social form of a Diné healing ceremony that works with the good will of the parties to reintegrate them into the community, in solidarity with it.

The Return of Other Nations to Traditional Peacemaking
The general outlines of the Navajo approach to dealing with wrongdoing are similar to the general traditions of most Indian nations in North America, although the details are specific to the tribe or band in question. Thus, a number of other nations are obtaining positive results with similar returns to tradition. The Hollow Water First Nation, an Ojibwa community of fifteen hundred in Manitoba, is a good example.[101] Having found that tribal members jailed by the criminal justice system for sexual offenses repeated their misconduct on release from prison, the nation initiated its own program, following traditional values, that brings together the victim, the offender, the community, and the justice system. Offenders who plead guilty work with specially trained community members and their families in a healing process that has considerably reduced recidivism. Four other First Nation communities in Manitoba who use similar approaches to local crime problems have also achieved high rehabilitation rates.

Several other reports of experiences of First Nation communities in Canada indicate that what is needed to re-create community harmony today is not simply duplicating old ways but rather applying core values that continue to be widely held in innovative ways that are appropriate for the current situation, with a view toward the future. Indeed, adoption of basic values to new circumstances is itself quite traditional. As E. Adamson Hoebel and Karl Llewellyn show, Cheyenne society developed many of its ways and institutions over time to meet specific problems and conditions.[102] Clearly, the arrival of the horse brought social and cultural changes in all the Indian nations that moved out onto the plains as a result, before direct contact with Europeans. It is recorded that the experience of the Cheyenne with the horse eventually caused the tribe to modify its custom that a man could borrow most anything from a friend that the friend was not using without prior permission: the custom was changed to require the asking of permission before borrowing a horse.[103]

Rupert Ross recounts that at the Alkali Lake Indian Reserve in British Columbia, beginning in 1972, the Alkali Lake Indian Band of the Secwepemc Nation undertook a major modification in their traditional healing approach to social problems in order to find an effective way of dealing with alcohol, and later sexual, abuse.[104] Previously, sessions to overcome wrongdoing and reharmonize a perpetrator with the community had spoken of improper acts indirectly, or hypothetically, in order to preserve the self-respect and interrelational respect of the individual and thereby promote responsibility, learning, healing, and reintegration. It then became important for those concerned "to open up to each other, to share their hurts and their sorrows, to express their discontentments as well as their dreams . . . gathering as a community to speak of such hidden things, to comfort each other, and to forgive and heal each other."[105] The extent of the unresolved grief that the community had to overcome to achieve healing from the physical and cultural genocide that underlies many similar social problems was unprecedented in Secwepemc tradition.[106] By 1979, 98 percent of the community was alcohol-free, and traditional spirituality and the subsequent creation of jobs increased the quality of life in the community. In 1985, a film, *The Honour of All: The Story of Alkali Lake*, was released, documenting the nation's development. Since 1998, the Betty Ford Center has had an expanding relationship with the still well-functioning Alkali Lake Indian Band, applying some of the principles and adopting some of the practices of its success to treating alcohol dependency in general, and for Native people in particular.[107] This success again demonstrates the relevance of traditional Native ways (when properly adjusted) to mainstream twenty-first century society.

Applying Indigenous Processes in Drug Courts
One area in which traditional healing and returning to harmony are increasingly being applied in Indigenous legal proceedings is in the institution of drug courts in the United States.[108] In 1989, in Dade County,

Florida, drug courts in the United States began the attempt to break addictions through problem-solving techniques and treatment fitted to the needs of the offender. The purpose of the process is to allow offenders to confront their substance abuse problems and undergo appropriate rehabilitation in an intensely supervised setting. By 2005, more than one thousand drug courts were operating around the country. In 1997, the DOJ's Drug Courts Program Office realized that to be effective, tribal drug courts would have to adapt to Indigenous culture, and the office established an assistance initiative with funding to help tribes establish and operate drug courts appropriately for their situation. By 2005, at least twelve tribal drug courts were functioning, and more than thirty more were planned.

At the Southern Ute Indian Reservation, the drug court was set up as the *Tuncai* or "well-being" court. Participation in the process by one charged with a drug offense is voluntary. The participants include the charged person, his or her family, the *Tuncai* judge, and various tribal agencies. Since Ute tradition varies somewhat from family to family, the court incorporates the ways of the family into the process, which aims to heal the substance abuser. The proceeding is an ongoing process with regular reviews over "four seasons" in the course of a year, during which time the offender is on probation. If the offender violates probation, he or she is immediately punished, with explanation. Good behavior is rewarded by praise and applause in a *Tuncai* meeting and, often, with gifts appreciated by the offender, such as movie passes or gift certificates. The program is holistic, treating body as well as mind. Assistance is provided as needed, such as arranging transportation or paying admission to a treatment facility, for example, or providing otherwise unavailable access to a basketball court. All is part of the *Tuncai*'s goal of helping an individual walk a good path with the support of family and friends, which involves uncovering talents and facilitating a person's finding his or her own positive way—not just discouraging negative behavior. The Indian drug courts, along with drug courts in the mainstream culture, have brought about significant reductions in drug use as participants have improved their lives while reducing costs in the criminal justice system, including savings realized from reduced jail time.

Other Kinds of Tribal Justice Practice

It should be noted that assistance to Indian nations for the development of tribally appropriate justice practices has been taking place in other kinds of peace-building courts. For instance, the Southwest Region of PeaceWeb in Tucson, Arizona, partnered with the Tohono O'odham Nation Justice Center in March 2006 to offer a three-day Peacemaking Circles training session for the Arizona Tribal Court System under a minigrant from the Victim Offender Mediation Association. The program trainers had previous extensive experience working with and for Native American tribes in Minnesota and in using Indigenous restorative justice practices, including sentencing circles and family group conferences. The training was intended to help tribal courts in Arizona design and implement Peacemaking Circles in their justice systems.[109]

Although most tribes do not have separate traditional court systems, such as the Navajo Peacemaking courts, set up within their tribal codes, they continue to carry out traditional justice processes. In many instances, these procedures function outside of formal tribal governments. Often, they are tied to the various tribes' ceremonial societies and operate in accordance with religious and cultural practices that predate formal tribal codes. In these ceremonial societies, membership requires the individual to recognize and honor the rules and authority of such societies. Internal disputes among ceremonial members are often settled by leaders of the societies in accordance with cultural norms and do not appear in the tribal court. In meeting this justice, the ceremonial communities maintain some of their traditions while making necessary accommodations given societal changes. For instance, in Muscogee stomp grounds, the violation of fasting requirements during certain ceremonies always resulted in grave punishment, which often included banishment. Specifically, prohibitions against ingesting any food or water during such ceremonies were absolute since time immemorial. However, given the realities of the diabetes epidemic among Native peoples and the fact that many ceremonial grounds members are under strict medication routines, some grounds have adapted rules to allow for the taking of certain nontraditional medications during ceremonies. In a few cases, such as that of the Hopi Nation, the roles of ceremonial societies are contemplated in tribal constitutions and codes, but most often they function informally, by custom.

Bringing Tribal Values into Tribal Courts: The Case of the Muscogee Nation

Most Indian nations whose current statutes and legal systems are similar to those of the federal and state governments because of colonial imposition have been bringing tribal values and ways into their law by utilizing the common law aspects of U.S. law. Tribal courts interpret and apply tribal law as mandated by a given tribe's constitution and code of ordinances or statutes. Like other court systems in the United States, where a given tribe's constitution and code is silent as to a particular legal issue, the tribal court has the duty to develop a common law consistent with that tribe's customs and values.

Drafters of most tribal codes and constitutions have included a mechanism for tribal courts to develop this common law: the choice-of-law ordinance. Tribal choice-of-law ordinances generally function in the same manner as state choice-of-law ordinances. Namely, these ordinances guide tribal courts to seek alternative sources of law when codified tribal law is lacking. In these choice-of-law ordinances, a hierarchy of appropriate alternate sources of law is usually set forth. Although the order of these alternate sources differs from tribe to tribe, almost all include "tribal customs and usage," "tribal traditions," or "traditional law" as appropriate sources of law.[110] A representative example of such an ordinance is that of the Muscogee Nation, which reads as follows:

> Law applicable
> A. Constitution and laws of the Nation. In all cases, the Muscogee Nation Courts shall apply the Constitution and duly enacted law of the Muscogee Nation, the common law of the Muscogee people as established by customs and usage, and the Treaties and Agreements between the Muscogee Nation and the United States.
>
> B. Federal law. [. . .]
>
> C. Applicability of Oklahoma law in limited circumstances. [. . .][111]

These choice-of-law ordinances have been specifically revised by many tribes to move reliance on tribal customs up in the hierarchy, so that tribal customs will be considered before any other sources of law. These ordinances provide both an opportunity and a duty to utilize tribal custom and culture in the interpretation and administration of tribal law. Before a tribal court ever considers federal or state law as persuasive authority in a given matter, tribal courts must apply tribal customs where these ordinances exist.

Despite this duty and obligation, the explicit mandate to use tribal custom and tradition is all too often overlooked by tribal courts and practitioners. Instead, where no specific tribal ordinance governs a dispute, practitioners often argue—and tribal courts often accept—that analogous federal or state laws should govern. This circumvention of the tribal custom mandate occurs for a variety of reasons, including the following:

1. Most traditions are oral, not written.
2. Many traditional practices are secret or meant only to be shared during certain ceremonies and therefore should never be written, shared with nontribal members, or shared outside appropriate settings.
3. Significant burdens on tribal courts exist, including lack of resources, time, and ability to investigate or verify the accuracy of proposed traditional solutions.
4. Several concerns related to the training of tribal judges and practitioners exist, including lack of familiarity with or exposure to tribal customs among some judges and many practitioners, the hiring of nontribal-member judges and attorneys/advocates familiar with those customs, and the failure of law schools to provide detailed training in tribal customary law.
5. There is a growing effort among some tribes to require tribal court judges to be attorneys, often to the exclusion of judges who may serve as valuable resources regarding tribal customs and traditions.
6. Many practitioners, given their familiarity with state and federal court settings, are often reluctant to investigate tribal traditions on a case-by-case basis. Sometimes this reluctance stems from genuine ignorance as to the sources of tribal customary law, and sometimes it is simply the result of laziness.
7. Often, there is a lack of consensus within a community about what the traditions are concerning a given topic.

A common situation in which this tribal custom mandate is bypassed involves determining whether certain activities give rise to justiciable causes of action.[112] Despite these challenges, it is imperative that tribes both recognize their duty and seize the opportunity to employ cultural norms and traditions in the formal judicial process. This is especially the case because federal courts are increasingly curtailing the scope of tribal jurisdiction.[113] But when federal courts review tribal court interpretations of federal law de novo, they generally defer to tribal courts on matters of internal tribal law. The result is that when tribal courts take time to explicitly state that their decisions are based on independent and adequate tribal grounds, such decisions are often insulated from federal review.

The responsibility to utilize the choice-of-law ordinance falls on both judges and practitioners. If the court is required to address tribal traditions before considering external laws, then practitioners have an obligation to advise the court of applicable traditional law. Likewise, the courts, under the choice-of-law mandate, can and should compel practitioners to advise the court of all relevant customs and tradition-based arguments. To do this, courts can require briefings of relevant issues or allow for a type of closed evidentiary hearing in which experts on tribal custom (such as recognized spiritual leaders) educate the court about relevant traditional solution to a given dispute. Such closed hearings can be designed to inform the court in the most respectful and discreet manner possible.

For example, the Muscogee Nation, whose choice-of-law ordinance we have referred to, has an ordinance specifically authorizing the court to consult with knowledgeable individuals regarding matters of traditional law.[114] The Muscogee District Court has used these ordinances on a number of occasions, particularly in regularly consulting traditional knowledge-bearers on divorce and child custody matters, as well as in disputes among members of the tribe's many ceremonial stomp grounds. For instance, after the divorce between a Christian mother and a father who belonged to a ceremonial ground, the question arose as to their child's standing within the tribe's ceremonial society. Creek society is matrilineal, and therefore ceremonial-ground membership is usually passed down from the mother. After consultation with ceremonial-grounds officials, the mother, who won custody, was able to establish that the child could remain a member of the father's grounds.

The effective use of choice-of-law ordinances is absolutely essential to the effort to develop strong tribal court systems and to ensure that tribal law adequately reflects tribal values. An additional benefit of the effective use of choice-of-law ordinances is that the ordinances allow for the consideration of customary law without the major redrafting of tribal codes or the creation of potentially costly separate court systems. Indeed, many traditional customs and rules are not meant to be written down or otherwise publicized. Whereas it would be absolutely inappropriate to codify such customs and rules, such customs and rules may potentially be discussed and implemented in a closed setting. Therefore, the proper use of choice-of-law ordinances allows a tribe to continue to apply its customary law to a limited extent without revamping its entire court system or divulging protected practices. Most important of all, choice-of-law ordinances allow tribal courts to do what they are supposed to do: namely, to utilize and administer tribal law in a manner that is as consistent as possible with the values and norms of their communities. If law is supposed to reflect, preserve, and promote values, then it is inexcusable for a tribe not to consider its values when applying its laws.

The Factors Involved in Successfully Applying Traditional Values to Native Dispute Resolution

Not all of the attempts to apply traditional values to develop Native justice or dispute-resolution systems have been successful. Bruce G. Miller's study of three such attempts and their divergent outcomes among Coast Salish peoples in the United States and Canada makes clear what is perhaps the most important set of factors in determining ultimate success.[115]

The Upper Skagit Tribe's Approach

The Upper Skagit Tribe in Washington state is a confederation of eleven bands, each recognized separately within the tribe but only collectively by the U.S. government. The tribe's 750 members, who live in close proximity with one another, have been involved since 1976 in the ongoing development of a tribal code and full justice system, with tribal police and a court, that recognizes the continuity both within the cultural and structural evolution of the nation and in its relationship to other governments. Gradually, the tribal council, local committees, and tribal membership, at general meetings and through individual input, have modified imposed generic codes and justice-system procedures to meet specific local needs and values.

Since prominent families, in somewhat modified ways since the old times, continue to be central to contemporary Upper Skagit relations, tribal leaders look to each of these families for guidance in developing tribal law and the legal system and to share in leadership responsibility. Constituent groups within the community have consistently contributed input into the ongoing development process, in which power is dispersed consistent with community values and the accepted social structure.

Competent specialists with technical skills and knowledge of community problems and views represent and are responsible to the community and play key roles in drafting new code and running the justice system. Respected elders participate as advisors during the case intake process, in trial or mediation, and in sentencing. Both as a matter of process and substance, the tribe has emphasized respect for the due process rights of all members and placing the good of the tribe above the interests of particular families. The latter is a sufficiently strongly internalized value across the community that when families have found that they are overrepresented on the tribal council, some of their members resign from it.

The system is flexible in its ability to resolve cases informally by a wide variety of means, including allowing parties to tell their stories and blow off steam with counseling or guidance and reaching settlement through traditional feasting ceremonies. Yet when necessary, cases are formally adjudicated through the Anglo-American adversarial process. Code is written to suit the wishes of the community, but with sufficient legal clarity that it can be understood by the local, state, and federal jurisdictions with which the nation interacts. Relations with adjacent jurisdictions are collaborative, including arrangements for extradition and the leasing of jail space. The Upper Skagit assert jurisdiction over the behavior of their members off as well as on the reservation. They have prosecuted major crimes cases within federal jurisdiction when the DOJ has failed to act.

Whatever its inadequacies, the code and the justice system of the Upper Skagit enjoy great legitimacy in the community and play a major role in restoring and maintaining harmony because they are the products of a community consensus system. The Upper Skagit revise their law and legal process according to their own values as new situations arise and their experience deepens, and they also gain understanding from others. They insist that they have not taken customary law from any other tribe or group, although they have adopted some code and concepts from other Coast Salish communities.

In the two Canadian cases that Miller studied, the federal government's failure to recognize broad tribal sovereignty meant that First Nations did not have their own justice systems and were limited to being granted diversionary sentencing systems by the Canadian courts without the communities' full participation in developing a culturally and structurally appropriate process. The Canadian exceptions arise from two developments that have also been occurring in the United States.

First is the growing recognition that mainstream justice often does not work well for tribal offenders, who are acculturated to more restorative approaches.[116] To the extent that this leads to truly culturally appropriate alternative sentencing for Native people, it is clearly a positive development. Second is the increasing perception that restorative and rehabilitative justice may be a better way to treat many mainstream offenders and that something can be learned about restoration and rehabilitation from traditional processes. This is a positive development in itself wherever mainstream alternative programs have been well conceived and carried out. It helps Native people to overcome the ill effects of being taught that their traditions are inferior to those of European origin and encourages them to find meaning and appropriate courses of action from their own heritage. There is a danger, however, that these developments may be applied in what continues to be an impositionist manner, so that programs that generally are appropriate in principle will continue to be imposed without adopting them to the specific circumstances and needs of the receiving community, causing the innovations to fail and at times causing harm to the recipients.

The South Island Justice Project
In the early 1960s, several Salish bands on Vancouver Island came together to form the First Nations of South Island Tribal Council, in order to lobby for mutual benefit.[117] By the 1980s, several provincially funded diversionary programs were in place in British Columbia that involved Indigenous organizations, including elders' groups. Following the Western Judicial Education Center's 1989 conference on Indigenous issues, representatives of the center, the First Nations of South Island Tribal Council, and other Indigenous leaders on Vancouver Island made a commitment to bring together elders and members of the justice system. Through a chain of interactions, this led ultimately to the creation of an elders' council "to receive referrals from the community, police, Crown, corrections and the court, and . . . recommend and supervise action to be taken within the traditional community in individual criminal and family law cases."[118] The resulting South Island Justice Project aimed to improve the response of the Canadian justice system to First Nations people and the delivery of justice in criminal, youth, and family cases, including applying traditional methods of resolution to those cases. It was hoped that this would lead to cross-cultural education for justice system professionals and Indigenous people. Although the project

was well intended, it was created without the input of the tribal council, band councils, or the concerned Salish population. The elders' council that the project created turned out to be but one faction of a divided population and thus was not considered legitimate to or representative of the membership of the bands composing the council. No mechanism was established for contending with the divisive issues and relations, nor was the project built upon a correct understanding of the culture of the people it applied to, including Coast Salish law ways. Hence, the project ultimately collapsed, having failed to achieve goals that members of the involved bands believed were important.

The Developing Stó:lō Experience

The experience of the Stó:lō is developing and has the potential to approach the level of success that the Upper Skagit Tribe has achieved.[119] The Stó:lō Nation consists of about five thousand Coast Salish people in several bands spread along the Frasier River in British Columbia. At the time of Miller's study, the Stó:lō were in a creative phase, working on the development of government and justice. They did not yet have civil or criminal jurisdiction over their members because they had entered into a diversion arrangement for sentencing with the Canadian government.

The Stó:lō Nation Tribal Council formed in 1994 by combining two former multiband tribal councils. The Stó:lō Council has taken responsibility for providing social, educational, health, and child welfare services for the nation. Its organizational structure is under development, but to facilitate the establishment of self-government, the Stó:lō mirrored the structure of the Canadian state, with a three-branch political arm and a bureaucratic arm housing tribal administration and services. The political arm includes the House of Respected Stó:lō Leaders, the main legislative body, which is made up of representatives of the member bands and selects a five-member cabinet, the Special Chief's council, which includes the Chief's Representative (the effective head of state, who is responsible to the chiefs) and the heads of the departments in the bureaucratic arm. The other two branches of the political arm are the House of Elders, which is equivalent to the Canadian senate and includes representatives from every band, and the not-yet-formed House of Justice. Still unresolved in 2000 were relations between far-flung and diverse Stó:lō bands and the tribal government. Discussion of how to develop all aspects of government has been ongoing throughout the nation, and the nation's newspaper publishes critiques of programs and branches and a diverse commentary.

Among the ongoing dialogues was a many-sided consideration of how Stó:lō justice should be properly carried out and what determined tribal tradition for handling trouble and resolving disputes. In the late 1990s, with the discussion about justice nowhere near completion, internal and external forces pressured for the immediate adoption of a pre-packaged and supposedly proven and appropriate justice program from the Māori in New Zealand. Others urged the use of the Navajo Nation Peacemaker Courts approach, but in 1996, provincial and Canadian government funding and legislative enablement precipitated adoption of family group counseling in the House of Justice family and youth services program.[120] After initial difficulties starting the project because of a lack of cooperation by the Royal Canadian Mounted Police and some parents, the partial program attained some successes by 1998. However, a Stó:lō justice worker found that the federal and provincial government agencies were focused on policy and procedure and thwarted creativity in planning.

To create a full diversionary justice program in 1999, the Stó:lō modified the family group counseling approach to follow the Māori program, on the grounds that to do so was the Stó:lō way. The diversion program operated with an advisory board to represent the Stó:lō and each of the Canadian government bodies involved in the program.

Meanwhile, discussion about the issues involved in developing an appropriate program continued throughout the Stó:lō nation. Many said that they wanted a program that re-created Stó:lō tradition (rather than adopting another group's system), and they exchanged views as to what that might be. One concern was the extent to which justice programs (as well as other services) should be managed at the national and band levels. To help the discussion process, in 1999 and 2000, a summer intern—a non-Native law student given an extensive orientation in Stó:lō ways—was hired under the direction of the nation's Aboriginal Rights and Title Department to record "the inherent and perpetual principles and values of the Stó:lō legal tradition."[121] This compilation was intended to assist the chiefs and elders in codifying Stó:lō law. At last report, the discussion process among the Stó:lō nation was continuing on the first stage of government development in general, and on justice and dispute resolution in particular.

3. Conclusion: Successful Governance and Peacemaking Requires Inclusive Participation

LaDonna Harris, Stephen M. Sachs, Benjamin J. Broome, and Jondodev Chaudhuri

The three Coast Salish cases demonstrate that whether an Indian nation is able to develop appropriate laws and justice and dispute-resolution processes that tribal members consider legitimate depends on decisions being made in an inclusive participatory manner that fits the culture and circumstance of the nation. Such appears to have been the case with the Upper Skagit, but clearly was not with the failed South Island Justice Project. Whether the Stó:lō Nation can achieve success, both with its justice arm and its government as a whole, remains to be seen.

Thus, we return to the focus of section 1 of this chapter. As of the last report, the Stó:lō process appears to be participatory and representative, although we do not know the full details and dynamics of the ongoing discussions. There are clear parallels between the Comanche and Stó:lō experiences that are suggestive. Both nations include fragmented tribes with a common cultural heritage and a population that is spread over local communities. In the Comanche case, a culturally appropriate, high-quality participatory discussion process was created whereby the people participated at the tribal and community levels in meetings in which they could discuss concerns until achieving consensus nationally and, in the community meetings, on their own local issues. This process appeared to work very well and achieved good-quality, well-supported decisions, moving the nation away from infighting to harmonious interchange so long as the Comanche used the process. In the Stó:lō situation, councils at the national and band levels already exist. If their process is sufficiently representative—inclusive of all the major views and parties—and if their internal processes are appropriate, with good enough communication between the levels (and across the communities), then some very fine program, governance, and community building will take place.[122]

Some key people will have important roles in developing and carrying out the process effectively. It is important that they are competent in their work as experts, specialists, or specific functionaries, as well as knowledgeable of the relevant problems and needs of the community. They also must be given sufficient direction that they can be focused on and work for the needs of the people in a proper manner. For the

Upper Skagit, the daily operation of the justice system and the drafting of codes was successful because well-oriented, competent personnel were willingly responsible to the people through a representative process. For the Stó:lō, an outside specialist (the law-student intern) appears to have been competent and was given considerable orientation to tribal ways in order to carry out the potentially valuable project of helping record views of traditional justice from a widely scattered community. We do not know how that project was undertaken or whether it was better, worse, or immaterial to have an outside person do the job. For the Comanche, the new tribal chair's unfamiliarity with the ILIS process and its role in the community brought about the collapse of tribal consensus building, returning the nation to disharmony.

As the Comanche, Upper Skagit, and Navajo experiences show, given the fundamental decisions that Native nations need to make and the extent of colonial harm they need to overcome, firmly institution-alizing major new ways requires considerable time, during the course of which events may occur that destroy the continuity of the development. When that happens, or when, as with the South Island Justice Project, the attempt is ill conceived to begin with and leads to collapse or poor results, the people can only learn from experience in order to better apply living, traditional values appropriately to the ongoing reality of their lives.

Notes

1. See also O'Brien, *American Indian Tribal Governments*, chap. 2; Sachs, "Transformational Native American Gift."
2. O'Brien, *American Indian Tribal Governments*, chap. 2; Sachs, "Transformational Native American Gift."
3. Trigger, *The Huron*, especially chap. 6.
4. Sachs, "Transformational Native American Gift," 1–3; O'Brien, *American Indian Tribal Governments*, chap. 2; Walker, *Lakota Society*, 17–18, 23–32; and Trigger, *The Huron*.
5. Wallace and Hoebel, *The Comanches*, chap. 9; O'Brien, *American Indian Tribal Governments*, 17.
6. Sachs, "Transformational Native American Gift," part 1, particularly 1n5; Hoebel, *Law of Primitive Man*, chaps. 5 and 7; and O'Brien, *American Indian Tribal Governments*, 37, 40.
7. LaDonna Harris letter, July 15, 1990, 1, 4–6, and fig. 1, Harris-AIO; Broome, "Promoting Greater Community Participation," 11, fig. 1. There is some discussion of this among the Utes and Shoshones in Jorgensen, *The Sun Dance Religion*, 139–41, 233–34, and 279–80. A recent difficulty resulting from factionalism among the Mohawk is discussed in Alfred, "From Bad to Worse." There is a brief discussion

of the factional difficulties at Pine Ridge and Rosebud Reservations in Mails, *Fools Crow*, 190–91, 194–95, 198–200, and 215–17.

8. For example, the lack of tribal courts and the absence of independence in tribal courts leaves unbalanced power in some tribal councils, in contrast to the dispersion of power in traditional tribal governments. See also O'Brien, *American Indian Tribal Governments*, 294–95; and Cornell, *Accountability, Legitimacy*.

9. The history of this development is outlined in O'Brien, *American Indian Tribal Governments*, parts 2 and 3. We discuss the background of the development of U.S. policy toward tribes and of tribal–federal, state, and local government relations in some detail in chapter 3.

10. O'Brien, *American Indian Tribal Governments*, 86–90; Foster, *Being Comanche*, 138.

11. For example, see Norell, "Chaos Continues," A6; Norell, "The Power That Divides," C1; Castile, *To Show Heart*, 129–33; and Alfred, "From Bad to Worse." See also Fowler, *Arapahoe Politics*, 1, 15: and Cornell, *Accountability, Legitimacy*.

12. Action was taken through the Navajo Nation Local Governance Act, 26 Navajo Nation Code, revised April 28, 1998. The Office of Navajo Government Development has been developing alternative means for chapters to improve the quality of their meetings, an undertaking for which author Stephen Sachs has been a consultant since 1997 and has instituted a process of sharing ideas for improving local meetings and governance among chapters. Much of the early work to develop decentralized government is discussed in the following documents, published by the Office of Navajo Government Development, PO Box 220, Window Rock, AZ, 86515; (928) 871–7214/7161: *The Commission on Navajo Government Development Report: Executive Summary of the Local Governance Act* (Spring 2000); Commission on Navajo Government Development, *Engaging the People of the Navajo Nation in the Process of Nation Building* (December 3, 2001); Commission on Navajo Government Development, *Executive Summary of the Agency-Wide Summits on Nation Building*; *Navajo Nation Statutory Reform Convention* (March 3, 2002); *Navajo Nation Statutory Reform Convention, Red Rock State Park, Church Rock, NM, May 14–15, 2002, Proposed Amendments*; Commission on Navajo Government Development, *Navajo Nation Statutory Reform Convention, Amendments and Policy Reasons for Them* (August 2002); Budget and Finance Committee of the Navajo Nation Council, in Coordination with the Office of Navajo Government Development and the Office of the Navajo Tax Commission, *Agency Wide Hearings on the Proposed Navajo Sales Tax Trust Fund, Plan of Operation for Distributing Funds* (September 24, 2002); Commission on Navajo Government Development, *Navajo Nation Statutory Reform Convention Amendments and Status of Those Amendments* (January 23, 2003); and Office of Navajo Government Development in Coordination with the Office of Navajo Tax Commission, *Navajo Nation Sales Tax Trust Fund Distribution Plan* (March 6, 2003).

13. Office of Navajo Government Development and Diné College Leadership Program, personal communication with author Stephen Sachs.

14. See *Navajo Times*, October 14, 2004, p. A12; and "Indian and Indigenous Developments: U.S. Developments" and "Tribal Developments," *Indigenous Policy* 16, no. 1.

15. On legislative measures, see Donovan, "Officials Put Brakes," A4. On action by the courts, see *Navajo Times*, October 10, 2004, A14. On off-reservation polling places, see *Navajo Times*, October 14, 2004, A4.

16. The Diné Policy Institute of Diné College *Navajo Nation Constitutional Feasibility and Reform Project* report is available as a PDF file at http://www.navajonationcouncil.org/Downloads/DPIupdated.pdf. The authors of the report are: Robert Yazzie, director; Moroni Benally, policy analyst; Andrew Curley, research assistant; Nikke Alex, research assistant; James Singer, research assistant; and Amber Crotty, research intern. On the reports being presented to the Navajo Council, see the press release from the Navajo Nation Council, Office of the Speaker, "Speaker Morgan to present report on feasibility of a constitutional government for Navajo Nation during 2008 Fall session," October 13, 2008. The report is available as a PDF file from the 21st Navajo Nation Council website's "Press Releases" page, at http://www.navajonationcouncil.org/Press%20Release/101308_DPI_Report_Speaker%20Morgan.pdf.

17. Diné Policy Institute, *Reform Project*. Further citations of this work are given in the text.

18. The four models and their authors are: "Model 1: Approaches for an Alternative Model Government" (which discusses general concerns and guidelines for all the alternative models but does not include keeping the current form of government with modification, which appears in the beginning of Model 2), Robert Yazzie; "Model 2: The Bicameral Parliamentary Model," James Singer; "Model 3: "Diné Political Philosophy," Moroni Benally; and "Model 4: Decentralization Model," Nikke Alex, Andrew Curley, and Amber Crotty.

19. The *Southern Ute Drum*, June 4, 1999, 2.

20. The facilitators reflected that the design team has helped the community to redefine and embrace a vision of healing. Given all that has been said about postcolonial dynamics of disharmony, the commitment, courage, honesty, and energy that the facilitators witnessed has been truly inspirational. According to one facilitator: "[S]etbacks, disappointment, and criticism are balanced by a passion for creating a better future for the tribe's children." See Hunt, Gooden, and Barkdull, "Walking in Moccasins." The three authors of this chapter, two of whom are Indian, although not Ute, have been the primary facilitating team at Southern Ute. Author Stephen Sachs, who has a long association with the Southern Ute Indian Tribe, was a participant at several meetings in 2000. On the 2003 and 2006 follow-up of the collaboration that began with the design team, see Brown, "A Meeting of Minds," 1.

21. Issues of the *Southern Ute Drum* in 2001 report announcements of the meetings. Author Stephen Sachs interviewed community members about the Sun Dance dispute and attended both the 2001 and 2002 Sun Dances.

22. For example, see "Indian and Indigenous Developments: U.S. Developments" and "Tribal Developments," *Indigenous Policy* 15, no 1; and Brown, "Tribal Government Reacts." See also the *Southern Ute Drum*, May 14, 2004, 1, 3, 7.

23. Peacock, "Tribal Official Calls," 3. For information about the Yurok Tribe's transportation plan, contact Outreach Coordinator Neil Peacock: 190 Klamath Blvd., Klamath, CA, 95548; (707) 482–1365.

24. In a May 1996 discussion at the Bahá í Faith office in Victoria, British Columbia, it was reported to author Stephen Sachs that several west coast Alaskan and Canadian tribes had adopted the Bahá í method of consultation. This is in essence a modified form of consensus decision making. Although it is undertaken with an elected council formally deciding by majority vote, a strong element of the process is that the decision makers gain a full overview of the issues from all perspectives

by listening carefully to the views of all parties. See John E. Kolstoe, *Consultation*, 81–83, 153–59, 169–72, 175–80. See also the dedication and chaps. 2, 3, and 5.

25. LaDonna Harris letter, July 15, 1990, Harris-AIO. The letter provides a report of the meeting to the participants and follows up on the points assigned to AIO to research at the February TIMS (now ILIS) session. This report, and other documents concerning the TIMS/ILIS process, are available from LaDonna Harris: AIO, 1001 Marquette, Albuquerque, NM, 87102; (505) 842–8677; ladonna@aio.org, aio@aio.org. See also Harris, Sachs, and Broome, "Returning to Harmony"; and Harris, Sachs, and Broome, "Wisdom of the People."

26. After its initial development, the TIMS/ILIS process was first used in design sessions with the Apache Tribe of Oklahoma, the Cheyenne and Arapaho Tribes of Oklahoma, and the Pawnee Nation of Oklahoma, in addition to the Comanche Nation. Results from these sessions are reported in Broome, "Collective Design," 205–28.

27. Wallace and Hoebel, *The Comanches*, 4.

28. Ibid.

29. Ibid., chap. 1; Foster, *Being Comanche*, 32–38; Rollings, *The Comanche*, chap. 1.

30. Hoebel, *Law of Primitive Man*, 128–29.

31. Wallace and Hoebel, *The Comanches*, chap. 1; Hoebel, *Law of Primitive Man*, 129; Foster, *Being Comanche*, 38–52.

32. Hoebel, *Law of Primitive Man*, 128–42; Wallace and Hoebel, *The Comanches*, 22–24, and chap. 9.

33. Wallace and Hoebel, *The Comanches*, 31.

34. Hoebel, *Law of Primitive Man*, chap. 9

35. This is the theme of Foster, *Being Comanche*. That being is relational for other tribes, see *Being Comanche*, chap. 6; and Sachs, "Transformational Native American Gift." For Lakota examples, see Stolzman, *The Pipe and Christ*, particularly 138–139; and Walker, *Lakota Society*, 5–6.

36. The Comanche signed a number of treaties with the United States between 1834 and 1875. The reservation was established under the Medicine Lodge Treaty of 1867. See *Comanche Indian Tribe*; Debo, *History of the Indians*, chap. 12; Wallace and Hoebel, *The Comanches*, chap. 12.

37. For a discussion of the reservation and post-reservation periods, see Wallace and Hoebel, *The Comanches*; and Foster, *Being Comanche*, chaps. 3 and 4.

38. The persistence of a relational sense of "being Comanche" and "living in a moral community regulated by a regard for mutual esteem" (167) is the main theme of Foster's work, *Being Comanche*. A discussion of what "being Comanche" is about runs through the book, and the overall impact of what that involves is summarized in chapter 6.

39. For information on the Kiowa-Comanche-Apache Business Committee, see Foster, *Being Comanche*, 105, 109–14, 135–37, 200n24, and 200n27.

40. Foster, *Being Comanche*, 137–39.

41. Ibid., 113. Broome, Christakis, and Wasilewski, "Designing the Future."

42. According to BIA statistics of November 1991, reported in Broome, "Promoting Greater Community Participation," 1, 14n3.

43. Ibid., 1–2.

44. Unless otherwise noted, information on Comanche tribal government is from Broome, "Promoting Greater Community Participation."

45. Foster, *Being Comanche*, 161.

46. Ibid., 204n79

47. Ibid., 138.

48. Ibid., 60.

49. LaDonna Harris letter, July 15, 1990, Harris-AIO. The letter, to participants in the ILIS (formerly TIMS) process, is available from AIO.

50. Numerous consensus decision-making, problem-solving, and strategic-planning processes have been developed, but most of these processes were not designed to deal with complex issues. The IM process on which ILIS is based deals specifically with difficult situations that have consistently resisted successful resolution, such as those confronting Native American tribes. An overview of IM can be found in Broome and Keever, "Next Generation Group Facilitation," 107–27. For more extensive descriptions of complexity and of the theory guiding IM, see Warfield, *Societal Systems*; and Warfield, *Science of Generic Design*.

51. The first experience using IM in work with Native Americans was during a three-day workshop in 1986 with twelve tribal leaders who met to define the system of problems facing tribal governance. An analysis of this workshop revealed that the participants perceived tribal issues to be approximately five orders of magnitude more complex than is the case for most other organizations to whom IM has been applied. See Broome and Christakis, "Culturally Sensitive Approach," 107–23.

52. See Broome and Cromer, "Strategic Planning," 217–35. The ILIS process as it was carried out with the Comanche is described in Broome, "Role of Facilitated Group," 27–52.

53. The phenomenon of empowering the membership through engaging in participatory process as a source of strengthening the community, increasing effectiveness of the leadership and the community in reaching its goals and objectives, and increasing support for the leadership has been demonstrated repeatedly in private, nonprofit, and public work organizations that build successful team process. For discussion of these points, see Simmons and Mares, *Working Together*; Blumberg, *Industrial Democracy*; Sachs, "Building Trust," 35–44; and Sachs, "Interest and Goal Structure." That the influence of managers (leaders) is strengthened through increasing participation in which the managers are supportive participants, see "Worker Participation and Influence," vol. 4.

54. Sachs, "Building Trust" and "Interest and Goal Structure."

55. In ILIS, idea generation is usually accomplished by first providing participants time to think about their answers to the triggering question and to write them down, then asking the participants to share one of their responses or pass each time it is their turn to speak in the oral round that follows the writing. This process of Nominal Group Technique is discussed in Delbeq, Van de Ven, and Gustafson, *Group Techniques*. Nominal Group Technique is used in situations in which uncertainty and disagreement exist about the nature of possible ideas. An alternative method of idea generation is Idea Writing, a methodology that allows a group to develop a list of ideas and explore their meaning. In this process, small groups of three to six people are formed from the general meeting. Following presentation of a triggering question, each participant writes down a list of answers to the question. Then the written lists of ideas are exchanged among the members, and each member has an opportunity to add ideas as she or he reads the others' papers. The group then discusses and clarifies the ideas, then reports and explains their group's list to the general meeting. Idea Writing is discussed in Warfield, *Science of Generic*

Design, 205–28. It is important to note that the selection of appropriate triggering questions is crucial to the success of ILIS processes. The question sets the agenda for the session and must be selected in a manner that is representative of the concerns of the participants. In the Comanche ILIS sessions reported here, the triggering questions were set by the participants with the assistance of the facilitators.

56. Sitting in a circle is a relational requirement for the process that helps enable participants to see themselves as equal participants and lets them see and speak to one another easily. Thus, a perfectly round seating arrangement is not required, although approximate roundness is preferred. Participants might sit around a square or oblong (or some other shape) table. Seating arrangements will be favorable for the process if the shape of the "circle" is not so distorted as to impair communications (including visual contact and perception) and the sense of equality and solidarity that the seating arrangement attempts to enhance. See Stolzman, *The Pipe and Christ*, 138–39 on this point in Lakota ceremonies.

57. In the Nominal Goup Technique process, five is the number of statements each person is allowed to select as most important from the larger set. This number has been found to result in optimal representation of the divergent opinions that exist in most groups dealing with complex issues. It should be noted that in other consensus decision-making processes, facilitators working with the participants have often adjusted the number of votes per person in unit voting as seems appropriate, offering anywhere from two to unlimited choices.

In the first Comanche ILIS meeting, all ideas receiving at least one vote were included in the structuring process. This was appropriate for the work at hand, especially as it reinforced the principle of inclusiveness, so that each person would feel that their ideas were included. In other consensus decision-making situations, it may be appropriate to consider those items that receive at least a higher number of votes agreed to by the group (i.e., all items receiving at least X number of votes will be considered), or the group might wait to see the pattern of voting and then decide by consensus what the minimum number should be, as is appropriate to the circumstances.

58. The computer-assisted process of Interpretive Structural Modeling is discussed in more detail in Warfield, *Societal Systems* and *Science of Generic Design*.

59. To operate successfully, all participatory processes require the building of trust among the participants: trust in one another, in themselves, and in the process. It is important to begin developing trust at the very beginning to launch the process on a proper footing. Afterward, good experience with the process itself, supported by occasional timely supporting intervention, tends to increase the process of trust, or team, building. In this and a number of other regards, the ILIS process is similar to most other consensus decision-making processes, including workplace participation processes. There is a considerable body of literature on this topic. See Sachs, "Building Trust."

60. For a discussion of tribal members' primary identity as being with their tribe, see Cajete, *Native Science*, 86–105.

61. Whereas larger tribes will be able to have their own facilitators, smaller tribes may find it useful to develop a common pool of facilitators.

62. A particularly glaring case of pseudoparticipation in the workplace as a method of employee manipulation initiated under the guise of employee empowerment through participation is reported in Grenier, *Inhuman Relations*. Other examples of

how participatory processes—that when appropriately and honestly applied benefit employees while increasing organization effectiveness—are sometimes misused are discussed in Parker, *Inside the Circle.*

63. Polyphony as employed by Johann Sebastian Bach is a harmony produced by the interaction of equal musical themes, as opposed to the more usual approach to harmony in Western music tradition in which secondary themes ("harmonies") accompany a main or dominant melody. The former is a democratic or equalitarian approach to harmony whereas the latter is an oligarchic or hierarchical approach.

64. Reported in LaDonna Harris letter, July 15, 1990, Harris-AIO.

65. The organizing and conducting staff consisted of a three-person conducting staff, a court reporter, a video crew of two, and two key people from AIO.

66. Demosophia, or "wisdom of the people," was used as a term for the ILIS process because one of the designers and facilitators of the ILIS process, Alexander Christakis, is Greek. The use of the Greek term is an example of Comanche inclusiveness. LaDonna Harris letter, July 15, 1990, Harris-AIO, 9 and 11.

67. Broome reports on these meetings in "Promoting Greater Community Participation."

68. Broome reports on these meetings in "Designing the Future."

69. In strategic-planning terms, the objectives of the sessions were: (1) to define the problems in the current situation, (2) to create a vision for the future with a set of prioritized goals to be attained, and (3) to establish a set of actions with objectives to attain the goals and realize the vision.

70. See Americans for Indian Opportunity, "Comanche Combined Structuring Forum."

71. Harris, *Final Evaluation.*

72. The Comanche have their own Protestant churches. See Foster, *Being Comanche,* 120–22.

73. Harris, *Final Evaluation,* 2.

74. Developing a well-established consensus process is a strategic matter that needs to be undertaken according to the circumstances. Generally, it is best to include all of the major parties from the beginning, lest those who are left out oppose and undermine the process. For example, failure by a firm to make the union an equal partner in an employee participation process has often led to union opposition and the demise of the process (Sachs, "Building Trust"). But if trying to bring all of the parties together at the beginning is too difficult, it may be advisable to start with the most important parties, then, once some level of trust and narrowing of differences has been achieved among the initial participants, it may be appropriate to bring in the other parties. This was done with some success in settling an eighty-year-old water rights debacle at the Pyramid Lake Paiute Tribe's Reservation, northeast of Reno, Nevada, although one of the parties dropped out of the negotiation and did not participate in the settlement (see Blomquist, "Improving Dispute Resolution"; Wilds and Gonzales, "On the Cutting Edge"; and Burton, *American Indian Water Rights*). Which issues to tackle first is also a strategic question. Often, trust in the process and among the parties can most safely and quickly be built by starting with relatively easy issues. But the process can be most firmly established if the largest issues can be settled first, as was done at Pyramid Lake. The Comanche, using a process designed to deal with complex issues, began with the central questions but set in motion processes to work with a

number of issues of different levels of difficulty according to timetables that seemed appropriate for each issue in the context of the perceived needs of the larger process and situation.

75. LaDonna Harris letter, July 15, 1990, Harris-AIO, 2.

76. Ibid. Stanley Paytiamo was part of the Indian leadership group that participated in the first Interactive Management session with tribal leaders that was held at George Mason University in 1986. After experiencing the Interactive Management process, these leaders recommended that it be applied to Native American issues generally, and some invited AIO and the university to hold sessions in their tribal communities. It was from these experiences that the decision was made to develop ILIS, then called TIMS.

77. Americans for Indian Opportunity, "Progress Report for 1993." ILIS is now a central process for AIO. Its more recent applications, including in international meetings, are reported in AIO's *Ambassador* newsletter. For example, Wheeler, "Bolivian Interactive Advisory Forum," discusses the application of ILIS in a meeting jointly run by AIO and Advancement of Maori Opportunity of New Zealand with Indigenous people in Bolivia, "to develop a working relationship with several Indigenous communities to further the leadership skills and self-determination capabilities of Indigenous people world wide." The same issue also carries a discussion, in "Staff Development," of Virtual ILIS, an ILIS application for Internet meetings.

78. As we discussed in chapter 1, section 2, an examination of Hoebel, *Law of Primitive Man*, particularly chaps. 5, 7, and 11, makes this clear, although readers might prefer something other than Hoebel's evolutionary anthropological terminology to explain his points.

79. Ibid., 146, 160–67, and 172–76.

80. Ibid., 87; Deloria, *Speaking of Indians*, 34.

81. Trigger, *The Huron*, 58–60

82. Hoebel, *Law of Primitive Man*, 143 and 150–156.

83. Ibid., 70, 88–91.

84. Ibid., 142–43, 156–60. Murder, however, was such a heinous act for the Cheyenne that the pollution never fully left the reformed killer, who was ever after perceived not to smell quite right and thus was not permitted to share in communal ceremonies, although he might otherwise participate in the life of the community.

85. Pommersheim, *Braid of Feathers*, 61.

86. Ibid., 62–64.

87. Ibid., 63–66.

88. For a discussion of the complex set of questions concerning the extent and limit of tribal court jurisdiction, see ibid., 79–98.

89. "Indian and Indigenous Developments: U.S. Developments" and "States, Localities, and Indian Nations," *Indigenous Policy* 17, no. 1; Graef, "Disenrollment"; Thompson, "Split Widens," 8; "American Indian and International Indigenous Developments"; and Sachs, "Need for More," 36. In 2008, nine banished members of the Snoqualmie Indian Tribe, including the tribal chairman, several council members, and a minister of the Indian Shaker Church, filed suit against the tribe on May 29 in U.S. District Court for the Western District of Washington, in Seattle. The nine banished members claimed that the tribe violated their civil rights by stripping them of their tribal identity, barring them from tribal lands,

and cutting them off from any tribal benefits, including health-care services, in a continuing struggle for leadership of the tribe ("Indian and Indigenous Developments: U.S. Developments" and "In the Courts," *Indigenous Policy* 19, no. 3). To date, the federal courts have refused to hear such suits on the grounds that the tribes have sovereign immunity from suit in matters of tribal membership. This case involves the Snoqualmie Indian Tribe of Washington. In late April 2008, the tribe banished former tribal chairman Bill T. Sweet, several of his family members, and their supporters (banishing a total of nine tribal members), and purged forty-three individuals from the tribal rolls for failing to meet the blood quantum requirement for membership. The action appears to have been taken over issues of tribal politics (as reported in "Indian and Indigenous Developments: U.S. Developments" and "In the Courts," *Indigenous Policy* 19, no. 1).

90. Dvorak, "Meskwaki Hope," 9. Another recent instance is that of the Hopland Band of Pomo Indians of California, which established its own tribal court in June 2004 to weigh civil disputes occurring on its Hopland Rancheria by applying both contemporary and traditional legal methods. For legal disputes best handled in traditional ways, the Hopland Band established a body of elders known as the Peace Makers Council to mediate. The Hopland Band Tribal Court stated that it was looking forward to working together with the local California court on a government-to-government basis ("Indian and Indigenous Developments: U.S. Developments" and "Tribal Developments," *Indigenous Policy* 15, no. 3).

91. See Miller, *The Problem of Justice*, 194–210, for a discussion of the difficulties that must be overcome to appropriately develop a tribal justice system.

92. Bluehouse and Zion, "Hozhooji Naat'aanii," 181–82.

93. Tso, "Process of Decision Making," 170–89.

94. Navajo Office of Government Development, personal communication with author Stephen Sachs.

95. Zion and Zion, "Hazho's Sokee,'" 170–78; and Kluckholm and Leighton, *The Navaho*, chap. 3. We have discussed some traditional Diné gender relations in chapter 1.

96. Zion and Zion, "Hazho's Sokee,'" 96–100. See also our discussion in chapter 2, including the impact of boarding schools, which is not discussed by Zion and Zion.

97. Zion and Zion, "Hazho's Sokee,'" 100.

98. Ibid., 96–97, 100–102.

99. Donovan, "Police Can't Lie," A3.

100. Ibid., 106–7; Tso, "Process of Decision Making," 170–73, 176–78; and Bluehouse and Zion, "Hozhooji Naat'aanii," 181–89.

101. Moon, "Aboriginal Justice," A3. See also Nielsen and Silverman, *Native Americans, Crime*, chap. 2, for a discussion of the causes behind the problems of sexual misbehavior at Hollow Water First Nation, which mirror those of Native peoples in the United States, including the removal of Native children to abusive boarding schools. For a more extensive discussion of the ill effects and inappropriateness of mainstream Western adjudicatory approaches for many Native people, see Ross, "Leaving Our White Eyes," 152–69, an edited version of the original article that appeared in *Canadian Native Law Reporter* 3 (1989), 1–15. Note that to date, in Canada, First Nations often have not been able to institute their own courts but have been allowed to establish diversionary sentencing-corrections programs.

102. In Hoebel, *Law of Primitive Man*, chap. 7; and Llewellyn and Hoebel, *The Cheyenne Way*.

103. Hoebel, *Law of Primitive Man*, 24, 146–50.

104. Ross, "Leaving Our White Eyes," 159.
105. Ibid. More recent information about Alkali Lake community development is available from "Journey Through Secwepemculew—Secwepemc Leaders" at: http://www.spiritmap.ca/chelseasl.html.
106. We discuss the nature of the problems to be overcome and some of the healing measures that have been effective in transcending them in chapters 2 and 5.
107. To learn more about the Betty Ford Center's relationship with the Alkali Lake Indian Band, see "Betty Ford Center Teams with First Nation Bands," on the Betty Ford Center website's "Addiction, Treatment and Recovery" page, available at http://www.bettyfordcenter.org/recovery/recovery/betty-ford-center-teams-with-first-nation-bands.php.
108. For a general background of drug courts, see Farole et al., "Applying," 40–42. For the use of drug courts by Indian tribes, see Sanvestian, "Southern Ute 'Tuncai,'" 1–2; and "Tuncai Court Success Story," 1–6. See also the U.S. Department of Justice Drug Courts Program Office pamphlet, *Healing to Wellness Courts: A Preliminary Overview of the Tribal Drug Courts.*
109. "Indian and Indigenous Developments: U.S. Developments" and "States, Localities, and Indian Nations," *Indigenous Policy* 17, no 1. For information about the work under this program at Tohono O'odham, contact: Genevieve Porter, Tohono O'odham Justice Center, (520) 383–6318; or Ann Yellott, PeaceWeb Southwest, (520) 670–1541, azyellott@aol.com.
110. The language that the various tribal choice-of-law ordinances use to describe customary law is extremely various. Various ordinances refer to "customary law," "tribal common law," "cultural norms and/or practices," and other variations. For purposes of this explanation, many of these terms, as well as the terms "rules," "values," "traditions," "norms," and "practices," are used somewhat interchangeably to describe the means by which traditional societies governed and continue to govern conduct.
111. Muscogee Nation Code Ann. Title 27 § 1–103.
112. For example, American jurisprudence, which grew largely out of English common law, developed the various causes of action for tort claims through a long series of court decisions rather than through any codified law. Whether a given activity gives rise to a justiciable cause of action is therefore dependent on a society's customs and values, which in turn shape that society's common law. Therefore, there is no reason why tribes should be bound by causes of action that grew out of nontribal common law.
113. Gone are the days when tribes were able to exercise complete adjudicatory authority over all activities within their borders. Instead, federal courts have developed an extremely murky and increasingly illogical set of rules to determine the types of disputes that tribal courts can hear and the types of parties over whom tribal courts have jurisdiction. Federal courts give almost no deference to tribal court interpretations of these federal rules and readily review the basis for tribal court jurisdiction when such authority is based on federal law. One last remaining stronghold of tribal court jurisdiction is that of a tribal court's ability to interpret tribal law.
114. Title 27, section 1–104 of the Muscogee Nation Code states, "[w]here any doubt arises as to the common law of the Muscogee people as established by custom and usage, the Court may request the advice of counselors familiar with these customs and usages."

115. Miller, *The Problem of Justice*. Summary descriptions and key findings about the three justice programs are particularly to be found on 38–40, 77–79, 121–22, 125–27, 133–62, 169–74, 194, 199, and 201–11, but important points are presented across the entire work.

116. As exemplified by Ross, "Leaving Our White Eyes," and by articles about the contemporary use of traditional Native processes for rehabilitation and re-creating harmony, including Zion and Zion, "Hazho's Sokee'"; and Tso, "Process of Decision Making."

117. Miller, *The Problem of Justice*, 175–99, details the background and development of the South Island Justice Project.

118. Ibid., 183.

119. Ibid., 121–62 discusses the Stó:lō Nation and its justice project.

120. Promoted by James Zion, counsel for the Navajo Court, ibid., 156.

121. Ibid., 157–58.

122. Ibid., 143, 150–56. Good communication appears to have been exemplified by the Stó:lō newspaper, which publishes representative discussions of the issues. This can be accomplished by a great many other means and media, eventually including the Internet, once the infrastructure and development of its use for the purpose spreads sufficiently through Indian country.

Five

Rebuilding the Circle

REESTABLISHING APPROPRIATE MEANS FOR OVERCOMING THE
ECONOMIC, EDUCATIONAL, PSYCHOLOGICAL, AND SOCIAL
PROBLEMS OF PHYSICAL AND CULTURAL GENOCIDE

Stephen M. Sachs, LaDonna Harris, Barbara Morris,
Gregory A. Cajete, and Phyllis M. Gagnier

Exercising sovereignty effectively, attaining tribal self-sufficiency, and returning communities to harmony require building an adequate economic base, educating tribal members, and overcoming the psychological and social wounds that colonialism has inflicted. This chapter focuses on what has been developing and how progress can be attained appropriately concerning these matters. In section 1, we discuss how to properly undertake Indian economic development holistically, so that it creates balanced community development. In section 2, we consider the creation of well-functioning Indian education that preserves culture, fosters a strong positive identity as a basis of confidence for achievement, and empowers tribal members to contribute effectively to their communities while functioning effectively in the wider world. In section 3, we consider how traditional principles can be and are being applied to heal the wounds inflicted by the colonial experience to make Native people and nations whole again.

1. Nurturing the Circle: American Indian Nation Sovereignty and Economic Development
Stephen M. Sachs

Adequate and appropriate economic development is a necessity if American Indian nations are to attain a high level of sovereignty and self-sufficiency in order to govern themselves and be equal participants in American federalism. But experience has shown that if it is not accompanied by sufficient sovereignty and a major say in how economic efforts are undertaken, Native economic development rarely succeeds.

As we discussed in chapter 2, despite considerable gains since the 1930s, and especially in the most recent decades, American Indians continue to rank near the bottom of measured groups in almost every social, health, and economic indicator, experiencing more than twice the average poverty and unemployment rates and the worst math and English achievement levels, while lagging in high school and college graduation rates. They also have the shortest life expectancy and suffer more from diseases than any other group. At the same time, Native Americans receive much less federal money per person for services than do Americans in general, with Washington spending more money for the health care of one federal prisoner than it does for one Indian.

To differing extents, most recognized Indian nations suffer from poverty, including high unemployment, low income, and low net personal worth. Although the situation is improving for many nations, most tribes experience a shortage of capital and income and suffer from extremely underdeveloped infrastructure, which restricts their ability to undertake economic and community development and provide jobs and sufficient housing of adequate quality, as well as appropriate and adequate health, education, police, and social services.

Although tribal economies generally have improved over the past few decades, they remain undercapitalized and underdeveloped. For many years, it was extremely difficult for tribes to obtain capital because tribal land was held in trust by the U.S. government and could not be used as collateral for loans, while neither the government nor the private sector provided loan guarantees. As Indian nations began to be able to make their own economic decisions, they realized that they could borrow against the value of future natural resource extraction, as well as gain capital through increasing that production and obtain better prices by negotiating their own deals. Thus, in 1970, during the gasoline shortages brought on by the Middle East oil embargo, a group of tribal leaders, who met for the purpose of having the tribes take over management of their gas and oil, formed the Council of Energy Resource Tribes (CERT).[1] To finance CERT initially, the organization met with government agencies that dealt with energy. Almost all, except the Bureau of Indian Affairs (BIA), assisted CERT in getting started. CERT, in combination with recent efforts and developments, has placed many tribes in a better economic position, but the preponderance of Indian nations and their members continue to be considerably less well off economically than the rest of the country. Additionally, lack of funding reduces the ability of tribes to govern themselves, and most Indian nations lack the resources to take over many federal programs, which makes it more difficult for tribal governments to collaborate with other governments and have an equitable say about public policy that affects them. Thus, there is an immense need for the expansion of tribal economies.

From 1990 to 2010, Indian nations as a group have made significant economic gains: a few tribes are very well off, some have made a little improvement, and most have significantly improved but are still way behind the rest of the country. For the 40 percent of the tribes that have them, casinos have played a role in fiscal improvement, but the most important factor in economic growth has come about because nations have gained control of their economic initiatives: from 1990 to 2000, tribes with casinos have increased economic development by 36 percent, and tribes without gaming have increased economic development by 30 percent.[2] At the same time, although there remain significant barriers to individual Indigenous business development, Native American business activity is growing rapidly on and around reservations. Among companies earning more than $50,000 annually, firms owned by Native Americans are outperforming other minority-owned ventures. Dun & Bradstreet reports that American Indian enterprises, which constitute 5 percent of minority-owned businesses, have a greater average sales volume and larger number of employees than their counterparts. However, particularly in states with large Indian populations, fewer Indigenous people own businesses than non-minority people do. From 1987 to 2000, the number of Indian-owned enterprises grew by 84 percent, seven times the national rate, to 197,000, with sales-rate growth double that of the U.S. average, so that Indian enterprise gross incomes have expanded by 179 percent to $34.3 billion.[3]

Wind and Solar Power: The New Casinos?

For a large number of tribes, particularly in isolated areas in the western United States, including Alaska, developing alternative sources of energy provides hope for substantial economic development as well as inexpensive energy, in some cases for homes that currently do not have electricity.[4] A large and growing number of Indian nations, particularly in the West, have been initiating alternative electricity generation, primarily wind farms but also the use of solar voltaic cells. So far, this development has been slow to grow for a combination of reasons: difficulty obtaining capital and large-scale power development expertise; the need to build working relationships with distant companies with different cultural backgrounds; a worldwide shortage of wind turbines as demand grows; the slowness of the federal bureaucracy—particularly the BIA—to approve development plans; and the distance of many reservations from much of the national power grid, which requires extensive infrastructure creation. Although many tribes have been in the process of developing wind power, some for a number of years, as of fall 2008, only one major wind farm was operating on Indian land: the 50-megawatt project on the Campo Reservation, near San Diego. Another major wind farm is finally about to come into being on the Rosebud Indian Reservation in South Dakota, one of the poorest reservations in the United States.

Sprouting a Wind Farm on the Rosebud

The project began in 2003. After erecting a 750-kilowatt turbine to power the Rosebud Casino near the Nebraska border, the Rosebud Sioux tribal council authorized building the Owl Feather War Bonnet Wind Farm, a 30-megawatt project that could power about twelve thousand homes and bring some $5 million to the tribe over twenty years. After five years of negotiations with a non-Indian developer, Distributed Generation Systems of Colorado, in the early fall of 2008, council president Rodney M. Bordeaux said that he expected to sign a deal with the firm to begin construction. The total estimated twenty-year income was about $1.7 million less than the developer's original offer because of an acrimonious last-minute dispute with the tribe, which seemed to be based in misunderstandings stemming from differences in culture and experience. The DOE is providing almost $450,000 in funding for the 50-acre wind farm. Construction was delayed initially because the BIA took eighteen months to sign off on the original agreement, which was approved by the tribal council in 2006. Under the terms of that agreement, the tribe would receive $280,000 in royalties during the first year of the wind farm's operation. The amount would have grown each year, with the twenty-year total topping $7 million.

Other Tribal Alternative Energy Developments

Among the many nations moving to launch sizable wind generation are the Mandan, Hidatsa, and Arikara Nation, known as the Three Affiliated Tribes, of North Dakota, which began operating its first wind turbine on the Fort Berthold Reservation in spring 2006. In California, the Morongo Band of Mission Indians were constructing a wind generation station to meet their own and the surrounding community's power needs in the summer of 2008. The Navajo Nation has included wind power in its energy development program and in a series of important smaller scale projects using photovoltaic cells and wind turbines to bring power to isolated homes well away from the U.S. electric grid. That development has been slow because of limited funding. As of June 2005, Laguna Pueblo designer Dave Melton and Sacred Power Corporation of Albuquerque, of which he is co-owner, had brought electricity to thirty isolated homes on the Navajo Nation. The Hopi Tribe is proceeding to develop both wind and photovoltaic electric-power generation. Honor the Earth, in coordination with Solar Energy International, the Western Shoshone Defense Project, American Spirit Productions, and the Battle Mountain Colony of the Te-Moak Tribe of Western Shoshone Indians, provided free training and installation of a photovoltaic system in Western Shoshone territory near Elko, Nevada, in April 2005. Honor the Earth continues to provide technical assistance to Indigenous nations using wind turbines and photovoltaic cells in New Mexico. The Intertribal Council on Utility Policy, a consortium of Northern Plains tribes, has been promoting tribal wind power both across some twenty Great Plains reservations that are all connected to the federal hydropower grid and on land owned by the nonprofit Alaska Village Electric Cooperative in Kasigluk, Alaska.

Tribal Sovereignty and Economic Development

Experience shows that tribal economic development needs to be controlled by tribes and their members, although appropriate outside expert advice and technical assistance is necessary. Studies of economic development on reservations demonstrate that imposed programs have largely failed, whereas those that have been successful have almost always been undertaken by Indian people themselves or in full partnership with others.[5] Only the members of a local community can fully understand their own situation, though outside experts with a sufficient knowledge of the particular people and place may be extremely helpful in partnering with community members to build understanding of the situation and identify realistic options for action.[6] The more the local culture differs from that of outside experts or decision makers—as Native cultures differ from the American mainstream—the more this is the case. Moreover, economic development is not merely a matter of providing jobs and income. It is part of community development and needs to be undertaken consistently with the values and goals of the community, both of which the community must determine for itself.

Inappropriate Government: A Barrier to Tribal Development

The process by which the community decides what its values and goals are must be consistent with the culture of the community members.[7] Tribal sovereignty is not the sovereignty of the tribal government or council, which is only an instrument for the expression of the sovereignty of the Native nation. Many Indian nations suffer from culturally inappropriate governments imposed by the United States that need revision as an essential step toward returning their communities to harmony and initiating effective economic and community advancement. Because most Native people continue to hold inclusive participatory values (although they may be frustrated by a lack of opportunity to participate in community decision making), in most instances it is essential to give tribal members ownership (and make them feel like owners) of their nation's economic processes and entities by involving them in economic decision making in ways that fit their traditions. Doing so will not only prevent economic development from being a divisive issue by moving the community toward harmony while increasing the quality and consistency of tribal economic policy, but it will also increase the ability of the tribal government to be a reliable partner with external entities and work for tribal economic advancement.

Similarly, many Indian nations either do not have judicial entities or have tribal courts that are not independent from the tribal councils. This situation has made it difficult for communities to achieve equitable resolution of conflicts and trouble cases within the community that are widely recognized as legitimate.[8] It has also been a deterrent to numerous outside businesses that undertake economic ventures with tribes by engendering fear that tribal courts will be partial to the nation should a dispute arise.[9]

In addition, although it is right for tribal governments and the tribal political process to set the goals and guidelines for tribally owned businesses and to review their operation, tribal businesses need autonomy in their day-to-day operations, so long as they function well within the purposes and guidelines set for them.[10] This interrelationship is necessary to ensure that tribal enterprises are run professionally and that the quality of their management is not undercut by politics, weighed down by bureaucracy, or overrun by turbulence from rapid shifts in policy or interpersonal conflict. It is also consistent with the traditional dispersion of power in Indian nations that promotes their participatory democracy.

Moving from Dependence to Independence

One set of concerns that many Native nations need to address as they grow their economies is how to do so in ways that increase the independence of nation citizens and overcome the dependence that colonialism has created. Tribal member participation in decision making, in education and other services, and in appropriately developed programs can and does play an important role in doing so. In addition, tribes need to find a good balance for their situation between sharing tribal income directly with members and investing it to increase member opportunity and empowerment through funding such vehicles as education, including scholarships; cultural exchanges and technical training; business financing; and creating meaningful employment.

In addition, author Phyllis Gagnier has noted in her education work that receiving sudden increases in income without having had previous training in managing money can be a source of trauma for some students, their parents or guardians, and their extended families. For some truant students, there is a perception that the current flow of money will continue indefinitely, which leads them to conclude that their education is not essential because they will not need an income. Thus, significant increases in funds are a disincentive to Native students to complete their education, a situation that contributes to poor academic performance and truancy. There is also evidence within tribal communities that with "sudden money," some youth will make significant expenditures to purchase disposable items such as "stuff" for self and friends, including large items such as cars, as well as take advantage of the ability to quickly enter into the purchase and experimental use of drugs.

Compounding the problems of a quick inflow of money for Indian youth is the fact that at eighteen years of age, the brain's frontal lobes, which govern decision making and planning for the future, are not yet fully developed, leaving young people vulnerable to predators, immediate gratification, and alienation. (We will discuss overcoming and preventing this situation in our discussion of education later in this chapter.) Students and their families may find their money is soon gone, leaving them feeling guilty. Thus, adequate financial literacy education is necessary to support a program of tribal income sharing.

Running Native Businesses with Culturally Appropriate Management

To promote the effectiveness of Native enterprises and reinforce tribal culture, it is extremely valuable to run tribal businesses in accordance with the nation's culture. Because the traditional values of most Native nations are participatory, in many instances, it would make sense to operate a nation's businesses as participatory organizations. Today, the wider world is increasingly discovering the advantages of using traditional tribal organization principles and methods in the operation of business, government, and nonprofit organizations.[11] Research shows that organizations, particularly in business, with properly structured and functioning employee participation, or team process, function better by every measure.[12] Well-functioning workplace participation engenders better organizational communication, more knowledgeable decision making, more understanding, greater care taken in carrying out decisions and functions, and increased commitment and morale among employees, bringing greater efficiency, productivity, and effectiveness to the organization. Thus, it would seem especially appropriate for Indigenous organizations, whose cultural values are participatory, to operate with organizational democracy. For tribally owned enterprises, this can mean developing an appropriate participatory or team process that is typically best reinforced by a parallel reward system that might include group productivity bonuses and profit sharing.[13] In businesses owned by tribal members, employee participation can be enhanced by structuring the enterprise for democratic worker ownership. This can be accomplished by employing a variety of strategies, including employee cooperatives and employee stock ownership plans (ESOPs), under which debt is separated from participation so that members of the organization can own varying financial stakes in an enterprise without limiting their right and ability to participate in decision making. The idea is to use financial reward in ways that reinforce the process of organizational operation while encouraging investment so that through participation in decision making and from financial compensation, employees feel like owners—and contributors to tribal welfare—in the course of advancing their personal (and family) interests.[14]

Applying Traditional Participatory Inclusiveness to Native Business and Economic Development

A fine instance of a participatory employee-owned Indian enterprise is Navasew, a garment-sewing business that began in an abandoned factory on the Navajo Nation reservation in December 2003.[15] The company, which manufactures dress shirts for the navy and combat uniform shirts for the army, began carefully with technical and planning assistance from the ICA Group, a venture capital firm with experience working with Native business; financing from Navajo Nation, Omega Apparel—a firm experienced in the garment field—and ICA Group's Local Enterprise Assistance Fund; and grants from the U.S. Department of Agriculture (USDA). Navasew's Navajo workforce is trained in all aspects of the apparel business, so that employees can effectively participate in the management of the firm. By late 2005, plans for expanding the operation were in progress.

The Mondragon Model

An excellent model of an alternative community-wide participatory organization that might be useful for Indian nations to consider is the Basque federation of worker cooperatives centered at Mondragon, in the Basque region of Spain. The Mondragon Cooperative Federation is in fact similar to the much more recent holistic development by tribes such as the Mississippi Choctaw and Southern Utes, which we discuss below. The Mondragon Corporation now owns participatory businesses and undertakes business ventures with partners all over the world.[16] It grew from a single workshop employing five people in 1956 to a federation of well over one hundred primary-producer cooperatives by the 1980s that employed more than twenty thousand people. The first cooperative, which began as a manufacturer of cookstoves, by the 1960s became Spain's leading manufacturer of household appliances and expanded in the 1980s to realize a quarter of its sales internationally, primarily in Latin America. The primary cooperatives are supported by secondary cooperatives, including an investment bank, educational cooperatives—one of which became Mondragon University in 1997—and a research and development unit that created its own robots for manufacturing. There are also retail, restaurant, and housing cooperatives, as well as Basque cultural organizations and activities, so that the federation functions very much as a community. As a whole, the Mondragon enterprises have been far more productive than conventional businesses in Spain; in the 1980s, Mondragon businesses realized a 25 percent greater return on investment than standard Spanish businesses did. By 2000, the cooperatives expanded to provide more than fifty-three thousand jobs, and they took advantage of developments in globalization to further internationalize their business to almost double sales and employment between 1995 and 2000.

An important element in Mondragon's success has been its financial arrangements. Co-op employees have individual accounts, similar to ESOPs in the United States, that pay out to them when they retire or otherwise leave federation employment. If their co-op makes money, a share goes into their accounts. If the enterprise loses money, the employees help support the business with deductions from their accounts. As with ESOPs, employees generally accumulate a large nest egg by the time of their retirement, which gives them an interest in the long-term performance of the firm. In the meantime, the capital in the employee accounts is available to the bank to support enterprise development, although some of the capital is invested outside the Mondragon cooperatives to provide the security of diversification. The entrepreneurial division at the co-op bank has been exceedingly careful in choosing new investments and appoints an incubation team of experts to nurture each new business until it is ready to operate on its own. In more than a half-century, no Mondragon cooperative has failed.

Commanding a large amount of capital, the co-op bank, whose board is composed of representatives of each cooperative, has acted in a tribal manner for both the good of each enterprise and the larger whole. It makes low-interest loans to new undertakings and to those that are going through hard times. When the market changes, the bank shifts its investment and loan activity. Similarly, because the federation has its own educational and training entities, when a cooperative needs fewer workers, the excess employees are supported in going back to school. When they have finished their training or educational advancement, they go back to their co-op; if it does not need them, they are placed in a federation firm that does.

As a result of these entrepreneurial and educational arrangements, when the recession of the 1980s hit Europe, the Mondragon Federation simply adjusted to it, financially supporting temporarily troubled businesses, retraining momentarily unneeded workers, and investing and marketing to expand business overseas, so that for Mondragon worker-owners, there really was no recession. In the 1980s, when European manufacturing began having difficulty succeeding against Asian competition, the federation bank shifted its investment priority into developing service industry. In the 1990s, taking advantage of globalization, the federation doubled its sales and employment by internationalizing further. Mondragon's automotive division, for example, whether by purchase, start-up, takeover, or joint venture, has acquired manufacturing plants close to its customers in Brazil, Mexico, India, Great Britain, and the Czech Republic, while the appliance cooperative, Fagor, which already had plants in Argentina and Morocco, has purchased facilities in Poland and the Czech Republic.

Appropriate Education, Training, and Technical Assistance

Because a high percentage of Indian people living on isolated, low-income reservations or in low-income urban neighborhoods lack business and effective personal finance experience, the need exists for business and financial education for Native Americans.[17] First, education in economic literacy is necessary, including how to deal with banks and other financial institutions; how to build, maintain, and understand credit; and how to access and use financial resources. Second, although entrepreneurship is compatible with traditional Indigenous culture, a high percentage of American Indians do not have knowledge of mainstream business and entrepreneurship practices and need education in such basic knowledge and skills as how to develop a business plan and how to understand investment, cash flow, marketing, and other general business practices. Similarly, without a business background, many Native American business owners need technical assistance and mentoring regarding many areas of their business operations.[18]

To be most effective, business, financial, and technical education and training need to be provided in appropriate ways to fit the culture and individual learning styles of those involved. Native nations can develop the capacity to offer this training themselves or can collectively provide incubators for Native-owned businesses. For example, four Indian nations in Maine operate the Four Directions Development Corporation, which offers technical assistance and funding to Native businesses.[19]

When tribes wish to start up businesses or manage exploitable resources, they might need to contract with experienced external firms to manage the enterprise or undertake the resource extraction. It is advisable in such cases for Indian nations to include in the contract that the external management firm will train tribal members to take over the enterprise. A number of tribes have done this, including the Southern Ute Indian Tribe, which arranged for training and the right to buy out the management contract from the company that helped it set up its casino.[20] When enough tribal members had attained sufficient training and experience, the nation exercised its buyout right and took over management of the casino, consequently increasing tribal income. Similarly, the Southern Utes arranged for training of tribal members when they organized their own natural gas distribution company. As gas leases with external production companies have expired, the tribe has taken over the gas production and distribution, significantly increasing the amount of money the tribe brings in from each cubic foot of distributed gas. With the increased income, the tribe was then able to invest in natural gas pipelines extending from Ignacio, Colorado, all the way to Texas. As of summer 2007, the Southern Utes controlled the distribution of roughly 1 percent of the country's natural gas supply. Natural gas revenues have been used to fuel tribal economic diversification. By mid-2007 the Southern Utes were worth nearly $4 billion.

Technical Assistance from Native Organizations

Technical assistance can be provided by Native organizations. There have long been state, regional, and national Indigenous chambers of commerce. A recent development is the American Indian Alaska Native Tourism Association, which hired its first director in September 2008 to oversee tribal tourism operations. In December 2007, Ron Erdmann, Travel and Tourism Industries deputy director of research in the U.S. Department of Commerce, stated that Native tourism markets are expected to grow as international visitors return to the United States after the greatest travel decline in U.S. history.[21]

Gaining Access to Capital and Financing at Reasonable Interest Rates

Many American Indian nations and tribal members who seek to become entrepreneurs, particularly on reservations, lack access to debt and equity capital and often are confronted with very high interest rates for the capital that is available. For tribal members on isolated reservations, there are often no financial institutions within very long distances, and the lack of electricity or telephone service can prevent electronic access to financial resources. Part of the problem of obtaining financing, and doing so at favorable rates, is that because land and resources are held in trust, they are not available as loan collateral. In the past, this often meant that tribes could not launch potentially successful businesses, such as tourist hotels, themselves and were reduced to leasing land to outside companies that would create and manage the businesses, forcing the tribes to accept a limited number of dead-end, low-paying jobs and a small portion of the enterprise income.

As Indian nations have gained more control of their economic affairs, including the ability to negotiate lucrative contracts for energy extraction and rights of way, this situation has begun to change, and more capital has become available. The potential profitability of casinos has made acquiring capital or investment to launch them relatively easy, and although the increased tribal income generated by gaming has typically been far less than what is required for full business and social service development, it has provided a significant new source of income. However, numerous tribes still lack the capital they need to begin to approach economic self-sufficiency and to develop education, housing, health, and other services, as well as the infrastructure necessary for all kinds of tribal development.

The money needed for tribal economic development can come from a number of sources such as grants, investments, and loans. The federal government can play a major role in meeting its trust responsibility, both with direct grants and with measures that encourage private investment, grants, and low-cost loans. Such measures can include loan guarantees and devices such as declaring low-income reservations "enterprise zones," which entitles private parties to receive federal tax reductions for on-reservation investments. A number of foundations have already provided some important assistance. For example, the Northwest Area Foundation provided the Lummi Nation of Washington a $200,000 grant in January 2004 to reduce the tribe's 18.3 percent poverty rate through wellness, education, and economic development efforts.[22] And Microsoft Corporation deposited $1 million in the Native American Bank to help make mortgages available to American Indians.[23]

Developing Tribal Development Organizations
Tribal institutions and tribes can also play an important role in providing

economic development funding to Native nations and Indigenous-owned businesses. One important event has been the rise of Native Community Development Financial Institutions.[24] As part of a conference hosted by Opportunity Finance Network in October 2007, a Community Development Financial Institutions meeting brought together thirty-five certified Native Community Development Financial Institutions funds, which provided their Native nations community-scale economic opportunity through financial literacy training, savings plans, business strategies, basic loans, informational networks, technical assistance with the general requirements of business and home ownership, and training in specific financial and administrative tasks. Six years earlier, only two Native Community Development Financial Institutions existed: First Nations Oweesta Corporation and the Hopi Credit Association. Oweesta at that time had just become independent from its mentor organization and current affiliate, First Nations Development Institute. First Nations Development had become the only national Native Community Development Financial Institutions intermediary, as certified by the Community Development Financial Institutions Fund of the U.S. Treasury Department (which means, among other things, that it can assist other organizations to become Community Development Financial Institutions Fund–certified). By February 2007, First Nations Development had directed $22 million to Native initiatives. Native Community Development Financial Institutions have done as much as gaming to advance Native economies. For example, Citizen Potawatomi Community Development Corporation in Shawnee, Oklahoma, has offered a combination of training, technical assistance, financial education for enterprises, and loans, including seventy-six micro business loans to members of the Citizen Potawatomi Nation, investing $5 million in Native-owned businesses and granting more than three hundred loans totaling over $300,000 to employees of the nation, greatly increasing the number of Citizen Potawatomi small businesses and jobs. Similarly, Four Directions Development Corporation of Orono, Maine, since its founding in 2001 has built a portfolio of $2 million in housing and small business loans while establishing a network of partners that range from Quakers to bankers as the organization's services have expanded to every Maine tribe.

The Lakota Fund has been making loans to small businesses on the Pine Ridge Reservation in South Dakota since 1986 and runs the Spirit Horse Gallery, an outlet for Oglala Lakota artists and artisans.[25]

Indian nations can also help their own members, as the Cherokee Nation Commerce Department has done by promoting tribal member savings for business development, education, and home ownership through offering individual development accounts, budget training, and credit counciling.[26] Federally recognized tribes, as governments, can issue bonds for economic development and other purposes, although current law limits tribal bonding power to strictly "governmental functions." Thus, it has been proposed that federal statutes be changed to make Indian nations fully equal to other governments in this regard.[27]

Native American Banking

The rise of Native American Bank has been a significant development. Native American Bank provides a variety of banking services to tribes and individual Indians, including loans for capitalization and business services.[28] A growing number of Indian nations have started their own banks, but not all of them have been doing well financially.

Indian-owned banks had mixed success during 2007. In California, the Borrego Springs Bank, owned by the Viejas Band of Kumeyaay Indians, lost $801,000 during 2007 after earning $5 million in 2006, with assets falling from $86 million to $81.3 million, and deposits flat at $67 million. Bank2 in Oklahoma City, owned by the Chickasaw Nation, showed a small gain in earnings in 2007, rising to $316,000 in profits from $210,000 in 2006. Bank2 grew in asset size, reporting $86.5 million in assets at the end of the year, up from $82.9 million in 2006. Deposits totaled $77 million on December 31, 2007, up from $72.8 million a year earlier; equity grew modestly as well, to $8.8 million from $8.2 million. Canyon Bancorp, in Palm Springs, California, owned by the Agua Caliente Band of Cahuilla Indians, posted a substantial profit of $3.6 million in 2007. Its Canyon National Bank earned $421,000 during the fourth quarter, down from $1.2 million in the fourth quarter of 2006, but it enjoyed a 15 percent increase in assets during the year, to $289 million. Net loans were up 22.5 percent to $248 million. Deposits increased slightly, from $226.4 million to $230.6 million as of December 31, 2007. Shareholder equity rose by 17 percent at the bank during 2007 to $28.6 million. The Woodlands National Bank in Hinckley, Minnesota, owned by the Mille Lacs Band of Ojibwe, made $1.3 million in 2007, down from $1.8 million in 2006. It reported $114.2 million in assets to the Federal Deposit Insurance Corporation at the end of 2007, down from $119.6 million in assets in 2006. Deposits also fell, from

$99 million at the end of 2006 to $94 million at the end of 2007. Equity increased during that time, from $15.5 million to $16.6 million. Bay Bank in Green Bay, Wisconsin, owned by the Oneida Nation of Wisconsin, saw a small increase in its earnings year over year. It made $836,000 in 2007, up from $700,000 in 2006. The bank also bought a parcel of land in Indio, California, to develop its fifth branch in the Palm Springs area. The Oneida's Bay Bank managed a small increase in assets, rising from $99.6 million at the end of 2006 to $102.4 million at the end of 2007. At that time, it had $78.6 million in deposits, down from $83.2 million in 2006. Equity stood at $11.1 million at the end of 2007, up a little from $10.8 million at the end of 2006.[29]

In some cases, the need for on-reservation banking has been filled by Native people. For example, in 2007, Turtle Mountain State Bank, a private bank partly owned by Native Americans, opened on the Turtle Mountain Band of Chippewa Indians' reservation in North Dakota. The question in November 2008 is how well Indigenous banking will emerge from the credit crunch of 2008, and how federal policy, particularly under the Obama administration, might affect Native banks and banking interests.

Intertribal Collaboration to Share and Leverage Economic Well-Being

Now that some Native nations have become economically self-sufficient and others are reaching that stage, economically advantaged Indian nations would do well to assist their less well off brothers and sisters through investment, grants, and technical assistance, either directly or through Indian economic institutions.[30] This process has begun to occur.

Intertribal coalitions and organizations are forming to finance development. For example, the Mashantucket Pequot Tribal Nation, with huge profits from its Connecticut casino, has been involved in a number of collaborative development ventures. In the summer of 2007, for instance, the Mashantucket Pequots and the Pauma Band of Luiseño Indians of California made plans to build a $300 million luxury resort and new casino at Casino Pauma in the hills of north San Diego County.[31] Earlier, the Yavapai-Apache Nation of Arizona assisted the La Posta Band of Mission Indians of California to fund, design, and build a casino east of San Diego.[32] The Mohegan Tribe's tribal council voted in April 2008 to return more than half a million dollars in federal grants to the BIA to be redistributed to tribes with greater needs, particularly other members of the United South and Eastern Tribes.[33]

A new economic initiative that would link land-rich, cash-poor tribes with wealthy gaming tribes was announced in February 2008 by Assistant Secretary for Indian Affairs Carl Artman, Mashantucket Pequot Tribal Nation Chairman Michael Thomas, Seminole Tribal Chairman Mitchell Cypress, and other United South and Eastern Tribes.[34] The purpose is to stimulate purchasing by the wealthy tribes from less financially well-endowed partner tribes. Officials of the National Tribal Development Association, which developed the "Join the Circle" tribal economic development and diversification model, said they were extremely pleased that someone had been listening and that another piece of the model was coming together. The National Tribal Development Association is an association of forty-nine tribes dedicated to creating and stimulating intertribal trade and commerce. The association model is based on a partnership between wealthy tribes, nongaming or "marginal" gaming tribes, private investors, current gaming vendors and service providers, and, in some cases, elements of the federal government. The model would establish collective marketing capability for existing tribal and Indian businesses and, more importantly, create and enhance incentives to bring distribution points, manufacturing, assembly, fabrication, and importation points to Indian country. The National Tribal Development Association and its partner, Native American Business Development, have drafted business plans under which the customers are the owners of the distribution networks, manufacturing facilities, service points, service companies, and importation centers, similarly to the Costco warehouse club model.

In 2008, the Indian gaming industry and tribal governments associated with Indian gaming are estimated to have spent perhaps $15 billion a year on goods and services. Less than 1 percent of this spending was estimated to go to Indian, tribal, or Native majority–owned companies. The National Indian Gaming Association (NIGA) created the goal of having its member tribes enforce Indian preference in hiring and contracting so that at least 10 percent of what the association purchases in goods and services would come from Indian country sources or Native majority–owned companies. NIGA Chairman Harold Monteau suggested that the non-Indian vendors, companies, and firms should be asked to do the same thing: "Tribes should demand that these companies not only hire Indians but they should be subcontracting with Indian and Native companies. They should be partnering with tribes or Native and Indian-owned companies to produce, assemble, distribute, and deliver the goods and services to our tribes and our Indian gaming industry consumers.

Without the full cooperation and participation of these non-Indian companies and firms, even NIGA's 'modest' goal of 10 percent will not be reached."[35]

In 2008, more than one hundred Alaska Native village corporations banded together for the first time to form the Alaska Native Village Corporation Association to stimulate their economic growth.[36] The Native corporations, formed by Congress under the 1971 Alaska Native Claims Settlement Act, range from some of the largest businesses in the state to tiny companies that make little or no money for their shareholders. The association encourages the larger companies to coach the smaller ones, according to Maver Carey, chief executive of the Kuskokwim Corporation, a leader in the effort to unite the village corporations. The association also aims to promote land management and development policies, lobby the government, and organize group purchasing to save money on corporate expenses.

The Need to Adequately Communicate Resource Availability

To be useful, financial and other resources for tribes and Native entrepreneurs must be readily available. Such information needs to be included in education, technical assistance, and public information venues, including the Internet. It should be regularly updated and made available by Indian nations and institutions, financial institutions, and government agencies.

Reducing Bureaucracy, Clarifying Rules and Processes, and Providing Necessary Infrastructure

Both tribal governments and the federal government can clarify policies and rules and reduce bureaucracy so that decisions affecting business can be made in a reasonable time frame. Currently, on a number of reservations, the process for gaining approval from the tribe or the BIA to allow a business to start up or move in a new direction takes several times longer than for a private business on private property.[37] Similarly, by developing clear land use and other enterprise policies and approval processes, tribes can direct development to fit tribal needs and values, reduce decision-making time to facilitate business development, and allow those affected by a decision to have a say about it. Also, the stability that is necessary for business development can be enhanced by establishing clear appropriate transaction-recording instruments (e.g., a method for recording a land-use agreement) and effective, low-cost enforcement and adjudication procedures.

Although to accomplish it requires capital that at times may only become available from economic expansion, a critical requirement for economic development is the creation of infrastructure, which is missing on many reservations. Necessary improvements include building and maintaining not only adequate roads and bridges but also electric, water and sanitation, telephone, and computer systems. Government, business, and nonprofit foundations have an important role to play in this effort. For example, a provision inserted into a 2006 highway bill allocated $3 million over five years to pave some of the seventy-six hundred miles of dirt roads on the Navajo Nation reservation.[38] Various public and private initiatives to increase computer availability and training on reservations are in existence, such as the $6 million grant to the Navajo Nation in 1998 to help the nation's chapters build their computer capacity. By fall 2005, each of the nation's 110 chapters had from three to fourteen computers wirelessly connected to the Internet, which were available around the clock to chapter members. OnSat, an international company that helps developing nations establish computer networks in rural areas, undertook much of the installation. The Native-owned firm Sacred Wind began providing cell phone service in isolated areas of the Navajo Nation early in 2005 and with the help of federal and state subsidies planned to supply twenty-five hundred Diné households with phone service by the end of the year.[39] By using newer technology, sometimes via satellite, communication can be improved without the expense and environmental damage connected with the construction of phone lines over vast distances.

A number of Indian nations have been moving to fill their need for electricity by using wind and other alternative technology that is consistent with their environmental values. The Hopi Nation is exploring developing wind-generated electricity and possibly solar power from photovoltaic cells in an effort to attain ecological and economic sustainability. The nation might partner with the Sterling Energy wind farm, replacing its association with the Mohave Generating Station, which uses Hopi coal from Black Mesa and coal slurry water from the N-aquifer, dangerously depleting the aquifer. In addition, pollution from the Mohave plant is contributing to global warming and high cancer rates in the area.[40]

Appropriate Development Planning

An important piece of economic development strategy is choosing economic enterprises that fit the geographic location of a tribe. The most profitable Indian casinos are located in populous areas. The Navajo

Nation, whose reservation lies within sparsely populated and scenically beautiful rural areas, has been attempting to increase tribal and tribal member tourist-related business. Some nations in isolated rural areas have provided outsourcing services to an increasing number of U.S. companies that prefer to outsource jobs to reservations rather than outside the United States. On four Utah reservations, between 150 and 180 jobs were created through commercial and government outsourcing. On the Pine Ridge Reservation, Lakota Express, an Indian-owned web design and marketing firm, secured a contract to check the accuracy of transcriptions of handwritten information in English recorded by an outsourcing operation in China.[41] Doing business over the Internet is another option for isolated tribes and Native entrepreneurs.

Finally, to be able to develop sufficiently with economic security for the long term, it is wise to diversify economic activity. Single lines of business have limited capacity, may have limited life spans, and are extremely likely to vary in success over time. A variety of ventures provides security as individual enterprises decline or need reorganization and can better fill community needs. Broad-based economic activity is also likely to build stronger ties with the surrounding community, which includes providing a wide range of employment opportunities and shared interest among tribal and neighboring governments and communities.

Diversification and Intergovernmental Cooperation: The Case of the Mississippi Choctaw

Although much remains to be achieved, there are numerous instances of successful diversified tribal business development. An excellent example of a tribe that made significant progress before the advent of Indian gaming and that has continued to expand with gaming's assistance, is the Mississippi Band of Choctaw Indians.

The Choctaws who remained in Mississippi after the tribe was removed to Indian territory—now Oklahoma—in the 1830s had to persist in a difficult struggle of survival as a people and as individuals.[42] With the government failing to fulfill its treaty obligation to provide allotments to most of those remaining in Mississippi, many tribal members were reduced to sharecropping on what had been their own land, for fifty cents a day. Amid poverty and harsh living conditions, the band's population declined to just over twelve hundred people in 1910. In 1918, the federal government finally acknowledged its responsibility and established the Choctaw Agency with a few sparsely funded programs. In 1921, the government purchased seventeen thousand scattered acres to create a reservation, which today contains seven communities. Yet conditions remained so desperate that it was only in the 1960s that the community's birth rate began to exceed the death rate, and the new federal politics allowed space for the tribe to assert its self-determination and begin its own process of holistic development, including building an economic base. Business efforts began with the sale of tribal timber, which allowed the tribe to hire one of its members as a business manager.

By the late 1960s, the Choctaw had established a construction company that built and renovated homes and an eighty-acre industrial park that by the late 1980s contained six manufacturing plants, three of which were owned by the tribe. One of these businesses was Chata Greeting Enterprises (now American Greetings), which near the end of the 1980s was the fourth largest producer in the world, by volume, of greeting cards. The plant was financed largely under a compact with the city of Philadelphia, Mississippi, through which the city passed the first industrial bond issue in the United States used for Indian economic development. Another of the manufacturing plants is Chata Enterprises, which began supplying General Motors with wire harnesses for automobile instrument panels in 1983. The plant expanded—also in collaboration with the city of Philadelphia, which passed a bond issue—to become the fourth largest employer in Mississippi, with many nontribal workers.[43] In 1999, Chata Enterprises opened a plant in Sonora, Mexico.

In 1985, the Choctaw set up a credit union to provide banking services to tribal members and three years later completed construction of the Choctaw Shopping Center, which houses a bank, grocery store, restaurant, barber and beauty shop, gas station, and other businesses. As of 2003, the nation owned and operated a broad portfolio of manufacturing, service, retail, and tourism enterprises throughout Mississippi, the Southeast, and Mexico, including two resorts anchored by casinos.[44] The Choctaw then provided more than eight thousand permanent full-time jobs, 65 percent of which were held by non-Indians. With an annual payroll of more than $123.7 million, the Mississippi Band of Choctaw Indians had become one of the ten largest employers in Mississippi. Tribal revenues have helped the Choctaw to reinvest more than $210 million in economic development projects in Mississippi. Some tribal enterprises, such as the Choctaw Farmers Market, are intended to provide some noneconomic benefits to tribal members, in the Farmers Market's case by enhancing nutrition, while increasing tribal farmers' incomes.

Economic Development Bringing Choctaw and Wider Community Development

On this economic base, the Choctaw have funded tribal and broader community development in collaboration with surrounding localities and governments for mutual benefit. Before the end of the 1980s, community development already included an education program from preschool through high school and a training and vocational center for adult education that provided learning in a culturally appropriate manner, including education in Choctaw culture, and that led to more than sixty tribal members earning college degrees by late in that decade. Also during the 1980s, the health program encompassed a 40-bed hospital with three satellite clinics, a 120-bed nursing home, mental health and substance abuse programs, an ambulance service, a community nursing and training program, and a sanitation and water-quality monitoring program.

Today, these and other tribal and collaborative programs have considerably expanded. The Mississippi Choctaw education system has grown to become the largest unified reservation school system in the United States, with 1,700–1,800 students. Newer programs included child care, post-secondary education, and all levels of post-secondary education counseling, scholarships, and student support services. Health services have been enhanced with a dental clinic, a diabetes management center, dietary and nutrition programs, nonemergency medical transportation, a women's health center; and a women, infants, and children nutrition program. The Choctaw Housing Authority now provides general maintenance, emergency maintenance, housing placement, resident services, and the holistic Drug Elimination Program.

Community Services now encompasses a full range of programs, including child welfare, foster care, handicapped and elderly services, domestic abuse, food and emergency services, and behavioral health programs. The Choctaw Department of Agriculture and Rural Development operates a number of programs that provide assistance and education to farmers and gardeners, along with education for homemakers. The department's conservation, nature, and education programs combine with those of the Environmental Program Office to manage and protect the environment and provide for sustainable development. The tribe monitors air and water quality, runs its own water treatment plant for drinking water, and undertakes solid waste treatment. Tribal government is well financed and has expanded to include a court system, corrections, and a police and fire department.

Tribal Development for the Oneida Nation of Wisconsin

The Oneida Nation of Wisconsin has also built a diversified economy to support tribal development that benefits neighboring communities.[45] Following a historic commitment to constructing a strong economy and improving quality of life, the Oneida Development Division has implemented a seven-generation planning concept—"a belief that what is said and done today effects the next seven generations, or 150 years"—using its initial gaming success to grow an expanded economy.

The Oneida Nation first entered the gaming industry in 1976. Initially, it began bingo games to subsidize the building expenses of a community recreation facility. The initial small, volunteer-run bingo operation has grown into a bingo and casino enterprise that generates millions annually for the Oneida Nation. Oneida Bingo and Casino is a facility with more than 3,200 slot and video poker machines and forty-six blackjack tables near Austin Straubel International Airport. It adjoins a comprehensive hotel and conference facility and is bolstered by a second casino and bingo hall.

The nation has created Oneida Industrial Park, a thirty-two acre development with eighteen retail stores. Oneida Printing is a state-of-the-art printing company equipped with an electronic prepress department, five presses, and binding capability. Oneida Nation Farms provides food and agricultural products to tribal members at a discount and to the general public at low cost. It includes a beef cattle operation, apple orchard, and feed crops that help sustain the agricultural operations. "Tsyunhehkwa," or "life's sustenance," is an organic farming operation that specializes in traditional farming methods and provides natural products and herbs. The tribe has built the Oneida Retail Enterprise, a retail chain of four convenience centers, over a quarter of a century. All of the nation's enterprises, except the retail businesses, employ a significant number of nontribal members.

The Wisconsin Oneida have broadened their economy with a number of investments. In some instances, the tribe granted charters to corporations pursuant to its constitution. In other cases, the tribe invested in public and private companies. Seven Generation Corporation is an Oneida limited liability corporation that has partnered with Management Enterprises to lease a health facility to Bellin Health Systems. The facility's primary purpose is family medicine patient care. Other services include sports medicine, physical therapy, fitness, diagnostic testing, and administrative and ancillary services. Chartered in 1985, the Oneida Airport

Hotel Corporation is responsible for the management and operation of the Radisson Hotel & Conference Center in Green Bay, Wisconsin. Baybank, a full-service bank located on the Oneida reservation, is fully owned by the nation. The Oneida Nation also has a partnership with the Green Bay Packers National Football League team, under which the tribe sponsors a gate named after the nation at the team's Lambeau Field. The sponsorship supports various forms of tribal advertising and the opportunity to provide education and awareness of the Oneida's cultural diversity by sharing their ideas and values with a seventy-thousand-person audience, and gives Oneida Nation youth opportunities to work with the Packers on community events.

Joint Ventures with Other Native Nations
The Oneida Tribe of Indians of Wisconsin has come together with three other nations seeking to build on their gaming success: the Forest County Potawatomi of Wisconsin and two Southern California tribes, the San Manuel Band of Mission Indians and the Viejas Band of Kumeyaay Indians. Together, the four nations form the investment partnership Four Fires. The partnership's first venture was the development of a $43 million, thirteen-story, 233-suite Residence Inn by Marriot in Washington D.C., which opened in September 2007.[46] The Wisconsin Oneida are a major shareholder in the Native American Bank, a bank focused on large business loans, agricultural operations, and community development, with a focus on loans to Indian tribes and Indian-owned businesses.

Oneida Tribal Development
The Oneida Nation has leveraged its extensive economic growth to create many community resources, including the Department of Public Works, Division of Land Management, Development Division, Planning Department, Geographic Land Information Systems, Engineering Department, and Zoning Department. Oneida Nation planning efforts, including functions such as zoning, environmental impact, and urban development, are coordinated with area municipalities through service contracts. One of the most aggressive planning efforts includes the Duck Creek Priority Watershed Project to revive Duck Creek, which flows through the center of the Oneida reservation. This ten-year project calls for setbacks, sediment ponds, and other preventive and restoration measures. The Oneida have also applied their financial gains to reacquire much lost reservation land. As of 2008, the tribe had regained nearly

25 percent of its original reservation, an area comprising 16,689 acres in Brown and Outagamie Counties. The Oneida's long-term goals include the purchase and recovery of all original reservation lands.

The Oneida Nation has invested heavily in services to improve the quality of life on its reservation by boosting the level and quality of services available to the tribal membership. To enhance efficiencies in administering nearly one hundred programs and services, the Nation has centralized accounting, computer, and maintenance programs. A priority has been to provide high-quality educational opportunities to all members, from infants to elders. Educational programming includes early childhood development, Head Start, Oneida Tribal School K-12, projects under the Job Training Partnership Act, a Community Education Center, and Higher Education division. Other educational resources encompass the Oneida Nation Museum and Oneida Library, as well as programs in recreation, repatriation, culture, and language.

In 2004, the Oneida Tribe signed a charter that details ways to preserve the Oneida language. The tribe's goal is to return the language to being a part of everyday life for the first time in three generations. The Oneida Language Charter Team is working to help the tribe's fifteen thousand members become fluent in the Oneida language, which will become the tribe's official language.

Oneida Health and Human Services
The tribe has enhanced community health, beginning by upgrading the Oneida Community Health Center, which offers comprehensive outpatient and inpatient medical services to tribal members, including dental and vision care, as well as X-ray, laboratory, pharmacy, and after-hours services provided by a full-time staff of physicians, nurses, and other healthcare professionals. Community Health Nursing offers a variety of public health services such as a home-visit program and nutritional, health promotion, disease prevention, reproductive, and other informational services. Additional Oneida community health services include audiology, physical therapy, and a medical benefits coordinator for tribal members needing medical assistance. A number of community sites have been established for elder care, which offers meal-assistance programs, referral services, recreational activities, and emergency aid.

Oneida Social Services provides a wide range of services for tribal members and employees. These encompass an extensive chemical dependency treatment and prevention program, family service programs, employee assistance, and counseling services. Additional social services include a boys and girls group home.

Providing for Security

The Oneida Nation operates its own police department, which patrols the reservation as well as the exterior boundaries under cross-deputization agreements with neighboring jurisdictions. In the field of fire and rescue services, many tribal members serve on local volunteer fire departments, and the nation has contributed to the purchase of new fire trucks and entered into service agreements with local municipalities.

Development by the Pokagon Band of Potawatomi Indians

As with numerous cases in which the improvement of tribal economies in rural areas helps neighboring communities, the Four Winds Casino Resort of the Pokagon Band of Potawatomi Indians, the first casino in southwestern Michigan, is transforming an area long considered just a gas and rest stop for out-of-state tourists into a vacation destination.[47] The rapid success of the casino resort has had an expansive effect on the life and economy of the New Buffalo area near Lake Michigan, where a ten-mile stretch along the lake includes many shops, restaurants, and choices of lodging. For the Pokagon Band of Potawatomi Indians, whose reservation is in Dowagiac, Michigan, business was strong enough by spring 2008 that the nation began planning an expansion that would add more lodging, restaurants, and parking spaces. The extent to which the economic downturn that began in 2008 will reduce business for the casino or increase it (as a closer alternative for Chicago-area customers) remains to be seen.

The Rise of Ho-Chunk, Inc.

The Winnebago Tribe of Nebraska's economic development division, Ho-Chunk, Inc., began by using casino profits and had one employee in 1995. By 2005, having used funds generated by its various businesses, Ho-Chunk, Inc., had developed into a $100 million business with more than five hundred employees in six states, Mexico, Iraq, and Afghanistan.[48] The company built sixteen subsidiaries whose only connection to gaming is receiving development capital from the tribe's casino operation, which has been reduced since 1994 by competition from nearby Iowa. Ho-Chunk posted revenues of $111.3 million in 2005, up from $22.9 million in 2000, and holds assets that grew to

$39.8 million from $8 million. It recorded nearly $691,000 in net profits in 2005. In 2007, with the addition of two subsidiaries in two years, sales revenue increased 7 percent to reach $121 million, net profits rose 66 percent to over a million dollars, and employment increased by 54 employees to total 638 people.

Ho-Chunk, Inc., included fifteen subsidiaries in 2005. All Native Systems, a telecommunications, computer, and networking company with a mix of government and private contracts, is based in Winnebago, Nebraska, with offices in Bellevue, Nebraska, and Washington, D.C. HCI Distribution Co., based in Winnebago, blends and sells gasoline and sells American Indian tobacco products. HCI Logistics, a division of HCI Distribution, is a transportation services provider. AllNative.com is an online American Indian gift shop and catalogue. AllNative Office Products markets office products and office furniture. AllNative Solutions markets computer hardware, software, and other products throughout the United States. Indianz.com is an American Indian Internet news and information site that receives approximately 9 million hits per month. Dynamic Homes, in Detroit Lakes, Minnesota, is a prefabricated housing manufacturer. HCI Construction is a general contractor based in Winnebago with offices in South Sioux City, Nebraska. Ho-Chunk Builders, an electrical services and construction management company, has offices in Winnebago and Bellevue, Wisconsin. AllNative Resources operates a variety of business services, including interior design, warehousing, marketing, and public relations. Native Plains Pharmacy is a national distributor of pharmaceuticals based in Winnebago. Blue Earth Marketing is a marketing and advertising agency. Rez Cars is a car dealer with locations in Winnebago and South Sioux City. WinnaVegas Inn is located near the tribe's WinnaVegas Casino. Ho-Chunk, Inc., also owns seven gasoline and convenience stores in Nebraska and Iowa and holds investments in more than fifty hotels and five thousand housing units in more than a dozen states.

Although the economic situation on the Winnebago reservation was improving, as of 2005, the median household income for the approximately 2,600 tribal members living on the reservation was around $20,000, and more than 40 percent of people lived below the federal poverty line. To meet the people's needs while continuing to further the tribe's economic development as part of tribal development, Ho-Chunk, Inc., helped start the Ho-Chunk Community Development Corporation in 2000. The corporation had raised $11 million by 2005 to help improve the reservation. The biggest development project has been Ho-Chunk Village, a mixed residential development with a village square surrounding a sculpture garden filled with twelve statues that represent the original clans of the Winnebago Tribe, a variety of retail stores, and the home office of several Ho-Chunk businesses. Walking trails lead through the village and connect the houses. The homes are sold at low interest rates with down-payment assistance for tribal members, some of whom have never before owned a home. Internships and jobs directly help the tribal members and help keep young people—especially those with an education—on the reservation, so that the whole community can move ahead and stay together. An important aspect of Ho-Chunk's organization is that it has a board of directors that acts independently of the Winnebago tribal council, which keeps short-term political ups and downs from undermining Ho-Chunk's progress.

Economic development has also empowered the nation to increase services, including scholarships. Among the nation's educational activities is Little Priest Tribal College, founded in May 1996, which is named after the last true war chief of the Winnebago Tribe. The major focus of the college is to provide two-year associate degrees and to prepare students to transfer and successfully complete a degree at a four-year institution. An equally important part of the college's mission is the commitment to offer language and culture classes that provide students with the opportunity to improve their knowledge of Winnebago language and culture and also help build self-esteem.

Economic Diversification by Oregon Nations

Tribes in Oregon are also moving well beyond casinos in their economic development and are coming to have a major role in how the economy of the state develops.[49] In 2005, tribal casinos of the state's nine federally recognized tribes had a direct $675 million effect on Oregon's economy, according to a study by the economic consulting firm ECONorthwest, which was commissioned by the tribes. The additional effect of the construction, manufacturing, wholesale, retail, and services industries brings the overall impact to at least $1.47 billion. Oregon's tribes employed 2,200 people in January 1995; by July 2007, that number had almost quadrupled to 8,700. Meanwhile, between 2000 and 2007, the number of American Indians living below the poverty level in Oregon dropped 23 percent, and the number of tribal members going to college increased by 88 percent.

Developments at Cow Creek

The Cow Creek Band of the Umpqua Tribe of Indians in Canyonville, Oregon, has used profits from its casino and resort, first launched in 1992, to build twelve tribal enterprises worth several million dollars: the Seven Feathers casino, a motel, an RV resort, a truck stop, a restaurant, a communications company, a graphic design and marketing company, a lodge, a cattle ranch and hay operation, Umpqua Indian Foods—where the tribe manufactures and sells jerky and gift items—and self-storage units. The band runs its own electric utility. The Cow Creek Tribe has become the second largest employer in Douglas County, employing about 1,270 people. It also built a series of dams so the tribe could be self-sufficient and also, in an emergency, supply the city of Canyonville with water. The Cow Creek Tribe has built a new sewer treatment facility and is undertaking a major expansion to the hotel portion of its resort. The tribe estimates it had a $142 million overall impact in Douglas County in 2006.

Increased Well-Being for the Coquille Indian Tribe, Confederated Tribes of the Umatilla, and Confederated Tribes of the Grand Ronde

The Coquille Indian Tribe, with a nearly $53 million impact in Coos County, Oregon, partnered with Home Depot in 2006 to create a $20 million shopping center. The nation operates an assisted living and Alzheimer's care facility, the Mill Casino, a fiber-optic telecommunications company, and Coquille Cranberries, the world's largest producer of organic cranberries. Providing more than 600 jobs, Coquille was the second-largest employer in the county in 2006, paying an estimated $15 million in wages and benefits a year—wages that the tribe's analysis indicated were 15 to 60 percent higher than those at comparable jobs elsewhere in Coos County.

The Confederated Tribes of the Umatilla Indian Reservation in Oregon have brought two Fortune 500 companies to a new business park outside of Pendleton: DaVita will build a kidney dialysis center, and the international outsourcing company Accenture will create Cayuse Technologies, a tech service provider offering software programming, digital document processing, and a call center. The Umatilla own Wildhorse Casino, a truck stop, an energy company, a market, a golf course, and a recreation area. Of the Umatilla's $145 million 2007 budget, the tribe reported that less than 20 percent of revenue came from casino profits; the rest derived from grants, contracts, interest earnings, utility taxes, and funding from the state and federal governments. The tribe employed 1,135 people in 2007 with a $35 million annual payroll, which made them the second-largest employer in their county. Cayuse Technologies was expected to create more than 250 additional jobs that pay more on average than other area jobs. This project may catapult the nation to become the largest employer in the county. After completing construction of the buildings for the first two tenants in the Umatilla's Coyote Business Park, the tribe began an effort to bring light manufacturing to the south end of the park in 2008.

The Confederated Tribes of Grand Ronde was already the largest employer in Polk County, Oregon, in 2007, with fifteen hundred employees. Several years earlier, the confederated tribes helped finance an office building in Portland. Then it teamed up with the Confederated Tribes of Siletz Indians on a $2.5 million business development project in Keizer, Oregon. The Confederated Tribes of the Coos-Lower Umpqua-Siuslaw Indians, which built its casino in 2004, estimated that an upcoming casino expansion would create 250 more jobs in the town of Florence, Oregon, population eight thousand.

The Tribes of Washington and the State Economy

American Indian casinos in Washington have been a major factor in the movement of the state's tribes: "in just a dozen years ris[ing] from poverty to enjoying comforts many others take for granted, from high-quality medical facilities to decent housing."[50] The Muckleshoot Indian Tribe, for example, just outside Auburn, Washington, with a population of about 2,100, bought the landmark Salish Lodge near Snoqualmie for $62.5 million. The tribe has invested in a hotel-condo project in downtown Seattle. And it is moving beyond entertainment and hospitality with a $3 million investment in a California manufactured-home company: in 2007, the Muckleshoots paid $3 million for the majority interest in Forma Home Systems in Danville, California, and secured the option to build the company's next factory in the Seattle area. The tribe has also invested in the Four Seasons Hotel and Residences in downtown Seattle. In 2007, the Muckleshoots were seeking a partnership with other tribes to buy seventy acres at the end of the Las Vegas Strip for that city's first Native-owned casino property. Possible partners include the Mashantucket Pequots of Connecticut, who run one of the world's largest casinos; the Seminole Tribe of Florida, which recently bought the Hard Rock Cafe chain; and the Shoshone-Bannock Tribes of Fort Hall, Idaho. The resort complex is envisioned as a modernist fantasy with an indoor ski park, Rodeo Drive–style shopping mall with air-conditioning under a clear plastic roof, and thirty-thousand-seat stadium with retractable roof. The project would have a sizable American Indian museum and a Native healing and spiritual center. Partnership with other tribes provides much more than capital to swing the Las Vegas deal. It would give the tribal partners access to one another's customer lists and other opportunities to build customer traffic to and from their own casinos and the Las Vegas venture. It is also envisioned as a major training opportunity for tribal members that would include a job-training facility with forty apartments and might include a recording studio for training purposes. Indeed all of the tribe's business ventures are considered for their training potential, as well as for profit.

The Tulalip Tribes in northern Snohomish County are turning prime land into retail and commercial success. The Puyallup Tribe of Indians, outside Tacoma, in 2007 were planning a deep-water seaport in partnership with SSA Marine on Tacoma's East Blair Waterway. The $300 million project, scheduled to open in 2012, was slated to be the largest recent private investment in Tacoma, creating a considerable number of jobs. It would increase shipping volumes on Commencement Bay with four new berths for ships from Asia and 180 acres of other facilities. SSA Marine will manage the seaport for fifty years, then the tribe will take over management. The Puyallup's casino, the Emerald Queen, grants full college scholarships and other social services to tribal members, and all thirty-five hundred tribal members receive two thousand dollars each month. The much smaller Jamestown S'Klallam Tribe of the Olympic Peninsula bought into a medical-supply company in California and took over an 18-hole golf course.

Development with Intergovernmental Collaboration by the Morongo Band of Mission Indians

Two California tribes exemplify how successful economic development in which tribal gaming plays an important role can bring intergovernmental cooperation. The first tribe, the Morongo Band of Mission Indians, has one of the largest reservations in the state, and the tribe had long used much of its 32,000 acres for fruit farming and cattle ranching.[51] The tribe also leased land for sand and gravel-mining operations or to various utilities, water districts, and rail lines. None of this, however, was enough to fully support the tribal community.

When it launched tribal gaming, the tribe made the strategic decision to use gaming revenue as a catalyst to diversify the tribal economy.

In 1997, the Morongo opened one of the largest Shell gasoline stations in the country and followed it up in 1999 with an A&W drive-in restaurant nearly twice the size of the national prototype, which became one of the country's most successful A&W franchises. Also in 1999, the Morongo opened the first Coco's Restaurant owned by an American Indian tribe. The Morongo then acquired Hadley Fruit Orchards, three retail stores, and mail-order operations. In 2003, the tribe opened a $26 million Arrowhead Mountain Spring Water bottling plant. All of this has made the Morongo the largest private-sector employer in the Banning Pass area with almost two thousand employees. The tribe is a major contributor to the regional economy with an annual payroll that exceeds $25 million, and millions more are generated in payroll taxes, unemployment benefits, employee benefits, and health programs.

Nearly two-thirds of the jobs created by tribal governments in California are held by residents of nearby communities. In 2003, the Morongo were spending an estimated $20 million per year for goods and services purchased from about twelve hundred outside vendors, about 25 percent of which are minority owned and operated. This figure does not include the sale of goods and services generated by patrons visiting the area or services and merchandise purchased by tribal employees. U.S. Department of Commerce research estimates that forty-two jobs are created for every million dollars spent on goods and services. As of late 2003, the Morongo were exploring how to provide clean, reliable, and low-cost energy to their businesses, tenants, and tribal members. In the course of becoming energy self-sufficient, the tribe will create another income stream and maintain its traditional role as a steward of the environment.

The Elk Valley Rancheria

By investing its casino profits, the Elk Valley Rancheria in Crescent City has been reviving one of California's poorest counties.[52] The tribe renovated the town's dingy bowling alley and gave the local golf course new carts and clubs. The golf course has since been expanded from 9 to 18 holes. In 2003, the tribe opened a sports bar and grill while operating Harborside Internet, the only Internet service provider serving the southern coast of Oregon, which the tribe purchased in 1999. The tribe has since acquired an RV park and is planning other new enterprises and improvements.

By the early 2000s, the tribe had become the county's largest private employer, with 250 workers on its payroll and 200 more anticipated with the projected oceanfront resort near the Oregon border. In addition to creating jobs, tribal investment has increased the wages and income of community members. In the fall of 2003, a bill was pending in the state legislature that would allow the tribe to partner with the city and county to finance a greatly needed $35 million wastewater treatment plant. For the tribe, its casino was a clear path out of poverty. As of 2003, none of the one hundred Elk Valley Rancheria tribal members remained on government assistance, and a college fund was putting thirteen students through school. The tribe planned to move its casino from a residential street to a major north-south highway. The Elk Valley Rancheria petitioned the BIA to put its newly acquired land in trust and made an agreement with the county to make up for the $2,800 in property taxes it would lose by pledging a share of bed taxes from the resort that could bring the county as much as $250,000 a year. The tribe has been contributing to fund what has been billed as the largest Fourth of July fireworks display between San Francisco and Portland. It also has loaned money interest-free to the county fair board. The tribe has taken the reins of the community's only Head Start program, which served sixty mostly nontribal children and hosts Native American motivational speakers at the local high school.

Indian Economic Development as of 2008

Thus, by early 2008, quite a number of Native nations had improved their economies substantially, raising tribal incomes and quality of life with tribal development. This, in turn, created significant benefits for surrounding communities. Although a few tribes had become wealthy, most still lagged behind Americans generally, and a number of reservations remained among the financially poorest communities in the United States. At the time, the general outlook was for continuing financial improvement for most Indigenous nations and people. The time, however, was just prior to a major U.S. and world economic crisis that began to unfold shortly thereafter.

Tribal Economies and the 2008 Economic Crisis

As of this writing, at the beginning of November 2008, it is clear that the first stages of a major economic recession that has been developing in the United States and the world will have a great impact upon everyone, including Indigenous people. It remains to be seen whether this financial decline will approach or exceed that of 1929 and what government and other institutions will do in response. For instance, might a newly elected President Obama institute another "Indian New Deal"? Everyone will be affected in some way, but just how and to what extent will vary. The trends in Indian economic affairs will change in ways that cannot yet be foreseen. However, as some aspects of the economic crisis began to be evident early in 2008, initial impacts on Indian country can be reported.

Writing in *Indian Country Today*, Rob Capriccioso reported some of the emerging effects coming from events in banking and on Wall Street on October 10, 2008: "With major bank closings and mergers taking Wall Street by storm, American Indian–focused investment programs and individual Indians who work in the finance sector have already ended up on the cutting block. Financial experts say the developments will likely add to problems already facing credit-crunched and economically ailing tribes."[53] "We've certainly seen some Native-focused banking teams take a hit," said Bill Lomax, president of the Native American Finance Officers Association. "At least two or three firms have cut back on their Native American banking groups." In March 2008, for example, after Bear Stearns, formerly one of the world's largest investment banks, was purchased by JPMorgan Chase for two dollars a share, officials with JPMorgan decided to shut down the company's Native-focused bond and investment banking crew. Meanwhile, Derrick Watchman (Navajo) continued to lead the Native American Banking Group, which was part of the commercial banking activities of Bear Stearns. At the same time, some firms, such as Merrill Lynch, were continuing to reach out to tribes. Merrill Lynch retained Frank King as managing director of tribal banking for the company; King's team has raised more than $6 billion in the capital markets from a broad range of investors for tribal governments and their enterprises. Bank of America was also known to be one of the largest lenders to Indian country and had developed relationships with several tribes. It was not yet clear what the impact of the merger between Merrill Lynch and Bank of America would be. The two firms were competitors for Indian business. "But one thing is for sure as a result of the merger: there will be less competition for tribal dollars. And less competition usually means higher rates for borrowing."[54]

What seems apparent in November 2008 is that credit will likely be harder to obtain for Indigenous nations and people, and this by itself will restrain Native development (which is also likely to be held back in many instances by reduced demand for goods and services, though this will not be universal, and even bad economic situations produce some opportunities for growth). One early casualty of the financial crisis was the Fort Yuma Quechan Indians: in October 2008, when the $155 million in bonds funding the tribe's new casino resort in the California Imperial Valley, west of Yuma, were downgraded to junk bond status, officials for a financial ratings company said the tribe faced the possibility of default if it could not secure $25 million in private funding for the $214 million project. Similarly, the Sault Tribe of Chippewa Indians, who had invested $47 million over ten months into the Greek Town Casino in Detroit, in which they were the largest stakeholder, were attempting to sell the financially troubled gaming operation, which was going through bankruptcy.

Although the subprime mortgage crisis, which set in motion much of the 2008 economic collapse, did not directly threaten large numbers of Native Americans with the loss of their homes, by late summer 2008, it had greatly reduced mortgage lending in Indian country when the closing of Capital One Financial Corporation's wholesale mortgage company shuttered its American Indian mortgage program, Tribal POINT Housing Partnership.[55] In response, three Native American financial institutions—Native American Bank, Sycuan Funds of California, and Seacrest Investment Management of South Dakota—agreed in August to form a marketing alliance to bring the full range of financial services to Indian country. This was expected to lessen the impact of reduced mortgage funding for many Indian people, but only to the extent that these institutions and tribal banks had available funds.

A critical effect of the economic meltdown was extensive reduction in the value of most investments. This reduction has affected tribes, at least on paper. For example, at the beginning of October 2008, Jason Begay reported: "Navajo Nation officials have seen $120 million of the government's investments go down the drain in one swoop during Monday's huge 777.68-point drop."[56] And the market continued to decline precipitously. However, even before the beginning of the crash, the Navajo Nation, like many others, was already being pinched: "The slumping stock market has taken a substantial toll on the Navajo Nation's Permanent Trust Fund—dropping the fund's overall value from $1.330 billion in December to $1.272 billion in March. By the end of June, it had declined further to $982 million."[57] How great the losses will be for Indian nations, and people, is for the future to determine.

The initial impact of the financial fall-off varied for Indian enterprises but by fall 2008 in many instances was substantial. For example, the Indian gaming industry grew by 5 percent in 2007, bringing in around $26 billion; however, as the economy worsened and gas prices rose, starting early in 2008, tribal gaming revenue growth began to slow, and in some cases drop, across the United States. Both of the existing tribal casinos in Connecticut saw sizable reductions in their slot revenues over the year. On September 22, the Mohegan Tribe announced that it was postponing the final phase of its $925 million expansion project at the Mohegan Sun for at least a year. On September 30, the Mashantucket Pequot Tribal Nation, owner of Foxwoods Resort Casino, announced it would lay off approximately seven hundred of eleven thousand employees. A week later, the nation's tribal council announced it had eliminated the executive position responsible for overseeing its business operations. As a whole, the Nevada gambling industry appeared to be headed for its worst year, with a 6.6 percent revenue decline through July, according to the Nevada Gaming Control Board. However, Florida's gambling industry, with several major Indian gaming facilities, remained strong despite the national economic crisis. Jim Allen, chief executive of gaming operations for the Seminole Tribe of Florida, said in early October: "The Florida gaming market has been showing double-digit growth all year."

Overall then, it is unclear whether, to what degree, and in what ways Indigenous economic development will be able to continue empowering tribal development and enhancing well-being, and how the state of reservation economics will affect neighboring communities and relations between tribal and neighboring governments.

Economic Development and Tribal Sovereignty

Where Indian nations have been able to develop their economies sufficiently, tribal sovereignty has been significantly realized and tribal governments operate effectively, running their own programs consistently with tribal needs and providing the infrastructure, education, training, and other services necessary to empower tribal members to be good citizens and employees. Externally, those tribes that have been able to build functioning economies have gained a degree of political power that enables them to fulfill their roles as governments in the American federal system. Doing so has involved not only collaboration between tribes and local governments but has also included Indian nations contributing more to decisions that affect them in some states and, to a lesser degree, at the federal level. This is especially the case in California, where Indian nations collectively are now the largest contributor to political campaigns and with heavy financing have been able to realize the passage of some ballot propositions.[58] As an active member of one California nation stated in the presence of author Stephen Sachs, before her tribe's financial rise, it was difficult for it to obtain any acknowledgement from inquiries to the state's U.S. senators. Since the nation's coming to economic prominence, when she calls Senator Feinstein's office, the senator often calls her back personally.

Large campaign donations, particularly at the federal level, do not necessarily bring about a desired policy action. Often, they provide more in the way of access than direct influence, and at times, Indian nations have been prompted by political operatives to make sizable contributions with no actual possibility of obtaining a policy gain, as has been made clear by the Abramoff scandal.[59] Nevertheless, although most Indian nations and most Native Americans still have much to attain to be reasonably well-off financially, there is no question that advances in tribal economics are increasing tribal well-being and sovereignty at home while empowering tribal governments to move toward becoming full partners in American federalism.[60] The key to successful tribal economic development is undertaking it as part of tribal development as a whole, understanding the necessity of transcending the overly narrow Western definition of economics and transforming it into the art and science of living well within the community and with the environment, human and nonhuman, all of which is part of nature. This is something the rest of the world may also find desirable.

2. The Spiral of Renewal: Appropriate Indian Education

Gregory A. Cajete, Stephen M. Sachs, and Phyllis M. Gagnier

Introduction

STEPHEN M. SACHS

Developing appropriate American Indian education and education policy is fundamental to returning Indian nations to sovereignty, self-sufficiency, and harmony. Such a policy encompasses learning from pre-school through college and graduate school to continuing education and affects related policy at every level, from tribal government through local and state governments to the federal government.

Although notable exceptions exist, the history of Indian education and policy has been marked by disaster whenever Indian people did not play a major role in its development. In the worst case, the federal government forced Indian children to leave their families and peoples to attend boarding schools, where the young people were not allowed to speak their own languages or follow traditional customs, all in the name of acculturating them into mainstream society. The result, as we discussed in chapter 2, was that Native children most often became alienated from both cultures. Their vocational and other education in "white man's ways" (with some important exceptions) was usually insufficient to help them succeed in the larger society. Young people often were cut off from learning much about their own culture, including acquiring traditional ways of parenting. Moreover, the considerable abuse that many Indians suffered in boarding schools tended to inculcate abusive patterns of behavior (to self and others), especially when the resulting alienation combined with racism and the failure by the federal government to live up to its promises to provide new ways of making a living to replace those that were destroyed by expansionist policies and military and economic warfare.

Indian education is much improved since the worst of the boarding-school days but unfortunately continues to suffer serious problems. The Meriam Report of 1928 brought movement in federal Indian policy in general, and education in particular, toward recognizing the rights of Native Americans to preserve their own cultures and run their own affairs. Limited movement in this direction occurred during the New Deal era and has slowly but incompletely developed under the policy of Indian self-determination since the 1960s. Yet as we detail in chapter 2, today, of all groups measured, American Indian students have the lowest achievement levels in mathematics and reading, the highest school dropout rates, and very low college completion rates (although some Native students have made remarkable achievements at every level). The continuing difficulties are severe for Native students in BIA and BIA-funded tribal and contract schools, public schools, tribal colleges and other Indian postsecondary school institutions, and at non-Indian institutions of higher learning. In order for Native people to achieve in school, in the community, and in the world at large, efforts to develop appropriate Indian education need to advance to the next level.

Contemporary Indigenous Education: Thoughts for American Indian Education in a Twenty-First Century World

GREGORY A. CAJETE

Creating consciousness and acting for the renewal of American Indian education is the essential message that underlies the work of many

Indigenous educators. The perception that there is a need to evolve a deeper consciousness of the issues, practices, and paradoxes of our collective involvement with Western education forms the impetus for this section. In addition, this work advocates the creation of Indigenous theories of education that will lead to various forms of praxis that support the renewal of Indigenous education. The perceived needs that underpin this call for developing Indigenous education theory may be summarized as follows:

1. The need for a contemporary perspective of American Indian education, which is principally derived and informed by the thoughts, orientations, and cultural philosophies of American Indian people themselves. The articulation and fulfillment of this need is an essential step in Indian educational self-determination.

2. The need for exploration of alternative approaches to education that more directly and successfully address the needs of American Indian populations during this time of "educational and ecological crisis." During such a time of crisis, it is essential to open up the field and to entertain the possibilities of new approaches in a creative quest for more viable and complete educational processes.

3. The need to integrate, synthesize, organize, and give focus to the enormous amount of accumulated materials from a wide range of disciplines about American Indian cultures and American Indian education toward the evolution of a contemporary epistemology for American Indian education that is Indigenously inspired and ecologically based.[61]

The purpose of contemporary American Indian education as it is currently interpreted has been to assure that American Indian people learn the skills necessary to be productive—or at least survive—in postindustrial American society. American Indians have been taught to be consumers in the tradition of the "American dream" and all that that entails. We have been encouraged to use modern education to "progress" by being participants in the "system." We have been conditioned to seek the rewards and benefits of success in the world that modern education purportedly provides. We are enticed from every direction to pursue careers in law, medicine, business, and the sciences, which form the pillars of Western thought and conditioning. Yet, in spite of the many

American Indian people who have succeeded by embracing Western education, many have not been very successful or have dropped out entirely. This is the paradox of modern education that American Indians must continually negotiate. In this negotiation, American Indian people must critically analyze the effects modern education has had on our collective cultural, psychological, and ecological viability. What has been lost and what has been gained by participating in a system of education that does not stem from, or really honor, our unique Indigenous perspectives? How far can we go in adapting to such a system before that system literally educates us out of cultural existence? Have we reached the limits of what we can do with mainstream educational orientations? How can we revision and establish once again the "ecology of education" that guided our tribal societies? Our collective response to these questions will guide the evolution of American Indian education in the twenty-first century.

The history of American Indian education has largely been characterized by a policy of assimilation combined with covert attempts at modernizing American Indian communities to "fit" them into the mainstream profile of American life. This has been, for the most part, a technical process of development, combined with intense indoctrination in the political and bureaucratic ways of the federal government. Educational development, like other extensions of "federal aid," has occurred through the actions of technicians, bureaucrats, and political manipulators who act to keep real decision-making power outside the parameters of the tribes and individuals affected. Many Indian educators, social reformers, businesspeople, and politicians continue to perpetuate this federal and mainstream paradigm either because they have never questioned their own educational conditioning within this system or because they have not found or explored alternatives. This situation has largely prevented Indian people from being the subject and beneficiaries of the exploration of their own transformational vision and educational process. As a result, Indian tribes are too often relegated to having to "react" to "their" administration by the federal government because of continued dependence on federal aid and extension services. Rather than being "proactive" and truly self-determined in their efforts to educate themselves, through themselves, too often, Indian people continue to struggle with modern educational structures that are not of their own making and are separated from, and compete with, their traditional forms of education. Despite recent advances, such as tribally initiated charter schools, there continues to be a kind of educational schizophrenia in the reality of American Indian education as it exists today.

A pervasive problem affecting the contemporary vision of American Indian education stems from the fact that its contemporary definition and evolution has always been largely dependent on the prevailing winds of American politics. Much of that which characterizes American Indian education policy is not the result of research predicated upon American Indian epistemological orientations but rather the result of "Acts of Congress," the history of treaty-rights interpretation through the courts, and the historic Indian–White relations unique to each tribal group or geographic region.

Historically, the views guiding the evolution of modern American Indian education have been predicated upon assumptions that are anything but representative of American Indian cultural mind-sets. In spite of such policy orientations, traditional educational processes paralleling mainstream education have continued to take place within the context of many Indian families and communities. While there has been progress in the last thirty years, the integration of these two approaches to education has been practically nonexistent.

The basis of much of contemporary American Indian education is the transfer of academic skills and content that prepares the student to compete in the social, economic, and organizational infrastructure of American society as it has been defined by the prevailing political, social, and economic order of vested interests. Much of contemporary American educational theory is devoid of substantial ethical or moral content regarding the means that are used to achieve its ends. The ideal curriculum espoused by a great deal of American education ends up being significantly different from the experienced curriculum internalized by students and the realities of American society, which many minority students experience as wrought with contradictions, prejudice, hypocrisy, narcissism, and unethical predispositions at all levels, including the schools. As a result, there have been educational conflicts, frustration, and varying levels of alienation experienced by many American Indian people following from their encounters with mainstream education.

To overcome these conflicts and frustrations, Indian people need to develop their own educational approach, at every level of schooling, and throughout their lives. In the conditions of the contemporary United States, this needs also to incorporate the best of Western thinking, in order that Native people can function comfortably and effectively in their own contexts and cross-culturally.

A fundamental obstacle to cross-cultural communication continues to revolve around significant differences in cultural orientations to the world and to the fact that American Indian people have been forced to adapt to an educational process that is essentially not of their own making. Traditionally, American Indians view life through a different cultural metaphor than that of mainstream America. It is this different cultural metaphor that is needed to frame the exploration of an appropriate Indigenous educational philosophy.[62]

Alienation from mainstream approaches to education has been one of the consistent criticisms leveled against modern education by American Indian students. They have been given relatively few choices of school curricula that truly address their alienation beyond compensatory programs, remediation, and programs that attempt to bridge the social orientations of students with those of the school. Rather, most of the attempts at addressing such issues have revolved around refitting the problematic American Indian student to the very "system" that caused the student's alienation and failure in the first place. Too often, the American Indian student is viewed as the problem, rather than the inherent and unquestioned approaches, attitudes, perspectives, and curricula of the educational system. The knowledge, values, skills, and interests that Native students possess are largely ignored in favor of strategies aimed at enticing them to conform to mainstream education. Few comprehensive attempts have been made to create a body of content and teaching models that are founded upon contemporary expressions of American Indian educational philosophy. The inherent worth and creative potential of American Indian students and American Indian perspectives of education have not been given serious consideration by mainstream education. Many of the brightest and most creative Indian students continue to be alienated from modern education.

The alienation of American Indian students from education and the resultant loss of their potentially positive service to their communities need not continue if American Indian people revitalize and reclaim their own deep heritage of education. Indigenous approaches to education can work if we are open to their creative message and apply a bit of creative thought to find ways to revitalize and reintroduce their inherently universal processes of teaching and learning. Indigenous educational principles are viable whether one is learning leadership skills through community service, learning about one's cultural roots through creating a photographic exhibit, or learning from nature by exploring its concentric rings of relationship.

A growing number of Indigenous educators have begun exploring the dimensions of Indigenous teaching and learning in creative ways. Teachers create "curricula" (circles of learning and teaching) through constantly creating models and applying them to actual teaching situations. Ideally, teachers constantly adjust their models to fit their students and the constantly changing realities of educating. Through such constant and creative adjustment, teachers and students engage in a symbiotic relationship and constantly form feedback loops around what is being learned. In this way, teachers are always creating their stories even as they are telling them. From this perspective, what is needed is a culturally informed alternative for thinking about and enabling the contemporary education of American Indian people. The task is to undertake a translation of traditional Indian concepts and foundational principles into a contemporary framework of thought and description. This leads to the development of a contemporized, community-based education process that is founded upon traditional tribal values, orientations, and principles but that simultaneously utilizes the most appropriate concepts and technologies of modern education.

American Indian cultures are among the most "studied" anywhere in the world. Access to this vast sea of content, facilitated by Indian educators and scholars, is an essential step to the creation of a contemporary epistemology of American Indian education. Because Native classrooms are integral parts of communities that are themselves revitalizing, this access to, and renewal of, the Indigenous bases of education must occur not only in the contemporary classroom but must include all dimensions of Indian communities as well. All American Indian people, young and old, professional and grassroots, must consider themselves participants in a process of moving forward to the "Indigenous basics" of education. Indian people themselves must introduce contemporary expressions of tribal education to their own people.

Ultimately, it is up to each community of American Indian people, whether they live in an urban setting or on a reservation, to decide how its needs regarding cultural maintenance or revitalization might be addressed through education, in order that the people take ownership of and identify with their educational process. Because every community is unique in its experience and needs, it is up to each community of Native people to decide what is appropriate to introduce through the vehicle of modern education and what should be imparted within the context of appropriate traditional mechanisms in the community.

Modern education and traditional education can no longer afford to remain as historically—and contextually—separate entities. Every community must learn to integrate the learning occurring through modern education with the cultural bases of knowledge and value orientations essential to the perpetuation of a community and its way of life. A balanced integration must be created. Over time, the emphasis on only modern education and Western-oriented curricula, by their nature and predisposition, will tend to erode an Indigenous way of life. In their embracing of modern education, American Indian educators and tribal leaders must understand that the unexamined application of modern education and its models essentially condition people away from their cultural roots, not toward them. Thus, for too many Native students, Western education creates a cultural schizophrenia that undermines their ability to achieve, in both their own communities and the broader world. Modern education provides tools essential to the survival of American Indian people and communities, but this education must be placed in the context of a greater whole. In support of cultural preservation, Indian educators and tribal leaders need to advocate culturally based education as one of the foundational goals of self-determination, self-governance, and tribal sovereignty. Indigenous education offers a highly creative vehicle for thinking about the evolving expressions of American Indian cultures as they develop in the twenty-first century, providing a basis for Native people to contribute more fully and effectively to their own community and nation, and to the wider world.

"Coming Back to Our Power"

The goal of Indigenous educational revitalization is really about coming back to our power. In contemporary terms, this is often referred to as "empowerment." But, "coming back to our power" is a phrase that I believe is more inclusive and descriptive of the multidimensional and multicontextual process of the consciousness, theory development, and applied practice toward transforming Indigenous education that is now taking place in the Indigenous world.

A primary goal of Indigenous education must be to educate for empowerment. For Indigenous people and communities, this must begin with essentially an inward transformation, a kind of "in-powerment" that emphasizes the internal work that "coming to our power" requires. This empowerment necessarily leads to the increase of personal, interpersonal, communal, and political power of Indigenous people. This is the type of empowerment that inherently forms a foundation for actions to change an oppressive situation toward healing and revitalization of individuals and communities.

The colonial history of America and its historic effects on American Indian tribes have included physical, political, economic, and social domination. This history has been based on the internalized notion of the superiority of American colonialism and its foundations in Eurocentric culture and racism. It is well known that the history of American colonialism involved exploitation, oppression, and control. This history included physical and cultural genocide and later cultural assimilation effected through the various social institutions of religion, education, government, law, and economics.

Long-term effects of colonization on American Indians include a host of collective and individual malaise (which we have outlined in chapter 2). Some of the most pronounced of these are: loss of traditional homelands, loss of traditional sustaining practices, and disintegration of traditional communities, economies, and languages. American Indian populations have been significantly reduced, personal and communal self-sufficiency has been lost in many communities, and personal freedom and family life have been consistently disrupted. At the personal level, there has been a loss of self-respect, honor, identity, and economic independence. All of this has been described under terms such as "historical trauma," "internalized colonization," and "ethno-stress." The historical and contemporary effects of colonization on Indigenous peoples have been well researched by postmodernist scholars. This research forms the informational foundation for the call by some Indigenous scholars and educators for the revitalization of Indigenous ways of knowing through a contemporary expression of Indigenous education. It is the history of colonization that guides Indigenous scholars and educators in their advocacy for a "coming back to our collective Indigenous power," for returning Indigenous communities to wholeness and enabling them to be strong participants with their neighbors for mutual benefit.

In order to begin this process, the dynamics of colonization must be further researched and understood, especially in terms of their continuation in educational, institutional, economic, and political structures and the "psychology" of both Native and non-Native alike. The injustices through history and at present need to be critically analyzed. The nature of prejudice and discrimination toward Indigenous peoples associated with colonization and its continuation in "hidden forms" need to be critically viewed. The inherent dehumanization of colonialism must be described and understood in both the historic and contemporary contexts in order to overcome its continuing pernicious effects. The modern denial of colonialism by many, with its accompanying tendency to blame the victims of colonization for their victimization, must be confronted. Likewise, the instances in which the victims blame themselves, and as a result act out various forms of self-abuse, need to be understood and addressed in their various expressions. The internalized shame and negative self-image that characterize the mind-sets of some Indigenous people need to be understood in their various expressions. Finally, the role of internalized colonization in its most pronounced expression as hopelessness and powerlessness among some Indigenous people must be understood and addressed.

Developing Conscientisation and Praxis for Culturally Appropriate American Indian Education

In the development of a critical consciousness and the active addressing of issues, the "praxis" required to evolve a contemporary expression of Indigenous education, it is important to understand the critical nature of the kind of work that is required.

The political grounds of Indigenous education today (which affect the content and context of Indigenous pedagogy) define the meaning of Indigenous educational theory for Indigenous people. Indigenous educational cultural studies combine an evolving and integrative theory and practice to affirm and demonstrate pedagogical practices in: (1) creating a new language; (2) transcending Western academic boundaries; (3) decentering the historic and contemporary consciousness and assimilative power of colonial authority; (4) rewriting the institutional and discursive story of Indigenous people; and (5) applying the essence of democracy as an active political principle for reasserting Indigenous rights, self-determination, and economic viability.

Based on this foundation, critical Indigenous educators and scholars work to develop a new language of and for Indigenous history. They critique the current situations found in Indigenous education contexts. This work is done toward the goal of presenting possibilities for new expressions of Indigenous thought and action.

This work is also done within a broader context of what can be termed a contemporary expression of Indigenous "cultural studies." Indigenous cultural studies attempt to demonstrate the broader implications of Indigenous cultural work and the evolving Indigenous pedagogy as a "new form" of Indigenous cultural production that takes place in a variety of educational, political, cultural, institutional, and community spheres. In doing this, Indigenous educators and scholars create a kind of space to explore the connection between Indigenous education and Indigenous cultural studies. At the same time, Indigenous scholars offer critical analysis of cultural, political, educational, institutional, economic, and postcolonial situations of Indigenous people.

In this work, there are two general categories of concerns that Indigenous educators and scholars attempt to address. First, they attempt to demonstrate a pedagogy of Indigenous "cultural studies." They undertake to make clear how Indigenous cultural studies can deepen Indigenous political possibilities by establishing pedagogical practices that inform and support Indigenous people in their social, political, economic, and spiritual struggles. Central to these concerns are issues of representation, the discourse of cultural difference, economic and environmental exploitation, cultural memory, art and creative expression, and Indigenous community, leadership, and self-determination. Second, Indigenous educators and scholars work to engage the body and production of Indigenous knowledge, values, and collective understanding that takes place within particular social, historical, cultural, institutional, and textual formations.

In Indigenous circles, this essential cultural work is facilitated and informed by gatherings and focused projects and efforts of Indigenous educators and scholars and committed non-Indigenous "allies." The forms that this work can take may include community-focused, political, social, artistic, environmental, curriculum-focused, institutional, leadership-focused, health-focused, and personal endeavor, to name only a few.

The Broader Relevance of Indian Education
Traditional Indian education represents an anomaly for the prevailing theory and methodology of Western education. What is implied in the application of "objectivism" is the assumption that there is one correct way of understanding education in general and, therefore, with minor adaptations, the dynamics of Indian education—with one correct methodology and way of understanding the reality of Indigenous educational philosophy. In this view, there is one correct policy for American Indian education. And that one way is the way of mainstream America. The mindset of "objectivism," stemming from the mainstream approach to science, when applied to the field of Indian education, excludes serious

consideration of the "relational" reality of Indian people, the variations in tribal and social contexts, and the processes of perception and understanding that characterize and actually form its expressions.[63]

For example, the No Child Left Behind Act exemplifies an oversimplified mainstream approach to education that misses the dynamics of many of the cultures that compose the United States today, and hence many of their members are not adequately served by this one-size-fits-all, reductionist assessment approach. Moreover, because of its narrowness, many mainstream students do not do well with mainstream education, as indicated by the substantial improvements in performance that occur when alternative educational approaches are applied. Instances of successful alternatives include varieties of the child-need-oriented education that, for example, helped turn East Harlem in New York City from one of the worst school districts in the country by every measure to one of the best, for many years, by every measure.[64] Similarly effective, in many instances, has been participatory and experiential progressive education as set forth by John Dewey.[65] Both of these approaches are closer to traditional Indigenous education than typical mainstream education in taking into account individual student needs and, in principle, dealing with the students holistically while building greater connections between the school and the community.[66] Most often, child-needs-centered education increases parent involvement in the school, as occurred in East Harlem. The emphasis in Dewey's approach of encouraging self-development and self-initiated development and of directly involving the student as an active participant in the learning process, which is viewed very broadly so as to encompass all facets of life, including involving students, to the degree appropriate for their age, in running the school, participating in decision making, and sharing physical work, has Native American roots.[67] In a related vein, other critiques of American education maintain that mainstream education in primary and secondary schools is too detached from, and seemingly irrelevant to, the world beyond the classroom, leaving students not planning to go to college with little preparation for life after secondary school. This view has resulted in some effective school programs that involve students in apprenticeship programs at businesses in the community during some school hours, combined with changes in some academic classes to make some of the work directly relevant to those apprenticeships.[68]

Reductionist educational research has contributed a dimension of insight to Indian education (and to education more generally), but it has substantial limitations in the multidimensional, holistic, and relational reality of the education of American Indian people. It is the affective elements—the subjective experience and observations, the communal relationships, the artistic and mythical dimensions, the ritual and ceremony, the sacred ecology, the psychological and spiritual orientations—that have characterized and formed Indigenous education since time immemorial. These dimensions and their inherent meanings are not readily quantifiable, observable, or easily verbalized and as a result have been given little credence in mainstream approaches to education and research. Yet it is these very aspects that form a profound orientation for learning through exploring and understanding the multidimensional relationships between humans and their inner and outer worlds. Progressive educators, and some other critics of standard American education, would argue that is a crucial missing piece of mainstream schooling.

For American Indian educators, a key to dealing with the conflict between the reductionist and relational orientations, the cultural bias, and the cultural differences in perception lies in the kind of open communication and creative dialogue that challenges the "tacit infrastructure" of ideas that have guided contemporary American Indian education. Education is essentially a communal social activity. Educational research that produces the most creatively productive insights involves communication within the whole educational community, not just the "authorities" recognized by mainstream educational interests. Education is a communication process that plays an essential role in every act of learning and teaching perception. There must be a flow of communication regarding the educational process among all educators as a result of individual internal dialogue, interactions among educators, publication, and discussion of ideas. Unfortunately, a serious blockage of communication and fragmentation of educational thought continues to be the rule rather than the exception, and communication related to American Indian education is no exception. This has had ill effects in both directions, although the losses are more obvious for Native people.[69]

Many ideas based on the established tacit infrastructure of mainstream American education have been embraced religiously by most educators. This situation, as it pertains to American Indian education, limits creative acts of perception. A free play of thought and opening up of the field that is not restricted by unconsciously determined social pressures and the inherent limitations of the currently established paradigms of Indian education needs to occur. It is only in realizing that there is a tacit infrastructure, and then questioning it, that a high level of creative thought regarding the possibilities and potentials of Indigenous educational philosophy can become possible. And only in realizing that American Indian perceptions of education have traditionally been informed by a different metaphor of teaching and learning can more productive insights into contemporary American Indian education be developed.[70]

These traditional metaphors of education derived their meaning from unique cultural contexts and interactions with natural environments. In turn, the collective experience of American Indian people and their elegant expressions of cultural adaptations have culminated in a body of shared metaphors and understandings regarding the nature of education and its "essential ecology." An intercultural dialogue concerning the differing educational perspectives and metaphors would be mutually beneficial.

Traditional Indian education involves a fundamentally different approach from that of mainstream American education, so that the two ways of learning differ not only in philosophy but in their entire gestalt, including in their carrying out of the learning process and its methodologies, and in the nature and dynamics of educational relationships. Because traditional Native education is holistically interrelational and not dualistic, it does not intrinsically separate theory and practice, human beings and nature, or the classroom (or learning process) from the world. This makes Native education eminently practical while simultaneously developing a higher, or more abstract, knowledge and worldview, emphasizing wisdom over scholarship (in the sense of formal learning). Thus, traditional Native societies were very effective in enhancing the development of skills. Furthermore, the traditional learning process is far more interactive than mainstream education has been (though the increased popularity of child-needs-centered education and similar approaches currently is reducing this difference), so that those who serve as educators are far like more facilitators and resource persons than like teachers or imparters. Moreover, although Indigenous cultures emphasize respect for elders and those who are skilled and knowledgeable, learning (and other) relations are more equalitarian and less hierarchical, collaborative, rather than competitive, in order to support the unique "student" in acquiring knowledge experientially and in participatory interchange, as opposed to essentially similar students being instructed by the teacher and the teaching materials. An important result of this set of differences is that many Indian students have been acculturated to function with very different learning styles than have the vast majority of mainstream Americans, and thus, for Native people to learn effectively, they require different teaching styles.[71]

To what extent and how this is the case varies across Native communities and with individuals, according to differences in traditional culture and the extent of intercultural impact, as well as for other reasons. Therefore, it is hardly surprising that there are numerous instances in which Indian students achieved poorly in schools run on a mainstream model but thrived when their communities became involved in designing and carrying out the schooling. The improvement in formal education occurred not only because learning was changed within the school but also because the community became involved with the students and the school, following continuing tradition. (This also highlights a difficulty with Indian boarding schools that are distant from students' homes, as contrasted with schools that are close enough to home to be centers of community activity).[72]

An exploration of the epistemology of Indigenous education develops insights into the community of shared metaphors and understandings specific to Indian cultures yet reflective of the nature of human learning as a whole. Ultimately, an exploration of traditional Indian education is an exploration of nature-centered philosophy. Traditional Indian education is an expression of environmental education par excellence. It is an environmental education process that can have a profound meaning for the kind of modern education that is required to face the challenges of living in the world of the twenty-first century. It has the potential to create deeper understanding of the collective role of caretakers of a world that Americans must share responsibility for throwing out of balance.

Ironically, a number of the most creative Western thinkers have embraced what are essentially Indigenous environmental-education views and are vigorously appropriating Indigenous concepts to support the development of their own alternative models. For example, cultural historian and philosopher Thomas Berry proposes a new context for education that is essentially a reinvention of the roles and contexts that are inherent to Indigenous education:

> The primary educator as well as the primary law giver and primary healer would be the natural world itself. The integral earth community would be a self-educating community

within the context of a self-educating universe. Education at the human level would be the conscious sensitizing of humans to the profound communications made by the universe about us, by the sun, the moon, and the stars, the clouds, the rain, the contours of the earth and all its living forms. All music and poetry of the universe would flow into the student, the revelatory presence of the divine as well as insight into the architectural structures of the continents and the engineering skills whereby the great hydrological cycle functions in moderating the temperature of the earth, in providing habitat for aquatic life, in nourishing the multitude of living creatures would be as natural to the educational process. The earth would also be our primary teacher of sciences, especially biological sciences, and of industry and economics. It would teach us a system in which we would create a minimum of entropy, a system in which there is no unusable or unfruitful junk. Only in such an integral system is the future viability of humans assured.[73]

Berry's comments mirror what might be termed a contemporized exposition of the Indigenous education processes of tribal societies. It is exactly within the light of such a vision that this story must unfold for Native and non-Native alike. If our collective future is to be one of harmony and wholeness, or if we are to even have a viable future to pass to our children's children, it is imperative that we actively envision and implement new ways of educating for ecological thinking and sustainability. The choice is ours yet, paradoxically, we may have no choice.

American Education from a Tribal Perspective

Learning is always a creative act. We are continuously engaged in the art of making meaning and creating our world through the unique processes of human learning. Learning for humans is instinctual, continuous, and simultaneously the most complex of our natural traits. Learning is also key to our ability to survive in the environments that we create and that create us.

Throughout history, human societies have attempted to guide, facilitate, and even coerce the human instinct for learning toward socially defined ends. The complex of activities for forming human learning is what we call "education" today. To this end, human societies have evolved a multitude of educational forms to maintain their survival and as vehicles for expressing their unique cultural mythos. This cultural mythos also forms the foundation for each culture's "guiding vision," that is, a culture's story of itself and its perceived relationship to the world. In its guiding vision, a culture sets forth a set of "ideals" that guide and form the learning processes inherent in its educational systems. In turn, these ideals reflect what that culture appreciates as the most important qualities, behaviors, and value structures to instill in its members. Generally, this set of values is predicated on those things it considers central to its survival.

The realm of cultural ideals from which the learning, teaching, and systems of education of Native America evolved present a mirror for reflecting on the critical dilemma of American education. For, although the legacy of American education is one of spectacular scientific and technological achievement resulting in abundant material prosperity, the cost has been inexorably high. American prosperity has come at the expense of the environment's degradation and has resulted in unprecedented exploitation of human and material resources worldwide.

American education is in crisis as America finds itself faced with unprecedented challenges in a global community of nations desperately struggling with massive and profound social, economic, and cultural change. American education must find new ways of helping Americans learn and adapt in a multicultural twenty-first-century world. It must come to terms with the conditioning inherent in its processes and systems of educating that contribute to the loss of a shared integrative metaphor of life. The loss of such a metaphor, which may ultimately lead to a social, cultural, and ecological catastrophe, should be a central concern of every American.

The orchestrated "bottom line, real world" chorus sung by many in business and government has become the all-too-common refrain of those who announce they lead the world. Yet what underlies the crisis of American education is the crisis of modern man's identity and his collective cosmological disconnection from the natural world. Those who identify most with the "bottom line" more often than not suffer from image without substance, technique without soul, and knowledge without context, the cumulative psychological results of which are usually unabridged alienation, loss of community, and a deep sense of incompleteness.

In contrast, traditional American Indian education historically occurred in a holistic social context that developed a sense of the importance of each individual as a contributing member of the social group. Essentially, education in tribal context worked at sustaining a life process. It was a process that unfolded through mutual reciprocal relationships between one's social group and the natural world. This relationship involved all dimensions of one's being while providing both personal development and technical skills through participation in the life of the community. It was essentially an integrated expression of environmental education.

Understanding the depth of relationships and the significance of participation in all aspects of life are the keys to traditional American Indian education. *Mitakuye Oyasin* ("we are all related") is a Lakota phrase that captures an essence of tribal education because it reflects the understanding that our lives are truly and profoundly connected to other people and the physical world. Likewise, in tribal education, knowledge is gained from firsthand experience in the world and then transmitted or explored through ritual, ceremony, art, and appropriate technology. Knowledge gained through these vehicles is then used in the context of everyday living. Education, in this context, becomes education for "life's sake." Education is, at its very essence, learning about life through participation and relationship to community, including not only people but also plants, animals, and the whole of nature.

This ideal of education directly contrasts with the predominant orientation of American education that continues to emphasize "objective" content and experience detached from primary sources and community. This conditioning for being marginal participants and perpetual observers involved with only objective content is a foundational element of the crisis of American education and the alienation of modern man from his own being and the natural world.

In response to such a monumental crisis, American education must forge learning processes that are for "life's sake" and honor the Native roots of America. A true transition of today's American educational orientations to more sustainable and connected foundations requires serious consideration of other cultural, life-enhancing, and ecologically viable forms of education.

Traditional American Indian forms of education must be given serious consideration as conceptual wellsprings for the "new" kinds of educational thought capable of addressing the tremendous challenges of the twenty-first century. Tribal education presents examples of models and universal foundations for the transformation of American education and the development of a new paradigm for curricula that will make a difference for "life's sake" in the world of the twenty-first century.

To begin such a process, orientations of American education must begin to move from a focus on only specialization to holistically contexted knowledge, from a focus solely on structures to an understanding of processes, from objective science to systemic science, and from building to networking as a metaphor for knowledge.

American education needs to rededicate its efforts to assist Americans in their understanding and appreciation of spirituality as it relates to the Earth and the "place" in which we live. It must engender a commitment to service rather than competition as an espoused social value. It must promote practiced respect for individual cultural and biological diversity. It must engage students in learning processes that fully facilitate the development of their human potentials through creative transformation. Along its margins, as I've mentioned, American education encompasses approaches and methods, some of which have Native roots, that together with leanings from Indigenous experience, can assist in the renewal of mainstream education for the exigencies of the twenty-first century.

American Indians have struggled to adapt to an educational process that is not their own with its inherent social, political, and cultural baggage. Yet, American Indian cultural forms of education contain seeds for new models of educating that can enliven American education as a whole, as well as allow American Indians to evolve contemporary expressions of education tied to their cultural roots.

Indigenous Education and Individual Transformation

In the context of the development of a basic conceptual framework of a viable Indigenous educational philosophy, it is essential that the relationship of Indigenous education to establishing and maintaining individual and community wholeness be seriously considered. Much of Indigenous education can be called "endogenous" education, in that it revolves around a transformational process of learning by bringing forth illumination from one's ego center. Educating and enlivening the inner self is the life-centered imperative of Indigenous education embodied in the metaphor "seeking life" or "for life's sake." Inherent in this metaphor is the realization that ritual, myth, vision, art, and learning the "art" of relationship in a particular environmental context facilitates the health and wholeness of individual, family, and community. Education for wholeness, by striving for a level of harmony between individuals and their world, is an ancient foundation of the educational process of all cultures. In its most natural dimension, all true education is transformational and Nature-centered. Indeed, the Latin root *educare*, meaning "to draw out," embodies the spirit of the transformational quality of education.

> A transformational approach to education is distinctly universal, integrative and cross-cultural because it is referenced to the deepest human drives. From this viewpoint all human beings concern themselves with self-empowerment and with whatever enables them to transform their lives and the conditions in which they live; such a viewpoint engenders the intent of people striving to create whole, happy, prosperous, and fulfilling lives.[74]

The goals of wholeness, self-knowledge, and wisdom are held in common by all the traditional educational philosophies around the world. Indeed, even through medieval times, all forms of European education were tied to some sort of spiritual training. Education was considered important in inducing or otherwise facilitating harmony between a person and the world. The goal was to produce a person with a well-integrated relationship between thought and action. This idealized outcome was anticipated as following naturally from the "right education."

The "right education" is, of course, a culturally defined construct, one of whose main criteria are socializing the individual to the collective culture of a group. However, this sort of socialization is only one dimension of education, a first step in a lifelong path of learning. In reality, "right" education causes change, which in time creates a profound transformation of self. This transformation is a dynamic creative process, which brings anything but peace of mind, tranquility, and harmonious adaptation. The exploration of self and relationships to inner and outer entities, requires a tearing apart in order to create a new order and higher level of consciousness. Harmony is achieved through such a process, but it lasts for only a short period of time before it again has to be revised as people and their circumstances change. This is the "endogenous" dynamic of tribal education.

The process begins with a deep and abiding respect for the spirit of each child from before the moment of birth. The first stage of Indigenous education, therefore, revolves around learning within the family, learning the first aspects of culture, and learning how to adapt and integrate one's unique personality in a family context. The first stage ends with gaining an orientation to place.

Education in the second stage revolves around social learning, being introduced to tribal society, and learning how to live in the natural environment. The second stage ends with the gaining of a sense of tribal history and learning how to apply tribal knowledge to day-to-day living.

The third stage revolves around melding individual needs with group needs through the processes of initiation, the learning of guiding myths, and participation in ritual and ceremony. This stage ends with the development of a profound and deep connection to tradition.

The fourth stage is a midpoint in which the individual achieves a high level of integration with the culture and attains a certain degree of peace of mind. It brings the individual a certain level of empowerment and personal vitality and maturity. But it is only the middle place of life.

The fifth stage is a period of searching for a life vision, a time of pronounced individuation and the development of "mythical" thinking. This stage concludes with the development of a deep understanding of relationship and diversity.

The sixth stage ushers in a period of major transformation characterized by deep learning about the unconsciousness. It is also a time of great travail, disintegration, wounding, and pain that paves the way for an equally great reintegration and healing process to begin in the final stage. The pain, wound, and conflict act as a bridge to the seventh stage.

In the seventh stage, deep healing occurs in which the self "mutualizes" with body, mind, and spirit. In this stage, deep understanding, enlightenment, and wisdom are gained. This stage ends with the attainment of a high level of spiritual understanding, which acts as a bridge to the finding of one's true center and the transformation to "being a complete man or woman in that place that Indian people talk about."

These stages of interrelationship form a kind of creative continuum, a "life way," which helps us to become more fully human as we move through the stages of our life. Indigenous education traditionally recognized each of the most important interrelationships through formal and informal learning situations, rites of passage, and initiations.

Inherent in Indigenous education is the recognition that there is a knowing Center in all human beings that reflects the knowing Center of the Earth and other living things. Indian elders knew that coming into contact with one's inner Center was not always a pleasant or easily attainable experience. This recognition led to the development of a variety of ceremonies, rituals, songs, dances, works of art, stories, and traditions to assist individual access and use the potential healing and whole-making power in each person. The connecting to that knowing Center was choreographed through specific ritual preparation to help each individual on the journey to his or her own source of knowledge. Through this process, the potential for learning inherent in each of the major stages of a person's life was engaged and set to the task of connecting to one's knowing Center. This was the essential reason for the various rites of passage associated with Indian tribes and various societies within each tribe.

Because the highest goal of Indigenous education was to help each person to "find life" and thereby realize a level of completeness in life, the exploration of many different vehicles and approaches to learning was encouraged. This was done with the understanding that all individuals would find the right one for themselves in their own time. But the process of finding one's self and inner peace with its usual implications of being "adjusted," as it is called in modern circles today, was not the central focus of Indigenous education. Seeking peace and finding self was seen to be a by-product of following a path of life, which presented significant personal and environmental challenges, obstacles, and tests at every turn. This kind of development should not be confused with "individualism," which is so highly prized in American society today. Rather, this is the developmental process of "individuation," as Jung called it.[75] It was a mature stage of human "being" that did not come easily. It had to be earned every step of the way. But in the process of earning it, one learned to put forward the best that one had—one learned the nature of humility, self-sacrifice, courage, service, and determination. Indian people understood that the path to individuation is riddled with doubt and many trials. They understood that it was a path of evolution and transformation.

> Individuation is a work, a life opus, a task that calls upon us not to avoid life's difficulties and dangers, but to perceive the meaning in the pattern of events that form our lives. Life's supreme achievement may be to see the thread that connects together the events, dreams and relationships that have made up the fabric of our existence. Individuation is a search for and discovery of meaning, not a meaning we consciously devise, but the meaning embedded in life itself. It will confront us

with many demands, for the unconscious, as Jung wrote, "always tries to produce an impossible situation in order to force the individual to bring out his very best."[76]

There are elemental characteristics that exemplified the transformational nature of Indigenous education. The following are a few of the most important elements that may provide points of reference for learning goals and the development of content areas.

First was the idea that learning happens of its own accord if the individual has learned how to relate with his or her inner Center and the natural world. Coming to learn about one's own nature and acting with accord to that understanding was a necessary preconditioning that prepared the individual for deep learning.

Second, there was the acceptance that, at times, experiences of significant hardship were a necessary part of an individual's education and that such circumstances provided ideal moments for creative teaching. A "wounding" or memory of a traumatic event and the learning associated with such events provide a constant source for renewal and transformation that enlarged the consciousness if individuals were helped to understand the meaning of such events in their lives.

Third was that empathy and affection were key elements in learning. Also, direct subjective experience combined with effective reflection was an essential element of "right" education. Therefore, mirroring behavior back to learners became a way that they might come to understand for themselves their own behavior and how to use direct experience to the best advantage.

Fourth came an innate respect for the uniqueness of each individual that gave rise to the understanding that ultimately each person was his or her own teacher as far as achieving an understanding and realization of their process of individuation. Indigenous education integrated the notion that there are many ways to learn, many ways to educate, many kinds of learners, and many kinds of teachers, each of which had to be honored for their uniqueness and their contribution to education.

Fifth followed that each learning situation is unique and innately tied to the creative capacity of the learner. When this connection to creative learning and illumination is thwarted, frustration and rigidity follow. Learning therefore had to be connected to the life process of each individual. The idea of lifelong learning was therefore a natural consideration.

Sixth was that teaching and learning are a collaborative cooperative contract between the "teacher" and learner. In this sense, the teacher was not always human but could be an animal, a plant, or other natural entity or force. Also, based on this perception, the "teachable" moment was recognized through synchronistic timing or creative use of distractions and analogies to define the context for an important lesson. The tactic of distract-to-attract-to-react was a common strategy of Indigenous teachers.

Seventh was that learners need to see, feel, and visualize a teaching through their own and other people's perspectives. Therefore, telling and retelling a story from various perspectives and at various stages of life enriched learning, emphasized key thoughts, and mirrored ideas, attitudes, or perspectives back to learners for impact. Reteaching and relearning are integral parts of complete learning. Hence the saying, "every story is retold in a new day's light."

Eighth followed that there are basic developmental orientations involved with learning through which we must pass toward more complete understanding. Learning through each orientation involves the finding of personal meaning through direct experience. The meaning that we each find is always subjective and interpretive, based on our relative level of maturity, self-knowledge, wisdom, and perspective.

Ninth understood that life itself is the greatest teacher and that each of us must accept the hard realities of life with the realities that are joyous and pleasing. Living and learning through the trials and pains of life are equally as important as learning through good times. Indeed, life is never understood fully until it is seen through difficulty and hardship. It is only through experiencing and learning through all life's conditions that one begins to understand how all that we do is connected and all the lessons that we must learn are related.

Tenth flowed that learning through reflection and sharing of experience in community allows us to understand our learning in the context of greater wholes. In a group, there are as many ways of seeing, hearing, feeling, and understanding as there are members. In a group, we come to understand that we can learn from another's experience and perspective. We also become aware of our own and others' bias and lack of understanding through the process of the group. We see that sometimes people do not know how to understand or use real innovation and that many times, people do not know how to recognize the real teachers or the real lessons. We see that a community can reinforce an important teaching or pose obstacles to realizing its true message. It is not until, as the Tohono O'odham phrase it, "when all the people see the light shining at the same time and in the same way," that a group can truly progress on the path of knowledge.

Creating A New Circle of American Indian Education

For American Indians, a new "circle" of education must begin that is founded on the roots of tribal education and reflective of needs, values, and sociopolitical concerns as Indian people themselves perceive them.

Such a new circle must encompass the importance American Indian people place on the continuance of their ancestral traditions. It must emphasize a respect for individual uniqueness in the diversity of expressions of spirituality. It must facilitate a strong and contextual understanding of history and culture. It must develop a strong sense of place and service to community and forge a commitment to educational and social transformation that recognizes and further empowers the inherent strength of American Indian people and their respective cultures.[77]

To understand how to accomplish this, Indian people must begin to exploit all avenues of communication open to them and establish a reflective dialogue about a contemporary theory for Indian education that evolves from them and their collective experience. In the past, Indian education has been defined largely by non-Indian educators, politicians, and institutions through a huge volume of legislative acts at the state and federal levels, which for decades have entangled Indian leaders, educators, and whole communities in the morass of the federal government's social-political bureaucracy.

Indeed, Indian education stems more from the U.S. government's self-serving political-bureaucratic relationship with Indian tribes than from any true process within cultural context that is rooted in tribal philosophies and social values. In fact, no contemporary theory of Indian education exists that can be said to guide the implementation or direction of educational curriculum development. Instead, what is called "Indian education" today is really a "compendium of models, methodologies and techniques gleaned from various sources in mainstream American education and adapted to American Indian circumstances, usually with the underlying aim of cultural assimilation."[78]

It is time for Indian people to define Indian education in their own voice and in their own terms. It is time for Indian people to allow themselves to explore and express the richness of their collective history in education. Among American Indians, education has always included a visionary expression of life. Education has been, and continues to be, a grand story, a search for meaning, and an essential food for the soul.

A contemporary expression of Indigenous education must be a viable "culturally-informed alternative" that includes the expression of the "universals" of the educational process as viewed from the perspective of traditional American Indian thought. Its foundation of credibility must lie in the applicability of the perspectives and models presented to the whole process of teaching and learning, not just that of American Indians. The universals, which are explored, may be viewed as "archetypes" of human learning and as part of the Indigenous psyche of all peoples and cultural traditions, including those of Western civilization. All relevant sources of thought and research and educational philosophy, regardless of cultural source, need to be considered to fully illuminate the future possibilities of a contemporary education that mirrors Indigenous thought and its primary orientation of relationship with the natural world.

I view the next phase of the development of American Indian education as requiring the collective development of transformative vision and educational process based on authentic dialogue. This requires that new structures and practices emerge from old ones through a collective process of creative thought and research. An ongoing and unbiased process of critical exchange between modern educational thought and practice and the traditional philosophy and orientations of Indian people can only generate these kinds of new structures and practices.

A new kind of educational consciousness, an "ecology of Indigenous education," must be forged that allows American Indian people to explore and express their collective heritage in education and to make the kinds of contributions to global education that stem from such deep ecological orientations. The exploration of traditional American Indian education and its projection into a contemporary context is much more than just an academic exercise. It illuminates the true nature of the ecological connection of human learning and helps to liberate the experience of being human and being related at all its levels.

From this perspective, education takes on the quality of a social and political struggle to open up the possibilities for a way of education that comes from the very "soul" of American Indian people. It also brings to the surface the extent and the various dimensions of the conditioning of modern educational processes that have been "interjected" into the deepest levels of their consciousness. They become critical observers of the modern education to which they have had to adapt and that demands conformity to a certain way of education that more often than not has been manipulated to serve only certain vested interests of American society. Through the exploration of Indigenous education they learn how to demystify the techniques and orientations of modern education. This understanding allows them to use such education in accord with their needs and combine the best that it has to offer with that of Indigenous orientations and knowledge. They cease to be "recipients" of modern education and become active participants and creators of their own education.

At a more inclusive level, exploration of Indigenous education liberates the American Indian learner and educator to participate in the kind of creative and transforming dialogue that is inherently based on equality and mutual reciprocity. This is a way of learning, communicating, and working of relationship that mirrors those ways found in nature. It also destigmatizes the American Indian learner as "disadvantaged" and the educator as "provider of aid." Rather, it allows both the learner and educator to cocreate a learning experience and mutually undertake a pilgrimage to a new level of self-knowledge. The educator enters the cultural universe of the learner and no longer remains an outside authority. By being allowed to cocreate a learning experience, everyone involved generates a kind of critical consciousness and enters into a process of empowering one another. And with such empowerment, Indian people become significantly "enabled" to alter a negative relationship with their learning process. Ultimately, with the reassertion, contemporary development, and implementation of such an Indigenous process at all levels of Indian education, Indian people may truly take control of their own history by becoming the transforming agents of their own social reality.

In the final analysis, American Indian people must determine the future of American Indian education. That future must be rooted in a transformational revitalization of our own expressions of education. As we collectively "Look to the Mountain," we must truly think of that seventh generation of American Indian children, for it is they who will judge whether we were as true to our responsibility to them as our relatives were to us seven generations ago. It is time for an authentic dialogue to begin to collectively explore where we have been, where we are now, and where we need to go as we collectively embark on our continuing journey "to that place that Indian people talk about."

Current Developments on the Path Toward an Indigenous Education

STEPHEN M. SACHS AND PHYLLIS M. GAGNIER

Currently, there are a growing number of examples of Indian people carrying out education on their own terms and providing a basis for developing a truly Indian education that roots students in their traditional culture, increasing their understanding of who they are and enhancing their ability to develop in their own context, while providing the integrative bridging necessary to function successfully in the wider society. This is particularly important today to overcome the alienation of too many Native young people from themselves, their families, their traditions, and their communities that is the major source of gang and drug problems, especially with methamphetamine use, which has become a serious problem across Indian country.

An example of a school that reestablished appropriate Indian education was the Rough Rock Community School, serving grades K–6, in the Navajo community of Chinle, Arizona. The school was turned over to a local school board organized as a nonprofit organization, Demonstration in Navajo Education, under grants from the Bureau of Indian Affairs and the Office of Economic Opportunity in 1966.[79] The school pioneered local Indian control and bicultural curriculum development, providing a center for the creation and collection of Navajo cultural materials. It also developed a parent dormitory program that brought community members to live with the children, and an open door policy that encouraged school visits and participation by people in the community. In 1983, Rough Rock obtained a federal grant to introduce a bilingual inquiry curriculum in Navajo studies for kindergarten through the ninth grade, on the basis of a survey of parents, students, and teachers that identified local needs related to educational goals. The program is built on Navajo values, developing concepts, ideas, and problem-solving abilities in the context of culturally relevant experience and topics while promoting competency in Navajo and English. A key part of the program was the development of the Navajo concept of interaction in relation to traditional notions of balance and harmony. The educational setting was a participatory classroom, with student discussions taking place in small groups and with the entire class, and issues were discussed to build consensus. Students were encouraged to "make their own unique generalizations and conclusions," and sustained high levels of active participation in the dialogue. Experiential learning also was used in other contexts, allowing students to use what they had learned and inspiring their participation by involving them with matters in their own lives and community.

The private Southern Ute Indian Academy was launched in 2000 by the Southern Ute Indian Tribe as a four-year primary school that would expand through eighth grade and possibly later encompass a high school.[80] The academy functions with a modified Montessori program because that program's flexible, student-centered approach is the closest Western educational model to traditional Native ways of educating. The first truly Indian-oriented curriculum administered by the BIA was a Montessori program.[81] The school learning activities are in Ute and English, include Ute culture along with mainstream school subjects, and involve community elders. In the school's first year, standardized testing indicated that all of the young people at the academy functioned at satisfactory or higher levels for their grade levels in math and English.

Hopi High School at Keams Canyon, Arizona, has achieved an 87 percent graduation rate, as compared with a 63 percent graduation rate for Indian students nationwide, and a 76 percent rate for all Arizona students.[82] This success is attributed partly to the school's teaching the Hopi and Navajo languages, culture, and Native tradition. Students participate in cultural activities, among which is a week of traditional celebration incorporating about twenty dance groups. Other factors are parent involvement, a 90 percent teacher retention rate, regular meetings with counselors, after-school tutoring with bus service to distant homes, and a Second Chance Program for students who do not complete English on the first attempt. Several programs encourage college attendance, and some classes offer college credit. The Upward Bound program takes students to the Northern Arizona University campus to meet college students and provides a five-week summer session. In 2003, ten students participated in the Hopi Harvard Summer, during which they attended classes at Harvard Medical School.

Two Indian Schools in the Southwest: The BIA School Program
A particularly interesting set of innovations involves the work of author Phyllis M. Gagnier with a BIA school and a tribal charter school in the Southwest. The center of Gagnier's work focuses on nurturing and honoring the intuitive awareness and creativity of each individual. According to Gagnier, "This elicits self-awareness and understanding, generating a

body, mind, spirit synergy within the individual and in the group as a whole."[83] The approach involves empowering students to become aware of and understand that they have a choice in how they see their situations and can take ownership for how they see things, shifting their perceptions, and self-managing their own behaviors. Because her premise is that parents, guardians, and community members are the first and the last teachers in the life of the child, her intention was to offer services that strengthened those relationships; created and sustained a nurturing school community in each classroom; built authentic student, parent, and teacher relationships; created understanding of the child's communication process; equipped the emotionally vulnerable child with self-empowerment skills; integrated strength-based emotional intelligence ("heart") and brain-based learning into life skills; and infused aspects of the program development into the existing infrastructure.

The principal of a BIA high school contacted Gagnier to provide conflict-resolution training to specific students, who were to assist their peers in problem solving. The assumption was that typical school-type peer mediation training would be provided. However, Gagnier, based on the findings of her previous work with eliciting the perceptions of the mediation model from a variety of Native peoples within different tribal communities, recommended that inclusive elicitive decision making and collaborative consensus-building processes be facilitated with the identified youth. The "elicitive process" is a specific type of facilitation that focuses on obtaining the perceptions of students, parents, and teachers. Through this process, a safe environment is created where each participant can access self-understanding and self-empowerment in order to take ownership of transforming his or her own perceptions. This provides each participant with the opportunity to address the emotional state of learned helplessness that is imposed by victimization. Subsequent training is designed based on the elicited facts of the students', parents', and teachers' perceptions. This decision to provide an open-process model, rather than a prescriptive model, proved to be more culturally appropriate for the selected youth, who early on disclosed their reluctance to "have the answers" for their peers, who were also their friends and family members. They preferred to develop their leadership skills and be role models for their peers. Thus, the Native students received one-on-one and small-group training as cofacilitators in elicitive group decision making and collaborative consensus-building processes to develop their leadership abilities.

Unfolding the Facilitation Process

From the onset, the students enthusiastically responded to the facilitated processes, taking charge of creating their learning environment by arranging furniture and materials to allow for individual space, community space, and a training area. They actively engaged in participatory decision making regarding the training content, interactions with one another, the facilitated processes, and the setting for the application of their learning. They chose to serve as visible role models for the younger students by designing and facilitating in-classroom interactive processes at the adjacent BIA elementary school, where the students and teachers reportedly were both appreciative and impressed with the older students' skill and service. Some teachers were amazed at some of the students they had previously taught. Thus, through their own decision-making processes, the students were able to establish authentic relationships with teachers, understand their own communication styles, and learn about the younger children's communication process. Some students applied their learning to their interactions with their peers, which they stated improved the relationship.

This endeavor led to the creation of a summer project in one of the Nation's villages, which the district's community developer cofacilitated. He stated, "When I work with the community, we can spend too much of the time in our heads—finger pointing or jealousy, that type of thing. In order to move forward, we need to knock down those barriers and work together more. . . . We are trying to reconnect back to ourselves." His desire is to "put traditional ways of the past into today's context."[84]

Thus, in the intense heat, youth of all ages, parents, and elders joined together in the community building to focus on their interactions with one another and to develop more trust through the use of emotional-intelligence "heart" processes and activities. Many stories emerged that demonstrated little adjustments in the children's perceptions toward the extended families of their community, and the adults' shifts in their perceptions toward the children. This perceptual transformation process is based on coaching students, parents, and guardians to their own awareness of how they are seeing things by discerning whether their responses are coming from their head, their heart, or their emotions. Thus, the person owns her or his perception, decides whether to choose to reframe the perception, and transforms the original perception. Problem solving, interactive communication, and relationship building takes place from the new perception.

Using the Heart Tools

Using heart tools as the universal connector to cut through the "stuff" and find a way to express their core selves, the youth learned that their heart intelligence can bridge the divisions of their established group interactions. For example, one day, a group of mixed-age youth were playing basketball. The trainer-coach kept calling out, "Play from your heart." Suddenly one of the older youth, whose group had been annoyed at the presence of the younger children, picked up a toddler who was watching and refusing to move. The older youth very gently made the young child part of his team, almost as if the little one was an extension of his body. In a short time, the kids switched from a game that was highly competitive between specific groups to a game that involved the younger children and, still later, some of the adults present. The movement by the youth in their awareness, understanding, acceptance, and ability to think outside their initial group to include other peers, parents, and elders demonstrated a change in their attitudes, an opening of their perceptions, a developing trust in and ownership of their choices in self-managing their own behaviors. The support provided by the presence and interactions of the parents and elders created genuine safety for the children amid the laughter and fun.

Originally contacted by the BIA elementary school principal to provide training to students and staff in conflict-resolution and communication styles, Gagnier, due to the children's responses in the village, spent a day in classrooms demonstrating teaching heart tools. The teacher of the gifted and talented program accompanied her and stated, "I observed a few of my students with Ms. Gagnier and was really impressed. . . . The kids were very genuine in their response to her message about working with both their hearts and their heads. . . . We decided to do some work with the students and emotional intelligence."[85] Very quickly, the special-education teacher became involved: "I observed her working with a few classes at school. The children connected, their faces glowed."[86]

Combining their classes, the two teachers and the tribal community developer received training and cofacilitated with the trainer-coach. According to Gagnier, "When we introduced the heart tools, the prevalent perception of the students about school was that everything was boring." Specialized "What puts you in your heart?" activities were initially facilitated and the results shared with the faculty, some of whom were surprised at the students' statements.

In every instance in the program, the students' work included family members regardless of their parents' situation. The students' perceptions brought increased awareness to the faculty of the need for meaningful involvement of the parents in the school. Also, initially, the mention of the word *feeling* would cause most of the students to shut down. It took time for trust to be built so that students felt safe enough to begin to disclose their feelings. Later, they were openly engaging in expressing themselves, including their feelings. When that stage of growth was reached, some students were overheard informing new students that the heart work is where "we sit around and discuss our feelings." This was a shock to the trainer-coach when she heard it because initially any reference to "feelings" resulted in silence and nonparticipation on the part of the students. The students' new expressed perceptions to the concept of feeling reinforced for Gagnier the value of the concept of eliciting students' perceptions prior to and during the offering of direct services. According to Gagnier,

> When we elicited from the students their perceptions of their experiences, they expressed labeling, violence, gangs, drugs, stupid, and bored. A list of the heart tools we had and could learn, including the science topics, were submitted as a summary to each student (3rd through 8th graders) with the request that they each choose the perceptions, heart tools, and science they wanted to work on for the year. The responses ranged from the first introduction of the program in 1997, where the main theme was boredom, to 1999 where the choices selected by the students were kindness, heart, truths, care, focusing, leadership, play, giving, appreciation, peace, respect, music, gangs, drugs and feelings. Boredom was not checked by any student!

Some of the students in the combined groups volunteered to cofacilitate in their respective classrooms. A presentation was made to the faculty, resulting in several teachers requesting the program. Later, every classroom except one was involved in the heart-centered, grade-specific, in-classroom training. On-site training and coaching services were provided to the teaching staff, support staff, bus drivers, and cooks through one-on-one, small-group, and in-classroom processes during time periods elicited from the respective personnel. The total amount of training time averaged eighteen days at intervals throughout the school year. During the absence of the trainer-coach, the students and staff sustained their learning, as demonstrated by their behaviors upon her return. The students would excitedly "send her heart," remind her of some of the activities they had learned, and share with her the creative ways they were implementing their learning. For instance, students created "heart caring" school bulletin boards, heart-community in-classroom activities, and special in-classroom discussion topics. Several teachers confidently reported that the faculty agreed to (and some teachers had insisted upon) including "kindness," which was taught in the project as a heart skill, in their school rules as a best practice for building effective schools.

The Teachers' Observations

The special-education teacher made the following statements about her observations and experience with the program:

> The children bring with them a deep and rich tradition and culture. They know about energy and spirit in a very special way. HeartMath tools add another way to make connections with who they are and make healthy choices and good decisions. After almost three years of implementing HeartMath, we are working harder, smarter, and happier. The students' test scores are up. They take better care of materials and equipment, are more polite and considerate, complete more assignments and retain more of what they learn. Their written work is more organized and legible and they say good morning back to me every morning. Their parents come to parent groups and have learned to "send heart" too. It has helped me create more inclusive ways to provide special education services to children. By giving kids the tools and knowledge to access their heart, I hope to see them continue to succeed, achieve and be happy. HeartMath has opened another door for me as a teacher and as a person. I enter my classroom each day with a renewed energy, intention and appreciation. I am fortunate to be teaching in a school where HeartMath is welcomed and supported.[87]

The gifted and talented program teacher made the following comments about the program:

> I think it changes the students' perspective of things. They feel more empowered to do what they know is right. And even when they do not always follow their heart's decisions,

they are conscious of them and might be more likely to pick those solutions in the future. They also realize that when they make a decision, they are responsible for it. If they get in an uncomfortable situation, they are not as likely to blame other people for being in that situation. This is especially powerful for the junior high school girls in their newfound ability to set boundaries in the area of what behaviors they will accept from other people. I would like to help enable them to make more intelligent choices. We talk, for instance, about "heart dreams"—things that your heart tells you, that you would really like to do. We try to get them to research that dream, asking how they are going to achieve their goal. The students have learned to use the HeartMath tools both in and outside of the classroom."[88]

Furthermore, states Gagnier, "We are seeing changes in the students' interactions with each other and the adults in their school, including individual students self-managing their own responses and making an effort to help others." In the words of a third grader, "We give heart to each other."

Student Participation in the NCPCR Conference
A significant outcome of the facilitated heart processes that elicited student perception and decision making involved several junior high school boys. In a circle activity, one student who previously never spoke in the group presented a creative intervention plan for eradicating drugs from the high school campus. Another student seriously desired to be a cofacilitator outside the arena of his school and community. Thus was born the idea that these two young men, accompanied by two volunteers, would participate in the National Conference on Peacemaking and Conflict Resolution (NCPCR) as cofacilitators. They interactively engaged in developing their leadership, critical-thinking, creative, communication, and negotiating skills through naming, writing, and submitting the description of their workshop to the conference, recruiting a parent chaperon and program cofacilitators, writing permission slips and gaining their parents' permission, obtaining funding from their school and districts, creating their training agenda, and practicing their facilitation processes. As the time for the conference grew near, their heart commitment was strong despite their fears, which they faced and transformed

through naming themselves the "Natural Heart People." They documented this shift in their perception about themselves and one another on T-shirts, which they wore for their presentation. They persistently encouraged each other and expressed their needs to the trainer-coach.

At the conference, they each stayed on task, kept their agreements, relaxed, and engaged in unplanned conference participation amid the overwhelming volume of people. They responsibly showed up at the designated time to help the trainer-coach and their teacher cofacilitators set up the training seminar environment and arranged their own training materials. Some of the conference participants were electrified by the happy heart energy that greeted them as they entered the room. Others told the boys they were choosing to stay "because of you." Meeting other presenters with whom they had to share their time, actually guiding their group participants through facilitated processes, and role playing a concept for the entire room provided the young men with the unique experience to learn and express the degree to which they had internalized the concepts of the heart intelligence training. When a distinguished academic in the group put them on the spot with a direct intrusive question, they immediately shifted to their hearts without a reactive response, sent her heart, and proceeded to explore their answers by interacting with each other through a spontaneous role play. Their authenticity moved the participants to applause, some of them standing in recognition of them.

Debriefing and cleanup occurred without an attitude, despite the boys' fatigue, demonstrating they were sustaining their heart-brain-coherent emotional state. In their free time, they chose to meet and participate in the elder circle. Phyllis Gagnier, as cochair of the Indigenous committee of the conference, was facilitating the Honoring of the Elders conference luncheon. The boys stepped up to assist her in a crowded room and the light of their pride and appreciation was felt by everyone when they were chosen to honor the vice chairman of their tribe and a retired teacher from their tribe and school. Two of the boys upon graduation from high school received scholarships to a junior college, which they both attended. Recently, one of the young men contacted Phyllis Gagnier and shared that he is continuing his education, working for his tribe, and building a house. During the conversation, he recalled some memories. He disclosed the impact that both the heart training and presenting at the conference had had on his self-esteem and self-confidence, helping him to persevere despite difficult times. One of the elders in peace and justice education has, on more than one occasion, reminded Gagnier of what she learned from the Natural Heart People in their conference presentation, to which Gagnier responds, "This all happened because of facilitating heart processes eliciting student perception and decision making, which I call listening to 'the voices of our children.'"

Re-creating an In-Classroom Heart Community as a School Community

At the BIA school, "the voices of the children" were spontaneously expressed, individually and collectively, when a closing activity eliciting heart was framed as "appreciating our teachers." Over three days, the students collaborated and communicated to organize, facilitate, and create a schoolwide appreciation program for their teachers, bus drivers, cooks, and administrative staff. Each student in the school created a traditional flower on which he or she wrote appreciation statements for a specific adult in the school. Students volunteered for the tasks of personally, or with a heart buddy, delivering the invitations, arranging for the food, designing the flower and seating arrangements, serving as hostesses, and cofacilitating the appreciation program presented to the personnel. The skills of self-direction, leadership, and self-reflection flowed in and out of expressions of delight, joy, fun, and beauty. Individual staff members who could not arrive on time stated they did not want to be left out and requested that their flowers remain so they could participate. Some children shared with Phyllis Gagnier that as the adults opened and read their flowers, "they had tears in their eyes!"

The children had successfully re-created an in-classroom heart community as a school community, making connections through sending heart to one another and sharing their learning. Also noteworthy is the student who demonstrated the most fear in the initial phase of the program. Always observing at a distance, preserving his safety on his own terms, he gradually eased into the circles with limited active participation. Later, he explained the "heart thing" to the new students. Still later, he requested that the group stay connected and advised the group how "we can stay connected to each other over the summer by sending heart." Later, after he moved on to high school, a teacher questioned him about his feeling towards high school, to which he responded, "Oh, they need that heart stuff here!"

For Phyllis Gagnier, the trainer-coach whom the children call the "heart lady," the credit goes to "the people." It is their perceptions, their participation, their expressions, their creativity, their actions that express their beingness, which moves the transformational process into the experience of the joy and fulfillment of relationships. (See the parallel discussion of working with Indian nations in "Facilitators and Resource Persons for the People: Consulting with Indian Nations as Collaborators," in chapter 6.)

> This HeartMath stuff is about learning more about your heart; how to get in it, and listen to what it is telling you because your mind can sometimes tell you bad things to do, like hurt people. The heart gives you good thoughts. Sometimes I practice getting in my heart when I'm in my room alone. (Boy, age 13)

> I like to shift to my heart when my friends make me mad. Shifting to my heart helps me get along better with my friends. (Boy, age 11)

> HeartMath is special and fun. It gets you in your heart. Makes you do better in school and feel better for the rest of the day. It helps you focus and it helps me get along with friends. After I get out of the HeartMath class, I go to science and I feel better for the rest of the day. (Girl, age 12)[89]

The Truancy Intervention Program

At the tribal charter school, the Native American principal and Phyllis Gagnier collaborated to create a Tribal Family Empowerment Program for truancy intervention. Students from the community who were in violation of the tribe's Truancy Ordinance were ordered by the court to attend the Saturday School program with their parents or guardians. Initially, students and their parents or guardians received twenty hours of training and coaching in specialized emotional intelligence processes, which included an academic reading component. The program's training and coaching hours were later increased to forty and offered on eight consecutive Saturdays.

Parents as the First and Last Teachers

Operating on the premise that parents are the first and the last teachers, the program posed questions (What do we want? What is in our way? What are we going to do about it? How are we going to sustain it?) to the truant students to facilitate self-discovery, with their parents and guardians functioning as "guiding hands." Gagnier perceives that Indigenous education programs such as the ones she has been facilitating (and other individual and community healing efforts that we will discuss in section 3 of this chapter) need to face the high degree of disconnect among Indian youth. She states that deep in the hearts of our Native children rests the potential for healing: healing the traumas of their parents' miseducation and healing the wounds inflicted systematically, day after day and year after year, on their growing bodies, brains, and spirits by administrative decisions that focus on replicating the mainstream culture's obsession with cognitive retention.

With the stifling of their self-discovery and creative expression, some of our Native children experience boredom. Stimulated by the need for excitement, they are resorting to truancy, gang activity, and more recently have found their way into the world of methamphetamine. With methamphetamine, Gagnier feels that a new child is being birthed in the culture of "tweekers." Rage, self-mutilation, and violence are expressed as the new humanity, allowing our youth to openly engage in and normalize elder abuse. This behavior of their precious child leaves parents and guardians at a loss, particularly if their own path is disconnected from their Native traditions. With meth, another layer of invisibility is created that is more deadly than the previous one. The cycle repeats at a core level, overshadowing the heart-intelligent wisdom. The path of balance is forgotten and in some situations remains forgotten, if it was ever known. The journey home is unrecognized, and home is a long, long, long distance away.

Gagnier has observed awe and puzzlement on the faces of many parents who are feeling the brunt of their child's rage. What is the basis of their children's anger? Is it their perception of entitlement? Is it their feelings of extreme sadness? Is it the latest peer standard? Is it their experience of control? Is it their intergenerational trauma remanifesting in the cruelest twist yet of history? Where will their unprocessed emotions lead our children? Will their reactions to their lives self-perpetuate to internal annihilation? Are their storm clouds forming a funnel of irreversible destiny? How will the processes presented in this book take our children by the hand and safely return them into the circle?

Improving Student–Parent Relations

The unique feature of the Tribal Family Empowerment Program is the required presence of the student with his or her parent or guardian. This has consistently resulted in the improvement of the relationship between the child and the parent or guardian. The students and parents are particularly responsive to their increased understanding and perceptual shifts about one another. They expressed appreciation that, through the program, they were healing their own relationships with one another and expressed the desire that the healing be sustained. A community member who served as the parent and community involvement coordinator for the school and cofacilitated in the Saturday School program stated, "The parents told us repeatedly how they especially enjoyed the time they had to relate to their child on a one-to-one basis."[90]

Pre- and post-testing of the students who completed the first run of the forty-hour truancy intervention training in Saturday School showed significant improvements in all but one area. The Family Comfort score rose 11 percent and represented "getting along with family members," which likely occurred because the program design specified that students and parents (or guardians) receive the training together and emphasized healing and building the relationship between student and parent, including learning skills to communicate with each other. The Self-reliance score increased by 8 percent and represented "self-control." The increase in this score probably occurred because of the emotional intelligence elicitive decision-making training and coaching that the program provided, which focuses on students learning to trust their own heart intelligence. These processes flow from the inside out and include consistently listening to the student's perceptions.

The Social Skills score increased by 13 percent, representing "ability to get along with others." This rise possibly resulted from both the respect and the trust the facilitators gave to the students through the processes, at the end of which the students, with their parents and the Saturday School facilitators, reported back to the whole group. In some instances, the students served as cofacilitators with the trainer-coach and as recorders. The students also engaged in a final elicitive celebration process in which they are acknowledged—by being affirmed through appreciation—and listened to for their recommendations and comments. The Ability to Complete Tasks score went up 7 percent, representing increased focus. This increase appeared to have resulted from the clear focus of the training and coaching as well as the emotional intelligence skills it taught.

The Anger Management score improved 5 percent, which was significant because the students and parents were already angry before being made angry about the court requirement to take and complete the training on Saturdays. The improvement in the ability to manage anger might have occurred largely because the program training and coaching focuses on perceptual transformation processes, which include always appreciating self and parents. It probably also followed from the facilitation of an appreciation circle for each student, in which he or she receives appreciation statements from the students, parents, and facilitators present in the circle.

The Distress Management ability score increased 8 percent, possibly as the result of the perceptual-transformation process training, which includes understanding emotional states, identifying present emotional states, experiencing an emotional state, learning ways to reframe the emotional state, becoming aware when the emotional state has shifted, and assessing whether the new state in fact feels better. Similarly, the Ability to Handle Anxiety score went up 4 percent, likely because the training facilitated learning the emotional intelligence skills of shifting emotional states and handling stress.

The one area that did not improve was the Ability to Be Empathetic score (which declined 1 percent). Phyllis Gagnier, who facilitated the program, believed that there was no improvement in this area and also that the ability to manage anxiety and anger showed the smallest increases because of unresolved traumas that are at or just below the surface for the students. She intuited that to shift a behavior to "empathetic" required the student to have needs-based awareness. During the initial training, students promptly denied any reference to individual needs and would shut down. Gagnier's observations of the correlation between the emotional states of trauma, pain, denial, and being in need led her to add the processing of feelings and needs by writing specific needs and feelings on cards and encouraging students and parents to choose from the cards. The card method has proven to be powerful, leading time after time to an understanding between parent and child when the trauma can be identified (although not yet processed or resolved), which results in the quality of the child–parent relationship improving markedly. In addition, the needs-based emphasis resulted in the identification of financial needs and directly led to the inclusion of First Nations Development Institute's "Building Native Communities: Financial Skills for Families" curriculum in the Saturday School training-coaching program.[91]

Establishing Interventions as Integral Parts of the Regular Process

An essential aspect of creating the program for Gagnier as consultant and trainer-coach has been integrating innovations into processes by gaining approval for them from the administration and establishing a basis for considering future truancy intervention strategies and curriculum development for the purposes of continued the program after she leaves it.[92]

The Tribal Family Empowerment Program continued at the tribal charter school, having evolved through several administrations and a change in the tribal truancy ordinance. The Saturday School, with the addition of a weekly Family Circle training-coaching component for individual families, was offered as a truancy-intervention school program to students and their parents or guardians before students were cited for chronic nonattendance. Offering intervention services at the school level prior to citation represented the recommendations of parents and guardians. The program had more latitude in offering the student and parent or guardian individualized needs-based truancy intervention services in which they engaged in the decision-making process. Gagnier, after reflecting on the program's needs, facilitated processes with the school's intervention team and recommended creating the role of coach-mentor for community members, which would allow them to be an integral part of the intervention team working directly with the truant student in the initial eight-step process that occurred prior to the student being referred to the tribal attendance officer for citation.

"Keys to Connectedness: Learning Is Cultural"

A central part of the Tribal Family Empowerment Program and the BIA school programs is Gagnier's "Keys to Connectedness: Learning Is Cultural" curriculum. In Saturday School and Family Circle facilitation, students and parents or guardians choose the curriculum aspect that each perceives she or he needs. The components of the program combine to form the acronym CULTURAL:

C = Caring. Shifting perceptions is an integral part of Saturday School and Family Circle. Acknowledging parents as both the first and the last teachers in the life of a child affects the parent–child relationship directly. In the training room, heads turn toward one another and smiles light up faces as each person becomes aware of the primary relationship. The fact that educators have the honor of being in their child's life for a sliver of time seems to affirm for the parent who the real teacher is. Although subtle, a shift in perception toward one another is initiated. Shifting the student's negative perception of school requires yet another set of strategies, each of which is situational. Students who are allowed to function on their own at an early age appear to experience positive and negative peer influences, making them susceptible to peer pressure that affects their personal preferences, tastes, and behaviors. Their early exposure and overexposure to external influences clouds their intuition and jabs the edges of their spoken and unspoken traumas. A high percentage of students disclose in Family Circle the barriers to their desire or lack of desire to learn. With each of these students, there are unresolved and unprocessed traumas of death, violence, and loss, all of which are affecting their present behavior. In Family Circle, this fact begins to raise the awareness of the parent's understanding of the need for the family to participate in traditional or counseling processes. Gagnier finds that trauma directly affects the attendance behaviors of the student. Conscious efforts are made to create and sustain a support team for each student and his or her parent or guardian.

U = Understanding the teenage brain. The Tribal Family Empowerment Program and the BIA school program's curriculum includes learning facts about, the necessity of, and the choices involved in growing a healthy brain. The students are curious about themselves and demonstrate an interest in what makes their brains grow and the effects certain behaviors have on their brain. The parents who have received the brain training have responded positively to the information that a brain can be made healthy. They have expressed relief in learning that their child's brain is still developing and that the needs of the brain (such as for sleep, nourishment, enrichment, and relationship) can account for some of their children's behaviors. Chronic sleep deprivation among students has surfaced as a truancy concern. Because the material is straightforward and based on scientific research, understanding is reached in a neutral tone. In Saturday School and Family Circle, students and their parents or guardians consistently choose to learn facts about the brain and its needs, and each chooses a healthy behavior to assist him or her in taking responsibility for the health of his or her brain. In the BIA school, a fourth grader eagerly asked for more of the handouts depicting the impact of drugs on the brain. He counted them out until he had five. Gagnier casually asked him what he was going to do with them. He looked her in the eyes and passionately stated, "I'm going to give them to my Dad, one a day. He's killing his brain and I want him to stop!" For Gagnier, the brain curriculum is an essential core step in facilitating motivation to develop self-care and self-responsibility.

L = Love and heart intelligence. The initial presentation of the emotional intelligence training in Saturday School resulted in a request from the mothers to "teach this to our kids. This is what they need." Both parents who are practicing their traditions and parents who are not expressed an understanding of the heart connection to their people. Some parents stated: "This is just practicing our tradition." Yes, says Gagnier: it is our tradition with science added. Using computer technology for biofeedback, some of the students who are actively engaged in self-labeling have discovered their ability to manage their emotions positively. Understanding and identifying fluctuating emotional states is key to the practice of the self-managing intervention strategies the program teaches. "Sending heart" originated with the students at the BIA school, where some enjoyed teaching the heart concepts to their parents during specialized parent trainings. Appreciation circles are always facilitated. For Gagnier, the heart training is learning to respect, listen to, and follow your own heart direction, which assists the students and their parents or guardians to shift their emotional state, handle stress, and trust their intuition.

T = Truth and reentering the circle. Attending school is the job of the student. Educators are the leaders who guide the truant student to reenter the circle. Knowing that the truant student needs to connect with the tradition of his or her tribe, function in present time, and prepare for the future, educators are called to be the leadership that connects the students' present to their past and to their future. Investing time, resources, energies, and creative courage is the fundamental commitment teachers can make to ensure that truant students and their parents or guardians are an integral part of the school community. Some truant students and their parents or guardians have indicated that financial literacy issues are of interest to them. Gagnier adapted the First Nations Development Institute's *Building Native Communities: Financial Skills for Families* by processing the information according to Native traditions in general, and according to the specific tribal cultures of the students in particular. Correlating the financial information to their particular school subjects, and showing the student's per capita loss because of truancy appears to be an effective intervention strategy for some truant students.

U = Understanding. Applying brain-based learning to taking notes and tests, developing the language of success, and self-managing negative thinking helps the students develop self-mastery and provides them with "in the moment" tools to manage stress and self-monitor behavior. These resources seem to have little impact on the unmotivated student whose desire to learn or attend school is diminished. Student-centered visual tools are introduced and used with the truant students and their parents or guardians to assist the students in organizing and understanding their thinking processes.

R = Relationship building. The heart of the Saturday School and Family Circle programs is building relationships. In a room filled with students and their parents, the trainer asked each to privately rank their first, second, and third choice among the following: all the money you want; do anything you want; have a meaningful relationship with a parent. Twenty-one students out of twenty-four ranked meaningful relationship as their first choice. More difficult to achieve and less perceived as a need is the relationship between student, parent, and teacher. Regardless of training, role playing, and facilitated interactive communication with truant students and their parents or guardians, the gap remains wide even in those situations where the teacher is willing, open, and goes the extra mile to communicate with truant students and their parents or guardians. The connection is fragile, if it exists at all. The degrees of alienation are high for truant students. Thus, a facilitated student, parent or guardian, and teacher conference is part of the Tribal Family Empowerment Program. Gagnier feels strongly that the creation of parental connections to the life of the school can occur through community-based empowerment models that will widen the educational circle and heal the distrust and alienation of truant students. Their parents and guardians also would benefit from a healthy educational exchange about the workings of a school and how to navigate their child through the educational system. She observed that when the facilitated communication activities are framed as building relationship, the most consistently resistant and passive truant students actively participate with their respective parents or guardians. Gagnier added the experience of working in the community's senior care center to assist students to "get outside themselves" and learn to connect with an elder through relationship building. The ultimate goal is to support truant students in learning to value themselves through positive relationships with parents and guardians, community members, teachers, and peers, and to learn that it is their presence that counts.

A = Awareness, healing–breaking the cycle, intergenerational trauma. In some situations, the reality of intergenerational trauma supersedes each intervention strategy provided to the student. The truant student remains frozen in the behavior pattern he or she uses to cope with and massage the pain of his or her feelings. Gagnier knows that unless the trauma is released, perceptual shifts and their consequential behavior changes cannot occur. Many educators are struggling in this glacial environment without permission, time, and the knowledge to facilitate a strategic trauma and renewal curriculum. Compounding the situation is the fact that many of the traumatized youth are unreceptive to tribal behavioral health and counseling services. Thus, the school behavioral therapist attempts to meet the needs of each truant student, which is contingent upon the student attending school. Then the truant student again falls into the abyss, taking with him or her the pain, hurt, anger, degradation, and shame of the traumas. Inertia sets in with an "I don't care" attitude. Gagnier feels there is a need for a community-based empowerment model at the school-system level. Strategies for trauma awareness and recovery are facilitated with the truant student and parent or guardian in the Family Circle component of the program.

L = Learning, ownership of choices. The bottom line in supporting the junior high or high school truant student in choosing and taking responsibility for his or her own life involves a redefinition of role for the student and his or her parent, with a clarification of the boundaries accompanying each role. The truant student usually does not see that it is his or her job to attend school and, in some cases, successfully makes the parent responsible for his or her nonattendance. The parent or guardian, who sometimes feels at the end of his or her endurance, takes ownership for their child's behaviors rather than redefining the parenting role as that of a guide, with setting boundaries and enforcing consequences as a priority. Also, adolescent truant students sometimes feel burdened by the weight of the expectations they perceive others have of them. Struggling to be in charge of his or her life, the student reacts to the imposed conditions without the inner safety of knowing his or her needs. Developing empathy based on needs rather than wants is a continuous learning process for the truant student, and Gagnier feels it is essential to the development of the student's imagination and inner will. Some perceptual shifts about learning and school have been observed in truant students when they have been supported in making choices that focus on their own boundaries. Both truant students and their parents and guardians have and are taking increased responsibility in monitoring their attendance.

The crucial reclaiming of our youth requires considerable educational reframing because many Native communities are experiencing the alienation of some of their young people due to a variety of factors. To see the need to intervene, stand up for, and take back our children appears in some school communities to be an idea dimly lit in the fog of commercialism, gangs, and present-day lifestyles. The hope that traditional practices will prevent the daily loss of yet another child to drugs, gangs, and violence runs thin in areas where traditional values lose their strength with the loss of the elders. A united cry for the health and welfare of the child is too often smothered by alcohol and fear of reprisal. The creation of a school community with intentional intergenerational community member representation increases the opportunity for wisdom to be passed on and mentoring to occur, particularly when elders are involved. In the safety of a nurturing school community, the child who may be on the verge of exploring drugs and gangs can experience fun, learning, and have the occasion to form friendships with other "heart buddies." For the child whose familial situation is stressful due to unresolved historical trauma, which many times results in parents seeking relief in drugs, the inter-generational nurturing school community can offer refuge. For the child whose parents are positive role models, the intergenerational school community can offer the experience of developing and sustaining empathy. Within the "intentional intergenerational school community," relationships can be strengthened, conflicts can be resolved, biases can be shifted, support can be received, traditions and Native language can be learned and respected, and listening and interactive sharing can occur. There are other successful ways, by applying traditional principles within current appropriate behaviors, to help tribal councils as they work diligently to fund their educational organizations and Indian educators as they contribute daily to the effort of positively affecting the life of the child.

Several other tribes in the Southwest utilized processes that Gagnier created. These include a tribal social services residential home for youth; a public school Indian education department; and tribal education, nutrition, health, and diabetes departments. A unique application of Gagnier's work occurred in a tribal social services department that addressed truancy through cooperative collaboration with the tribal court and tribal departments, particularly the education department. The Brain–Emotional Health Program focused on truancy prevention and intervention as an educational process, thus cutting through the punitive treatment of truancy.

An all-out effort to reclaim the child on his or her way to the drug deal, the gang gathering, the thrill ride, the creation of a life that is beyond our grasp, is needed within our schools, our communities, and our Native families to ensure that our children are an integral part of the circle. Participating in Indigenous education is a privilege for Phyllis Gagnier, a "journey to the heart of the child."

Indian Education Off-Reservation

Most Native students attend public schools off-reservation, a situation about which Indian people had very little say for many years and that, for the most part, provided inappropriate education in classrooms that Indian young people often found unfriendly. In some cases, parents' frustration with the schools and the inadequate support for their children in a difficult environment made schooling lose legitimacy for Indigenous students, lowering their academic performance.[93] The federal government might provide money for public schools to teach Native students under the Johnson-O'Malley Act of 1934 or as Impact Aid to compensate school districts for teaching students who lived on federal or federal trust land that was exempt from local property taxes. But federal funding did not bring with it any requirement to give concerned Indians a say about their children's education.[94] Sometimes, such as for Ute Mountain Utes in Colorado, the schools were at some distance from tribal land.[95] In other cases, public schools were in the middle of where Indians lived but, because of allotment, which led to checkerboarding of reservations, or because of a reservation's total elimination, as happened in most of Oklahoma, outnumbered Indian parents in a school district had little impact on the school board or administration. Members of the Southern Ute Indian Tribe in Ignacio, Colorado, could sometimes elect one or two members of the school board, but never near a majority, and the tribe often had no elected representation on the board.[96] It is only in very recent years, since the Southern Ute nation has become an important economic force in the area and the tribe has opened its own school, that the Ignacio school board has begun to have regular meetings with the Southern Ute Tribal Council about improving the school experience for Southern Ute children.

Developing Appropriate Indian Education Policies in Public Schools

The increase in Native political power over the past few years that largely flows from growing Indian economic development and political organization has provided a significant boost to collaboration between at least some local school boards and Indian nations. For example, in 2004, the Ukiah Unified School District in California approved an Indian education policy that was developed over a year's time in negotiations between representatives of local tribes and school officials.[97] The policy, endorsed by the Mendocino County Tribal Chairs Association and several local tribes, acknowledges that federally recognized tribes are sovereign nations and have an inherent authority over the formal education of their members and recognizes the unique government-to-government relationship between tribes and federal and state governments. To support and strengthen educational opportunities for Native American students in the school district, the district will work closely with the tribes to provide programs that will help to support equal access to a quality education for all Native American students. Major areas of concern that are identified in the policy include encouraging parent and family involvement; improving student attendance; and recognizing values, philosophies, expectations, and attitudes and how they affect the education of Native Americans.

Similar improvements are needed for the growing number of Indian young people living at a distance from reservations. Support for these students can be enhanced by local and state Indigenous organizations working with local schools, school boards, and governments, and by state governments and departments of education, with assistance and coordination from some of the vehicles for providing Native input to state policy that we discussed in chapter 3, section 2. Montana provides examples of helpful state action. In 2004, two bills were introduced in the Montana State Legislature (H.B. 423 and H.B. 424) that would allow preference to hiring Indian teachers, where qualifications are equal, in schools on reservations or in which at least half the students are Indian, on the principle that Indian students generally learn better with Indian teachers.[98] Similarly helpful are efforts led by Indian organizations for the development of curricula to meet the requirements of Montana law that public schools teach about the Indian nations in the state. This kind of measure not only helps Indigenous young people directly by teaching the value of their own culture and making classrooms more friendly, but it also helps to build public understanding about Native people. As we discussed in chapter 3, a deeper realization of government-to-government relations between tribal and other governments would exist if history and government textbooks explained the place of Indian nations and their governments in American federalism.

EAGL in Portland Greatly Boosts High School Graduation and College Entrance

Indian efforts in a pair of programs in Portland, Oregon, have enabled very high high-school graduation and college entrance rates for their students.[99] The year-round Excellence in Advancement toward Graduation and Leadership (EAGL) program has seen 85 percent of its Indigenous students graduate from high school, compared with a 53 percent graduation rate for all Portland high school students. EAGL was instituted in response to a high percentage of Native students dropping out as an increasing number fell behind math and science benchmarks. The program was launched "in response to an unmet community need for a culturally specific, innovative, college preparatory educational program based on 9th–12th grade American Indian/Alaska Native Students."[100]

The center of EAGL's achievement has been individualized education: each of the seventy-five students in the plan is assigned an advocate to work as a team facilitator with the student, parents, and school staff. The advocates, most of whom are Native, help the students identify and carry out specific goals. Students and parents are provided with services such as tutoring, educational assessment, transcript evaluation, school advocacy, and parent-teacher conferences. Advocates assist in identifying appropriate opportunities for each young person as well as possible barriers, then help the student and family by setting an individual education plan that leads the student to programs and services and, as needed, opportunities for educational improvement. The program is designed to empower students to complete high school ably and transition to a community college, university, or trade school.

Advocates also help students with problems outside of school. This has been important in overcoming the high Native youth substance abuse rate and frequency of trouble with the juvenile justice system, in part by linking young people to needed services. Many of these services are offered by the Native American Youth and Family Center (NAYA Family Center), including housing, talking circles, and parenting classes. NAYA Family Center provides a positive atmosphere for developing healthy relationships. Referrals are provided for substance abuse treatment and health care to Native clinics that provide culturally appropriate services.

NAYA Family Center runs an early-college-experience summer program that has resulted in 91 percent of its participants going on to college. The intensive program has twenty-five young Natives taking community college classes for eight weeks to familiarize them with higher education as they earn college credit. Each day after class, students meet with tutors who help them with homework, understanding course material, and improving study skills. Not least important is that NAYA Family Center enhances cultural pride and understanding by incorporating Native arts and culture classes in all its programs. NAYA Family Center, which has grown from a volunteer-staffed organization at its outset in 1974 to serving more than three hundred youth each year from more than three hundred tribal backgrounds, in 2008 received a $425,000 grant from the Bill and Melinda Gates Foundation to expand its programs.

Building Native Youth Interest and Pride in Culture and History Through Archaeology

Because pride in culture is important for tribal people in building personal confidence and is a strong basis for success in life and school, programs that involve Indian youth in their history and culture in culturally appropriate ways are important educational vehicles. One traditional way of providing Indigenous youth with hands-on experiential participation and learning is involvement in appropriate archaeology. The Crow Canyon Archaeological Center in southwestern Colorado does precisely that, involving two hundred Indian students from fourth grade through high school in one-day to three-week projects to learn about and assist in archaeological fieldwork.[101] Students are involved both in classroom learning, made experiential with simulations, and field explorations of the Native past. Students are supported by counselors, and the center also provides distance learning on its website, http://www.crowcanyon.org.

Education Beyond K–12: Colleges and Universities

Improvement of postsecondary Indigenous education is necessary. A 2003 American Indian Higher Education Consortium survey found that only 10 percent of Native Americans who enter mainstream four-year colleges and universities directly from high school earn a degree, whereas the graduation rate jumps to more than 90 percent for those who have first attended a two-year tribal college.[102] Likewise, Indian-owned and run Native American Educational Services College (NAES), with campuses in Chicago and on several Indian reservations, has reversed the failure rates for Native students.[103] Enrollment at the fifty-eight tribal colleges, mostly located in the Great Plains states and the Southwest, has doubled to more than thirty thousand since their creation in the late 1960s, and appropriate new development is needed. Some of this is already in progress: seven tribal colleges have expanded from two- to four-year degree-granting colleges, and several offer master's degrees. New Indian colleges and college programs are in the process of starting up, including a new $40 million Diné College campus in Shiprock, New Mexico.[104] Leaders of the Creek, Choctaw, Chickasaw, Cherokee, and Seminole Nations in Oklahoma and Oklahoma State University have agreed to look into establishing Oklahoma American Indian University, initially to be a two-year institution of higher learning overseen by a new Creek board of regents. Officials and students at the University of Denver held preliminary discussions in spring 2004 with representatives of the Southern Ute and Ute Mountain Ute tribes about the possibility of establishing a program focusing on American Indian law. Meanwhile, United Tribes Technical College in Bismarck, North Dakota, has been accredited to offer degrees to students who complete their classes online.

Innovation at Tribal Colleges

Tribal colleges have long been extremely important in Indian higher education by providing, often near home, friendly and confidence-building learning opportunities incorporating cultural learning and participation. Recently, tribal institutions of higher learning have been providing innovative programs that preserve culture and language and link to tribes to offer needed education for Indian nation development, sometimes with student internship and job opportunities. These efforts have been strongly boosted by the Lilly Endowment, which in 1999 awarded grants totaling $30 million to tribal colleges for capital improvements that will upgrade the poor condition of at times dilapidated buildings and infrastructure. The endowment has also made available $17.5 million to twenty-one tribal colleges between 2007 and 2012, through the multifaceted approach of the Woksape Oyate ("Wisdom of the People") Program. The program's purpose is to "dramatically enhance recruitment, retention and development of tribal college faculty, staff, and students. Leadership development programs, increased fellowship, and sabbatical opportunities for staff and pipeline programs to bring the best and brightest students back to teach at their tribal college will all be developed during this initiative. Institutional capacity will also be enhanced by creation of development offices and recruitment of highly qualified faculty."[105] The initiative is designed to allow tribal colleges to tailor their programs to address their individual needs while strengthening the entire tribal college system.

One of many examples of innovative Indian higher education, the College of Menominee Nation (CMN) in Wisconsin offers degree programs that include traditional knowledge in sustainable development and tribal legal studies and makes available a free Menominee language course.[106] Under the Woksape Oyate Program, CMN is developing a new bachelor's degree program in public administration that will provide graduates with a strong academic background in the government, public, and nonprofit sectors and will place a special emphasis on serving rural communities. The new public administration program will address the needs of a large and growing student population that works for county government, tribal government, and other tribal entities. CMN augments its own program with an agreement with the University of Wisconsin, which offers CMN courses at two of its campuses.

In addition, CMN is among the many tribal institutions of higher education that are working with the Science, Technology, Engineering, and Mathematics (STEM) Education Coalition to make STEM accessible to all students.[107] A key to the tribal approach to science and math is finding ways to integrate STEM into the tribal curriculum, blending Western science with traditional knowledge. CMN is collaborating with the Menominee Nation to broaden its economic base, particularly through its program of sustainable development that incorporates traditional values of living in harmony with one's environment. Through the school's Sustainable Development Institute, students are encouraged to participate in research projects, internships, or the organization of one of many conferences that are regularly held at the college and bring in Native scholars from around the world. Every student is required to take at least one sustainable development course, and the classes include practical applications of math, science, and technology, which includes researching and solving problems in the Menominee community, creating enthusiasm for STEM. Entering students without adequate math and science backgrounds engage in a first-year math and science program that improves success and retention. Because students are expected to study full-time, they are offered a stipend so that they do not need to secure employment while in school.

As at many tribal colleges and institutions, being in harmony with all beings, including the environment, goes beyond sustainable development to encompass every aspect of CMN's operation—from making buildings energy efficient to instituting respectful labor practices to purchasing green and fair trade products as much as possible. The college motto is applied across the curriculum: sustaining the forest, sustaining the nation, sustaining the spirit. The interaction between the concrete world and the community that occurs in the sustainable development classes and that makes CMN's academic work exciting, practical, and service-oriented is applied in many other programs and courses, in part by incorporating case studies that are both complex enough to be challenging and interesting, and relevant to the particular class and the tribal community. Similar development across tribal higher education was greatly enhanced by a 1995 grant from the Luminia Foundation for Education to Evergreen State College, Gray's Harbor College, Northwest Indian College, Salish Kootenai College, and Bainbridge Graduate Institute to develop Native case studies for engaging and relevant teaching.[108]

Oglala Lakota College: Another Example of Growing Tribal College Innovation

On the Pine Ridge Indian Reservation in South Dakota, the Oglala Lakota College Department of Nursing applies a teaching model that reflects Lakota values and philosophy.[109] The model is doubly beneficial, providing an appropriate framework for student learning while ensuring that those who complete the nursing program and choose to work on the Pine Ridge reservation or in other Native communities with similar traditions will provide appropriate care. As do other tribal colleges, Oglala Lakota College offers STEM programs. The STEM Education Coalition also provides science and math curricula in elementary and secondary education that is making it possible for Lakota students to go on to teach in the technical school on the reservation. Similarly, the Oglala Lakota College's Environmental Sciences Program fills community needs. For example, program graduates populate the environmental programs of the Pine Ridge Indian Reservation and several agencies in the surrounding area.

Lifelong Education—Preserving Language and Culture

Both because learning is a lifelong process and because many Indigenous people have been separated from their own culture, to varying degrees, by assimilation efforts that have often lowered their confidence in their culture and themselves, continuing education is an important area of tribal education. Most Indian nations offer adult education programs of various kinds on useful topics such as health, in vocational training, and in culture and language that need to be further developed.

Of special importance is preserving, and in many cases restoring, tribal language, which is the main element in traditional culture. Many Native populations have lost their languages, and the vast majority of Indigenous languages are declining to the point that they may no longer be spoken. Among the Southern Ute, for example, only an estimated 15 percent of the total tribal population of 1,316 still converse in their tribal tongue.[110] Thus, expanding programs to preserve and teach tribal languages is essential. An example of such efforts is the Kodiak, Alaska, Alutiiq Museum's expansion of a master-apprentice language program aimed at preserving the Alutiiq language, under a $171,000 federal grant.[111] Indiana University's American Indian Studies Research Institute collaborates with schools in North and South Dakota to help preserve the Lakota language in a sixteen-year project that will rewrite the curricula of thirty-eight school systems to teach eighteen thousand students.[112]

Oglala Lakota College has been working to help preserve the Lakota language and strengthen Lakota families with the assistance of a three-year, $419,189 grant from the U.S. Department of Health and Human Services (HHS).[113] The program includes incentives to college staff to learn and use Lakota. The college has been expanding its language program under a Lilly Foundation Woksape Oyate grant, developing a Center of Excellence for Lakota language by expanding and sustaining the Lakota Language Institute, upgrading the Lakota studies and education departments, and collaborating with Head Start and K–12 schools so that "Everyone will speak Lakota."[114] In addition, the Lakota Language Institute was organizing to become a repository for the research and study of the Lakota language while adapting and developing the necessary processes and materials for the infusion of Lakota language into all levels of education and life.

In 2008, Diné College of the Navajo Nation began working with a Woksape Oyate grant to

> recover the Diné Universe through language, intellectual knowledge, and collective wisdom in publications and media that can be shared throughout the Navajo Nation. The wealth of documentation and people brought together through this project will retain traditional knowledge in the Navajo community. The collective knowledge of the Navajo people will serve as the foundation for four-year bachelor's degrees in Diné Studies and Diné Teacher Education. The funding will allow for the development of five Diné Studies textbooks, multi-media tools, Songs and Leadership Instruction, a Diné Summer Leadership Institute, and a collection of monographs and curricular publications. Project activities will result in dynamic academic programs and professional development

opportunities that ensure recruitment and retention of Diné College community members. The activities of the initiative will create educational materials and institutional philosophy critical for achieving accreditation for a four-year bachelor's program in Diné Studies, and ultimately building this program to the master's and PhD levels. The tangible outcomes for the project—textbooks, research, archives, songs and instructions, and leadership—will benefit the Navajo Nation as Diné College strengthens its abilities to prepare students with life skills and cultural knowledge to be successful human beings in body, mind and spirit.[115]

Other tribal colleges are engaged in preserving and teaching tribal languages, including Blackfeet Community College and Chief Dull Knife College, which is serving as a repository for the collection, archiving, and publication of Northern Cheyenne history and language.[116]

Several language and culture preservation programs are using film. In 2008, filmmaker Ben Levine and language specialist Julia Schulz were in the middle of producing an eight-part film series, *The Language Keepers*, to record and teach Passamaquoddy language and culture.[117] On Kodiak Island, Alaska, the Qik'rtarmiut Alutil language preservation and education program is similarly using film to record elders undertaking cultural actions in the language.[118] A number of school programs have found that the best way to preserve a language is to immerse students in it, using it for as much of the day as possible, which includes teaching subjects such as math and science in a nation's language.[119] English, including literature and composition, can then be taught as a second language.

Developing Tribal Educational Institution Collaboration

Tribal government and organization collaboration with educational institutions is extremely important, both for enhancing Indigenous education and for catalyzing tribal development. Indeed, this is a model that could be a general one for connecting institutions of higher learning to communities in virtually all contemporary societies, for mutual benefit.[120] An especially interesting example is the Applied Indigenous Studies Program at Northern Arizona University, which was launched after two years of discussions with all of the state's tribes to determine how the program could best serve their needs, and collaboration on program development is ongoing.[121] The program works to attain a balance among the academic, practical, cultural, and spiritual needs of its students. It provides some on-reservation services and has a concern for building Native nations. Applied Indigenous Studies is globally focused, based in the American Southwest, and recognizes that indignity is a global phenomenon. The program has taken a number of steps to enhance student experience and retention, including providing mentoring and resident elders.

A growing number of specific collaborations are sprouting between colleges and universities and tribes or tribal organizations. A pair of instances involving gaming management and education are illustrative. In the first case, San Diego State University initiated a program in the fall of 2008 on tribal gaming management that considers all aspects of tribal gaming.[122] San Diego is a prime location for such a project, with seventeen tribes and ten gaming facilities in San Diego County. Much of the start-up funding for the program came from endowments from the Sycuan Band of the Kumayaay Nation and the Sycuan Institute on Tribal Gaming. In the second instance, the Nisqually Red Wind Casino, in Olympia, Washington, arranged with Tacoma Community College to provide the Tribal Enterprise Gaming Certificate, with courses taught at the casino. The casino encourages its employees to take the classes for their own and the gaming facility's advancement.[123]

Increasing the Number of Native American Advanced Degrees in Science, Engineering, and Agriculture

In October 2003, the University of Arizona announced a fellowship program aimed at increasing the number of Native American recipients of master's and PhD degrees in science, engineering, and agriculture. The fellowships offer a total stipend of $30,000 for master's and $36,000 for PhD students and carry in-state and out-of-state tuition waivers and individual health insurance for each year in the program. Students can supplement these funds with tribal and other scholarships as well as with research and teaching assistantships offered by their graduate programs. Tutoring, social and cultural programs, and limited travel funds for family emergencies and ceremonial events are available, as is the use of the American Indian Graduate Center.[124] This program includes some of the features that are necessary to increase Indigenous student success rates at non-Indian institutions of higher learning and that have been undertaken across the curriculum at Arizona State University.[125]

Nurturing Leadership: The Ambassadors Program

An educational undertaking of broad importance for American Indians has been operated for more than a decade by Americans for Indian Opportunity. AIO's two-year American Indian Ambassadors Program, a leadership nurturing program (which is equivalent to an applied master's degree program, but without the academic entrance requirements for a standard master's degree), was launched to help young Native community leaders increase their inner strength and enhance the development of their own leadership style through experiences that reconcile their traditional Indigenous values with contemporary global reality.[126] Ambassadors are selected on the basis of their track record of giving back to their community, their potential to grow from their experience in the program, and their demonstrated leadership qualities. One aspect of the program is that each participant develops a project designed to help her or his community. Recent examples include Michelle Anderson's research to address the problem of violence committed against Native women living in the Ahtna region of Alaska; Darius Smith's development of a financial literacy curriculum that combines Native beliefs and values with successful economic principles; Lisa Brown's project to preserve six Chickasaw burial sites in Oklahoma; and Judy Winchester's work with Western Michigan University and a series of Pokagon Band of Potawatomi Indians town meetings to institute a halfway house for tribal members who complete substance abuse treatment programs. The Ambassadors Program also facilitates participants developing a sense of identity while it enhances their ability to participate in inclusive participatory decision making, particularly by using the ILIS strategic planning system we discussed in chapter 4.

Ambassador alumni, who are now working in every major national Indian organization and every federal agency with significant Native American activity, remain in the Ambassador network, helping AIO in decision making and providing information and ideas for Indian country. The network was formalized in 2006 by the formation of the Ambassadors Alliance. Some recent Ambassador alumni include Madona Yawakee (Turtle Mountain Chippewa), who served as president and CEO of Turtle Island Communications, which provides telecommunications engineering and technical consulting services to tribal governments and organizations, for which she was one of six women honored as rural leaders by Minnesota Futures in April 2006.[127] Michelle Anderson (Athabascan), while continuing her work at the Denali Commission representing HUD, created the Denali Commission website as part of her project work for the Master of Fine Arts in Rural Development degree from the University of Alaska, Fairbanks.[128] Ivan Posey (Eastern Shoshone) was appointed Wyoming's first tribal liaison between the state's Indian nations and state government. Jamie Goins (Lumbee) has been involved with her tribe's Boys and Girls Clubs and is on the tribal youth council. Richard Blue Cloud Castaneda (Pima-Maricopa) has created the American Indian Youth Art Program in San Francisco. Linda Ogo's (Yavapai) community-initiative project of creating a junior board of directors across her nation's three communities has expanded into a one-year Yavapai Ambassador's program for people of Yavapai ancestry across Arizona. The program's inaugural class participated in the National UNITY Conference in San Diego, and the World Indigenous Peoples Congress on Education meeting in New Zealand.

The Ambassadors program includes an international component. Building upon Ambassador interchanges with Māori in New Zealand in 2001, an AIO group held a meeting with Māori contacts that was hosted by Wānanga o Aotearoa, the largest Māori institute of higher education, to share ideas for the formation of Advancement for Māori Opportunity.[129] The assembled Māori found that they held the same core values as did their American colleagues, as that general way of seeing is almost universal among Indigenous thinkers around the world. Advancement for Māori Opportunity was established and now runs its own Ambassadors program. AIO and Advancement for Māori Opportunity have since launched Advancement of Global Indigeneity to: (1) assist local Indigenous communities in maintaining cultural identity in the face of globalization; (2) actively participate in the globalization process in order that Indigenous peoples can control how it effects them; (3) influence policy and public opinion; and (4) contribute Indigenous wisdom, values, and worldview to the emerging world order. "These self-determined communities will be able to rely on a worldwide network of Indigenous leaders who successfully weave their core cultural values into their decisions and institutions and who recognize that they have something unique and vital to share with the world. . . . It is important to remember that although there is a great diversity among Indigenous communities, there is a strong, spiritual inter-connectedness that is key to our collective vision."[130]

Education Policy Impacts and Needs

Because the federal government provides educational funding for state educational programs, with requirements that state governments and local schools must follow to receive the funding, developing and maintaining of appropriate federal Indian policy is extremely important to Indian education. For example, the No Child Left Behind Act of 2001 established requirements for student accomplishment on standardized tests that are difficult for many Indigenous students, as well as students of other cultures, to meet, particularly if they are bilingual or English is not their first language.[131] Schools not meeting the standards over time are penalized, and efforts to teach to the tests take away from other educational goals. Thus, it is of note that on April 30, 2004, President Bush issued an executive order establishing the Interagency Working Group on American Indian and Alaska Native Education, which consisted of the heads of the Departments of Education, Interior, Health and Human Services, Agriculture, Justice, Labor, and such other executive branch departments, agencies, or offices as the cochairs of the working group may designate.[132]

The working group was charged with developing a federal interagency plan within ninety days that recommends initiatives, strategies, and ideas for future interagency actions to assist American Indian and Alaska Native students to meet the student academic standards of No Child Left Behind in a manner that is consistent with tribal traditions, languages, and cultures. The secretary of the Department of Education, in coordination with the working group, was charged with conducting a multiyear study of American Indian and Alaska Native education in order to improve the students' ability to meet the student academic standards of No Child Left Behind. The study was to identify and disseminate research-based practices and proven methods in raising the academic achievement, and in particular the reading achievement, of American Indian and Alaska Native students. The study also was intended to assess the effect and role of Native language and culture on the development of educational strategies to improve academic achievement, to develop methods to strengthen early childhood education so that American Indian and Alaska Native students enter school ready to learn, and to develop methods to increase the high school graduation rate and develop pathways to college and the workplace for American Indian and Alaska Native students.

The secretaries of education and the interior were ordered to consult with the working group and tribally controlled colleges and universities to seek ways to develop and enhance the capacity of tribal governments, tribal universities and colleges, and schools and educational programs serving American Indian and Alaska Native students and communities in order to carry out, disseminate, and implement education research, as well as to develop related partnerships or collaborations with nontribal universities, colleges, and research organizations. The secretaries were also charged with jointly convening, in collaboration with the working group and federal, state, tribal, and local government representatives, a forum on the No Child Left Behind Act to identify means to enhance communication, collaboration, and cooperative strategies to improve the education of American Indian and Alaska Native students attending federal, state, tribal, and local schools. The working group was established to exist for as long as five years, which could be extended by the president. On paper, this process appears favorable. It is hoped that it will be carried out with sufficient consultation with culturally knowledgeable Native educators to produce positive improvements. Similarly, because most decisions concerning education are made at state and local levels, it is essential that the growing dialogue between state and local governments on the one hand, and Indian tribal governments, organizations, and people on the other, continue to expand, increasingly encompassing issues of Indigenous education.

The Problem of Underfunding

A major problem for federally funded Indian schools and other educational entities, including tribal postsecondary colleges and programs, is serious underfunding: Indian schools receive considerably less money per student than the national average. Appropriations for important programs have often been short-lived and uncertain; for example, the Rough Rock Community School's successful inquiry-based curriculum, which we discussed above, was largely shut down after two years because monies could not be found to continue the program following the completion of its foundational grant. The financial problem is apparent in the physical condition of many school facilities, which are seriously overcrowded, underequipped, old, and deteriorating (at times to the point of being dangerous). Underfunding affects every aspect of the operation of both BIA-funded schools and of public schools that receive federal impact funding for teaching Native students.[133] Increases in state and local funding for appropriate Native education are also necessary. Gains in Indian economic development and growth in foundation grants has helped reduce the serious financial gap, but much more needs to be done, especially on the part of governments, to make Native American education adequate to return U.S. Indigenous communities to sovereignty, self-sufficiency, and harmony.

Appropriate Indigenous Education

As essential as adequate funding is to developing well-functioning Indian education, it is important to remember that the most important aspect of educational development is its appropriateness. Whereas the Southern Utes of Colorado have been able to operate a very fine Indian school with a considerable amount of money, the Northern Utes of Utah have made significant gains in their charter school with far fewer dollars by including cultural elements in the curriculum and by working with parents to involve them, with increased effectiveness, in their children's education.[34] Providing high-quality Indigenous education from kindergarten through college requires considerable money, but more important is how those dollars are spent.

It is clear, then, that although there is still a long way to go, both in terms of providing adequate funding and designing truly appropriate Native education for the specific needs of each community and each learner, a number of promising Indian education processes exist that, if developed well, can eventually become a system of Indigenous learning. That this occurs is crucial for the full development of Indian communities and individuals. It will also benefit the wider society, both in terms of the direct positive effects to neighboring areas and by providing useful alternative models that can be used to improve mainstream education.

3. Re-creating the Circle: Healing the Wounds and Returning to Harmony: Healing Historical Trauma and Grief: Transforming the Wound to Medicine
Stephen M. Sachs, LaDonna Harris, and Barbara Morris

The restoration of harmony in Indian communities requires a multifaceted approach that will address collective wounds created by physical and cultural genocide. Culturally responsive methods that acknowledge the effects of the American Indian holocaust are needed to help heal the wounds at the personal, family, and community levels. During this era of Indian self-determination, there are active efforts both on and off reservations to re-create the circle and overcome the damaging effects of colonialism and oppression. Many culturally appropriate programs are now being designed and implemented to help tribes and descendants of Indigenous people heal the effects of unresolved historical grief. Healing can be contagious. In healing the grief, the strength and pride of cultural identity can be reclaimed and can provide the impetus to move forward with economic and political sovereignty. Much of this healing can be accomplished through appropriate education (as we discussed above) and services, and through returning tribal institutions, including governments, to functioning in ways that are consistent with each nation's values (as we discussed in chapter 4).

Historical Trauma and Unresolved Grief

The unrelenting chain of assaults by the U.S. government on American Indian people and cultures is well documented in this volume and elsewhere. American Indian people have survived trauma from colonization, extermination, civilization, and assimilationist policies. The spiritual, physical, and cultural losses to tribal people have been tremendous. Unresolved grief has accumulated across generations and continues to be experienced in the present through racism and oppression.[135] At the same time, core values of the grandmothers and grandfathers have managed to survive these historical traumas. These values have provided a buffer of resiliency as well as the strands of tradition necessary to re-create the circle and restore harmony to families and communities.

The generational transmission of traditional values was severely impeded when the children were violently removed from their homes and communities to boarding schools. Here, the children were not only removed from the source of their cultural identity, but they were severely punished for any expression of their culture. This loss of the children created the greatest grief in the hearts of the people because hope for the future was lost. Furthermore, in separating children from their tribes, the federal government disrupted the natural bonding and modeling required to pass on healthy parenting to the next generations.[136] This has led to subsequent generations being at risk for neglect and abuse and removal from their homes under child welfare laws. Although all forms of abuse are being passed on from boarding school experiences, most referrals for child protection in Indian country are made for neglect and abandonment.[137]

Identity and Culture

In effect, this forced assimilation left several generations of American Indians confused about their identity, alienated from their traditional culture, and marginalized citizens of both worlds.[138] Erik Erikson

recognized the importance of culture in the formation of personal identity. He conducted studies of Sioux and Yurok people in the late 1940s
and early 1950s. In his schema of human development, the fifth stage
occurs in adolescence and is referred to as

> identity versus identity confusion. In Erikson's work, identity
> was seen as a fusion of past family identifications, cultural issues
> and future hopes and dreams. Successful identity formation
> was by necessity embedded in the social and familial context.
> The young individual must learn to be most himself where he
> means the most to others—those others, to be sure, who have
> come to mean most to him. The term identity expresses such a
> mutual relation in that it connotes both a persistent sameness
> within oneself (self-sameness) and a persistent sharing of some
> kind of essential character with others.[139]

The negative resolution of this stage of development for Erikson resulted
in identity confusion due to being separated or alienated from one's traditional culture or being unclear about one's self-image.

Whether one finds the terminology of Erikson and of mainstream
psychology helpful or prefers a more Indigenous way of framing the
issues, identity is clearly a major problem for many Native and other
people who have been told repeatedly by the colonizing culture that their
ways are inferior or outmoded. Thus, the AIO Ambassadors Program has
found it important to make sure early in the program that participants
have clarified any identity questions that they may have.

Cultural alienation is directly related to the spiritual, physical,
and emotional health of American Indian youth today. Several studies
have linked absence of traditional acculturation with subsequent risk.
For example, E. R. Oetting and F. Beauvais have shown a relationship
between weak family bonding, lack of spiritual foundation, weak Indian
cultural identity, and substance abuse in American Indian youth.[140]

Shame and Alienation
Many Indian people today continue to try to escape the generational
pain and internalized shame of cultural alienation with alcohol and
drugs. It is clear that substance abuse is the major symptom of unresolved grief from the cultural losses under colonization and continuing
oppression. Tribal women report that drinking and suicide was never a

problem until the government took away the children.[141] For example, at the recent National Indian Child Welfare Association meeting, an Anishinabe MSW student told the story of her grandmother applying for welfare and immediately having her children taken away and placed in foster care. Her grandmother started drinking and became an alcoholic.

Other documented effects of generational trauma include depression, self-destructive behavior, substance abuse, identification with the ancestral pain, fixation on trauma, somatic symptoms, anxiety, guilt, and chronic bereavement.[142] The resolution of all the aspects of historical grief was further inhibited by federal prohibition of traditional ceremonies of culturally prescribed grief rituals.

Before healing of loss can occur, several stages must be completed. Elizabeth Kubler-Ross pioneered work in healing grief and loss.[143] She observed five stages of grief. The stages include numbness and denial, bargaining, depression, anger, and acceptance. These stages are dynamic and can fluctuate over long periods of time depending on a number of factors, including the presence of support and opportunity to mourn.

The inadequate expression of grief leads to a sense of powerlessness to heal and move on. This powerlessness can lead to a continuous movement between depression and anger.[144] In this cycle, anger justifies the hurt and may feel better than the emptiness of unresolved grief. Since emptiness is not a natural state, experiencing it leads to a feeling of shame. In response, there is a tendency to either project blame to an external source or, conversely, to blame one's self. Anger turned against the self is the classic Freudian definition of depression. When the hurt, shame, and internalized anger of grief remain unresolved, identity can be negatively affected. For example, Hillary Weaver and Maria Yellow Horse Brave Heart observe a group identity among the Lakota people being formed upon the status of being persecuted and oppressed that is directly related to historical trauma.[145] Thus, a perpetual sense of unworthiness to receive the good can occur. Often, the only release from the pain is self-destruction.

Evidence of shame and unresolved pain among Indian people includes disproportionate rates of suicide, alcohol and drug abuse, child abuse, and domestic violence. Indian-to-Indian violence results in high rates of incarceration of Indian men.[146] Preliminary research on the use of traditional methods indicates that strengthening cultural identity can assist Native people in healing historical grief and thus breaking free of the victim's identity.[147]

Transforming the Wound into Medicine: Bridging the Worlds

Walking "between the worlds" has created pain, grief, and loss. It has been strongly argued that cultural loss and forced assimilation have created marginality and self-destruction.[148] For example, Laurence A. French contends that for the survivors in Indian country, the twentieth century has been a long, rough road on which they have been forced to walk in two worlds without belonging fully to either. This is the most devastating element of cultural genocide.[149] Therefore, the healing of historical grief in Indian country requires acknowledging the losses but also nurturing the strength, resilience, pride, and unity in cultural identity. Reclaiming core cultural values becomes the medicine that promotes the healing of historical grief.

Some elders have taught that everything happens for a reason and that personal actions can affect the whole. One elder teaches that at a "crossroads," there is at once the most vulnerability and the most openness to healing.[150] At these times, it becomes possible to let go of old pain and to shift to a new level of personal power. This process requires listening carefully and setting ego aside and embodies the magic of the "in between." Many traditions teach that human beings are "hollow bones," capable of walking between the physical and spiritual worlds in order to bring healing medicine to the physical plane. Approaching this process humbly and with an open heart can illuminate the ways and times to act and to be still. This may require "taking on the energy of the enemy," or intentionally facing the dark side. When this work is consciously done, it is thought to be capable of shifting the whole toward balance.[151]

This is an approach used in many spiritual and psychological traditions. For example, many of the contemporary theorists and practitioners of transpersonal psychology use the work of psychologist Carl Jung. Jung's teachings emphasize working through the "dark night of the soul," where "shadow" parts of the psyche have been disowned. In essence, any of life's crises are opportunities to open to spirit guidance and come to a higher level of knowledge, truth, and action. At these times, human beings are most capable of facing the dark side of themselves: fears, pride, and attitudes that have hurt them and other people.[152] Jung's conception of the dark night might be equated with the Native concept of "in-between." In "walking between," there exists an opportunity to incorporate the energy of that which has been denied. In this way, the wounds may be transformed into healing medicine and brought back to the people in a good way.

This transformation of the wound occurs when the historical grief and loss are faced and resolved. Thus, although marginalization can be the effect of forced assimilation, it can also present beneficial opportunities. Several studies show positive aspects of multiple cultural identification.[153] Weaver and Brave Heart argue that identification with multiple cultures need not equal assimilation and need not be construed automatically as negative.[154] They identify the strength of having more than one cultural identity as the capacity to function effectively and appropriately within any given social or cultural context. In particular, the orthogonal model of cultural identification disputes the linear model of acculturation, which moves along a single dimension from traditional to acculturated to assimilated.[155] Rather, the orthogonal model posits the possibility of multiple and independent identifications with cultures. In this view, it is not necessary to give up any part or all of one heritage or relationship to the immediate cultural context.[156] Another term for this process might be *parallel identification*. Indeed, there is only one world, with numerous cultural situations and contexts. If one knows who she or he is, it is possible to function quite confidently and competently in all of them.

In addition to forced assimilation to mainstream ways, it is important to remember that the majority of Native people today are of mixed-blood descent. In addition, tribal members are literally dual citizens of the United States and their nation. Therefore, for Indian people, there are multiple levels of relationships in the two worlds that need to be acknowledged and validated. For healing to occur, models are needed that allow all people to self-identify without having to diminish or deny any part of themselves. All people need to walk in balance and be supported and fairly witnessed as whole, not splintered, human beings.

Much of cultural identification occurs through a process of social learning. Children gain an identity by modeling those persons they perceive to be like themselves and by being reinforced for appropriate behavior and discouraged from culturally incongruent behavior. In this way, core values and core identity emerge that will guide and sustain the individual throughout life and through many challenges. It is traditional that a child's special qualities are generally identified early by tribal elders.[157] These children are called to be leaders, healers, or teachers and are set apart in specific ways, according to tribal custom. All children are watched and witnessed carefully, but not necessarily protected from ordinary childhood lessons. Often, they are taught through natural consequences and corrected through natural shame. In the early stages, much learning can come about the hard way. Protection comes from witnessing the child continuously, by guarding the psychological and spiritual perimeters. When the child or the apprentice is too far out on the limb or when supernatural forces are greater than the person's ability to respond, the teacher, elder, or wise person steps in to create safe boundaries. At appropriate times, specific rituals, ceremonies, and teachings are given to empower the receiver. This is usually a lengthy process, requiring the entire community's support and participation.[158]

In order to fully incorporate the wound of the generational forced walk between the worlds and subsequent alienation, shame, and marginalization, American Indian families and communities must be strengthened so that the adults can begin to witness the children. This means moving beyond depression and anger and transforming the pain into the medicine of knowledge and power of moving between cultures. Many Native people today are physically and culturally blended products of diverse ancestors. Thus, the core strengths of all ancestral traditions can be reclaimed to build the cultural bridges to healing. The circle can be strengthened by embracing core cultural identities and thereby moving in the "in-between" with ease.

Culturally Competent Practice

Culturally competent methods are needed to facilitate the resolution of historical grief and the re-creation of the circle. To be a culturally competent practitioner is a complex process that requires knowledge, skill, and self-awareness. First, one must have a working definition of the notion of culture. Culture is defined as a stable pattern of beliefs, attitudes, and behaviors transmitted from generation to generation for the purpose of successfully adapting to other group members and to the environment.[159] These are incorporated into a person's everyday life, across many dimensions.

Understanding and valuing culture as a crucial aspect of the whole person, community, or organization is the next step toward cultural competence. It is hoped that in learning about history and cultural norms and values, sensitivity to the issues of social injustice and oppression is increased.[160] Without an understanding of historical traumas, practitioners risk blaming the victim, thus reinforcing the internalized oppression and reinflicting the trauma.[161]

In addition, the truly culturally competent practitioner should attempt through scrupulous self-reflection to identify the degree of privilege and power differentials between client and practitioner. Depending on the degree of acculturation to the center versus the margin of social, economic, and political power, each partner in the helping process will have varying amounts of unearned privilege as well as knowledge, skills, and other resources. According to Mary E. Swigonski, "Privilege refers to the unearned advantages enjoyed by a particular group simply because of membership in that group. Privileges accrue to those who (consciously or not) oppress others who are generally invisible to those who enjoy them."[162] Therefore, whether Native or non-Native, the practitioner needs to examine his or her own degree of privilege as well as cultural identifications, historical issues, and biases and consider how these will interact with the values and meanings of the client.[163]

Of most importance, culturally responsive practice would build on sensitivity and self-awareness and actively seek the input of the recipient regarding the definition and solutions applied to the identified concerns. This is essential because every culture and every individual has a unique way of defining and addressing problems. Thus, interventions that are not based upon a culturally appropriate assessment are likely to be ineffective and may compound trauma. Therefore, appropriate practice requires listening to clients' hopes, aspirations, and views while setting aside interpretation.[164] For this to occur, the practitioner must learn to build trust and draw out the stories of historically silenced and marginalized people. These stories, when carefully attended to, reveal the cultural values and meanings that have survived the generational holocaust. Next, cultural meanings derived from listening to clients' stories can contribute to mutually developing strategies that will empower those seeking help.[165] During such a process, people can be truly witnessed in their grief and enabled to transform the energy of unresolved trauma into healing and development. This can occur through traditional means, including in ceremonies and interacting with elders, or in appropriate services.

For empowerment to really occur, the practitioner or agency must truly view the recipient of service from the strengths-based perspective. This means acknowledging the resiliency and creativity required in surviving difficult circumstances. To be truly culturally competent, practitioners must always show respect to families as the experts on their unique situations and relationships within their communities.[166] In other words, solutions must include seeing the recipient of service as equally capable and important in the process.[167]

For American Indian individuals, families, and communities, the causes of the concerns presented encompass the impact of generational losses and unresolved grief.[168] This may include the assessment of the psychosocial effects of historical oppression, including loss of control, personal power, freedom, and independence. These effects are caused by violations of the client's space, time, energy, mobility, bonding, or identity due to membership in a marginalized population group.[169] A subsequent effect of oppression is alienation. The degree of alienation and lack of acceptance and belonging can be identified by negative self-image and lack of connection to one's culture, estrangement from significant others and others in general, feelings of loss, and detachment from social roles and activities.[170] We propose here that the strength of cultural identification may be indicative of the degree of resolution of historical grief.

Good practice includes assessing the individual, family, and community history regarding developmental disruptions, unresolved loss, and patterns of interaction that affect the current situation. Completing a genogram and culturegram, which physically portray generational events, myths, and relationship patterns, almost immediately normalizes the current functioning. Deborah Esquibel Hunt has noted in clinical experience that personal shame can be reduced by connecting the current struggles with historical loss, social marginalization, and racism. When one's history is witnessed fairly, an understanding begins to emerge about why things are the way they are now. There can be an audible catharsis of emotion that says, *No wonder things feel so crazy*. Looking at history is often the first experience of being witnessed. In this way, strength, courage, and resilience in survival can be validated. This is both a crucial aspect of assessment and an empowerment intervention.[171]

Another important part of assessment is to determine the degree and nature of cultural identification. For those seeking to reclaim cultural identity, predictable stages have been observed. Rebecca Van Voorhis identified four stages that were synthesized from a variety of models.[172] These are developmental in the process of reclaiming cultural identity and might apply both to American Indian individuals as well as to tribes and communities. It is not surprising that the stages of grief as outlined by Elisabeth Kubler-Ross correspond to the stages of cultural identity for marginalized and oppressed people. In the beginning stage, there is a minimal owning of group membership and striving to pass as belonging to the group at the center of power of society. This corresponds to denial in the first stage of grief. The second stage is termed adolescence and involves some acknowledgment of identity, limited disclosure and contact with one group, and a continuation of some passing behaviors. In the grief model, this relates to bargaining as well as depression because the loss must be acknowledged, and there is experimental movement away from denial. In the third stage, identity pride, there is an exhibition of public identity through dress, language, and activities, an immersion in one group and an avoidance of contact with people outside the group. This could involve the energy of the anger stage as one firmly and defiantly sets boundaries to limit the hurt of the grief. Finally, in identity synthesis, there is a full embracing of one identity (or identities), a positive internalization with the marginalized group, and the ability to comfortably interact with both groups. This stage exemplifies acceptance by reclaiming the strengths gained from the initial losses of cultural alienation.

Coping patterns should also be examined and validated as creative responses to oppression. These can include acknowledging family and community as teachers of coping with racism, as well as the personal qualities and skills developed in reaction to struggle. Van Voorhis identified three major coping patterns of historically oppressed people. She defined them as:

- capitulation, which involves conforming to the expectations of the population at the center and disconnecting from experiences on the margin;
- revitalization, which involves rejecting the center and its expectations and defending one identity on the margin; and
- radicalization, which involves claiming one identity, choosing to stand on the margin, and seeking change in conditions that oppress.[173]

Throughout the years of contact with the federal government, the circle has been fractured. Again, these coping strategies can be seen as developmental stages of healing grief. Capitulation can be seen and understood as an essential reaction for survival in any given era of U.S. policy toward American Indian nations prior to the self-determination era of the 1970s. It is easy to trace the movement toward revitalization and radicalization that is helping American Indian nations progress toward strengthening identity and sovereignty. Thus, there is an interactive process between changes in the social environment and strengthening of cultural identity.[174] As the social and political environment continues to grow to support sovereignty of tribes, nations will be required to call upon the best of the traditional and mainstream methods to heal the effects of cultural genocide and historical grief. Renewal of Indian nations in the political, economic, and educational spheres, as well as rising acceptance of Native people, nations, and ways by outside communities and people, will continue to help the process of healing but cannot fully achieve a return to individual and community harmony without appropriate traditional or contemporary actions toward the remnants of historical repression.

Return to the Circle: Healing the Effects of Oppression

It is clear that great diversity of experience and culture exists among Native people. In particular, there are differences in levels of acculturation and traditionalism depending on a number of historical, tribal, geographic, and cultural factors. In attending numerous national meetings regarding American Indian families, author Deborah Esquibel Hunt has observed an awareness of the need to strengthen tribal identity as a core of problem-solving efforts. It is evident through political activism and specific healing interventions that meaningful change is beginning to occur in the hearts of many American Indian people and communities. Indeed, healing is beginning in the hearts of many non-Indian people as well.

In one Native tongue, the spirit of the Ghost Dance is: "that which moves, moves." In other words, as the people heal, the people heal. Shared power can be contagious and results in ongoing positive cycles of people helping people. As participants are empowered by community solutions, they invite others who share similar life concerns to join their newfound successes.

Terry Cross (Seneca), executive director of the National Indian Child Welfare Association, admonished the participants at the association's 1999 national conference by stating, "Don't let the guilt of what you don't know get in the way of what you do know."[175] Throughout the conference, elders of various tribes admonished those in attendance to have compassion for one another, let go of past hurts, and be careful with words. One elder reminded people that in the old way, living in the heart was first. Today, he said, people are trying to live in the mind through the heart and it's not working. The people need, he said, to live again in their hearts, to listen to the connections, and to make offerings in love and respect to the elements as extensions of themselves. This elder reminded the people to love and forgive themselves and others as wounded children. Then, he said, the people can open to love, to tradition, and become whole.

Culturally Appropriate Interventions
Learning to listen with the heart and helping people remember how to live from the heart should form the basis of all culturally appropriate interventions with Native people. Despite intertribal differences, there are core spiritual principles that are common to most tribes that can inform strategies for healing. Several authors have delineated a set of "pan-Indian" values. These have included generosity, respect for elders, respect for women as lifegivers, regarding children as sacred, harmony with nature, self-reliance, respect for choices of others, accountability to the collective, courage, sacrifice for the collective in humility, recognizing powers in the unseen world, and stewardship of the earth.[176]

Contemporarily Appropriate Applications of Traditional Healing Principles
Several examples illustrate the use of pan-Indian concepts in healing interventions. With the help of the affected community, James Moran designed an alcohol prevention program for urban Indian youth called the Seventh Generation. The name reflects the traditional concept of actions affecting future generations. The first step in the process was to have the community identify "traditional" Indian values. A list of twenty values was narrowed to seven and included harmony, generosity, respect, courage, wisdom, humility, and honesty. With the help of local elders, the program culminated in a ceremony of "staking" to secure the youth's commitment to sobriety. The ceremony was created in an organic fashion. Although not an actual traditional or historical ceremony, it resembled the intent of traditional ceremony and gave the participants a sense of cultural connection. Similarly, a parenting program on a Lakota reservation utilized traditional Lakota spiritual principles as the foundation of parenting.[177]

Indian Brotherhood Twelve Steps Toward Sobriety
White Bison, a national consulting company headed by Don Coyhis (Mohawk), in one of the numerous and growing examples of applying

traditional values and methods appropriately to achieve contemporary healing, re-formed the Twelve Steps of Alcoholics Anonymous to be culturally relevant to American Indian people.[178] The Indian Brotherhood Twelve Steps Toward Sobriety are worded to align with pan-Indian spirituality. For example, steps 2 and 3 state: "We believe now that the Great Spirit can help us regain our responsibilities and model the life of our forefathers," and "We rely totally on the ability of the Great Spirit to watch over us." Coyhis has also consulted with tribes about utilizing traditional methods to solve community problems. In 1996, White Bison called for a national gathering of Native men. More than five thousand men, women, and children attended this camp in Estes Park, Colorado. Elders spoke about the need for the return of the warrior to families and communities. Sweat Lodges, Talking Circles, and other traditional ceremonies were held for teaching and healing. The gathering culminated in a "Wiping of the Tears" ceremony, which welcomed U.S. military veterans home and honored their service. An enormous circle of people performed an honor dance, which included passing under a large Medicine Wheel to which were tied more than one hundred eagle feathers sent by people from around the world. Most participants were moved to tears. The men created seven principles to live by and committed collectively to bring honor back to the people. (See also our discussion in chapter 4 of the success the Alkali Lake Indian Band of the Secwepemc Nation achieved in overcoming alcoholism as a community effort and of the adoption of some of its methods by the Betty Ford Clinic, demonstrating the relevance of Indigenous healing principles for mainstream America and beyond.)

Indian Health Service Encompassing Traditional Medicine: A Navajo Example

In recent years, the Indian Health Service (IHS), recognizing that there are psychological and cultural aspects of wellness and healing in both physical and mental health, has been open to including traditional medicine in health services.[179] A good example is the Navajo traditional healing program that began in 1996 with Substance Abuse and Mental Health Services Administration funds from IHS and became established on the Navajo Nation reservation in 2000 with federal funds. The traditional program complements the Western medicine program, and it is the patient's option whether or not to participate in it. But on the Navajo lands, where 50 percent of the people still speak Navajo, "Sixty percent of the clients come in requesting traditional practices or services," according to Carolyn Morris, a licensed clinical psychologist with Navajo health services. Navajo Director of Behavioral Health Herman Largo says that many Diné turn to traditional practices as a way to revive their lives after a period of substance abuse.

Typically, a course of treatment begins with a purification ritual, often a Sweat Lodge, and Diné songs that focus on moving from one place (or condition) to another. Diagnosis and prescribing a course of treatment in consultation with the patient follows with one of the traditional practitioners on staff. The third phase involves carrying out the treatment, often in a Beauty Way ceremony, and the fourth and final, or after-care, phase is a Blessing ceremony, always with lots of support from family and extended family. The treatment is tailored to the needs of the particular patient and often includes prayers and faith-based services, usually in the Navajo language. Morris noted that "it's a variety of interventions" that emphasize holistic, community-wide treatment, rather than Western individual-focus treatment. The one difficulty, now that IHS has recognized the value of traditional medicine, is that the agency tries to apply its traditional bureaucracy to it, in particular, by wanting traditional healing practitioners to be certified. Morris commented that the government needs to become more respectful of "cultural competency" in traditional healing practice because the practices have been effective for "years and years in the community," and traditional practitioners undergo a long and extensive training. Madan Poudel, a Navajo health services administrator, noted that the IHS system has come to "honor the sensitivities" around traditional healing practices. "It's in the process of educating them. . . . It's getting better for the past few years."

The Healing Aspects of Ceremonial Participation

Participation in traditional ceremonies has become an important part of the healing of many Native people—in overcoming substance abuse, mental health difficulties, and patterns of inappropriate behavior. In numerous instances, it has brought physical healing as well. Author Stephen Sachs has spoken with a number of longtime participants in plains Sun Dances, some of whom have become helpers (assisting leaders), who have stated how their becoming involved in traditional ceremonial life turned their lives around and helped them overcome substance and behavioral abuse. They have testified that involving themselves in ceremonial life, which continues through the entire year—encompassing long preparation, the ceremony itself, and living out the gifts and teachings of the annual ritual—has given them a new sense of identity and purpose, returning them to harmony with themselves, other people, their heritage, and the universe. Sachs has also observed that at some reservations, such as the Southern Ute Indian reservation, support of traditional ceremonies is part of the healing process employed by tribal substance abuse programs.

Indian Organizations Promoting the Use of Traditional Ways in Their Daily Operations

In addition, there are numerous national organizations that seek to empower American Indian people and that promote the use of traditional principles in their daily operations. These include the National Indian Child Welfare Association, AIO, National Congress of American Indians (NCAI), and many others. The national conferences of the National Indian Child Welfare Association and NCAI, for example, always seek the input of local elders in the cities where gatherings are planned. The meetings are opened with an elder's prayer and blessing.

Respecting Diversity and Emphasizing Empowerment as Part of Good Practice

However tempting it is to apply culturally based interventions, careful assessment of the degree and multiplicity of cultural identification is essential. In addition, it is important to remember the diversity among and within tribes. Good practice involves first and foremost building a trusting, respectful relationship based on discerning, understanding, and accepting the ways of seeing of the person being supported. Building trust takes time. Some people have no association with their historical cultures and would not appreciate interventions grounded in traditional concepts. Many others have sufficient connection to or yearning to connect with their cultural roots that traditionally based healing practices are empowering and transformative.

For those who are able to acknowledge and face historical grief, interventions that strengthen cultural identities should be considered. For example, Laurence French contends that the most crucial therapy issue for any Indian child or youth is the positive reinforcement of their Indianness.[180] French recommends two strategies in particular: storytelling (by a tribal elder or American Indian adult), or analyzing a story for its message of cultural value, and the Talking Circle. The Talking

Circle is a group discussion led by an adult Indian role model that provides an opportunity for insight and emotional catharsis. The Medicine Wheel is another concept that is used as a basic structure for conceptualizing causes of problems and designing ceremonial interventions. The Medicine Wheel is the physical representation of the circle of life and balance. This four-directional symbol is the foundation for the Sweat Lodge, which has been effectively used to heal historical grief.[181]

Because culturally responsive work with Indigenous people includes examining generational trauma and cultural genocide, this work might not be openly welcomed. Denial of pain and shame is a central coping mechanism when parents abuse alcohol or when other forms of parental abandonment and dysfunction are chronic. Patterns of dysfunction might include chronic poverty, domestic violence, sexual and physical abuse, and physical and emotional illness. In affected families, rules have developed to guard against the pain. These are: don't trust, don't talk, don't feel. Therefore, identity must be reframed as a normal response to extreme trauma as well as the normal first step in grief work.[182] When there is an unwillingness to look at historical grief issues, it is still possible to indirectly acknowledge the relationship between history and current functioning. Storytelling is the method used by elders to show what people cannot or will not see in their situations. In the course of being treated respectfully by practitioners or elders, messages may be rejected or incorporated without shame.

Whether traditionally based or Western methods are used, healing historical grief requires creating a safe context in which families and communities can trust, feel the emotion, and express the grief. Community healing rituals and ceremonies where all persons are witnessed as sacred and essential to the circle can move people from victims to survivors, to teachers and healers. Indirect methods such as play, sand, or art therapy may also be used. One student in a graduate class in social work created a community intervention program to help heal historical grief. Her intervention included the use of dramatic plays that were to be guided and informed by elders and written, produced, and directed by children.[183] Giving voice to the children and honoring the knowledge of elders can create the generational bridges that strengthen identity and give meaning to the future.

All methods need to emphasize empowerment, or regaining belief in the power to make choices that support the good of the whole. This might include reclaiming the center on one's own terms through self-definition, development of identity pride, and development of mutually supportive and empathetic relationships.[184] The hoped-for results are reduction of alienation and increase in self-worth and dignity.

Completing the Circle of Healing

Healing historical grief can mobilize the energy to overcome oppressive conditions of historical dependency and replace victim identification with a clear sense of cultural identity and strength. The Indigenous peoples of this land have undergone hundreds of years of devastating loss at all levels and have survived with courage, dignity, faith, and resilience. Author Deborah Esquibel Hunt has found strength in her own traditional Tsalagi (Cherokee) ancestors, who modeled strength in adaptability while never relinquishing traditional values. It is told that the people cried tears of grief on the Trail of Tears, and the grandmothers also accepted the fate of being victims in a dark time in human history. They never lost faith and did what they could to survive. They adapted to change by incorporating new forms but never relinquishing traditional values. As they marched, they sang Christian hymns in the Tsalagi language, asking Creator not to forsake them. More than a hundred years before the Indian Reorganization Act, the Tsalagi Nation adopted a Western form of government so that they would be able to work in the same arena as the state and federal governments. However, the men elected to the new governments always consulted the clan mothers. Theda Purdue points out that although intermarriage with whites eventually diminished the role of matriarchal clans, the mothers continued to pass on the values of the people.[185] Similarly, LaDonna Harris believes that the key to the future success of tribal America and its leaders is the ability to reweave traditional tribal values into a contemporary reality.[186]

The wounds of personal and cultural shame, alienation, and marginality can be transformed into medicine by reclaiming the strengths of culture and incorporating the skills taught in white institutions in ways that fit the contemporary Indigenous context. In deliberately choosing to walk between cultures, victims of historical trauma become the healers and the teachers. The capacity to operate from multiple worldviews can empower the people to greater sovereignty. While undeniably cruel and heinous, the forced walk between the worlds may be by choice transformed into medicine. There can be no other purpose for wounding than healing and returning the medicine with compassion. Mainstream culture has much to learn about resilience from Native peoples. Humanity is facing extermination from the effects of disrespecting the earth and her resources. Survival depends upon strengthening tribal sovereignty and identities and embracing traditional models of cooperation and community. When all people are restored to health and dignity, respect and harmony in all relationships are more likely to prevail.

Notes

1. Nordhaus, "30 Years"; LaDonna Harris at AIO, June 2006 personal communication with author Stephen Sachs.
2. Taylor and Kalt, *American Indians on Reservations*.
3. Corporation for Enterprise Development, *Entrepreneurship Development*, 1.
4. *Indigenous Policy* has reported on these developments since spring 2005; see also Sachs, "Climate Change"; Barrenger, "Indian Tribes See Profit"; Moses, "Seeking Solutions"; and Gray, "Windfall."
5. Cornell, "Politics, Business"; and Cornell and Kalt, *Reloading the Dice*.
6. On the problem of decision making and consulting with outsiders, see Sachs and Hunt, "Appropriate Consulting with Indian Nations." We discuss this further in chapter 6, section 2.
7. As we discussed in chapter 4. See also Cornell and Kalt, *Reloading the Dice*, 17–23.
8. Sachs, "Need for More," 36. See also chapter 4, section 2.
9. Cornell and Kalt, *Reloading the Dice*, 27–33.
10. Ibid., 33–38.
11. For a discussion about the development of employee participation and ownership, see Sachs, "Interaction of Forces."
12. Simmons and Mares, *Working Together*; Bernstein, *Workplace Democratization*, especially chap. 5; Blinder, *Paying for Productivity*; Lawler, Mohrman, and Ledford, *Employee Involvement*; and Nalbantian, *Incentives, Cooperation*.
13. Bernstein, *Workplace Democratization*, especially, chap. 5; Blinder, *Paying for Productivity*; Lawler, Mohrman, and Ledford, *Employee Involvement*; and Nalbantian, *Incentives, Cooperation*.
14. Bernstein, *Workplace Democratization*, especially, chap. 5; Blinder, *Paying for Productivity*; Lawler, Mohrman, and Ledford, *Employee Involvement*; and Nalbantian, *Incentives, Cooperation*.
15. *ICA News and Events: A Report from ICA's Community Jobs Program*, fall 2005. ICA is located at 1 Harvard Street, Suite 200, Brookline, MA, 02445; (617) 232–8765, ica@ica-group.org. Another worker cooperative development group with Native experience, particularly in Latin America, is led by Warner Woodworth, Department of Organizational Leadership and Strategy, Marriott School of Management, Brigham Young University, 786 TNRB, PO Box 2307, Provo, UT, 84602; (801) 422–6834, warner_woodworth@byu.edu.
16. Discussed in Thomas and Logan, *Mondragon*; Campbell et al., *Worker Ownership*; Mollner, *A Third Way*; Gutierrez-Johnson and Whyte, "The Mondragon System," 18–30; Gutierrez-Johnson, "Compensation, Equity," 267–89; Oakeshott, "Mondragon: Spain's Oasis," 290–96; Medanie, "Mondragon: Your Add"; and Kohler, "What Happens."
17. Corporation for Enterprise Development, *Entrepreneurship Development*, 2.
18. Ibid.

19. Ibid., 4. Another example is the Native Financial Education Coalition, a group of local, regional, and national organizations and government agencies working together to promote financial education in Native communities. The Department of the Treasury started the coalition in 2000, but it is now independent. It seeks to exchange information, forge partnerships, identify and develop strategies for outreach and training, and identify gaps in information about financial education needs. The coalition has trained nearly eight hundred instructors to teach financial education courses in Native communities by using the "Building Native Communities: Financial Skills for Families" curriculum. The coalition held a policy briefing in Washington, D.C., in April 2003 to stress the need for Native Americans to increase their financial understanding. The press release announcing the briefing is available on the U.S. Department of the Treasury "Press Room" page at: http://www.treas.gov/financialeducation.

20. The Sky Ute Casino and Resort is run by the Southern Ute Division of Gaming. Information about the extent of natural gas pipeline ownership and tribal net worth is from "Indian and Indigenous Developments: U.S. Developments" and "Tribal Developments," *Indigenous Policy* 18, no. 3 .

Red Willow is part of the Southern Ute Energy Group, which includes several different entities. Each has its own management team and business objectives, but all share elements and the opportunity to collaborate on a variety of projects. Red Willow Production Company is an oil and natural gas exploration and production company that operates predominantly in the western United States, the Gulf of Mexico, and western Canada. It is regarded as a world leader in the extraction of methane gas from coal-bed deposits, although the company is also actively engaged in conventional oil and gas exploration and production. Red Cedar Gathering Company treats and processes natural gas and delivers treated gas to intrastate and interstate gas pipelines. The operation is a joint venture with Kinder Morgan Energy Partners and is the largest gas gatherer and processor in the state of Colorado. Aka Energy Group processes and transports natural gas and natural gas liquids in six states. Aka identifies, acquires, and operates midstream assets that are underutilized or underperforming but that possess attractive growth potential.

In the 1980s and 1990s, the Southern Ute Indian Tribe aggressively developed its natural resource base, adopting in 1999 an official financial plan to separate its core government from its various business and related investment activities, and in 2000, a growth fund to operate and manage its business and investment activities. The financial plan provides the tribe with an economic strategy that ensures that a core government and baseline cash distributions will exist in perpetuity, while at the same time optimizing available investment resources to provide for the long-term security of the tribe and its members. More information is available on the Southern Ute Indian Tribe Growth Fund website, at http://www.sugf.com/energy.htm.

21. "Indian and Indigenous Developments: U.S. Developments," *Indigenous Policy* 19, no. 1.

22. "Indian and Indigenous Developments: U.S. Developments," *Indigenous Policy* 15, no 1.

23. "Indian and Indigenous Developments: U.S. Developments," *Indigenous Policy* 16, no. 1.

24. "Indian and Indigenous Developments: U.S. Developments" and "Economic

Developments," *Indigenous Policy* 19, no. 1. An Internet portal to information about Native community development resources has been established on the "Our Native Circle" website, at http://ournativecircle.org.

25. Corporation for Enterprise Development, *Entrepreneurship Development*, 4–5, includes a larger list of sources of Native business technical assistance and funding.

26. Ibid., 4.

27. Proposed by National Congress of American Indians (NCAI) President Tex Hall in his third annual State of Indian Nations Address, February 3, 2005. Reported in "Indian and Indigenous Developments: U.S. Developments" and "Ongoing Activities," *Indigenous Policy* 16, no. 1.

28. More information is available on the Native American Bank website: http://www.nabna.com.

29. The source of information about Indian banks in this paragraph is "Indian and Indigenous Developments: U.S. Developments" and "Economic Developments," *Indigenous Policy* 20, no. 1.

30. Giago, "It Is Time."

31. "Indian and Indigenous Developments: U.S. Developments" and "Tribal Developments," *Indigenous Policy* 18, no. 3.

32. "Indian and Indigenous Developments: U.S. Developments" and "Tribal Developments," *Indigenous Policy* 15, no. 1.

33. "Indian and Indigenous Developments: U.S. Developments" and "Economic Developments," *Indigenous* Policy 20.

34. "Indian and Indigenous Developments: U.S. Developments" and "Economic Developments," *Indigenous* Policy 19, no. 1.

35. Ibid. Harold Monteau, Chippewa-Cree, is an Indian attorney and former chairman of NIGA.

36. "Indian and Indigenous Developments: U.S. Developments" and "Economic Developments," *Indigenous* Policy 19, no. 1.

37. For a lengthy discussion of additional economic policies and strategies that Indian nations might consider, and for an explanation of how to develop clear and easily applied policies and procedures, see Rosser, "This Land."

38. The bill passed the Senate in May 2006. ("Indian and Indigenous Developments: U.S. Developments" and "Economic Developments," *Indigenous Policy* 16, no. 2.)

39. Ibid.

40. Ibid.

41. "Indian and Indigenous Developments: U.S. Developments" and "Economic Developments," *Indigenous Policy* 16, no 2.

42. O'Brien, *American Indian Tribal Governments*, chap. 1. The Mississippi Band of Choctaw Indians provides updates on tribal affairs, including economic development, on the tribe's website: http://www.choctaw.org/index.htm.

43. See Mississippi Band of Choctaw Indians, *Choctaw Industrial Park*; and Peterson, "Three Efforts at Development."

44. "Indian and Indigenous Developments: U.S. Developments" and "Economic Developments," *Indigenous Policy* 14, no. 2.

45. Information on the Oneida Nation of Wisconsin is available on the nation's website, at http://www.oneidanation.org; on "The Oneida Tribe of Indians from Wisconsin" website, at http://www.jefflindsay.com/Oneida.shtml; and on *Wikipedia*, at http://en.wikipedia.org/wiki/Oneida_tribe.

46. "Indian and Indigenous Developments: U.S. Developments" and "Tribal Developments" *Indigenous Policy* 18, no. 3.

47. For more information about Four Winds Casino Resort, visit the resort website: http://www.fourwindscasino.com.

48. "Indian and Indigenous Developments: U.S. Developments" and "Economic Developments," *Indigenous Policy* 19, no. 1. Information about Ho-Chunk, Inc., is available on the corporate website: http://www.hochunkinc.com and includes the 2007 Ho-Chunk, Inc., Annual Report in a PDF file.

49. Information about Oregon tribal development is from "Indian and Indigenous Developments: U.S. Developments" and "Tribal Developments" *Indigenous Policy* 18, no. 3.

50. Mapes, "New High Rollers."

51. "Indian and Indigenous Developments: U.S. Developments" and "Economic Developments," *Indigenous Policy* 14, no. 2. The article's source was a statement by Morongo Band of Mission Indians Tribal Chairman Maurice Lyons, reported in the email newsletter *Digest of Indigenous News* (from Andre Cramblit: andrekar@ncidc. org). Reports on economic development by additional Indian nations are found in Wilkinson, *Blood Struggle*, part 4.

52. "Indian and Indigenous Developments: U.S. Developments" and "Economic Developments," *Indigenous Policy* 14, no. 2. See also the Elk Valley Rancheria website: http://www.elk-valley.com/index.html.

53. Rob Capriccioso, "Wall Street Crisis."

54. Ibid.

55. "Indian and Indigenous Developments: U.S. Developments" and "Tribal Developments," *Indigenous Policy* 18, no. 3.

56. Begay, "Hold Steady on Investments."

57. Snyder "Wall Street Woes."

58. For example, by October 2003, California Indian nations were the largest contributor in the recall election of the state's governor, having contributed more than $11 million and expecting to contribute more. By that date, Indian money accounted for one of every six dollars of the $66 million contributed to candidates or spent by independent committees on the recall effort. See "Indian and Indigenous Developments: U.S. Developments," *Indigenous Policy* 14, no. 2.

59. For example, see "Abramoff Pleads Guilty," 1, 5; and "Documents Show," 5, 8.

60. For an extensive discussion of tribal governments and American federalism, see Sachs, Harris, and Morris, "Native American Tribes"; Morris, Sachs, and Harris, "Strategy and Choice"; and Sachs, Harris, and Morris, "Honoring the Circle."

61. Cajete, *Look to the Mountain*.

62. Peroff, "Doing Research."

63. For a critique of Western science that shows its strengths and the weaknesses of its limitations, illuminated by an examination of the Native equivalent of science, see Cajete, *Native Science*.

64. Osborne and Gaebler, *Reinventing Government*, 5–8, 17, 38, 93–113, 148–49, 169, 264–67, 271, and 290. See also Smith, *Rethinking America*, chap. 6.

65. As operated by Dewey's inspiration in the public schools in Gary, Indiana, early in the twentieth century in Dewey, *Schools for Tomorrow*, and in some progressive schools more recently, including the Putney School in Putney, Vermont. Some of the more permissive applications of progressive education in the 1950s and 1960s that allowed students freedom to make choices permitted them wide latitude to do whatever they

wanted, including not following through on choices or fulfilling obligations, whereas Dewey's approach involved giving young people maximum positive freedom to make reasonable choices in their education, on which they were expected to follow through unless student–teacher discussion worked out a change of plan. Dewey's experiential and participatory approach to education emphasizes students having a wide variety of positive experiences, as well as coming to understand all viewpoints on issues. Too much permissiveness can lead to negative experiences, in terms of the individual's development. See Sachs, "The Putney School."

66. It was precisely because progressive education was closer to traditional Indian education than most European American approaches to teaching and learning that it was employed in Indian education reform during John Collier's administration of the BIA during the New Deal. See Szasz, *Road to Self-Determination*, chaps. 4–6. Dewey's philosophy itself had Native American roots, as is developed in Pratt, *Native Pragmatism*.

67. Pratt, *Native Pragmatism*.

68. Smith, *Rethinking America*, particularly chaps. 5 and 7, includes descriptions of business–school partnerships, including apprenticeships, and teaching mathematics and English relevant to them in Wisconsin and other places, as well as the dual education system in Germany.

69. Cajete, *Look to the Mountain*, 20.

70. Ibid.

71. For example, see Fuchs and Havighurst, *American Indian Education*, chaps. 11 and 12; McCarty et al., "Call for Reassessment," 42–59; and Woods, "Diverse Learning Styles," 26–30.

72. Cajete, *Look to the Mountain*, 20; and Fuchs and Havighurst, *American Indian Education*, 232–33.

73. Berry, "The Viable Human," 79.

74. Waterman, *Introduction to Transformation*, 5.

75. For a discussion of individuation, see Jung, *Memories, Dreams, Reflections*; Jung, *Archetypes*; and Jung, *Structure and Dynamics*.

76. Sanford, *Healing and Wholeness*, 22.

77. Hampton, "Toward a Redefinition."

78. Deloria, "The Perpetual Indian Message."

79. Fuchs and Havighurst, *American Indian Education*, 252–56; and McCarty, et al., "Classroom Inquiry." The Center for Education Reform in Washington, D.C., reported on December 21, 2004, that the number of Indian tribes using charter schools is increasing and that there were at least thirty Indian charter schools in the country. Arizona has the most with twelve, followed by California with six. Indian charter schools have also opened in Minnesota and Michigan. Some have achieved positive results quickly. The San Diego–area Barona Indian Charter School, for example, posted substantial increases in student performance on standardized test scores in 2003–2004, with the school ranking higher than the state average. Not all Native charter schools have been unqualified successes, however: one Arizona Indian charter school had to shut down after trouble with an audit and federal special education requirements. Additional Native charter schools are being planned, including one in Alaska. See "Indian and Indigenous Developments: U.S. Developments" and "Educational and Cultural Developments," *Indigenous Policy* 16, no. 1.

80. Brown, "Ribbon Cutting Marks Opening," 1; Brown, "Academy Students ZAP,"

1, 3; Brown, "Southern Ute Academy," 1; Brown, "Academy to Offer," 1; Bear, "Academy Embraces Outdoor Education," 1; and Brown "Academy Class Asks." Southern Ute tribal officials, personal communication with author Stephen Sachs.

81. Szasz, *Road to Self-Determination*, chaps. 4–6.

82. Nichols, "Cultural Focus Credited," 8.

83. Gagnier, *Keys to Connectedness* (forthcoming). The author may be contacted at phyllisgagnier@gmail.com.

84. Goelitz, "Feature Interviews," 5–6.

85. Ibid., 6.

86. Ibid., 7.

87. Ibid. HeartMath® is a national research and training organization that helps people handle stress, regulate emotional responses, and employ heart-brain communication. More information is available on the HeartMath website, http://www.heartmath.com.

88. Goelitz, "Feature Interviews," 6.

89. Ibid., 7.

90. Goelitz, "Successful Truancy Program," 3.

91. First Nations Development Institute/Fannie Mae Foundation, *Building Native Communities: Financial Skills for Families*, "Instructor's Guide" and "Participant's Workbook," 2nd ed.

92. Gagnier, *Keys to Connectedness*.

93. Southern Utes in discussion with author Stephen Sachs.

94. Federal funding also comes to Native students under Title IX. The U.S. Department of Education funds applications that carry out a local educational agency's comprehensive plans for Indian students that address the language and cultural needs of Native students and supplement and enrich the regular school program. The Indian Education Formula Grant Program supports local education agencies, schools funded by the BIA, and certain tribal schools in their efforts to reform elementary and secondary school programs that serve American Indian and Alaska Native students. Programs are based on challenging state or local content and performance standards used for all students and are designed to assist Indian students to meet those standards. Participation by parent committees are required in the development of grant applications, as are open consultations with parents of Indian children, teachers, and, where applicable, Indian secondary students. The applicant must obtain the parent committee's written approval on all new and continuation applications. The comprehensive plan also requires the applicant to provide assessment results to the parent committee and the community served by the local education agency. (See "Overview of Issues in American Indian Education," Digest for IndigenousNewsNetwork@topica.com, available from Andre Cramblit, andrekar@ncidc.org.)

95. Young, *Ute Indians of Colorado*, 160–61, 234–35, and 265–67.

96. Ibid. Southern Utes and their neighbors in discussion with author Stephen Sachs.

97. "Indian and Indigenous Developments: U.S. Developments" and "Educational and Cultural Developments," *Indigenous Policy* 15, no. 3.

98. "Indigenous Developments: Economic Developments" and "Educational and Cultural Developments," *Native American Policy* 14.

99. Hansen, "Innovative Program," 13–14.

100. Ibid., 12.

101. Woodard, "Rethinking the Past," 23–25.

102. "Indian and Indigenous Developments: U.S. Developments," "Economic Development," and "Educational and Cultural Developments," *Indigenous Policy* 14, no. 2. It is reported elsewhere that American Indian students have a 15 percent completion rate at state-supported institutions of higher learning.

103. Former NAES College Dean of Admissions David Beck, in discussion with author Stephen Sachs. NAES College can be contacted at 2838 W. Peterson, Chicago, IL, 60659; (773) 761–5000.

104. "Indian and Indigenous Developments: U.S. Developments" and "Educational and Cultural Developments," *Indigenous Policy* 15, no. 1.

105. Information about the Woksape Oyate Program, which is carried out through the American Indian College Fund, and about each of the twenty-one tribal college applications of the program, is available on the "Tribal Colleges" page of the American Indian College Fund website: http://www.collegefund.org/colleges/projects08.html.

106. Information about CMN is available on the college's website: http://www.menominee.edu. 107. The STEM curriculum is presented in Boyer, *Tribal College*, vii–xvi, 30–31; and Pember, "The Red Road."

108. The development of Native case studies for Indigenous education is presented in Smith, "Understanding of Sovereignty." For more on the value of participatory teaching for virtually all students with actual or simulated cases, see Sachs, "Bringing the Case"; and Sachs, "The Uses and Limits."

109. For more information about Oglala Lakota College, see the college's website at http://www.olc.edu.

110. Information about the Utes' tribal language is available on the "Tribal Language" page of the Southern Ute Indian Tribe website: http://www.southern-ute.nsn.us/government/language.html.

111. "Indian and Indigenous Developments: U.S. Developments" and "Educational and Cultural Developments," *Indigenous Policy* 15, no. 3.

112. Without such a program, it is estimated that within a decade, only one in twenty Lakotas might speak their language and that it might cease to be a living language within a generation. "Indian and Indigenous Developments: U.S. Developments" and "Economic, Educational, and Cultural Developments," *Indigenous Policy*, 13, no. 2.

113. More information is available on the Lakota Language Consortium website: http:www.lakotalanguage.org.

114. Oglala Lakota College's work under the Lilly Grant is discussed at: http://www.collegefund.org/content/woksape_oyate.

115. This quotation's source is a now-defunct web page of the American Indian College Fund. For current information from the fund about Diné College and the Woksape Oyate Program, go to http://www.collegefund.org/content/woksape_oyate.

116. For information about the Blackfeet and Dull Knife developments, go to http://www.collegefund.org/content/woksape_oyate.

117. Toensing, "Film Project Helps Passamaquoddy," 56–58.

118. Woodard, "Speak Like a Person," 100–101.

119. Peterson, "Staving Off Extinction."

120. This is becoming more common in the United States. For instance, on November 14, 2008, the recently organized Consortium for Collaborative Public Policy at the University of New Mexico hosted a symposium, "Exploring Collaborative Governance in New Mexico," with panelists from the Policy Consensus Initiative and university-based governance centers in Oregon and

Colorado, to explore cooperative ways of developing public policy and expanding university community collaboration. For more information, contact Paul Biderman, UNM Institute of Public Law: biderman@law.unm.edu.

121. For more information about the program, go to the Applied Indigenous Studies website at http:// www.ais.nau.edu, or contact Octaviana Trujillo, PhD, chair of Applied Studies, Northern Arizona University, PO Box 15020, Flagstaff, AZ, 86011; (928) 523–6624, Octaviana.Truillo@nau.edu.

122. Marales, "New Program," 114–15.

123. Herrmann, "College Credit Certificate Program," 120–21.

124. For more information about the fellowships, contact Maria Teresa Velez, PhD, associate dean, Graduate College, Administration #322, University of Arizona, Tucson, AZ, 85721; (520) 621–7814, mvelez@u.arizona.edu. See also "Indian and Indigenous Developments: U.S. Developments" and "Educational and Cultural Developments," *Indigenous Policy* 14, no, 2.

125. Peterson Zah, former advisor to the Arizona State University president on American Indian Affairs, in discussion with author Stephen Sachs.

126. More information about the Ambassadors Program is available on the AIO website at http://www.aio.org, and on the Ambassador's Alliance website, at www. aioambassador.com. See also back issues of AIO's newsletter, *The Ambassador*; Beams, "Ambassadors Meet," 17; and the December 1, 2002, AIO press release, "1984 University of New Mexico Graduate Takes Over the Helm of a Thirty-Two Year Legacy." Reports about the AIO Ambassadors Program appear in the "Ongoing Activities" column of *Indigenous Policy*.

127. The Turtle Island Communications website is available at http://www. turtleislandcom.com.

128. The Denali Commission website is available at http://www.denali.gov.

129. Information about Advancement for Mōari Opportunity is available at http://www. amo.co.nz, and in the "Ongoing Activities" column of *Indigenous Policy*. See also Sachs, "Circling the Circles," 14–35.

130. Sachs, "Circling the Circles." See also Bausch, et al., *Designing A Transitional*; Harris, "Letter from the President," 2. Author Stephen Sachs observed and participated in the meeting.

131. The requirements of the No Child Left Behind Act are creating difficulties for many schools in Alaska, especially in the western part of the state. Schools that for decades have taught and helped preserve Native Yup'ik and other Indigenous languages will likely have to test children in English. The act allows for some testing in languages other than English, but little money is available for that purpose, and even if it were, taking written tests in specified subjects in many Native languages is not practical. For example, mathematics to American children is based on units of ten, whereas increments of twenty are used in Yup'ik math, and numerous English words have no Yup'ik counterparts. Similar difficulties have been noted for Native students elsewhere in the United States. In the winter of 2005, the Department of Education relaxed some of the No Child Left Behind requirements, including those for students whose first language is not English, but the exact effect of the changes is not yet clear. Many BIA schools do not meet the standards of the No Child Left Behind Act; nineteen BIA schools fall in the lowest category. In January 2005, the BIA planned to provide more money to the schools with the biggest problems. In a report to the Navajo Nation council in March, delegate Wallace Charley stated

that Navajo Nation schools are always underfunded by the federal government, and seven of the fourteen schools that are on the BIA construction list because of serious structural deficiencies—to the point that they are literally crumbling—are located in Navajo Nation. According to Charley, "I would give them [the federal government] a D." One positive development was that Tse Ho Tso Intermediate Learning Center began the 2004–2005 school year at its new school building in Fort Defiance, Arizona, that was dedicated on April 30, 2004. See "Indian and Indigenous Developments: U.S. Developments" and "Educational and Cultural Developments," *Indigenous Policy* 14, no. 1.

132. "Indian and Indigenous Developments: U.S. Developments," *Indigenous Policy* 15, no. 1.

133. Since 1993, states do not have to distribute impact aid equally to school districts on the basis of the number of eligible students in each district. When the state of New Mexico changed its funding formulas, the Gallup-McKinley County Schools, with a large Indian population, dropped from a ranking of second to seventy-sixth (close to the bottom) in teacher salaries statewide. School officials say the reduced funding has lowered the quality of education. The Zuni Public School District reported essentially the same kinds of losses in funding and quality of education following the change in funding formula. New Mexico's action in changing funding formulas was upheld by the Tenth Circuit Court of Appeals in early January 2005. See *Navajo* Times, "N.M. Can Shortchange Schools," A10.

134. Forrest S. Cuch (Northern Ute), executive director, Division of Indian Affairs, Utah Department of Economic Development, in discussion with author Stephen Sachs. Executive Director Cuch is a former director of the Northern Ute charter school.

135. Weaver and Brave Heart, "Examining Two Facets," 19–31. Section 3 of chapter 5 was developed from a portion of a paper initially drafted by Sachs et al., "Recreating the Circle," Part 3, A.

136. Brave Heart, "*Oyate Ptayela*."

137. Cross, "Opening Remarks."

138. French, *Counseling American Indians*.

139. Erikson, "Identity," 102.

140. Oetting and Beauvais, "Epidemiology and Correlates," 239–67.

141. Middleton-Moz, "From Legacy to Choice."

142. Brave Heart, "*Oyate Ptayela*," 111.

143. Kubler-Ross, *On Death and Dying*.

144. Middleton-Moz, "Wisdom of Elders."

145. Weaver and Brave Heart, "Examining Two Facets," 23.

146. Brave Heart, "*Oyate Ptayela*," 111.

147. Lewis, *Quantitative Study in Two Places*.

148. Van Voorhis, "Culturally Relevant Practice," 121–33.

149. French, *Counseling American Indians*, 6–7.

150. As experienced by author Deborah Esquibel Hunt, who is of Tsalagi (Cherokee) descent.

151. On this point, see the discussion in Duran and Duran, *Native American Postcolonial Psychology*, 147–49.

152. For example, see Rice, *Ella Deloria's The Buffalo People*, 184, 189–92, and 196; and von Franz, *Alchemy*.

153. McFee, "The 150% Man," 1096–1103; and Polgar, "Biculturation," 217–35.

154. Weaver and Brave Heart, "Examining Two Facets."

155. Oetting and Beauvais, "Orthogonal Cultural Identification Theory," 655–85.

156. On multicultural identification, see McFee, "The 150% Man"; Polgar, "Biculturation"; Weaver and Brave Heart, "Examining Two Facets"; and Oetting and Beauvais, "Orthogonal Cultural Identification Theory." Author Deborah Esquibel Hunt has coined the term *parallel identifications*.

157. For examples, see Black Elk and Lyon, *Black Elk*, part 1, chaps. 1 and 2; Mails, *Fools Crow*, chaps. 3–5; and Crow Dog and Erdoes, *Crow Dog*, chap. 9. Insight into traditional Indian child upbringing that generally follows the principles we've given here can be found in Deloria, *Waterlily*; and Riley, *Growing Up Native American*.

158. Author Deborah Esquibel Hunt personally observed this process.

159. Carballeira, "Live and Learn Model," 4–6, 12.

160. Weaver, "Indigenous People," 203–10.

161. Ibid.

162. Swigonski, "Challenging Privilege," 153.

163. Weaver, "Indigenous People."

164. Van Voorhis, "Culturally Relevant Practice."

165. Leigh, *Communicating for Cultural Competence*.

166. Ibid.

167. Ibid.

168. Weaver, "Indigenous People"; and Weaver and Brave Heart, "Examining Two Facets."

169. Van Voorhis, "Culturally Relevant Practice," 124.

170. Ibid.

171. This point is discussed throughout Duran and Duran, *Native American Postcolonial Psychology*, 42–53, 180, and chap. 4. See also Sachs, "LaDonna Harris," 77–85.

172. Van Voorhis, "Culturally Relevant Practice," 126.

173. Ibid., 121–23.

174. Levine, "Prevention and Community," 189–206.

175. Cross, "Opening Remarks."

176. See Tolman and Reedy, "Implementation," 382–93.

177. See Moran, "Seventh Generation Program," 51–68; and Brave Heart, "*Oyate Ptayela*," 106–26.

178. Gurnee et al., "Urban Treatment Program," 17–26. Another example of applying traditional values and ways to attaining healing today is Pine Ridge Reservation mental health specialist Iron Cloud-Two Dogs, who treats emotionally disturbed and suicidal children by using a spiritual assessment followed by healing ceremonies at a Lakota purification (sweat) lodge under a federally funded Native American mental health program called *Nagi Kicopi*, "Calling the Spirit Back." The program often blends Western allopathic treatments, including medications, with traditional methods, including ceremonies. See *News from Indian Country*, "Reservation Program Blends," 23; *News from Indian Country*, "Program Blends Conventional," C4; and Vedantam, "Healers Prescribe Tribal Tradition," A11.

179. Reynolds, "Traditional Approach to Healing."

180. French, *Counseling American Indians*, 36.

181. Duran and Duran, *Native American Postcolonial Psychology*, 42–53, 180, and chap. 4.

182. Tafoya and Del Vecchio, "Back to the Future."

183. Medina, "Community Mental Health Intervention."
184. Van Voorhis, "Culturally Relevant Practice."
185. Purdue, *Cherokee Women.*
186. See Sachs, "LaDonna Harris," 77–85. Loretta Fowler reports that from 1851 to 1978 the Northern Arapaho "resolved problems of legitimation of authority and advocacy of tribal interests by interpreting new social realities in ways that were culturally acceptable as well as adaptive. Symbols emerged that worked to revitalize or reassert traditional values and relationships, yet at the same time reassured whites that the Arapahoes were neither dangerous or uncooperative. At the same time, old symbols took on new meanings that both reinforced traditional understandings and motivations and made innovation culturally acceptable" (*Arapahoe Politics*, 5). In his foreword to the book, Fred Eggan states that because of this, "the Northern Arapahoes have made the most successful adjustment to white culture of any plains tribe, . . . The Northern Arapahoes have managed to avoid serious factional divisions and particularly those between the generations, and have been able to maintain a united front against the Bureau of Indian Affairs and other agencies of government" (xvii).

Part Three:

Completing the Circle Through Appropriate Leadership and Collaboration and an Overview of the Re-creation Process

Six

Working in the Circle

APPROPRIATE LEADERSHIP, COLLABORATION, AND CONSULTING
TO APPLY TRADITIONAL VALUES APPROPRIATELY FOR THE TWENTY-
FIRST CENTURY

*LaDonna Harris, Stephen M. Sachs, Barbara Morris,
Deborah Esquibel Hunt, Gregory A. Cajete, Benjamin
Broome, Phyllis M. Gagnier, and Jondodev Chaudhuri*

Traditionally, leadership in American Indian society was largely a matter of inclusively facilitating the forming of community consensus while providing guidance for reinforcing traditional values and applying them in the current context.[1] Out of the core value of respect, leaders had responsibility to make sure that everyone's views were heard and, so far as practicable, included in finalizing decisions. To preserve respect for all and to keep decision making representative of the community, power was dispersed among a variety of leaders, who often could be changed with the shifting consensus of the populace. Additionally, because it was understood that everything is interrelated with and affects everything else, courses of action were considered holistically. The traditional forms of leadership and the processes through which they functioned varied from tribe to tribe. Within each tribe, leadership also changed over time to meet changing circumstances. The general nature of traditional Native American leadership, however, was virtually universal across North America, with some exceptions in those societies that grew large enough that they began to become states.

As a colonial power, the United States forced Indian nations to function with more fixed and central leaders who most often could respond only reactively to U.S. policy. Moreover, the federal bureaucracy, especially in the Bureau of Indian Affairs (BIA), forced tribal leaders to deal with policy issues narrowly, in isolation from their broader contexts. Although there was an advantage to centralizing leadership in order to deal with the colonizers, the imposed culturally inappropriate Western forms of governance, in which leaders decided for those who were used to participating in decision making, often became major sources of disharmony in Native communities.[2]

As Indian societies regain self-determination, external respect, and an appreciation for tribal sovereignty, we believe that it will be most helpful for them to return to more traditional modes of leadership, including being proactive and holistic in policy development. The career of LaDonna Harris (Comanche), founder of Americans for Indian Opportunity (AIO) and a major catalyst in the development of Indian affairs for four decades—whom *Ladies' Home Journal* in 1979 declared Woman of the Year and the Decade—is an excellent example of the kind of leadership and activism that is necessary to overcome the inequality imposed on Native peoples. By bringing parties together in an inclusive and respectful manner, she has facilitated major advances in Indian legislation and in developing government-to-government relations between tribal and other governments. By applying traditional values appropriately to new circumstances, she has sparked the development of Indian leadership and organization and collaborated with Native communities as they return to harmony through inclusive consensus building. Returning to traditional Indigenous leadership in the context of the twenty-first century is the focus of the first section of this chapter.

Similarly, those working with Indian nations as allies or consultants are most helpful when they act inclusively, as facilitators and resources. The history of failed programs being imposed on tribes is long. But when outside experts have collaborated with Indians in developing their own solutions, success has been far more frequent.[3] Appropriate consulting and collaboration with Indian nations is the main concern of the second section of this chapter. The third section of the chapter pulls together the strands that run through the entire book to form an overview of developments to date, of what still needs to be done to complete the circle of Native peoples, and of how this is relevant today to Native nations and the wider world.

1. Returning to Traditional Leadership in Indian Nations: The Example of LaDonna Harris

Stephen M. Sachs

LaDonna Harris, Comanche, founder and president of AIO, has been a strong voice for the advancement of all Native Americans for over four decades.[4] Her role in developing Native American leadership, improving tribal governance, and developing government-to-government relationships between tribal governments and federal, state, and local governments in the United States exemplifies the application of the traditional American Indian values of respect and inclusive participatory leadership appropriately to contemporary circumstances.

Raised during the Great Depression on a farm in the Comanche community around Walters, Oklahoma, by her maternal grandparents—an Eagle medicine man who also worked with peyote medicine and a devout Christian woman—Harris learned the traditional principles of relating to people on the basis of mutual respect and freedom of personal choice.[5] Combined with those traditional values, her bicultural upbringing—she spoke only Comanche at home while learning English and mainstream American ways at school—contributed to her developing an abiding belief that there is room for all traditions. Both by temperament and personal philosophy, following the traditional Comanche preference for collaborative endeavor, Harris strives to attain goals through focusing on the positive and by relating to others from the heart, although she can be tough when necessary.[6] Her heart energy is such, that when author Stephen Sachs first visited her home in Washington, D.C., for a gathering in 1991, he experienced so much warmth that he found it almost physically impossible to leave.

Organizing in Oklahoma: Founding OIO

LaDonna Harris first came into national prominence in 1963, when she began to organize Native Americans in western Oklahoma, following a meeting with members of the Southwest Center for Human Relations Studies at the University of Oklahoma. Starting with a meeting of Comanches in her living room, her organizing expanded to seven communities with assistance from the center faculty members. Angie Debo reported on one of these local efforts:

In Lawton a successful program was launched, mainly through the leadership of two gifted women of the Comanche tribe: Mrs. Iola Taylor, county home demonstration agent for Indian work, and Mrs. LaDonna Harris, the wife of the rising young politician Fred R. Harris.

The result of all this was a called meeting of Indians and non-Indians at the University [of Oklahoma] on June 14, 1965. It turned out to be the most important gathering of Oklahoma Indians since the last intertribal council met in 1888 to fight dissolution. Nineteen tribes were represented. They discussed their problems and organized a committee with Mrs. Harris (her husband was now in the [U.S.] Senate) serving as chairman. The Unity of the diverse tribes was "downright astounding," a Seminole participant reported; and looking back, the leaders agreed that it was largely due to the ability and enthusiasm of Mrs. Harris. Quickly she appointed key persons to report to their tribes, learn their wishes, and prepared an agenda for a statewide meeting.[7]

At that meeting, held at the university on August 7, 1965, with more than five hundred Native Americans attending, Oklahomans for Indian Opportunity (OIO) was formed as a nonprofit organization. Harris was elected president and a group of forty-one directors was selected "that reads like a roll call of Oklahoma tribes."[8] In a manner that has been typical of Harris's inclusive style, OIO, with Iola Taylor (now Iola Hayden) as full-time director, developed a network of community interests and relationships with existing agencies throughout the state to begin reversing the stifling socioeconomic conditions that were affecting Indian communities. With the help of an initial grant from the Office of Economic Opportunity, OIO put together an office and field staff (of people who lived in the areas they served) that grew with the expansion of its activities. OIO quickly developed projects in community development, which were carried out collaboratively at the grassroots level by Native and non-Native Americans; in work orientation, which connected Native Americans with employers for training and apprenticeships; and in youth development, which included a strong focus on helping Native American high school students acquire leadership character and skills, and on helping schools provide education in Native American heritage and history through such activities as supplying books to the libraries of public schools with large Native American enrollments.

With a strong traditional recognition that young people are the future, OIO undertook considerable effort in youth activities, including establishing statewide annual Indian Achievement Conferences. The first of these conferences was held in October 1966 with 750 Native Americans participating and Secretary of Health, Education, and Welfare (HEW) John W. Gardner as keynote speaker. Following OIO's philosophy of empowering Indians in their own self-development and individual achievement and building understanding and acceptance in the white-oriented community, the conference awarded individuals and the town that had done the most to involve Native Americans in community life. The following March, OIO produced the first of its annual Oklahoma Youth Conferences, in which one thousand students participated from forty high schools and Senator Robert Kennedy was the principal speaker. OIO continues to be active in Oklahoma today; its primary current focus is assisting individual Indians to develop their own business.

Harris continued to be reelected president of OIO each year. In 1968, she became chairwoman of the National Woman's Advisory Council of the War on Poverty. This was the first of several national bodies on which she served with distinction.[9]

On to D.C.: Work in the Johnson Administration

On arriving in Washington, D.C., Harris undertook considerable effort to advance the traditional principle that those who are affected by decisions should be involved in making them. Her method was to share views respectfully, clearly explaining the advantages to those concerned about a policy. When it was appropriate, she could express herself forcefully. Her style was to collaborate with others who were interested in an issue, drawing in the people who would support a coalition. Thus, with the collaboration of others, she succeeded in persuading President Johnson to establish the National Council on Indian Opportunity by executive order on March 6, 1968, to move American Indian policy forward in a coordinated manner with representative input from Indian nations. The council consisted of the vice president, then Hubert Humphrey, serving as chair, the six cabinet members whose departments were concerned with Indian land and people, the director of the Office of Economic Opportunity, six elected Native American chairmen, and Ms. Harris. Vice President Humphrey chaired the first meeting. Because of the tumultuous events that followed its establishment (including Robert Kennedy's entering the presidential race, Johnson's withdrawal from the race, President John F. Kennedy's assassination, and Humphrey's obtaining the Democratic Party's nomination for president), the council did not meet again when Richard Nixon became president. Because President Nixon agreed with President Johnson on the need to improve the lives of Native Americans through developing self-determination without fear of termination, he had promised the National Congress of American Indians (NCAI) during the election campaign that he would "fully support the National Council on Indian Opportunity."[10] However, "it was not activated until January 26, 1970, when Vice President Spiro Agnew called the first meeting at the angry insistence of Mrs. Harris."[11]

Facilitating the Progress on Indian Issues
Indeed, for a number of years, LaDonna Harris, working with a small group of American Indians that included Ada Deer (Menominee), Pat Locke (Yankton Sioux), Alma Patterson (Tuscarora), Minerva Jenkins (Mojave), Mary Jo Butterfield (Makah), Helen Sherbeck (Lumbee), and Lucy Covington (Colville), was able to keep Native American issues on the national agenda. This forward movement was supported by increased Native American political activity, an improving American Indian public image, favorable presidents, and the interest of some key members of Congress. In some of her activity, she partnered with her husband, U.S. Senator Fred Harris (among other milestones, she became the first senator's wife to testify before a congressional committee). For example, she helped achieve the return of Taos Blue Lake to the people of Taos Pueblo, helped obtain a settlement of Native Alaskan claims that was in line with the thinking of Native Alaskan leaders, and assisted in the return of federal recognition to the Menominee Tribe (which led to the end of the federal government's policy of tribal termination). More generally, she played an important role in guiding the development of virtually all the major Native American reform acts that passed Congress in the 1970s.

An important factor in Harris's success is her ability to bring together virtually all of the most important people, including representatives of all but the most extreme positions, to talk through an issue, and to help the parties to understand one another's concerns and reach at least something of an initial consensus for a policy proposal. That meant that Indian interests would have to compromise on some issues initially but had a fair chance of achieving what was important to them. Though later amendment by Congress or executive agencies would often reduce Indian gains, without the initial consensus building, in most cases, considerably less would have been achieved. Within the Indian community in Washington, Harris also played an important role in bringing together its members for gatherings on a regular basis. When Harris left the city, she was much missed as the hub of the Indian community.[12]

Working in the same way, LaDonna Harris has made a concerted effort to realize the development of true government-to-government relations between tribal governments and federal, state, and local governments (and agencies). This has included work to bring about institutional development to facilitate making Indian nations partners in federalism and day-by-day efforts to lift the consciousness and change the culture of policy makers. Concerning the federal government, it is significant that virtually every one of the structural innovations that have been undertaken since 1968 to improve coordination of federal Indian programs and decentralize government functions to empowered tribal governments had been previously advocated by Harris (although the results have often been somewhat less than what she was striving for). These innovations include the initiation of American Indian advisory committees in federal agencies under President Johnson; the establishment of Indian Desks in agencies that interact with the tribes under President Nixon; and the establishment of annual meetings at the White House with tribal leaders, the creation of an interagency working group with representation in the White House Office of Intergovernmental Relations, and extensive decentralization of Indian programs to tribal governments under President Clinton. Moreover, she was instrumental in the adoption of government-to-government–oriented official Indian policies by the Environmental Protection Agency (EPA), the Department of Energy (DOE), and the Department of Agriculture. Thus, she has played a major role in the slow evolution from the paternalistic virtual-monopoly control of Indian programs by the Department of the Interior (prior to the New Deal reform efforts lead by John Collier from 1933 to 1945) to a partnership in federalism that is considerably improved, but not yet fully achieved, today.

Acting with Traditional Understanding of Uncertainty amid Complexity

One aspect of traditional inclusiveness that has marked Harris's approach to leadership is the long-held Indigenous view, similar to contemporary chaos and complexity theory, that in a complex world of considerable uncertainty, one is wise to create and keep as many friends and allies as possible in the short run, while looking for opportunities to move toward long-term goals as they arise.[13] This involves the view that small, timely changes can have large effects and that one can be effective by looking for moments of opportunity and acting properly in them when they arise. Thus Harris was able to build upon her position as wife and political ally of Oklahoma senator Fred Harris and upon her inclusiveness and ability to sense developing relations and circumstances—and how they relate to long-term goals—to facilitate effectively among and for Indians on many issues in the federal government and to continue to do the same in many other contexts afterward. As she interacted in her naturally and tradition-ally nurtured friendly way, she noted people with skills and resources she could later call on, when they could be most helpful. For instance, Harris related to author Stephen Sachs that when Oklahoma politics pre-vented OIO from receiving funding for one of its first projects through the University of Oklahoma, OIO found a faculty group at an out-of-state university that would and did obtain a grant for the work.

This traditional approach to leadership, which emphasizes main-taining a view of the big picture while remaining firmly grounded in the situation of the current moment—requiring a deft sense of timing and openness to finding creative solutions—has made many contempo-rary Indian leaders extremely effective. Vine Deloria, for example, while president of NCAI and in other positions, was able to seize the moment when necessary to suggest to a member of Congress that a small but important change—such as adding "and Indian Tribes" after "authoriz-ing States"—be placed in a bill when there was no opposition to the pro-posal. Particularly to the point, Deloria stated that it was not a bad thing being a "token Indian," if one remembered who one was. As the sole Native American for several years on the board of what later became the National Museum of the American Indian, Deloria saw that a moment of opportunity existed during a board meeting just before a press con-ference launching an important exhibit opening. Seizing this moment enabled him to force the appointment of more Indians to the board—under threat of embarrassing the board with a statement at the press con-ference—with backing from other Native leaders who were prepared to publicly support his statement. That began the turnover of board mem-bers that soon brought Native people into the majority, setting the stage for the eventual development of the national museum.

This kind of incisive leadership, of taking the long view while acting knowledgably in the present, is not only a proper approach for Indian leaders but would be quite helpful in the mainstream, as well. A good case can be made that President George W. Bush and his advisor Carl Rove made impressive initial gains for the Republican Party by dividing people but in the longer term greatly weakened the party, contributing significantly to its major losses in the 2006 and 2008 national elections.

Developing AIO

The primary vehicle for LaDonna Harris's work after her first coming to Washington, D.C., has been AIO, which she founded in 1970 and for which she continues to serve as president. Since its inception, AIO has been engaged in a wide variety of activities and a series of projects in a number of fields to enhance the cultural, social, political, and economic self-sufficiency of tribes. These efforts include working to strengthen tribal governance, promoting the rise of government-to-government relations, and nurturing up-and-coming Native American leaders.

In all of this, AIO has served as a catalyst for new concepts and opportunities for Indian people. In working to strengthen tribal governance, Harris and AIO have collaborated directly with the Winnebago, Poarch Band Creek, Cheyenne-Arapaho, Comanche, and Menominee tribes. AIO has assisted these nations in assessing how they can reincorporate traditional dispute-resolution methodologies and methods for building community consensus and harmony into contemporary tribal government. The Indigenous Leadership Interactive System (ILIS) was developed for this purpose by AIO in collaboration with Alexander Christakis of George Mason University.[14] Harris and AIO have found ILIS to be a useful procedure for considering complex issues with tribal people in the United States and internationally. For example, in May 2003, AIO facilitated an inclusive participatory ILIS forum for the United Nations of All Tribes Foundation conference, Strengthening Children and Families: Networking Urban Indian Centers in the U.S., in Seattle. Similarly, the process was used for Indigenous meetings in Bolivia in October 2007, and in Japan in July 2008.[15]

Working on a Variety of Projects in Numerous Contexts to Move Forward on Basic Goals

In the course of working to make tribal governments equal partners in American federalism, AIO, under Harris's leadership, has conducted hundreds of forums and workshops, from small meetings to large national and international conferences; published a number of significant papers; and engaged in several important projects.[16] For example, to assist the EPA in developing tribal government capability to operate environmental protection programs, AIO first engaged in the Messing with Mother Nature Project to comprehensively assess the environmental problems and concerns of federally recognized tribes in the United States. AIO then undertook To Govern or Be Governed: American Indian Tribes at the Crossroads (known as the Governance Project) to assist tribal governments in developing their capability to improve their own policies and run their own programs so as to act as effective partners with the EPA and other federal agencies.[17] In helping tribes plan for the future, AIO has created INDIANnet, the first Indian-owned and operated computer telecommunications network, which is dedicated to establishing and developing free public access and communication services for Native Americans, and which is now a part of Native American Communications.

The Ambassadors Program

AIO's leadership development efforts have been carried out primarily through the vehicle of its American Indian Ambassadors Program. Medicine Pathways to the Future is an example of one program sponsored by the Ambassadors Program that brings young Americans Indians together to learn to use traditional tribal values in a contemporary setting. Participating in decision making by using the ILIS process and following traditional inclusionary principles, Ambassadors Program alumni continue to be involved in an active network and to participate in ILIS-process discussions of new directions for AIO and of how best to approach broader Indian concerns. Because there are now Ambassador Program alumni in every major national Indian organization and every federal agency that deals significantly with Indians and Indian issues, this network and discussion process have been valuable communication resources for Indian country. Sharing information and ideas beyond one's immediate organization applies the traditional value of generosity as an aspect of collaboration for the general good. It also applies the idea that the long-run results are better for all if reciprocity is maintained through mutual give-and-take, rather than through marketplace competition.

Broader Projects

In the course of working on a variety of Native American concerns, Harris and AIO have launched a number of other national Native American organizations. These include the National American Indian Housing Council, the Council of Energy Resource Tribes (CERT), the National Tribal Environmental Council, and the National Indian Business Association.

In addition, Ms. Harris is an active participant in the broader civil rights, environmental, women's, and world peace movements. One of OIO's first projects in the 1960s was cooperating with African American organizations to integrate Oklahoma. As the vice presidential candidate on the Citizens Party Ticket with Barry Commoner in 1980, she collaborated in making environmental issues a permanent area of major concern in presidential election campaigns. She was a founding member of Common Cause and the National Urban Coalition and has served on many national boards and advisory committees.[18] Harris's breadth of concern for and collaboration with a wide variety of organizations and efforts is part of a traditional, holistic tribal outlook that understands that everything is related and places one's own interests in the context of the long term, over which one gains the most through fostering collaboration and supporting others' goals whenever it is possible to do so.

Harris's work has extended to the international arena. She was an original member of the Global Tomorrow Coalition and served as U.S. representative to the Organization of the American States Inter-American Indian Institute. More recently, she has been a member of the board of Women for Meaningful Summits. Currently, she is engaged in developing Advancement of Global Indigeneity as a networking vehicle for international indigenous cooperation for improving the globalization process for the benefit of all peoples. Advancement of Global Indigeneity held its first board meeting in Crete in July 2003 in conjunction with its founding organizations, AIO and Advancement of Maori Opportunity, and participated in the Agoras of the Global Village annual conference of the International Society for Systems Sciences. During the conference, AIO and Advancement of Maori Opportunity facilitated the indigenous Wisdom of the People Forum by using the ILIS process. In recognition of her far-reaching contributions, *Ladies' Home Journal* declared LaDonna Harris "Woman of the Year and the Decade" in 1979.[19]

For almost four decades, LaDonna Harris has been, as she continues to be, an amazing activist of the heart, demonstrating that traditional inclusive and collaborative ways of relating are especially appropriate in the contemporary world. Her compassion, vision, and sense of justice have gifted us with a deeper and richer understanding of the true meaning of public service. She is helping the world to see that traditional tribal ways need to be integrated with modern technologies if all the people of this planet are to survive and prosper as we enter the new millennium. In so doing, she has provided an excellent model for contemporary American Indian leadership.

2. Facilitators and Resource Persons for the People: Consulting with Indian Nations as Collaborators
Stephen M. Sachs and Deborah Esquibel Hunt

Indian nations currently are struggling to return to harmony by replacing culturally inappropriate forms of tribal government imposed by the U.S. government with culturally appropriate government forms and processes.[20] Indeed, as we discussed in chapters 2 and 3, from the late nineteenth century to the 1930s, the thrust of U.S. Indian policy was to attempt to force culturally inappropriate polices on Indians in the hope of assimilating them into the mainstream culture.[21] That entire set of policies was a failure.[22] Indians were not assimilated but rather were forced into extreme poverty and suffered considerable, still often unresolved, historical grief, as the Meriam Report pointed out in 1928.[23]

Although U.S. policy toward Indian nations has improved since 1928, most notably since the current policy of Indian self-determination was instituted in the 1970s, many programs and initiatives continued to be largely imposed and hence were not effective. This has particularly been the case with economic development. In this field, the results have been disappointing, except where Indians have had a large say in their own development. One exception is the establishment of casinos, which have not always been designed and managed in culturally appropriate ways but typically still have been profitable. Even with tribal casinos, the operations have run more effectively when managed by Indians or in consultation with tribal personnel. For tribes with self-directed economic development, the results have not only consisted of increased income, but have also included improvement in services, education, employment, and other aspects of social well-being.[24] Similarly, as we developed more fully in chapter 5, when Indian nations have been able to run their own social service programs, the programs have become far more effective, particularly in overcoming the difficulties created by outside providers who ran health, education, substance abuse, and other service programs in ways that conflicted with tribal culture.

So it is that the ineffectiveness of imposed forms of tribal governance along with the accompanying decrease in individual political power are major contributors to the serious economic and social problems that beset Indian reservations, including underdevelopment, high unemployment, poverty, extremely high rates of suicide, drug and alcohol abuse, and various forms of violent behavior.

As a result of this history, a major concern for Indian nations today is how to return tribal governments to operating according to their own traditional values, applied appropriately for contemporary circumstances. There are three interrelated aspects to this concern. First is finding ways to return tribal decision making to a participatory process that is inclusive and respectful and that fits the particular culture and situation of each Indian nation. Second is insuring that programs function appropriately for tribal people, both in terms of their goals and in the way in which tribal agencies and personnel interact with tribal members. Third is developing programs holistically, so that they take into account the full range of tribal needs over time while providing interactive coordination of projects and their administration, in order to keep all aspects of development in balance. In all of these undertakings, an essential factor is that although Indian nations have a common set of core values, each nation has its own specific culture and ways of applying those values.[25] To be effective, social science and academic professionals, whether tribal members or outsiders, who are invited to collaborate with Indian nations in efforts to strengthen tribal sovereignty and community well-being, must be prepared to work in culturally responsive ways.

Appropriate Consulting in Collaboration with Indian Nations

Recent experience has begun to demonstrate that Indian nations can benefit from consulting with appropriate external experts. Appropriate consulting (and provision of services) involves respectful collaboration with equals to facilitate attaining their goals in ways they find culturally harmonious. It also depends on collaborators being aware of a nation's history and culture and on listening carefully and speaking in a supportive manner to assist tribal participants to draw on their own strength and knowledge. When this is accomplished, trust can be facilitated, and other useful information and networking can be provided. A crucial element of appropriate consultation is helping Indian people to take ownership of the project so that as early as practicable, the consultant is no longer needed. On some occasions, consultants have asked representatives of tribal governments whether the tribe had the capability to handle the project on its own, which, on reflection, was found to be the case. When consultants keep tribal self-direction at the heart of the process, true empowerment occurs. Some may argue that using outside consultants undermines tribal sovereignty. This is effectively the case when nations give their power away by doing what outsiders (or a narrow group of tribal members) tell them to do, without inclusively reflecting on the courses of action given to them, making sure that what is proposed really is in the long-term tribal interest. But whenever experts or consultants, whether internal or external, are employed in a way that empowers the nation to make its own decisions more knowledgably or in a better way, tribal sovereignty is increased.

The goal of all culturally responsive work is to support empowerment. In the broadest sense, empowerment is defined as "increasing personal, interpersonal or political power so that individuals, families and communities can take action to change their situations."[26] For that change to be beneficial, the process of deciding what is to be done needs to take into account the full range of relevant community needs and concerns, both at the moment and for the future. Each project that is undertaken needs to fit appropriately into the larger set of goals and be administered to harmonize with the rest of the nation's undertakings. Thus, good consultants, and those who employ them, will question how a particular project best fits into the whole of the tribe's vision and activities.

Assumptions, Attitudes, and Skills for Empowerment

A number of assumptions, attitudes, and skills are necessary for empowerment. The first assumption is that oppression is destructive to the whole. In the Native way, everything is related. The pain of one is the pain of all. All humanity shares common ground and has common needs. Therefore, we need one another to attain empowerment. In other words, both the oppressor and the oppressed are afflicted and bound when any person is unable to have a reasonable degree of direction over her or his own daily life. In healing oppression, relationships must be based on equality and mutual respect. This respect is reflected in the attitude that people empower themselves. Therefore, people must define their own reality, in their own terms and language. Problems must be articulated and solutions must be designed by those most directly affected by the situations at hand.[27]

The interaction of personal and political realities affects individual relationships, community relationships, and relationships between the community and the outside political and social environments. On a personal and community level, empowerment requires a particular consciousness. For Native people and communities, this consciousness includes an awareness of the effects of colonization and historical trauma.[28] When one is aware of one's own history and remembers the pain and grieves for the losses, it is possible to reduce self-blame by normalizing and validating one's responses to trauma.[29] Community and self-empowerment can be enhanced by assuming responsibility for change, thereby increasing confidence and skill.[30] Self-aware and responsible partners in the political process of change can help to realistically assess the opportunities and barriers in external and internal social structures. Proactive advocacy by people who display sovereign confidence is more likely to affect and modify social structures to reallocate power and resources.[31] Control of power and resources must return to the hands of Indigenous people on their own terms for true sovereignty to be realized.

Current empowerment concerns in Indian nations include strengthening sovereignty and increasing self-determination. This is particularly true in the era of devolution and decentralization of programs and funding to states, counties, and tribes. The challenge for Indian nations is to restore harmony and balance from within while simultaneously building government-to-government relations with states and local entities. Culturally competent consultants can help facilitate the achievement of these relationships that call for increasing mutual respect. No matter what the consulting or provision of services involves, consultants can be helpful in maintaining, if not increasing, sovereignty and self-determination by functioning in a culturally conscious and empowering manner.

The Importance of Building Trust

It is important to realize that building relationships requires trust, and that takes time to accomplish. An essential requirement for non-Native consultants is an understanding of the history of betrayal of Indian nations by the U.S. federal government and the culturally inappropriate way in which many, even well-meaning, non-Indian individuals and institutions have interacted with Native people and peoples. History is the foundation for what people believe to be possible in future relations. If outside governments, economic-development interests, service providers, and consultants truly wish to work with Indian people, it is important for them to truly listen for understanding regarding the hurt, distrust, and anger over past efforts to destroy Native people and culture and the ongoing lived experience of racism. Whenever possible, governments need to reconcile past hurts with sincere apologies, and nongovernment people and organizations need to act with compassionate understanding. It is really all right to say, in effect, "What happened was not right. The U.S. federal government was dishonorable in its approach to the Indigenous people of this land." It is good to express sincere regret for the actions of one's ancestors and bring one's own heart into a humble and empathetic place. In working responsively with traumatic histories, validating the grief is essential.

The importance of understanding colonialism cannot be overemphasized in culturally responsive work with American Indian people. Colonialism is based on the notion of racial superiority, as in the belief in Manifest Destiny. Colonialism requires political, economic, and social domination of one group by another. This is acted out through deliberate exploitation, oppression, and control. The mechanisms of control are prejudice and discrimination, dehumanization, and blaming the victim. One of the marks of a colonized people is internalized shame and negative self-image, hopelessness and powerlessness and internalizing the characteristics of the oppressor. Sadly, in all oppressed groups is seen the phenomenon of the "oppressed become the oppressor," whereby oppressed persons commit crimes against members of their own group and work to keep their own people down.[32] The goal of colonialism is complete cultural genocide and assimilation of the natives into the dominating culture. To accomplish this end, history belongs to the colonizer. Thus, not only do the descendants of the colonizer fail to recognize their ancestral "karma" in the perpetuation of oppression, but the oppressed are denied access to the reason for their grief.

Each tribe has a unique experience with European colonizers and with the evolving policy positions of the U.S. government. Therefore, consultants from outside the nation should also actively learn about tribal history before and after first contact.[33]

Fortunately, a passionate renaissance of traditional values and methods of governance is emerging in Indigenous nations. This resurgence of cultural strength is bolstered by a growth in opportunities for Native nations to administer their own programs under federal devolution, increasing economic development that is culturally appropriate, and a movement toward government reform that is more responsive to the people. Culturally aware, sensitive, and responsive consultants are playing a vital role in this movement.

In summary, consultants can be most helpful when they are prepared to collaborate with tribes for optimal empowerment. A humble heart and mind is aware of a people's historical trauma and oppression. Really listening without interrupting or interpreting allows trust to develop, especially when the strengths and resiliency in survival are validated. It is extremely important to recognize levels of power and privilege and the ongoing effects of racism and living on the margins of power. When the consultant is of European ancestry, it is important to acknowledge that privileges exist and that he or she does not share certain experiences that tribal community members have undergone. Not only does trust take time, an open heart and mind, humility, and self-awareness, but it also takes keeping commitments and investing for the long term. It means making lifetime relationships. It means "working to dismantle structures of inequality."[34] It means being willing to be tested on that commitment by the community the consultant wishes to serve.[35]

Cases of Collaboration in Returning Indian Governance to the Wisdom of the People

Three useful cases illustrate the application of traditional participatory and inclusive values based upon mutual respect in ways that are appropriate for the current, developing situation of the Indian nation concerned. The three Indian nations involved are the Comanche Nation of Oklahoma (and several other Oklahoma tribes), the Navajo Nation, and the Southern Ute Indian Tribe. The first case involves the Comanche Nation's use of ILIS.[36] The appropriateness of ILIS as a process for tribal decision making began with its development. AIO selected consultants who were sensitive to the need to adapt any intervention method to the culture and requirements of the people involved, and who were working with an interactive strategic planning process that was consistent with Indian values and a good fit with the situations of many Indian tribes at that time. The existing process was then refined over two years to make it a good vehicle for Indians in general. Then, when the process was applied, ILIS was specifically adapted for the people who would be working with it.

The strengths of ILIS for Indian people include its mirroring of traditional participatory decision making in honoring the concerns of all participants. As is traditional, in ILIS, the group sits in a circle, and each person has the chance to speak and have a say in whatever is decided. ILIS is organized to build the competence of the participants to solve complex problems collaboratively as they work through their own community's concerns. This is particularly important in returning people to trusting one another and themselves to work together communally in societies that have been fractured by the destruction of harmonizing and interactive consensus-building mechanisms. Moreover, ILIS allows Indian people to deal holistically and on their own terms, as is traditional, with the full range of often very complex problems confronting them as they build their own future. Thus, ILIS is not based on the consultant's values, as happens too often in interventions, or limited to deal only with narrow concerns, which would be insufficient to empower the community to reach and resolve the fundamental complex of problems that blocks its progress.[37] Rather, ILIS is designed to aid participants with diverse viewpoints to get below the symptoms at the surface of discussion to explore the deeper logic of issues, thereby enabling a tribe to create a vision of its own future and then empower itself to embody that vision.

Functioning Consistently with Tribal Social Relations

One of the strengths of ILIS for tribal use, both structurally and procedurally, is that it functions consistently with the psychology and cultural manifestations of tribal social relations. A number of mechanisms are built into the process that recognize the crucial role tribal identity and tribal values can play in discovering new ways out of complex and deeply rooted problems. This begins with the opening of an ILIS session with a locally appropriate tribal ceremony. Other practices are added that are important in the specific culture of the participants and that enhance the strengthening of tribal identity. Practices that have been used, when appropriate, include gift giving, blessings, pipe ceremonies, and prayers that draw the attention of tribal participants to the richness of their common bond. Following the tradition of sitting in a circle equalizes the participants in the discussion.

In addition, the bonding necessary for a successful process is often enhanced by calling on each participant to track her or his kinship ties to the rest of the group, since tribal cultures heavily emphasize kinship relations. Cross-links between individuals and their inherent relational obligations immediately begin drawing the group together and help make tribal values and identity the focus of the group's attention. Often, the strongest component of the tribal vision statement that the process develops is the continuation of "the people." Group identity is synonymous with being tribal, and where group identity is strong, preserving the group and its value system becomes all-important. The reiteration of kinship terms calls forth those values and practices that set the group apart and immediately bonds the group around a common cause.

Furthermore, participants are often asked to express what being a member of the tribe means to them, which brings forth a deep affirmation of cultural values that are commonly expressed subliminally. These values, if captured and clarified, become a useful reference point during all the subsequent steps of the process. In ILIS sessions, as much as one-third of the time spent together is dedicated to these preliminary activities whose chief function is to bind the participants together into a single collaborative group. This percentage of time is far greater than is the practice with other issue-management models, but it provides extremely crucial groundwork in most Indian settings. It tends to create a spirit of optimism about the potential for overcoming the immediate set of problems, given all that the participants and the Indian nation have overcome in the past. These bonding activities are implemented at the beginning of the process but, even more importantly, before the potentially controversial period of generating options for dealing with problems that the group has identified.

Giving Everyone a Chance to Express Her or His Views Prior to Discussion

It is also important that ILIS forums develop the issues to be considered and give all participants an opportunity to voice their views as to what these issues are, then record and prominently post the individual views before discussion of possible solutions begins. This process takes account of the fact that in many tribes, much of the discussion that takes place during the early stages of public meetings involves a strategy by various participants to position themselves and establish a role in the group. This is partly a reflection of the importance of honor and of the relational sense of identity of traditional tribal cultures. It is also a reflection of the importance of feeling in Native American cultures and of the fact that many people feel strongly about the issues under consideration (or the background concerns related to the discussion). Thus ILIS provides an often necessary opportunity for participants to vent their feelings and establish their place in the dialogue, opening the way for them to engage in open discussion and consensus building. Having their views honored in their initial contributions and included in the later consideration of issues frees Native participants to go beyond their first expressions and join in consensus building. So it is, that instead of emphasizing Western conceptions of time and efficiency and winning and losing, its creators designed ILIS to meet the Native need to develop relationships prior to, and as a basis for, truly collaborative decision making.

Appropriately Facilitating the Process

The application of ILIS and the facilitation of the process with the Oklahoma Comanches were carried out quite appropriately. From the very beginning, the outside consultants made clear that their function was to collaborate for the benefit of the entire tribe and not just for the interest of the Comanche Business Committee members, even as they obtained the invitation of the committee and the tribal chairman, which was necessary to legitimize the process. In setting up each of the tribal-level sessions, care was taken to include representatives of all the major groups in the communities. Since the Comanches live primarily in four towns, once the tribal level process was functioning, each of the localities set up its own meetings, and discussion of issues went back and forth between the tribal and community levels. The regular ILIS sessions required a computer and trained operator to map the decision making. This technology was not always readily available to each of the localities, so these communities adapted the process so that it would function well without computer mapping but would still maintain the same participatory consensus-building principles.

The facilitation of the sessions seems to have been quite good in providing necessary education in the process and enough appropriate neutral intervention to keep the sessions moving well without being overbearing. Moreover, Comanche facilitators were trained early on, so that the nation could take over the process. Also extremely helpful to the Comanches in making the process their own and ensuring that the sessions developed well in accordance with Comanche culture was the facilitation by traditional community leaders, who provided a historical overview and reminded the participants of tribal values at key points in the dialogue, consistent with the traditional practice of elders exhorting fellow Comanches to act properly. In addition, care was taken to have the central, "triggering" questions for each meeting thoughtfully selected by the Comanches.

Evaluation and Feedback

Finally, the process was evaluated by the participants at the completion of each session, and the feedback was employed to make it function better. For example, participants in the first session commented that when breakout groups returned to share their ideas with the entire meeting, they did so one group at a time. Since several groups often came up with the same ideas, those who reported first appeared to receive more of the credit for the ideas and to be making a larger contribution to planning for the future of the tribe. Following the participants' suggestions, a greater sense of equality of participation was achieved by having each group in turn present one of its ideas and continuing in that fashion until all the thoughts had been offered. In addition, as each idea was presented, the facilitators asked whether other groups had produced the same thought, so that no matter who voiced an idea first, each person's effort was equally honored.

The Results of the Process

The results of the 1990–1992 launching and incubating of the Comanche ILIS process showed its introduction to be a valuable collaboration. A number of important tribal and community projects were initiated, and in June 1992, the four communities formalized the two-level ILIS process in the "Comanche Community Participation Units Articles of Voluntary Association," which was officially made part of the tribal governance process in a resolution of the Comanche Business Committee of July 11, 1992. Those who participated in the Comanche ILIS meetings were unanimous in their enthusiasm for returning to inclusive consensus decision making.[38]

The broader impacts of the return to consensus decision making were considerable for the Comanche. Factional fighting declined and relations in the nation improved. Political processes became more harmonious and efficient. The annual meeting of the people, Comanche Tribal Council, was better attended than it had been for many years, and for the first time in a decade, a tribal chair was reelected. Meanwhile, proposals that had been developed through the participatory discussion process, having gained a broad consensus, easily passed the Business Committee, whereas those that had not been taken up by the nation typically continued to fail to pass, regardless of their merits, for lack of consensus.

Overall, the design and carrying out of the ILIS process over three years was a fine example of appropriate consulting. It was a collaboration with Indian people that fit their values and needs, functioning very well in producing important direct and secondary positive results. The project created only a few relatively minor problems, which inevitably occur in the course of any action for change, and these difficulties were success-fully overcome.[39] However, even the best and most needed social inno-vation is difficult to achieve in a single effort. The external consultants clearly worked well with the Comanches, enabling them to take over the process while continuing to support its development until it was fully established. However, a new tribal chair, elected after the establishment of the Comanche ILIS process, did not appreciate the process and discon-tinued the consensus-building dialogues. This returned the Comanches to political infighting, which included causing difficulties for the tribal chair. Although the localities continued to use their version of ILIS for some time—three of them were still doing so as of 2002—Comanche community participation had not functioned long enough to gain the needed support for reinstituting ILIS at the tribal level. If, as the authors of this book believe, returning to appropriate forms of participatory con-sensus building is timely for Native peoples, it is hoped that the success-ful, though short-lived, Comanche experience with one form of inclusive participation will be an illuminating forerunner for future development, as has occurred in the unfolding of other forms of participation.[40]

Decentralization at Navajo Nation

The Navajo Nation has been working continuously to decentralize power to its 110 local chapters, with the goal of improving the quality of political discourse and decision making by developing ways of proceeding appro-priately in communities whose people have varying levels of traditional and adaptive culture. Spread over three states—Arizona, New Mexico, and Utah—the Navajo Nation is the largest Indian tribe in the United States both in terms of population and geographical reach. Traditionally, the Diné, whom the Spanish during their conquest of North America in the seventeenth century named "Navajo," lived in widely dispersed autonomous bands. Their decision making was extremely democratic and based on consensus. This was often achieved through extensive network-ing discussions in which families and clans played a major role. Bands often cooperated with one another because they were relatives and allies, but they had no overarching government.[41] Living across a wide expanse where they interacted with different peoples, the Diné developed a degree of cultural diversity, although they shared a core culture and identity.

Over time, in response to pressure from the U.S. government and mainstream society, the Navajo Nation developed a tightly centralized government of three branches that mirrors the U.S. government and created 110 chapters that provide local governance. This government system, although it is now familiar, does not fit Diné tradition and has been very bureaucratic, slow, and unwieldy, and the national government is often isolated from many local people. For a number of years, partly in response to local and popular expressions of concern, the Navajo Nation has been working to improve its government system, and the Office of Navajo Government Development has assisted the national legislature to design change while facilitating implementation on various levels. As with virtually all Indian nations, the process of creating appropriate government processes in the wake of the cultural devastation of the past several centuries has been complex and is not a simple matter of restoring the old ways. The conditions of life and governing have changed substantially, and the culture has become more diverse as Navajo people have responded, in different ways and to different degrees, to contact with other cultures. Thus, there is disagreement about just what is traditional, as well as over what aspects of tradition to apply now and how to implement them in current circumstances.

Consulting to Increase Sovereignty and Participation

Consistent with the practical, political, and psychological need to be sovereign and self-determining, the Navajo Nation has been independently undertaking the work of government improvement and has attempted to be responsive and inclusive in the course of redeveloping the tradition of participatory governance. There has been some place for external consultants in this process, and author Stephen Sachs has collaborated with the Office of Navajo Government Development on some matters.[42]

The office first assisted the Navajo legislature in preparing measures to decentralize many government functions to the chapters. When this was achieved with the passage of the Navajo Nation Local Governance Act (26 N.N.C.) in 1998, the office began working on ways to help chapters improve their decision-making process because some chapters ran very well, with strong community participation, but others did not. In addition, the office has been engaged in helping develop ways to make the national Navajo government operate less bureaucratically and with more citizen participation. All of this work has involved research into Diné traditional ways, current conditions, and the experiences of other Indian nations, including discussions with elders and traditional medicine people (some of whom are directly involved in the work), national government leaders, chapter leaders, and a sampling of Navajo people.

Some of the discussions with Navajo people have been done in focus groups. The process is a continuing one, and the Navajo legislature has passed new legislation and amendments and taken advice from the Office of Navajo Government Development, other Diné executive agencies, the chapters, and the Diné public to meet problems in realizing the decentralization. For example, it has been found necessary to adjust accounting procedures and rules to empower chapters—some of which have very small staffs and little government fiscal experience—to become certified to receive discretionary funding for self-governance, while ensuring fiscal competence and accountability.

Meanwhile, the leadership program at Diné College has assisted implementation by working with individual chapters on improving their community discussion and decision making and by teaching Diné philosophy. The outside consultants have collaborated with the office and the leadership program, joining in brainstorming sessions, sharing information and the experiences of other Indian nations and available resources, and raising concerns about questions that seem important for the Diné to consider. In a few instances, it has been useful to rely on outside experts to provide technical assistance or to provide specific pieces of the training process. However, this has been done only when the outside providers have been willing and able to do so appropriately for the specific situation and culture of Navajo Nation and its chapters.

Making Sure Consultants Really Are Functioning Appropriately
Making sure that external consultants and technical experts really are oriented toward the needs and wishes of the nation often takes vigilance and effort by tribal officials. Indeed, it is a too-common occurrence, in all settings, that many consultants become overly focused on their own agendas and do not take sufficient note of the realities of the particular circumstances in which they are working or of the needs, wishes, and values of their clients. A common difficulty is for consultants to be overly concerned about what worked well in another setting or about theory that developed under circumstances that may not be the same as those of the current situation. Thus it is critical that outside experts observe and listen well, check and double-check that they understand the goals and observations of those they are working with, and continually review that the project is developing well in accordance with the clients' goals, with willingness to make adjustments in dialogue with those with whom they are collaborating.[43]

The Design Process at Southern Ute

In the late 1990s, the Southern Ute Indian Tribe of southwest Colorado began a return to inclusive and cooperative governance by augmenting general quarterly meetings with monthly tribal forums. This was followed by the introduction of monthly opportunities for tribal members with concerns or complaints about tribal government or services to meet individually with the tribal council. Then, in 1999, the Southern Utes became the first Indian nation to participate in a project funded by the U.S. Department of Health and Human Services (HHS) Children's Bureau. At the request of the tribal chair and council, a consulting team from the Social Research Institute at the University of Utah was asked to help facilitate the Southern Ute Design Team. This project allowed the tribe to create a community collaboration to build teamwork and coordinate programs among their social service agencies. The intent was to overcome the narrow focus of individual agencies that often failed to meet the full range of needs of those they served, and sometimes took conflicting actions. Professionals and administrators, community consultants who were former service recipients, and elders worked to fulfill their self-defined mission "[t]o provide culturally relevant, supportive and integrated services to insure that all Southern Ute children are successful in school and in life."

The Design Team has helped the community to redefine and embrace a vision of healing. Given all that has been said about postcolonial dynamics of disharmony, the commitment, courage, honesty, and energy witnessed by the facilitators has been truly inspirational. According to one facilitator, "setbacks, disappointment and criticism are balanced by a passion for creating a better future for the tribe's children."[44]

The design project was organized so that it would be carried out on a regular basis by the Utes. The external consulting team facilitated the organization of the process at its inception, sharing professional expertise as part of the dialogue leading to decisions by the local community participants. Then, for over a year, the facilitating team returned to moderate monthly meetings in which they could collaborate in the development of the project by raising important issues and sharing concerns and information that the Ute team could take into account as it moved the process forward. By being involved at frequent regular intervals over an extended period, the consultants provided a supportive incubation period during which the Utes could firmly establish their interagency collaboration.

Consulting as Collaboration

As the American Indian experience makes clear, participation by outside experts in institutional and process development can be helpful only when such participation is undertaken as a true collaboration in which the outside consultants serve knowledgeably and appropriately as resource people for their partners. This means that consultants must understand the history, culture, and situation of their clients and act to empower by carefully listening to and speaking directly to the needs of their clients.[45] Because innovations can be effective only when they are compatible with the system they are being applied to or developed for, they must be adapted to the situation and culture of the users in ways by which the users can take ownership of them for their own purposes. Thus, the job of consultants is to collaborate in facilitating their partner's process of becoming more fully who they already are.

Unfortunately, too often consultants around the world do not operate in a collaborative manner. In far too many instances, consultants simply take what has worked in one location and attempt to apply it in another without adequate (if any) adaptation. Because every community has its own subculture and conditions, the "canned" approach often creates problems when consultants work in their own culture. But when external experts go to other cultures, these problems are compounded. Moreover, in far too many instances, consultants merely assume that they know what the needs and wants are of the people on whose behalf they are intervening, and they are often mistaken, leading to very inappropriate interventions. In too many instances, outside specialists come with little or no preparation in the needs and conditions of the location in which they are working, undertake the intervention quickly, and then go away, leaving it to the people who were supposed to be helped to try and make an ill-fitting program work as best they can. This is a worldwide difficulty, and some very fine people in organizational development and related fields call for interventions to be done appropriately and collaboratively, as has been undertaken in the Indian cases presented here. Indeed, it would behoove all who attempt to consult to take an Indigenous perspective: to look at situations and issues holistically to understand all the factors and relationships that are involved, take the time to closely observe before acting, include the views of all concerned, consider the long-term effects before acting, and because the world is sufficiently complex and changing that not all outcomes can be known, give time for processes to be fully established and adjusted while providing for ongoing review to make changes for shifting circumstances.

Returning to the Traditional Wisdom of the People in Facilitating the Progress of Indian Nations in the Twenty-First Century

It is clear that both internal leaders and outside consultants and experts need to act as collaborating facilitators and resource sharers in cooperative decision-making partnerships if Indian nations and their citizens are to be successful in returning to effective sovereignty, self-sufficiency, and harmony. It has been shown that traditional values centered on mutual respect, which require that everyone affected by a decision have a say in it, are still widely held in most Native American communities. Enacting these values requires processes that, regardless of their specific forms, build community consensus inclusively in some version of a participatory manner that fits the culture and circumstances of the people involved. Participation in deciding about community affairs cannot function effectively unless leaders and experts act in a participatory way that retains the respect of the members of the community. Indeed, as the Comanche experience with the ILIS process demonstrates, leadership in the form of good facilitation that keeps the process of community discussion and decision making participatory and reminds participants to function with respect is necessary for the dialoguing process to function in a positive way. If the members of a community are to really hear one another and take one another's views into account, their leaders need to be able to function in just that manner. To the extent that leaders listen accurately and compassionately, speak knowledgably of the circumstances and issues, and speak consistently with the values of the community, they can have an effective positive influence as advisors to the people. It is also helpful if leaders remind the people to view issues holistically and are prepared to act proactively. The same can be said of those who act as advisors to the people in sharing expertise.

In many Native communities and contexts today, it is especially important that leaders and consultants act as inclusive participatory facilitators. In traditional times, if they did not do so, the people would replace them as leaders and advisors. Today, when communities are attempting to return to deciding through the wisdom of the people, it is necessary to have leaders and advisors who will build, reinforce, and incubate such ways. It takes time to reestablish these processes, and where, as happened with the Comanche, new leaders come to office who do not understand

and continue the consensus building, the processes collapse, resulting in loss of community harmony.

Moreover, where a group of people are attempting to overcome fractious factionalism and to reconcile long-unresolved differences, which is the case in many Indian communities, a special effort at respectful, compassionate, and inclusive facilitation is needed. Fortunately, many elders are very skilled at and oriented toward doing just that. They are good role models and teachers for younger Native people, who may also learn such skills from mainstream experiences, now that Western society is being forced to deal with fragmentation by instituting Indigenous methods, and teamwork is becoming essential in postindustrial organizations.[46] Additionally, if Indian communities are to bridge the range of divergent values and views that have developed over the course of colonialism and in the face of modern communication and transportation, it will be necessary for Native communities to dialogue openly and inclusively to find common ground in approaching these issues, with leaders inclusively and respectfully facilitating the discussion.

American Indians today, as individuals, as communities, and as nations, are engaged in renewal and healing. One of the results of the application of ILIS with the Comanche Nation was that by being able to participate in working for the good of the tribe with which they identify, tribal members felt better about themselves and their nation. By participating in a well-facilitated, inclusive consensus-building process, members achieved a significant measure of personal and community healing. Thus, it is clear that inclusive and participatory leadership can play an essential role in the recovery and advancement of Indian nations.

This is not to say that there is not a time and place for other styles of leadership and action. It was extremely helpful for the usually collaborative LaDonna Harris to speak angrily in order to get the Nixon administration to take notice that it was more than time to initiate the National Council on Indian Opportunity. The American Indian Movement made some important political gains for Indian people in the 1970s with confrontational demonstrations, which assisted the negotiations of Native leaders functioning with more collaborative styles of interaction. Internally, when leadership fails to include everyone's concerns in making decisions, it may be useful for those left out to act confrontationally in order to call the community's attention to injustices. But once the necessary awareness has been gained, it will be necessary for leaders to be inclusive, conciliatory, and collaborative, in order to rebuild the harmony of the community and facilitate its moving ahead, for its own welfare, and to contribute to the well-being of the wider world, which traditional wisdom says is in the long-term interest of the community and each of its members. Indeed, as Indian nations return to functioning from a holistic perspective, with their leaders respecting the interconnectedness of all interests, all people, and all that is, they can assist the world at large in returning to such an understanding, and they can re-create ways to realize mutual and ecological respect, which, increasingly, the wider world struggles to do every day.[47]

3. Completing the Re-creation of the Circle: An Overview of the Process

LaDonna Harris, Stephen M. Sachs, Barbara Morris, Deborah Esquibel Hunt, Gregory A. Cajete, Benjamin Broome, Phyllis M. Gagnier, and Jondodev Chaudhuri

As we have shared across the six chapters of this book, Native nations are engaged in a many-faceted process of renewal in overcoming the vestiges of colonialism. That process requires appropriate leadership and collaboration with others to complete the regaining of sovereignty, self-sufficiency, and harmony, and to fully realize self-determination. In the view of the authors, in a world in which the interconnection of everyone and everything is becoming increasingly clearer, this is a matter of developing the necessary independence to be collaborators in interdependence. On the political level, it involves completing the empowerment of tribal governments to be true partners in American federalism, which is necessary for American Indian and Alaskan and Hawaiian Native economic, social, and cultural development to go forward for the mutual benefit of the communities and people directly involved, and for the advancement of the wider society.

Returning to Effective Sovereignty

As we discussed in chapter 3, the return to realized sovereignty by Indian nations, with tribal governments as partners with federal, state, and local governments, has four primary aspects. First, the federal legal structure needs to fully recognize that tribal governments are governments in the United States, as are states and municipalities, and that tribal governments must have the necessary legislative, executive, and judicial powers to run their own affairs and to have an adequate say in the actions of other jurisdictions that affect them. This is both a matter of honoring the general power of tribal governments and of structuring federal programs with adequate control of tribal programs given directly to tribes. There must be sufficient incentive for states and localities to collaborate fairly with tribal governments in endeavors of mutual concern, as, for example, with the delivery of services to Indian people by state and local governments. On the legislative front, a great deal has been accomplished at the federal level and in some states. But more needs to be done to properly fill in many details in executive orders. In some cases, what has been established by executive order needs to be more firmly institutionalized in legislation.

There are two problems, however, that have arisen with the move in recent years toward increasing states' rights by some presidents and members of Congress, and even more so by a bloc of justices on the U.S. Supreme Court. To the extent that this involves an evenhanded decentralization of power to all governments below the national level, including tribal governments, Indian nations would be empowered by it in most cases, although the increase in state authority might undercut or limit tribal sovereignty in some instances, depending on the details of the decentralization. The devolution of federal authority by Congress has partially included increasing tribal power, but not sufficiently in comparison with the increased authority of the states. This situation is exemplified in welfare reform, which we discussed in chapter 3, that was passed during the Clinton presidency, under which tribal governments can run their own programs (although most often are not able to do so, for reasons we will discuss). There are some, but not sufficient, incentives in the legislation for states to cooperate fairly with tribal governments in providing an equivalent level of services, in an appropriate manner, when states supply services to Indian nations and people. Under the Bush administration, which was less concerned with Native Americans, the orientation of devolutionary legislation and budgets was less favorable toward tribal government and the needs of Indian people.[48]

The Supreme Court: "The Gang of Five"

The states' rights tendencies of "the gang of five" at the Supreme Court to date has been much more damaging to tribal sovereignty.[49] For example, under Chief Justice William Rehnquist's leadership, the court found that Indian tribes do not have the same status as other domestic sovereigns, and hence are barred by the Eleventh Amendment from suing states in federal court, which states and the federal government have the constitutional

power to do.[50] Similarly, tribal courts have been denied criminal jurisdiction over non-Indians committing misdemeanors on tribal land, and
Alaska Native villages have been declared not to have the same governmental powers as tribal governments in the lower forty-eight states.[51] If
the line of decisions sampled here is not stopped and reversed, the ability of Indian nations to govern themselves will be seriously undermined.
John G. Roberts Jr. as chief justice has brought no essential change in the
Supreme Court's approach to Indian affairs as of November 2008.

Adequate Structures to Appropriately Coordinate Indian Policy

Second, adequate and appropriate structures and processes need to be in
place to coordinate federal and state Indian policies, as well as the policies
of each department or set of departments that has a major effect upon
Native Americans, with adequate and appropriate input from Indian
people and tribal governments. (One example is New Mexico Governor
Bill Richardson designating the head of the State Commission on Indian
Affairs a cabinet position.) To be meaningful, this must be undertaken
through a high-quality dialoguing process. In addition, Indian nations
and people need to have their own intertribal structures to consider and
coordinate approaches to policy.

For structures and processes to function so that federal, state, and local
governments communicate with one another knowledgeably and respectfully in a true collaboration, the personnel of each Indian and other government entity need to be educated to interrelate cooperatively and need
to have sufficient knowledge of one another's needs and concerns. This is a
considerable problem throughout American federalism. For example, state,
local, and tribal personnel frequently complain that what is announced as
"consultation" is in reality a one-sided presentation by federal staff of their
agency's perspective.

The Need for Adequate Funding

Moreover, adequate funding to make all of this possible is necessary. On
the one side, this means enough funding for the operation and training
of staff persons of federal-, state-, and local-government Indian-related
programs and coordination and communication entities. On the other
side, and in practice more important, this requires sufficient resources
that tribal governments can set up and administer their own programs
appropriately and effectively, with high-quality intertribal and intergovernmental communication.

The Almost-Complete Model of the Clinton Administration

We have seen that a good, but not complete, model of the executive branch of the federal government coordinating Indian policy in dialogue with tribal governments and Indian organizations was put into place in the Clinton administration, which built on the experiences of earlier presidencies. Each agency that dealt significantly in Indian affairs functioned with an Indian Desk, and there were Native American coordinating bodies in the larger agencies with extensive Native concerns, and in the federal government as a whole. In addition, the president met twice yearly with tribal and other Indian leaders. Structurally, the most important improvement needed in the Clinton administration's approach would have been to move the federal coordinating body from the cabinet level, where it was headed by the secretary of the interior (who was hampered by the conflicts of interest and constituencies within his own department), to the Office of Intergovernmental Relations in the Executive Office of the President. In addition, although the Clinton administration did well in recognizing tribal sovereignty by communicating regularly with tribal government leaders, more representation of off-reservation, or urban Indians, who now make up more than 60 percent of the Native population, was needed to ensure that those making decisions and carrying out federal policy affecting Native people understood the concerns and needs of the urban Native population. Finally, these arrangements needed to be institutionalized by an act of Congress. If the Indian coordinating bodies and positions had been established by law, then on coming to office, President Bush, rather than dropping these arrangements and leaving Indian affairs coordination and consideration to the distant BIA, would probably have eventually made appointments, including at least some Native people, to these posts, so that the White House would have continued to have some direct communications with Indians. President Barack Obama appeared to be oriented toward returning to the Clinton model and expanding upon it, but what his administration will ultimately do is not yet clear.

Developing a Proper Administrative Culture

In terms of developing an administrative culture, and the education to support it, with knowledge about and openness toward the concerns of Indian nations and people, some achievements were made in the Clinton years that developed from earlier accomplishments. Some agencies, exemplified by the EPA, employed a number of Native people in important positions involving Indian issues, operated with Indian-issue coordinating bodies, and provided relevant training for personnel concerned with Native matters, which resulted in more knowledgeable decision making in the midst of considerable positive dialogue between the agency and those affected by its actions.

A great deal more, however, needs to be established in the matter of Native American education, not only across the branches of the federal government but in state governments as well. LaDonna Harris regularly expresses her frustration at the never-ending necessity to teach officials on every level "Indian Affairs 101" all over again every time there is a change in personnel because of a pervasive ignorance in the mainstream culture about Indian nations, Native people, and Indian policy. Knowledgeable attorneys and legal scholars frequently complain that the Supreme Court often makes bad Indian law because the justices do not understand it and its background. The ultimate solution to the problem is for textbooks and teachers from primary school through the university level, and especially in political science literature and classes, to give a full and accurate portrayal of Indian nations and people, including the place of tribal governments, as governments, in U.S. federalism. Until that can be sufficiently accomplished, appropriate on-the-job orientation and education is needed throughout every level of government in the United States.

The Role of Congress

Concerning Congress, the existence of a permanent Committee on Indian Affairs in the Senate has shown that chamber to be considerably more active in Indian legislation and oversight of Indian policy in the executive branch and more informed about Indian affairs and better representative of Indian nations and people than is the House, which relegates Indian affairs to a subcommittee. Therefore, it would seem wise to create an Indian Affairs committee in the House to complete the federal Indian Affairs structure.

Improving Tribal Government Relations with State and Local Governments

Regarding the subnational level, we presented examples in chapter 3 of states that have good government structures for knowledgeably and representatively dealing with Indian affairs in dialogue with tribal governments, organizations, and people that have their own intertribal vehicles of communication. These models need to be enhanced and spread to other states as appropriate for the circumstances in each location. In Indiana, for example, where no federally recognized tribe has a reservation, it was appropriate that in establishing the Indiana Native American Affairs Commission, the governor included representation of members of non-federally recognized nations. More broadly, the trend toward increased collaboration between Indian tribal governments and state and local governments, of which we have presented many examples in virtually every policy field, needs to be expanded to become the overwhelmingly predominant practice. In saying this, and in speaking of collaborative approaches to Indian affairs in general, we understand that there will always be differences of interest and opinion in the course of dealing with sometimes difficult issues. Our point is that there need to be inclusive attitudes and methods for communication about the issues in order to solve problems equitably, and thereby usually with overall efficiency, for the mutual benefit of everyone concerned.

Returning to Appropriate Tribal Governance

For Indian nations, there are two primary internal governance concerns that also have wider aspects and external facets. The first, which we discussed briefly above and in detail in chapter 4, is for Indian nations to return in both process and substance to culturally appropriate and effective governance. Many tribes are struggling to overcome government forms imposed by the U.S. government that conflict with their cultures, creating frequent deadlock and community infighting while compounding other problems created by colonialism. Progress is being made in this area by numerous nations, and the sharing of concerns and experiences in this regard will be most helpful in moving ahead.

Adequately Funding Tribal Governments and Economic Development

The second internal concern is adequate funding. Although the Clinton administration virtually completed the process of turning over the authority to run tribal programs to tribes that were willing and able to do so, either directly or by contracting or compacting out tribal programs, relatively few Indian nations elected to do so because little and often no funding was provided for cash-strapped tribes to pay for the administrative, start-up, and training costs. As a result, in many cases where tribal governments do take over responsibility for programs, they end up with less program money than the federal government had to run the program. If the program is one of those involving matching federal and state funding, in which the federal government puts up part of the money and the states the rest, tribes taking over programs receive only the federal share and must either put up the rest, which few Indian nations can afford to do, or provide less service. In some instances, as has been shown with some housing programs, many tribes run the program more cheaply than the federal government previously did, providing better housing more quickly for less money.[52] But the savings, however great, are often insufficient to cover all of the increased costs to the tribe of taking over the program. So even if the tribe can provide better services, in terms of the needs of its members, and do so more economically, the tribe may not be able to afford to do so. Thus, there is a clear need for federal funding to cover the full range of costs until Indian nations have the financial capability to carry their share of administering the programs.

The unfunded financial needs just for tribal government go even further, however. Concerning the first aspect, funding is necessary for improving tribal governance, and it is not always available. The Navajo Nation, for example, has not been able to move as quickly as it would like to empower chapters to run their own programs because there has not been enough money to provide anywhere near the amount of training and support necessary to assist chapters to move rapidly to gain the competencies they need to function properly with the new responsibilities. The federal government has a responsibility here because it began by breaking up well-functioning tribal government and replaced it with poor government systems that now need to be replaced, revised, or enhanced.

The need for adequate funding, of course, goes much further. Once self-sufficient and independent peoples, having had their traditional sources of livelihood destroyed, are struggling to raise themselves from poverty and break out of dependence. The federal government, to date, has failed to live up to its trust responsibility to those peoples. As a result, Native people receive far less money per capita than other Americans do for education, health, housing, and the whole range of services and developments that communities need to live decently with adequate incomes and to be economically competitive while competently staffing their governments and preserving their cultures, thus enabling them to have the esteem for themselves and their nations that underlies all other success.

Ultimately, Indian tribes need more than funding for government, services, and decent living. They need economic development for self-sufficiency. Some movement has been made in that direction through various means, including tribal gaming. But while a few Indian nations have become prosperous and the situation for others is improving, most tribes and their members are in need of considerably more income than is likely to be available in the foreseeable future, and some remain in dire financial straits. Under its trust responsibility, the federal government has a duty to enable the accomplishment of a fundamental level of economic development, whether it provides the necessary resources directly, or facilitates private collaboration and assistance. This is not only a matter of providing sufficient capital but includes the creation of infrastructure (as we discussed in chapter 5). Gains are being made on this set of matters, but significantly more needs to be undertaken at a faster rate to foster general self-sufficiency for Native peoples in the reasonably near future.[53] Also, wealthier tribes can do more to assist less prosperous Indian nations in moving forward. But the wealthier Indigenous nations have investment resources that can only partially enhance Native development. The main portion of what is needed must come from sources external to Indian communities.

Economic Development for Tribal Development and the Need for Appropriate Services

Economic development is but one prerequisite for human development. To live decently and to enjoy good governance, Indian people require adequate education, health, social, and other services. As we have seen, particularly in chapter 5, to be effective, economic development, education, and the services required to assist the healing and advancement of Native communities must fit the values and culture of each of those communities. Appropriate development and service provision has rarely taken place except when it has been undertaken by the Native people involved or by those who collaborate closely with them. Thus, there is a vicious circle of relationships in which tribal sovereignty cannot be fully realized without appropriate development, education, and other services, whereas appropriate development, education, and other services cannot be secured without effective tribal sovereignty.

Development, particularly economic development, does not take place without difficulties. Infusing significant increases in money into any community will exacerbate existing problems and infighting. In most cases, however, Indian nations have handled increasing income very well by diversifying their economy, improving education, preserving culture, increasing government capability, and enhancing the appropriateness, quality, and availability of services for the general welfare of the people, as we discussed in chapter 5.

As we have seen, the renewal of Native nations has been of benefit to their surrounding communities. Economic advancement on reservations has produced more jobs for non-Indians than for Indians. Economic studies have shown that Indians contribute significantly to the general economies of their areas and states, and as Native economies have improved, benefits for the wider economy also accrue. Moreover, following traditional values, Native communities have been generous in contributing to civic undertakings and charitable causes among their neighbors. As we showed in chapter 3 and chapter 5, when dealt with respectfully and fairly, tribal governments and communities, understanding that their well-being is related to the well-being of those around them, have been good partners and collaborators with surrounding jurisdictions, assuring mutual benefit.

As part of their traditional relational understanding, Native people see contributing to the welfare of the country and the world as an important aspect of their responsibility and sphere of concern, as the Comanche Nation's strategic planning goals, which we discussed in chapter 4, reflect. Currently, the world is moving more and more toward tackling problems and viewing issues in ways that approach that of the worldviews of traditional Native Americans (as we discussed in chapter 1, section 2). Native people increasingly have contributions to make to the entire planet in developing ways of better dealing with a wide range of concerns, from living in better balance with the environment to finding improved ways of working with diversity and handling globalization. Thus, the renewal of Native American self-determination, the returning of American Indian nations to realized sovereignty, self-sufficiency, and harmony as partners in American federalism, is very much to the advantage of all Americans and all the citizens of the world.

The Broader Relevance of Re-creating the American Indian Circle

Moreover, the principles underlying successful Native American renewal are the same principles that are needed for the rejuvenation of Native peoples around the planet in this the Second International Decade of the World's Indigenous People. Indeed, what we have said in these pages about American Indian development lays the foundation for a more appropriate approach to development in general, an approach that holistically takes into account the full range of needs, concerns, and perspectives of all those who are affected, so that actions for advancement are successful and for the mutual benefit of all concerned.

Finally, throughout the book, we have shown that the traditional principles of Native ways, which need to be applied appropriately for American Indian renewal in the twenty-first century, increasingly have relevance for the wider world, as more and more communities around the earth are challenged by problems similar to those that faced traditional Indigenous peoples. Had the world's leaders of the past three centuries thought and acted according to Indigenous values, climate change, pollution, and other environmental problems would not now be threatening the earth with major crises. As a planet, we need to return to understanding that we are intimately connected to all that is, to each other and everything in our environment. It is incumbent upon us to recall that our every action affects everyone and everything and can have long-term effects and, with that holistic understanding, to act appropriately.

Originally, all cultures and societies were tribal. We need to remember our indigenousness, realizing that everything is relational and that it is in our own interest to collaborate with others in achieving their interests. We need to see that all our relationships must be brought into balance and that we must work continually on every level, from interpersonal interactions to global relations, to restore the world to harmony and beauty.

Notes

1. Chapter 1 develops this theme. See also O'Brien, *American Indian Tribal Governments*, chap. 2; and Sachs, "Remembering the Circle."
2. Harris, Sachs, and Broome, "Wisdom of the People."
3. Sachs and Hunt, "Appropriate Consulting."
4. Portions of section 1 are excerpted from Sachs, "LaDonna Harris."
5. Except where otherwise noted, LaDonna Harris biographical information is taken from her undated AIO biographical statement, and from Klein, *Reference Encyclopedia*, 537; Rollings, *The Comanche*, 103; Schwartz, *Contemporary Native Americans*; and author Stephen Sachs's personal communications and experience with Ms. Harris since 1990.
6. About the Comanche preference for collaborative endeavor, see Hoebel, *Law of Primitive Man*, 131.
7. Debo, *History of the Indians*, 408–9.
8. Ibid., 409–10.
9. She was appointed by President Johnson to the National Council on Indian Opportunity; by President Nixon to the White House Fellows Commission; by President Ford to the U.S. Commission on the Observance of International Women's Year; by President Carter to the Commission on Mental Health and as a

representative of the United States on the United Nations Educational, Scientific and Cultural Organization; and by President Clinton to the Institute of American Indian Arts Advisory Board. During the Clinton administration, she was appointed by Secretary of Energy Hazel O'Leary to the Secretary of Energy's Advisory Board and by Secretary of Commerce Ron Brown to the Advisory Council on the National Information Infrastructure.

10. President Nixon's Indian policy is set forth in his Special Message on Indian Affairs of July 8, 1970, reported in part in Prucha, *United States Indian Policy*, 256–58. See also Debo, *History of the Indians*, 413.

11. Debo, *History of the Indians*, 413.

12. Comments of several Indian leaders who were in Washington, D.C., at the time to author Stephen Sachs.

13. The effectiveness of LaDonna Harris, Vine Deloria, and other contemporary Native leaders by acting from the traditional approach to the complexity and uncertainty in the world, and the approach's similarity to chaos theory, is discussed in Sachs, "Power and Sovereignty"; and Sachs, "Cutting Edge of Physics."

14. We discuss ILIS in detail in chapter 4. ILIS was originally called the Tribal Issues Management System (TIMS). A technical description of TIMS and ILIS is provided in Broome, "Collective Design," 205–28. A short report about ILIS use by the Comanche appears in Harris, Sachs, and Morris, "Native American Tribes." An extensive analysis of ILIS as used by the Comanche, with short descriptions of its application by three other Oklahoma tribes, appears in Harris, Sachs, and Broome, "Recreating Harmony." Christakis and his participation decision-making consulting firm have continued to collaborate with AIO.

15. Wheeler, "Bolivian Interactive Advisory Forum"; and "Calendar 2008," in the AIO *Ambassador* 11, nos. 1, 5 and 17. AIO's applications of ILIS are often reported in the *Ambassador*.

16. Among LaDonna Harris's AIO papers are: "To Govern or Be Governed: Indian Tribes at a Crossroads," "Partnerships for the Protection of Tribal Environments," "Indian Business Opportunities and the Defense Sector," "Alternatives for Agriculture: Successful Tribal Farms," "Hard Choices: Development of Non-Energy and Non-Replenishable Resources," and "Tribal Governments in the U.S. Federal System."

17. See "A Proposal Submitted to the U.S. Environmental Protection Agency by Americans for Indian Opportunity, Inc.," LaDonna Harris Papers.

18. National boards on which she has served include Girl Scouts of the USA, Independent Sector, Council on Foundations, National Organization for Women, National Urban League, Save the Children, the National Committee Against Discrimination in Housing, and the Overseas Development Corporation. Boards upon which she currently serves include the Native American Public Broadcasting Consortium, the National Indian Business Association, Partners for Livable Communities, Women for Mutual Security, and the Jacobson Foundation. She also serves on the following advisory boards: the National Museum of the American Indian, National Institute for Women of Color, National Institute for the Environment, Pax World Foundation, Delphi International Group, National Organization on Fetal Alcohol Syndrome, and Every Child by Two.

19. Schwartz, *Contemporary Native Americans*, 35–36.

20. Many of the issues addressed in section 2 of this chapter are discussed in Sachs and Hunt, "Appropriate Consulting with Indian Nations."

21. See Debo, *History of the Indians*, chaps. 16 and 17. The effect of the assimilation policy is considered in Meriam, et al., *Problem of Indian Administration*, discussed in Debo, 336–37; and Olson and Wilson, *Native Americans in Twentieth Century*, 100–112, 193. A representative excerpt is published in Prucha, *United States Indian Policy*, 219–21. For a perspective on how badly Indian policy was applied, see Cahn, *Our Brother's Keeper*.

22. See Weaver and Brave Heart, "Examining Two Facets"; Brave Heart, "*Oyate Ptayela*"; and Sachs et al., "Recreating the Circle," parts 2 and 3a.

23. Meriam, et al., *Problem of Indian Administration*, discussed in Debo, *History of the Indians*, 336–37; and Olson and Wilson, *Native Americans in Twentieth Century*, 100–112, 193. For perspective on the problems of overcoming unresolved historical grief, see Sachs et al., "Recreating the Circle"; and Duran and Duran, *Native American Postcolonial Psychology*.

24. Cornell and Kalt, *Successful Economic Development*.

25. See Tolman and Reedy, "Implementation," 382–93.

26. Gutierrez, "Beyond Coping," 201–19.

27. Lee, *Empowerment Approach*.

28. On the effects of colonization, see Yellow Bird, *Deconstructing Colonialism*; and Duran and Duran, *Native American Postcolonial Psychology*. On historical trauma, see Brave Heart and DeBruyn, "So She May Walk," 345–68.

29. Sachs et al., "Recreating the Circle."

30. Gutierrez, "Beyond Coping."

31. Miley, O'Melia, and DuBois, *Generalist Social Work Practice*.

32. Friere, *Pedagogy of the Oppressed*.

33. An excellent resource for understanding the experiences of many tribes is Miller, *From the Heart*.

34. Gutierrez and Nagda, "Multicultural Imperative," 203–13.

35. Gutierrez and Lewis, "Community Organizing," 23–44.

36. See the extensive discussion of the use of the ILIS process by the Comanche and several other Indian nations in chapter 4. Also see Harris, Sachs, and Broome, "Returning to Harmony."

37. Numerous consensus decision-making, problem-solving, and strategic-planning processes have been developed, but most of these processes were not designed to deal with complex issues. The Interactive Management process on which ILIS is based was specifically developed to deal with difficult situations that have consistently resisted successful resolution, such as those confronting Native American tribes. An overview of Interactive Management can be found in Broome and Keever, "Next Generation Group Facilitation," 107–27. For a more extensive description of complexity and of the theory guiding Interactive Management, see Warfield, *Societal Systems*.

38. As reported in Broome, "Promoting Greater Community Participation."

39. These problems are discussed in chapter 4. The most prominent example involved the ILIS-catalyzed initiative whereby one of the communities undertook an extended series of discussions across the Comanche nation to develop a new tribal constitution. Sometime well into the community dialogue, a former tribal chair who had been critical of the Comanche political system since being defeated for reelection, proposed his own revised constitution and obtained enough signatures to call a special election on the measure. Because of poor communication, many Comanches thought that this constitutional revision was the one they had been

discussing in the ILIS process, and the measure passed. It was quickly discovered, however, that many Comanches had voted mistakenly, and a new balloting took place that repealed the erroneous enactment.

40. For example, early achievements in employee participation were often of short duration. But whether they served as mere indicators of a needed development or as inspirations and educational experiences for that development, those achievements have been followed by an increasing application of workplace participation. Over time, the extent of participation generally has grown in both theory and practice, in what has become a revolution in management that is currently in the midst of shifting from a top-down to a participatory paradigm. See Sachs, "The Interaction of Forces."

41. Kluckhohn and Leighton, *The Navaho*, 111–23. Young, *Political History of the Navajo*, 15–16, 25–27, reports that according to Diné legend, the people lived in independent, self-sufficient camps, in which, like other band societies, decisions were made by the community by consensus, and headmen (*Hozhooli Naat'aah*) acted only as advisors. They usually were proficient in leading at least one ceremony, governed by persuasion,

> expounded on moral and ethical subjects, admonishing the people to live in peace and harmony. With his assistants he planned and organized the workday life of his community, gave instruction in the arts of farming and stock raising and supervised the planting, cultivating and harvesting of the crops. As an aspect of his community relations function, it was his responsibility to arbitrate disputes, resolve family difficulties, try to reform wrong doers and represent his group in its relations with other communities, tribes and governments. He had no functions whatsoever relating to war because the conduct of hostilities was the province of War Chiefs.

> A headman was a man of high prestige chosen for his good qualities and remained a leader only "so long as his leadership enlisted public confidence or resulted in public benefit."

42. In one instance with author Deborah Esquibel Hunt, with whom Sachs has previously written on this topic, and who involved him in the Southern Ute Design Project, for which she was a member of the facilitating team.

43. Several examples of the unfortunate results that occurred when external experts did not do their homework in advance of a project and failed to sufficiently dialogue with those for whom they were working are related in Sachs and Hunt, "Appropriate Consulting."

44. Hunt, Gooden, and Barkdull, "Walking in Moccasins." These three authors, two of whom are Indian but not Ute, have been the primary facilitating team at Southern Ute. Stephen Sachs, who has a long association with the Southern Ute Indian Tribe, was a participant at several meetings in 2000.

45. For example, to assure that that would be the case, when author Stephen Sachs consulted with the economic analysts at the Czech Confederation of Trade Unions for three months in 1993, the analysts spent the first several weeks educating him about their situation and the details of the Czech economic condition. They were aware of the necessity for beginning in this fashion after having experienced too

many foreign consultants who arrived with incorrect preconceptions about the Czech situation and simply presented their inappropriate proposals based on those misconceptions, without ever sounding out or dialoguing with their clients about their actual needs and circumstances. A more complete discussion of consulting appropriately, and the problems of intervening improperly, is presented in Sachs and Hunt, "Appropriate Consulting." 46. On instituting indigenous methods to address fragmentation, see Sachs, "Acknowledging the Circle," part 2. For an overview of teamwork as essential in postindustrial organizations, see Sachs, "Interaction of Forces."

47. We developed this point in chapter 1. The ecological perspective is further developed in Sachs, "Climate Change."

48. As can be seen in the reports of presidential and congressional action in the spring and fall issues of *Native American Policy* (now *Indigenous Policy*); issues from spring 2001 to fall 2002 are accessible online at http://www.indigenouspolicy.org.

49. Nowak, "The Gang of Five." Some examples of recent Supreme Court decisions undercutting tribal sovereignty are *Cotton Petroleum Corp. v. NM*, 490 U.S. 163 (1989); *Brendale v. Confederated Tribes and Bands of the Yakama Indian Nation*, 492 U.S. 408 (1989); *County of Yakama v. Confederated Tribes and Bands of the Yakama Indian Nation*, 502 U.S. 251 (1992); *Seminole Tribe of Florida v. FL*, 517 U.S. 44 (1996); and *Strate v. A-1 Contractors*, 520 U.S. 438 (1997), in Wilkins, *American Politics*, 317n41.

50. In *Blatchford v. Native village of Noatak*, 501 U.S. 775 (1991), discussed in LaVelle, "Rise of the 'New Federalism.'"

51. *Oliphant v. Suquqmqsh*, 435 U.S. 191 (1978), and *Alaska v. Alaska Native Village of Venetie Tribal Government*, 522 U.S. 520 (1988).

52. For example, San Juan Pueblo had taken over its own housing program by 1996. That year, it was able to build a new house in fifty-five days for one-third the average cost HUD paid to build an inferior house that typically required much longer to plan and complete. It was then conceivable that the new program would eventually be able to make up for the 9.1 percent cut in the 1996 housing budget that was not returned in 1997, and that in the long run, with even less money, might provide more housing of better quality than HUD had previously provided. Part of the greater cost for HUD's lower quality housing was the agency's use of one home design everywhere in the United States—and that the agency didn't consider other designs that would be more appropriate for specific locations, or which building materials would be most suitable, readily available, and economical at specific construction sites. See Brambach, "Building for Bertha," C7–C8.

53. A good short statement of the needs and proposals for meeting them is included in Hall, "State of the Nations," 8–9.

Bibliography

Archival Material

LaDonna Harris Collection. Americans for Indian Opportunity, Albuquerque, NM. [Harris-AIO]

LaDonna Harris Collection. Native American Community Education. Chicago, IL, moved to University of New Mexico Library. Albuquerque, NM. [LaDonna Harris Papers]

Senator Fred Harris Papers. University of Oklahoma, Norman, OK.

Books and Periodicals

Adams, David Wallace. *Education for Extinction: American Indians and the Boarding School Experience, 1875–1928*. Lawrence: University of Kansas Press, 1995.

Alfred, Gerald. "From Bad to Worse: Internal Politics in the 1990 Crises at Kahanewake." *Northeast Indian Quarterly* (Spring 1991).

Allen, Paula Gunn. *The Sacred Hoop: Recovering the Feminine in American Indian Traditions*. Boston: Beacon Press, 1986.

Allenan, Bradley. "Homosexuality in the Navy." *Time*, July 1994.

"American Indian and International Indigenous Developments, Lower Federal Courts." *Indigenous Policy* 15, no. 3 (Fall 2004).

Americans for Indian Opportunity. *Comanche Combined Structuring Forum: Lessons Learned.* Washington, D.C.: Americans for Indian Opportunity, 1991.

———. *Progress Report for 1993.* Bernalillo, NM: Americans for Indian Opportunity, 1993.

———. *We the People, In Order to Promote the General Welfare for Ourselves and Our Posterity.* Washington, D.C.: Americans for Indian Opportunity, 1979.

Andrews, N. L. "Deregulation: The Failure at EPA." In *Environmental Policy in the 1980s: Reagan's New Agenda,* edited by Norman J. Vig and Michael E. Kraft, 143–80. Washington, D.C.: Congressional Quarterly, 1984.

Archambault, William G. "Government Reductionism and Academic Bias in Criminal Justice Research on American Indian Crime and Justice Issues." *Indigenous Policy* 19, no. 3 (Fall 2008).

Bachman, Ronet. "An Analysis of American Indian Homicide: A Test of Social Disorganization and Economic Deprivation at the Reservation County Level." *Journal of Research in Crime and Delinquency* 28, no. 4 (November 1991).

Barber, Benjamin. *Strong Democracy: Participatory Politics for a New Age.* Berkeley: University of California Press, 1984.

Bardy, Kevin. "Improvement Strategy for Homosexuals in the U.S. Military." *Communications Monograph* 13, no. 3 (August 1994): 221–34.

Barreiro, Jose, ed. *Indian Roots of American Democracy.* Ithaca, NY: Cornell University Press, 1992.

Barsh, Russel Lawrence. "The Nature and Spirit of North American Political Systems." *American Indian Quarterly* 10, no. 3 (Summer 1986): 181–98.

Bausch, Kenneth C., Alexander N. Christakis, Diane S. Conway, LaDonna Harris, Laura Harris, and Bentham Ohia. *Designing a Transitional Indigenous Leaders Interaction in the Context of Globalization: A Wisdom of the People Forum (Co-Laboratory of Democracy), Final Report.* Bernalillo, NM: Americans for Indian Opportunity/Institute for 21st Century Agoras and Advancement for Maori Opportunity, 2002.

Bayer, Laura. *Santa Ana: The People, the Pueblo, and the History of Tamaya.* With Floyd Montoya and the Pueblo of Santa Ana. Albuquerque: University of New Mexico Press, 1994.

Bernstein, Paul. *Workplace Democratization: Its Internal Dynamics*. New Brunswick, NJ: Transaction Books, 1980.

Berry, Thomas. "The Viable Human." *Revision* 9, no. 2 (1987): 79.

Bilharz, Joy. "First Among Equals? The Changing Status of Seneca Women." In *Women and Power in Native North America*, edited by Laura E. Klein and Lillian A. Ackerman. Norman: University of Oklahoma Press, 1995.

Black Elk, Wallace, and William S. Lyon. *Black Elk: The Sacred Ways of a Lakota*. New York: Harper and Row, 1990.

Blinder, Alan S., ed. *Paying for Productivity: A Look at the Evidence*. Washington, D.C.: Brookings Institution, 1990.

Blomquist, William. "Improving Dispute Resolution." In *Planning to Govern*, U.S. Advisory Commission on Intergovernmental Relations, report no. M-191. Washington, D.C., 1994.

Bluehouse, Philmer, and James Zion. "Hozhooji Naat'aanii: The Navajo Nation Justice and Harmony Ceremony." In *Native Americans, Crime, and Justice*, edited by Marianne O. Nielsen and Robert A. Silverman, 181–82. Boulder, CO: Westview Press, 1996.

Blumberg, Paul. *Industrial Democracy: The Sociology of Participation*. New York: Schocken Books, 1968.

Bohm, David, and B. J. Hiley. *The Undivided Universe: An Ontological Interpretation of Quantum Theory*. London: Routledge, 1993.

Bottomore, T. B. *Karl Marx: Selected Writings in Sociology and Social Philosophy*. New York: McGraw-Hill, 1964.

Bowers, Alfred W. *Hidatsa Social and Ceremonial Organization*. Lincoln: University of Nebraska Press, 1992.

Boyer, Paul. *Tribal College and University Profiles: New Directions in Math and Science*. Pablo, MT: Salish Kootenai College Press, 2008.

Branegan, Michael. "Restoring Community to Restorative Justice." *Research and Creative Activity, Indiana University* 11 (January 1997).

Brave Heart, Maria Yellow Horse. *"Oyate Ptayela:* Rebuilding the Lakota Nation through Addressing Historical Trauma among Lakota Parents." In *Proceedings of the 1999 American Political Science Association Meeting*. Washington, D.C.: American Political Science Association, 1999.

———, and L. DeBruyn. "So She May Walk in Balance: Integrating the Impact of Historical Trauma in the Treatment of American Indian Women." In *Racism in the Lives of Women: Testimony,*

Theory, and Guides to Antiracist Practice, edited by J. Adelman and G. Enguidanos, 345–68. New York: Haworth Press, 1995.

Broome, Benjamin J. "Collective Design of the Future: Structural Analysis of Tribal Vision Statements." *American Indian Quarterly* 19, no. 2 (1995): 20–28.

———. *Designing the Future of the Comanche: Report of Planning and Design Sessions Held in Lawton, Oklahoma, July 12–13 and September 27–28, 1991*. Fairfax, VA: Department of Communications, George Mason University, 1991.

———. *Promoting Greater Community Participation in Comanche Tribal Governance: Planning Sessions Held March 26–28 and May 13–15, 1991*. Fairfax, VA: Department of Communications, George Mason University, 1991.

———. "The Role of Facilitated Group Process in Community-Based Planning and Design: Promoting Greater Participation in Comanche Tribal Government." In *Innovations in Group Facilitation: Applications in Natural Settings*, edited by L. R. Frey, 27–52. Cresskill, NJ: Hampton Press, 1994.

———, and A. N. Christakis. "A Culturally Sensitive Approach to Tribal Governance Issues Management." *International Journal of Intercultural Relations* 12 (1988): 107–23.

———, Alexander Christakis, and Jackie Wasilewski. *Designing the Future of the Comanche Tribe*. Report for the Comanche TIMS [now ILIS] Process, March 21, 1990.

———, and I. L. Cromer. "Strategic Planning for Tribal Economic Development: A Culturally Appropriate Model for Consensus Building." *International Journal of Conflict Management* 2 (1991): 217–35.

———, and D. B. Keever. "Next Generation Group Facilitation: Proposed Principles." *Management Communication Quarterly* 3 (1989): 107–27.

Brown, Joseph Epes. *The Sacred Pipe: Black Elk's Account of the Seven Rites of the Oglala Sioux*. Norman: University of Oklahoma Press, 1953.

———. *The Spiritual Legacy of the American Indian*. New York: Crossroads Publishing, 1988.

Burton, Lloyd. *American Indian Water Rights and the Limits of the Law*. Lawrence: University of Kansas Press, 1991.

Cahn, Edgar, ed. *Our Brother's Keeper: The Indian in White America*. New York: New American Library, 1969.

Cajete, Gregory A. *Look to the Mountain: An Ecology of Indigenous Education*. Skyland, NC: Kivaki Press, 1994.

———. *Native Science: Natural Laws of Interdependence*. Santa Fe, NM: Clear Light Publishers, 2000.

California Indian Oversight Hearings: Hearings before the Subcommittee on Interior and Insular Affairs, 93rd Congress (1974). Washington, D.C.: Government Printing Office, 1974.

Campbell, Alastair, Charles Keen, Geraldine Norman, and Robert Oakeshott. *Worker Ownership: The Mondragon Achievement*. London: Anglo-German Foundation for the Study of Society, 1977.

Campbell, John Kennedy. *Honour, Family and Patronage: A Study of Institutions and Morals*. Oxford: Clarendon Press, 1970.

Campbell, Joseph. *The Masks of God: Primitive Mythology*. New York: Viking Penguin, 1959.

———. *Transformations of Myth Through Time*. New York: Harper and Row, 1990.

Capra, Fritjof. *The Tao of Physics*. 2nd rev. ed. Toronto: Bantam Books, 1984.

Carballeira, N. "The Live and Learn Model for Culturally Competent Family Services." *The Source* 6, no. 3 (Summer 1996): 4–6, 12.

Castile, George Pierre. *Taking Charge: Native American Self-Determination and Federal Indian Policy, 1975–1993*. Tucson: University of Arizona Press, 2006.

———. *To Show Heart: Native American Self-Determination and Federal Indian Policy, 1960–1975*. Tucson: University of Arizona Press, 1998.

Champagne, Duane. "Organizational Change and Conflict: A Case Study of the Bureau of Indian Affairs." In *Native Americans and Public Policy*, edited by Freemont J. Lyden and Lyman H. Legters. Pittsburgh: University of Pittsburgh Press, 1992.

Chaudhuri, Jean, and Joyotpaul Chaudhuri. *A Sacred Path: The Way of the Muscogee Creeks*. Los Angeles: UCLA American Indian Studies Center, 2000.

Child, Brenda, and Tsianina Lomawama, eds. *A Hard Lesson: The Indian Boarding Schools*. Santa Fe: Museum of New Mexico Press/ Heard Museum, 2000.

Citizens Action Coalition. *Citizens Power* 18, no. 2 (Fall 1992).

Clark, Wilson. *Energy for Survival*. Garden City, NY: Anchor Books, 1975.

Collier, John. *Indians of the Americas.* New York: W. W. Norton, 1947.

Comanche Indian Tribe. *The Comanche Indian Tribe.* Lawton, OK: Comanche Tribal Office, 1991.

Cornell, Stephen. *Accountability, Legitimacy, and the Foundation of Native Self-Governance.* Harvard Project on American Indian Economic Development, Malcolm J. Weiner Center for Social Policy, John F. Kennedy School of Government, PRS93–1. Cambridge, MA: Harvard University, 1993.

———. "Politics, Business, and Nation Building: Self-Governance and Economic Development in *Indian Country Today.*" Paper presented at the 4th Annual Arizona Economic Summit, Phoenix, AZ, 1997.

———, and Joseph P. Kalt. *Reloading the Dice: Improving the Chances for Economic Development on American Indian Reservations.* Harvard Project on American Indian Economic Development, Malcolm Wiener Center for Social Policy, John F. Kennedy School of Government, PRS92–1. Cambridge, MA: Harvard University, 1992.

———, and Joseph P. Kalt. *Successful Economic Development and Heterogeneity of Government Forms on Indian Reservations.* Harvard Project on American Indian Economic Development, Malcolm Wiener Center for Social Policy, John F. Kennedy School of Government. Cambridge, MA: Harvard University, 1995.

Corporation for Enterprise Development. *Effective State Policy and Practice: Entrepreneurship Development in Native American Communities* 4, no. 2. Washington, D.C.: Corporation for Enterprise Development, 2005.

———. *Entrepreneurship Development in Native American Communities* 4, no. 2. Washington, D.C.: Corporation for Enterprise Development, 2005.

Cross, Terry. "Opening Remarks." Address at National Indian Child Welfare Association conference, *Family Preservation the Indian Way: Bringing It Back*, Washington, D.C., 1998.

Crow Dog, Leonard, and Richard Erdoes. *Crow Dog: Four Generations of Sioux Medicine Men.* New York: Harper Collins Publishers, 1995.

Davies, J. Clarence. "Environmental Institutions and the Reagan Administration." In *Environmental Policy in the 1980s: Reagan's New Agenda*, edited by Norman J. Vig and Michael E. Kraft, 143–80. Washington, D.C.: Congressional Quarterly, 1984.

Davis, Charles. *The Politics of Hazardous Waste*. Englewood Cliffs, NJ: Prentice Hall, 1993.

Davis, Mary V., ed. *Native America in the Twentieth Century: An Encyclopedia*. New York: Garland Publishing, 1993.

Debo, Angie. *A History of the Indians of the United States*. Norman: University of Oklahoma Press, 1989.

Delbeq, A. L., A. H. Van de Ven, and D. H. Gustafson. *Group Techniques for Program Planning: A Guide to Nominal Group and DELPHI Processes*. Glenview, IL: Scott, Foresman, 1975.

Deloria, Ella. *Speaking of Indians*. Lincoln: University of Nebraska Press, 1998.

———. *Waterlily*. Lincoln: University of Nebraska Press, 1981.

Deloria, Vine, Jr. *American Indian Policy in the Twentieth Century*. Norman: University of Oklahoma Press, 1985.

———. "The Evolution of Federal Indian Policy Making." In *American Indian Policy in the Twentieth Century*, edited by Vine Deloria Jr. Norman: University of Oklahoma Press, 1985.

———. "The Perpetual Indian Message." *Winds of Change* 7, no. 1 (Winter 1992).

———, and Clifford Lytle. *Nations Within*. New York: Pantheon Books, 1984.

———, and Daniel R. Wildcat. *Power and Place: Indian Education in America*. Golden, CO: Fulcrum Resources, 2001.

———, and David E. Wilkins. *Tribes, Treaties, and Constitutional Tribulations*. Austin: University of Texas Press, 1999.

DeMallie, Raymond, and Douglas Parks, eds. *Sioux Indian Religion*. Norman: University of Oklahoma Press, 1987.

"Department of the Interior, Bureau of Indian Affairs, Notice of Schedule of Regional Consultation Sessions on Tribal Shares." *Federal Register* 62, no. 95 (Friday, May 16, 1997), 27064.

Dewey, John. *Schools for Tomorrow*. Boston: Heath, 1906.

Dooling, D. M., and Paul Jordan-Smith. *I Become Part of It: Sacred Dimensions in Native American Life*. San Francisco: Harper Collins, 1992.

Doss, Michael P. "The American Indian Policy Review Commission: A Case Study and Analysis of an Attempted Large Systems Change by a Temporary Organization." PhD diss., Harvard University, 1977.

Downes, James F. *The Navajo*. New York: Holt, Rinehart and Winston, 1972.

Driver, Harold. *Indians of North America.* Chicago: University of Chicago Press, 1969.

Duran, Eduardo, and Bonnie Duran. *Native American Postcolonial Psychology.* Albany: State University of New York Press, 1995.

Eastman, Charles A. (Ohiyesa). *The Soul of the Indian: An Interpretation.* 1911. Reprint. Lincoln: University of Nebraska Press, 1980.

Eastman, Charles A. (Ohiyesa), and Elaine Goodale Eastman. *Wigwam Evenings: Sioux Tales Retold.* Lincoln: University of Nebraska Press, 1990.

Easton, David. *The Political System.* New York: Alfred A. Knopf, 1953.

Eccles, W. J. *The Canadian Frontier, 1534–1760.* Albuquerque: University of New Mexico Press, 1983.

Elizar, Daniel. *American Federalism.* New York: Thomas Crowell, 1973.

Erikson, Erik. *Identity and the Life Cycle.* New York: International Universities Press, 1959.

Farole, Donald J., Jr., Nora Puffett, Michael Rempel, and Francine Byrne. "Applying the Problem-Solving Model Outside of Problem-Solving Courts." *Judicature* 89, no. 1 (July–August 2005): 40–42.

Foster, Morris W. *Being Comanche.* Tucson: University of Arizona Press, 1991.

Fowler, Loretta. *Arapahoe Politics, 1851–1978: Symbols in Crises of Authority.* Lincoln: University of Nebraska Press, 1982.

Fox, Edward J. "Tribal/State Health Policymaking in the Northwest States of Oregon, Washington, and Idaho: Institution Building for Policymaking." In *Proceedings of the 1998 Annual Meeting of the American Political Science Association.* Washington, D.C.: American Political Science Association, 1998.

Francke, Linda Bird. *Ground Zero: The Gender Wars in the Military.* New York: Simon and Schuster, 1997.

Freeman, J. Leiper. *The Political Process: Executive Bureau–Legislative Committee Relations.* New York: Random House, 1966.

Freesoul, John Redtail. *Breath of the Invisible: The Way of the Pipe.* Wheaton, IL: Theosophical Publishing House, 1986.

Friends Committee on National Legislation. "Federal Indian Spending: A Sinking Trust." *Indian Report* 1, no. 55 (Summer 1997).

Friere, Paolo. *Pedagogy of the Oppressed.* Rev. ed. New York: Continuum Publishing, 1993.

French, L. A. *Counseling American Indians.* Lanham, MD: University Press of America, 1977.

French, Laurence Armond. *Legislating Indian Country: Significant Milestones in Transforming Tribalism*. New York: Peter Lang Publishing, 2007.

Fritschler, A. Lee. *Smoking and Politics: Policy Making and the Federal Bureaucracy*. New York: Appleton-Century Crofts, 1969.

———, and James M. Hoefler. *Smoking and Politics: Policy Making and the Federal Bureaucracy*. 5th ed. Upper Saddle River, NJ: Prentice Hall, 1995.

Fuchs, Estelle, and Robert J. Havighurst. *To Live on This Earth: American Indian Education*. 1972. Reprinted with a new introduction by Margaret Cornell Szasz. Albuquerque, NM: University of New Mexico Press, 1983.

Garment, Leonard. *Crazy Rhythm: My Journey from Brooklyn, Jazz, and Wall Street to Nixon's White House, Watergate, and Beyond*. New York: Random House, 1997.

Garrett, Michael. "To Walk in Beauty: The Way of Right Relationship." In *Medicine of the Cherokee: The Way of Right Relationship*, edited by J. T. Garrett and Michael Garrett. Santa Fe, NM: Bear and Company Publishing, 1996.

Gebser, Jean. *The Ever-Present Origin*. Athens: University of Ohio Press, 1986.

Giago, Tim. "It Is Time for Gaming Tribes to 'Think Indian.'" *Indigenous Policy* 16, no. 1 (Spring 2005).

Gill, Sam. "It's Where You Put Your Eyes." In *I Became Part of It: Sacred Dimensions in Native American Life*, edited by D. M. Dooling and Paul Jordan-Smith. San Francisco: Harper Collins, 1992.

Goelitz, Jeff. "Feature Interviews: Working with a Bureau of Indian Affairs School in Southern Arizona." *Quality Classroom Newsletter* (Fall/Winter 2000): 5–6.

———. "Successful Truancy Program Involves Parents and HeartMath." *A Change of Heart: A Newsletter from the Institute of HeartMath* 1, no. 4 (Winter 2003): 3.

Goldberg, Carole, and Duane Champagne. *Law Enforcement and Criminal Justice under Public Law 280*. Los Angeles: UCLA Native Nations Law and Policy Center, 2007. http://www.law.ucla.edu/home/index.asp?page=1984.

Goldman, Irving. "The Kwakiutl of Vancouver Island." In *Cooperation and Competition Among Primitive Peoples*, edited by Margaret Mead. New York: McGraw-Hill, 1937.

———. "The Zuni Indians of New Mexico." In *Cooperation and*

Competition Among Primitive Peoples, edited by Margaret Mead. New York: McGraw-Hill, 1937.

Gray, Christine. "The More Things Change . . . : Contracts, Compacts, Evolution, and Stasis in the Tribal-Federal Relationship." In *Proceedings of the 1999 Annual Meeting of the American Political Science Association*. Washington, D.C.: American Political Science Association, 1999.

Gray, Megan. "Windfall." *Cultural Survival Quarterly* 32, no. 2 (August 2008).

Grenier, Guillermo. *Inhuman Relations*. Philadelphia: Temple University Press, 1988.

Grinde, Donald A., Jr. "Iroquois Political Theory and the Roots of American Democracy." In *Exiled in the Land of the Free: Democracy, Indian Nations, and the U.S. Constitution*, edited by Oren Lyons, John Mohawk, Vine Deloria Jr., Laurence Hauptman, Howard Berman, Donald Grinde Jr., Curtis Berkey, and Robert Venables. Santa Fe, NM: Clear Light Publishers, 1992.

Grinde, Donald A., and Bruce E. Johnson. *Exemplar of Liberty: Native America and the Evolution of Democracy*. Los Angeles: American Indian Studies Center, UCLA, 1991.

Grinnell, George Bird. *By Cheyenne Campfires*. 1922. Reprint, Lincoln: University of Nebraska Press, 1971.

———. *The Cheyenne Indians: Their History and Way of Life*. 2 vols. 1923. Reprint, Lincoln: University of Nebraska Press, 1972.

Gurnee, C. G., D. E. Vigil, S. Krill-Smith, and T. J. Crowley. "Substance Abuse Among American Indians in an Urban Treatment Program." *American Indian and Alaska Native Mental Health Research* 3, no. 3 (1990): 17–26.

Gutierrez, L. M. "Beyond Coping: An Empowerment Perspective on Stressful Life Events." *Journal of Sociology and Social Welfare* 21, no. 3 (1994): 201–19.

Gutierrez, L., and E. Lewis. "Community Organizing with Women of Color." *Journal of Community Practice* 1, no. 2 (1994): 23–44.

———, and B. Nagda. "The Multicultural Imperative in Human Services Organizations." In *Future Issues for Social Work Practice*, edited by P. Rafford and A. McNeece, 203–13. Boston: Allyn and Bacon, 1996.

Gutierrez-Johnson, A. "Compensation, Equity, and Industrial Democracy in the Mondragon Cooperatives." *Economic Analysis and Workers' Self-Management* 12: 267–89.

————, and William Foote Whyte. "The Mondragon System of Worker Production Cooperatives." *Industrial and Labor Relations Review* 31, no. 1 (October 1977): 18–30.

Hampton, Eber. "Toward a Redefinition of American Indian/Alaska Native Education." Analytic paper, Harvard Graduate School of Education, 1988.

Harris, LaDonna. *Comanche Governance Community Involvement Project: Demosophia: The Wisdom of the People, Final Evaluation.* Washington, D.C.: Americans for Indian Opportunity, 1992.

————. "Letter from the President." *The Ambassador* (Winter 2002): 2.

————, Stephen M. Sachs, and Benjamin Broome. "Recreating Harmony through Wisdom of the People: The Case of the Comanche and Other Oklahoma Tribes, Summary Version." In *Proceedings of the National Gathering on Aboriginal Peoples and Dispute Resolution: "Making Peace and Sharing Power."* Victoria, BC: University of Victoria, 1997.

————. "Returning to Harmony through Reactivating the Wisdom of the People: The Comanche Bring Back the Tradition of Consensus Decision Making." *Native Americas* 12, no. 3 (Fall 1996).

————. "Strategy and Choice: Opting for Cooperation or Competition, Investigation of Tribal and Sub-National Government Relations." In *Proceedings of the 1998 American Political Science Association Meeting.* Washington, D.C.: American Political Science Association, 1998.

————. "Wisdom of the People: Potentials and Pitfalls in Efforts by the Comanches to Re-create Traditional Ways of Building Consensus." *American Indian Quarterly* 25, no. 1 (Winter 2001).

————, Stephen M. Sachs, and Barbara Morris. "Native American Tribes and Federalism: Can Government to Government Relations between the Tribes and the Federal Government Be Institutionalized?" In *Proceedings of the 1997 American Political Science Association Meeting.* Washington, D.C.: American Political Science Association, 1997.

Hart, John. *The Presidential Branch.* Chatham, NJ: Chatham House Publishers, 1995.

Hassrick, Royal B. *The Sioux.* Norman: University of Oklahoma Press, 1964.

Hensen, Eric, and Jonathan B. Taylor. *American Indians at the Millennium.* Harvard Project on American Indian Economic Development, Malcolm Wiener Center for Social Policy,

John F. Kennedy School of Government. Cambridge, MA: Harvard University, 2005.

Hoebel, E. Adamson. *The Cheyennes: Indians of the Great Plains.* New York: Holt, Rinehart and Winston, 1960.

———. *The Law of Primitive Man.* New York: Atheneum, 1976.

Holm, Tom. "The Crises in Tribal Government." In *American Indian Policy in the Twentieth Century,* edited by Vine Deloria Jr. Norman: University of Oklahoma Press, 1985.

Hopcke, Robert H. *A Guided Tour of the Works of C. G. Jung.* Boston: Shambala, 1997.

Hunt, Deborah Esquibel, Myrna Gooden, and Carenlee Barkdull. "Walking in Moccasins: Indian Child Welfare in the 21st Century." In *Innovative Practices with Vulnerable Children and Families,* edited by Katharine Briar-Lawson, Hal A. Lawson, and Alvin L. Sallee. Dubuque, IA: Eddie Bauer Publishing, 2000.

———, Stephen M. Sachs, and Barbara Morris. "Devolution of Welfare Programs: The Impact on Indian Nations and on Tribal Government–State and Local Government Relations." In *Proceedings of the 2000 American Political Science Association Meeting.* Washington, D.C.: American Political Science Association, 2000.

"Indian and Indigenous Developments." *Native American Policy Network Newsletter* 17, no. 1 (Spring 2001).

"Indian and Indigenous Developments: U.S. Developments." *Indigenous Policy* 14, no. 1 (Spring 2003).

"Indian and Indigenous Developments: Economic Developments." *Indigenous Policy* 20, no. 1 (Spring 2009).

"Indian and Indigenous Developments: Economic Developments," and "Educational and Cultural Developments." *Indigenous Policy* 14, no. 2 (Fall 2003).

"Indian and Indigenous Developments: Economic Developments," and "Tribal Developments." *Indigenous Policy* 19, no. 1 (Spring 2008).

"Indian and Indigenous Developments: Economic Developments," "Tribal Developments," "Educational and Cultural Developments," and "Ongoing Activities." *Indigenous Policy* 16, no. 1 (Spring 2005).

"Indian and Indigenous Developments: Economic, Educational, and Cultural Developments." *Indigenous Policy,* 13, no. 2 (Fall 2002).

"Indian and Indigenous Developments: Educational and Cultural Developments," and "Tribal Developments." *Indigenous Policy* 15, no. 1 (Spring 2004).

"Indian and Indigenous Developments: Educational and Cultural
     Developments," and "Tribal Developments." *Indigenous Policy*,
     18, no. 3 (Fall 2007).
"Indian and Indigenous Developments: In the Courts." *Indigenous Policy*
     19, no. 3 (Fall 2008).
"Indian and Indigenous Developments: Tribal Developments," and
     "Economic Development." *Indigenous Policy* 16, no. 2 (Fall 2005).
"Indian and Indigenous Developments: Tribal Developments," and
     "Educational and Cultural Developments." *Indigenous Policy* 15,
     no. 3 (Fall 2004).
"Indian and Indigenous Developments: Tribal Developments,"
     "Ongoing Activities," and "U.S. Activities." *Indigenous Policy* 18,
     no. 1 (Spring 2007).
"Indian and Indigenous Developments: Tribal Developments," and
     "States, Localities, and Indian Nations." *Indigenous Policy* 17,
     no. 1 (Spring 2006).
Indian Health Service. *Trends in Indian Health, 1993.* Rockville, MD:
     U.S. Department of Health and Human Services, 1993.
Indian Nations at Risk Taskforce. *Final Report, Indian Nations at Risk:
     An Educational Strategy for Action.* Washington, D.C.: U.S.
     Department of Education, 1991.
"Indigenous Developments: Economic Developments," "Educational
     and Cultural Developments," and "Ongoing Activities." *Native
     American Policy* 14, no. 1 (Spring 2003).
"Indigenous Developments: Tribal Developments." *Native American
     Policy* 13, no. 2 (Fall 2002).
Irwin, Lee. *The Dream Seekers: Native American Visionary Traditions of
     the Great Plains.* Norman: University of Oklahoma Press, 1994.
Jackson, Camille. "A Summer of Violence in the Navajo Nation: A
     Discussion Activity: Teaching Tolerance." A Project of the
     Southern Poverty Law Center. November 2006.
Jefferson, James, Robert Delaney, Gregory Thompson, and Floyd
     O'Neill. *The Southern Utes: A Tribal History.* Ignacio, CO:
     Southern Ute Tribe, 1972.
Johnson, Bruce. *Forgotten Founders: How American Indians Helped Shape
     Democracy.* Boston: Harvard Common Press, 1982.
Jones, Lilias. "Neither Fish Nor Fowl: Federalism, Native Americans,
     and United States Institutions." In *Proceedings of the 1997
     Annual Meeting of the American Political Science Association.*
     Washington, D.C.: American Political Science Association, 1997.

Jorgensen, Joseph G. *The Sun Dance Religion: Power to the Powerless.* Chicago: University of Chicago Press, 1972.

Jung, Carl. *The Archetypes and the Collective Unconscious.* Princeton, NJ: Bollingen, 1967.

———. *Carl Gustav Jung: Basic Writings*, edited by Violet Staub de Laszlo. New York: Modern Library, 1959.

———. *Memories, Dreams, Reflections*, edited by Aniela Jaffe. Princeton, NJ: Bollingen, 1965.

———. *Psychological Types.* New York: Harcourt Brace, 1923.

———. *The Structure and Dynamics of the Psyche.* Princeton, NJ: Bollingen, 1965.

"Keeping Current." *Labor Relations Today* (November/December 1990).

Kehoe, Alice B. "Blackfoot Persons." In *Women and Power in Native North America*, edited by Laura E. Klein and Lillian A. Ackerman. Norman: University of Oklahoma Press, 1995.

Keirsey, David, and Marilyn Bates. *Please Understand Me: Character and Temperament Types.* Delmar, CA: Prometheus Nemesis Book, 1984.

Kier, Elizabeth. "Homosexuality in the U.S. Military." *International Security* 35 (1998): 36–56.

Klein, B. T. *Reference Encyclopedia for the American Indian.* 6th ed. West Nyack, NY: Todd Publications, 1993.

Klein, Laura E., and Lillian A. Ackerman, eds. *Women and Power in Native North America.* Norman: University of Oklahoma Press, 1995.

Kluckhohn, Clyde, and Dorothea Leighton. *The Navaho.* Cambridge, MA: Harvard University Press, 1974.

Kohler, Holm-Detlev. "What Happens to Successful Cooperatives in Capitalist Globalization: Some Notes on Recent Trends in the Basque Mondragon Cooperative Corporation (MCC)." *GEO: Grass Roots Economic Organizing*, no. 50 (February 2001).

Kolstoe, John E. *Consultation: A Universal Lamp of Guidance.* Oxford: George Ronald, 1985.

Kubler-Ross, Elizabeth. *On Death and Dying.* New York: Macmillan, 1969.

Lame Deer, John (Fire), and Richard Erdoes. *Lame Deer: Seeker of Visions.* New York: Washington Square Press, 1972.

Landes, Ruth. "The Ojibwa of Canada." In *Cooperation and Competition Among Primitive Peoples*, edited by Margaret Mead. New York: McGraw-Hill, 1937.

Lasswell, Harold *Politics: Who Gets What, When, How.* New York: McGraw-Hill, 1936.

LaVelle, John P. "The Rise of the 'New Federalism' from the Destruction of Indian Rights: A Meditation." In *Proceedings of the 26th Annual Indian Law Conference of the Federal Bar Association: The New Tribalism Meets the New Federalism.* 2001.

Lawler, Edward E., III, Susan Albers Mohrman, and Gerald E. Ledford Jr. *Employee Involvement and Total Quality Management: Practices and Results in Fortune 1000 Companies.* San Francisco: Jossey-Bass Publishers, 1992.

Laszlo, Violet Staub de, ed. *Carl Gustav Jung, Basic Writings.* New York: Modern Library, 1959.

Lee, J. A. B. *The Empowerment Approach to Social Work Practice.* New York: Columbia Press, 1994.

Leigh, J. W. *Communicating for Cultural Competence.* Needham Heights, MA: Allyn and Bacon, 1998.

Levine, M. "Prevention and Community." *American Journal of Community Psychology,* no. 26 (1998): 189–206.

Lewis, Lorre. *American Indian and Alaska Native Sex Offenders: A Quantitative Study in Two Places.* PhD diss., University of Utah, 1998.

Llewellyn, Karl, and E. Adamson Hoebel. *The Cheyenne Way.* Norman: University of Oklahoma Press, 1941.

Locke, John. *The Second Treatise on Civil Government.* Buffalo, NY: Prometheus Books, 1986.

Luna-Firebaugh, Eileen M., and Delphine Redshirt. "The Impact of the Criminal Justice System on the Higher Education of American Indian Juveniles." Paper presented at the Western Social Sciences Association Meeting, Denver, CO, April 2008.

Lyden, Freeman J. and Lyman H. Legters, eds. *Native Americans and Public Policy.* Pittsburgh: University of Pittsburgh Press, 1992.

Lyons, Oren. "The American Indian in the Past." In *Exiled in the Land of the Free: Democracy, Indian Nations, and the U.S. Constitution,* edited by Oren Lyons, John Mohawk, Vine Deloria Jr., Laurence Hauptman, Howard Berman, Donald Grinde Jr., Curtis Berkey, and Robert Venables. Santa Fe, NM: Clear Light Publishers, 1992.

———, John Mohawk, Vine Deloria Jr., Laurence Hauptman, Howard Berman, Donald Grinde Jr., Curtis Berkey, and Robert Venables, eds. *Exiled in the Land of the Free: Democracy, Indian*

Nations, and the U.S. Constitution. Santa Fe, NM: Clear Light
Publishers, 1992.

Mails, Thomas E. *Fools Crow.* Lincoln: University of Nebraska Press,
1979.

———., and Dan Evehema. *Hotevilla: Hopi Shrine of the Covenant,
Microcosm of the World.* New York: Marlowe and Company,
1995.

Maltz, Daniel, and JoAllyn Archambault. "Concluding Remarks." In
Women and Power in Native North America, edited by Laura
E. Klein and Lillian A. Ackerman. Norman: University of
Oklahoma Press, 1995.

Marsh, Charles S. *The Utes of Colorado: People of the Shining Mountains.*
Boulder, CO: Pruett Publishing, 1982.

Marshall, Joseph M., III. *The Lakota Way: Stories and Lessons of Living.*
New York: Viking Compass, 2001.

Mason, W. Dale. "Tribal-State Relations: A New Era in
Intergovernmental Relations." Paper presented at Southwest
Political Science Association Meeting, 1999.

Mathes, Valerie Sherer. "Native American Women in Medicine and the
Military." *Journal of the West* 21 (1982): 44.

McCarty, T. L., Regina Hadley Lynch, Stephen Wallace, and AnCita
Benally. "Classroom Inquiry and Navajo Learning Styles: A
Call for Reassessment." *Anthropology and Education Quarterly* 22
(1991): 42–59.

McCool, Daniel. "Intergovernmental Conflict and Indian Water Rights:
An Assessment of Negotiated Settlements." *Publius: The Journal
of Federalism* 23, no. 1 (Winter 1993): 85–101.

———, and Laura Kirwin. "Environmentalists, Tribes, and Negotiated
Settlements." In *Proceedings of the 1995 American Political Science
Association Meeting.* Washington, D.C.: American Political
Science Association, 1995.

McDonnell, Janet A. *The Dispossession of the American Indian, 1887–1934.*
Bloomington: Indiana University Press, 1991.

McFee, M. "The 150% Man: A Product of Blackfeet Acculturation."
American Anthropologist 70, no. 2 (1968): 1096–1103.

Mead, Margaret, ed. *Cooperation and Competition Among Primitive
Peoples.* New York: McGraw-Hill, 1937.

Medanie, Germal. "Mondragon: Your Ad Is About to Run Out."
Grassroots Economic Organizing Newsletter 10, September/
October, 1983.

Medawar, Mardi Oakley. *Death at Rainy Mountain*. New York: Berkeley Prime Crime, 1996.

———. *Murder at Medicine Lodge*. New York: St. Martin's Press, 1999.

———. *The Witch of Palo Duro*. New York: Berkeley Prime Crime, 1977.

Medicine, Beatrice. "Indian Women and the Renaissance of Traditional Religion." In *Sioux Indian Religion*, edited by Raymond DeMallie and Douglas Parks. Norman: University of Oklahoma Press, 1987.

Medina, G. "A Community Mental Health Intervention in Mora, New Mexico." Paper prepared for New Mexico Highlands University School of Social Work, Las Vegas, NM, 1998.

Meriam, Lewis. *The Problem of Indian Administration*. Baltimore: Johns Hopkins University Press, 1928.

Metoui, Jessica. "Returning to the Circle: The Reemergence of Traditional Dispute Resolution in Native American Communities." *University of Missouri Journal of Dispute Resolution* (2007): 517–40.

Meyers, Isabel. *Gifts Differing*. Palo Alto, CA: Consulting Psychologists Press, 1980.

Middleton-Moz, J. "From Legacy to Choice: Healing the Effects of Generational Trauma and Effects on Individuals, Families, and Communities." Keynote address at the National Indian Child Welfare Association Conference, Minneapolis, MN, 1999.

———. "The Wisdom of Elders: Working with Native American and Native Alaskan Families." In *Growing in the Shadow*, edited by Robert Ackerman. Pompano Beach, FL: Health Communications, 1986.

Miley, Karla K., Michael O'Melia, and Brenda L. DuBois. *Generalist Social Work Practice: An Empowering Approach*. Needham Heights, MA: Allyn and Bacon, 1998.

Miller, Bruce G. *The Problem of Justice: Tradition and Law in the Coast Salish World*. Lincoln: University of Nebraska Press, 2001.

Miller, Lee. *From the Heart*. New York: Random House, 1996.

Mirsky, Jannette. "The Dakota." In *Cooperation and Competition Among Primitive Peoples*, edited by Margaret Mead. New York: McGraw-Hill, 1937.

Mississippi Band of Choctaw Indians. *Choctaw Industrial Park*. Philadelphia, MS: Mississippi Band of Choctaw Indians, 1982.

Mohatt, Gerald, and Joseph Eagle Elk. *The Price of a Gift: A Lakota Healer's Story*. Lincoln: University of Nebraska Press, 2000.

Mohawk, John. "Indians and Democracy: No One Ever Told Us." In *Exiled in the Land of the Free: Democracy, Indian Nations, and the U.S. Constitution*, edited by Oren Lyons, John Mohawk, Vine Deloria Jr., Laurence Hauptman, Howard Berman, Donald Grinde Jr., Curtis Berkey, and Robert Venables. Santa Fe, NM: Clear Light Publishers, 1992.

Mollner, Terry. *Mondragon: A Third Way*. Shutesbury, MA: Trustee Institute, 1984.

Moon, Peter. "Aboriginal Justice Cited As Way to Combat Crime." In *Native Americans, Crime, and Justice*, edited by Marianne O. Nielsen and Robert A. Silverman, 146–47. Previously published in (Toronto) *Globe and Mail*, October 2, 1995. Boulder: CO: Westview Press, 1996.

Moran, James A. "Preventing Alcohol Use Among Urban American Youth: The Seventh Generation Program." *Voices of First Nations People: Human Service Considerations*, edited by H. N. Weaver, 51–68. New York: Haworth Press, 1999.

Morgan, Lewis Henry. *Ancient Society*. New York: H. Holt, 1877.

———. *League of the Iroquois*. Secaucus, NJ: Citadel Press, 1996.

Moris, C. Patrick. "Termination by Accountants: The Reagan Indian Policy." In *Native Americans and Public Policy*, edited by Fremont J. Lyden and Lyman H. Legters, 63–84. Pittsburgh: Pittsburgh University Press, 1992.

Morris, Barbara, Stephen M. Sachs, and LaDonna Harris. "Placing Tribes in the Context of American Federalism." Paper presented at Western Political Science Association Meeting, 2000.

———. "Strategy and Choice: Opting for Cooperation or Competition: Investigation of Tribal and Sub-National Government Relations." In *Proceedings of the 1998 American Political Science Association Meeting*. Washington, D.C.: American Political Science Association, 1998.

Morrisette, P. I. "The Holocaust of First Nation People: Residual Effects on Parenting and Treatment Implications." *Contemporary Family Therapy* 16 (1994): 381–92.

Nabokov, Peter. *Where the Lightning Strikes: The Lives of American Indian Sacred Places*. New York: Viking, 2006.

Nagel, Joane. *American Indian Ethnic Renewal: Red Power and the Resurgence of Identity and Culture*. New York: Oxford University Press, 1996.

Nalbantian, Haig R., ed. *Incentives, Cooperation, and Risk Sharing: Economic and Psychological Perspectives on Employment Contracts.* Totowa, NJ: Rowman and Littlefield, 1987.

National Congress of American Indians Nuclear Waste Program. "Tribal Radiological Emergency Preparedness: Transporting Radioactive Waste through Tribal Lands: Protecting the People and Resources." Washington, D.C.: National Congress of American Indians, 1996.

National American Indian Housing Council. *Sustaining Indian Housing: An Evaluation of Tribal Economic Development and Its Impact on Housing in Four Case Studies.* http://www.naihc.net/uploads/research/2004_Economic_Dev_Report.pdf.

National Tribal Gaming Commission. "Growth in Tribal Gaming Revenues, 1996–2006." Gaming Revenue Reports. http://www.nigc.gov/Default.aspx?tabid=67.

Neihardt, John G. *Black Elk Speaks.* New York: Pocket Books, 1959.

Nelson, Robert A., and Joseph F. Sheley. "The Bureau of Indian Affairs Influence on Indian Self-Determination." In *American Indian Policy in the Twentieth Century*, edited by Vine Deloria Jr. Norman: University of Oklahoma Press, 1985.

New York Stock Exchange. *People and Productivity.* Homewood, IL: Dow Jones-Irwin, 1985.

Nichols, Roger L. *American Indians in U.S. History.* Norman: University of Oklahoma Press, 2003.

Nielsen, Marianne O., and Robert A. Silvermen, eds. *Native Americans, Crime, and Justice.* Boulder, CO: Westview Press, 1996.

Nordhaus, Bob. "30 Years of Indian Law Practice." Unpublished paper, 2006.

Nowak, John E. "The Gang of Five and the Second Coming of an Anti-Reconstruction Supreme Court." *Notre Dame Law Review* 73 (2000): 1091.

Oakeshott, Robert. "Mondragon: Spain's Oasis of Democracy." In *Self-Management: The Economic Liberation of Man*, edited by Jaroslav Vanek, 290–96. Baltimore: Penguin Books, 1975.

O'Brien, Sharon. *American Indian Tribal Governments.* Norman: University of Oklahoma Press, 1989.

Oetting, E. R., and F. Beauvais. "Epidemiology and Correlates of Alcohol Use Among Indian Adolescents Living on Reservations." In *Alcohol Use Among U.S. Ethnic Minorities*,

239–67. NIAAA research monograph no. 18. Rockville, MD: U.S. Public Health Service, 1989.

———. "Orthogonal Cultural Identification Theory: The Cultural Identification of Minority Adolescents." *International Journal of the Addictions* 25, nos. 5A, 6A (1991): 655–85.

Olson, James S., and Raymond Wilson. *Native Americans in the Twentieth Century*. Urbana: University of Illinois Press, 1984.

Opler, Morris Edward. *An Apache Way of Life: The Economic, Social, and Religious Institutions of the Chiricahua Indians*. Lincoln: University of Nebraska Press, 1996.

Osborne, David, and Ted Gaebler. *Reinventing Government: How the Entrepreneurial Spirit Is Transforming the Public Sector*. Reading, MA: Addison-Wesley, 1992.

Osburn, Katherine M. B. *Southern Ute Women: Autonomy and Assimilation on the Reservation, 1887–1934*. Albuquerque: University of New Mexico Press, 1998.

Page, Jake. *In the Hands of the Great Spirit: The 20,000 Year History of the American Indians*. New York: Free Press, 2003.

Parker, Alfred L. *The Economic and Fiscal Importance of American Indians in New Mexico*. Bernalillo, NM: Americans for Indian Opportunity, 1993.

Parker, Michael. *Inside the Circle: A Union Guide to QWL*. Boston: South End Press, 1985.

Patterson, Victoria D. "Evolving Gender Roles in Pomo Society." In *Women and Power in Native North America*, edited by Laura E. Klein and Lillian A. Ackerman. Norman: University of Oklahoma Press, 1995.

Pember, Mary Annette. "The Red Road to Green: Tribal People's World Views Preceded 'Green' Trend." *Tribal College Journal of American Indian Higher Education* 20, no. 2 (Winter 2008).

Peristiany, J. G. *Honour and Shame: The Values of Mediterranean Society*. Chicago: University of Chicago Press, 1966.

Peroff, Nicholas C. "Doing Research in Indian Affairs: Old Problems and a New Perspective." Kansas City: University of Missouri/ L.P. Cookingham Institute of Public Affairs, 1989.

———. *Menominee Drums: Tribal Termination and Restoration: 1954–1974*. Norman: University of Oklahoma Press, 1982.

Perry, Barbara. "Nobody Trusts Them! Under- and Over-Policing Native American Communities." *Critical Criminology* 14 (2006): 411–44. http://www.springerlink.com/index/8414017173KU5500.pdf.

Peterson, John H., Jr. "Three Efforts at Development Among the Choctaws of Mississippi." In *Southeastern Indians Since the Removal Era*, edited by Walter L. Williams. Athens: University of Georgia Press, 1979.

Pettit, Jan. *Utes: The Mountain People*. Colorado Springs: Century One Press, 1982.

Polgar, S. "Biculturation of Mesquakie Teenage Boys." *American Anthropologist* 62, no. 1 (1960): 217–35.

Pommersheim, Frank. *A Braid of Feathers: American Indian Law and Contemporary Indian Life*. Berkeley: University of California Press, 1995.

"Poverty Status, by Race/Ethnicity, 1980 and 1990." In *Statistical Record of Native North Americans*, edited by Marlita A. Ready, 814. Detroit, MI: Gale Research, 1993.

Powers, William K. *Oglala Religion*. Lincoln: University of Nebraska Press, 1977.

Pratt, Scott L. *Native Pragmatism: Rethinking the Roots of American Philosophy*. Bloomington: Indiana University Press, 2002.

Price, Catherine. *The Oglala People, 1841–1879: A Political History*. Lincoln: University of Nebraska Press, 1996.

Proceedings of the 1997 Annual Meeting of the American Political Science Association. Washington, D.C.: American Political Science Association, 1997.

Proceedings of the 1999 Annual Meeting of the American Political Science Association. Washington, D.C.: American Political Science Association, 1999.

"Proposed List of Inherently Federal Functions and Non-Inherently Federal Functions of the Bureau of Indian Affairs, May 1997." *Federal Register* 62, no. 95 (Friday, May 16, 1997): 27064.

Prucha, Francis Paul, ed. *Documents of United States Indian Policy*. 2nd ed. Lincoln: University of Nebraska Press, 1990.

Purdue, T., *Cherokee Women: Gender and Culture Change, 1700–1835*. Lincoln: University of Nebraska Press, 1998.

"Recommendations for Indian Policy, Message from the President of the United States Transmitting Recommendations for Indian Policy." Referred to the Committee on Interior and Insular Affairs, House of Representatives, 91st Cong., 2nd sess., document no. 91–363. July 8, 1970.

Reichard, Alice. *Navaho Religion*. New York: Pantheon Books, 1950.

Rice, Julian. *Ella Deloria's The Buffalo People.* Albuquerque: University of New Mexico Press, 1994.

Richardson, James. *Law and Status Among the Kiowa Indians.* Seattle: University of Washington Press, 1966.

Riley, Patricia, ed. *Growing Up Native American: An Anthology.* New York: William Morrow, 1993.

Robinson, Robert F. *The Economic and Fiscal Importance of Indian Tribes in Arizona.* Phoenix: Arizona Commission of Indian Affairs, 1993.

Rollings, Willard H. *The Comanche.* New York: Chelsea House Publishers, 1989.

Ross, Rupert. "Leaving Our White Eyes Behind: The Sentencing of Native Accused." In *Native Americans, Crime, and Justice,* edited by Marianne O. Nielsen and Robert A. Silverman, 152–69. Boulder, CO: Westview Press, 1996.

Rosser, Ezra. "This Land Is Your Land, This Land Is My Land: Markets and Institutions for Development of Native American Lands." *Arizona Law Review* 47, no. 10.

Rousseau, Jean Jacques. *The Social Contract.* New York: E. P. Dutton, 1950.

Rusmich, Ladislav, and Stephen M. Sachs. *Lessons from the Failure of the Communist Economic System.* Lanham, MD: Lexington Books, 2003.

Sachs, Stephen M. "Acknowledging the Circle: The Impact of American Indian Tradition upon Western Political Thought and Its Contemporary Relevance." In *Proceedings of the 2002 American Political Science Association Meeting.* Washington, D.C.: American Political Science Association, 2002.

———. "Bringing the Case into the Classroom, or One Up on Simulation." *Social Science Record* 10, no. 2 (1973).

———. "Building the World Team: Getting to Peace Through Developing a Collaborative Culture." *Organization Development Journal* 8, no. 1 (Spring 1990).

———. "Building Trust in Democratic Organizations." *Psychology* 31, no. 2 (1994).

———. "Circling the Circles: Indigenous Movements Towards an Alternative Appropriate Globalization." *Indigenous Policy* (Summer 2004), 14–35.

———. "Climate Change, Environmental Decay, and Indigenous People: Indigenizing the Greening of the World." *Indigenous Policy,* 18, no. 3 (Fall 2007).

————. "Concerning the Interest and Goal Structure of Self-Managed Organizations." Paper presented at the Second International Sociological Conference on Participation, Workers Control and Self Management, Paris, 1977.

————. "The Cutting Edge." *Workplace Democracy* 12, no. 2 (Fall 1985).

————. "The Cutting Edge of Physics: Western Science Is Finally Catching Up with American Indian Tradition." In *Proceedings of the American Indian Studies Section of the 2007 Western Social Science Association Meeting*. Also published in *Indigenous Policy* 18, no. 2 (Summer 2007).

————. "Employee Participation: The Next Stage." *Workplace Democracy*, no. 61 (Summer 1988).

————. "Global Focus: Beyond the Workplace." *Workplace Democracy*, no. 57 (Summer 1987).

————. "Global Warming and What Can Be Done About It." *Nonviolent Change* 22, no. 1 (Fall 2007).

————. "The Interaction of Forces for and Against Political and Social Transformation." In *Proceedings of the 1997 American Political Science Association Meeting*. Washington, D.C.: American Political Science Association, 1997.

————. "LaDonna Harris, Founder of Americans for Indian Opportunity: Leadership in the Tradition of American Indian Women's Voices." *A Leadership Journal: Women in Leadership— Sharing the Vision* 3, no. 1 (Fall 1998): 77–85.

————. "Learning the Pedagogy of Peace: or Living the World Team into Existence." Paper presented at the Consortium on Peace Research Education and Development (COPRED) 16th Annual Conference, Milwaukee, 1987.

————. "Need for More Indian Nations to Develop Independent Courts." *Indigenous Policy* 16, no. 2 (Fall 2005): 36.

————. "Power and Sovereignty: The Changing Realities of Indian Nations." In *Proceedings of the 2008 Western Social Science Association Meeting, American Indian Studies Section*. Also published in *Indigenous Policy* 19, no. 2 (Summer 2008).

————. "The Putney School: John Dewey Is Alive and Well in Southern Vermont." *Democracy and Education* 6, no. 3 (Spring 1992).

————. "Remembering the Circle: The Relevance of Traditional American Indian and Other Indigenous Governance for the Twenty-First Century." Paper presented at the Western Social Science Association Meeting, Reno, NV, 2001.

————. "Returning the World to Harmony: Getting to Peace in American Indian Tradition." *Nonviolent Change* 10, no. 3 (Spring 2006).

————. "Termination by Budget: Impact of the 1996 Federal Budget on Native Americans." In *Proceedings of the 1996 Meeting of the American Political Science Association*. Washington, D.C.: American Political Science Association, 1996.

————. "A Transformational Native American Gift: Reconceptualizing the Idea of Politics for the 21st Century." In *Proceedings of the 1993 American Political Science Association Meeting*. Washington, D.C.: American Political Science Association, 1993.

————. "The Uses and Limits of Simulation Models in Teaching Social Sciences and History." *The Social Studies* 51, no. 4 (1970).

————. "Workplace Democracy, Education, and Self-Management." In *Proceedings of the 1991 American Political Science Association Meeting*. Washington, D.C.: American Political Science Association, 1991.

————, and Deborah Esquibel Hunt. "Appropriate Consulting with Indian Nations: Facilitating Returning to the Wisdom of the People." In *Proceedings of the 2000 American Political Science Association Meeting*. Washington, D.C.: American Political Science Association, 2000.

————, LaDonna Harris, and Barbara Morris. "Devolution of Federal Authority to the States: The Growth of Tribal Government Authority and the Development of Tribal–State and Local Government Relations." Paper presented at the Southwest Political Science Association Meeting, San Antonio, TX, 1999.

————. "Honoring the Circle: Developing Government to Government Relations between Indian Tribal Governments and Federal, State, and Local Governments." Paper presented at the Western Social Science Association meeting, Albuquerque, 2002.

————. "Native American Tribes and Federalism: Can Government to Government Relations between the Tribes and the Federal Government Be Institutionalized?" In *Proceedings of the 1997 American Political Science Association Meeting*. Washington, D.C.: American Political Science Association, 1997.

————, LaDonna Harris, Barbara Morris, and Deborah Esquibel Hunt. "Recreating the Circle: Overcoming Colonialism and Returning to Harmony in American Indian Communities." In *Proceedings of the 1999 American Political Science Association Meeting*. Washington, D.C.: American Political Science Association, 1999.

Sahlins, Marshall. *Stone Age Economics.* Chicago: Aldine-Atherton, 1971.

Sandoz, Mari. *Crazy Horse: The Strange Man of the Oglalas.* Lincoln: University of Nebraska Press, 1942.

Sanford, Donald. *Healing and Wholeness.* New York: Paulist Press, 1977.

Sattler, Richard A. "Women's Status among the Muscogee and Cherokee." In *Women and Power in Native North America,* edited by Laura E. Klein and Lillian A. Ackerman. Norman: University of Oklahoma Press, 1995.

Saunders, Nicholas J. *Ancient Americas: The Great Civilisations.* Stroud, UK: Sutton Publishers, 2004.

Schwartz, M. *Contemporary Native Americans: LaDonna Harris.* Austin, TX: Steck-Vaughn, 1997.

Sharp, Lauriston. "Steel Axes for Stone Axes in Australia." *Human Organization* 11, no. 2 (1952): 17–22.

Simmons, John, and William Mares. *Working Together.* New York: Alfred A. Knopf, 1983.

Simmons, Virginia McConnell. *The Ute Indians of Utah, Colorado, and New Mexico.* Boulder: University Press of Colorado, 2000.

Singleton, Sara. "Dividing a Shared Resource: Creating Institutions for Intertribal Allocation of Pacific Salmon." Tucson, AZ: Western Political Science Association, 1997.

Smith, Barbara Leigh. "Understanding of Sovereignty and Identity Improved by Learning with Cases." *Tribal College Journal of American Indian Higher Education* 20, no. 2 (Winter 2008).

Smith, Hedrick. *Rethinking America.* New York: Random House, 1995.

Smith, Paul Chaat, and Robert Allen Warrior. *Like a Hurricane: The American Indian Movement from Alcatraz to Wounded Knee.* New York: The New Press, 1996.

Smith, Zachary. *The Environmental Paradox.* Englewood Cliffs, NJ: Prentice Hall, 1992.

Standing Bear, Luther. *My People, the Sioux.* Lincoln: University of Nebraska Press, 1975.

Stein, Harold, ed. *Public Administration and Policy Development.* New York: Harcourt, Brace and World, 1952.

Stiffarm, L. A., and P. Lane Jr. "The Demography of Native North America: A Question of American Indian Survival." In *The State of Native America: Genocide, Colonization, and Resistance,* edited by M. A. James. Boston: South End Press, 1992.

Stolzman, William, SJ. *The Pipe and Christ.* Chamberlain, SD: The Tipi Press, 1989.

Storm, Heyemeyohsts. *Seven Arrows*. New York: Ballantine Books, 1972.

Stringer, William L., with Charles Blackwell. *The Economic Impact of Tribal Tax and Expenditure Programs in the State of Oklahoma*. Washington, D.C., and Oklahoma City: George Washington University Center for Native American Studies and Indian Policy Development/Oklahoma Indian Affairs Commission, 1992.

Strong, G., and C. Morris. "Family Wellness: A Path to Wellness for Clients and Helpers." Presentation at the National Indian Child Welfare Conference, Minneapolis, MN, 1999.

Szasz, Margaret Connell. *Education and the American Indian: The Road to Self-Determination Since 1928*. 3rd ed. Albuquerque: University of New Mexico Press, 1999.

Tafoya, N., and A. Del Vecchio. "Back to the Future: An Examination of the Native American Holocaust Experience." In *Ethnicity and Family Therapy*, edited by M. McGoldrick, J. Giordano, and J. Pearce. New York: The Guilford Press, 1996.

Taylor, Jonathan, and Joseph Kalt. *American Indians on Reservations: A Data Book of Socio-Economic Changes between the 1990 and 2000 Census*. Harvard Project on American Indian Economic Development, Malcolm Wiener Center for Social Policy, John F. Kennedy School of Government. Cambridge, MA: Harvard University, 2005.

Taylor, Theodore W. *The States and Their Indian Citizens*. Washington, D.C.: United States Department of the Interior, Bureau of Indian Affairs, 1972.

Thomas, Henk, and Chris Logan. *Mondragon: An Economic Analysis*. London: Allen and Unwin, 1982.

Tiler, Veronica E. *The Jicarilla Apache Tribe: A History*. Lincoln: University of Nebraska Press, 1983.

"Tobacco, Alcohol, and Other Drug Use Among High School Students in Bureau of American Indian Affairs–Funded Schools: United States 2001." *MMWR Weekly* 52, no. 44 (November 7, 2003): 1070–72. http://www.cdc.gov/mmwr/preview/mmwrhtml/mm5244a3.htm.

Toelken, Barre. "The Demands of Harmony." In *I Become Part of It: Sacred Dimensions in Native American Life*, edited by D. M. Dooling and Paul Jordan-Smith. San Francisco: Harper Collins, 1992.

Tolman, A., and R. Reedy. "Implementation of Cultural-Specific Interventions for a Native American Community." *Journal of Clinical Psychology* 5, no. 3 (1998): 382–93.

Toms, Michael. *The Wisdom of Joseph Campbell: In Conversation with Michael Toms.* Carlsbad, CA: New Dimensions/Hay House, 1997. Audiobook.

Trigger, Bruce G. *The Huron: Farmers of the North.* Fort Worth, TX: Holt, Rinehart and Winston, 1990.

Tso, Tom. "The Process of Decision Making in Tribal Courts." In *Native Americans, Crime, and Justice*, edited by Marianne O. Nielsen and Robert A. Silverman, 170–89. Boulder, CO: Westview Press, 1996.

Two Years after the President's Meeting with Tribal Leaders: Annual Report of the Administration Working Group on Indians and Alaska Natives. Prepared by the Administration Working Group on Indians and Alaska Natives. Washington, D.C., 1996.

U.S. Census Bureau. *March Current Population Survey (CPS), 1994 to 2003.* Washington, D.C.: U.S. Census Bureau.

U.S. Department of Housing and Urban Development. *Annual Report to Congress: FY1979: Indian and Alaska Native Housing and Community Development Programs.* Washington, D.C.: U.S. Department of Housing and Urban Development, 1979.

U.S. Department of the Interior, Bureau of Indian Affairs. *Strategic Plan 2000–2005.* Washington, D.C.: U.S. Department of the Interior, 2000.

U.S. Department of Labor, Bureau of Labor Management Relations and Cooperative Programs. *ARMCO Steel's Quality Plus Program at Ashland Kentucky.* Washington, D.C.: U.S. Department of Labor, 1990.

Utley, Robert M. *The Lance and the Shield: The Life and Times of Sitting Bull.* New York: Ballantine Books, 1994.

Van Biema, David. "Bury My Heart in Committee." *Time*, September 18, 1995.

Van Voorhis, Rebecca M. "Culturally Relevant Practice: A Framework for Teaching the Psychosocial Dynamics of Oppression." *Journal of Social Work Education* 23, no. 1 (1998): 121–33.

Venables, Robert W. *American Indian History: Five Centuries of Conflict and Coexistence.* Vol. 2, *Confrontation, Adaptation, and Assimilation.* Santa Fe, NM: Clear Light Publishers, 2004.

―――. "American Indian Influences on the Founding Fathers." In *Exiled in the Land of the Free: Democracy, Indian Nations, and the U.S. Constitution*, edited by Oren Lyons, John Mohawk, Vine Deloria Jr., Laurence Hauptman, Howard Berman, Donald Grinde Jr., Curtis Berkey, and Robert Venables. Santa Fe, NM: Clear Light Publishers, 1992.

von Franz, Marie-Louise. *Alchemy: An Introduction to the Symbolism and Psychology*. Toronto: Jung Foundation of Ontario, 1991.

Walker, David B. *The Rebirth of Federalism: Slouching Toward Washington*. 2nd ed. New York: Chatham House Publishers, 2000.

Walker, James R. *Lakota Belief and Ritual*, edited by Raymond DeMallie and Elaine A. Jahner. Lincoln: University of Nebraska Press, 1980.

―――. *Lakota Myth*, edited by Elaine A. Jahner. Lincoln: University of Nebraska Press, 1983.

―――. *Lakota Society*, edited by Raymond DeMaillie. Lincoln: University of Nebraska Press, 1982.

Wall, Steve. *To Become a Human Being: The Message of Tadodaho Chief Leon Shenandoah*. Charlottesville, VA: Hampton Roads Publishing, 2001.

Wallace, Ernest, and E. Adamson Hoebel. *The Comanches: Lords of the Plains*. Norman: University of Oklahoma Press, 1952.

Warfield, J. N. *A Science of Generic Design: Managing Complexity through Systems Design*. Ames: Iowa State University Press, 1995.

―――. *Societal Systems: Planning Policy and Complexity*. New York: Wiley, 1976.

Waterman, Robert. "Introduction to Transformation." Unpublished manuscript, 1992.

Waters, Frank. *The Man Who Killed the Deer: A Novel of Pueblo Indian Life*. Athens: University of Ohio Press, 1970.

Weaver, Hillary N. "Indigenous People in a Multicultural Society: Unique Issues for Human Services." *Social Work* 43, no. 3 (May 1998).

―――, ed. *Voices of First Nations People: Human Service Considerations*. New York: Haworth Press, 1999

―――, and Maria Yellow Horse Brave Heart. "Examining Two Facets of American Indian Identity: Exposure to Other Cultures and the Influence of Historical Trauma." In *Voices of First Nations People: Human Service Considerations*, edited by Hillary N. Weaver, 19–31. New York: Haworth Press, 1999.

————. "Facets of American Indian Identity: Implications for Social Work Practice." *Journal of Human Behavior in the Social Environment.* In press.

Weise, Allan O., and Autumn Stewart. "Intergovernmental and Economic Impacts of Grand Casino and Mystic Lake Casino." In *Proceedings of the 1993 American Political Science Association Meeting.* Washington, D.C.: American Political Science Association, 1993.

Wheeler, Nathan, and Emily Ronald. *Research Report: Navajo Community and Farmington, New Mexico (2006).* The Pluralism Project at Harvard University. http://www.pluralism.org/research/profiles/display.php?profile=74198.

Wheeler, Nicole. "Bolivian Interactive Advisory Forum." *The Ambassador* 11, no. 2 (Summer 2008): 5, 17.

Wilds, Leah, and Danny Gonzales. "On the Cutting Edge: Overcoming Obstacles to the Resolution of Water Resource Conflicts in the West." Paper presented at the Western Political Science Association Meeting, Seattle, 1991.

Wilkins, David E. *American Politics and the American Political System.* Lanham, MD: Rowman and Littlefield, 2002.

————. "Renouncing Jurisdiction: Tribes, States, and Constitutional Disclaimers." In *Proceedings of the 1998 Meeting of the American Political Science Association.* Washington, D.C.: American Political Science Association, 1998.

Wilkinson, Charles. *Blood Struggle: The Rise of Modern Indian Nations.* New York: W. W. Norton, 2005.

Williams, Walter L., ed. *Southeastern Indians Since the Removal Era.* Athens: University of Georgia Press, 1979.

Wilson, Jon. "Real Justice." *Hope Magazine,* no. 20 (Fall 1999).

Woods, J. Cedric. "Diverse Learning Styles Among Native Students." *Red Ink* 4, no. 2 (Fall 1995): 26–30.

Yazzie, Robert, Moroni Benally, Andrew Curley, Nikke Alex, James Singer, and Amber Crotty. *Navajo Nation Constitutional Feasibility and Reform Project.* Diné Policy Institute of Diné College, Tsaile, Navajo Nation, AZ, September 2, 2008.

Yellow Bird, Michael J. "Deconstructing Colonialism: A First Nations Social Work Perspective." Unpublished manuscript, 1998.

Young, Richard K. *The Ute Indians of Colorado in the Twentieth Century.* Norman: University of Oklahoma Press, 1997.

Young, Robert W. *A Political History of the Navajo Tribe.* Tsaille, AZ: Navajo Community College Press, 1978.

Zahran, Hatice S., Rosemarie Kobau, David G. Moriarty, Matthew M. Zack, James Holt, and Ralph Donehoo. *Health-Related Quality of Life Surveillance: United States, 1993–2002.* Atlanta, GA: Center for Disease Control, Division of Adult and Community Health, National Center for Chronic Disease Prevention and Health Promotion, 2005. http://www.cdc.gov/mmwr/preview/mmwrhtml/ss5404a1.htm.

Zehr, Howard, *Changing Lenses: A New Focus for Crime and Justice.* 3rd ed. Scottsdale, PA: Herald Press, 2005.

Zelio, Judy, ed. *Promoting Effective State-Tribal Relations.* Denver: National Conference of State Legislatures, 1990.

Zion, James, and Elsie B Zion. "'Hazho's Sokee'—Stay Together Nicely: Domestic Violence under Navajo Common Law." In *Native Americans, Crime, and Justice,* edited by Marianne O. Nielsen and Robert A. Silverman, 17–18, 96–102. Boulder, CO: Westview Press, 1996.

News Articles

ACLU of Northern California. "ACLU Protects Native American Children in Landmark School Settlement." http://www.aclunc.org/issues/racial_justice/aclu_protects_native_american_children_in_landmark_school_settlement.shtml.

ÈAmericans for Indian Opportunity. "1984 University of New Mexico Graduate Takes Over the Helm of a Thirty-Two Year Legacy." Press release, December 1, 2002.

Barrenger, Felicity. "Indian Tribes See Profit in Harnessing the Wind for Power." *New York Times,* October 10, 2008. http://www.nytimes.com/2008/10/10/us/10wind.html?_r=2&ref=environment&oref=slogin&oref=slogin.

Beams, Lillian. "Americans for Indian Opportunity Ambassadors Meet." *News from Indian Country,* mid-June 1995.

Bear, Tahlia. "Academy Embraces Outdoor Education." *Southern Ute Drum,* December 26, 2003.

Begay, Jason. "Hold Steady on Investments, Advisors Say." *Navajo Times,* October 2, 2008.

Bindell, Stan. "Southwest Native Tourism Conference Provided a Forum." *News from Indian Country,* mid-June 1994.

Brambach, Steve. "Building for Bertha: San Juan Pueblo Housing Puts It All Together Without HUD." *Indian Country Today*, June 4–11, 1996.

Brasher, Phillip. "Audit Finds Tribal Governments Run Own Programs Better." *News from Indian Country*, late May 1995.

———. "Indians' Crime Risk Is More Than Twice the Norm, Study Says." *Indianapolis Star*, February 15, 1999.

Brokaw, Chet. "Indian Tribes Allege Government Slow to Act on Crumbling Schools." Associated Press, June 19, 2005.

Brown, Dave. "Academy Class Asks about G F Building." *The Southern Ute Drum*, March 19, 2004.

———. "Academy Students ZAP the CSAP Test." *The Southern Ute Drum*, May 18, 2001.

———. "Academy to Offer Parenting Circle." *The Southern Ute Drum*, October 17, 2003.

———. "A Meeting of Minds over Social Services." *The Southern Ute Drum*, March 3, 2006.

———. "Colorado House Passes DUI Revocation Power on Tribal Lands." *The Southern Ute Drum*, March 9, 2001.

———. "Ribbon Cutting Marks Opening of Academy." *The Southern Ute Drum*, September 8, 2000.

———. "Southern Ute Academy Begins Third Year." *The Southern Ute Drum*, September 6, 2002.

———. "SUIT and Herald Find Common Ground." *The Southern Ute Drum*, October 8, 1999.

———. "Tribal Government Reacts to Focus Groups." *The Southern Ute Drum*, September 30, 2005.

Brown, David. "Family/Community Centers and Tribal School Location Selected by Tribal Council." *The Southern Ute Drum*, February 12, 1999.

Burch, Chairman Leonard C. "Briefing Paper on Animas–La Plata ('A/LP') Project Alternatives." March 19, 1993.

Capriccioso, Rob. "Wall Street Crisis Clouds Rez Road." *Indian Country Today*, October 10, 2008. http://www.indiancountrytoday.com/national/30803129.html.

Clay, Catherine A. "EPA Proposes to Work with Tribes in Same Way It Works with States." *News from Indian Country*, late October 1994.

Deer, Ada. "1997 Budget: GOP Cuts Threaten BIA Funding; Impact Deep at Reservation Level." *Indian Country Today*, May 27–June 4, 1996.

Dishneau, David. "Drill Sergeant in Sex Scandal Begs for Mercy, Gets 6 Months." *Indianapolis Star*, May 31, 1997.

Donovan, Bill. "Officials Put Brakes on Legislative Process." *Navajo Times*, February 10, 2005.

———. "Police Can't Lie to Obtain Confession, Court Rules." *Navajo Times*, December 20, 2004.

Dvorak, Todd. "Meskwaki Hope New Court Will Help Avoid Disputes of the Past." *News from Indian Country*, September 20, 2004.

Fisher, Maria Sudekum. "Haskall, Tribal Colleges, Serve Struggling Population with Less." *Native American Times*, February 8, 2005.

Frosch, Dan. "In Shadow of 70's Racism, Recent Violence Stirs Rage." *New York Times*, September 17, 2006. http://www.nytimes.com/2006/09/17/us/17navajo.html.

Gouras, Matt. "American Indian Legislators Hear Sobering Statistics." *News from Indian Country*, September 2007. http://indiancountrynews.net/index.php?option=com_content&task=view&id=1585&Itemid=33.

Graef, Christine. "Disenrollment: 'We're not alone any more.'" *News from Indian Country*, July 11, 2005.

Gray, Louis. "Indians Remain Poorest under Bush, Study Says; Urban Indians Suffer in Great Numbers, Report Claims." Editorial, *Native American Times*, September 1, 2004.

———. "Weak Economy Hurting American Indian Families." *Indian Country Today*, September 22, 2004.

———, and Matt Kelley. "Critics: BIA Too Slow in [Saginaw Chippewa] Crises." *News from Indian Country*, mid-September, 1999.

Haase, Eric. "Tribal Housing Singled Out for Major Cuts." *Indian Country Today*, June 29, 1995.

Hall, Tex. "State of the Nations Address, National Congress of American Indians," January 21, 2004. *News from Indian Country*, February 9, 2004.

Hamilton, Candy. "$28 Million Turned Back by BIA; Lack of Funding Means Unsafe Buildings at Loneman School." *News from Indian Country*, mid-May 1996.

———. "Governor Janklow Meets with Oglala Tribal Leaders." *News from Indian Country*, late August 1995.

Hansen, Terri C. "EPA Establishes Offices to Strengthen Tribal Operations." *News from Indian Country*, late October 1994.

———. "Innovative Program Results in Success for Native Students." *Indian Country Today Education '08–'09.*

———. "People for Salmon Project Takes Off." *News from Indian Country,* late April 1999.

———. "Three Sovereigns Fish Management." *News from Indian Country,* mid-April 1998.

Herrmann, Babette. "College Credit Certificate Program Held at Casino." *Indian Country Today Education '08–'09.*

Howell, Randall. "Tribes Writing Regs on Housing: New HUD Law Effective Oct. 1." *Indian Country Today,* December 23–30, 1996.

Indianapolis News. "EPA, Quayle, Committee Head for Showdown." November 21, 1991.

Indian Country Today. "Casino Profits Going Down." December 14, 1995.

———. "DA Signs with Acoma Pueblo." May 4–11, 1998.

———. "Housing and Urban Development Inspector General Addresses Congressional Committees about Findings." March 31–April 7, 1997.

———. "NIGC Numbers Tell No Lies." July 28, 2004.

———. "Policy Center to Participate in National Forum." September 16–23, 1996.

———. "Standing Rock–State Tax Compact Can Be Tribal Model." January 25–February 1, 1999.

———. "Tribal Housing Susceptible to Economic Stress." June 29, 1995.

———. "Tribal Leaders Zero in on Treaty Obligations at Summit Meeting." Week of May 4, 1995.

———. "Trust Funds Gone." May 7–14, 1996.

———. "Ute Child Welfare Gains Support." September 29–October 6, 1997.

Jawort, Adrian. "Tribes Work Together to Fight Youth Suicide." *Indian Country Today,* December 19, 2007. http://www.indiancountrytoday.com/archive/28142004.html.

Kelley, Matt. "Tribal Schools—Decaying Death Traps under Feds." *News from Indian Country,* mid-September, 1995.

Kent, Jim. "Montana Governor Wants Improved Relations with Tribes." *News from Indian Country,* mid-March 2001.

Krol, Debra Utacia. "Tribes Work to Clean Up Their Indoor Air Act." *News from Indian Country,* July 8, 2004.

Mahesh, S. U. "Tribes Fail to Report DWI Cases: Many Tribal Members Escape State Penalties." *Albuquerque Journal,* April 30, 2000.

Mapes, Lynda V. "Tribes Are State's New High Rollers—In Business." *Seattle Times*, February 17, 2008. http://seattletimes.nwsource. com/html/localnews/2004186688_tribes17m.html.

Marales, Victor. "New Program Emphasizes Tribal Gaming Management." *Indian Country Today Education '08–'09.*

May, James. "California AG Creates Native American Affairs Office." *Indian Country Today*, March 29, 2000.

Melmer, David. "$850 Million Needed to Repair BIA Schools: No Relief in Sight." *Indian Country Today*, August 5–12, 1996.

———. "BIA Financial Reports Leave Some Questions Unanswered." *Indian Country Today*, February 1, 1996.

———. "'Bribes for Tribe': Fuel Tax Rebate Paid; Some Tribes Say at the Price of Sovereignty." *Indian Country Today*, March 24–31, 1997.

———. "Casino Tax Shelved but May Rise Again." *Indian Country Today*, November 23, 1995.

———. "Native American Families and Winner School District Announce Settlement in Case Alleging Discrimination." American Civil Liberties Union press release, June 18, 2007. http://www.aclu.org/crimjustice/juv/30155prs20070618.html.

———. "School District Settles Lawsuit with Conditions." *Indian Country Today*, published June 25, 2007, updated September 10, 2008. http://www.indiancountrytoday.com/archive/28147099. html.

———. "Statistics Show Prosecution in Indian Country Is Lacking." *Indian Country Today*, November 30, 2007.

Morrison, Joan. "Chippewa Rap EPA on Trust Responsibilities." *Indian Country Today*, May 12–19, 1997.

Moses, Sarah. "Seeking Solutions for Global Warming." *Indian Country Today*, December 8, 2006.

Mukluk Telegraph, April–June, 2008.

"Native Americans Find Little Progress Made between 1974 and 2006." Race Relations blog from About.com, Sunday, September 17, 2006.

Native American Times. "Study: Natives Suffer More from Kidney Disease, Less Likely to Receive Transplants." March 2, 2005.

———. "Trifecta for Pro-Indian Legislation." May 25, 2005.

Navajo Nation Council, Office of the Speaker. "Speaker Morgan to Present Report on Feasibility of a Constitutional Government for Navajo Nation During 2008 Fall Session." Press release, October 13, 2008. http://www.navajonationcouncil.org/press.htm.

Navajo Times. "N.M. Can Shortchange Schools, Court Rules." January 6, 2005.

News from Indian Country. "Abramoff Pleads Guilty, Promises to Help in Probe." January 23, 2006.

———. "Dakota Agree to Split Sales Tax with State [Minnesota]." Late March 1997.

———. "Documents Show Lobbyist Took $14 Million from Mississippi Choctaw." January 23, 2006.

———. "Governor Invites Native Leaders to Discussion." Mid-June 1994.

———. "Locke Signs Cigarette Tax Bill." Late May 2001.

———. "Montana Joint Law Enforcement Proves Beneficial." Mid-January 2000.

———. "North Dakota and Lakota Sign Cooperative Agreement." Mid-March 1996.

———. "Program Blends Conventional Treatment with Tradition." December 30, 2004.

———. "Reservation Program Blends Conventional Treatment with Tradition." February 7, 2005.

———. "Study Says American Indian Students Falling Behind." September 2007.

———. "Tribes Set Own Goals." Late July, 1996.

Nichols, Judy. "Cultural Focus Credited for Graduation Rate." *Native American Times*, June 9, 2004.

Norell, Brenda. "Chaos Continues for San Carlos." *Indian Country Today*, August 31–September 7, 1998.

———. "The Power That Divides: San Carlos Conflict Isn't Resolved with New Council." *Indian Country Today*, January 4–11, 1999.

Peacock, Neil. "Tribal Official Calls for Input: Developing Transportation Plan." *Native American Times*, January 12, 2005.

Prichard, James. "New Casino Boosts Tourism in Michigan's Southwestern Corner." Lakes Entertainment, Inc. http://indiancountrynews.net/index.php?option=com_content&task=view&id=3563&Itemid=109.

Priest, Diana. "Admiral, Army Lawyer Face Sexual Allegations." *Indianapolis Star*, May 31, 1997.

Rector, Leta. "Comanche Nation Conflict Question: Who Chooses Chairman?" *Indian Country Today*, October 5–12, 1998.

Reeves, Tracy A. "The Big Game Returns to the Reservation." *Indianapolis Star*, December 11, 1994.

Rehorn, John T. "Red Willow Branch Replaces Olive Branch in County, Tribe Tax Talks." *The Southern Ute Drum*, December 22, 1995.

———. "Tax Dispute Ends with Governor's Signature." *The Southern Ute Drum*, June 7, 1996.

———. "Tax Talks—County, Tribe Make Headway." *The Southern Ute Drum*, February 2, 1996.

———. "The Tribal Gaming Controversy." *The Southern Ute Drum*, April 16, 1993.

———. "Tribe Becomes Player Among Local Governments." *The Southern Ute Drum*, October 11, 1996.

Reynolds, Jerry. "Traditional Approach to Healing Encouraged." *Indian Country Today*, November 21, 2007.

Rolo, Mark Anthony. "Tribes, Government Differ on Definition of Consultation." *Indian Country Today*, Wednesday, March 1, 2000.

Rowley Jill. "Dollar Impact of Tribes Greater Than Air Base [in South Dakota]." *Indian Country Today*, June 15, 1995.

Sanvestian, Beth. "A Tuncai Court Success Story in the Making." *The Southern Ute Drum*, August 5, 2005.

———. "Southern Ute 'Tuncai' Court a Success Story." *The Southern Ute Drum*, July 8, 2005.

Siskiyou Daily News. "Tribes Gather to Discuss Highway Safety." July 19, 1996.

Smith, Jeff. "Traditional Foes Agree on Gasoline Formula." *Indianapolis Star*, March 14, 1991.

Snyder, Jim. "Wall Street Woes Drive Trust Fund below $1 Billion." *Navajo Times*, September 4, 2008.

Southern Ute Drum. "Animas–La Plata Project Chronology of Events." March 9, 1993.

———. "Good Neighbors Meet at Rolling Thunder Hall." March 23, 2001.

———. "SUIT [Southern Ute Indian Tribe], LaPlata County Happy with Tax Agreement on Lands." March 12, 1997.

Swanson, Holly. "Oregon Natural Resources Specialist Takes EPA Post." *Indian Country Today*, February 3–10, 1997.

Thompson, Don. "Split Widens between Haves, Have-Nots Among Indian Tribes." *Native American Times*, July 21, 2004.

Toensing, Gale Courtney. "Film Project Helps Passamoquoddy Languages Ford 'The River of Time.'" *Indian Country Today Education '08–'09*.

Urbinato, David. "Nebraska Tribes, State Pledge Cooperation." *News from Indian Country*, late August 1995.

Vedantam, Shankar. "Healers Prescribe Tribal Tradition: 'White Man's Medicine' Is Secondary to Time-Honored Customs." *Washington Post*, June 26, 2005.

Woodard, Stephanie. "Rethinking the Past: American Indians, Archaeologists Collaborate at Crow Canyon." *Indian Country Today Education '08–'09*.

———. "Speak Like a Person." *Indian Country Today Education '08–'09*.

Selected Internet Sources

Americans for Indian Opportunity: http://www.aio.org

Commission on Indian Services, Oregon State Legislature: http://www.leg.state.or.us/cis

Fellowship of Reconciliation Peacemaker Training Institute: http://www.forusa.org/programs/pti/default.html

Harvard Project on American Indian Economic Development: http://www.ksg.harvard.edu/hpaied/res_main.htm

Indigenous Policy Journal: http://www.indigenouspolicy.org

Native Financial Education Coalition: http://www.nfec.info/

National American Indian Housing Council: http://www.naihc.net/

National Congress of American Indians: http://www.ncai.org

National Indian Gaming Association: http://www.indiangaming.org/

National Indian Gaming Commission: http://www.nigc.gov/

Native American Bank: http://www.nativeamericanbank.com

Nonviolent Change Journal: http://www.nonviolentchangejournal.org

Our Native Circle: http://ournativecircle.org

Restorative Justice: http://www.restorativejustice.org

Southern Ute Tribe Education Center: http://www.southern-ute.nsn.us/education/index.html

The Ambassador: http://www.aio.org/news/ambassador_newsletter

Urban Indian Health Institute: http://www.uihi.org/

U.S. Census Bureau Educational Attainment: http://www.census.gov/population/www/socdemo/educ-attn.htm

Index

Page numbers in *italic* text indicate illustrations.

Abourezk, James, 115
Abramoff scandal, 317
abuse, 55, 103n88, 381. *See also* substance abuse
acculturation, 17–18, 76, 112, 114, 141, 380, 385, 388
ACLU. *See* American Civil Liberties Union
activism, Indian, 114–16, 185n15
adaptability, 33, 38–39, 50n108; in application of core values, 34
administrative culture development, 439–40
Advancement for Māori Opportunity, 277n77, 375
Advancement of Global Indigeneity, 375
AIO. *See* Americans for Indian Opportunity
air quality programs, 128
Akicita, 12
Alaska–British Columbia inclusiveness, 217–18

Alaska Native Claims Settlement Act, 115, 188n29, 298
Alaska Native Village Corporation Association, 298
Alaska Reorganization Act of 1936, 205
Albuquerque–Pueblo arrangement, 197n127
alienation, 109–10, 318, 344, 380–82, 386; education and, 322
Alkali Lake Indian Reserve, 258, 279n107
Allen, Jim, 316
allotment, 109, 185n8
alternative energy, 299; development, 284–85; on Rosebud Indian Reservation, 284–85
"Alternative Governance Models," 209–15, 272n18
Alutiiq Museum (Kodiak, Alaska), 371
Ambassadors Alliance, 374
American Civil Liberties Union (ACLU), 62–63
American dream, 319

American Indian Advisory Group, 123
American Indian Alaska Native Tourism Association, 292
American Indian Ambassadors Program, AIO, 374–75, 380, 416–17
American Indian College Fund, 66
American Indian Environmental Office, EPA, 127
American Indian Health Commission for Washington State, 178
American Indian Higher Education Consortium, 66, 367–68
American Indian Housing Council, 418
American Indian Movement, 435
American Indian Policy Review Commission, 150
American Indians and Alaska Natives with Cancer, 73–74
Americans for Indian Opportunity (AIO), 100n173, 118–20, 125–26, 161, 185n13, 375, 409; American Indian Ambassadors Program and, 374–75, 380, 416–17; developing, 416; Governance Project of, 190n56; ILIS and, 218, 223–24, 232, 277n77; projects, 416–17
Anderson, Michelle, 374–75
anger, 381
Animas–LaPlata Project, 166–68, 197n139
Apache, 162–63, 220; bands, 103n85; community, 243. *See also specific bands*
Applied Indigenous Studies Program at Northern Arizona University, 372–73
apprenticeship programs, 328

archaeology, 367
Arizona economy, 156–57
Arizona Tribal Court System, Peacemaking Circles training for, 260
Armco Steel, 48n88
Artman, Carl, 297
assimilation, 54–55, 76, 109, 112, 203, 379–80, 383; education and, 320; U.S. Indian policy and, 419
authority, traditional, 15, 23
autonomy, 182; in business activities, 287; in decision making, 116; individual, 16
awareness, healing–breaking the cycle, intergenerational trauma, 361–62

Bahá í Faith consultation method of decision making, 217, 249, 272n24
Baker, Archie, 199n161
balance, 17–18, 31, 43n19, 445; Navajo notion of, 212
balanced reciprocity, 46n63
banking, Native American, 295–96; economic crisis and, 314
Beauvais, F., 380
Begay, Jason, 315
behavior: abusive patterns of, 318; dysfunctional, 55; patterns of dysfunction, 393
Bellin Health Systems, 303
Berry, Thomas, 331–32
Betty Ford Center, 258, 279n107
BIA. *See* Bureau of Indian Affairs
bicameral parliamentary model for government revision, 210–11
binge drinking, 77
Bishop Paiute Tribe, 63
Black Elk, 50n112
Black Elk Speaks, 50n112

block grants, 130–31

Blue Lake, 115

boarding school, 54–55, 109, 317–18, 379

Board of Indian Appeals, 118

Bordeaux, Rodney M., 284

border security, 146

Bowles, Erskine, 193n86

brain-based learning, 346

Brain–Emotional Health Program, 363

bridging worlds, 382–84

Brown, Lisa, 374

Brownlow Committee, 142

Building Native Communities: Financial Skills for Families, 357

bureaucracy, 298–99

Bureau of Indian Affairs (BIA), 55–56, 132; bookkeeping audits, 112–13, 186n21; business startups and, 298; Collier and, 110–11; as colonial agency, 111–14; complaints concerning, 185n15; control, 95n12, 134; decentralization of authority, 113–14; devolution of, 114; dominance of Indian affairs, 107; education and, 153; -funded schools, 62, 64, 68, 318, 377; government form, 222; hiring Native Americans at, 112; Law and Order Code, 255; leadership and, 409; monopoly, 204; oversight, 189n46; reform, 114; Road Program, 2003, 82; school programs, 345–54, 358; Southern Ute relations with, 141; strategic plan, 143; transformations, 141; Tribal Housing Authority, 81; trustee role, 187n24

Bureau of Indian Affairs Road Program, 2003, 82

Bureau of Indian Affairs' strategic plan, 143

Bureau of Indian Affairs Tribal Housing Authority, 81

Bureau of Indian Education, 64

Bush, George H. W., 27

Bush, George W., 27, 130, 139–40, 147, 416; developments during administration, 142–46; environmental policy, 26

business, Native American, 283; autonomy and, 287; with culturally appropriate management, 288–89; development, 289; education and, 291–92

business–school partnership, 399n68

By Cheyenne Campfires (Grinnell), 49n101

Cache community, 243

cacique, 16

California, 168, 179, 205

campaign donations, 189n31, 317, 398n58

Campbell, Joseph, 50n112

Campo Reservation, 284–85

Canada, 278n101; courts, 265–66; peacemaking in, 257

cancer, 73–74

capital, gaining access to, 292–93

capitulation, 387

Capriccioso, Rob, 314

Carey, Maver, 298

caring, 358–59

Carson River, 168

Carter, Jimmy, 119, 124–25

casino gambling, 195n111, 283, 419; economic development and, 170–73; income generated from, 293; industry spending, 297–98;

profits, 87–88; Southern Ute, 174; taxation, 170–71. *See also* gaming industry; *specific casinos*

Cason, James, 140

Castaneda, Richard Blue Cloud, 375

CDC. *See* Centers for Disease Control and Prevention

Cederstrom, Thoric, 75–76

Census Bureau, U.S., 58, *58, 64, 86*

Center: as direction, 35–36, 50n112; in education, 337–38

Centers for Disease Control and Prevention (CDC), 72

ceremonial participation, 391–92

CERT. *See* Council of Energy Resource Tribes

Chapman, Michael, 193n86

chapter governments, 206–7

Charley, Wallace, 67

Chaudhuri, Jean, 5–6, 43n19

Chaudhuri, Jonodev Osceola, ix, 5–6

Chaudhuri, Joyotpaul, 5–6, 43n19, 46n63

Cherokee Nation: kinship and, 19; Oklahoma collaboration with, 175–76. *See also specific bands*

Cherokee Nation Commerce Department, 295

Cheyenne, 14, 49n101, 250, 257–58; adaptability and, 33–34; authority, 23; hunting, 31–32, 251; murder among, 277n84

The Cheyenne Indians (Grinnell), 49n101

The Cheyennes (Hoebel), 49n101

The Cheyenne Way (Hoebel & Llewellyn), 49n101

children: abuse of, 103n88; alienation, 109–10, 318, 344; under poverty line, 57; social services, 216, 268, 366–67, 412, 432; welfare and, 163, 381. *See also* youth

Chippewa, 191n64

Chiricahua Apache of the Southwest, 7–8

Choctaw. *See* Mississippi Band of Choctaw Indians

Choctaw Agency, 300–301

choice-of-law ordinances, 261–64; language, 279n110

Christakis & Associates, 218

Christianity, 204

circle as symbol, 35–36

Citizen Potawatomi Community Development Corporation, 294

Civil Rights Commission, U.S., 70–71

Clan Mother, 21

clans, 8

Clean Water Act, 162

Clinton, Bill, 122, 128, 138–42, 147; Department of Education under, 150; Indian policy and, 439

CMN. *See* College of Menominee Nation

Coast Salish communities, 265–67, 269

Cobell, Elouise, 187n21

Cobell v. Kempthorne, 187n21

code development, tribal, 255–56

Code of Federal Regulation Courts, 252

collaboration, 17–18, 38; appropriate, 420–21; consulting and, 433–34; contemporary application of, 25–26, 48n88; coordination for developing, 176–82; cross-cultural, 159–60; educational institution, 372–73; environmental protection and, 161–62; external, 204; federal

agency efforts in, 124–29; in
federalism, 151; government-to-
government, 149; intertribal,
296–98; regulation and, 161–62;
repression compared to, 30;
services delivery and, 161–63;
tribal governance and, 424–26.
*See also specific examples of
collaboration*
collective bargaining, 48n88
collective rituals, 20
"Collective Vision Statement for
Comanche Future," 239–40,
240–41
college: degree, 60, 64; entry rates,
discrimination as factor in,
61–64; graduation rates, 282
college, tribal, 367–68; BIA-funded,
318; facilities, 66; funding,
65–66; innovations, 368–70
college enrollment: advanced
degrees and, 373; American
Indian and Alaska Native, *64*;
EAGL and, 365–67
College of Menominee Nation
(CMN), 368–70
Collier, John, 110–12
colonialism: impact on Native
Americans, 53, 56; modern
denial, 326; traditional
leadership and, 409;
understanding, 423
colonization, 76, 109; long-term
effects of, 325–26, 422
Colorado, 166–68, 172, 174
Colorado Ute Settlement Act
Amendments, 2000, 198n140
Columbia River Inter-Tribal Fish
Commission, 127, 191n59
Columbus, Christopher, 3–4, 41n7
Comanche, 8, 20, 94n6, 185n13,
269–70, 446n14; community

development, 242–43; complex
issues, 276n74; experience to
1990, 219–22; governance,
220; identity, 232, 273n38;
institutions, 232; leaders, 219–
20; nation establishment, 221;
political system, 447n39; power
dynamics, 47n72; social life, 219;
social services, 222; weapons
and, 103n85; women, 22–23
Comanche Business Committee,
234, 243–44, 427; ILIS and, 223–
24; role in Comanche relations,
221–22
Comanche Community
Participation Units Articles of
Voluntary Association, 243–44
Comanche ILIS, 424, 427, 434–35;
application by, 218–19, 221, 223–
24; "Collective Vision Statement
for Comanche Future," 239–40,
240–41; critical issues map,
230–31; evaluation and feedback,
427–28; experience, 229–32;
first meeting, 275n57; impacts
on tribal level, 243–45; influence
map of barriers to Comanche
Tribal Governance, 234–35;
July and September meetings,
238–42; March and May 1991
meetings, 232–38; results of
process, 428
The Comanches (Wallace &
Hoebel), 47n72
Comanche Tribal Council, 428
Comanche tribal governance:
barriers to, 233, *234–35*;
community participation
implementation options for,
236–37
Commission on Indian Services, 177
communication, 176; cross-cultural,

322; in education, 329;
institutionalization of, 180;
tribal–federal government,
135–38
Communism, 3, 40n2
community, 3, 23; -based education
process, 323; -building
processes, 185n13; consensus,
5–6; education, 353–54, 363;
empowerment, 422; esteem, 55;
fragmentation, 55–56; honor
and, 91; individual united to,
17, 52–53; involvement, 249;
relations, 29–30; traditional, 203;
tribal courts, 252–53
community development, 101n62,
242–43, 302–4; appropriate, 129;
economic development and, 302;
education and, 335–411
community participation, 234,
248–50; barriers to, 239;
implementation options for,
236–37. See also Indigenous
Leadership Interactive System
Companion, Michele, 76
competitiveness, 176; contemporary,
26; cooperation and, 17–18;
decision making and, 26–27;
resource, 163–65
computer availability and training,
299
Confederated Tribes of Grand
Ronde, 310
Confederated Tribes of the
Umatilla Indian Reservation,
309–10
conflict management, 39n1. *See
also specific approaches to conflict
management*
conflict-resolution training, 346;
facilitation process, 347; heart
tools, 348–50; NCPCR and,

351–53; nonviolent, 28; teachers'
observations, 350
Congress, U.S., 150, 182; critics of,
24; role of, 440; water rights
and, 167
consensus-based decision making,
17–18, 28, 48n91, 50n119, 272n24,
428, 447n37; of band societies,
5–8; developing, 276n74; at each
organizational level, 202. *See also
specific approaches*
consensus politics, 9–13
Constitution, U.S., 15, 153; on
president, 14
consulting, 429, 448n43;
appropriate, 420–21;
collaboration and, 433–34;
leaders and, 434–36; orientation
of members, 431; sovereignty and
participation and, 421, 430–31;
trust building, 422–24
cooperatives, 289–90
coping patterns, 387
Coquille Indian Tribe, 309
Cornell, Stephen, 85
Council of Energy Resource Tribes
(CERT), 283, 418
courts: Canadian, 265–66; federal
jurisdiction, 279n113. *See also*
Supreme Court
courts, tribal: community and,
252–53; drug, 258–59; federal
review of, 263; independence
needed in, 253–54; jurisdiction,
279n113; tribal values in, 260–
64. *See also* Peacemaker Courts
Courts of Indian Offenses, 252
Cow Creek, 309
Coyhis, Don, 389–90
Crevecoeur, John, 4
crime: against Native Americans,
68–69; prevention, 179;

punishment and, 250–51; rate,
68; victimization from, 68–72
criminal justice system, 31–32;
traditional, 250–51
Cross, Terry, 388
Crow, 205
Crow Canyon Archaeological
Center, 367
Crow Creek tribal high school, 67
CULTURAL, 358–63
cultural alienation, 380
cultural awareness: of government
personnel, 182; lack of, 117
cultural genocide, 54, 88, 94n6
cultural ideals, 333
cultural identity, 379–80, 386;
interventions and, 392; multiple,
383
cultural maintenance, 323–24
cultural schizophrenia, 324
culture, 5–24, 384; guiding vision
of, 333; modern education effects
on, 320; preserving, 370–72
curricula, 323–24
Cypress, Mitchell, 297
Czech Confederation of Trade
Unions, 448n45

Dartmouth Medical School, 75
Dawes Allotment Act in 1887, 109,
153, 185n8
death rate, 72
decentralization, 129–31, 437;
of BIA authority, 113–14;
educational guidance for, 131–32;
for empowerment, 132–33; of
federal agencies, 130; in housing
programs, 132; HUD, 129–30;
model of government revision,
213–15, 272n18; at Navajo Nation,
206–7, 429–30
decision making, 420; authority

to tribes, 113; autonomy in,
116; Bahá í Faith consultation
method of, 217, 249, 272n24;
competitive processes, 26–27;
Diné, 429; process of dialogue,
26–27; returning to culturally
appropriate forms of, 201–50;
student process, 347. See also
consensus-based decision
making; specific methods
Deganawidah, 21–22
Deloria, Ella, 18–19, 94n6
Deloria, Vine, Jr., 415
demographic profile highlights, 58
Demonstration in Navajo
Education, 344
denial, 393
Department of Agriculture, 123, 414
Department of Commerce, 27
Department of Communication at
George Mason University, 218
Department of Defense, 193n89
Department of Education,
143, 400n94, 414; Clinton
administration, 150
Department of Energy (DOE), 128
Department of Health and Human
Services (HHS), 123, 305–6;
Children's Bureau, 432
Department of Health, Education,
and Welfare (HEW), 123
Department of Housing and
Urban Development (HUD),
130–31, 138, 188n27, 449n52;
decentralized, 129–30
Department of Justice (DOJ), 128,
138, 160
Department of Labor, 137
Department of the Interior, 55–56,
110–11, 132, 138, 188n27; funding
agreements, 140
depression, 381, 387

development planning, 299–300
Dewey, John, 328, 398n65
diabetes, 77–78
dialectical model for government revision, 211–13, 272n18
dialogue, process of, 26–27; federal agencies and, 150; with tribal governments, 149
Diné, 31, 44n26; decision making, 429; legal development, 255; legend, 448n41. *See also* Navajo Nation
Diné College, 207, 367, 431; Woksape Oyate grant, 371–72
Diné Policy Institute of Diné College, 208–15, 272n16
disharmony, contemporary, 202–3, 205–6
displacement, 93n2, 103n85
dispute resolution, 250–68; traditional, 250–52; traditional values applied to, 264; Upper Skagit Tribe, 264–66
Distributed Generation Systems, 284
diversification: economic development, 300–301, 303–4, 308–9; intergovernmental cooperation and, 300–301
diversity: respecting, 392; unity in, 29–30, 34–35
DOE. *See* Department of Energy
DOJ. *See* Department of Justice
Domestic Policy Council, 138
domestic violence, 255–56, 381; Peacemaker Court and, 256–57
Dorgan, Byron, 71
dream societies, 20–21
drug: courts, 258–59; use, 76–77, 344, 355, 363
Drug Courts Program Office, DOJ, 259

dual citizenship, 383
Dubray, Christine, 73
Duck Creek Priority Watershed Project, 304

EAGL. *See* Excellence in Advancement toward Graduation and Leadership
Earth as Mother, 46n66
Eastern Band Cherokees, 101n65
Eastern Europe, 3, 40n2
economic crisis, 2008, tribal economies and, 313–17
economic development: alternative energy for, 284–85; barriers to, 286–87; bureaucracy, 298–99; casino development and, 170–73; community development and, 302; diversification, 300–301, 303–4, 308–9; education, training, and technical assistance for, 291–92; financing and capital for, 292–93; funding and, 292–93, 441–43; infrastructure and, 299; intergovernmental cooperation and, 311–12; Mississippi Band of Choctaw Indians, 300–301; Navajo Nation, 209; need for, 86–88; overcoming poverty and, 56–59; participatory inclusiveness in, 289; on reservations, 101n65; self-determination and, 152; self-governance and, 152; service availability and, 443–44; Southern Ute, 292; sovereignty and, 282–83, 285–86, 316–17; as of 2008, 313; Winnebago Tribe of Nebraska, 306–8
economic order theory, 211–12
economic problems, 92
economic structures, traditional, 202

economies, tribal, 282; economic crisis and, 313–17; gains from 1990 to 2010, 283

education, 54, 104n89, 120, 332–33, 399n66; alienation and, 322; assimilation and, 320; budget, primary and secondary, *68*; Bush, G. W., and, 143–46; business and, 291–92; Center in, 337–38; child-needs-centered, 328; communication in, 329; community-based process, 323; community development and, 335–411; cultural maintenance through, 323–24; for decentralization, 131–32; distribution of eighth-grade students by level of performance in math and, *61*; economic development and, 291–92; financial literacy, 287–88, 291–92, 294; funding, 376, 402n133; for government-to-government relations, 149–50; harmony achieved through, 336; healing and, 379; in Indian affairs, 123–24; individualized, 366; learning goals, 339–40; lifelong, 370–72; objectivism in, 327–28, 334; participation, 334; participatory and experiential progressive, 328; policy impacts and needs, 376–77; poverty and, 65; racism and, 195n110; reductionist, 328; relational orientations, 329; transformational approach to, 336. *See also* college; high school; public school; *specific programs and schools*

education, Indian, 302; achievement rates, 60–62, 195n110, 282; appropriate, 378; archaeology and, 367; BIA and, 153; boarding school, 54–55, 109, 317–18, 379; broader relevance of, 327–32; contemporary, 318–84; creating new circle of, 341–43; current developments, 344–78; defining, 341–42; developing conscientisation and praxis for culturally appropriate, 326–27; ecology of, 342; endogenous dynamic of, 336–37; funding, 65–68, 142, 189n34; gaming industry management, 373; goals, 338; history, 317–18; holistic, 329, 333–34; in-classroom heart community in, 353–54; institution collaboration, 372–73; intergenerational school community and, 363; intervention, 357–58; as model, 334–35; NCLB and, 402n131; off-reservation, 364; policy, 321; political grounds of, 326; programs, 345–54, 355, 358; public school policy, 153, 364–65; reasons for low performance in, 64–68; revitalization goals, 324–26; in Southwest, 345–46; traditional, 330–31; traditional Indian governance and, 204; transformation and, 335–41; underfunding problems, 377–78; urban, 364. *See also* Indigenous education theory; *specific school programs; specific schools*

education, modern American, 320; crisis, 333; critical observation of, 343; infrastructure, 329–30; theory, 321; traditional Indian education compared to, 330–31; transformation of, 334–35; tribal perspective of, 332–35

educator–learner relationship, 343
educators, Native American, 65, 318–19, 323
elections: participation in, 89–90, 189n31, 203; urban participation, 207
electoral systems, tribal, 203
elicitive process of facilitation, 346
Elk Valley Rancheria, 312–13
emotional-intelligence, "heart," 346, 355, 359–60
employee: co-op, 290; participation, 448n40
employee stock ownership plans (ESOP), 288–89
employment, 57; of Native Americans at BIA, 112; through participatory process, 274n53; Pine Ridge Reservation, 84; program funding cuts, 137; urban Indians, 84
empowerment, 20–21, 33, 324–26, 385–86, 392–94; assumptions, attitudes, and skills for, 421–22; decentralization for, 132–33; ILIS and, 247; self-, programs, 346; self-governance, 183; to tribe, 131
energy conservation, 26
Engels, Friedrich, 4, 93n3
environmental protection, 125–27, 188n27; tribal–state and local collaboration and, 161–62; in U.S., 25–26
Environmental Protection Agency (EPA), 25, 116, 149, 180, 188n27, 414; gasoline-content, 27; Indian affairs model, 124–29; programs, 190n58; tribal governments and, 126–28; trust responsibility, 191n64. See also specific offices
equity theory, 211
Erdmann, Ron, 292

Erikson, Erik, 379–80
Eskimo leadership, 6
ESOP. See employee stock ownership plans
Excellence in Advancement toward Graduation and Leadership (EAGL), 365–67
external experts. See consulting

Farmington, New Mexico, 69–71
federal agencies, 139–40; advisory committees, 121; collaborative efforts, 124–29; decentralizing, 130; education in Indian affairs, 123–24; Indian sovereignty and, 133–35; personnel, 148, 182; programs dialogue, 150; service delivery systems, 117–18; tribal–federal government relations developments within, 121–22
federal budget, 194n108; cut, 137; education, 68
federalism, 106–7, 147; collaborative, 151; sovereignty and, 129–31; tribal governments and, 183–84; in U.S., 24
federally recognized tribes, 140, 194n104
federal policy making: coordination in, 135–38; inclusive approach, 26–27; Native American input into, 121–22
feminine, 46n65
financial literacy training, 287, 291–92, 294
financing, 292–93
First Nations Development, 294
food access, 75–76
Food and Consumer Services, 123
Ford, Henry, 136
Forest County Potawatomi of Wisconsin, 304

Fort Berthold Reservation, 285
Fort Yuma Quechan Indians, 315
Four Directions, 35–36
Four Directions Development
    Corporation, 291–92, 294
Four Fires, 304
Four Winds Casino Resort, 306
Fowler, Loretta, 405n186
French, Laurence A., 382, 392–93
funding, 155–56; economic
    development and, 292–93,
    441–43; education, 65–68,
    142, 189n34, 376, 402n133;
    employment program cuts in,
    137; for housing, 82; for Native
    American programs, 116; need
    for, 438–39; for self-governance,
    140–41; under-, 60–62, 377–78
funding, federal Indian, 56–57;
    agreements, 140; Bush, G. W.,
    cuts, 144–45; direct, 130; levels,
    96n19; lost, 112–13
fur trade, 93n2

Gaffney, Susan, 192n73
Gagnier, Phyllis M., 287, 345–55, 357,
    363; "Keys to Connectedness:
    Learning is Cultural"
    curriculum, 358–63
gaming industry, 303; economic
    crisis and, 316; management
    education, 373; in Washington,
    310. See also casino gambling;
    specific organizations
"the gang of five," 437
Garment, Leonard, 135–36
Garrett, Michael, 19
gays, military treatment of, 111, 186n16
gender dynamics, 46n65; domestic
    violence and, 255–56; power,
    46n63, 47n72; Southern Ute,
    47n73

General Motors, 173
generational trauma, 381
generosity, 37
genocide. See cultural genocide;
    physical genocide
gifted and talented program,
    348–50
global warming, 30–31
Goins, Jamie, 375
Gorpospe, Kathy, 191n59
Gorton, Slade, 115
governance, tribal, 441;
    collaboration and, 424–26;
    contemporary use of traditional,
    205; education on traditional,
    204; imposed forms of, 419–
    20; inclusive participation,
    269–70; revision models,
    210–15; traditional values to
    improve, 206; traditional vs.
    contemporary, 201–6. See also
    self-governance
government, U.S., 182; as
    culturally inappropriate,
    88–90; encouragement of
    government cooperation, 179–
    80; undermining of traditional
    peacemaking, 252–53, 255–56
governments, tribal, 89–90;
    authority, 203–5; autonomy to,
    182; dialogue with, 149; EPA
    and, 126–28; federalism and,
    106–7, 183–84; funding and
    economic development for, 441–
    43; government partnerships,
    436–37; law enforcement and,
    196n120; service delivery systems
    to, 117–18; training, 131
government-to-government
    relations, 90, 106, 121, 180, 182,
    184, 188n27, 365, 409, 436–37;
    collaborative, 149; development

of, 116; education and, 149–50;
EPA and, 124–29; Harris, L.,
and, 414; ILIS and, 248. *See
also* tribal-federal government
relations; tribal-state and local
government relations
"Government-Wide Responsibility
to Native Americans: An
Implementation Strategy," 117–18
Governors' Interstate Indian
Council, 154
Governor's Office of Indian Affairs,
178
Great Peace, 24
grief, five stages of, 381, 387
grief, historical, 90–91, 392–93;
culturally competent methods to
facilitate resolution of, 384–88;
transformation, 383; unresolved,
379; validating, 423
Grinnell, George Bird, 49n101
group: empowerment of, 20–21;
identity, 226, 425–26

Hall, Tex, 57, 64, 73, 83
harmony, 39n1, 43n19; of circle,
52–53; through education,
336; of individual with whole,
17–20; maintenance and
reestablishment, 31–33; with
nature, 30–31; restoring, 92, 378
Harris, Fred, 115, 413, 415
Harris, LaDonna, 47n72, 100n173,
150, 188n29, 196n127, 246,
394, 409, 435, 440, 445n9;
government-to-government
relations and, 414; Johnson
administration and, 412–13;
leadership approach, 414–16;
national boards, 446n18; OIO
and, 410–12; traditional values
and leadership of, 409–19

Harvard Project on Pluralism,
69–71
Haudenosaunee, 21, 29
HCI Distribution Co., 307
healing, 54, 393–94; ceremonial
participation and, 391–92;
contemporary application of
traditional, 389–92; education
and, 379; oppression, 388–89
health, American Indian, 72–80;
compared to other ethnicities,
78–80; housing and, 81–82;
infrastructure and, 83; U.S.
policy and, 110. *See also specific
health conditions*
health maintenance organization
(HMO), 246
Health-Related Quality of Life
(HRQOL), 78–80
health services, Indian, 58–59, 73;
agencies, 176–78; cuts in, 144–
46; of Oneida Nation, 305–6;
urban Indian, 77–78. *See also
specific services*
heart-intelligent wisdom. *See*
emotional-intelligence, "heart"
HeartMath, 345–54
hepatitis C infection rate, 73
HEW. *See* Department of Health,
Education, and Welfare
HHS. *See* Department of Health
and Human Services
Hickok, Eugene, 143
Hidatsa, 9–10
high school: dropout rates by ethnic
group, 1989, *60*; equivalency
degrees, 62
high school graduation rates,
60–63, 195n110, 282;
discrimination as factor in,
62–64; EAGL and, 365–67
HIV/AIDS infection rates, 75

HMO. *See* health maintenance organization
Hobbes, Thomas, 3, 30
Ho-Chunk, Inc., 306–7
Ho-Chunk Village, 308
Hodel, Donald, 118
Hoebel, E. Adamson, 31–32, 47n72, 49n101, 257–58
holistic development, 444–45
Hollow Water First Nation, 257, 278n101
home mortgages, 102n65
The Homestead in Hot Springs, Virginia, 27
honor, dark side of, 90–91, 103n84
Honor the Earth, 285
The Honour of All: The Story of Alkali Lake, 258
Hoopa Valley Indian Tribe, 141
Hopi, 94n6, 260; alternative energy projects, 285, 299
Hopi High School at Keams Canyon, 345
Hopland Band Tribal Court, 278n90
horse, 91, 258
House of Justice, 268
House of Respected Stó:lō, 267
housing, 80–82, 100n61, 101n62; alternative energy and, 284; development, 101n65; federal funding for, 82; health and, 81–82; infrastructure development with, 83; tribal authorities, 129–30; tribal programs, 131
Housing Act, U.S., of 1996, 129
housing programs, 192n73, 449n52; decentralization in, 132; San Juan Pueblo, 188n27, 449n52. *See also specific programs*
HRQOL. *See* Health-Related Quality of Life

HUD. *See* Department of Housing and Urban Development
Humphrey, Hubert, 412–13
Hunt, Deborah Esquibel, 386, 388, 394, 448n42
Huron, 13–15, 202, 251
hurt, 381

ICA Group, 289
Idaho, 176–78
idea generation, ILIS, 274n55
Idea Writing, 274n55
identity: Comanche, 232, 273n38; confused, 379–80; culture and, 379–80; group, 226, 425–26; identity confusion vs., 380. *See also* cultural identity
Ignacio (city), 172
IHS. *See* Indian Health Services
ILIS. *See* Indigenous Leadership Interactive System
IM. *See* Interactive Management
inclusive approach: to governance and peacemaking, 269–70; policy making, 26–27; requirements, 27–28
inclusiveness, 29, 43n19, 414–16; Alaska–British Columbia, 217–18; economic development and, 289; principle of, 20–21; at Southern Ute, 215–17; Yurok Tribe, 217
income: from casino, 293; demographic profile highlights, 58; demographics and, 57–59; mean Native American, 58–59
"Income, Poverty, and Health Insurance Coverage in the United States," 2003, 58
Indian affairs, 134; BIA dominance of, 107; BIA monopoly on, 204; conflict of interest in, 152;

education in, 123–24; EPA model of approach, 124–29; resources in, 137; state coordination body, 181–82; Supreme Court approach to, 438; White House and, 135–38

Indiana Native American Affairs Commission, 441

Indiana University's American Indian Studies Research Institute, 371

Indian Brotherhood Twelve Steps Toward Sobriety, 389–90

Indian charter schools, 320, 399n79

Indian Country Today (Capriccioso), 314

Indian Desks, 122, 123, 139, 414

Indian Education Act, 120

Indian Education Formula Grant Program, 400n94

Indian Health Care Improvement Act, 145–46

Indian Health Services (IHS), 59, 193n92; traditional medicine and, 390–91

Indian Health Services Act, 144–45

Indian Housing Act, 144

Indian policy, 151; BIA application of, 111; coordination at, 438; department level coordination, 122–23; education and, 153, 321, 364–65, 376–77; evaluations, 148–49; federal agencies and, 121; of self-government, 110–11. *See also* Indian policy, U.S.

Indian policy, U.S., 54–55, 116, 183; assimilation and, 419; Bush, G. W., and, 143; Clinton administration, 439; as destructive, 54–56; on health, 110; self-determination and, 116

Indian Policy Review Commission, 115

Indian Policy Statement, 1983 (Reagan), 125

Indian Reorganization Act of 1934, 88, 131, 153, 205, 252, 394

Indian rolling, 69

Indian Self-Determination and Education Assistance Act of 1975, 65, 132, 137

Indian Trust Counsel Authority, 122, 189n46

Indian trust fund, 187n21

Indian Work Group, EPA, 125, 190n52, 191n59

Indian Working Group, 139

Indianz.com, 307

Indigenous cultural studies, 326–27

Indigenous education theory, 319, 326

Indigenous Leadership Interactive System (ILIS), 218–19, 223–24, 232–34, 274n50, 277n77, 416, 446n14; advantages and disadvantages, 248–49; applied use of, 248; consistent with social relations, 425–26; critical issues map, *230–31*; empowerment and, 247; facilitation, 427; failure to institutionalize, 245–47; government-to-government relations and, 248; idea generation, 274n55; key roles in process, 226; kinship tracking, 226; participation, 426–27; problem-definition, 224–25; process, 417; seating arrangement, 275n56; stages of, 224–27; strengths, 424; tribal level impacts of, 243–45; value of, 247–48. *See also* Comanche ILIS

indigenousness, 445

individual: autonomy, 16; ceremonies, 20; community

and, 17, 52–53; empowerment of, 20–21; harmony with whole, 17–20

individualism, 3

individualized education, 366

individuation, 338–39

infighting, 52–53, 205–6

infrastructure, 82–85, 101n62; Alaska, 83–84; economic development and, 299; housing, 83; Indian country, 82–85; mainstream American education, 329–30; tribal–state and local government relations and, 154

Interactive Management (IM), 223, 274n50, 274n51, 277n76, 447n37

Interagency Working Group on American Indian and Alaska Native Education, 144, 376

Intercultural Cancer Council, 73–74

interest group, Indians seen as, 133–35

interest rates, 292–93

intergovernmental cooperation, 300–301, 311–12

Intergovernmental Personnel Act, 137–38

International Affairs and Commodity Programs, 123

International Relief and Development, 75

Interpretive Structural Modeling, ILIS, 225

Inter Tribal Council of Arizona, 81

interventions, 354–55, 357–58; appropriate, 385, 389; cultural identification and, 392

Intradepartmental Council on Native Affairs, 123

Inuit, 6, 251

Iron Cloud-Two Dogs, 404n178

Iroquois, 4, 22, 93n3

itancan, 11

Janklow, Bill, 157, 196n125

job training, 132

Job Training Partnership Act, 144–45, 243

Johnson, Lyndon, 114, 121, 135; Harris, L., and, 412–13

Johnson-O'Malley Act of 1934, 153, 364

Join the Circle, 297

Jones, Lovell, 74

judicial authority, 154

judicial process, indigenizing, 250–68

Jung, Carl, 36, 338, 382

jurisdiction, 158–60, 196n120; authority, 252; cooperative approach, 159–60; environmental protection and, 161–62; Indian country, 68–70, 128–29; tribal and federal, 279n113

jurisprudence, 279n110

justice: restorative and rehabilitative, 266; tribal practices, 259–60

Kalt, Joseph, 57–59, 62, 63, 85

Kaur, Judith Salmon, 74–75

Kennedy, Robert, 115

"Keys to Connectedness: Learning is Cultural" curriculum (Gagnier), 358–63

Kilburg, Bobbie, 135–36

Kindle, William, 84

King, Frank, 314

kinship, 18–19, 425; obligations, 241–42; tracking for ILIS, 226

Kiowa, 16–17, 250

Kiowa-Comanche-Apache Business Committee, 220

Kluckhohn, Clyde, 8–9
Kohner, Lisa, 179
Kubler-Ross, Elizabeth, 381, 386
Kuskokwim Corporation, 298
Kwakiutl, 17

Laguna Pueblo, 16
Lakota, 103n85, 251; application
    of Center direction, 50n112;
    consensus politics and,
    9–13; four virtues, 17;
    interconnectedness, 30; kinship,
    18–19; language, 371, 401n112;
    Sacred Pipe of, 23–24; Sun
    Dance, 13, 20, 50n112; women,
    22–23
Lakota Fund, 294
land, Native American and Alaska
    Native, 207, 211; environmental
    policy for, 125–26; ownership,
    115; rights, 119
language, 402n131; choice-of-law
    ordinances, 279n110; Lakota,
    371, 401n112; preserving, 370–72
The Language Keepers, 372
La Plata County, 172; social service
    agencies, 216
La Plata County Board of
    Commissioners, 172
La Posta Band of Mission Indians,
    296
law, traditional, 250–51
Law and Order Code of BIA, 255
law enforcement, 68–72, 179,
    196n120, 306; Oneida Nation,
    306; tribal–state and local
    government relations in, 158–60.
    See also jurisdiction; police
Lawton community, 243
leaders, Indian, 202; Ambassadors
    Program, 374–75; Comanche,
    219–20; consultants and, 434–36;

exemplified by Harris, L., 409–
    19; 1960s, 115; traditional, 5–8
leadership: BIA and, 409;
    centralizing, 409; traditional
    Indian, 408–9; U.S., 14
Leadership Program at Diné
    College, 207
learning, 343; goals, 339–40;
    ownership of choices, 362; social,
    337, 383–84
legal codes, indigenizing, 250–68
Leighton, Dorothea, 8–9
Letters of an American Farmer
    (Crevecoeur), 4
Levine, Ben, 372
Liberal tradition, 40n3
life expectancy, 72–73, 282
Little Priest Tribal College, 308
Llewellyn, Karl, 49n101, 257–58
Local Enterprise Assistance Fund,
    289
Local Governance Act Community
    Land Use Plan, 207
Locke, John, 3–4, 37, 40n3, 93n3
Locke, Patricia, 120, 121
Lomax, Bill, 314
Loneman School, 66
love, 359–60
Lumberman, Alex J., 84
Luminia Foundation for Education,
    370
Luna-Firebaugh, Eileen M., 62

Maarse, Ted, 120
malnutrition, 75
man, traditional Native American,
    46n63, 47n72. See also gender
    dynamics
Mankiller, Wilma, 175
Maoli, Kanaka, 144
Māori, 268, 375
Marshall, Clifford Lyle, 141

Marx, Karl, 4, 93n3
masculine, 46n65
Mashantucket Pequot Tribal
  Nation, 296, 316
medical services, 57
Medicine Wheel, 35–36, 393
meetings, national Indian, 138–42
Menominee Tribe, 115
Meriam Report, 53, 110
Meskwaki court, 253–54
Miller, Bruce G., 264
mineral rights, 119
Minnesota Tribal and County
  Government Summit, 179
Mississippi Band of Choctaw
  Indians, 102n75, 173, 302;
  economic development,
  300–301
Mohave Generating Station, 299
Mohegan Tribe, 296, 316
Mondragon Cooperative
  Federation, 289–91
Mondragon University, 289–90
Monteau, Harold, 297
Montessori program, 345
Moore, Rebecca, 50n108
Moran, James, 389
Morgan, Lewis Henry, 4, 93n3
Morongo Band of Mission
  Indians, 285, 311–12
Morris, Barbara, 142–43
Morris, Carolyn, 391
mortality rates: infant, 72–73; after
  surgery, 75
Muckleshoot Indian Tribe, 310
Muscogee: creation story, 43n19;
  tribal courts, 260–64
Muscogee District Court, 263
Muscogee Nation Code, 279n114
mutual respect, 30, 33, 36–37, 174,
  202

naat'aanii, 256
NAES. See Native American
  Educational Services College
National Conference of State
  Legislatures, 180
National Conference on
  Peacemaking and Conflict
  Resolution (NCPCR), 351–53
National Congress of American
  Indians (NCAI), 57, 115, 180, 413
National Council on Indian
  Opportunity, 121, 135, 412–13, 435
National Indian Business
  Association, 418
National Indian Child Welfare
  Association, 381
National Indian Gaming
  Association (NIGA), 146, 297
National Indian Gaming
  Commission, 87, 102n76
National Indian Housing Council,
  101n65
National Indian Listening
  Conference, 138
National Indian Opportunity
  Council, 114
National Museum of the American
  Indian, 415
National Tribal Development
  Association, 297
National Tribal Environmental
  Council, 418
Native American Bank, 295
Native American Business
  Development, 297
Native American Church, 204
Native American Educational
  Services College (NAES), 367
Native American Programs, 137
Native American Youth and Family
  Center (NAYA Family Center),
  366–67

Native Community Development Financial Institutions, 294

Native Financial Education Coalition, 396n19

"Natural Heart People," 352

nature: -centered philosophy, 331; relations to, 30–31; society and, 37–38

Navajo Court of Indian Offenses, 255

Navajo Government Commission, 206–7

Navajo Nation, 8–9, 193n93, 270, 424, 442; "Alternative Governance Models," 209–15, 272n18; balance and, 212; computer capacity, 299; decentralization and participation at, 206–7, 429–30; economic development, 209; education, 344; energy development programs, 285; Farmington and, 69–71; governance, 206, 210–15; IHS and traditional medicine, 390–91; Peacemaking Court, 255–56; reservation, 82; schools, 66–67, 402n131; tribal code development, 255–56. See also Diné

Navajo Nation Constitutional Feasibility and Reform Project report (Diné Policy Institute), 208–15; "Alternative Governance Models," 209–15, 272n18

Navajo Nation Council, 255

Navajo Nation Judicial Conference, 256

Navajo Nation Local Governance Act, 271n12, 430

Navasew, 289

Navy Tailhook scandal, 186n16

NAYA Family Center. *See* Native American Youth and Family Center

NCAI. *See* National Congress of American Indians

NCLB. *See* No Child Left Behind

NCPCR. *See* National Conference on Peacemaking and Conflict Resolution

Nevada, 168

Nevada Gaming Control, 316

New Mexico, 166–68; collaborative efforts in, 161; economy, 156–57; Farmington, 69–71

New York, environmental regulation in, 162

NIGA. *See* National Indian Gaming Association

Nixon, Richard, 122, 135–36, 413

No Child Left Behind (NCLB), 62, 144, 328, 376, 402n131

Nominal Group Technique, 274n55, 275n57

Northern Arapaho Tribe, 34

Northern Ute Indian Tribe, 163, 378

Northwest Indian Fisheries Commission, 164–65, 197n136

Northwest Portland Area Indian Health Board, 176–78

nuclear waste, 128

Numunuh, 219

Obama, Barack, 314

obesity, 77–78

objectivism, 327–28, 334

Oetting, E. R., 380

Office of Economic Opportunity, 411

Office of Indian Education, 143

Office of Intergovernmental Affairs, 136

Office of Management and Budget, 116, 145

Office of Native American Affairs, 179

Office of Navajo Government
Development, 206–7, 271n12,
430–31
Office of Public Liaison, 136
Office of Solid Waste Management,
EPA, 248
Office of Tribal Operations, EPA,
127
Office of Tribal Relations, 191n59
Office of Water Regulation
Standards, EPA, 191n61
off-reservation tribal members. *See*
urban Indians
Oglala Lakota College, 370–71
Ogo, Linda, 375
OIO. *See* Oklahomans for Indian
Opportunity
Ojibwa, 8
Oklahoma, 179; Cherokee Nation
collaboration with, 175–76;
economy, 156; tax commission,
169–70
Oklahoma American Indian
University, 368
Oklahoma Indian Affairs
Commission, 155
Oklahoma Indian Welfare Act of
1936, 88, 205
Oklahomans for Indian
Opportunity (OIO): founding,
409–12; ILIS and, 218, 223–24,
232
Oklahoma Youth Conferences, 412
Oneida Development Division,
303–4
Oneida Nation of Wisconsin:
community development, 303–4;
health and human services,
305–6; intertribal ventures, 304;
law enforcement, 306; tribal
development, 304–5
OnSat, 299

oppression, 421–22; healing, 388–
89; responses to, 387
oral history, 42n14
Oregon, 176–78; economic
diversification of nations in,
308–9
Oregon Commission on Indian
Services, 181
organizations, Indian, 115; cultural
promotions, 392; technical
assistance from, 292; tribal
development, 293–95. *See also*
specific organizations
Osburn, Katherine M. B., 47n73
Owl Feather War Bonnet Wind
Farm, 284

Pacific Northwest, 176–78. *See also*
specific places
Paige, Rod, 143
participation, 434; ceremonial,
391–92; consulting and, 430–31;
decentralization and, 206–7,
429–30; educational, 334;
election, 88–90, 189n31, 203,
207; employee, 448n40; ILIS,
426–27; inclusive, 269–70; in
NCPCR, 351–53; workplace, 288.
See also community participation
Patterson, Bradley, 135–36
Pauma Band of Luiseño Indians, 296
Paytiamo, Stanley, 248, 277n76
Peacemaker Courts: domestic
violence and, 256–57; Navajo
Nation, 255–56
Peace Makers Council, 278n90
peacemaking: in Canada, 257;
inclusive participation, 269–70
peacemaking, traditional:
development, 254; return
to, 257–58; U.S. government
undermining of, 252–53, 255–56

Peacemaking Circles training, 260
peace pipe. *See* Sacred Pipe
Pechanga Band of Luiseño Indians,
   253
People for Salmon Project, 197n136
Perry, Barbara, 69
peyote rituals, 34
Philadelphia (Mississippi), 173
physical genocide, 53, 88
Pine Ridge Reservation, 66–67,
   80–82, 84, 404n178
Poarch Band of Creek Indians, 159
police, 256; activity in Indian
   country, 69; cross-deputizing
   arrangements, 159–60; racism
   and, 69; state and local, 158–60;
   tribal, 158–60
political institutions, Indian impact
   on, 93n3
politics, traditional American
   Indian, 5–24; contemporary
   politics and, 24–39
polyphony, 276n63
population: demographic profile
   highlights, *58*; European and
   European American growth, 91;
   Native American, 53, 94n4
Portland, Oregon, 176–77, 365–67
Posey, Ivan, 375
poverty, 54, 59, 86–87, 114,
   203–4, 282; children and, 57;
   demographic profile highlights,
   58; economic development and
   overcoming, 56–58; education
   and, 65; food insecurity and, 76;
   reservation vs. urban, 59
power, 5; check of, 212–13;
   concentration, 203–4; gender
   dynamics, 46n63, 47n72;
   political, 155; U.S., 24, 109; of
   woman in traditional Indian
   societies, 21–23

powerlessness, 381
Presidential Executive Order 13270,
   143–44
President's Board of Advisors on
   Tribal Colleges and Universities,
   143
privilege, 385
problem-definition, ILIS, 224–25
problem-solving, 168–69, 447n37;
   ILIS, 233–34; traditional
   strategies, 247–48
property, 211
pseudoparticipation, 275n62
psychological problems, 92
Public Law 280, 154, 196n120
public school, 64–65, 153, 377; BIA-
   funded, 318; Indian education
   policy in, 153, 364–65
Pueblos, 16, 103n85
Purdue, Theda, 394
Puyallup Tribe, 311
Pyramid Lake Paiute Reservation,
   168, 276n74

Quayle, Dan, 27

racism, 54; institutional, 204; police
   and, 69; in schools, 195n110;
   violence and, 69–71
radicalization, 387
raids, 39n1
rape, 71
Reagan, Ronald, 125, 136; budget
   cut, 137, 193n82
reciprocity, 37, 50n116, 211
"Red Alert," 118
Redshirt, Delphine, 62
Rehnquist, William, 437
relational view, 36–37
relationship building, 361
religion, 10
relocation, 109

Reno, Janet, 160
representation theory, 211
resource: competitiveness and, 163–65; extraction, 282–83; in Indian affairs, 137; mineral rights and, 119
resource development, 87, 298; tribal–state and local government relations and, 163–65
respect, 43n19. *See also* mutual respect
respiratory illness, 83
revitalization, 387
Ritter, Troy, 83
Roberts, John G., 438
Robertson, Bob, 135–36
Robertson, James, 187n21
Roosevelt, Franklin, 110–11, 113
Rosebud Indian Reservation, 84; lawsuit, 61–62; wind farm on, 284–85
Rosebud Sioux Tribe, 84
Ross, Rupert, 258
Rough Rock Community School, 344
Rousseau, Jean Jacques, 4, 93n3

Sachs, Edgar, 100n173
Sachs, Stephen, 23, 46n63, 89, 103n87, 141, 250, 271n12, 272n20, 317
A Sacred Path (Chaudhuri, Jean & Chaudhuri, Joyotpaul), 43n19
Sacred Pipe, 23–24
Sacred Wind, 299
San Carlos Apache high school, 162–63
San Juan Pueblo housing program, 188n27, 449n52
San Manuel Band of Mission Indians, 304

Saturday School program, 354–55, 358; improvement scores, 356–57
school–business partnership, 399n68
school-to-prison pipeline, 63
Schulz, Julia, 372
Schwartz, Stephanie M., 81
science, contemporary, 49n100
Science, Technology, Engineering, and Mathematics (STEM), 369
Scott County Public Affairs Coordinator, 179
Search for Common Ground, 27
Second International Decade of the World's Indigenous People, 444
The Second Treatise on Civil Government (Locke), 4
Secwepemc Nation, 258
self-determination, 90, 106–7, 132, 137, 182, 419; economic development and, 152; federal Indian policy toward, 116; institutional problems in recognition of, 116–20; policies, 188n26
self-discovery, 355
self-esteem, 55; honor and, 91; in students, 65
self-governance, 110–11, 193n92; allowable costs, 141; economic development and growth of, 152; empowerment, 183; of federally recognized tribes, 140; funding for, 140–41; 1960s, 114; right of, 108
Senate Select Committee on Indian Affairs, 111–13, 150–51, 185n15
services, 216; Comanche Nation, 222; deficiencies, 59; economic development and availability of, 443–44; of Oneida Nation,

305–6. *See also* health services, Indian; *specific services*

services delivery: collaboration and, 161–63; to Southern Utes, 216; systems to tribal governments, 117–18

Seven Arrows (Storm), 49n101

Seven Generation Corporation, 303

Seventh Generation, 389

shame, 103n84, 380–82

Shiprock Agency Local Government Support Center, 207

shirtwearers, 12–13

Sierra Pacific Power Company, 168

Six Nations. *See* Iroquois

Six Nations Confederation, 21–22

skin infections, 83

Sky Ute Casino and Resort, 396n20

slavery, 39n1

Smith, Darius, 374

Smith, Greg, 145–46

smoke shop taxation, 169–70

smoking, 77–78; secondhand smoke, 82

Snake, Ruben, 247

Snoqualmie Indian Tribe, 277n89

Snyder Act, 145

The Social Contract (Rousseau), 4

social learning, 337, 383–84

social roles, 386

society, traditional, 5–24; quality of life, 3–4

solar power. *See* alternative energy

South Dakota, 196n125; education in, 61; smoke shop taxation in, 170

Southern Ute, 23, 172, 193n93, 198n140, 199n161, 364, 378, 424; BIA relations with, 141; design process, 432; drug courts, 259; economic development, 292;

gambling facilities, 174; gender dynamics, 47n73; inclusiveness at, 215–17; local government collaborative relations, 174–75; Sun Dance, 31, 37, 216; Tribal Council, 172

Southern Ute Design Team, 216, 272n20, 432

Southern Ute Division of Gaming Information, 396n20

Southern Ute Energy Group, 396n20

Southern Ute Indian Academy, 345

Southern Ute Indian Tribal Information Services Department, 216

Southern Ute Women (Osburn), 47n73

South Island Justice Project, 266–67, 269

South Island Tribal Council, 266

Southwest American Indian Tourism Conference, 157

Southwest schools, 345–46

sovereignty, 108; consulting and, 421, 430–31; difficulty for, 132; economic development and, 282–83, 285–86, 316–17; federal agencies and, 133–35; federalism and, 129–31; returning to, 436–37

Sovereignty Symposium, 179

special-focus coordination, 179

spending: casino industry, 297–98; direct, 155–56; per Indian, federal, 57, 95n16, 282

spending, tribal, 155–56; state economy and, 173, 196n123

spirituality, 19–20

spiritual practice, traditional, 55

state economy: Indian contributions to, 155–57; tribal

spending and, 173, 196n123; of
    Washington, 310–11
status quo model for government
    revision, 210, 272n18
STEM. *See* Science, Technology,
    Engineering, and Mathematics
Sterling Energy, 299
Stó:lō, 267–69, 280n122
Stó:lō Nation Tribal Council, 267
Storm, Heyemeyohsts, 49n101
student: decision making
    process, 347; feelings, 349;
    in-classroom heart community,
    353; parent relations, 354–57;
    participation in NCPCR, 351–
    53; performance in math, *61*;
    self-esteem, 65
Subcommittee on Indian Affairs of
    the House Interior Committee,
    185n15
substance abuse, 76–77, 380–81,
    393; alcoholism rate, 103n88;
    overcoming, 391; support, 59
sudden money, 287
suicide, 381
Sun Dance, 89; importation of,
    204; Lakota, 13, 20, 50n112;
    Southern Ute, 31, 37, 216
Supreme Court, 438
Sustainable Development Institute,
    369
Sweet, Bill T., 277n89
Sweetwater Chapter, 207
Swigonski, Mary E., 385
Synar, Mike, 118

Tahontaenrat Tribe, 14
Talking Circle, 392–93
Taos Blue Lake, 413
Taos Pueblo, 115, 413
Taualii, Maile, 77–78
taxation: casino gambling on

reservations, 170–71; tribal, state,
    and local, 169–70
Taylor, Iola, 411
Taylor, Jonathan, 57–60, 62, 63
team building, ILIS, 226
teamwork, 38; interorganizational,
    51n119
technical assistance, 291–92
Thomas, Michael, 297
Thompson, Morris, 120
Three Affiliated Tribes, 285
three-branch government, 205–6,
    208
Three Sovereigns Fish and Wildlife
    Governance Process, 197n136
tiyospaye, 11
Tohono O'odham Community
    Action, 76
Tohono O'odham Community
    College, 76
Tohono O'odham reservation, 76
town meeting participation, 89–90,
    203
tradition, Indian: contemporary
    knowledge of, 42n14;
    revitalizing, 2–3
traditional medicine, 390–91
Trail of Tears, 394
transaction-recording instruments,
    298
trauma, historical, 379
treaties, 108, 195n114
tribal development organizations,
    293–95
Tribal Family Empowerment
    Program, 355–56, 358
tribal–federal government relations,
    106–51, 155, 436–37, 440–41;
    communication and, 135–38;
    completing the circle of, 146–51;
    federal agencies and, 121–22;
    Indian activism and, 114–16;

Roosevelt and Collier and, 110–
11; unfolding of, 108–10. *See also*
specific tribes
Tribal Gaming Coordinating
Committee, 175, 199n161
Tribal Housing Authority, 81
Tribal Law and Order Act of 2008,
71–72, 96n46
Tribally Controlled Schools Act of
1988, 65
Tribally Designated Housing
Entity, 129
Tribal Priority Allocation, 140
tribal shares, 133
Tribal Shares Process, 132
tribal–state and local government
relations, 151–84, 436–37,
440–41; child welfare and,
163; cooperation in, 158–63;
coordination for collaboration,
127, 174–82; environmental
protection and, 161–62; future
factors in, 182–84; infrastructure
and, 154; in law enforcement,
158–60; resources and, 163–65;
Southern Ute, 174–75; taxation
and, 169–70; U.S. government
encouragement of, 179–80;
water rights and, 165–69. *See also*
specific tribes
Tribal Transportation Plan of
Yurok Tribe, 217
tribal vision statement, 425
tribe as state, 127–28, 155
Trigger, Bruce G., 13–14
truancy intervention program,
354–55
Truancy Ordinance, 354–55
Truckee-Carson-Pyramid Lake
Water Settlement, 168–69
Truckee River, 168
trust, 212, 276n74; -building

process, 198n148, 275n59, 422–
24; relationship, 109, 136, 160
trust responsibility, 132, 147, 158,
443; EPA, 191n64
truth, 360
Tsalagi Nation, 394
Tulalip Tribes, 311
Tuncai, 259

Ukiah Unified School District in
California, 364
Unalit, 6
uncertainty principle, 50n112
understanding, 360–61; teenage
brain, 359
unemployment, 59, 84–86, 282;
U.S. rates among ethnicities, *86*
Union Elementary School District,
63
United States (U.S.), 59; as colonial
power, 109; criminal justice,
32; environmental protection
regulation, 25–26; federalism,
24; judicial system, 251; justice
system, 50n102; leadership, 14;
power, 24; prior to invasion,
2; unemployment rates among
ethnicities, *86*. *See also* tribal–
federal government relations
unity in diversity, 29–30, 34–35
Upper Skagit Tribe, 267, 270;
dispute resolution, 264–66
urban Indians, 138; education,
364; election participation, 207;
employment, 84; health and
health care, 77–78; poverty and
service deficiency among, 59
U.S. *See* United States
Utah Division of Child and Family
Services, 163
Utes of Rocky Mountains, 8

values, traditional Native: adaptability in application of, 34; common core, 2; dispute resolution and application of, 264; incorporated into government, 208–9; modern application of, 409–19; pan-Indian, 39n1; in tribal courts, 260–64; tribal governance improved by, 206

Van Norman, Mark, 146

Van Voorhis, Rebecca, 386–87

Viejas Band of Kumeyaay Indians, 304

violence, 381; racism and, 69–71. *See also* domestic violence

Wakiconza, 11–12

Wallace, Ernest, 47n72

Walters community, 243

war, 39n1; increased, 103n85; intensity, 91

War on Poverty, 114, 203–4

warrior, 91, 103n85

Washington, 164–65, 176–78, 197n135; state economy, 310–11

Washington, Newman, 78

Watchman, Derrick, 314

Water Quality Act of 1987, 127–28

water quality standards, 127–28

water rights, 119, 191n61, 197n137, 276n74; Congress and, 167; tribal–state and local government relations in, 165–69

water services, 101n62; to homes, 83

weapons, 91, 93n2

welfare, 88, 123, 163, 205, 381, 444; reform, 130–31, 141–42, 180, 192n70

Wendat. *See* Huron

White Bison, 389–90

White Buffalo Calf Woman, 22, 24

White House: developing coordination of policy and communication within, 135–38; working group and national Indian meetings, 138–42

White House Office of Intergovernmental Relations, 414

wildlife conservation, 164–65

Williams, Terry, 191n59

Winchester, Judy, 374

Window Rock, 206, 208

wind power. *See* alternative energy

Winnebago Tribe of Nebraska, 306–8

Wisconsin, 191n64

Woksape Oyate program, 368–72

women: European, 21; military treatment of, 111, 186n16; mythical figures, 22, 24

women, Native American and Alaska Native: hepatitis C infection rate among, 73; rape against, 71

women, traditional Native American and Alaska Native, 47n72; collective voice of, 23; as mother, 46n66; power held by, 21–23

Workforce Investment Act, 144–45

working group, 138–42; under Bush, G. W., 142–43. *See also specific working groups*

Working Group on American Indian and Alaska Natives, 138, 147

workplace: mutual empowerment use in, 33; participation, 288; pseudoparticipation in, 275n62

World War II, 110, 114

wound to medicine transformation, 378–95

Yakima, 6–7, 205
Yarihawa, 13
Yavapai-Apache Nation, 296
Yawakee, Madona, 374
Youngdahl, Luther, 154

youth: archaeology and, 367; reclaiming, 362–63; sudden money and, 288
Yurok Tribe, 217